TORAH

Society of Biblical Literature

The Bible and Women
An Encyclopaedia of Exegesis and Cultural History

Edited by Jorunn Økland, Irmtraud Fischer,
Mercedes Navarro Puerto, and Adriana Valerio

The Bible and Women
Hebrew Bible/Old Testament
Volume 1.1: Torah

TORAH

Edited by

Irmtraud Fischer and Mercedes Navarro Puerto,
with Andrea Taschl-Erber

Editor of English Edition: Jorunn Økland

Society of Biblical Literature
Atlanta

TORAH

Publication made possible by the support of the Fondazione Valerio
per la Storia delle Donne and the Research Council of Norway.

Library of Congress Cataloging-in-Publication Data

The Bible and women : an encyclopaedia of exegesis and cultural history.
        v. cm.
    Set published simultaneously in English, German, Italian, and Spanish.
    Includes bibliographical references and index.
    Contents: 1. Hebrew Bible/Old Testament: 1.1 Torah / edited by Irmtraud Fischer,
Mercedes Navarro Puerto, with the collaboration of Andrea Taschl-Erber — 1.2.
Writings / edited by Irmtraud Fischer and Athalya Brenner — 1.3. Prophets / edited
by Nuria Calduch-Benages and Christl Maier
    ISBN 978-1-58983-564-1 (v. 1.1 : pbk. : alk. paper) — ISBN 978-1-58983-565-8 (v. 1.2
: pbk. : alk. paper) — ISBN 978-1-58983-634-1 (v. 1.3 : pbk. : alk. paper)
    1. Bible—Feminist criticism. 2. Bible and feminism. I. Society of Biblical Literature.
BS521.4.B54 2011
220.6082—dc23   2011044084

Printed on acid-free, recycled paper conforming to
ANSI/NISO Z39.48-1992 (R1997) and ISO 9706:1994
standards for paper permanence.

Contents

PREFACE TO THE ENGLISH EDITION

The current volume is the first in a series published simultaneously in Spanish, Italian, German, and English. Its aim is to present a history of the reception of the Bible as embedded in Western cultural history and to focus particularly on gender-relevant biblical themes, biblical female characters, and women recipients of the Bible.

The first volume of this encyclopedic project in cultural history and exegesis presents the entire project ("Introduction—Women, Bible, and Reception History: An International Project in Theology and Gender Research," 1–30) and explains the reasons for its layout. In particular, the adoption of the basic structure of the Jewish canon and a strong focus on tradition is defended. This volume also sets the standard for our way of addressing canonicity, social, historical, and legal backgrounds, and iconography.

In a project of this scale, the first volume is exemplary of the further ones; on the other hand, it is also a "practice volume" where the editors learn what will need special attention in future volumes. As examples we could first mention that this English version is published some time after the German version (the editorial language of this particular volume). Second, there is a certain discrepancy between the reality of this volume and the principles of the project as outlined in the introduction, where it is a stated aim to include as many nationalities, linguistic backgrounds, genders, and religious/confessional affiliations as possible—not just in the project as a whole but in each volume. The fact that in this volume there are only two scholars outside of Continental Europe, Mercedes García Bachmann (Argentina) and Carol Meyers (United States), and only one male contributor, Thomas Hieke, was not according to plan. We are still grateful that scholars from ten different countries (more than most volumes of a similar size!) have helped us to produce a representative overview over the gender-relevant questions with regard to the Torah and its sociohistorical context, and we want to thank them all for constructive collaboration! It will be clear to readers that the contributors who are present in this volume represent the widest possible range of methodological and hermeneutical approaches. Not all approaches will be equally familiar within all linguistic contexts. For example, the psychoanthropological-narratological approach to the creation narratives, which also betrays a strong systematic interest, will be less familiar to an Anglophone audience, whereas the liberation theological approach to Miriam may be less familiar to an Italian audience. Such is the nature of a multilingual, multicultural project.

On behalf of all the general editors I want to express also in this English version our deepest thanks and gratitude to the sponsors who have made the project and this volume in particular possible: the Mary Ward sisters in Madrid; the Karl-Franz University of Graz and its vice-rector and the Dean of the Faculty of Theology for hosting the colloquium in preparation of the chapters presented here; the City of Graz and the County of Steiermark, whom we also want to acknowledge; and Fondazione Pasquale Valerio per la Storia delle Donne, who have sponsored most of the translations.

Our deepest thanks also go to the four publishing houses for taking on this project. Through their publishing and sale of the volumes, they further contribute to securing the volumes to follow this one. We want to thank Kohlhammer, represented by Jürgen Schneider, who has advised us along the way and sponsored the launch conference for editors in Naples in 2006. Above all, in this English version we want to thank the Society of Biblical Literature, especially Kent Richards, who championed the project. We also want to thank SBL's publications program, directed by Bob Buller, for help and advice with the English edition.

Dr. Andrea Taschl-Erber, based in Graz, has borne nearly all of the practical organization of this large-scale publication project in a very impressive way since 2008. She has been responsible for contracts, production of style sheets, correspondence with volume editors, general editors, and, for this particular volume, the chapter authors. In addition, she has also put in countless hours in the editorial process. We want to thank Dr. Antonio Perna for translation of information at short notice and for helping us to track the translations.

For the English version, the editorial process and some translation has been sponsored by the University of Oslo's Centre for Gender Research and the Norwegian Research Council. I, Jorunn Økland, would finally like to thank my wonderful assistants, Chantal Jackson and Stefanie Schön, for working extremely hard and diligently on this English version of the volume jointly with me.

Oslo, August 2010   Jorunn Økland

Introduction—Women, Bible, and Reception History: An International Project in Theology and Gender Research

Irmtraud Fischer – Jorunn Økland –
Mercedes Navarro Puerto – Adriana Valerio

The idea of this large-scale project originated in the European Society of Women in Theological Research (ESWTR). Irmtraud Fischer and Adriana Valerio have both been presidents of this twenty-five-year-old association of women theological scholars (2001–2003 and 2003–2007, respectively). From the start, the society has had members in America as well as in northern and southern Europe, but it was for a long time dominated by the "northwestern belt" of the German-, English-, and Flemish-speaking regions. In our work, it became increasingly clear that the northwestern belt's scant reception of gender research conducted in the Romance countries—and vice-versa—was only partly due to a difference in mentality and research tradition.[1] Above all, it was due to a linguistic problem.

In December 2004, on the way to a colloquium on gender research at the Centro per le Scienze Religiose in Trento, Italy, Adriana Valerio and Irmtraud Fischer decided to undertake a reception-historical research project on women that, through the connection of the Bible, history, art history, philosophy, and the letters, would include not only the greatest possible number of women scholars but also establish better connections for theological gender research in Europe. With this intention, an Italian historian (Valerio) and a German-speaking Old Testament scholar (Fischer) asked Mercedes Navarro Puerto, who has published studies on both the Old and the New Testaments

---

1. These differences still become evident in the personality differences between the editors, and they can be traced in this introductory chapter. We have attempted to exemplify particular issues from each linguistic context. The various chapters of this volume put in relief the different linguistic domains with their respective horizons of thought and research traditions.

and specializes in the psychology of religion, and Norwegian Jorunn Økland, who was at that time teaching New Testament studies in Sheffield, England, to collaborate as editors for the Spanish- and English-speaking regions. All four series editors, united by their common interest in the Bible and its reception history, came together for their first meeting in Naples in December 2006.

1. Description of the Project

1.1. A Vast Network of Linguistic Domains and Groups of Recipients

This project is ground-breaking not only in its focus on feminist-exegesis-*cum*-reception-history but also in its large scale of international cooperation and multilingual character. The general editors entrust the responsibility for the various volumes to internationally recognized scholars. They, in turn, solicit contributions from researchers who are already distinguished through publications in their respective fields.

Each volume will be evaluated approximately one-and-a-half years before its publication in a dedicated research colloquium, where the contributions will be critically discussed. This will, on the one hand, guarantee their quality and, on the other hand, promote the creation of new networks of scholars working in the field of gender research in scientific communities of different linguistic regions.

The work will appear more or less simultaneously in four languages: English, Italian, German, and Spanish. This decision was a topic of hot discussion because some thought an English publication would suffice. Nevertheless, for several reasons we believe that the translations are useful even though they constitute the most costly aspect of this project.[2] By publishing in four languages, we hope to extend the reception of the scientific literature appearing in each of the four linguistic areas into the other regions. Now, certainly, scholarly literature in English is noted internationally, while this cannot be generally said (any longer) about sound scholarship in the other three languages. Moreover, publications in the *lingua franca* are read more commonly in the scientific context than in the fields where theological research is applied in practice. So, in order to make the results of research on women also truly accessible to the general public interested in theology, translations are necessary.

---

2. We thank the Fondazione Valerio per la Storia delle Donne for spearheading the translation of this project.

These four languages represent linguistic communities in which gender research is already well underway. Certainly, it would also be useful to add French or at least one of the Slavic languages. However, it is a sad fact that thus far few scholars doing gender research in theology have published in these languages. The reasons for this situation are found in university systems that relegate the subject of theology almost exclusively to educational institutions (seminaries) supported by religious communities. Be that as it may, we make our best efforts to invite scholars from these linguistic areas to also contribute.

1.2. A Project in the History of Theology and Culture

Every research project has an academic context, with regional, historical, and sociological limitations. However, this cannot imply that the formulation of the research question is limited to this geographical, temporal, and social space.

1.2.1. An *International* Project of *Western* Religious History

From its emergence, this project has been conceived with a focus on European theological research on women but, of course, with an international extension. Yet a research interest centered on Western culture can neither ignore the past five hundred years in North and South America nor exclude women and gender scholars of worldwide significance. The global outlook must above all be present in studies of biblical reception during the past two hundred years. We are conscious that "global" is a magic word that can in reality never be reached in the field of scholarship, since "global" in distinct questions can only be conceived regionally. Whoever is not conscious of this fact runs the risk of promoting a new form of colonialism. Europe has a colonial past and is still privileged in many ways, but the tiny continent of Europe is no longer the center of the world. Thus the mention of "Europe and the West" in this project is a sobering acknowledgement of our own limitations, not a self-celebratory form of universalism. We need to explore new, decentered understandings of what Europe and the West is in a global context where the centers of gravity have shifted to the opposite side of the globe, above all to China. This situation frees us up to think more self-critically about our own history, also in gender terms.

The project was from the beginning envisioned as an ecumenical one, that is, with the possible collaboration of all main Christian denominations as well as Judaism. Given the history of its emergence, The Bible and Women is carried on by four Christian theologians from the different linguistic and scientific traditions in whose languages the work will be published. With respect to Judaism, American biblical scholar Adele Berlin is the advisor for the entire series. Furthermore, there will be three volumes of reception history relative to the Hebrew Bible in Judaism, which also grounds the decision in favor of the canonical distribution and the order of the books as presented in the Hebrew Bible. Certain volume editors come from the Jewish tradition, and the attribution of the articles in the other volumes should, according to the principle of the greatest possible diversity, be made not only with respect to the linguistic regions but also with regard to religious denominations.

Who in the end becomes involved in this project thus depends on factors such as the distribution among different countries, linguistic groups, and religious contexts. Male scholars who openly address the questions of gender research and have conducted pertinent studies are also invited to collaborate. However, should some volumes nevertheless give more importance to a particular region or context or contain only a small number of contributions from men, this may be because of different research specializations or because of refusals due to the impossibility of collaboration within a set time limit.

1.2.2. *The* Book of Western Culture as an Object of Research

The Bible is considered *the* book of Western culture. Undoubtedly, no other written work has so fundamentally influenced this culture as the Bible, which originated mainly in Israelite/Jewish cultures in the southwestern corner of Asia and in the Mediterranean world. From ethics through to legal conceptions to philosophy and art, this book has had an imposing effect. Each generation, region, and epoch actualizes different aspects of the Bible's meaning potential, and these actualizations have in turn accumulated to an extremely variegated reception history. Some of the actualizations may appear to be episodic curiosities, while others have formed the mainstream of biblical exegesis. Nevertheless, for almost all periods and contexts, it is possible to recognize that biblical actualizations by women are numerically few and that, in most cases, women's traditions were marginalized or even interrupted. Even a brilliant biblical exegesis such as that represented by Christine de Pizan's *City of the Ladies* received opposition in its own time, and, although it certainly remained present for a long time in discussions about the history of interpretation and culture, it was finally intentionally forgotten, and feminist researchers had to recover it anew in the modern period.[3]

---

3. One of the most outstanding projects in the history of exegesis is the series of volumes edited by Giuseppe Barbaglio, La Bibbia nella Storia (Bologna: Edizione Dehoniane, 1985–), whose most recent volume is Adriana Valerio, ed., *Donne e Bibbia: Storia ed Esegesi* (La Bibbia nella Storia 21; Bologna: Edizione Dehoniane, 2006).

1.2.3. Women's History is No Independent Chapter but an Integral Part of History

This research project aims to bring to light the reception by women that has either been ignored or marginalized by the malestream history of exegesis or only considered to be of regional significance; it does not, however, intend to write a history that merely compensates for the exclusions of previous male-stream scholarship. In fact, that would mean simply adding one distinctive chapter—albeit a long one—to the reception history that has already been established. Biblical interpretation by women and the exegesis of biblical texts concerning women do not represent compensations to a global vision largely developed as "his-story."[4] Actually, this "reception his-story" excludes large bodies of relevant material and must therefore be fundamentally rewritten: reception history, like general history, may only bear this title if it does not exclude half of the population as a priori insignificant. The present project, therefore, is not satisfied with exploring some niches; it enters into main-stream research discussions, for instance by introducing archive materials that have been neglected for a long time (in part even because access to them was denied), by raising necessary gender-relevant questions and hermeneutic discussions, or by pointing out the areas where religious communities seem to want to avoid inculturation. They are all too frequently the areas that con-stitute the cornerstones of an egalitarian order with respect to gender, social status, and ethnic background.

1.2.4. The Inculturation of the Bible in Societies with Gender Democracy

Until this day, the theological argument for maintaining gender inequality in many religious contexts (especially in the Catholic Church) draws on bib-lical texts *and* church tradition. It has gradually become clearer, thanks to highly developed hermeneutics and historical research on the Bible, that the Bible cannot be used to legitimize oppression of women and/or marginaliza-tion of their concerns. At best, some of its individual texts can be applied to such purposes. Since this is also becoming progressively clear to the churches that reject the equality of the sexes, the legitimization of the prevalence of the

---

4. This term, borrowed from feminist historiography, has already been introduced into the discourse of feminist-theological historiography by Charlotte Methuen. See her "Stranger in a Strange Land: Reflections on History and Identity," in *Feministische Zugänge zu Geschichte und Religion* (ed. Angela Berlis and Charlotte Methuen; Jahrbuch der Europäischen Gesellschaft für theologische Forschung von Frauen 8; Leuven: Peeters, 2000), 41–68.

male gender is increasingly based on "the weight of the tradition." Of course, certain traditions are widespread and in many ways more effective than the biblical texts themselves, for example, the exegesis of the paradise narrative. The entire development of tradition, which is an integral part of divine revelation both in Judaism and in some parts of Christianity, has nevertheless still been insufficiently exposed to critical analysis. In the absence of such in-depth scrutiny and analysis, the formulation of generalizing arguments that apply constantly throughout history in favor of a seamless patriarchal tradition proves very problematic.

The project The Bible and Women accordingly understands itself as that contemporary part of reception history that attempts to actualize the Bible and its history of exegesis for societies with gender democracy and to track biblical views of the relation between the genders as well as their cultural development. From this point of view, the project is an attempt at inculturation, which inquires the possibilities of a gender-fair, biblically reasoned theological anthropology, and in the process critically considers Scripture and tradition because each one of them cannot alone eradicate invalid arguments used, especially in ultraconservative circles.

Now, Scripture and tradition certainly do not have the same value in all churches. The Protestant Christian denominations that do not operate with a clear notion of "tradition" (or even reject tradition as authority) still *function* as traditions when analyzed in an etic (i.e., from the outside) perspective. Even when studying reception history in a narrow sense, as a sequence of authoritative biblical interpretations, it is clear that also the authoritative interpreters in the Protestant tradition who all claim to adhere to *sola scriptura* have read this Scripture in radically different ways and that their differences can be partly traced back to reading conventions—that is, traditions for dealing with the text—as well as to the interpreters' historical contexts.

1.2.5. Without the Pretension of Encyclopedic Exhaustiveness

The Bible and Women is not only an ambitious project through its international elaboration of the subject matter but also because it seeks to cover all the periods of reception history primarily in Western culture. Of the projected volumes, following the logic of the distribution of the canon, five in all will deal with the Bible, three with the Hebrew Bible and two with the New Testament. The subsequent volumes will attempt to cover, without gaps, the history of inculturated biblical reception, particularly in the four linguistic regions. This enterprise explains the subtitle "Encyclopedia" present in some versions of this work. It refers to the *integral* and *continuous* nature of the historical treatment of the *subject matter*, not, however, to a pretension to cover everything exhaustively. The separate volumes will assemble neither all the biblical interpretations of a given period nor pretend to study geographically all the centers of exegesis. The term "encyclopedia" expresses the common concept of the volumes, that they are *not* a series of feminist essays on the topic of reception history.[5] The Bible and Women is neither an encyclopedia with entries on individual women of the Bible[6] or individual woman exegetes[7] nor a series aiming at making women of the Bible visible and reading them from a gender-critical perspective;[8] moreover, it is not a feminist commentary on the Bible[9] with an attached *Wirkungsgeschichte*, nor is it a reception history of the female biblical characters[10] throughout different periods. The project indeed intends to present in an *exemplary way* the entire history of the Bible and its interpretation with regard to women and gender-relevant questions for the cultural regions dealt with. While the volumes will cover the first millennium of reception history mainly in the geographical regions of the Mediterranean and to a certain extent Europe, in the course of the second millennium the perspective constantly widens, from the *conquistadores* who in their own particular way brought the Bible to today's South America, then in the nineteenth century, when European missionary societies brought the Bible to Africa and Eastern Asia. A fully global view is reached with volume 9, which will deal with academic feminist exegesis in the twentieth century.

---

5. In contrast to the volumes in the Feminist Companion to the Bible series edited by Athalya Brenner (18 vols.; Sheffield: Sheffield Academic Press, 1993–2001).

6. In contrast to Carol Meyers, Toni Craven, and Ross S. Kraemer, eds., *Women in Scripture: A Dictionary of Named and Unnamed Women in the Hebrew Bible, the Apocryphal/Deuterocanonical Books, and the New Testament* (Grand Rapids: Eerdmans, 2001).

7. The volumes of Elisabeth Gössmann, ed., *Das wohlgelahrte Frauenzimmer* (8 vols. and a special volume; Archiv für philosophie- und theologiegeschichtliche Frauenforschung; Munich: Iudicium, 1984–2004), are devoted to writings of individual women who also commented on the Bible.

8. Collections of this kind exist in all four languages. See, for example, in Spanish, the different volumes of the collection En clave de mujer, edited by I. Gómez-Acebo, and Aletheia, edited by ATE (Asociación de Teólogas Españolas).

9. In contrast to Carol A. Newsom and Sharon H. Ringe, eds., *The Women's Bible Commentary: Expanded Edition with Apocrypha* (Louisville: Westminster John Knox, 2003), as well as to Louise Schottroff and Marie-Theres Wacker, eds., *Kompendium Feministische Bibelauslegung* (3rd ed.; Gütersloh: Gütersloher Verlagshaus, Sonderausgabe, 2007), who comment on the biblical books. All these works are invaluable resources for our project.

10. On this, see, for example, Andrea Taschl-Erber, *Maria von Magdala—erste Apostolin? Joh 20,1–18: Tradition und Relecture* (Freiburg im Breisgau: Herder, 2007); and John L. Thompson, *Writing the Wrongs: Women of the Old Testament among Biblical Commentators from Philo through the Reformation* (Oxford: Oxford University Press, 2001).

1.2.6. The Reception of the Bible Does Not Occur Only in Exegesis

Bible reception does not, however, take place only in theological research. *Reception in art* has been at least as influential as that in exegesis. We are thinking above all of visual arts, paintings and statuary, although also of music and literature. Apart from some particular periods and cultural locations, biblical texts that have formed part of the (often subconscious) cultural code of the West until today have not been directly influential in their own right but rather exercised their influence through their own emulations, interpretations, and configurations in such other media as art, literature, liturgies, and sermons.

Throughout the majority of the history of Christianity, ordinary Christians have not personally owned a Bible or even been able to read the Bible. Even fewer have had the education needed to access the exegetical literature produced by and for the experts. Images, on the other hand, were available everywhere, and they taught illiterate believers the stories of the Bible. Furthermore, if much of the Bible is imaginative and visual, artists have often been better interpreters of such expressive forms than scholars. Some genres and media make certain readings possible that the other genres do not, and on this basis the preferred genres and media have also changed over time.

Accordingly, a section on iconography is planned for each period. For the volumes dealing with the Bible, this section will be predominantly archaeological; from the Middle Ages on, all the volumes contain a chapter about the reception in either art history, literature, or music. American professor of art history Heidi Hornik and Spanish conservator María Leticia Sánchez Hernández have taken on the supervision of art history in this encyclopedia, and, with regard to reception in literature, the project is advised by German literary scholar Magda Motté.

The contributions are conceived with historical and philological precision. They have a scholarly rather than a popular-scientific orientation and consider the relevant research publications, especially in the area of women's and gender research. In order to serve the goal of better networking and facilitate access to the results of gender researchers within the different linguistic fields, the contributions nevertheless aim to be understandable for a larger public and composed in a scholarly rigorous but still accessible style also for readers who are not theologians or biblical scholars.

1.3. A PROJECT IN WOMEN'S AND GENDER RESEARCH

Religion is a central factor that has shaped gender relations throughout the centuries and today continues to exert influence even in secular societies. As the canonical text of once-dominant religion(s), the Bible became a reference text that not only exerted influence on the organization of social relations but also profoundly formed the jurisprudence, moral standards, and philosophical questions of Western culture.

1.3.1. The Bible Emerged in a Patriarchal Society

Neither the biblical texts nor their interpretations are unique inventions that fell from the sky. They have emerged in a cultural context. They strive to communicate to the people of their time and hence inevitably have to be "children of their time" themselves. This embeddedness in social conditions will have to be considered throughout the entire reception history. Therefore, various contributions elucidate the living conditions of men and women in the different periods, social contexts, and regions; they will also attempt to shed light on the standard legal norms, anthropological and philosophical concepts, or standards of iconographic representation.

The Bible originated in a patriarchal culture that discriminated not only on the basis of gender but also on the basis of other social characteristics:[11]

CRITERIA FOR THE DEFINITION OF SOCIAL STATUS IN THE PATRIARCHAL SOCIETIES		
Criterion	**Positive**	**Negative**
Status of citizen in the ancient Near East	free	slave
Gender	masculine	feminine
Age in the ancient Near East: free	old	young
Age in the ancient Near East: slave	young	old

11. Elisabeth Schüssler Fiorenza, *In Memory of Her: A Feminist Theological Reconstruction of Christian Origins* (New York: Crossroad, 1983), has further developed these criteria for biblical studies on the basis of liberation theological concepts. For the following table and explanations, see Irmtraud Fischer, "Was kostet der Exodus? Monetäre Metaphern für die zentrale Rettungserfahrung Israels in einer Welt der Sklaverei," *JBTh* 21 (2006): 25–44, here 29.

Ecumenical status	rich	poor
Ethnicity	indigenous	foreign
Religion	dominant	foreign/deviant

The most important distinction for the determination of social status in the ancient Near East (and in antiquity in general) was that of freedom versus slavery. This distinction decides whether one has personal rights or whether these rights, in the case of slaves, belong among the possession rights of the master or the mistress. Gender becomes a criterion only to determine priority within the same social class. Women are subordinated as children to their father and, after his death, if unmarried, to their oldest brother or, if married, to their husbands. However, patriarchy did not simply mean male domination; rather, it is to be seen as a pyramid of social hierarchy in which free women naturally were also superior to male members of lower social classes. Old age is a positive distinction, since the elderly have authority over younger individuals. On the other hand, for the role of patriarch within an extended family, age is a relative criterion: the oldest man of the hereditary line is head of the family; upon his early death a twenty-year-old can inherit his position. Only in the case of male and female slaves is age a negative criterion, since they are valued according to their full labor potential. Religion must be mentioned as another criterion for social status. It can be a negative criterion if it is foreign or deviant within the society's own symbolic system. Foreignness, like poverty, is ipso facto until today a negative criterion in most societies. Precisely the economic status, which today is probably the most determinant criterion for social status, has throughout history tended to trump all the other criteria and has therefore been considered a positive criterion in itself. In every age, the rich could most easily arrange things to their advantage.

1.3.2. Biblical Texts Are Both Descriptive and Prescriptive

In reception history, special attention must be given to the interplay between the theological and ideological positions regarding gender and to the social status of the men and women. It must be supposed that many of the texts dealt with in this project do not describe the living conditions of women but rather aim to present a prescriptive reality.[12] To better understand the texts' correlation to their social environment and real-life conditions, archaeological

---

12. This has already been indicated by Schüssler Fiorenza, *In Memory of Her*, 167–68.

findings will be presented and cross-cultural historical comparisons included (e.g., jurisprudence in the history of the ancient Near East). Furthermore, a sort of comparative control vis-à-vis other cultural products of the respective period will be effected, which may also reveal traces of possible "losses" or radical changes in the tradition (e.g., the *Haustafeln* [household codes] put into circulation in the Roman Empire).

2. WHOEVER SAYS A MUST ALSO SAY B: WHOEVER DEALS WITH THE BIBLE MUST ALSO ACCOUNT FOR THE CANON

The Bible and Women is a historical project in as much as it deals with both the emergence and the reception history of ancient texts. So, it would seem reasonable to study and explicate texts of a certain period with respect to their gender relevance. However, the project has decided not to consider the reception of "antiquity" or "the ancient Near East" but rather that of the *Bible*. This implies accepting a canon,[13] a list of writings that a community considers holy, binding, and authoritative.

2.1. WHY A FEMINIST HISTORICAL PROJECT ACCEPTS THE CONCEPT OF A (CLOSED) CANON

In feminist theology, the problem of a closed canon of the Bible was discussed early on, since this canon perpetuates an androcentric restriction of which writings are considered holy and binding.

2.1.1. Opening of the Canon: Yes or No?

Research constantly made it clearer that early Christianity was a far more multifaceted movement than hitherto realized. Many small groups or sects existed that also left their traces in writing, and among these groups there were still other texts in circulation with a much more friendly attitude toward women than some of the texts later qualified as "New Testament writings." There were also works attributed to women that did not find their way into the canon. However, in the fourth century, when Christianity became the official religion of the Roman Empire, one particular strand of Christianity was seen as especially useful for that purpose. Consequently, priority was given to the writings

---

13. What the "canon" is, the origin of the different forms of canon, and their role in the research of their different periods is presented in detail by Donatella Scaiola in her article in this volume.

of this particular strand when a canon of Christian writings was formed.[14] It could be argued, then, that the selected New Testament texts emerged within a shorter time span and within a relatively narrow strand of early Christianity and that this accounts for its relatively narrow range of gender models compared to the wider variety found in the Hebrew Bible.

A canon concept also refers to the community through whom, up to today, we have continuously received these texts, and thus a modern recovery of them is unnecessary (as in the case of some other ancient texts). As an organizational principle of texts, the canon is certainly not relevant in an equal sense throughout the developing stages of the texts in question. Indeed, at the moment of their redaction it was not yet decided what their rank among the holy texts was and which social group would be able to impose its texts as *holy* texts.[15] The decision for a closed canon, to which nothing is to be added or taken away (see Deut 4:2; 13:1), implies the exclusion of many other texts on the same topic and written at the same time and to which henceforth the highest authority is denied.

Such decisions reflect the constellations of power in the religious communities concerned. Above all, the closure of the Christian canon seems to have been effected in the wake of a reduction of female participation in the leadership of the communities of early Christianity. Therefore, in recent decades Elisabeth Schüssler Fiorenza has urgently called for the opening of the canon, so that, on the one hand, woman-friendly texts would be authorized as holy scriptures and, on the other hand, the further reception of misogynous texts would cease.[16] With respect to the writings of the Hebrew Bible, no similar process of marginalization can be shown; this may be so because the redaction of Hebrew writings cedes in favor of Greek after 300 B.C.E. and thus becomes

---

14. See, above all, Bart D. Ehrman, *The Orthodox Corruption of Scripture: The Effect of Early Christological Controversies on the Text of the New Testament* (New York: Oxford University Press, 1996); idem, *Lost Christianities: The Battle for Scripture and the Faiths We Never Knew* (Oxford: Oxford University Press, 2005); Karen L. King, *What Is Gnosticism?* (Cambridge: Harvard University Press, 2005).

15. On the categorization of holy and canonical texts, see Maurice Halbwachs, *The Collective Memory* (New York: Harper & Row, 1980), as well as the work by Jan Assmann (very influential in the German-speaking biblical scholarship), *Das kulturelle Gedächtnis: Schrift, Erinnerung und politische Identität in frühen Hochkulturen* (2nd ed.; Munich: Beck, 1997), 103–29 (also available in English translation).

16. This wish appears throughout all her writings. See, above all, Elisabeth Schüssler Fiorenza, ed., *Searching the Scriptures, Volume 1: A Feminist Introduction* (London: SCM, 1994); eadem, ed., *Searching the Scriptures, Volume 2: A Feminist Commentary* (London: SCM, 1995), especially eadem, "Introduction: Transforming the Legacy of *The Woman's Bible*," in *Searching the Scriptures, Volume 1*, 8–11.

more meager or stops completely. However, certainly even in advanced Hellenistic times the book of Esther does not suggest a similar procedure. On the contrary, the books of women in the Hebrew Bible—Ruth and Esther—are of postexilic origin; as extracanonical continuation, the book of Judith, which is marked by a dominant feminine figure, may also be mentioned here. In conclusion, for the Hebrew Bible the opening of the canon would not have the same effect of offering larger variety of gender models as it would in the case of the New Testament writings.

2.1.2. The Whole Is More Than the Sum of Its Parts

The acceptance of the concept of canon is further recommended, since it concerns texts that became important as a *collection* and not only as independent books or texts in the preliminary stages of their emergence. To arrange all the materials of a single period in the temporal succession of its redactional history[17] would imply choosing a hypothesis for categorization that in many cases would not extend beyond a decade[18] and, already for this reason alone, would not be recommendable for a long-term project such as this. So, in the case of the Torah, whose origin is at present envisioned by extremely divergent hypotheses with regard to its redactional history, a historical criterion for the arrangement of the texts would be inconceivable in the present state of research. Even if the same historical contexts are in part discussed in different volumes (e.g., there are Jewish writings from the Hellenistic period both in the canon and in the Apocrypha), it is advisable to afford special treatment to the late canonical writings because they alone became binding as norms and still retain this character today. So, the biblical texts became relevant in the course of history in such a way that a privileged position must be awarded to them in a history of reception—even if they do not need to retain a special status in directly religious contexts.

---

17. See Claudio Moreschini and Enrico Norelli, *Handbuch der antiken christlichen Literatur* (Gütersloh: Gütersloher Verlagshaus, 2007).

18. Thus, for example, the attempt made by Hanns-Martin Lutz, Hermann Timm, and Eike Christian Hirsch, *Altes Testament: Einführungen, Texte, Kommentare* (8th ed.; Munich: Piper, 1992), or the commentary by Hermann Gunkel, *Genesis* (9th ed.; Göttinger Handkommentar zum Alten Testament 1; Göttingen: Vandenhoeck & Ruprecht, 1977), who arranges the order of the biblical texts according to the sources.

2.2. A Project in a Tradition of Research Burdened by Anti-Judaism

Since the international project The Bible and Women originated historically in the European Society of Women in Theological Research, it is published by women theologians of Christianity in a university context. So, one would assume that the Bible is defined as the two-part Holy Scripture of Christianity. However, the publishers have made a different decision and base their history of the Bible's reception on the extent, the organization, and—as far as this may be clearly defined[19]—the canonical succession of the different books of the *Hebrew Bible*. This certainly requires a detailed explanation.

Although the project originates in a context shaped by Christianity, it is inevitable that a culturally and historically oriented theological project considers Jewish reception history as well—not only because it substantially influenced Christian cultural history but also because it received insufficient attention in the tradition of historical-critical research during the last centuries, given that such research developed particularly within Christian university theology. When Jewish reception entered into research, it was frequently used as a negative foil for the presentation of an even brighter Christian tradition.[20] In this way, the inclusion of Jewish tradition was frequently made in Christian exegesis from an *anti-Jewish* point of view.

Likewise, the beginnings of feminist exegesis constituted no exception to this more than problematic "use" of Jewish exegesis as "proof" that early Christianity had been much friendlier toward women than contemporary Judaism.[21] However, a painful process of consciousness-raising has led most Christian feminist theologians to a reorientation. In the meantime, in many fields this process of reconsideration and reorientation gave rise to a fruitful dialogue that still remains very delicate due to the excessively long and problematic tradition of research and also because of the power and majority/minority issues involved. The Bible and Women considers itself a part of the

---

19. Peter Brandt, *Endgestalten des Kanons: Das Arrangement der Schriften Israels in der jüdischen und christlichen Bibel* (BBB 131; Berlin: Philo, 2001).

20. Classic is, for example, Hermann L. Strack and Paul Billerbeck, *Kommentar zum Neuen Testament aus Talmud und Midrasch* (4 vols.; Munich: Beck, 1922–1928).

21. See Leonore Siegele-Wenschkewitz, *Verdrängte Vergangenheit, die uns bedrängt: Feministische Theologie in der Verantwortung für die Geschichte* (Kaiser Taschenbücher 29; Munich: Kaiser, 1988); Katharina von Kellenbach, *Anti-Judaism in Feminist Religious Writings* (AAR Cultural Criticism Series 1; Atlanta: Scholars Press, 1994); Judith Plaskow, "Christian Feminism and Anti-Judaism," *Cross Currents* (Fall 1978): 306–9; eadem, "Blaming the Jews for the Birth of Patriarchy," in *Nice Jewish Girls: A Lesbian Anthology* (ed. Evelyn Torton Beck; New York: The Crossing Press Trumansburg, 1982), 298–302; Annette Daum, "Blaming the Jews for the Death of the Goddess," *Lilith* 7 (1980): 12–13.

inevitable and necessary—for Christianity, which has its roots in Judaism—process of reconciliation, and its decision concerning the canon is one element in this process. The dialogue, however, is still like walking a tightrope because during the last two decades Jewish researchers have resisted legitimately against an all-too-violent Christian "embrace." The attempt to integrate Jewish interpretation into a predominantly Christian context in fact risks collecting once again Jewish elements for Christian interests. The Bible and Women is aware of this difficult starting point; nevertheless, it has intentionally chosen this way, which certainly holds some traps in store, and so from the beginning takes the risk of leaving a flank open for criticism. Despite this, the editors believe that the heightened value of a closer dialogue that takes both the temporal and theological historical priority of the Hebrew Bible seriously in its reception as Christian "Old Testament" makes this risk worthwhile.

2.3. Jewish Order of the Canon in a Predominantly Christian Context

If we commit ourselves, in a context of Christianity, to including the Jewish tradition in a history of biblical exegesis, we actually no longer have a choice regarding the extent of the canon and its order. The decision to include the Jewish tradition, not only as further illustration of the periods of the Christian Bible's exegesis but as acknowledgement of the independent value that it has retained, necessarily leads to the subsequent decision to give priority to the Jewish canonical order. The latter is characterized by the prominent position of the Torah, which is followed by the two-part Prophets and the Writings. From a theological point of view, the Prophets and the Writings form, as it were, an actualizing commentary on Torah and already thereby represent, in a certain way, its interpretation and/or reception.

2.3.1. Visualization of the Double Outcome of the Hebrew Bible

The choice of a Christian extent and order of the canon, with prophecy at the conclusion and as transition from the Old Testament to the New Testament, would leave the Jewish exegetical tradition to perish as just one "special history" in relation to the Christian "regular history." For The Bible and Women, the Hebrew Bible has a "double outcome."[22] The Hebrew Bible continues to be effective in Jewish exegesis, and emerging Christianity is

---

22. Erich Zenger, *Das erste Testament: Die jüdische Bibel und die Christen* (Düsseldorf: Patmos, 1991), 140–44.

understood as part of the latter. Consequently, the writings of the New Testament are, on the one hand and to begin with, Jewish interpretations of the Hebrew Bible; on the other hand, in Christianity, New Testament writings very soon became Holy Scriptures in their own right. However, Christians never abandoned any of the canonized books in the Hebrew Bible.[23] Actually, Christians did receive the latter as the first part of its Bible, as the "Old Testament"—although almost exclusively and for a long time in the Greek translation of the Septuagint, which was originally produced in a Jewish context. The Septuagint's extended canon also included writings transmitted only in Greek.[24] On this basis, the present project understands the New Testament writings, on the one hand, as reception of the Hebrew Bible and, on the other hand, as new contributions to Holy Scriptures that have reception histories of their own.

The decision in favor of the extent and order of the Hebrew canon makes it possible to demonstrate a twofold exegesis history[25] of one and the same set of biblical writings. It allows a proper space for the continuation of an equally legitimate Jewish reception history within a project that originates in a predominantly Christian context. Therefore, three volumes will be dedicated exclusively to Jewish reception history. With the volume on the Jewish deuterocanonical and pseudepigraphical writings[26] and the three biblical volumes, there are seven volumes in all consecrated to Jewish texts. Some apocryphal writings only became authoritative and efficacious in Judaism, whereas the biblical texts attained this validity in both religions; conversely, some Jewish writings have become substantially more influential within Christian theology.[27]

---

23. Although the discussions already began in the second century, when Marcion raised the issue, the Old Testament was never rejected as a part of the Bible by Christianity.

24. This affirmation does not concern the question of a Hebrew original (cf. the book of Sirach, whose text was transmitted in the Greek translation of a Hebrew original, of which fragments have been recovered).

25. Since this project is limited to the Jewish and Christian reception history, initially the third reception line in the Qur'an will not be considered.

26. According to its etymology, "apocryphal" means "hidden, secret," while "pseudepigraphical" implies that a text is "falsely" attributed to an author. Today's use of these terms results from the discussions of the Reformation. The Protestant churches use the term "apocryphal" to designate extracanonical writings, while the Roman Catholic Church applies it to the "deuterocanonical" writings. See David Satran, "Apocrypha/Pseudepigrapha. II. Old Testament," *RPP* 1:308.

27. An example is the book of Jesus Sirach, which received the title "Ecclesiasticus" because in Christianity it was used for learning to read.

2.3.2. Separate and Common Paths

The Bible and Women will not, however, follow the entire history of exegesis on the separate paths of Jewish and Christian interpretation, rather only in the formative and authoritative periods of Jewish interpretation. The different traditions will be reunited after the volume dealing with the periods of the Jewish Middle Ages and the early modern period. Each volume will contain at least one article on Jewish exegesis of the particular period. To a certain degree, it makes no sense to separate the Jewish heritage from the Christian one, for instance with regard to the reception of biblical themes in literature and art from the twentieth century until today. At least since the Enlightenment, the prevailing trends affect both Jewish and Christian exegesis; an eloquent example of this is given by the biblical interpretations in the nineteenth- and twentieth-century women's movements, which discussed the access of women to offices and/or functions in Judaism as well as Christianity.

Choosing the canon of the Hebrew Bible further makes more sense with regard to the reception history in the churches that emerged from the Protestant Reformation. Through their return to the *hebraica veritas*, they have attributed canonical status only to the books transmitted in Hebrew. Consequently, the decision in favor of the Jewish extent of the canon also has analytical advantages for the history of exegesis in Protestant Christianities, since it ensures that the canonical and deuterocanonical books are not mixed.

Thus, in conclusion, the decision in favor of the Jewish extent of the canon both makes sense ecumenically and is also more analytically advantageous when studying the reception of the Bible in Judaism and Protestant *as well as* Catholic Christianities.

2.3.3. A Historical Project Chooses a Canonical Form Attested at an Early Period

Even though the three-part division of the Hebrew Bible was not adopted by Christianity, since it did not assume the two-part Prophets,[28] this canon form can be considered the historically original one. Around 180 B.C.E. the prologue of the book of Sirach, only canonical for some Christian churches, mentions a three-part division of the canon: "Law, Prophets and the other Writings."

---

28. The Hebrew Bible has a two-part division (Former Prophets: Joshua–2 Kings; Latter Prophets: Isaiah–Malachi), whereas the Christian Bible only considers the books of the "prophetic authors" (Isaiah–Malachi + Daniel) as prophecy.

Naturally, since Christianity only authorized the books attributed to individual prophets as prophecy and placed them toward the end of the Old Testament as "transition" to the New Testament, it did not assume this three-part division, although it does recognize the succession Torah-Prophets in its Holy Scriptures with the designation "the Law and the Prophets." Since the Writings of the third part of the canon are predominantly more recent than those of the Torah and Prophets and the discussion concerning their canonicity has already been going on for a long time, a two-part designation of the canon without any specification of the third part, the Writings, could leave the canonicity of the latter open to further questioning.

In the course of Christianity's history, the books of the Former Prophets are, however, received as historical books. The *Luther Bibel*, even in its most recent revision, still places the Torah side by side with the latter and, in this way, perpetuates a historicizing interpretation of those books considered prophetic by the Jewish tradition. This inconsistency in the canon of the Reformed churches, who by adopting the *range* of the Hebrew Bible simultaneously accepted the Catholic *order* of the canon, is exemplified by this abolition of the Torah's privileged position.

2.4. GENDER-RELEVANT ASPECTS OF THE CANON'S ORDER, FORM, AND LIMITATION

The three-part canon model of the Hebrew Bible is not only historically the earliest attested but is also suggested by the hermeneutical-theological structure of the writings.

2.4.1. The Torah as Connecting Theologoumenon of the Three-Part Hebrew Bible

The Torah, as normative text, shapes the other parts of the Hebrew Bible canon in so far as the understanding of prophecy presupposed in the so-called office law in Deut (16:18–18:22)—as an actualizing interpretation of the Torah—determines the sequence of the books Joshua–2 Kings. According to Deut 18:14b–22, the prophetic office was awarded immediately after God gave the gift of the Decalogue to the people through direct revelation at Mount Horeb (Deut 18:16–18 takes 5:23–33 into account). After this fear-inducing meeting, the people ask for an intermediary, whom God does indeed grant by appointing Moses. Among the offices, only prophecy is directly assigned by YHWH, Israel's God (18:15, 18); consequently, it is considered the highest office. All prophets are therefore, in some sense, successors of Moses (God will raise up people with the prophetic gift like Moses; Deut 18:15, 18), the prophet and mediator of divine legislation par excellence.

With the literary connection of Deuteronomy, originally transmitted in the narrative context of Joshua–2 Kings, to the sequence of books from Genesis to Numbers, the canonical sequence of Torah and Prophets is constructed. Deuteronomy, conceived as law for life in the land, where prophecy is considered the most important office, announces that the gift of the land is permanent only if the people, when in the country, let themselves be led by prophecy and so listen to the actualized prophetic word of the Torah and live according to it. The Jewish canon thus structures the writings that Christianity labels "Historical Books" as Prophets. *Historical* is, accordingly, seen as the history guided by prophecy and categorized as a *theological* representation of history. The understanding of the Former Prophets as well as that of the Torah as historical books lends support to the sort of (Christian) fundamentalist interpretation that arose in an era (post-Darwin) when it became clear to most people that the Torah and the Prophets are not history books at all. Law and Prophets are rather hermeneutical categories: they give clues about what we should read these texts *as*. The categories themselves are naturally also to be explained from their historical contexts, but the point is this: their individual texts do not claim to represent primarily historical but theological truth.

Another consequence of the separation between the Former and Latter Prophets in the Christian forms of the canon is that the texts relative to women prophets also became marginalized and removed from the (relatively speaking) more central place that they hold in the Jewish canon. Klara Butting has pointed out that both the first and the last prophetic figures of the part of canon entitled Former Prophets are women. Deborah (Judg 4–5) and Huldah (2 Kgs 22) thus frame this part of the canon, and they are themselves framed or modeled (according to Butting) on the example of the woman prophet Miriam (Exod 15).[29] This literary style figure of inclusion has decisive influence on the understanding of prophecy as a whole, since it means that in all

---

29. Klara Butting, *Prophetinnen gefragt: Die Bedeutung der Prophetinnen im Kanon aus Tora und Prophetie* (Erev-Rav-Hefte: Biblisch-feministische Texte 3; Wittingen: Erev-Rav, 2001), 77, 99–100. Irmtraud Fischer, *Gotteskünderinnen: Zu einer geschlechterfairen Deutung des Phänomens der Prophetie und der Prophetinnen in der Hebräischen Bibel* (Stuttgart: Kohlhammer, 2002), represents the premise that the feminine figures are also in Moses' following. This interpretation is suggested precisely by the phenomenon of cross-gender intertextuality in the case of the later female figures, who are modeled after the great male figures of Israel's narrated history (e.g., Esther as "new Joseph," Ruth as "new Abraham," Judith as "new David"). For more details on this and the following presentation, see Fischer, *Gotteskünderinnen*, 16–38.

the books in between, all notes relative to the "prophets" must be understood as referring to "men and women prophets." Consequently, the grammatically masculine designation "prophet," and/or the functional indicator "prophet," must be translated (whenever no concrete male figures are connected with it) as "humans with the gift of prophecy," since women can be, and were, included everywhere.

2.4.2. The Order and Structure of the Canon Influences the Status of Women in the History of Interpretation

The Jewish concept of canon with its emphasized status of the Torah has further consequences for research on women, in as much as it increases the significance of both the creation narratives and the gender-specific legislation for an anthropology justified by the Bible. The foundation narrative of God's people, told in Genesis principally through narratives about women, highlights the importance of women as Israel's mothers, who determine the succession in each generation and thereby decisively influence the fate of the people. Thus the term "patriarchal narratives" is to a large extent avoided here, as the term reinforces patriarchy and conceals the ambiguity found in the texts. It is a fundamental task for feminist biblical interpretation to explore this ambiguity.

Whether biblical women are visible or not, and whether and how they are received in the history of interpretation, thus also depends on the form of the canon agreed upon by the reception community. Some further examples are as follows.

The women in the ancestral narratives have a very high status in Judaism, since they are the founding figures of the people, whereas the Christian tradition frequently received them only as the wives of the founding fathers, without—in contrast to their husbands—attributing any historical importance to them.[30]

There have been many women prophets in the Christian tradition, but they have not necessarily seen themselves as the successors of Deborah and Huldah, since these women in the Christian canon had fallen out of the biblical section of prophetic books. Thus they were often replaced, such as by the Sibyls in the history of art. The Talmud, on the other hand, mentions seven biblical prophetesses (b. Meg. 14a).[31]

---

30. Martin Noth, *A History of Pentateuchal Traditions* (trans. Bernhard W. Anderson; Englewood Cliffs, N.J.: Prentice-Hall, 1972).

31. The number seven indicates perfection, even if the names of the prophetesses do not coincide with those named in the Bible: b. Meg. 14a mentions Sarah, Miriam, Deborah,

A further example in this regard is the very different reception of those passages of the Torah that deal with cultic ability. While the gender-relevant categories of clean and unclean play a central role in Judaism even today, they were very selectively received as primarily moral categories in Christianity, with a clear emphasis on sexuality.

The option for the Jewish canon and the associated elimination of the deuterocanonical books leads to the loss of a woman's book such as Judith. But, on the other hand, it means that misogynistic passages and receptions, as found, for instance, in the book of Sirach, are also excluded. The neutral designation Writings for the third part of the canon better accommodates the diversity of the books in question than the designation frequently used in Christian exegesis: "wisdom books." Furthermore, the explicitly "woman-centered" books, Ruth, Song of Songs, and Esther, are better highlighted within the context of the relatively small collection of the Megilloth,[32] or "scrolls," where they form the largest part.

3. Scriptural Exegesis, Tradition, and Reception

The existence of a canon distinguishes texts from one another on the basis of their differing degrees of importance. Central to a notion of canon is that nothing should be further added or omitted. This means that the actualization of biblical texts[33] and continued progress of the tradition is possible only outside of the delimited canon. Due to the normative status canonical texts have in religious communities, they need to be continuously interpreted so that in each epoch their significance can be represented anew and accepted. The cultural phenomenon initiated by this process of actualization can be designated as the formation of tradition. According to the different meanings of "tradition" in Catholic and Orthodox contexts, on the one hand, and in

---

Hannah, Abigail, Huldah, and Esther as prophetesses. For more details on this subject, see Fischer, *Gotteskünderinnen*, 35–37.

32. A selection of five Hebrew Bible books (thus a canon extracted from a wider canon) that are used for liturgical purposes.

33. Quotations of biblical texts in later passages, as well as generally intertextual connections, can already be presented as beginnings of a creative exegesis of texts in the Bible; they are to be understood as the expression of a reception process that began within the Bible and, outside of it, continues with the canon. On this subject, see the more detailed presentation in Irmtraud Fischer, "Erinnern als Movens der Schriftwerdung und der Schriftauslegung: Woran und warum sich Israel nach dem Zeugnis der Hebräischen Bibel erinnert und wieso dies für unsere heutige Erinnerung relevant ist," in *Erinnern: Erkundungen zu einer theologischen Basiskategorie* (ed. Paul Petzel and Norbert Reck; Darmstadt: Wissenschaftliche Buchgesellschaft 2003), 11–25.

Protestant Christianities, on the other, the term *tradition* plays a more crucial role in feminist discussions of the linguistic areas predominantly shaped by Catholicism (i.e., Spanish, Italian), since in this research context tradition is placed side by side with the Scriptures. What follows thus applies primarily to those contexts.

3.1. Tradition as Reception History of the Faith

The category of tradition is very closely tied to that of *reception*.[34] Both must be discussed by The Bible and Women. Reception history of the Bible is also a history of *the reception of faith*, which especially in Catholicism is based on the passing on of *the* tradition, whose only legitimate carriers (for a long time) were men.

3.1.1. On the Status of Women in the Formation of Tradition

To transmit does not mean continuously conveying something that is eternally the same; on the contrary, what is passed on is exposed to a necessary process of change. This applies both in terms of the selection of what is passed on and in terms of the direction of the actualization throughout the process, which is driven at all times by the governing forces of the group passing on the tradition.[35] Which perspectives in the Bible and in its interpretation become dominant and which become marginalized is, when it comes to gender relations in religious communities, above all a question of power.

Since women in Western culture were not legal subjects until hundred years or so ago (and in some countries even later), they were hardly able to leave memorable traces in the official historiography or as interpreters of the Bible. Nevertheless, some women did read and interpret the Bible and became focal points for traditions, since they defied the "property right" of men, who as the guardians of orthodoxy selected some traditions that today are seen as *the* tradition. The current editorial project intends to bring to light and analyze the traditions of many women, constructed and passed on at the margins of the official tradition. In biblical studies, *traditio* is understood to be

---

34. Tradition, from the Latin *tradere*, composed of *tra* (beyond, the other side) and *dere* (give), replaces the concept *mancipatio* in the Roman law, first in reference to the transmission of property and then to the rights.

35. The fact that the poor do not have a historiography has been considered a problem since the beginning of feminist theology and its adoption of the concepts of liberation theology; see Elisabeth Schüssler Fiorenza, *Bread, Not Stone: The Challenge of Feminist Biblical Interpretation* (Boston: Beacon, 1984), 102–4.

an oral and/or written process that passes on, from generation to generation, one's predecessors' fundamental recollections of the faith. This process, with a pretext of faithfulness, always developed within a particular community and its culture. In the meanderings of this process, as in the course of rivers, there are many tributaries, some of which supply while others drain. In the transmission of collective memory, in the narratives and in the habits, there are hidden emotional, political, and ideological aspects that determine what must or must not be remembered and transmitted, who can be responsible for the transmission, what must be done and with what aim, which pieces of transmission should be legally binding and which should remain peripheral. This process carries with it traces of strife and resistance and leads the term *tradition* back to its double meaning: the act of transmission itself and the transmitted contents.

3.1.2. The Act of Transmission: Women as Agents

Even when the act of transmission was for a long time officially attributed to men, women in fact also participated in transmission, since the act of transmission is closely related to the psychosocial process of *identity* formation. The patriarchal system considers the act of transmission as *cultural* formation. Accordingly, tradition is identified with the guiding lines of a culture that, until just a few centuries ago, were inseparable from religion. Such a patriarchal understanding of an official transmission hides yet another unofficial aspect of the act of transmission, the one that is carried out by women. In this living process of transmission we find two apparently contradictory lines. According to the first one, the women, as products of a socialization into patriarchy, carry patriarchal culture, identity, and tradition. According to the second one, women *simultaneously* transmit *as tradition* also particular traditions that are usually identified with women. The critical feminist perspective seeks, with great analytical force, to distinguish between these two lines, to relate them to each other, and, in some cases, to oppose them to one another. Feminist biblical exegesis of the past century well accounts for this and, consequently, also of the history of women within the studies of gender and of feminist theory.

3.1.3. Who Transmits What? Women as Active and Passive Subjects of Tradition

Exegetes and feminist historians of the Bible have, already for decades, worked hard to identify the traces of women and their resistance in the main traditions and to use these traces against women's invisibility and marginalization in face of these same traditions. They have sought to analyze critically the processes of transmission and reception that gave the biblical texts the form in which they reached us today. It appears that women have been active agents as biblical texts emerged, as well as in their reception, even if their traces are not easy to recover.

The role of women in the processes from the emergence of the texts, through the process of definition of canonical scriptures, and to the adaptation of traditions into authoritative tradition is today the subject of great controversy. Athalya Brenner and Fokkelien Van-Dijk-Hemmes have used the distinction of male-voices and female-voices, which appear in the biblical texts, to analyze the social groups passing on biblical materials.[36] With this notion, they have detached the question of the emergence of the biblical texts from questions about particular authors and their gender. We wonder whether such hermeneutical attempts could not also be useful for a larger part of the biblical reception that was not initially conceived as *Autorenliteratur* (literature by authors).

The project The Bible and Women is particularly interested in critically analyzing the androcentric processes of the transmission and thereby itself becoming a part of the chain of transmission. The roles of women in the creation and reception of the biblical traditions of Judaism and Christianity should no longer be concealed. The project wants to relate, in detail, the story of women's reception with its bright notes and more obscure dimensions. So, it is meant to be a lucid guide for those who want to see themselves as part of the chain of transmission in which both women and men have participated. We believe that in this way, on the basis of our critical scholarly contribution with its multilingual, international, multicultural, and interconfessional facets, we will contribute to the creation of a more egalitarian tradition and a more complete and adequate reception of our very rich cultural heritage.

3.1.4. Fragile and Strong Traditions

The traditions of a culture, a people, or a religion are certainly part of a collective human capital. Their shared characteristics are their historical conditioning and, hence, their capacity to develop. This capacity, as history shows, is paradoxical. A solid tradition with deep roots is not immobile; it is not a fragile treasure exhibited for passive contemplation and under the protection of those who preserve it from ruin. A solid tradition is, on the contrary, one that

---

36. Athalya Brenner and Fokkelien van Dijk-Hemmes, *On Gendering Texts: Female and Male Voices in the Hebrew Bible* (Biblical Interpretation Series 1; Leiden: Brill, 1997).

does not fear the moves that its own historical condition pushes it to make. When we speak about tradition with regard to the Bible, we are referring to this concept of necessary adaptation. In the Bible there is not one unified tradition but rather several great lines of tradition, and the greater they are, the more frequently they have been exposed to—and integrated—modifications and changes. Consequently, a really strong tradition is characterized by its paradoxical nature because it grows stronger as it adjusts to new situations that imply change, and through change it acquires the capacity to stimulate further mutations.

The Bible and Women acknowledges the studies both of women inside the traditions who see tradition as support and also of those who regard the tradition as an enemy and opponent. It analyses those basic elements of tradition that originated with women and that have endured changes because they are, and have been, promoters of further transformations in the Bible as well as in the entire history of reception.

3.2. Exegesis as Reception

The interpretation of Scripture was, for a long time, a field for those religious communities who recognized the Bible as authoritative Scripture. Exegesis as scholarship is today, in most cases, still confessionally tied on a personal or institutional level; however, it does not interpret texts primarily according to pastoral needs but according to scholarly, transparent rules.

3.2.1. From the Prehistory of the Text to Its Aftermath

If the Western tradition of research during the past couple of centuries above all dealt with the prehistory of the biblical text, starting from the postulated oral beginnings and ending with the emergence of the final form of the canonical text defined with all the rules of the exegetical art, over the past decades the research questions have shifted more and more toward an area largely neglected for a long time: *reception research*. This research is interested not only in what the biblical texts might have meant in their original context and how they interact with the ideologies of the time of their emergence (historical-critical research) but also in what they have been taken to mean and how they have been used, inculturated—and abused. It is clear that interest in reception history is finally also establishing itself more firmly in biblical studies (after colleagues in literary and art history have been pursuing this approach for a long time), from the emergence of a great many new multivolume reference works and series such as The Bible through the

Centuries[37] and *The Encyclopedia of the Bible and Its Reception*.[38] Reflections on the reception history of a text are now regularly included even in mainstream traditional biblical commentary series.[39]

The term that now gradually reaches consensus, "reception history," is usually understood as wider than the previous notions of "history of exegesis" or "history of interpretation," which mainly meant the academic understanding and appropriation of the texts in question, something in the direction of "history of research." The term *Wirkungsgeschichte* (the German term is used even in English, or alternatively "effective history") presupposed, to a too great extent, that the Bible was the source of clear and identifiable effects in culture and society. With the development of the field in question, it was, on the one hand, gradually realized that if we mean that the Bible has "effects," then we need measures to pin down and demonstrate the extent to which something is an effect of the Bible rather than of a myriad of other factors. Without such measures, the term will be too slippery to be a useful analytical tool.[40] On the other hand, this is a lot to ask if one wants to *understand* the

---

37. David Gunn, Judith Kovacs, Christopher Rowland and John Sawyer are editors of the series The Bible through the Centuries (Oxford: Blackwell, 2003–). Since the focus is on historical readings and the uses and effects of biblical texts, this series constitutes a radical departure from the norms of the biblical commentary tradition. Still, typical of a more Protestant Christian tradition, the series is structured like a biblical commentary series, in that one volume is devoted to each of the books of the Bible (with some exceptions for minor books/letters). In other European languages, there is an Italian series with an encyclopedic scope currently being published under the title La Bibbia nella Storia, edited by Giuseppe Barbaglio for the publishing house Dehoniane in Bologna. In French, already in the 1980s (1984–1989) the publishing house Beauchesne in Paris published the eight-volume encyclopedia *Bible de tous les temps*, structured according to historical periods.

38. Hans-Josef Klauck et al., eds., *The Encyclopedia of the Bible and Its Reception* (Berlin: de Gruyter, 2010–).

39. See, e.g., Herders Theologischer Kommentar zum Alten Testament, whose concept was developed over a ten-year period, and whose volumes now appear successively by Herder-Verlag, Freiburg. See also some of the volumes of the Evangelisch-Katholischer Kommentar (Neukirchen-Vluyn: Neukirchener), esp. Ulrich Luz, *Das Evangelium nach Matthäus* (EKKNT 1; 4 vols.; Neukirchen-Vluyn: Neukirchener, 1985–2002), and Wolfgang Schrage, *Der erste Brief an die Korinther* (EKKNT 7; 4 vols.; Benziger: Zürich 1991–2008) and the NIGTC (Grand Rapids: Eerdmans), esp. Anthony Thiselton's volume on 1 Corinthians.

40. See, e.g., Heikki Räisänen, "The Effective 'History' of the Bible: A Challenge to Biblical Scholarship," *Scottish Journal of Theology* 45 (1992): 303; Ulrich Luz, *Mt 1–7* (vol. 1 of *Das Evangelium nach Matthäus*; 5th ed.; EKKNT 1.1; Neukirchen-Vluyn: Neukirchener, 2002), 106–8; John Sawyer, "The Place of Reception-History in a Post-Modern Bible Commentary." Online: http://www.bbibcomm.net/news/sawyer.html.

workings of authoritative texts in historical societies. Colleagues from disciplines other than biblical studies especially have particularly made it clear that a study of history *as* an effective history of the Bible can easily develop into a rather reductionist historical project. In illiterate cultures, as well as in modern cultural expressions, biblical books are rarely experienced as discrete entities. In a Christian setting at least, it would be extremely difficult to pin down the effects of the book of Genesis as distinct from the effects of the Gospel of Matthew. An adequate reception history must allow for this fact instead of continuing to beg for consistency in messy material. Although the term "reception history" may be analytically less sharp, it is more sensitive to the nuances of the workings of the biblical text in different social and cultural areas, which is probably the reason why the term has been preferred in the most recent and most ambitious reference works, including works also of aesthetic, legal, or representative value. This term is furthermore acceptable to scholars outside the discipline of biblical studies. The term is, finally, particularly apt when working on women's encounters with biblical texts: since through long periods women have not had access to formal training or formal office, their readings would not then count as "interpretation" or "exegesis." As women have had limited access to power, their readings would seldom result in measurable social, political, or cultural effects. Still, women have read and used the Bible, and some have been privileged enough to leave traces in print and paint, or otherwise. All of this can be studied under the inclusive concept of "reception history."

3.2.2. On The Multiple Meanings of the Texts and the Role of Readers in the Creation of Meaning

Thus we see how the changing terminological choices reflect developments and an accumulation of knowledge in the field as such. Greater knowledge of the variety of ways historical readers have responded to the biblical texts has expanded our understanding of the history of the texts. Indeed, it has also expanded our understanding of the texts themselves, their meanings, and their workings. First, the more one sees how real audiences have responded, the better guesses scholars will be qualified to make concerning how original audiences may have responded. For this reason, scholars with a primary interest in the origins of the text in question should also pay more attention to its reception history. Second, it has become clearer that the meaning of canonized texts is a result of interaction between the texts and their readers and that even if one operates with a closed concept of canon there can never be a completion or closure of meanings of this canon. When we take all the different things readers and recipients can do to the Bible into serious consideration, it becomes clear that it is not a closed, separate entity that has had separate and identifiable effects but rather a living text kept alive by the recipients' constant re-creation of it. For this reason, the term "reception history" and the notion of text, canon, and tradition that it entails bring to the fore a range of methodological questions and challenges that will not be consistently pursued in this interdisciplinary project proper, because the challenges will be different according to the disciplinary angle and because the most urgent need is to present the *material*. Instead, the theoretical and methodological questions are relegated to specialized forums associated with the project and further discussed there.[41] Reception history, then, is not an exercise in cataloguing; it is not reductionist and mono-causal history-writing; nor is it merely a descriptive overview of the authoritative readings of particular biblical texts by pillars such as Rashi, Aquinas, or Luther. These obviously deserve a place, but the picture is much larger and far more complicated than that.

Even if reception history gives us a better and more concrete grasp of how the biblical texts have worked to produce meaning historically, we do not see a reception-historical endeavor as primarily a way of getting at what the biblical texts' original intention was. This encyclopedia could rather be seen as a gender-inclusive display room of what the reception history of the Bible might *also* be if we include a focus on the reception of gender-relevant texts and interpretations generated by women. Some of the interpretations considered here might be written off as exotica by some, but we maintain that they can contribute to new gender-inclusive syntheses. They represent, in fact, an untapped world that we believe biblical scholars should pay more attention to, rather than continuing to inhabit only a small part of the "museum" and interacting only with a limited range of male interpreters usually considered authoritative.

Thus far, all larger-scale reception-historical encyclopedias, series, and projects have failed to include gender among the basic structuring categories of the project in question[42]—if it has been reflected upon at all. This is partly

---

41. See, e.g., the proceedings of the Norwegian Research Council–funded project Canonicity, Gender and Critique: The Hermeneutics of Feminism and Canon Transformations, which sponsored parts of the encyclopedia but especially focuses on theory and method: http://www.stk.uio.no/English/canonicity.html. See further William John Lyons and Jorunn Økland, eds., *The Way the World Ends? The Apocalypse of John in Culture and Ideology* (Sheffield: Sheffield Phoenix, 2009). In the introduction to that volume (1–30), Økland expands further on many of the points presented in short form here.

42. A structural exception is the series edited by Giuseppe Barbaglio mentioned above, La Bibbia nella Storia, in which a volume edited by Adriana Valerio has appeared, *Donne e Bibbia: Storia ed esegesi* (La Bibbia nella Storia 21; Bologna: Edizione Dehoniane, 2006), to which also the other three general editors of this research project contribute. In

due to the reception historians' sources: through most of European/Western history, it was predominantly men who had access to reading, writing, and positions of interpretive authority. Mainly men's interpretations of the Bible were transmitted, and the result of the elimination of the corrective voice that women might have represented is that the body of preserved interpretations contains an inevitable androcentric focus. This androcentric focus has consequences both for the way reception historians approach "women-texts" (biblical texts with particular relevance for women) and also for if and how they present women as exegetes. A feminist reception history of biblical texts of particular relevance to women has yet to be written, likewise a history of women's biblical readings.

3.3. Questions for Further Research

The Bible does not have a uniform model of sexed human existence, nor has it just one conception of how the relationship between the sexes should be organized. In order to account for different views, can social places be reconstructed in which discussions around gender roles and models took place? How do changes in social conditions affect the reception of such texts? When and under which conditions are egalitarian concepts actualized and when are hierarchical ones? Can the developments of theological anthropologies and their legitimizing reference to the Bible be incorporated into social history? Reception history does not follow a straight course. Some topics are especially popular in certain periods only to then disappear again completely. Particularly eloquent examples are the queen of Sheba in the Middle Ages or the representation of Judith in Italian baroque painting. How do such "fashions" arise, and why do they disappear?

These tasks and questions, to which the project will have to dedicate itself, make it clear that the history of interpretation of biblical texts is not simply the history of influence or tradition but rather a reception history. What is judged relevant and what is left aside, which topics or literary figures are used and which message is to be mediated in each case, all of this depends on the determinations of particular periods and is neither simply an effect of great texts nor the product of a tradition never closed or broken off.

Finally, we are also aware of the ecclesiological and theological consequences of this project. Although the project does not directly address problems of this kind, we cannot ignore that the kind of exploration of the sacred

---

this volume, a history of women's biblical interpretation is presented separately from "general" history, and thereby the volume defends a compensationalist claim.

texts and of tradition presented here reopens central questions that should occupy theological research at large: the relation between revelation and history; the issue of a more gender-inclusive liturgical language; ecclesiological questions about the lived relations between men and women within faith communities; delicate and intimate ethical and pastoral matters that in the past have received a biblical justification that is no longer considered a viable answer in today's gender-democratic societies. Finally, even the question of how to adequately "narrate" the biblical God must be posed again if the human as man and woman, with equal worth, was created in God's image.

Through this project, a thematically closed overview of gender-relevant questions with regard to the Bible and its reception history is presented for the first time. We are conscious of the problem that many of the fields on which we depend have in no way been scientifically treated yet and that, as the work progresses, new questions for research arise. But this challenging situation can also be seen in a positive light, in that it can initiate new research projects. We hope that, through the international and interdisciplinary network established, this large-scale project will also recruit many young scholars into theological and cultural historical gender research. We want to close with the Norwegian feminist author Aasta Hansteen, who when faced with the new and vast oceans of possibilities in feminist interpretation exclaimed already in 1870 (lecture published some years later):

> I am not a woman of letters, and I do not pretend to be one. I am a settler instead. As a woman forcing myself upon the religious-philosophical terrain … I therefore possess the settler's great advantage: I can acquire thousands of acres of land, yes, enormous stretches, just by drawing a line in the ground.[43]

---

43. Aasta Hansteen, *Kvinden skabt I Guds Billede* (Kristiania: Foredrag i Studenters-amfundet, 1878), 4-32, translated by Jorunn Økland.

Ancient Near Eastern Pictures as Keys to Biblical Texts

Silvia Schroer
Institut für Bibelwissenschaft, Universität Bern

The biblical texts are testimonies of an ancient Near Eastern culture. Palestine/ Israel was not an island in the ancient Orient but rather a constitutive part of it, implicated in the lively exchange with the great surrounding cultures in Mesopotamia, Anatolia, Syria, and Egypt. Following expeditions and excavations in the nineteenth century that rediscovered these cultures, biblical scholarship found itself challenged to study the multiple relations between these cultures and the biblical text.[1] Scholars discovered, for example, that the story of the flood (Gen 6–9) had literary predecessors in Mesopotamian mythology. The work of the schools of religious history, created at the end of the nineteenth century, which devoted their efforts especially to studying the religions in the Near East and their influence on the Bible, was virtually halted by the two World Wars in the twentieth century. New interest in the elements common to the biblical and old oriental traditions only reappeared in the 1960s. Alongside the texts, pictures now entered the researchers' field of vision.

Religious sentiment and ideas are documented exclusively by images for a few periods that predate writing. A majority of the population, in all probability, did not have access to literature, but people did wear pendants around their necks, brought small images of the gods home from the temples, or placed amulets for their dead in the tombs. Even if the monumental and majestic art in a relatively small and poor country such as Palestine/Israel was not widespread, miniature art forms were in many hands. The images became popular, and, since arts and crafts in the entire ancient Near East were

---

1. For a more detailed presentation of this development, see Othmar Keel and Silvia Schroer, *Schöpfung: Biblische Theologien im Kontext altorientalischer Religionen* (2nd ed.; Göttingen: Vandenhoeck & Ruprecht, 2008), 15–19.

principally the work of artisans, they were closely tied to tradition. Art influenced not only art but also writing. Biblical texts refer to concrete imagery, for example, the golden calf (Exod 32) or the serpent of bronze (Num 21).[2] Yet such references can be subtle; that is, we need to know the images being cited in order to understand the allusion in the text. In Isaiah's vision of Israel's God surrounded by six-winged seraphs (Isa 6), the sense of this image becomes clear only in the light of the four-winged seraphs on Judean seals at this time.[3] In the case of the description of God as shepherd and Lord of five pairs of wild animals in the book of Job (38–39), an ancient Near Eastern tradition picturing the "Master of the animals" represents an important approach for understanding God's discourse.[4] Let us note that our approach does not concern the illustrations of everyday life—equally revealing and very important—and of the Israelite culture in general as depicted in the contemporary art (on this, see Carol Meyer's contribution) but rather normative pictorial conceptions that can throw light on the biblical texts.

The keys to a deeper understanding of the texts contained in the imagery are particularly important for women and gender-conscious readings of the Bible.[5] Biblical texts are often androcentric. Hence, they do not present the reality of an ancient culture and the experiences of humans but at best glimpses of life, culture, and religion. They are, above all, reflections of the conceptions and projections of the authors, or circles, that transmit a particular writing. The pictures can relativize, complete, or even contradict the texts' assertions. For example, the First Testament always mentions goddesses in a polemical sense or rejects them. Only with the help of iconography does it become possible to reconstruct the cults to goddesses in Palestine/Israel in the first millennium B.C.E.[6] On the other hand, the condition for an exact

---

2. See Silvia Schroer, *In Israel gab es Bilder: Nachrichten von darstellender Kunst im Alten Testament* (OBO 74; Fribourg: Universitätsverlag; Göttingen: Vandenhoeck & Ruprecht, 1987).

3. Othmar Keel, *Jahwe-Visionen und Siegelkunst: Eine neue Deutung der Majestätsschilderungen in Jes 6, Ez 1 und 10 und Sach 4* (SBS 84/85; Stuttgart: Katholisches Bibelwerk, 1977).

4. Othmar Keel, *Jahwes Entgegnung an Ijob: Eine Deutung von Ijob 38–41 vor dem Hintergrund der zeitgenössischen Bildkunst* (FRLANT 121; Göttingen: Vandenhoeck & Ruprecht, 1978).

5. See Silvia Schroer, "Gender and Iconography from the Viewpoint of a Feminist Biblical Scholar," *lectio difficilior* 2 (2008); online: www.lectio.unibe.ch/08_2/Silvia_Schroer_Gender_and_Iconography.html.

6. See the ground-breaking work of Urs Winter, *Frau und Göttin* (2nd ed.; OBO 54; Fribourg: Universitätsverlag; Göttingen: Vandenhoeck & Ruprecht, 1987). There are

understanding of the biblical polemics is the precise description of demarcation processes of Israelite monotheism.

The following contribution will consider a selection of texts from the Torah whose historical religious background can be illuminated with the help of iconography, which in turn allows us to recognize more clearly the theological accentuation, developments, or restrictions in the texts.

1. Let the Earth Put Forth ... (Gen 1:11–12)

The Bible's first account of creation is simultaneously a summa of biblical creation theology, an ancient Israelite cosmology, and a hymn to God the Creator.[7] This brilliant opening text is attributed to the Priestly writer (P)—the priestly circle of the late exilic or early postexilic period—who tried to formulate new foundations for the faith in the unique God after a catastrophic loss of the homeland and the temple. Genesis 1 tells how God created the inhabitable world in six days and then rested. If we compare this creation narrative to the well-known traditions of creation in the ancient Near East, the following characteristics emerge:

(1) The text takes for granted that *one* God (Elohim) is the world's creator.

(2) Through his word, God calls the ordered world, the cosmos, forth from darkness and from the *tohu wabohu* of the primordial chaos.

This model of creation, according to which the world was created through the magic of words, appears only rarely in the Bible. Nonetheless, it is also fundamental in a central account of creation attributed to the Egyptian priest of Ptah from Memphis, in the so-called Memphite Theology. Other modes of creation are not, at first sight, considered in Gen 1, neither are engenderment, birth, growth, and development (biological concepts) nor are craftsmanship (an artistic concept) or combat. Yet a second look reveals that, in the model "creation through the word," other certainly more ancient aspects from non-monotheistic models have, so to speak, endured.

The creation of light and the separation of the waters and land masses are at the beginning of God's work of creation. Hence the conditions for life are

---

methodical hermeneutical continuations in Othmar Keel and Silvia Schroer, *Eva—Mutter alles Lebendigen: Frauen- und Göttinnenidole aus dem Alten Orient* (3rd ed.; Fribourg: Academic, 2010).

7. The topics dealt with here in the context of the theology of creation are more fully presented in Keel and Schroer, *Schöpfung*, with many references to other biblical texts, scholarly publications, etc. It is not possible to give detailed references here.

prepared for plants, animals, and humans. The creation of the vegetation in 1:11–12 is not introduced, as one might expect, with a simple "Let there be"; instead, it is stated:

> Then God said, "Let the earth put forth vegetation: plants yielding seed, and fruit trees of every kind on earth that bear fruit with the seed in it." And it was so. The earth brought forth vegetation: plants yielding seed of every kind, and trees of every kind bearing fruit with the seed in it. And God saw that it was good. And there was evening and there was morning, the third day.

Here Elohim does indeed speak and command, but God then orders: "Let the earth bring forth vegetation." With the "earth," the mythical background of an "earth-goddess" clearly comes into play. In this passage, P has recourse to the goddesses of the earth and vegetation, the sovereigns of the world of vegetation, who were extremely important in Palestine/Israel. There are goddesses of vegetation with sprouting branches on the cylinder seals (fig. 1) as early as the third millennium B.C.E. They seem to be rising from the earth.

Fig. 1. Cylinder seal from Shadad near Kerma, Iran (ca. 2500 B.C.E.). In the center of the seal impression, we can see an earth-goddess; the upper part of her body rises from the earth, and, at the same time, branch-like growths sprout from her, where the animals (left-hand side of the picture) live (see Gen 1:11–12:24). On the right side, the same goddess may well be represented with her full human physique. (Keel and Schroer, *Schöpfung*, fig. 18)

The typical Canaanite tree-goddess of the first half of the first millennium B.C.E. also practically rises from the earth. She is either surrounded by branches or holds them in her hands, and sometimes her genitals are decorated with leaves or branches (fig. 2). The underlying tradition of an earth-goddess, fecundated by a sky-god, so that she may give birth to the plants, is well-attested in texts from Mesopotamia. In the Sumerian Debate between Tree and Reed, the birth of the vegetation is still clearly a consequence of the copulation of the earth with the sky-god:

Fig. 2. Scarab from Gezer (1650–1550 B.C.E.). The stamp seal shows a naked goddess, with a side view of her head. Both to the right and to the left she holds aloft a branch or tree. The branches seem to rest directly on the feet of the goddess. The prominent aspects of this picture are the navel, the necklace, the girdle, and the two branches that sprout from her pudenda. The association of the pubic triangle and the branch is attested by the imagery from the Near East since approximately the third millennium B.C.E. (Keel and Schroer, *Schöpfung*, fig. 22)

6. And, the sublime sky-god, copulated with broad earth ...
9. the earth stepped forth joyful to bear "the plants of life."[8]

The biblical text includes this biological conception but dexterously subordinates it to Elohim's creating word. Nevertheless, the power of the older conceptions remains apparent in the fact that the earth is the subject of the bearing.

2. THE MOTHER OF ALL THE LIVING (GEN 1:24; 3:20)

After the rhythm of day-night was established with the sun and the luminaries of the night on the fourth day, and after the creation of all the living beings in the waters on the fifth day of creation, the creation of the animals of the earth begins in Gen 1:24: "And God said, 'Let the earth bring forth living creatures of every kind.'" However, in contrast with Gen 1:11–12, it is not simply stated that the earth brought forth living beings; rather, the description unexpectedly includes God himself "making" the animals. This "making" is reminiscent of how YHWH, in 2:19, creates the animals by forming them out of clay. Despite this inconsistency, it cannot be denied that the earth as "mother of all the living" is still present in these verses. Goddesses are often depicted as patrons of flocks or sovereigns of animals (fig. 3; see below on

Fig. 3. Ivory relief from Minet el-Beida, the port of Ugarit (fourteenth century B.C.E.). A mountain goddess feeds two wild billy goats that flank her or stand up at the goddess's throne on the mountain. (Keel, *Deine Blicke sind Tauben*, fig. 11)

---

8. Quoted and translated into English from Willem H. P. Römer, "Der Prolog des Streitgespräches zwischen Holz und Rohr" (lines 1–29), *TUAT* 3.3:357–60.

Deut 28:4). In Gen 3:20, the honorific title "mother of all the living" is given to Eve, the first woman created. The great consciousness and importance, in the Priestly text, of growing and thriving, of engendering, conceiving, and giving birth as the background for the creation of the world and the transmission of life is attested by the caption at the end of the first story of creation (Gen 2:4): "These are the generations [תולדות] of the heavens and the earth."

3. God as Potter and Artisan, or Woman as Art Product (Gen 2:4–25)

Genesis 2:4–25 contains a creation narrative that has been traditionally identified with the label "Yahwist" (J). The mode of creation chosen here is craftsmanship: God works as potter. Technical conceptions of creation appear quite often in the First Testament. Israel's God is, for example, also occupied as master builder, erecting columns and laying a roof; God already forms or weaves humans in the womb. Likewise, in Mesopotamia, the participating deities use clay to create humans. Yet how does clay become a living being? In the Mesopotamian Atrahasis Epic, from the eighteenth century B.C.E., the blood of a murdered god is the life-giving elixir. According to Gen 2:7, YHWH breathes the breath of life into the nose of the being formed from the dust of the earth in order to make it a living being. This transformation cannot happen without divine input. Egyptian depictions show the creator-god Khnum making the royal child and its *ka* (life-force) on a potter's wheel even before it reaches maturity in the womb. The vivification is then the work of the goddess Hathor, who places the symbol for life, *ankh*, directly under the nose of the child (fig. 4).

The second creation story is not a general cosmology but rather the story of the creation of humans in the context of a short narrative of the world's

Fig. 4. Part of a relief, dated in the Roman period, from the maternity house in Dendera. Still in the Roman period, the god Khnum is represented making the royal child, whom the queen conceived from the god Amun, upon the potter's wheel, while the enthroned goddess Hathor extends the sign of *ankh* to him in order to make him a living being. (Keel and Schroer, *Schöpfung*, fig. 105)

Fig. 5. Neolithic statue (6700 B.C.E.) from 'Ain-Ghazal in Jordan, clay-lime mixture over reed or rush with traces of paint. The materials attest to the attempt to imitate human bones and flesh. The discovery of this, along with other similar virtually life-size sculptures in a deposit of the settlement, is almost certainly related to the cult of the ancestors, which was central in this period. (Schroer and Keel, *Vom ausgehenden Mesolithikum bis zur Frühbronzezeit*, no. 45)

creation. The main accent is on the creation of the woman. When God himself is obliged to recognize that the earthling Adam (without specification of gender) is alone and lonely, the creation of animals is intended to help. This attempt ultimately fails, and only the creation of the woman is greeted with jubilation by Adam. She is not formed, like the animals, out of clay; instead, God takes a part of Adam's body and uses it to build the woman. This procedure evokes the production, in the Neolithic period, of clay figures that were often sculptured around a cane framework (fig. 5). The relationship between the two human beings is then sealed: "This at last is bone of my bones and flesh of my flesh" (Gen 2:23).

4. Eve, the Serpent, and the Sacred Tree (Gen 3)

The story of the so-called fall of humanity in Gen 3 has a history of persistent misogynistic interpretation. In the first centuries of Christianity, particular attention was already paid to the rapport between Eve and the serpent. Both are demonized and appear as Satan's helpers, although the latter does not figure in the biblical account of the transgression. The *Wirkungsgeschichte* concerning this point cannot be discussed in this chapter.[9] However, it must be asked whether iconography provides indications as to why the woman in this story is placed in a closer rapport with the serpent than the man. Which traditions made this proximity plausible at the time the text was written? It is

9. On this subject, see Helen Schüngel-Straumann, *Die Frau am Anfang: Eva und die Folgen* (2nd ed.; Exegese in unserer Zeit 6; Münster: LIT, 1997).

notable that, in the Near East, serpents often appear with goddesses (fig. 6). The Canaanite Qudshu/Qedeshet, "the Holy One," frequently holds serpents; on Egyptian stelae, she holds them out to the god of healing, Resheph (fig. 7).

Fig. 6 (below left). Golden pendant from Minet el-Beida, the port of Ugarit (ca. 1350 B.C.E.). A largely frontal representation of an erotic goddess, with a pretty, curly, shoulder-length hairstyle. She is standing on a lion that is stepping to the left. In the pose of the mistress of animals, she lifts two goats up onto their hind legs. Two serpents cross behind her broad hips. (Keel, *Deine Blicke sind Tauben*, fig. 20)

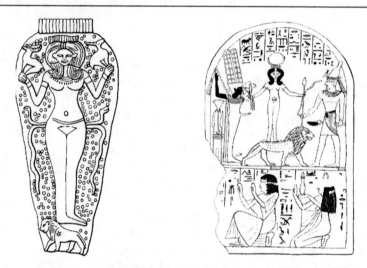

Fig. 7 (above right). Egyptian stela from Deir el-Medina. The naked goddess, with a Hathor hairstyle, upon the lion (according to the inscription Qudshu/Qedeshet, "the Holy One") extends lotus flowers to the fertility god, Min, and a serpent to the martial god, Resheph. Resheph, like Qudshu, was not Egyptian but originated in the Near East and was considered not only a dangerous bringer of epidemics but also a powerful aide against disease. The serpents embody the same ambivalence: they can become lethal yet, at the same time, effectively protect against danger. In the lower part of the picture, the person donating the stela and his wife are represented in a gesture of admiration. (Keel, *Deine Blicke sind Tauben*, fig. 22)

Serpents in symbolism are ambiguous: they incarnate vitality as well as danger, healing as well as death.[10] The biblical narrative also permits the serpent to act with ambivalence: it proclaims God's omniscience but, finally, provokes great damage and restricts human living conditions.

---

10. On the symbolism of the serpent in Palestine/Israel, see Othmar Keel, *Das Recht der Bilder gesehen zu werden* (OBO 122; Fribourg: Universitätsverlag; Göttingen: Vandenhoeck & Ruprecht, 1992), 195–266.

The (sacred) tree is another motif in the story that evokes themes in art. The tree in the middle of the garden is made taboo by YHWH. Consequently, it is especially sacred. Any forbidden direct contact with the sacred can be deadly (cf. the story of the holy ark and Uzzah in 2 Sam 6:1–11). The first human couple transgresses this taboo, but they do not die immediately. In contradiction to the serpent's prediction, they find themselves definitively in the state of mortality and subject to heavy sanctions. We can imagine that Gen 3 refers to representations depicting the goddess and her partner, the weather-god, as protectors of the stylized tree of the cosmic order (fig. 8). While the weather-god kills the menacing serpent of chaos, the goddess blesses the tree that symbolizes the world to be protected, especially the vegetation. In the biblical narrative, Adam and Eve fail; they do not sanctify and protect the tree, nor do they ward off the serpent.

Fig. 8. Classical Syrian cylinder seal (1850–1700 B.C.E.). An aggressive god with a horn crown crosses over two mountain peaks. In his left hand, he holds a dagger aloft; with his right hand, he drives his spear down the throat of a half-erect serpent. His partner, the naked goddess, stands on a pedestal, at the same height as the god. She lifts a protective hand over the stylized world-tree in the center. The tree may embody the ordered world, whose existence is guaranteed, on the one hand, by the protection of the goddess and, on the other hand, by the weather-god, who successfully fought off chaos in the form of the threatening serpent (Rahab, Leviathan). The serpent symbolizes the threatening flood waters that the weather-god brings under control. (Keel and Schroer, *Schöpfung*, fig. 20)

5. Justice or Compassion? The Gender Sign of Divine Conduct

YHWH, the God of Israel, is experienced as just but also as compassionate. It is evident that these two characteristics can enter into strong competition in concrete circumstances. Should God accomplish justice, that is, punish malefactors, or place grace before justice and renounce punishment one more time? The tension in the image of God persists throughout the entire Bible, including the New Testament. In the book of Genesis, two traditions in particular elucidate each of these traits of God.[11]

Genesis 19 tells how Lot was saved. The malice and violence of the inhabitants of Sodom literally cry up to heaven and provoke God's intervention and decision to destroy the city. At sunrise, God's messengers strongly advise Lot, the sole righteous man, to hurriedly flee the city with his wife and children. Fire and sulfur quickly destroy Sodom and the entire surrounding region. YHWH appears in this narrative in the tradition of the sun-god Shamash, the ancient Near Eastern god of rights and justice. When he appears in the morning, malefactors are destroyed; the sun-god throws devouring fire upon the earth. Shamash is depicted on the seals of the Akkadian period (ca. 2300 B.C.E.) as triumphant between mountain peaks (fig. 9) or seated on his throne at the doors of heaven (fig. 10).

Fig. 9 (left). Cylinder seal of the Akkadian period (2350–2150 B.C.E.). With a powerful bound, the sun-god Shamash appears between the mountaintops. He is characterized by flames radiating from his shoulders and by his typical feature, the saw. The mountains are mythicized by the two gate posts decorated with lions. Three divine aides function as gate guards. Two of them throw open the gates of the east for Shamash. (Keel and Schroer, *Schöpfung*, fig. 50)

Fig. 10 (above). Cylinder seal of the Akkadian period, found in Jerusalem (2350–2150 B.C.E.). This important scroll seal was found in a Jerusalemite grave (eighth–sixth century B.C.E.). By that time, the valuable engraving was already an antiquity. In the center of the pictorial composition, the sun-god Shamash is again represented; here, however he is depicted as a sovereign between the opened sky gates, sitting upon a throne, an attitude typical of Shamash as judge. (Keel and Schroer, *Schöpfung*, fig. 51)

---

11. See Keel and Schroer, *Schöpfung*, 77–80, 192–95.

He is also frequently represented as presiding in scenes of judgment and sometimes shown with the scale of justice that is still proverbial today (fig. 11).

In the version of the flood narrative in Gen 6–9, written by the same group of authors as the second creation story, YHWH finds the wickedness of humankind to have become excessive (Gen 6:5–6) and decides to destroy virtually all life on earth. Humans, animals of the earth, and birds perish in the flood. We are very familiar with this narrative under other titles and with differing details in Mesopotamia. There the belligerent Enlil, the father of the gods, causes the deluge because he is annoyed by the noise of the humans, who are multiplying. All the stories of the deluge contain a "Noah" who can save himself in an ark because he has an ally in the divided community of the gods. In the biblical version, YHWH offers salvation to this single righteous man. Noah, with his family and the rescued animals, survives the deluge. Subsequently, God surprisingly takes an oath never again to destroy the earth in such a manner because of humans, who remain wicked, just as before (Gen 8:21–22). What provoked this change? The ancient Babylonian sources indicate that the goddess Ishtar made a similar oath because, as creator of humans, she never again wants to see them lying dead in the waters. The impulse reflects an affection often mentioned in the biblical texts with respect to humans, that is, the compassion that is attributed primarily to women because they give life. Such gender attributions are problematic from a feminist point of view. However, this biblical text, among others, attests to the fact that characteristics attributed to masculine and feminine deities in the surrounding polytheistic world were introduced into the Israelite image of God. God punishes (like Enlil), makes exceptions (like Ishtar), and regrets his action (like Ishtar). The feminine part, solicitude for life and compassion, endures in the

Fig. 11. Cylinder seal of the Akkadian period (2250–2150 b.c.e.). On the right-hand side, the sun-god is enthroned on a pedestal. He is holding his attribute, the saw. From the left, a priest approaches with the balance of justice in the hand, which he presents to the god upon a small altar. Behind him stands a worshiper with a kid in his arms, intended as a sacrifice. We cannot recognize what the smaller shape behind the worshiper is doing. (Keel and Schroer, *Schöpfung*, fig. 53)

representations of goddesses depicted with the womb sign. Life comes from their wombs; they nourish and certainly continue to care for beings, including those who do not come into the world and who quickly return to the earth (figs. 12–13). Inanna-Ishtar is a typical mother-goddess in the third to second millennium B.C.E. In First Testament anthropology, the womb (רחם) is associated with compassion (רחמים). It takes hold not only of women but also of men at times—and even God. Compassion for a creature or the people of Israel shakes his innermost organs and keeps YHWH from executing justice.[12]

Fig. 12. Old Babylonian terracotta relief from Tell Asmar (ca. 1800 B.C.E.). The relieved plate shows a goddess, pacing to the left, wearing a so-called tiered garment with a headdress that resembles the entry of a shrine or temple. She carries a baby at her right breast, which is not covered by the dress. In her lifted right hand, she holds an unidentifiable article. Above her shoulders, on each side, a human being, possibly a child, raises his or her head. The goddess can be associated with types of the mother goddess attested to in the texts, such as Ninhursanga or Nintu(r) because she is flanked by two large Ω-shaped signs and two shrunken childlike shapes, sitting at her feet. The latter are possibly embryos, miscarriages, or premature births. Their wandering spirits were greatly feared in ancient Mesopotamia. Perhaps the Ω signs above them bear their disastrous effects. (Winter, *Frau und Göttin*, fig. 390)

Fig. 13. Scarab from Tell el-Farʻa north (ca. 1750 B.C.E.). In north Syrian Anatolia and in Palestine, very small faience stamp seals were found; their lower surface is worked in raised relief, not, as is usual, in sunken relief. The Ω sign is an important motif of this group. It could be a very simplified representation of the female uterus, which was simultaneously a symbol of birth and of mother goddesses. As the seals were frequently found in graves, and twice in the graves of children, it is likely that the motif was intended to guarantee protection of pregnant women, mothers, and children from these goddesses or to give the dead some of the security of the womb on their final jour-

ney. The Ω sign still seems to symbolize this maternal security for people in ancient Israel. In the biblical texts, the word for womb (רחם) corresponds to the symbol, so important for anthropology and the picture of God. (Keel and Schroer, *Schöpfung*, fig. 88)

12. See Silvia Schroer and Thomas Staubli, *Body Symbolism in the Bible* (Collegeville, Minn.: Liturgical Press, 2001), 71–81.

6. Women and the (Divine) Ancestors (Gen 31)

In Gen 31:19, 34–35, Rachel steals the teraphim belonging to her father Laban when she secretly leaves her parents' home with her husband Jacob and sets out for Canaan. The teraphim in this story, also called "god" (אלהים, 'ĕlōhîm), is most likely a representation of a highly respected family ancestor. Strikingly, several biblical stories presuppose that it is women who handle these teraphim in a quite uncomplicated manner. Rachel hides the teraphim in the camel's saddle and sits on it. Michal saves her husband David from her father's messengers by putting the teraphim into David's bed as a dummy (1 Sam 19:11–16). Other biblical texts show that teraphim were used for consultations. People readily sought information and advice from their dead, probably precisely in family affairs, and women may well have been particularly active in such consultations.

The teraphim cannot be identified archeologically. Many of them were probably simple wooden figures of varying sizes. Perhaps masks were also hung on wooden poles; the existence of such masks as representations of ancestors has been attested in Palestine/Israel since the Neolithic period.[13] As early as the first half of the second millennium B.C.E., standards with one or two heads to whom in many cases women seem to offer libations appear on ancient Hittite and Syrian scroll seals (fig. 14). These standards were readily

Fig. 14. Classical Syrian cylinder seal (eighteenth–seventeenth century B.C.E.). In the main scene, a worshiper steps, with a sign of greeting, before an enthroned god. Between both figures sits a small representation of a musician playing a lyre. In a collateral scene, a woman is seen sitting on a bolster; she greets a standard with two heads or masks. This may depict the consultation of the divine being represented by the standard. (Winter, *Frau und Göttin*, fig. 72)

---

13. Silvia Schroer and Othmar Keel, *Vom ausgehenden Mesolithikum bis zur Früh-bronzezeit* (vol. 1 of *Die Ikonographie Palästinas/Israels und der Alte Orient*; Fribourg: Academic, 2005), nos. 41–42.

identified with the *semeion* mentioned by Lucian in the temple of Hierapolis; however, this argumentation, based as it is on a text from the second century B.C.E., is not compelling.

According to 1 Sam 28, competent women practiced necromancy in Israel; the teraphim ought to be situated in the context of this religious practice, which did not take place in the temple.[14]

7. With Blessings of the Breasts and of the Womb
(Gen 49; cf. Deut 33:13–14)

Life and all its good gifts come from God. The first creation narrative confirms, with a kind of refrain, that God himself found the created works to be very good. God blesses his creatures and orders the animals in the water and the humans to "be fruitful and multiply themselves." Consequently, all things created are "very good" from the outset; everything that grows and flourishes expresses God's will as Creator. The Hebrew word "blessing" (root ברך; "blessing" as noun: ברכה) is often used to refer to that which is good, about the goods of the creation.[15] The blessing is present when the harvest ripens, the hoards of small animals multiply themselves, the women are pregnant, the children are numerous, enough water is available, sleep is good, the land is at peace, and the Sabbath invites people to rest (see the concentration of blessings and maledictions in Lev 26; Deut 28). When humans bless, they acknowledge the blessing they experience themselves in all these concrete gifts, and they try to strengthen it. They bless either other people or the life-giving deity.

Genesis 49:25–26 contains an ancient benediction that Jacob uses to bless his son Joseph:

> by the Shaddai who will bless you
> with blessings of heaven above,
> blessings of the deep that lies beneath,
> blessings of the breasts and of the womb.[16]

On the one hand, the blessing comes through the rain and the spring water that irrigate the land and permit the fields to ripen. Already in the third millennium B.C.E., rain was considered the product of the collaboration of the

---

14. Silvia Schroer, "Häusliche und außerhäusliche religiöse Kompetenzen israelitischer Frauen—am Beispiel von Totenklage und Totenbefragung," *lectio difficilior* 1 (2002); online: http://www.lectio.unibe.ch/02_1/schroer.htm.

15. Keel and Schroer, *Schöpfung*, 92–97.

16. See also Deut 33:13–16 and then Luke 11:27.

earth-goddess and the weather-god; the rain was associated with the goddess and not with the god. In Syria, too, the divinities of springs are generally feminine rather than masculine. On the other hand, the blessing is associated with the breasts and the womb that can bring forth life. Full breasts have a central significance in the art of the ancient Near East from the Neolithic period onward (fig. 15). Countless feminine idols are represented presenting their breasts. This pose is primarily erotic. The breasts, independently from (one's) children, symbolize the fullness of life, the overabundance, the available nourishment.[17] Shriveled breasts are, in the First Testament, a symbol of horror (Hos 9:14). The womb, which God alone can open or close, is the guiding line in the book of Genesis. The stories of the forefathers are conducted by the theme "fertility," the desire for children, the problem of childlessness. In addition, it is striking that, before the Persian period, women are hardly ever depicted as mothers with infants. Although pregnancy was rarely and only ever discretely depicted in the ancient Near East before the Persian period, representations that unmistakably allude to conception and fertility are frequently found, as the cast figurine (fig. 16) from Revadim shows, for example.

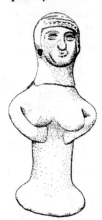

Fig. 15 (left). Small pillar figurine from Judah (eighth/seventh century B.C.E.). The blessing symbol of the Jewish population of the Iron Period IIB–C that is best attested by archaeology is the so-called pillar figurine. It represents a woman with a strongly schematized abdomen who presents her full breasts. In biblical texts, breasts are also the expression of abundant food and life. The figurines were found in many houses. Occasionally, however, they were also placed in the darkness of the tomb with the dead as a final blessing. (Keel and Schroer, *Schöpfung*, fig. 75)

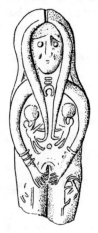

Fig. 16 (right). Clay figurine from Revadim (1250 B.C.E.). Parts of small figurines of goddesses were found at three different places in Palestine/Israel. These seem to come from the very same molding press; the most complete one, from Revadim, is shown here. The naked goddess is depicted frontally, with long hair hanging down, a moon sickle or Ω necklace and bracelets. Her hands open her pudenda. Two babies suckle at the breasts of the goddess. On both thighs, beside the vulva, palm trees figure with climbing caprids (see fig. 3). Here again, the tree is close to the pudenda of the goddess. The motif of the goats grazing on the tree is associated simultaneously with the nurturing aspects of the divine mother. (Keel and Schroer, *Schöpfung*, fig. 26)

17. Schroer and Staubli, *Die Körpersymbolik der Bibel*, 66–68.

The hoped-for fertility manifests itself in the opened pudenda of the woman, the goats beside the trees on her thighs, and the children at her breasts. Twins are also a symbol of fertility.

8. The Midwife as Companion to Life (Exod 1:15–22)

Pregnancy and birth entailed great danger for women. The fact that midwives were not only valued experts (wise women) but also had power over life and death is reflected in the biblical texts as well as in many depictions, especially from Egypt. Exodus 1 tells about the midwives Shiphrah and Puah, who disobey Pharaoh's deadly order and ingeniously find a way to save the baby boys of the Hebrew women. Some Cypriot terracotta figurines from the fifth/sixth century B.C.E. represent women in childbirth and midwives (fig. 17). The midwife was a potential savior for many women in the ancient world and, hence, also become a manifestation of a helping deity. In Egypt, birth goddesses such as the Heqet and the midwives appear in the cycles around the king's birth (fig. 18), and even the goddess of heaven, Nut, gives birth to the sun with the assistance of two midwives. Like the mourning women, midwives are not simple "earthly" figures; they receive their wisdom and their charge from the great divine powers of life. Each midwife is invested with a dignity that she does not personally produce.

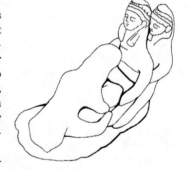

Fig. 17. Terracotta group from Karavas, Cyprus (seventh/sixth century B.C.E.). From the Cypriot Phoenician area, some terracotta pieces originate that represent women in childbirth and their midwives. The woman giving birth appears to kneel here; her back is supported by one midwife, and another sits before her. Sometimes women in childbirth are also depicted standing. (Sketch by Ulrike Zurkinden Kolberg after Ganslmayr, *Aphrodites Schwestern und christliches Zypern*, 85 above)

Fig. 18. Part of a relief from Erment near Luxor, Roman period. The queen, on her knees, gives birth to the prince, the future king. Behind her stands a midwife who holds her; in front of her, another midwife, kneeling, receives the child. The winged scarab above the newborn child symbolizes the rising sun, the sun-god. With the birth of the royal and divine child, a new sun rises over the land of Egypt. (Keel, *Die Welt der altorientalischen Bildsymbolik*, fig. 337)

9. With a Strong Hand and an Outstretched Arm: The Warring God of Exodus and the Drums of the Women (Exod 15:20–21)

In contrast to the book of Genesis, where the flourishing of the tribe and of the flocks is central, time and again, the book of Exodus tells the story of a small band of Hebrews who carry out hard labor in Egypt and miraculously flee the increasing oppression of the Pharaonic state. YHWH intervenes against the supremacy of the Egyptian king and his armed forces "with a strong hand and an outstretched arm." Thus God assumes the imperious triumphant pose of Pharaoh as he is depicted in countless Egyptian pictures (fig. 19).[18] He does not fight the Egyptian gods but the sovereigns authorized by the gods, whose violence and arrogance crumble before YHWH and the leading figures, Moses, Aaron, and Miriam, in whom he trusts. The confrontation, which is probably founded on the historical basis of a successful flight, assumes a cosmic mythological dimension in the book of Exodus and in the retrospective of many other biblical texts. In Exod 15, Aaron's sister celebrates the victory over Pharaoh by singing, thus adopting the classical role attributed to the women of Israel at the conclusion of successful wars.[19] She takes up the tambourine and stimulates jubilation, singing and dancing joyfully (Exod 15:20–21):

Fig. 19. Part of a relief from one of the rock temples in Abu Simbel (thirteenth century B.C.E.). The exaggeratedly large Pharaoh Ramses II is celebrated as victorious warrior. With a long stride, he walks over a fallen enemy who can only raise his arms in defense or perhaps in admiration. The left hand of the king seizes another adversary with an iron grasp, whose bow can no longer help him. In his right hand, drawn far back, he bears the baton or the lance. (Keel, *The Symbolism of the Biblical World*, fig. 404)

18. Othmar Keel, *The Symbolism of the Biblical World: Ancient Near Eastern Iconography and the Book of Psalms* (trans. Timothy J. Hallett; London: SPCK, 1978), esp. 291–306.

19. Instead of "intoning" the song, Miriam's response could also represent that of the entire people; see Irmtraud Fischer, *Gotteskünderinnen: Zu einer geschlechterfairen Deutung des Phänomens der Prophetie und der Prophetinnen in der Hebräischen Bibel* (Stuttgart: Kohlhammer, 2002), 65–66.

Then the prophet Miriam, Aaron's sister, took a tambourine in her hand,
and all the women went out after her with tambourines and with dancing.
And Miriam sang to them:
Sing to YHWH, for he has triumphed gloriously;
horse and rider he has thrown into the sea.

When the men do not return home and the cities are besieged and conquered,
in other narratives, once again it is women who publicly announce the catastrophe; they do so by standing in the streets and on the city walls and raising
cries of lamentation. The tambourine players are frequently found on terracotta artworks in Palestine/Israel during the first millennium B.C.E. (fig. 20).[20]
They probably had an important function in the cult as well, although the biblical texts do not mention such a cultic role. We can well imagine that, for the
authors of the biblical texts, the women's cultic drumming had a problematic
rapport with the warring goddess Anat or Ashtart or with erotic goddesses
such as Asherah or Hathor and was therefore silenced.

Another picture of belligerent power, evoked in the context of a decisive
passage in the exodus narrative, is the bull. Exodus 32 relates the apostasy of
the people, who even fashion a sacred image of a young bull bursting with
strength in order to then worship it as god. Bull-worship existed in Canaan
long before "Israel," in close relation with the weather-god, whom the biblical
texts call Baal. Originally, the bull represents
the power of generation and its fertility. The
weather-god had already assumed, in the
Late Bronze and Early Iron epochs, that is,
in the second half of the second millennium

Fig. 20. Terracotta figurine from Gezer (probably
eighth/seventh century B.C.E.). A woman with large,
emphasized eyes, ear and neck decorations, and
wearing a beautifully embroidered cloth holds a tambourine before her left breast. Nearly one hundred
figures of female drummers come from the Levante.
Sometimes they press the instrument flat against
their bodies; sometimes they also "play" in the correct position (Winter, *Frau und Göttin*, fig. 62)

20. See the two relatively recent monographs on this topic, with differing interpreta-
tions of the terracotta tambourine players, by Sarit Paz, *Drums, Women, and Goddesses:
Drumming and Gender in Iron Age II Israel* (OBO 232; Fribourg: Academic; Göttingen:
Vandenhoeck & Ruprecht 2007); David T. Sugimoto, *Female Figurines with a Disk from the
Southern Levant and the Formation of Monotheism* (Tokyo: Keio University Press, 2008).

B.C.E., the aggressive features and aspects of the Egyptian Seth, an assistant of the sun-god. The pictures of bulls then accentuated their strength rather than their fertility (figs. 21–22).[21]

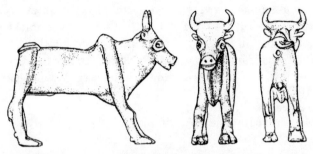

Fig. 21. Bronze bull from the mountain country near Dotan, the so-called "Bull Site" (twelfth/eleventh century B.C.E.). Small images of bulls, made out of metal, can be found in Palestine/Israel since the first half of the second millennium B.C.E. These may be valuable cult images, some of which were located in small clay chapels. This piece was originally fixed to a base. The depicted bull, a zebu, does not appear very dangerous; only the strutting forelegs betray his latent power. (Keel, *Das Recht der Bilder*, fig. 146)

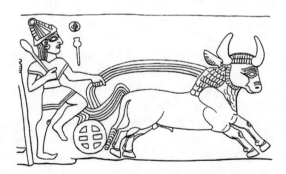

Fig. 22. Relief from the temple of the weather-god of Aleppo (tenth/ninth century B.C.E.). The Syrian weather-god drives in a chariot pulled by a powerful bull with enormous horns. Both the galloping movement of the animal and the pose of the god (who appears to jump lithely onto the chariot, strongly seizing the reins with a slack hand, while the other holds his scepter) express power and dynamics. (Keel and Schroer, *Schöpfung*, fig. 44)

---

21. On bull worship in Palestine/Israel, see Keel, *Das Recht der Bilder*, 169–93.

10. Israel's God as a Vulture Caring for Its Young
(Exod 19:4; Deut 32:11)

Although in earliest times the Egyptian gods and goddesses are represented in the form of animals or as combinations of human forms with animal heads, the First Testament maintains a very reserved attitude, perhaps even an explicit rejection of the apparition of YHWH in the form of an animal (see above, the image of the bull in Exod 32). In the end, only one of the diverse representations of divine animals remains: the vulture.[22] In Exod 19:4, YHWH has Moses deliver the following message to the Israelites at Mount Sinai:

> You have seen what I did to the Egyptians,
> and how I bore you on vultures' [נשר] wings
> and brought you to myself.

In his song, in Deut 32:10–11, Moses recalls how YHWH picked up his people in the desert:

> He found him in a desert land, in a howling wilderness waste;
> he shielded him, cared for him, guarded him as the apple of his eye.
> As a vulture [נשר] stirs up its young (its nest),
> and hovers over its young;
> as it spreads its wings,
> takes them up, and bears them aloft on its pinions.

YHWH's sheltering protection and care is compared to the behavior of birds in relation to their young, specifically not that of the eagle—as the captions indicate—but of the vulture. In Mic 1:16, the Daughter of Zion is ordered to make herself bald as the נשר. This kind of baldness is characteristic of the vultures. In the ancient Near East, these imposing birds as scavengers were certainly associated with the sphere of death, but they were also admired. Clearly, seeing that the vulture cared for the dead was also in some way comforting. They became the symbol for becoming and dying. The symbolism of the vulture has a long tradition in the Middle East as well as Egypt. In Egypt, the gyp represents the motherly goddesses such as Mut and Nekhbet. The name of the goddess Mut, who wears only a vulture-crest, was written with the picture of the griffon. *Mwt* was an ideogram for motherhood. The

---

22. See Silvia Schroer, "'Under the Shadow of Your Wings': The Metaphor of God's Wings in the Psalms, Exodus 19.4, Deuteronomy 32.11 and Malachi 3.20, as Seen through the Perspectives of Feminism and History of Religion," in *Wisdom and Psalms* (ed. Athalya Brenner and Carol R. Fontaine; FCB 2/2; Sheffield: Sheffield Academic Press, 1998), 264–82.

vulture-goddesses in Egypt protect the king above all else; they nourish him by letting him drink from their breasts (fig. 23). Vulture-goddesses protect the dead (fig. 24), but also future mothers as well as mothers with small children. Although the biblical text does not refer to this particular mythology and symbolism of the vulture, we can recognize how traditional aspects and representations from the ancient Near Eastern heritage could enrich Israel's picture of God, which did imply selection. Images of God as mother could also be integrated into the prophetic tradition (Hos 11), whereas other feminine images could not be used.

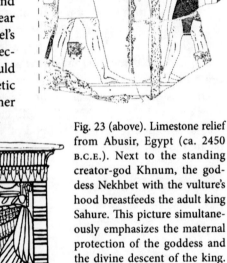

Fig. 23 (above). Limestone relief from Abusir, Egypt (ca. 2450 B.C.E.). Next to the standing creator-god Khnum, the goddess Nekhbet with the vulture's hood breastfeeds the adult king Sahure. This picture simultaneously emphasizes the maternal protection of the goddess and the divine descent of the king. (Schroer and Keel, *Vom ausgehenden Mesolithikum bis zur Frühbronzezeit*, no. 144)

Fig. 24. Golden pectoral, with lapis lazuli and glass (ca. 1320 B.C.E.). The precious breast decoration was placed on the mummy of Pharaoh Tutankhamun. The vulture-goddess takes the deceased under her spread wings and so leads him into the new life. Decay and becoming, birth and death are confidently left under the protection of the goddess. (Sketch by Ulrike Zurkinden-Kolberg after Wilkinson, *Ancient Egyptian Jewellery*, pl. 54)

11. No Kid in Its Mother's Milk (Exod 23:19; 34:26; Deut 14:21)

In several passages of the Pentateuch, prohibitions are formulated prohibiting separation of young animals from their mothers immediately after birth or boiling a kid in its mother's milk:

When an ox or a sheep or a goat is born, it shall remain seven days with its mother, and from the eighth day on it shall be acceptable as YHWH's offering by fire. But you shall not slaughter, from the herd or the flock, an animal with its young on the same day. (Lev 22:27–28; cf. Exod 22:28b–29)

You shall not boil a kid in its mother's milk. (Exod 23:19; 34:26; Deut 14:21)

This last prescription was a cultural movement, for it is the basis of Jewish kosher cooking with its instructions to separate milk and meat products. However, originally this law had a different sense: it is a transgression of nature's order to cook a young animal in its mother's milk, which is intended to nourish it.[23] The union of mother and child is inviolable because it incarnates divine care, the love for the engendered and growing life. The Egyptians visibly had compassion for the cow whose calf was taken away so that her milk could be collected (fig. 25). Scroll seals, Phoenician ivory, and seal amulets from Palestine/ Israel represent the cow with a drinking calf or the goat with a suckling kid (figs. 26–27). The motif can certainly express divine care; the picture is found in the royal temples of the Middle East from the third until the first millennium.

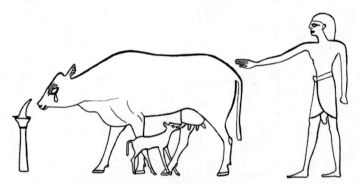

Fig. 25. Part of a sacrophagus relief from Deir el-Bahari (ca. 2000 B.C.E.). The cow and the calf represent benediction. The cow cries, probably because someone will take its calf away. The incense stand before the animal and the hand of the man on the right side, stretched out in protection or a blessing, indicate that this is not a purely agricultural scene. The mother and the young animal more likely represent a divine icon. (Schroer, *Mittelbronzezeit*, no. 306)

---

23. See Othmar Keel, *Das Böcklein in der Milch seiner Mutter und Verwandtes* (OBO 33; Fribourg: Universitätsverlag; Göttingen: Vandenhoeck & Ruprecht, 1980).

Fig. 26. Ivory plate from Fort Shalmaneser in Nimrud (eighth century B.C.E.). When people could afford to have expensive cattle and luxurious ivory sculptures, as was occasionally the case in Phoenicia and in Israel's northern kingdom, the feeding goats were replaced by the motif "cow and calf" as representations of the divine protecting power over herd animals. (Keel and Schroer, *Schöpfung*, fig. 41)

Fig. 27. Conic stamp seal from Taanakh (1000–900 B.C.E.). In the Early Iron period of Palestine/Israel, the most popular icon, which represents divine motherliness, is the nursing caprid (goat, game goat, or stone nanny-goat), which, through its care, lets life grow and prosper. On this amulet seal, the mother goat with kid is accompanied by a scorpion, which expresses the aspect of sexuality. (Keel and Schroer, *Schöpfung*, fig. 40)

12. The Mirrors of the Women at the Entrance of the Sanctuary (Exod 38:8)

A very short and truly enigmatic notice[24] inserted in the description of the holy tent mentions that the artisan Bezalel made instruments of bronze and clearly melted or otherwise used the bronze mirrors of the women serving in the temple: "He made the basin of bronze with its stand of bronze, from the mirrors of the women who served at the entrance to the tent of meeting" (Exod 38:8). From the outset, the Hebrew word מראת in the sense of "mirror" is peculiar, although it is well-attested to in the ancient translations. We can only speculate whether or not these mirrors originally had a cultic function. Founding or secondary uses of objects made of precious metal are mentioned in relation to the cultic inventory and new images of deities, for example, in the narrative of the golden calf, which Aaron cast in a mold with the jewelry of the impatient people (Exod 32:2–3). The offerings of gold and jewelry donated by Israelite men and women as sanctuary equipment are also mentioned in 35:21–22. Mirrors as cosmetic instruments in the hands of women appear in many

---

24. See Winter, *Frau und Göttin*, 58–65; Fischer, *Gotteskünderinnen*, 105.

depictions from Egypt (fig. 28), the Near East, and Greece. However, they are not infrequently represented in a patently cultic context: as gifts for goddesses such as Hathor, in cultic dances, or as attributes of goddesses (fig. 29).[25]

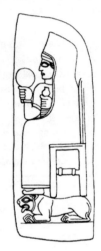

Fig. 28 (left). Bronze mirror from Akko (second half of second millennium B.C.E.). In the manner of the Egyptian tradition, the handle of the mirror represents a young woman, who (here) presents a breast in a Near Eastern manner. She is, at the same time, the bearer of the "sun disk" (mirror). Cosmetics and "beautiful things" have belonged since time immemorial to the array of the goddess Hathor, who was responsible for love, music, and merry celebrations. (Winter, *Frau und Göttin*, fig. 51)

Fig. 29 (right). Late Hittite cornerstone from Carchemish (ninth/eighth century B.C.E.). The enthroned woman, in a long garment and a high headdress, represents a goddess or a sovereign. The lion beneath her throne indicates that she is a goddess. She carries a scepter in one hand and a mirror in the other. (Winter, *Frau und Göttin*, fig. 5)

13. The New Mother under Control (Lev 12) and the New Mother as Queen

Birth, according to the ancient Israelite concept, carries with it conditions of impurity. Like most kinds of impurity (touching a corpse, bleeding, ejaculation, and so on), the impurity of birth ceases after a certain time period. The duration of this period differs for the birth of boys and girls: one week and thirty-three days or two weeks and sixty-six days, respectively.

25. Studies of the Egyptian tradition of mirrors can be found in Christine Lilyquist, *Ancient Egyptian Mirrors from the Earliest Times through the Middle Kingdom* (Münchener Ägyptologische Studien 27; Munich: Deutscher Kunstverlag, 1979); and in Claire Derricks, *Les miroirs cariatides égyptiens en bronze* (Münchener Ägyptologische Studien 51; Mainz: Zabern, 2001). On this difficult Old Testament text, see already Winter, *Frau und Göttin*, 58–65, and most recently Fischer, *Gotteskünderinnen*, 95–108.

Fig. 30. Limestone fragment from Deir el-Medina (1300–1000 B.C.E.). On ostraca, childbed scenes are occasionally represented. Here the woman who has given birth sits on a bed with her newborn child while a maid cares for her. The maid hands a mirror to her lady. The bed is protected by Bes figures. (Brunner-Traut, *Die altägyptischen Scherbenbilder*, pl. XXV, no. 65)

Leviticus 12 gives the impression that a new mother and a woman whose postpartum flow (lochia) has not yet stopped in the weeks following birth must only be controlled in regard to their purity. The postnatal period is presented very differently in Egyptian iconography. Ostraca, for example, show the new mother and the child placed under a special shelter, where they were clearly pampered (fig. 30). The protection for the mother and the child was in the foreground, hence the typical Egyptian helpers at birth and the protecting deities responsible for mothers and small children are present, especially Bes and Thoeris, who, since the Middle Empire, appear on magic sticks and amulets. Aside from measures of control, the Israelite legislative texts do not exclude other quite different aspects of the postnatal period, which possibly closely resembled those in Egypt. Yet nothing is said of these, and so the *Wirkungsgeschichte* increasingly considered the new mother to be a problem that responsible ecclesiastics finally resolved with misogynic purification rituals (absolution).[26]

The offering at the end of the period of purification is affixed, according to Lev 12:6–8, to a lamb and a turtledove or, for poor people, two turtledoves. In art works, the male bearers of these offerings are represented with lambs or kids. Women in Phoenician and Cypriot terracotta art more typically hold doves in their hands (fig. 31).

Fig. 31. Terracotta figure from Kamelarga on Cyprus (sixth/fifth century B.C.E.). From Cyprus and Phoenicia come small clay figurines of women who hold a dove either in their hand or before their chest. This dove is most likely a sacrificial animal. (Schroer, *In Israel gab es Bilder*, fig. 103)

26. See Thomas Staubli, *Die Bücher Levitikus und Numeri* (Neuer Stuttgarter Kommentar zum Alten Testament 3; Stuttgart: Katholisches Bibelwerk 1996), 106–14.

Fig. 32 (left). Scarab from Tell el-'Ajjul (1700–1550 B.C.E.). Only the head of a goddess, identified with Hathor because of the hairstyle, is flanked here by two kneeling, admiring female worshipers. (Schroer, *Die Mittelbronzezeit*, no. 302)

Fig. 33 (right). Gold jewelry from Tell el-'Ajjul, south of Gaza (1550–1480 B.C.E.). A small branch grows from the navel (on the interchangeability of pudenda and navel, see also Song 7:3). The strongly stylized representation of the goddess, with a beautiful shoulder-length, curly hairstyle and the pendant, have the character of a devotional picture owing to the attentive expression of the divinity (icon). (Keel and Schroer, *Schöpfung*, fig. 25)

14. YHWH MAKE HIS FACE TO SHINE UPON YOU (NUM 6:24–26)

Numbers 6 transmits a benediction that still directly touches us today, pronounced by a priest in the name of YHWH over the participants of the cult. This blessing is also attested outside of the Bible. It was placed on the tombs of deceased priests, inscribed on silver foil, and laid as an amulet on the forehead in a tomb in Jerusalem (Ketef Hinnom; sixth/seventh century B.C.E.).[27] The face of YHWH shines and turns with friendliness toward humans. In this alone resides the blessing. When the divinity turns away and shows its back, no life is possible. The deity with its face turned toward humans is a central theme in ancient Near Eastern religions. Representations of gods in temples show this regard, but especially figures on small amulet seals with devotional pictures. These almost always feature the face of a goddess who is looking directly at the worshiper (figs. 32–33).

Also, in the case of small pillar figurines that were placed in Jewish houses, the head and face are sculptured with particular care. Friendliness cannot be

---

27. A summary of the findings is given in Othmar Keel and Christoph Uehlinger, *Gods, Goddesses and Images of God in Ancient Israel* (trans. Thomas H. Trapp; Minneapolis: Fortress 1998), 367–72.

discerned in the expression, since ancient Near Eastern art generally did not detail facial expressions, but rather in the openness and the attentiveness of the face. The fundamental anthropological experience showing that a person cannot grow without this attentive face of the mother, grandmother, father, and other persons stimulated the transfer to the divine image.[28] Interestingly, gender-marking plays a role here as well. The biblical text actually does not make this explicit, although it is evident in the background and was introduced into the biblical image of God. In all probability, those blessed by YHWH's face imagined it with feminine features, even though, in other contexts, this same God assumed masculine roles.

15. Prohibited Cults of All Kinds

The prohibition of images in both redactions of the Decalogue has provoked a great deal of movement in Judaism as well as the Christian religion. Regarding a widespread misunderstanding, it must be made clear that this was originally a prohibition of devotional images and that there was no intention to prevent people from making mental representations of God. The fabrication of an image with the aim of worshiping it was prohibited. Detailed explanations of the prohibition of images in Deuteronomy, especially in 4:16–19, more graphically present the spectrum of the prohibition: there shall be no images of any created reality, no pictures of the stars, no pictures of plants, animals, or human figures. Likewise, it is forbidden to worship a tree, a bull, a king, or a queen. According to passages such as Deut 7:5; 12:3; and 16:21–22, just as images are forbidden, so also is an Asherah or a *massebah*, that is, a sacred tree and a sacred stone.

You shall not plant any Asherah as a sacred pole beside the altar that you make for YHWH your God, nor shall you set up a *massebah*—things that YHWH your God hates. (Deut 16:21–22)

Even without an actual picture, we know that these personify divine powers (fig. 34). Iconogra-

Fig. 34. Tyrian bronze coin (third/fourth century c.e.). It represents a small sanctuary, which is still completely in the Canaanite tradition. Two erect stones most likely embody a goddess and a god. The tree also indicates the presence of the goddess, and a small incense stand on the left suggests the holiness of the entire cultic district. (Keel, *The Symbolism of the Biblical World*, fig. 247)

28. See Schroer and Staubli, *Body Symbolism in the Bible*, 85–91.

phy helps one get a concrete understanding of what the prohibition of pictures actually involved. From this point of view, we can recognize the contours of the Canaanite religion—at home in this land—polemically described in the First Testament. We can deduce from many texts that women worshiped Asherah or her uranian apparition, the goddess of heaven (Jer 44); they danced around the golden calf (Exod 32) or venerated the image of the serpent, the Nehushtan, at the temple of Jerusalem (2 Kgs 18:4; cf. Num 21:4–9). However, they did not do this alone but with their husbands and families. If we nevertheless pay special attention to the prohibition of imagery here, it is because women in particular were blamed by certain groups of biblical authors for transgressing the prohibition against foreign gods and images (Deut 7:1–4; 1 Kgs 11:1–8).

16. No War against Trees and Other Prescriptions Relative to the Numina (Deut 20:19–20)

If the Torah speaks of concrete blessings, the flourishing of vegetation, animals, and humans, it also declares the holiness of life, the respect for the divine in all of creation. The fact that God is Creator does not mean, in the First Testament, that he is a manufacturer. Rather, he should be seen as an artist because that which God creates bears the marks of his fingers (Ps 8:4) or even his image, where humans are concerned. The creation and the divine in it are approached by the Israelites with piety.[29] One does not simply seize what is sacred; on the contrary, products of the field are left in the field, fruit is not immediately harvested from young trees, the mother of fledglings is left alive (Deut 22:6–7), animals are not castrated, and fruit trees are not ineffectively chopped down:

> If you besiege a town for a long time, making war against it in order to take it, you must not destroy its trees by wielding an ax against them. Although you may take food from them, you must not cut them down. Are trees in the field human beings that they should come under siege from you? You may destroy only the trees that you know do not produce food; you may cut them down for use in building siegeworks against the town that makes war with you, until it falls. (Deut 20:19–20)

The fact that cutting down trees was a brutal practice in warfare is shown by Neo-Assyrian reliefs. The soldiers of the victorious Assyrian army fell the fruit trees of a besieged town and destroy the basis of nourishment of the inhabitants (fig. 35). There is a transition from a polytheistic world of gods to a monotheistic faith behind the bans in the ancient Israelite laws, which did not

---

29. Keel and Schroer, *Schöpfung*, esp. 37–91.

Fig. 35. Part of a relief from the southwest palace of the Assyrian king Sennacherib (704–681 B.C.E.) in Nineveh. After conquering the city, Assyrian soldiers are felling its date trees. (Keel and Schroer, *Schöpfung*, fig. 9)

have to regard the world as having entirely lost its sacred character. Here iconography also serves the purpose of reconstruction and the search for traces.

17. THE INCREASE OF YOUR CATTLE (DEUT 7:13; 28:4, 18, 51)

In the Deuteronomic expression שְׁגַר־אֲלָפֶיךָ וְעַשְׁתְּרֹת צֹאנֶךָ ("the increase of your cattle and the issue of your flock"; Deut 7:13; cf. 28:4, 18, 51), the names of a north Syrian deity and a Canaanite deity of fertility, Shagar and Astarte are still to be found. The goddess protector of the herds, who was responsible for young animals thriving and the health and fertility of animals, was gradually replaced by YHWH as protector of the flocks. In Latin, too, there is a designation for the issue of the small animals: *veneres gregis*, "the Venusses of the flock." Scroll seals from Mesopotamia (fig. 36) and Syria (fig. 37) testify to the enduring close relation of goddesses with the herd animals.

Fig. 36. Cylinder seal of the late Uruk period from Chafadshi in Iran (ca. 3000 B.C.E.). Below a convoy of cattle in the upper section of the seal, the lower section depicts cattle approaching a hut in the center of the picture. Three staff and ring symbols of the goddess Nintu(r), "the lady of birth," stand upon its roof. Two calves spring out of the hut, from the left and the right; a manger lies before each of them. The composition may express the following message: Nintur, the lady or goddess of birth, produces animals, especially cattle. In the pictography of Uruk, hut has the sound value *tut/tur* "birth." (Keel and Schroer, *Schöpfung*, fig. 86)

Fig. 37. Classical Syrian cylinder seal (ca. 1750 B.C.E.). A naked goddess cares for a martial prince or (divinized) king who holds a club. The goddess and the prince look in the same direction. She strikes back her garb with an unmistakable intention; with one hand, she seems to touch him and to draw attention to herself; perhaps she also offers him a piece of fruit. At the bottom of the detailed collateral scene, which is divided into two parts by a braid, are two mating deer, a nursing domestic goat, and two mating fat-tailed sheep. Above there is a squatting lion striking down a domestic goat and two sphinxes. The lower scene represents the life-giving aspects of the goddess, the upper her dangerous and frightening side. (Keel and Schroer, *Schöpfung*, fig. 37)

Conclusion

In these selected examples, we have largely dealt with the lost heritage of the goddesses and pictures of feminine deities. Israelite monotheism developed in polytheistic surroundings and from the roots of these polytheistic religions. Israel's image of God came into being partly through the exclusion of aspects from the polytheistic world of the gods and partly through adaptation, modification, and processes of integration. Many biblical texts permit us to recognize such processes, that is, both exclusion and integration. Pictures—and the extrabiblical testimonies that we have not expressly discussed here—can be employed to graphically elucidate the dynamic and dramatic development of monotheism. According to Gen 1:27, the image of God is imprinted in women and men, and while God himself is neither "man" nor "woman," he is present in both masculine and feminine pictures and metaphors as well as in men and women.[30]

---

30. Lastly, on the abundance of feminine divine images in the ancient Orient, which are still conserved in part in the biblical texts, see Othmar Keel, *Gott weiblich: Eine verborgene Seite des biblischen Gottes* (Fribourg: Academic, 2008).

Archaeology—A Window to the Lives of Israelite Women

Carol Meyers
Duke University

Not long ago an elderly American woman who lived much of her adult life in Afghanistan was talking to a radio interviewer about her experiences there and her impressions of the country. The interviewer asked her to comment on "gender and the plight of the poor Afghan women." Her answer was surprising, for she explained that the concept of Afghan women as "abused" and "downtrodden" is a stereotype that does not apply uniformly to the population. In the rural areas where she lived at various times, she found a "tremendous amount of trust and respect between men and women in the household because they depend on one another." Women and men share the same experiential world, she explained. Women as well as men know the crops and the animals and have the same concerns about eking out a living. But, she continued, the situation in urban areas is different. When men work outside the home and when women and men live in separate realms during the day, dominance and distrust frequently appear. Those urban settings, she pointed out, create the stereotypes.[1]

In today's world we are fortunate to have ethnographers, travelers, journalists, and scholars to tell us about the reality in the agricultural villages of a struggling country in South Asia. For ancient Israel, we have no such direct witnesses to village women. The notions we have about them are based on interpretations of a text, the Hebrew Bible, which was produced mainly in an urban context by male authors. How can we find out if those notions are stereotypes that are at odds with social reality? Perhaps the only recourse for answering that question lies in turning to archaeological data, which help to

---

1. "An Afghan Love Affair," interview with Nancy Hatch Dupree on *The Story*, American Public Media (16 May 2007). Online: http://thestory.org/archive/the_story_251_An_Afghan_Love_Affair.mp3/view.

create a window through which we can glimpse some aspects of the everyday lives of Israelite women.

This essay will have four parts. (1) It will begin by noting why using the Hebrew Bible alone as a source of information about the lives of Israelite women is problematic. (2) Then the possibilities as well as the problems in using archaeological information, especially with respect to Israelite households, will be discussed, and the interpretive strategies for using archaeology will be considered. (3) Next, specific examples of archaeologically retrieved data relevant to women's lives will be presented. (4) Finally, an evaluation of women's lives in light of these archaeological data will be provided.

1. THE HEBREW BIBLE: A PROBLEMATIC SOURCE FOR WOMEN'S LIVES

For generations, people interested in women's lives in biblical antiquity have turned to the Hebrew Bible for information. However, using the Bible alone has led to assessments that have not taken into account the problems of using only one source.

1.1. COMMON ASSESSMENTS, USING THE HEBREW BIBLE, OF ISRAELITE WOMEN'S LIVES

One of the first studies of women in the Hebrew Bible in contemporary feminist scholarship,[2] Phyllis Bird's essay on "Images of Women in the Old Testament," mentions women as indistinct background figures, without names, voices, or status. Her analysis of biblical texts leads her to conclude that women were dependent on men in economic, religious, and political spheres and that they are presented as inferior to men.[3] Decades later, similar perceptions—some based on general cultural notions, others on readings of biblical passages without consideration of social context—still are common. In a course that I teach on "Women in Biblical Tradition," I ask students at the beginning of the term to write down their ideas about women in the period of the Hebrew Bible. Nearly all of them, both those with strong religious back-

---

2. Feminist biblical scholarship emerged in North America in the eighteenth and nineteenth centuries in relation to the suffrage movement and reemerged in the 1970s as a spin-off of the civil rights movement, but women's engagement with problematic biblical texts can be found earlier in Europe, in documents from the Middle Ages to the eighteenth century.

3. Phyllis Bird, "Images of Women in the Old Testament," in *Religion and Sexism: Images of Women in Jewish and Christian Traditions* (ed. Rosemary Radford Ruether; New York: Simon & Schuster, 1974), 49–50.

grounds and those who have never read the Bible, believe that women were "not as important as men," "subservient to men," "meant mainly for procreation," "inferior to men," "marginalized."[4]

These views are also found in more recent feminist scholarship, despite the advances that have been made in recovering little-known or underappreciated women's stories and in understanding the literary dynamics of biblical passages mentioning women. Because of their distress about the way certain biblical texts have been used, or misused, to subjugate women, as many essays in this project (The Bible and Women: An Encyclopedia of Exegesis and Cultural History) demonstrate, some scholars sharply critique certain biblical passages as misogynist or sexist. In so doing, they tend to equate Israelite women with biblical women. They thereby claim marginality and secondary status for our Iron Age female forebears, whom they see as under the power of men in all respects.[5]

These allegations are made by scholars who respect the authority of the Bible as well as by those who approach it from a secular viewpoint. In both instances, their claims are the result of using only texts—the Bible and other ancient Near Eastern documents—to understand what life was like for most women in ancient Israel. However, can texts alone provide the kind of accurate and balanced information that should be used for assessing women's lives? The answer to that question is no, for a number of reasons.

1.2. Problems in Using the Hebrew Bible as a Source for Women's Lives

1.2.1. Relatively Few Women

The first problem is a quantitative one. The Hebrew Bible is hardly balanced in the information it provides about women and men. Male figures far outnumber female ones. This is evident in the disproportionately small number of women who are mentioned by name. Only 135 women are named in the Hebrew Bible; this number is less than 10 percent of the total number of named individuals. Moreover, the named and unnamed female figures who do appear tend to have significantly less important roles in biblical narratives,

---

4. These are quotes from the statements that students write at the beginning of the course; at the end of the course, their perceptions are radically different.

5. See, for example, Kathleen M. O'Connor, "The Feminist Movement Meets the Old Testament," in *Engaging the Bible in a Gendered World: An Introduction to Feminist Biblical Interpretation in Honor of Kathleen Doob Sakenfeld* (ed. Linda Day and Carolyn Pressler; Louisville: Westminster John Knox, 2006), 13.

laws, and poetic imagery than do their male counterparts. This imbalance of attention to women means a dearth of information about them.

1.2.2. Mainly Exceptional Women

Another problem is that the most prominent female figures in the Hebrew Bible are exceptional women. The few women appearing in extended narratives—for example, Sarah and Rebekah, Miriam and Deborah, Bathsheba and Jezebel, Esther and Ruth—are leaders, wives of patriarchs or kings, or narrative heroes. As such, they are hardly representative of ordinary women and can be used only with the utmost caution in the search for information about women's lives.

1.2.3. National Orientation

A further consideration that explains the relative paucity of female figures and the fact that exceptional women dominate is the national orientation of much of the Hebrew Bible. It is concerned with the corporate existence of the Israelites and thus with the leaders, largely male, responsible for or critical of various aspects of its national life. Once we leave the family stories of Genesis, we encounter a series of public figures, most of them men: judges, kings, warriors, prophets, priests, and sages. Consequently, there is very little direct information about the everyday lives of ordinary women or, for that matter, of ordinary men.

1.2.4. Emphasis on Patrilineages

An additional problem is that the Hebrew Bible is concerned with family lineages; and those lineages are *patrilineages*, for society was organized along male descent lines.[6] Even the family stories in Genesis, as well as the preceding genealogies, are meant to show the establishment of lineages that eventually represent, as a literary construct if not a social reality, the entire people. Women are important for those lineages largely in relation to their biological function as progenitors of the descent lines. The matriarchs of the Genesis narratives may emerge as important characters in their own right and as major actors in the creation of the house of Israel,[7] yet their role in overcom-

---

6. For a discussion of Israelite society with its kinship structure and its patrimonial inheritance system, see Paula M. McNutt, *Reconstructing the Society of Ancient Israel* (Library of Ancient Israel; Louisville: Westminster John Knox, 1999); also, see §3.2 below.

7. See, in this volume, Thomas Hieke, "Genealogy as a Means of Presenting History in the Torah and the Role of Women in the Genealogical System."

ing barrenness and producing offspring to continue the lineage is central to the stories about them.

1.2.5. Orientation of Legal Materials to Men

The biblical concern for patrilineages creates a problem in using the legal materials in the Pentateuch for information about the "status" of women, for the laws are addressed primarily to the men who were heads of the households in which most Israelites lived. This can be seen in the fact that the Hebrew verbs in biblical laws are masculine in gender. To be sure, the male form of the verbs is sometimes gender inclusive, but in general women (and men other than heads of households) are probably not intended as the direct audience for the stipulations and rulings that comprise biblical law.[8]

1.2.6. Existence and Utilization of Legal Materials

A related problem concerning the use of legal materials to evaluate the status and role of Israelite women is whether the laws as they exist in the Pentateuch were operant for the Israelites. For one thing, very few if any of the laws existed in the form in which we have them until the very end of the Israelite monarchy, at the earliest. Thus it is anachronistic to suppose that the Pentateuch's laws were in effect for the entire Iron Age population of ancient Israel. To be sure, some of the legal materials may reflect customary laws emerging from the adjudications of village elders. However, others were formulated in political centers and served the interests of the Israelite elites; and the legal codes of a central authority in the premodern world rarely extended fully into the surrounding countryside. Another consideration is that many of the laws deal with specific and problematic cases and are not normative statutes; such laws intrinsically emphasize prohibition and thus do not reveal typical practices. Finally, many of the biblical laws dealing with women focus on reproductive issues. The stringency of laws dealing with sexuality may reflect general matters of honor, but it is likely that they are rooted in attempts to provide assurance that men were the biological fathers of their heirs. Such assurance was critical, especially for men with considerable property, in a society in which lineages were very important. Consequently, the laws show that a woman's reproductive potential was guarded by her father until she was married, and

---

8. David E. S. Stein, "Dictionary of Gender in the Torah," in *The Contemporary Torah: A Gender-Sensitive Adaptation of the JPS Translation* (ed. David E. S. Stein; Philadelphia: Jewish Publication Society, 2006), 403.

then it belonged to her husband. Adultery and premarital sex were treated stringently because they would compromise a man's confidence that his wife or bride was the mother of his children. However, the dynamics of household life are complex, and male control of female sexuality does not mean generalized male control of women in all household activities.[9] In short, the legal materials of the Hebrew Bible may be useful in considering the postexilic community but must be used with utmost caution for earlier periods; further, sexuality laws that restrict or punish women more than men cannot be taken as signs of general discrimination.

1.2.7. Urban Setting of the Hebrew Bible

Another issue derives from the fact that most of the Hebrew Bible was produced in an urban setting. Some of it may have come from the capital (Samaria) of the northern kingdom; but much more emanated from Jerusalem, with its priestly authors and royal scribes. Prophetic voices, too, are heard addressing people, often leaders, in the capital(s). However, especially after the eighth century B.C.E., when it became a major urban center, Jerusalem was hardly typical of the communities in which most people lived. As an agrarian people, most Israelites lived in farmsteads, small agricultural villages, or walled agricultural towns. Indeed, until relatively recently, the number of people living in truly urban centers within agrarian societies was relatively small.[10] The great majority of people in agricultural societies were peasant farmers, and urban dwellers were a tiny minority. The Hebrew term עִיר, often erroneously translated "city," appears frequently in the Hebrew Bible—over one thousand times—to designate a settlement of any size; it rarely denotes a truly urban center such as Jerusalem.[11] Thus the literature produced in Jerusalem is more reliable as a source for the urban few than for the rural majority.

---

9. Carol Meyers, *Discovering Eve: Ancient Israelite Women in Context* (New York: Oxford University Press, 1988), 33–36.

10. For example, in fourteenth-century England only 5.5 percent of the population lived in urban centers, and only about 3 percent of Russia's population was urban as recently as the eighteenth century; see Gerhard E. Lenski, *Power and Privilege: A Theory of Social Stratification* (Chapel Hill: University of North Carolina Press, 1984), 199–200.

11. Baruch A. Levine, "The Biblical 'Town' as Reality and Typology: Evaluating Biblical References to Towns and Their Functions," in *Urbanization and Land Ownership in the Ancient Near East* (ed. Michael Hudson and Baruch A. Levine; Peabody Museum Bulletin 7; Cambridge: Peabody Museum of Archaeology and Ethnology, Harvard University Press, 1999), 421–453. See also Yuval Portugali, "'Arim, Banot, Migrashim, and Haṣerim: The Spatial Organization of Eretz-Israel in the Twelfth–Tenth Centuries BCE according to the Bible" [Hebrew], *ErIsr* 17 (1984): 282–290.

1.2.8. Disconnect between Literary Images and Social Reality

Finally, the reality of at least some aspects of daily life for women (and men) in traditional cultures typically differs to some degree from the gender images appearing in the conventional notions and literary sources produced by those cultures. Anthropologists have documented this for living communities,[12] and there is no reason to think the case would have been any different for the Israelites. Thus we cannot assume a one-to-one correspondence between the biblical word and the Israelite world.

2. ARCHAEOLOGICAL DATA AND INTERPRETIVE STRATEGIES: THE PROBLEM OF HOUSEHOLDS

Information from extrabiblical sources dating to the period of the Israelites (the Iron Age, ca. 1200–600 B.C.E.; see §3) provides an independent witness to their daily lives and is thus essential for achieving a more balanced view of women's lives than can be obtained from using the Bible alone. Archaeological materials are the main source of such extrabiblical information. Although less plentiful or reliable than might be expected, a variety of archaeological data are relevant and will be presented in §3. Epigraphic (written) remains are especially helpful, but the information they provide pertains more often to elite or well-to-do women than to the majority of women who were part of peasant farming families.[13] Perhaps the most important kinds of evidence are the data that represent peasant households. As the primary unit of society, the household was the setting in which most women and men worked and lived. The challenges to the task of obtaining and using the vitally important information about the dwellings and artifacts that constituted the household must be examined.[14]

---

12. A classic study is Susan Carol Rogers, "Female Forms of Power and the Myth of Male Dominance: A Model of Female/Male Interaction in Peasant Society," *American Ethnologist* 2 (1975): 727–56. For a more recent and nuanced discussion, see Roberta Gilchrist, *Gender and Archaeology* (London: Routledge, 1999), 32–36.

13. "Peasants" are understood to be people who own and work small farms; what they produce is mainly for their own consumption, not for commerce or profit. See Robert Redfield, *Peasant Society and Culture: An Anthropological Approach to Civilization* (Chicago: University of Chicago Press, 1956), 26–30.

14. The problems with other kinds of evidence are noted below in the sections in which they are discussed.

2.1. DEFINING THE HOUSEHOLD

A household was not simply a family or a dwelling; it was both. It can be defined as a built environment that consists of not only persons and their "hardware" (that is, their material culture, which includes the house in which they live and also all its installations and artifacts) but also their activities and other aspects of their daily lives.[15] To put it another way, a household in a premodern agricultural society is a task-oriented domestic unit; and it is a unit of consumption as well as production.

To be sure, the persons who lived in an Israelite household are no longer visible; and the items that comprised their material culture are not inherently gendered. However, because a division of labor by gender is present in virtually all traditional societies, the activities that the people carried out in household space with the use of household artifacts *were* gendered.[16] Consequently, a household's gender-linked activities can be reconstructed through a series of analytical steps (involving ethnographic, iconographic, and textual data) that will be described below in §2.3. Connecting specific artifacts and the household space in which they were used with women allows us to understand women's economic tasks as well as other kinds of household behaviors (including social, political, and religious ones) and then to make judgments about the social relations and values embedded in those activities. In short, investigating households in all their material and organizational complexity offers the possibility of acquiring information available in no other way about the average Israelite woman's roles and the accompanying social dynamics and values.

2.2. AVAILABILITY AND USABILITY OF THE ARCHAEOLOGICAL REMAINS OF HOUSEHOLDS

No other place on earth has been so extensively surveyed and excavated, for nearly two centuries, as the land of the Bible. One would think that masses of data would be available for recovering the gendered lives of the Israelites. Unfortunately, that is not the case, especially for the study of households. The paucity of information lies in the very factor that has drawn archaeologists to ancient Palestine, namely, the Bible.[17] From its earliest days, archaeology in

---

15. Amos Rapoport, "Spatial Organization and the Built Environment," in *Companion Encyclopedia of Anthropology* (ed. Tim Ingold; London: Routledge, 1994), 461.

16. Note that the division of labor by gender is almost never absolute, and there is always some crossover in gendered tasks. See Sarah Milledge Nelson, *Gender in Archeology: Analyzing Power and Prestige* (2nd ed.; Walnut Creek, Calif.: AltaMira, 2004), 64–87.

17. The traditional goals of Syro-Palestinian archaeology and the difficulty in using

biblical lands has been driven by the possibility of a biblical connection. Some archaeologists were, and still are, motivated by pietistic hopes that some discovery or other would "prove" the Bible or at least verify its basic historicity. Many others are less concerned with such issues but nonetheless hope to find information that will shed light on biblical texts and their interpretation. Whether driven by conservative agendas or more liberal ones, archaeologists have let the agendas of the text set the agendas of the field projects and have thus limited the material useful for recovering women's lives. This is so in several ways.

2.2.1. Site Selection

For one thing, archaeologists have been drawn to the places mentioned most often in the Bible—Jerusalem and the larger walled towns—and have rarely turned to the rural sector, that is, the small agricultural settlements in which most people lived. To be sure, many hundreds of rural sites have been identified and examined, especially in the last decade and a half. However, most of those sites have been analyzed through salvage digs (excavations carried out when modern development threatens archaeological sites), which rarely include the systematic excavation of a sample of dwellings; and most of them have never been published or have been only partially reported.[18] The available information about these rural sites is concerned largely with dating them; it is useful for reconstructing settlement history but not for reconstructing household life.

2.2.2. Focus on the Remains of Communal Life

Another problem, typical for the archaeology of larger sites, is that excavation strategies tend to favor the structures and artifacts that represent communal life and male elites rather than those representing the daily lives of average folk. That is, the excavations often focus on fortifications and palaces, on temples and shrines, rather than on domestic buildings and their environs. Thus they pay attention to the structures associated more with men's roles than those of women. The same is true for artifacts. Weapons, objects made

---

its discoveries for analysis of the gendered life of biblical antiquity are discussed in Carol Meyers, "Recovering Objects Re-visioning Subjects: Archaeology and Feminist Biblical Study," in *A Feminist Companion to Reading the Bible: Approaches, Methods, and Strategies* (ed. Athalya Brenner and Carole Fontaine; Sheffield: Sheffield Academic Press, 1997), 270–284.

18. The limitations of salvage digs are noted in Avraham Faust and Ze'ev Safrai, "Salvage Excavations as a Source for Reconstructing Settlement History in Ancient Israel," *PEQ* 137 (2005): 153–154.

of precious metals and materials, and cultic objects—from military, royal, and religious contexts—rather than the more mundane objects of daily human existence similarly attract an inordinate amount of interest.

The significant exception to this privileging of objects associated with male activities is the enormous consideration given to the most mundane objects of all: the ceramic vessels used for the storage, cooking, and serving of most foodstuffs and beverages in ancient Israel. Fired in kilns, pottery is virtually indestructible; the vessels may shatter, but the pieces survive. Because the styles of ceramic vessels change over time, a typological sequence can be established. Broken potsherds are carefully saved and analyzed, for they are invaluable for dating the buildings in which they are found. In this way they serve the important chronological aspect of archaeology—the dating of buildings and their nonceramic contents. This in turn serves the purpose of linking the buildings and artifacts to specific periods of "biblical history." Once dated, the construction and also the destruction of the superimposed levels of the excavated sites can, it is hoped, be associated with the activities of monarchs and armies mentioned in the Bible. These diachronic concerns, generated by information in biblical texts, drive the archaeological enterprise at the expense, all too often, of other excavation and publication strategies that might better allow researchers to investigate other aspects of life in the biblical past. In short, investigating national political history is all too frequently a dominant motivation for excavation.

Syro-Palestinian archaeology has historically favored, and currently still favors, research on the "macro" level, the large-scale social and political organizations that existed in the Holy Land. It thus tends to give relatively little attention to the "micro" level, the small-scale life processes that take place in households and the settlements in which they are located. A case in point is a recent and well-regarded publication: *The Archaeology of Society in the Holy Land*. In the preface, the editor notes that most of the book is about the macro level because of the great interest in looking at large-scale sociopolitical structures and how they changed over time.[19]

To be sure, archaeologists rarely dig *only* for monumental structures and the pottery used to date them, and domestic buildings have long been uncovered in their excavations. Moreover, in recent decades, there has been a concerted effort to explore the more modest structures associated with the peasant farmers inhabiting the highlands of ancient Palestine and the areas east of the Jordan in the Iron Age.

---

19. Thomas E. Levy, "Preface," in *The Archaeology of Society in the Holy Land* (ed. Thomas E. Levy; New York: Facts on File, 1995), xiv.

2.2.3. Recovery and Publication of Relevant Data

Even with the best of intentions and research designs, the nature of archaeological remains sometimes precludes the recovery of data—the exact spot in which artifacts were used—essential for reconstructing gendered work patterns (see §2.1). For example, not all dwellings are abandoned with its artifacts left in place. People who flee from or desert their homes often take many of their tools and vessels with them. Even if some possessions are left behind, subsequent inhabitants, in occupying or rebuilding a dwelling, typically shove aside or remove whatever was left on living surfaces. Just as problematic are the gradual disturbances brought about by natural forces—wind, rain, animals, and so forth—if a structure is left abandoned. Tragically, the ruins that provide the best evidence for ancient household life are those produced by sudden, unexpected military conquest in which dwellings are hastily abandoned and then burned, with no subsequent rebuilding. Virtually all of a family's possessions, at least those on the ground floor, are thus left *in situ* and are preserved in their original behavioral context by the quantities of ash and debris from the collapsed walls, second story, and roof. As much as a meter of such debris can accumulate immediately, sealing the artifacts in their original locations. But this "ideal" situation does not always obtain.

Another problem lies in the nature of archaeological publications—the preliminary and final reports in which the results of fieldwork are presented. Unfortunately, relatively few publications are user-friendly for researchers interested in assessing household objects in relation to gender. The manner of analyzing ceramics has spilled over into all artifact categories. That is, archaeological publications usually publish stone, bone, and metal objects according to their typological or stylistic qualities. Consequently, it is often very difficult, if not impossible, to tell from the publications how many of a given type of artifact were found and where each was found. Yet knowing the precise find spots of objects is critical for analyzing the kinds of work that was done in households and for interpreting that work with respect to gender. There are notable exceptions; but all too often the information provided by field reports is incomplete, frustrating the attempts of interpreters who are interested in identifying gendered activities in household spaces.[20]

Fortunately, several sites with Iron Age dwellings destroyed with their artifacts left *in situ* have been excavated by projects that have taken great pains

---

20. P. M. Michèle Daviau, *Houses and Their Furnishings in Bronze Age Palestine: Domestic Activity Areas and Artifact Distribution in the Middle and Late Bronze Ages* (JSOT/ASOR Monograph Series 8; Sheffield: Sheffield Academic Press, 1993), 26–27), exposes the poor excavation and publication practices that preclude recovery of household activity areas.

to record and publish the materials exactly as they were found. One project is significant in this regard, for the excavators also collected debris samples containing micro-artifacts.[21] Micro-artifacts, which are the primary refuse that accumulates on floors, include tiny fragments of animal and fish bones, seeds, cereal remains, flint chips, mortar fragments, tiny pieces of metal slag, and red ochre. Close analysis of them contributes further to the understanding of household activity areas.

In sum, although for many decades archaeologists did not seek information about micro-level processes taking place in households nor adequately report relevant artifacts, the recent attention to domestic structures and their contents means that information about households and the economic processes that took place within them is now available and will be presented below (§§3.2–3).

2.3. INTERPRETING HOUSEHOLD DATA: AN INTERDISCIPLINARY PROCESS

Archaeologists provide information about structures and artifacts, not about social units and their members.[22] Thus archaeological data, even when well-excavated and published, are not immediately accessible for use in assessing women's activities. A number of interpretive steps must first be performed. The recovery of Israelite women's household lives is an interdisciplinary project involving a variety of sources and methodologies. The mundane objects of daily life, as recovered by archaeologists, can be engendered and contextualized (see §3). Then, women's activities can be evaluated in terms of what they meant in their own societies—not in relation to the values and expectations of the twenty-first century (see §4).

2.3.1. Establishing the Function of Archaeological Remains

To begin with, even before gender is considered, the function of artifacts and structures must be established. Sometimes the interpretive processes identifying function are intuitive, but they are nonetheless always present. For example, a wide variety of ceramic forms have been discovered in excavations of Syro-

---

21. Arlene A. M. Rosen, "1992 Field Season Report on Micro-artifact Analysis" and "1993 Field Season Report on Micro-artifact Analysis," both limited circulation reports cited in James W. Hardin, *Households and the Use of Domestic Space in Iron II Tell Halif: An Archaeology of Destruction* (Lahav Research Project 2; Winona Lake, Ind.: Eisenbrauns, 2010).

22. Penelope M. Allison, "Introduction," *The Archaeology of Household Activities* (ed. Penelope M. Allison; London: Routledge, 1999), 2.

Palestinian sites, and they are given different names in the publications: cooking pot, water jug, storage jar, goblet, and so forth. Yet none of these vessels is found with a label; the designations all come from analogies with forms used in existing traditional cultures that still use locally produced ceramic vessels for most of their household needs. Information from ethnographic research is essential for understanding how ancient artifacts were used.[23] Only then can the use of space in ancient domestic structures be inferred on the basis of the kinds of objects found in various rooms of the dwellings. Identifying activity areas also relies to a certain extent on analogy with household usage patterns observed by ethnographers studying traditional societies.

Archaeologists are thus heavily dependent on ethnographic research for understanding and evaluating what they unearth. The use of analogies with observable cultures for interpreting excavated materials involves a specialized kind of ethnography called *ethnoarchaeology*. This term refers to investigations of living traditional communities, preferably done by archaeologists themselves, in order to find data relevant to their questions about artifacts and structures that have been archaeologically retrieved. Some scholars question the legitimacy of this interpretive move, claiming that the practices of recent cultures may be quite different from those of ancient ones. Nonetheless, it is generally accepted that analogies provide an invaluable role in determining the function of ancient artifacts and identifying the use of architectural spaces under certain conditions. One is that the contemporary culture should be in the same general geographic area as the ancient one. Another is that the same level of society should be examined; that is, information about ancient peasant households must come from observing peasants still living in traditional ways rather than elites living in more modern urban contexts.[24] Several classic ethnoarchaeological projects in Iran have been particularly useful in analyzing the use of household objects and space in ancient Palestinian dwellings, as have many smaller projects in Israel, Cyprus, Jordan, and Syria.[25]

---

23. How the functional identities of the artifacts described below (in §§3.3–5) were established will not be explained; that information is not germane here.

24. The value and limitations of ethnoarchaeology are summarized by Charles E. Carter, "Ethnoarchaeology," *OEANE* 2:280–284. See also the pioneering work of Carol Kramer, *Ethnoarchaeology: Implications of Ethnography for Archaeology* (New York: Columbia University Press, 1979).

25. The Iranian projects are those of Patty Jo Watson, *Archaeological Ethnography in Western Iran* (Tucson: University of Arizona Press, 1979); and Carol Kramer, *Village Ethnoarchaeology: Rural Iran in Archaeological Perspective* (New York: New York Academic Press, 1982).

2.3.2. Engendering Archaeological Remains

For the purposes of engendering archaeological remains—that is, determining the gender of those who used them—additional analytical steps are needed. Artifacts are not intrinsically "gender noisy"; just as they are not labeled with respect to their function, they also are not labeled with respect to the gender of their user. The division of labor by gender may be nearly universal, but there is wide variation across cultures in the assignment of various tasks to either women or men.[26] Archaeologists dealing with prehistoric materials have devised ways to attribute gender to artifacts, and those of us dealing with historic periods must do likewise. Iconographic materials must be consulted, for they sometimes depict a woman (or a man) doing a certain task. Relevant textual sources are also important. The Hebrew Bible is helpful in this regard, for it occasionally alludes to a woman or a man carrying out a household activity. Although biblical evidence is problematic for evaluating female status, its references to aspects of daily life help us assign gender to activities involving the objects recovered by archaeology.

2.3.3. Using Archaeological Data to Reconstruct Women's Roles
and Relationships

One final kind of interpretation entails assigning meaning to women's activities, once they have been ascertained. A number of questions can be posed. If women's tools can be identified, and if their location in household space can be determined, can that information be used for understanding women's economic contributions to the household? Can it help in reconstructing their social interactions? That is, what are the economic and social realities reflected by the material culture? Also, what might female control of certain household technologies tell us about the dynamics of women's relationships with other members of their households and with members of other households? What might certain artifact groups tell us about women's role in household religious life? Answers to these and other similar questions can be suggested by engaging information from *anthropological archaeology*. Gendered archaeology carried out by anthropologists in the past several decades has provided paradigms, based on the direct observation of human behavior in traditional

---

26. A landmark study analyzes data from 186 societies and indicates the ratio of male and female participation in basic economic activities; see George P. Murdock and Catherine Provost, "Factors in the Division of Labor by Sex: A Cross-Cultural Analysis," *Ethnology* 12 (1973): 203–25. Women dominate in most maintenance activities, which are defined below in §3.3.

settings (that is, using ethnography), that help us determine, at the very least, the range of possibilities for reconstructing various aspects of women's lives.[27]

3. EXAMPLES OF RELEVANT ARCHAEOLOGICAL DATA

A number of different kinds of archaeologically recovered materials, many of which can be considered part of household life, are sources of information about women's lives. Remains of their bodies provide information, albeit limited, about their physical health and life spans. The domestic structures in which they and their families lived indicate their subsistence patterns and the spatial parameters of their daily interactions. Certain implements, especially those used in food and textile production, help us reconstruct women's daily activities. Items of personal use and adornment illuminate their aesthetic sensibilities and also certain religious practices. Iconographic remains, which are examined in another chapter of this project,[28] must be mentioned briefly in that they are perhaps witness to certain aspects of women's religious lives. Certain epigraphic remains provide additional information, probably about elite rather than peasant women. Finally, local community shrines indicate a context for religious life more accessible than the distant central shrines of the kingdoms of Israel and Judah.

The data presented here come from sites that can be associated with Israelites of the premonarchic and monarchic periods. In archaeological terms, the premonarchic period is called Iron Age I (or Iron I) and dates from about 1200 to 1000 B.C.E. The monarchic era, known as Iron Age II (or Iron II), begins in the tenth century B.C.E. and continues to the early sixth century, when the Babylonians conquer Jerusalem and Judah in 587/6 B.C.E. Most of the sites are in the central hill country of Palestine, from Galilee in the north to the northern Negev in the south; but some information also comes from sites east of the Jordan that perhaps can be associated with the tribe of Reuben in the premonarchic period. Some of the epigraphic remains are from the exilic period, which dates to the sixth century and is sometimes called Iron III, or from the postexilic Persian period, which dates from the late sixth century to the beginning of the Hellenistic Period (520–332 B.C.E.); they are

---

27. Resources for engendering Syro-Palestinian archaeology are presented in Carol Meyers, "Engendering Syro-Palestinian Archaeology: Reasons and Resources," *NEA* 66 (2003): 185–97. For a recent summary of theoretical advances and case studies, see Sarah Milledge Nelson, ed., *Handbook of Gender in Archaeology* (Lanham, Md.: AltaMira, 2006).

28. Silvia Schroer, "Ancient Near Eastern Pictures as Keys to Biblical Texts," in this volume.

included because they arguably reflect conditions that would have obtained in earlier periods.

3.1. HUMAN SKELETAL REMAINS

Direct information from the analysis of mortuary remains from Iron Age sites is virtually nonexistent for several reasons. For one thing, the study of human skeletons has not been possible at Israelite sites for several decades because of Israel's 1978 Antiquities Law, which forbids the excavation of "Jewish" burials. Even studies of burials excavated prior to 1978 contain little relevant evidence, for many of them were more concerned with measuring crania and ascertaining racial differences than with determining mortality rates or assessing ancient pathologies. Also, accurate determination of the sex and age of the skeletal remains usually requires the presence of most of the skeleton. This condition is rarely met in Iron Age human remains, most of which are found in the rock-cut tombs that were the dominant type of Israelite burial.[29] In those tombs, the desiccated bones of deceased ancestors were often moved aside or collected in repositories to make room for new burials. Moreover, because the rock-cut tombs were costly to make, they were probably the final resting places of the well-to-do, who would have enjoyed somewhat longer lives and better health than did the average subsistence farmers, who were most likely laid to rest in simple cist graves or perhaps communal graves (Jer 26:23; 2 Kgs 23:6) that have not survived. Another problem is that grave robbers, both ancient and modern, have greatly disturbed skeletal remains while gathering their spoils. Overall, gender and age have been determined for a very small and unrepresentative sample of the skeletal remains.

Because direct evidence about the longevity of Israelite women is so sparse, indirect evidence—from several tomb groups of the Bronze Age, which preceded the Iron Age, and also from the study of skeletal remains of other Mediterranean peoples—must be used. These data are relevant (for the average length of life did not vary significantly in the last three millennia B.C.E.), and they indicate short life spans. For example, analysis of Bronze Age skeletal remains from Lachish suggests that the average age at death for males was between 30 and 40 years and between 20 and 30 years for females;[30] the Iron Age remains show an even shorter life span. The average life expectancy

---

29. Elizabeth Bloch-Smith, *Judahite Burial Practices and Beliefs about the Dead* (JSOT-Sup 123; Sheffield: JSOT Press, 1992), 41–52, 137. Most of the evidence is from the southern kingdom (Judah); it is not clear why so few burials from the northern kingdom have survived.

30. Madeline Giles, "Human and Animal Remains. Appendix B," in *Lachish IV (Tell*

in an Iron Age tomb group from the western Mediterranean is estimated to be 23 years (for males and females combined),[31] a figure similar to that suggested for ancient Rome.[32] Of course, these figures are averages that take into account high infant mortality, with as many as one in two children dying in the first year or two of life. Thus some people survived into middle age and even beyond. Still, many women probably predeceased their spouses.

The short life spans and high infant mortality rate make it likely that, if not infertile, women were pregnant or nursing for much of their adult life. (It is important to note that the maternal functions of bearing children and caring for them are integrated into household life in traditional societies; they were not considered discrete roles and so would not have created the work-versus-family dichotomy that many contemporary women face.[33])

Virtually no studies of mortuary remains of the biblical period from Palestine have sought to understand population health. However, an overview of the musculoskeletal development in prehistoric and early historic Levant suggests that women and men had similar activity patterns, with similar amounts of stress on muscles and joints, until the advent of agriculture, when female musculature becomes more robust. Presumably this shift derives from the emerging division of labor by gender and the increased number of female tasks involving strength and repetitive motion, especially those involving the muscle groups used in grinding grain.[34] Data from a Syrian site reveal significant gender-linked abnormalities in skeletal structure.[35] Adult females have certain deformities—collapse of the last dorsal vertebra and severely arthritic big toes—understood to result from a demanding and injurious physical activity, namely, grinding grain while on one's hands and knees. This position appears in Egyptian iconography depicting a servant bent over a grinding stone, toes curled forward to provide leverage.[36] Because women were responsible for grinding grain in ancient Israel (see below, §3.3.1), some likely

ed-Duweir): The Bronze Age (ed. Olga Tufnell et al.; London: Oxford University Press, 1958), 318.

31. Alicia Alsean, Assumpcio Malgosa, and Simo Carles, "Looking into the Demography of an Iron Age Population in the Western Mediterranean. I. Mortality," American Journal of Physical Anthropology 110 (1999): 285–301.

32. Bruce W. Frier, "Roman Life Expectancy: Ulpian's Evidence," HSCP 86 (1982): 249.

33. Meyers, Discovering Eve, 167–68.

34. Jane Peterson, Sexual Revolutions: Gender and Labor at the Dawn of Agriculture (Walnut Creek, Calif.: AltaMira, 2002).

35. Theya Molleson, "The Eloquent Bones of Abu Hureyra," Scientific American 271 (1994): 70–75.

36. James H. Breasted Jr., Egyptian Servant Statues (Bollingen Series 13; Washington, D.C.: Bollingen Foundation, Pantheon Books, 1948), pl. 16b.

suffered repetitive stress injuries, which would have been painful if not debilitating, similar to those present in the Syrian examples.

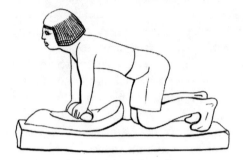

Fig. 1. Woman grinding. This small statue, in the Boston Museum of Fine Arts (accession number 21.2601), is from Giza, Egypt, and dates to the Old Kingdom. It depicts the way grinding stones were used, with the woman kneeling and bent forward, her toes curled under. (Schroer and Keel, *Die Ikonographie Palästinas/Israels*, vol. 1, no. 151).

3.2. ISRAELITE DWELLINGS: THE PILLARED (OR FOUR-ROOM) HOUSE

The typical Israelite dwelling is sometimes called the "four-room house" because of the four distinct rooms of the ground plan in many of the Iron Age dwellings that have been excavated.[37] However, there are many variants. Some examples have five rooms, and others have only three or two. In some instances extra rooms are added on, or the main rooms are subdivided. In addition, many probably had second stories with additional rooms. Thus a more suitable designation is "pillared house" because of the rows of pillars separating the longitudinal spaces of the ground floor in most examples. The description presented here is of a typical example, but there are many variants.

Fig. 2. Pillared house. A typical Israelite dwelling, often but not always with three longitudinal rooms and one transverse room at the rear, was suited to the needs of farming families. It had spaces for work and storage on the ground floor and probably also on a second story and on the roof. Room 2, the main longitudinal room, was the major, but not only, work space. (Adapted from a Tall al-'Umayri field plan, courtesy of Douglas Clark, Madeba Plains Project).

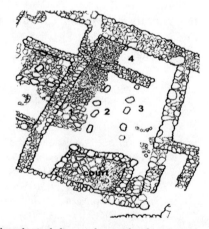

37. For descriptions that engage ethnoarchaeological data and consider function as well as architecture, see especially Lawrence E. Stager, "The Archaeology of the Family in Ancient Israel," *BASOR* 260 (1985): 1–35; and John S. Holladay Jr., "House, Israelite," *ABD* 3:308–18.

The ground-floor plan features a large, rectangular central space with a beaten earth floor; this space, or part of it, may have been open to the air, forming a small interior courtyard. The longitudinal room on one side of the central space is often paved with flagstones or cobbles. The longitudinal room along the other side and the transverse room across the back—both often subdivided—have beaten-earth floors. The dwelling is usually entered through the front wall of the central space. The walls are made of sun-dried mud bricks set upon stone foundations, usually two-three courses high; they appear to have been plastered on both inside and outside surfaces. The roof, which would have been flat, provided additional workspace and was probably used for sleeping space in the hot summer months.

The arrangement of space on the ground floor seems to be an adaptation to the needs of self-sufficient farm families in the hill country west of the Jordan River, in the northern Negev, and at some sites east of the Jordan. It provided a place for the stabling of animals, probably in the longitudinal room with the stone flooring. Storage vessels are commonly recovered from the transverse room (or rooms), indicating that the space was used for the storage of foodstuffs to be consumed from one harvest to the next; farming and food-processing implements are also stored there. However, in some instances food-processing activities were also carried out there, judging from the analysis of micro-artifacts.[38] The large central space as well as the longitudinal room with the earthen floor were the main activity areas; they provided room for transforming the family's crops into edible form and for producing the various utilitarian items, including cloth and tools, needed for daily life. These areas may also have been leisure-time space as well as eating space. That is, all the ground-floor rooms of the pillared dwellings were probably multipurpose spaces, changing function during the day according to the tasks or activities of the moment. Their usages would also have varied according to the season, for in cold or inclement weather, many activities that took place in nearby outdoor space were moved indoors. Rooms in the second story (or roof) provided sleeping areas (1 Kgs 17:19; 2 Kgs 4:10) as well as additional space for maintenance tasks[39] (Josh 2:6) or storage, judging from items recovered in the debris layers formed by the collapse of upper stories.

The extensive scholarship on pillared houses has focused mainly on architectural and functional aspects and has paid little attention to the behavior patterns of its inhabitants. Yet the dwelling was a major part of the Israelite household (see §2.1). Thus, as in traditional cultures everywhere,

---

38. Hardin, *Households*.
39. See §3.3 for a definition of "maintenance" activities.

the different areas of the Israelite house can also be considered "social" space, which in turn can be gendered.[40] That is, certain areas were relegated to activities performed by one gender rather than the other. This does not necessarily mean gender-segregated space; rather, it indicates a fluidity of spatial usage and allows for the possibility of crossover in gendered activity. Moreover, some household space at times was used by both genders simultaneously, as when family groups gathered for meals or special events. Except for activities carried out solitarily—and there would have been relatively few within the dwelling itself—household space, as the location of human interaction, thus had social properties. Sometimes it involved women interacting with women, as will become clear when the specific artifacts and associated tasks are examined; sometimes it meant the interactions of female and male family members with each other and perhaps also with guests of either gender. The identification of spatially located activities has implications for understanding the social relations of household members with each other and also with people from other households (see §4.3).

The amount of roofed space in pillared dwellings has been used to calculate the average size of Israelite families, using ethnoarchaeological information about space per person. The results are much debated.[41] Most calculations suggest that a nuclear family consisted of a conjugal pair with three or four children; this would have entailed at least six pregnancies for most women, given infant mortality rates. Whether real or constructed, biblical genealogies and narratives that mention many offspring do not represent a typical family. Rather, they signal elite families, where nutrition and life circumstances would have been more favorable to the survival of children. Similarly, polygyny, which could increase the number of offspring, was rarely possible except in elite families.

At some sites several pillared dwellings are linked together, sometimes with one exterior wall serving two adjacent buildings and with shared outdoor or courtyard space. This pattern has been interpreted as an indication of family complexity.[42] These groups of dwellings, with each individual unit occupied by a nuclear family, would represent a compound or extended

---

40. Carol Meyers, "Material Remains and Social Relations: Women's Culture in Agrarian Households of the Iron Age," in *Symbiosis, Symbolism, and the Power of the Past: Canaan, Ancient Israel, and Their Neighbors from the Early Bronze Age through Roman Palaestina* (ed. William G. Dever and Seymour Gitin; Winona Lake, Ind: Eisenbrauns, 2003), 426–30.

41. The issues are summarized in Avraham Faust, "Differences in Family Structure between Cities and Villages in Iron Age II," *TA* 26 (1999): 235–36.

42. Stager, "Archaeology of the Family," 18–20.

family, likely represented by the biblical term בית אב "house[hold] of one's father" (but see §4.5), which was the fundamental unit of Israelite society. Presumably it included a senior couple, unmarried offspring, and married sons with their spouses and children.[43] In this scenario, the opportunities for interaction among members of neighboring dwellings in the family compound would have been numerous, as the location of implements used in household tasks suggests. However, even if adjacent dwellings were occupied by nuclear families *not* related to each other, as was probably the case in larger settlements, opportunities for daily interaction among occupants of neighboring dwellings were likely numerous. In smaller communities or solitary farmsteads, the pillared houses were much larger—as much as twice the size of those in towns. In addition, their rooms are frequently subdivided. In those cases, the single structure itself perhaps housed a multigenerational family.[44] Interaction among family members under those circumstances would inevitably have been part of the normal course of daily life.

It is important to note that, whether living in smaller adjacent buildings or larger individual buildings, extended families were not isolated units but rather were enmeshed in the larger communities (villages or towns) in which they were situated. Moreover, these larger communities were not random collections of families but rather comprised related family units perhaps represented by the biblical term משפחה, which is often translated "clan." Perhaps the term "lineage," or better "patrilineages," is more appropriate, for patrilineage indicates that the groupings of families in a village or town are related to a real or putative common (male) ancestor. Local political affairs would have been managed by lineage leaders (elders). The larger towns likely contained several such lineages.[45]

This information about households in relation to larger community structure has implications for appreciating the social relations among women in Israelite settlements. Those female social relationships can be identified by analyzing the archaeological record of various household maintenance activities carried out on the ground floor of excavated buildings and assigning gender to those activities. (No second stories have survived.)

---

43. See n. 95.

44. Avraham Faust, "The Rural Community in Ancient Israel during Iron Age II," *BASOR* 317 (2000): 17–39.

45. See Faust, "Rural Community," for a summary of the extensive scholarship, using biblical and sometimes archaeological data, on Israelite social structures. See also McNutt, *Reconstructing the Society*, 85–90.

3.3. Artifacts of Maintenance Activities

The large pillared house (or adjacent smaller ones) was the basic economic unit for most Israelites; all able-bodied family members, including young children, would have been part of the work force necessary for obtaining the basic necessities of life. Artifacts discovered within pillared buildings testify to the fundamental maintenance activities—the production of food and clothing—carried out in those dwellings. "Maintenance activities" is a technical term denoting practices providing for the sustenance and welfare of the members of a social group.[46] It often refers to female technologies necessary to sustain life—including those that transform plant or animal materials into a form that can be consumed or stored and that convert fibers into fabrics.

Note that, although ceramic vessels are ubiquitous at all archaeological sites dating back to the Neolithic, they will not be considered here because pottery types used for storage and consumption were used by both women and men. Moreover, gender attribution to pottery used in the preparation of some foods, while perhaps possible, would not be helpful for determining gender-specific use locations because those vessels would have been transferred from one space to another for storage, cooking, and serving. It should be noted, however, that while men may have been potters in commercial workshops (Jer 18:1–4), ethnography suggests that women in villages may well have produced pottery.[47] Installations and vessels used for making wine and oil are also sometimes found in households but will not be considered; although the different stages of oil and wine production may have been single-gendered tasks, it is likely that some aspects involved both female and male labor.[48] Either way, attributing gender remains speculative.

---

46. Margarita Sánchez Romero, "Women, Maintenance Activities, and Space," in *SOMA 2001: Symposium on Mediterranean Archaeology: Proceedings of the Fifth Annual Meeting of Postgraduate Researchers, the University of Liverpool, 23–23 February 2001* (ed. Georgina Muskett, Aikaterini Koltsida, and Mercourios Georgiadis; BAR International Series 1040; Oxford: Archaeopress, 2002): 178.

47. Gloria London, *Women Potters of Cyprus* (video; Nicosia, Cyprus: Tetraktys Film Productions, 2000).

48. Larger installations for crushing olives or grapes to make oil or wine would have been used by large-scale commercial producers. Also, ordinary households perhaps shared communal presses or paid to use commercial ones in large settlements; see Faust, "Rural Community," 22–23. However, attributing gender to the workers in commercial or communal installations may not be possible.

3.3.1. Grain-Processing Implements and Installations and Their Locations[49]

The basic diet of the Israelites is well-known, mainly from biblical texts. The archaeological recovery of plant (grains, seeds, beans, pits) and animal remains (bones) generally confirms the textual information. The most important component of the Israelite diet was grain, with approximately half of a person's daily calorie consumption coming from grain-based foods. Cereal products—porridges or gruel but more commonly bread—were such an important part of the Israelite diet that לחם, the Hebrew word for "bread," sometimes means "food" in general in the Hebrew Bible. However, only the seeds, and not the husks, of cereal products are edible. Also, the nutritional starch in the seeds cannot be easily digested in its raw form. Consequently, transforming grains into edible forms involves a complex series of procedures—drying or soaking, grinding, sifting, kneading, heating, and often leavening—with grinding the most prominent (Isa 28:28). The preparation of edible grains would have been a daily activity in Israelite households. Crushing grain to provide enough flour to supply bread or gruel for a nuclear family would have required two to three hours of grinding time each day. No other activity took up so much household time and space as did the preparation of cereal-based foods.

Identifying and engendering the grinding tools and ovens used for processing grains thus tells us about a major component of women's work. Just as important, establishing the location of these archaeological remains provides information about the social interactions of women at work.

Grinding Tools. Evidence of grinding appears in the archaeological record in the form of grinding stones, probably indicated by the biblical word רחים, which is a dual form and thus represents a pair of stones. The lower grinding stone, sometimes called a quern or grinding slab, has a concave surface, a flat bottom, and is usually twice as long as it is wide. The smaller, upper grinding stone has convex surfaces and is called a grinder or handstone. The Hebrew term for the upper stone is from the root רכב, which means "to ride" and indicates that the handstone "rides" on the lower stone. The handstone is held in both hands and is moved back and forth across grains placed upon the lower stone, which rests on the ground. The repetitive movement requires both strength and stamina; unfortunately, the body position of the person grinding is potentially damaging to the lower back, knees, and curled-under

---

49. For the sources of the information in this section, see Carol Meyers, "Having Their Space and Eating There Too: Bread Production and Female Power in Ancient Israelite Households," *Nashim* 5 (2002): 14–28.

toes (see the end of §3.1) unless, as is occasionally the case, the lower stone was set upon a raised platform.

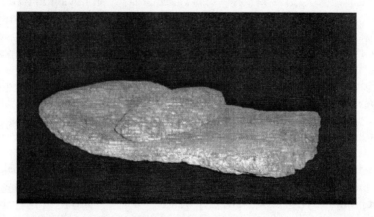

Fig. 3. Pair of grinding stones. Grains were placed on the larger bottom stone, and the smaller upper stone was moved back and forth over the grains to reduce them to flour. Only a few grains could be crushed at one time, making this a time-consuming and laborious task. (Zwickel, *Frauenalltag im biblischen Israel*, fig. 6).

Can gender be attributed to this task? Ethnographic evidence points to women as grinders in household contexts, and several biblical texts mention women in relation to grinding. According to Exod 11:5, Egyptian girls labor at the grinding stones. In Isa 47:2, Babylon is personified as a royal woman who will become a working woman, taking up the handstone to produce flour when God overcomes her country. Job alludes to the possibility of his wife being unfaithful by saying she will "grind for another" (31:10), a double entendre alluding to sexuality as well as flour production; Eccl 12:3 refers to women doing household labor as "women who grind." Also relevant is the story of the woman of Thebez (Judg 9:53–54; 2 Sam 11:21), who throws an upper grinding stone from a tower to kill the upstart king Abimelech.

Ovens. The remains of ovens, the other major archaeological correlate of household grain processing, are more fragmentary. Made of a mixture of clay and straw, ovens were built on a foundation of small stones. There were two variants, both shaped like a beehive with an opening at the top. The wood fire that provided heat for one kind, probably indicated by the biblical term רונת(Exod 8:3 [Heb. 7:28]), would be inside, with the loaves slapped against the interior walls to bake once the coals were hot enough. In the other version, burning fuel (dung cakes) was packed against the outside of the oven, and loaves were placed on the pebbled floor of the interior. Bread could also be baked on baking trays or griddles (see Lev 2:5, 7; 7:9) placed over an open hearth; these are very difficult to identify in the archaeological record.

Not surprisingly, household ovens are associated with female labor by ethnographic data and according to several biblical texts. The medium of Endor prepares unleavened cakes, presumably by baking them (1 Sam 28:24), as well as meat from a calf that she slaughters. Women as bakers appear in Samuel's famous warning (1 Sam 8:13) to the people that having a monarchy would mean losing the labor of many offspring. That passage also refers to women as cooks, indicating that other food-processing artifacts, notably stone mortars and pestles for grinding herbs or other foodstuffs and perhaps for loosening the outer hulls of grains, were mainly women's tools.

Location of Grinding Tools and Ovens. The location of the grinding stones and other food preparation tools in pillared dwellings indicates where women did much of their daily work. This information is essential for understanding the social interactions of the women who used them. Unfortunately, as already noted, archaeological reports do not always report all those artifacts, nor do they indicate their find-spots, when they have been discovered *in situ* rather than in secondary deposits. Yet data from the few excavation projects that have provided this information make it quite certain that grinding stones as well as plastered installations and smaller food-preparation tools are generally found in one of the large longitudinal rooms, typically but not exclusively the central one, of pillared buildings, suggesting that grinding took place in covered areas.[50]

Looking more closely at the location of upper and lower grinding stones at many sites reveals that several sets of them are often found near each other, with none being found *in situ* outside houses. For example, at 'Izbet Sartah, a small village on the western edge of the central hill country, multiple grinding stones were found in virtually every dwelling, especially in the large central room of the buildings. The number of upper stones tends to be greater than those of lower stones, perhaps reflecting the fact that the former were cheaper and could be more easily moved. The discovery of several sets of tools in the same household space indicates that grinding was not a solitary activity; rather, two or three women processed grain at the same time. Ethnographic information supports this interpretation: when simple tasks are time-consuming and repetitive, it is common for women from nearby households

---

50. See Philip J. King and Lawrence E. Stager, *Life in Biblical Israel* (Library of Ancient Israel; Louisville: Westminster John Knox, 2001), 67.

to perform these tasks together. Note also that in the New Testament Jesus speaks of two women grinding together (Matt 24:41).

The location of ovens is less consistent. Although often found in the main longitudinal room of a pillared dwelling, usually near a door to let smoke escape, in other cases they are located outside the building in open space or in a small adjacent building. The ones outside the homes arguably served several families. A biblical text supports this possibility. Leviticus 26:26 describes a time of near starvation, when a single oven can be used for the loaves of ten women; presumably fewer women—but more than one—would use a single oven in normal times. This would be an ecologically sound practice, saving on fuel in areas that were not heavily wooded. A postbiblical rabbinic text quotes a sage as saying that three women knead together but use a single oven (y. Pesaḥ. 3.30b). Although kneading implements were usually made of organic materials—wooden boards, baskets, or pieces of cloth—and do not survive, this passage suggests that kneading, like grinding and baking, was carried out by women working together in ancient Israel, as in many traditional societies. Indeed, a mud-brick installation preserved at Tel Dor appears to be a kneading trough, and a terracotta statuette from Boetia shows several women kneading dough together in a trough similar to the one at Tel Dor. Ethnographic data also indicate the use of a single oven by the women of several families. Thus, the information about ovens and perhaps kneading installations indicates that, like grinding stones, they were likely to have involved women working together.

3.3.2. Textile-Producing Tools[51]

Next to providing grain-based cereals and loaves for food, the production of textiles from wool, cotton, and flax is probably the most important maintenance activity; and it is well-represented in the archaeological record. Transforming fibers into fabric requires a complex series of steps. The fibers must be washed, carded, spun into thread, and then woven into fabric, which was then sewn into garments or other items. Israelite men may have produced the fibers—note that Gen 38:12 and 1 Sam 25:4 mention men shearing sheep. However, other biblical texts indicate that, as in most cultures, women performed the subsequent steps. They bring special yarns for the tabernacle's textiles (Exod 35:25–26) and weave fabrics for the temple (2 Kgs 23:7); Rahab

---

51. Except for the data from Beth-shan and Batash, the sources of the information in this section are given in Meyers, "Material Remains," 432–34. For a comprehensive discussion of women and textiles in antiquity, see Elizabeth Wayland Barber, *Women's Work: The First 20,000 Years—Women, Cloth, and Society in Early Times* (New York: Norton, 1994).

dries flax on the roof of her house (Josh 2:6); Delilah weaves Samson's hair into the warp threads of her loom (Judg 16:13–14); and the woman of Prov 31 spins, works in wool and flax, makes cloth, and also markets some of what she produces (31:13, 19, 22, 24). Iconographic and written remains from other ancient Near Eastern societies and the east Mediterranean provide additional evidence that household textile production was woman's work.

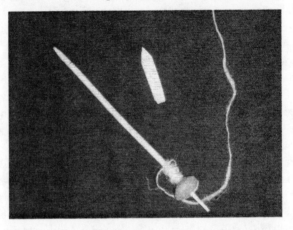

Fig. 4. Spindle, set in a stone spindle whorl, and piece of bone shuttle. Fibers were spun into thread using the spindle, and the shuttle was used to lift the warp threads and facilitate passage of the weft threads under and over them on the vertical frame-looms used in the Iron Age. (Zwickel, *Frauenalltag im biblischen Israel*, fig. 11).

Rarely do any of the fibers or fabrics survive, but archaeologists have found the tools of three different stages of textile work. First, evidence of making thread is provided by the discovery of many small stone or clay discs, called spindle whorls, which were used to stabilize the wooden spindles on which fibers were twisted together to form threads. Second, although the looms themselves were made of wood and have not survived, two tools linked with the weaving stage—loom weights and bone spatulae—are often found. The former are rounded chunks of stone or clay that are perforated with a hole so that a thread can be attached to it; the warp (vertical) threads of a loom are tied to these objects to keep them taut.[52] The latter are used to guide the weft threads in and out of the warp threads. Third, the final stage of textile produc-

---

52. The presence of loom weights attests to the Israelite use of vertical (warp-weighted) looms, for weights were unnecessary in the other kind of loom used in the ancient Near East, the horizontal ground loom.

tion, sewing fabric into a garment or some other item, is represented by the many bone or bronze needles found by archaeologists.

Not all of the extant textile tools are found *in situ* or intact. The original usage spots of the smaller, lightweight tools—spindle whorls, needles, and spatulae—can rarely be recovered; they have typically been displaced from their original usage location when the pillared building was destroyed or abandoned. Moreover, textile tools were not used every day and were stored away when not in use, perhaps on a shelf; thus the rooms in which they are discovered may not have been the rooms in which they were used. Also, because bone objects are somewhat fragile and often found in fragmentary condition, they are not always identifiable. The perforated weights, however, were part of a loom; and once the loom was set up, with its warp and weft threads in place, it would have been relatively stationary. Examining the find spots of the loom weights thus provides important information about where women wove fabrics.

Like grinding tools, the weaving tools are not always published in ways that allow us to identify where they were used. Fortunately, there are some notable exceptions. At some sites there are actually hundreds of the weights, perhaps indicating commercial production. This would not be surprising, given that Israelite textiles, at least during the more developed economy of the later monarchy, were an important trade item. But the recoverable remains of household textile production provide important information about this female task.

For example, about one hundred loom weights were discovered against the eastern wall in the main longitudinal room of a large eighth-century B.C.E. dwelling at Tell Beth-shan in the northern Jordan Valley.[53] Found in two concentrations, they represent two or possibly three looms. Amazingly, charred remains of two wooden shafts, probably beams of one of the looms itself, were also recovered. Household ceramic vessels and grinding tools were found nearby, attesting to multiple usage of this space. The disposition of loom weights of the Iron II period at Tel Batash (biblical Timnah), on the western edge of the highlands, shows a similar pattern.[54] A concentration of forty-one weights was found along one wall of the main room of a dwelling, where they had been set into the loom. Several spindle whorls were also found

---

53. Amihai Mazar, *From the Late Bronze Age IIB to the Medieval Period* (vol. 1 of *Excavations at Tel Beth-Shan 1989–1996*; Jerusalem: Israel Exploration Society and Institute of Archaeology, Hebrew University of Jerusalem, 2006), 220.

54. Deborah Cassuto, "Bringing Home the Artifacts: A Social Interpretation of Loom Weights in Context," in *The World of Women in the Ancient and Classical Near East* (ed. Beth Alpert Nakhai; Newcastle-upon-Tyne: Cambridge Scholars, 2008), 72–76.

nearby, as were grinding tools and cooking pots. Again, the artifacts indicate an activity area that included food preparation in addition to weaving and spinning. These concentrations of artifacts would be expected.[55] Unlike grain processing, textile work was not a daily task. However, it also was time-consuming and tedious; thus it would often have been a social task. Ethnographic evidence supports what the archaeological data suggest and also indicates a pragmatic reason for several women to do textile work together: setting up the warp and weft threads was normally a two-person job.

3.3.3. Interpreting the Artifacts of Maintenance Activities

Three important conclusions result from examining the archaeological record of maintenance tools: (1) Food processing and textile production were women's tasks. (2) Several sets of grinding stones or loom weights are often recovered from the same room, indicating that several women were grinding or weaving at the same time. Other artifacts of food preparation (mortars and pestles, cooking vessels, etc.) and of textile production (spindle whorls, needles, etc.) are found in the vicinity of grinding stones and loom weights, further suggesting that several people were working near each other. Women's labor was thus frequently social: their workspace was a gender-specific social space. (3) Food-processing and textile tools tend to be found in one of the main longitudinal rooms, typically a multiuse space, of a pillared building, where other family members would come and go during the course of a day. The implications of these features of maintenance activities will be discussed below in §4.2.

3.4. ARTIFACTS FOR PERSONAL USE

Items for personal use sometimes appear in the archaeological record,[56] although it is not always certain whether they belonged to women or men. For example, because long beards and hair for men were valued, the bone combs discovered by archaeologists are probably not gender-specific. The same is true for small bone or ivory pins, probably used to secure garments. However, some of the pins may have been used, at least by elite women, to secure long hair into a "well-set" coil or knot (see Isa 3:24). Small pottery vessels thought to contain expensive salves and perfumes (which were oint-

---

55. Cultic objects are sometimes also present; see §4.4.
56. For examples, see Michal Dayagi-Mendels, *Perfumes and Cosmetics in the Ancient World* (Jerusalem: Israel Museum, 1989).

ments, not liquids, in biblical days) can probably be associated with elite women. But ordinary women, as part of their food-processing tasks, would have worked with herbs and aromatics and prepared simple fragrances and unguents that they would have kept in such containers. Scents were used mainly by women (and perhaps some elite males), according to biblical data: they are frequently associated with the woman but not the man in the Song of Solomon (1:12–14; 4:6, 13–14; but cf. 3:6–7), and the women of the harem use them in Esth 2:12. Aromatic substances served not only as cosmetics but were also used for medicinal purposes (Jer 46:11; 51:8), and in the form of incense they served air-freshening and religious purposes. Women were surely involved in such activities, for Samuel (1 Sam 8:13) mentions women as "spice-makers" or "ointment-mixers" (Hebrew רקחות, often translated too narrowly as "perfumers") in his warning about the loss of female labor should the people decide to have a monarchy. Moreover, because perfumes and spices were used in burials (see 2 Chr 16:14), at least of elites, women would have contributed aromatic substances as well as laments (see Jer 9:17–19) to Israelite funerary practices.

Jewelry is fragile and valuable. Thus very few items have survived in household space; most come from tombs. Also, since both women and men wore jewelry, gender identification is a problem. However, some kinds of jewelry, especially beads and pieces made of shiny metal, were not simply items of personal adornment. Ethnographic evidence as well as ancient texts from other Near Eastern cultures suggests that women, especially those who were pregnant or who were new mothers, wore light-reflecting jewelry for apotropaic reasons. That is, shiny jewelry was considered protective against demonic forces that might threaten their lives or the lives of their unborn or infant children. Given the high infant mortality rate and the dangers of pregnancy and childbirth, it is likely that ancient Israelite women wore such jewelry.[57] Bone amulets with circles on them are also occasionally found, and the circles apparently were a magical symbol meant to deter the "evil eye" from harming the wearer. Perhaps the most striking amulets ever discovered are two tiny (3.9 cm long; 9.7 cm. long), rolled silver plaques, dating to the late Iron II period, from a tomb outside Jerusalem.[58] Both mention the name of God and

---

57. Carol Meyers, *Households and Holiness: The Religious Culture of Israelite Women* (Facets Books; Minneapolis: Fortress, 2005), 35, 51–52. See Schroer, "Old Oriental Pictures as Keys to Biblical Texts," in this volume for a discussion of the amulets depicting the Egyptian god Bes, who was thought to offer protection to pregnant women and newborn children.

58. Gabriel Barkay, Marilyn J. Lumberg, Andrew G. Vaughan, and Bruce Zuckerman,

a text, similar to Num 6:24–26, seeking divine protection; however, the gender of their owners is unknown.

3.5. Epigraphic (Written) Remains Mentioning Women

Most of the documents produced by the people of ancient Israel were written on perishable materials. Therefore, in contrast to the many thousands of inscriptions on stone or on clay tablets that have been discovered in Egypt and Mesopotamia, there are relatively few epigraphic remains from ancient Israel. However, several kinds of inscribed objects—ostraca and stamp seals—have survived and provide some information about women's lives. Most of the ostraca have been recovered from excavations, but relatively few of the seals—only 12–15 percent of the total—were discovered by archaeologists. The rest are "unprovenanced"; that is, they turn up on the antiquities market, and their place of origin is unknown. Unfortunately, many unprovenanced inscriptions may be forgeries. This is especially true if the inscription includes a name mentioned in the Bible, for those inscriptions bring high prices on the antiquities market. Some of the items mentioned in §§3.5.1–2 may be forgeries but are included here because there is no scholarly consensus about their inauthenticity.

One other kind of epigraphic material, letters written on papyrus, were discovered at Elephantine in Egypt and are also relevant. These Elephantine papyri include legal texts concerning the marital status of women as well as their business dealings.

3.5.1. Ostraca

"Ostracon" is a term referring to a shell, piece of stone, or, most often, potsherd with a brief inscription. Occasionally the text is incised, but most often it is written in ink. Unlike perishable materials, broken sherds were plentiful and cost nothing; thus they were used for keeping records or sending brief messages. Ostraca from the Iron II period attest to administrative aspects of the kingdoms of Judah and Israel.

Widow's Plea Ostracon. One ostracon, dating to the seventh century b.c.e., has been named "A Widow's Plea to an Official."[59] A woman calling

---

"The Amulets from Ketef Hinnom: A New Edition and Evaluation," *BASOR* 334 (2004): 41–71.

59. Pierre Bordreuil, Felice Israel, and Dennis Pardee, "King's Command and Widow's

herself "your maidservant" (a polite form of address toward an official) and identifying herself as a childless widow addresses an officer about rights to at least some of the property of her deceased husband 'Amasyahu:

> May YHWH bless you in peace. And now may my lord the official listen to your maidservant. My husband has died (leaving) no sons. (I request politely that the following) happen: (let) your hand (be) with me and entrust to your maidservant the inheritance about which you spoke to 'Amasyahu.

The case is somewhat similar to that of Zelophehad's daughters in Num 27:1–11; both claim inheritance rights for women, who would not ordinarily have them under ancient Israel's patrilineal system. This inscription implies that the widow's situation would be difficult without access to her husband's property; it also suggests that her claim is not an unreasonable one and is likely to have been honored.

Samaria Ostraca. Additional information about Israelite women comes from a corpus of some sixty-six ostraca dating to the mid-eighth century B.C.E. and recording the delivery or disbursement of oil and wine between Samaria and places in the tribal area of Manasseh.[60] The names on the ostraca include clan districts and people. Some of the districts correspond exactly to the female and male offspring of Manasseh listed in biblical genealogies. Two of them, each appearing in three different ostraca, are Hoglah (in nos. 45, 47, 66) and No'ah (in nos. 50, 52, 64). For example, ostracon 45 begins, "In the fifteenth year, from Ḥogl[â] to Ḥanan [son of] Ba['ar]ā," and ostracon 50 begins "In the fifteenth year, from No'ah to Gomer." The names Hoglah and No'ah correspond to two of Zelophehad's daughters, all of whom are presented in Josh 17:3–6 as part of tribal allotments. In these allotments, the ancestors' names probably represent eponymous founders of settlements. The appearance of Hoglah and No'ah in the ostraca suggests that the daughters-of-Zelophehad traditions in Num 27:1–11 and 36:1–12 reflect the historical reality of women as inheritors of territory in northern Manasseh and perhaps even as clan leaders.

Plea: Two New Hebrew Ostraca of the Biblical Period," *NEA* 61 (1998): 2–13. These scholars are confident that this ostracon is authentic, but others are dubious.

60. First published by the excavators: George A. Reisner, Clarence S. Fisher, and David G. Lyon, *Harvard Excavations at Samaria, 1908–1910* (2 vols.; Cambridge: Harvard University Press, 1924), 1:227–46.

Other Ostraca. Three administrative notations on potsherds, all dating
to the late seventh or early sixth century B.C.E., mention women as recipients or owners of commodities, thus indicating that women were involved
in economic transactions. One unprovenanced ostracon records the names
of six people—five men and a woman named "Mᵉšullemet the daughter of
'Elikon"—who were apparently to receive a ration, or perhaps a payment or
salary for services rendered, from a public official.[61] The woman's name is
known from the Bible (2 Kgs 21:19) and also appears on an unprovenanced
seal (see below, §3.5.2), but her father's name is otherwise unattested. The
authenticity of the other two ostraca is not in doubt, for they were discovered
in excavations at Jerusalem.[62] One designates three women whose names have
not survived as recipients of certain amounts of grain; they are each listed as
"[name] wife of [name]." The other is an inscription on a jar (and thus is not
technically an ostracon); it indicates that the jar belonged to a woman called
"daughter of Ya'ama" and contained good quality wine.

3.5.2. Seals and Bullae with Women's Names

Several stamp seals or their impressions (called bullae) attest to women's roles.
Seals are small stones (5–10 cm) with a design, an inscription, or both carved
in intaglio on its flat surface. Dating to the Iron II and Persian periods, they
almost always bear the names of their owners and were probably used in economic or legal transactions. Because seals were impressed on a lump of wet
clay that was affixed to documents, they served as a person's "signature" in
business dealings. The text of seals generally follows this form: "belonging to
NAME, son/daughter of NAME"; often the person's title, rank, or occupation
is added. More than twelve hundred West Semitic seals and bullae, mostly
unprovenanced, are known; and women's names, several of which are found
in the Bible, appear on about 3 percent of the Hebrew ones.[63] For example, a
seal of unknown origin and date reads: "Belonging to Abigayil daughter of

---

61. Robert Deutsch and Michael Heltzer, *New Epigraphic Evidence from the Biblical
Period* (Tel Aviv: Archaeological Center Publications, 1995), 83–88.

62. Joseph Naveh, "Hebrew and Aramaic Inscriptions," in *Inscriptions* (vol. 6 of *Excavations at the City of David 1978–1985 Directed by Yigal Shiloh*; ed. Donald T. Ariel; Qedem
41; Jerusalem: Institute of Archaeology, Hebrew University of Jerusalem, 2000), 3–5.

63. For a full corpus of seals, see Nahman Avigad and Benjamin Sass, *Corpus of West
Semitic Seals* (Jerusalem: Israel Academy of Sciences and Humanities, Israel Exploration
Society, and Institute of Archaeology, Hebrew University of Jerusalem, 1997); the seals with
women's names have been collected in Hennie J. Marsman, *Women in Ugarit and Israel:
Their Social and Religious Position in the Context of the Ancient Near East* (OtSt 49; Leiden:
Brill, 2003; repr., Atlanta: Society of Biblical Literature, 2009), 643–58.

Elḥanan."[64] Another seal also of unknown origin and date bears the inscription "Belonging to Meshillamot/Meshullemet"; it is possible, although not certain, that the owner was female.[65] An eighth-century example, reading "Belonging to Hannā (?) daughter of 'Azaryah," comes from excavations and is thus genuine; a second Hannah seal of the late eighth–early seventh century, reading "Belonging to Hannā," is probably from Lachish and may also be genuine.[66]

Fig. 5. Hannah seal impression. The impression, on a jar handle from a seventh-century B.C.E. context in Jerusalem, bears the inscription "Belonging to Hannah, daughter of 'Azaryah." Both names appear in the Hebrew Bible and on other seals. Hannah likely used her seal in a business transaction to "sign" the handle of the jar (of wine or oil) she was selling. (Courtesy of the Israel Exploration Society).

Scholars infer from the presence of their names that some women, probably from the upper classes, carried out business dealings in their own right;[67] the woman of Prov 31, who sold her textiles, may have been such an individual. Moreover, the elaborate decorative style on many of the women's seals suggests that their owners were women of means.[68] Whether women could read these seals—or whether they could have written letters such as the one on the widow's ostracon—is much debated. At least some experts believe that a modicum of literacy was relatively widespread among Israelites and not just among the upper classes; others disagree.[69] In any case, the seals

---

64. Avigad and Sass, *Corpus of West Semitic Seals*, no. 31. Abigail appears in 1 Sam 25.

65. Avigad and Sass, *Corpus of West Semitic Seals*, no. 255. Meshullemeth is a wife of King Manasseh (2 Kgs 21:19).

66. Avigad and Sass, *Corpus of West Semitic Seals*, nos. 37, 664. The biblical Hannah of 1 Sam 1–2 would date to centuries earlier.

67. Avigad and Sass, *Corpus of West Semitic Seals*, 30–31.

68. Marsman, *Women in Ugarit and Israel*, 658.

69. See Christopher A. Rollston, *Writing and Literacy in the World of Ancient Israel: Epigraphic Evidence from the Iron Age* (SBLABS 11; Atlanta: Society of Biblical Literature, 2010), 127–35.

attest to women's economic roles—the ability to buy or sell commodities or property—that transcend the household.

Several other seals are important as indications of women's political power. The first is an elaborately decorated (but unprovenanced) seal bearing the name Jezebel.[70] Because some date it to the ninth century (the era of the biblical Jezebel) and because it is quite large, it is plausibly a seal of the powerful Israelite queen Jezebel (1 Kgs 16:31; 18:4; 19:1–3; 21; 2 Kgs 9:30–37). However, for epigraphic reasons, an eighth-century date is more likely; but even if it were earlier and authentic, neither the identification of this Jezebel with the biblical queen nor the owner's female gender can be proved.[71]

Fig. 6. Shelomith seal. Discovered in Jerusalem and dating to the Persian period, the seal's inscription, "Belonging to Shelomith, maidservant of Elnatan the governor," refers to a woman of high status, perhaps a government official. (Courtesy of the Institute of Archaeology, Hebrew University of Jerusalem).

Two other seals—dating to the seventh century B.C.E. but of uncertain origin, if not forgeries—may also refer to women with administrative power. One reads "Belonging to Ma'adanah daughter of the king" and features a depiction of a lyre with a rosette in the middle of the sound-box.[72] The other, actually a bulla, is undecorated and reads "Belonging to Noiyah daughter of the king."[73] "Daughter of the king" is not simply a relational designation but, as is indicated by evidence from other ancient Near Eastern monarchies, may also be the title of a royal daughter as a functionary.[74]

Finally, two seals dating to the early Persian period (late sixth–early fifth century B.C.E.) may denote a woman in public office. One comes from

---

70. Avigad and Sass, *Corpus of West Semitic Seals*, no. 740.

71. Christopher A. Rollston, "Prosography and the יזבל Seal," *IEJ* 59 (2009): 86–91.

72. Avigad and Sass, *Corpus of West Semitic Seals*, no. 30.

73. Robert Deutsch, *Messages from the Past: Hebrew Bullae from the Time of Isaiah through the Destruction of the First Temple* (Tel Aviv: Archaeological Center, 1999), no. 14.

74. Elna K. Solvang, *A Woman's Place Is in the House: Royal Women of Judah and Their Involvement in the House of David* (JSOTSup 349: Sheffield: Sheffield Academic Press, 2003), 16–70, 78–79.

Jerusalem and reads "Belonging to Shelomith, maidservant of Elnatan the governor."[75] "Maidservant" can be an honorific term referring to a woman of high status, perhaps the governor's wife. But it can also be a title for a female public servant, a woman who is an official in her own right. This Shelomith was conceivably a descendant of the Davidic family and perhaps co-regent with Elnatan—if she is the Shelomith (of 1 Chr 3:19) who was a daughter of Zerubbabel.[76] A scion of the royal Davidic family, Zerubbabel was Elnatan's predecessor as governor of the postexilic community known as Yehud, serving from approximately 530 to 510 B.C.E. The other seal, only recently discovered (in an excavation), apparently reads just "Shelomith" and may be a seal of the same woman.[77]

3.5.3. Seals and Other Inscriptions Relating to Women's Lives

Although not bearing women's names, many seals and other inscriptions attest to the hopes of Israelites for successful childbearing. This information is obtained by examining the names on the inscriptions.[78] A person's name, which signified her or his existence and identity, was very important in Israelite culture. Some 1,630 different names are found on seals and other inscriptions; of those, 399 (24.5 percent) allude to some aspect of reproduction. The names are often compound words consisting of two or more elements: one of them the name of God (YHWH) or a shortened form of it (YAH), and the other a noun or verb. In combination, these elements form a phrase or short sentence. For example, Nedabyah means "Gift of YHWH," and Yonatan (Jonathan) means "YHWH has given." The fact that so many names found on the epigraphic remains (and also in the Bible) allude to the belief that God was instrumental in bringing about safe pregnancy and birth attests to the religiosity of women as well as men, especially in their hopes to have offspring. Of course, the frequency of names relating to childbirth also signifies the importance of reproduction. The Bible contains no ritual texts associated

---

75. Nahman Avigad, *Bullae and Seals from a Post-exilic Judean Archive* (Qedem 4; Jerusalem: Institute of Archaeology, Hebrew University of Jerusalem, 1976), pl. 11:14.

76. Eric M. Meyers, "The Shelomith Seal and the Judean Restoration: Some Additional Considerations," *ErIsr* 18 (1985): 33–38.

77. Michael Faust, comp., "Archeological Find Linked to Another Obscure O.T. Figure," *Baptist Press* (1 February 2008). Online: http://www.bpnews.net/bpnews.asp?id=27307.

78. Rainer Albertz, "Ritual Setting and Religious Significance of Birth in Ancient Israel" (paper presented at the Annual Meeting of the European Association of Biblical Studies, Piliscaba, Hungary, 7 August 2006). Note that mothers as well as fathers named their children—almost two-thirds of the name-giving narratives in the Hebrew Bible assign that role to the mother (e.g., Gen 30:22–24).

with pregnancy and birth, but these names show the religious dimension of women's reproductive roles (see §4.4). With infant-mortality rates so high, it is no wonder that the names given to many children acknowledged God's role in the birth of a child, as in the two names mentioned above.

3.5.4. Elephantine Papyri

Elephantine, an island in the Nile River opposite Aswan, was settled by emigrants from the southern kingdom of Judah in the early sixth century B.C.E. or before (see Jer 43–44). The Persians made it a military garrison in the late sixth century, and it survived until about 400 B.C.E. Written in Aramaic and dating mostly to the fifth century, the documents of this community include letters, legal documents, and administrative texts. They provide invaluable extrabiblical information about the religious and social practices of the sixth to fourth centuries B.C.E., and many of them attest to aspects of women's lives.[79] This information arguably reflects otherwise unknown practices of the Judeans who founded the colony, and it may even preserve some elements of the culture of the southern kingdom.

Information from family archives indicates that women could inherit from their fathers or husbands, buy and sell property, lend money, and divorce. The marriage contract for the third marriage of a woman named Mibtahiah, for example, shows that the property she brought to the marriage would remain hers and that either she or her husband could initiate divorce. The marriage contract of another woman, Tamut, similarly states that either partner could seek divorce and also indicates that the one who initiated divorce would have to bear the financial consequences:

> If tomorrow or another day Anani rises up on account of her (?) and says, "I divorce Tamut my wife," the divorce money is on his head. He shall give to Tamut in silver 7 shekels, 2 R., and all that she brought in in her hand she shall take out, from straw to thread. If tomorrow or another day Tamut rises up on account of her (?) and says, "I divorce my husband Anani," a like sum shall be on her head. She shall give to Anani in silver 7 shekels, 2 R., and all which she brought in in her hand she shall take out, from straw to thread.[80]

---

79. Summarized by Tamara Eskenazi, "Out from the Shadows: Biblical Women in the Postexilic Era," *JSOT* 54 (1992): 27–31.

80. Emil G. Kraeling, *The Brooklyn Museum Aramaic Papyri: New Discoveries of the Fifth Century BC from the Jewish Colony at Elephantine* (New Haven: Yale University Press, 1953), no. 2, lines 7–10.

The contract also stipulates that Tamut would gain control of her husband's property if he predeceased her.

These documents suggest that women had rights similar to those of men with respect to property. They also help challenge traditional interpretations of Deut 24:1–4, which deals with a case of a man divorcing his wife and seems to imply that only men could seek divorce. It is likely that at least some of the rights of women evident in the Elephantine papyri continued practices, undocumented in the Bible or other sources from Judah, that the Judean colonists brought to Egypt with them.

3.6. Religious Shrines

With its overwhelming interest in one national shrine (the wilderness tabernacle and the Jerusalem temple), the Hebrew Bible provides little information about women's roles in religious life. A sacrificial ceremony is mandated for women after childbirth in Lev 12:6–8, and the woman suspected of adultery is brought to the tabernacle for priestly adjudication in Num 5:11–28. Traveling to the central shrine (Jerusalem) for the celebration of major festivals is mandated for "all your males" in Deut 16:16, although women are apparently included in the stipulations for celebrating the Festivals of Weeks and Booths (Deut 16:11, 14), although not the Passover (16:1–8). But nothing is said about other women's rituals. Moreover, it is not certain that these priestly and Deuteronomic texts reflect religious customs widely in effect throughout Israelite history (see above, the sixth point in §1.2). In any case, these texts all concern the central shrine and give the impression that religious activities occurred mainly in Jerusalem. Narratives in Judges and Samuel reflect the existence of other shrines, but they depict a period prior to the construction of the Jerusalem temple. However, they are instructive in showing that sacrifices and prayer were offered to seek divine help in family issues, notably female infertility. Samson's mother and father offer a sacrifice in a field when they learn she will conceive (Judg 13:23). Hannah's petition asking that she conceive and also her sacrifice after she succeeds take place at the Shiloh shrine (1 Sam 1–2). In addition, the story of Micah's mother commissioning an idol for her household shrine reveals the existence of such shrines as well as a woman's involvement in equipping one (Judg 17:4–5).

The Bible also alludes to local shrines coexisting with the Jerusalem temple (e.g., 1 Kgs 14:23; 2 Kgs 17:9–10; Jer 2:20; Ezek 20:28–29; Hos 4:13). Those passages condemn them but in the process attest to their presence. Further, the passages about Hannah and Samson's mother indicate that women would have visited such shrines. Thus, although archaeological remains of shrines cannot reveal the gender of those who used them, the texts suggest that women as well as men participated in religious activities outside of the central shrine.[81] Archaeology provides information about the location of shrines, which in turn suggests their accessibility to women.

In general, no specific architectural form signifies a place of cultic or ritual activity, although the presence of one or more raised benches in a building is a strong indicator. More often, shrines are identified as such by the presence of cultic artifacts such as incense stands or votive figurines.[82] A surprisingly diverse set of cult structures has been recovered by archaeologists. These include cult rooms or corners of rooms built in a village, presumably for use by people living nearby. For example, one such room was discovered for the early Israelite period at Ai, northeast of Jerusalem; others from the period of the monarchies were found at Dan, Lachish, Megiddo, and Kedesh. At Iron Age Beersheba, most dwellings had small assemblages of cultic objects or vessels, suggesting that rituals took place at home; at least one dwelling at Tell el-Far'ah (biblical Tirzah) featured a similar assemblage in the large central room. At Tel Halif, remains of cultic activity—including the head of a pillar figurine—were recovered in a room used for group "living" activities, namely, the serving and consumption of food.[83] In addition, there were cult centers, open-air cult complexes, and various other cultic sites, some featuring standing stones that were probably the מצבות or "pillars" mentioned (and often but not always condemned) in the Hebrew Bible.

These discoveries suggest that Israelites carried out religious practices in their homes, villages, and towns, not only at the Jerusalem temple. Some rituals at regional shrines, such as seasonal festivals, likely included all family members; but others may have been particularly suited to women's needs.[84] Indeed, certain rituals were likely performed exclusively by women, probably in relation to their reproductive roles, as the stories of Hannah and Samson's mother and also evidence from ethnography and from other Near Eastern

---

81. Carol Meyers, "Contributing to Continuity: Women and Sacrifice in Ancient Israel," in *Women and the Gift: Beyond the Given and the All-Giving* (ed. Morny Joy; Bloomington: Indiana University Press, forthcoming).

82. For the procedures for identifying ritual places, see Ziony Zevit, *The Religions of Ancient Israel: A Synthesis of Parallactic Approaches* (London: Continuum, 2001), 80–83. The information in this section is based on Zevit's presentation of the full range of Israelite shrines.

83. Hardin, *Households*.

84. Phyllis Bird, "Israelite Religion and the Faith of Israel's Daughters," in *The Bible and the Politics of Exegesis: Essays in Honor of Norman K. Gottwald on His Sixty-Fifth Birthday* (ed. David Jobling, Peggy Day, and Gerald T. Sheppard; Cleveland: Pilgrim, 1991), 100–103.

cultures suggest. Archaeological evidence supports that possibility with respect to household religious practice, for some of the iconographic items in household cultic assemblages—female figurines holding their breasts, Bes amulets, beads or plaques representing the eye of Horus—suggest reproductive concerns.[85] The presence of ceramic vessels for food or liquids in cultic assemblages is an indication of food and drink offerings; because preparing food was a female role, women were surely involved in making those offerings. That women were among the practitioners of religious rituals everywhere is also indicated by Deut 13:6, which includes "daughter" and "wife" in the list of people who might be worshiping unauthorized deities.

4. Evaluating Women's Lives Using Archaeology

4.1. Cautionary Considerations in Analyzing a Premodern Society

Perhaps the greatest obstacle to using archaeological remains for evaluating women's lives is the tendency to read the present into the past.[86] Thus reconstructing the dynamics of women's lives cannot proceed without noting some ways in which what is familiar to us in the contemporary world leads to problematic assumptions about life in ancient societies.

For one thing, it would be misguided to assume clear and fixed boundaries between private life and public realms. Anthropological research into premodern cultures suggests otherwise. Anthropologists as well as feminist historians point out that the conception of the "domestic sphere" as female and passive and as marginal to and separate from the active, public male sphere is based on developments in Western society since the industrial revolution and is not universally applicable.[87] Indeed, in small-scale traditional societies, especially those organized along kinship lines, household boundaries are porous. Social, economic, religious, and political aspects of community life play out in interactions and transactions within as well as outside individual households. Therefore, analyzing the gendered aspect of household activities represented by the archaeological materials described here must resist the idea of categorical distinctions between "public" and "private" and also the accompanying gender binaries that devalue women.

It is also important to resist the contemporary tendency to undervalue household work. Because the economic center of life in developed societies

---

85. Meyers, *Households and Holiness*, 29–35; see also Schroer, "Ancient Near Eastern Pictures as Keys to Biblical Texts," in this volume.
86. Nelson, *Gender in Archaeology*, 9.
87. Summarized in Meyers, "Material Remains," 434–35.

today lies outside the household, women's unpaid labor at home is considered less important than paid labor outside the home. But in biblical antiquity there was no disjunction between home and work. The household was the center of economic life, with women's and men's labor *together* providing the materials—food, shelter, clothing, and basic tools—essential for the survival of a family. Moreover, assuming that male contributions to household tasks were valued more highly than those of women may be our own ethnocentric perspective and thus inappropriate for considering the inhabitants of the ancient Israelite household, where the contributions of both genders were essential for survival.[88] Instead, we need to consider the real value of women's tasks, designated maintenance activities, in their own, premodern context; contemporary evaluations cannot be applied to biblical antiquity.

A related issue is the tendency to devalue the household work of both genders in relation to the institutions and accompanying leadership roles that transcended households. Attaching greater value and prestige to community roles may be a construct based on contemporary perspectives but not directly applicable to traditional societies in which household life was central to existence. Prestige, of course, existed; but devaluing peasant labor was not necessarily its concomitant.[89] At the same time, it is important to recognize that women were not absent from community life; no fewer than seventeen suprahousehold "professional" roles for Israelite women appear in biblical texts and would have afforded prestige to the women in those positions.[90]

Keeping in mind these instances of how different life in ancient Israel was from what we know in today's industrialized world, analyzing the social interactions of women in relation to their gendered activities can give us insight into their lives. Central to this endeavor is focusing on several important features of women's maintenance work in grain-processing and textile production.

4.2. IMPORTANT FEATURES OF GRAIN PROCESSING AND TEXTILE PRODUCTION

Anthropological research allows us to reconstruct what these maintenance

---

88. See Almudenda Hernando, "¿Por qué la Historia no ha valorado las actividades de mantenimento?" in *Dones i activitats de mantinement en temps de canvi* (ed. Paloma González Marcén, Sandra Montón Subías, and Marina Picazo Gurina; Treballs d'Arqueologia 11; Barcelona: Universitat Autònoma de Barcelona, 2005), 115–33.

89. Much of John R. Jackson's "Enjoying the Fruit of One's Labor: Attitudes toward Male Work and Workers in the Hebrew Bible" (PhD. diss., Duke University, 2005) also applies to women too.

90. Summarized in Carol Meyers, "Women in the OT," *NIDB* 5:891–92.

activities would have meant for women individually, in relation to men's tasks, and also as participants in labor carried out in the company of others.

4.2.1. Women's Economic Contributions[91]

The production of food and textiles, among other aspects of household life, represented an essential contribution to the household economy and to the very survival of the family. Because the economic activities of a household were at the very core of its functional identity, women's control of the production of food and textiles would have meant considerable power in household life. Moreover, as ethnographic studies have shown, women can experience considerable prestige when they contribute substantially to household labor.

4.2.2. Women's Labor Compared with Men's[92]

Technological knowledge and technical skills were required for many of the steps in producing cereal foods and cloth. The ability to carry out these procedures typically provides a considerable amount of personal gratification. In addition, because women's tasks were slightly more complex than were those of men, performing them would have afforded somewhat greater satisfaction. Also, the products of women's work differed from the products of male labor, which centered on growing field crops.[93] Women produced items that were immediately consumable or usable—they gave their families food in its edible form, and they transformed fibers into wearable garments. This kind of productivity is essentially different from the outcomes of male fieldwork, for crops are harvested only seasonally, and even then conditions such as drought and pestilence may bring men very little satisfaction for their labor.[94] Thus women again had the opportunity for personal satisfaction and self-esteem, perhaps to a greater degree than did men, from their role in the household economy.

---

91. See Meyers, *Discovering Eve*, 169–173.

92. The information in this section is based on Carol Meyers, "The Family in Early Israel," in Leo G. Perdue, Joseph Blenkinsopp, John J. Collins, and Carol Meyers, *Families in Ancient Israel* (Louisville: Westminster John Knox, 1997), 22–27.

93. Male agrarian tasks (plowing, sowing, harvesting, shearing) appear in many biblical texts, e.g., Gen 26:12; 31:19; 1 Sam 8:11–12; 25:2–4; 1 Kgs 19:19; 2 Kgs 4:19; Job 31:8; cf. Ruth 2:2, 8–9.

94. See Deut 28:38–41; Isa 5:10.

4.3. Women's Shared Labor and the Resulting Informal Networks[95]

As noted in §3.3.3, women often worked in the company of others. Women from one household and probably adjoining households almost certainly joined together on a regular if not daily basis as they performed the tedious and time-consuming activities necessary to provide food and clothing for their families. Conversation and song typically ease the tedium of repetitive tasks and make the time more pleasant. Moreover, spending time with other women no doubt eased the emotional difficulty for young wives of being separated from their birth families when they married and moved to their husband's households.[96]

But another feature of shared time and work, although less clear to us from our twenty-first-century vantage point, was perhaps even more important. Ethnographers have shown that women working together on a regular basis over extended periods of time form informal social networks. Women not only amuse each other but also forge bonds with each other. The existence of these female alliances in ancient Israel is suggested by the archaeological evidence of shared female labor and also may be reflected in several biblical passages. In Ruth, the women of Bethlehem are the ones to greet Naomi when she comes home after a long sojourn in Moab (1:19), and "women of the neighborhood" come to be with Ruth when her son is born (4:17; see also 4:14). Similarly, 1 Sam 4:20 mentions women who gather to help Ichabod's mother when she goes into labor.

4.3.1. Functions of Women's Networks

The importance of female networks lies not only in what they provide for the women themselves but also in how they serve their communities. When women spend time together as they work, they share information about each other and each other's families and even about other nearby households. This sharing of knowledge would have served several functions in ancient Israel.

---

95. Except for materials published after 1999, the information in §4.3 about women's networks, including reference to relevant ethnographic research, is drawn from Carol Meyers, "'Women of the Neighborhood' (Ruth 4.17): Informal Female Networks in Ancient Israel," in *Ruth and Esther* (ed. Athalya Brenner; FCB 2/3; Sheffield: Sheffield Academic Press, 1999), 110–127.

96. Ancient Israel was generally patrilocal; when a woman married, she moved to her husband's household or to that of his parents.

Socioeconomic Functions. Women's intimate familiarity with each other's lives creates a kind of social knowledge that helps solve certain economic and family problems. This is particularly true in traditional societies such as ancient Israel, which lacked government agencies or service organizations to help families experiencing difficulties. Ethnographic observations show how informal alliances of women across households serve as the mechanisms for carrying out the mutual aid necessary for people in premodern settlements to survive. That is, women in these informal networks help solve sporadic economic problems. They know when a family is having difficulties harvesting its crops or preparing its food because of illness or a death in the household. Thus they are typically adept at deploying labor—older children, for example—to help out, or they can arrange to supply food or other resources, or they can provide childcare for an ailing mother. As already noted, women also gather to help each other in the intimate circumstances of childbirth, providing emotional support and physical help to the new mother, which in turn increases their solidarity. In short, informal networks of Israelite women would have facilitated helping others in ways that served community needs, provided emotional support, and also entailed personal gratification for those who arranged or provided aid.

Sociopolitical Functions. When Israelites deliberated about matters affecting the place of a household in the community or about issues relating to the community as a whole, those discussions did not take place in some remote city hall, as in today's world, but rather in households. Those political interactions may have been dominated by men; but, as anthropologists have shown, men typically rely on information, often unavailable to them directly, gathered by women in their informal, supra-household networks. The fact that most tools associated with women's tasks have been found in the large central room of their dwellings is relevant to this. Working in the main space of a dwelling, women were not sequestered; and they were not cut off from the comings and goings of male household members or from the issues that concerned them. Conversely, what women learned from each other was readily transmitted to their male relatives. Indeed, in traditional societies the household is frequently a place in which political life is carried out by both women and men.[97]

---

97. See Brenda Bowser and John Q. Patton, "Domestic Spaces as Public Spaces: An Ethnoarchaeological Case Study of Houses, Gender, and Politics in the Ecuadorian Amazon," *Journal of Archaeological Method and Theory* 11 (2004): 157–81. Similar information comes from Middle Eastern countries.

For example, arranging marriages was in many cases a political act for the Israelites, as a kinship-based society. Marriages were potentially alliances between kin groups and not, as today in industrialized societies, the individual relationship of a woman and a man. In fact, the biblical word for "bridegroom" (חָתָן) is related to the term for "father-in-law" (חֹתֵן), indicating that marriage links two families, not just two people.[98] In this regard, the information acquired by women in their informal associations would have been an integral part of the process by which parents selected mates for their daughters and sons. Also, because women moved to their husbands' households when they married, they had two sets of kin relationships—their birth families and their marital ones—and thus could serve as intermediary figures helping forge alliances between two kinship groups. Men may have negotiated the terms of a marriage, but the input of women was frequently invaluable.

Leadership Functions. Opportunities for leadership were present for women who arranged, via informal networks, to help others. Even in the modern world, women frequently exercise effective leadership in informal positions that lack institutional authority. Leadership does not always involve certain personality types or formal positions but rather lies in the actual process of getting something done.

The technologies and techniques of women's economic tasks also provided opportunities for leadership. Women who work together share information about how to do one task or another more skillfully or how to carry out some procedure more effectively. Women with greater expertise become mentors to others, probably younger women or their own daughters or daughters-in-law; in so doing, they garner the respect of those whom they help and experience the satisfaction of transmitting their skills to others. In providing instruction to others—just as in organizing help for other families—some women would have had the opportunity for informal leadership. This would also have been true for women's expertise in areas such as midwifery, prophecy, sagacity, musical performance, and lamenting the dead that have not left traces in the archaeological record but are known from passages in the Hebrew Bible.[99]

---

98. Note that there is no word in the Hebrew Bible for marriage as an institution, nor is there a verb meaning "to marry." Rather, marriage is expressed by statements that a man "takes" a woman, probably reflecting the fact that a man took his bride from her parent's house and brought her to his own family's household. E.g., Gen 24:67 reports that Isaac "took Rebekah" to his mother's tent and that she thereby "became his wife."

99. For biblical references, see Meyers, "Women in the OT," 891–92.

4.3.2. Importance of Women's Networks

Informal women's networks in traditional communities are not usually visible to outsiders. In the ancient world, they rarely appear in documents. The possible references to female cohorts in the Bible (see §4.3) are far fewer and certainly less prominent than the frequent and central mention of men's formal associations in military, political, and religious institutions. But their informality and lack of biblical visibility must not be understood to mean that women's networks were not important to the well-being of Israelite communities. They would have been genuine "institutions" in their own right, gaining legitimacy by the unspoken and probably unconscious acquiescence of their members. Although more diffuse than formal organizations, they were probably more flexible in responding to a variety of needs. Formal connections among Israelite families and settlements were established by lineages and marital ties and were marked by the constructed relationships laid out in genealogies. The relationships formed by women working together would have been a source of social, economic, and political energy that facilitated many essential aspects of family and community life. Seen in this way, it becomes clear that private and public indeed were not separate domains for the Israelites and that women played a vital part in community as well as household life.

4.4. WOMEN'S RELIGIOUS LIVES

Although the biblical text remains an important source for reconstructing women's religious lives, archaeological remains contribute additional information. The access of women to shrines in their communities or homes (see §3.6) indicates regular female participation in local celebrations. In addition, the discovery of cultic objects together with women's maintenance tools in household contexts[100] suggests that Israelite women had their own household rituals, some of which may have been related to their reproductive function. Childbearing was an essential part of women's lives; choosing to remain childless would not have been an option. Offspring were needed to provide labor, to care for elderly parents, and, in the case of male offspring, to continue a family's lineage and maintain ownership of its property. It is no wonder that barrenness is presented as a grave problem in many biblical narratives and poetic passages. Indeed, attempts to have safe childbirth

---

100. Elizabeth A. R. Willett, "Women and Household Shrines in Ancient Israel" (PhD. diss., University of Arizona, 1999).

are evident in certain kinds of jewelry women wore (see §3.4); and the religious aspect of childbirth appears in many of the names given to infants (see §3.5.3). Because successful childbirth was essential for family and community survival, women's household rituals would have been considered instrumental in securing reproductive success; like medical interventions in the modern world, women's pregnancy and childbirth rituals can be considered strategies deemed essential for the creation and survival of new life. Archaeological materials thus point to a major religious role for women otherwise unmentioned in the Bible.

4.5. CONCLUDING COMMENTS

This overview of archaeological materials as sources of information about Israelite women has shown them to have had more control over their lives and a larger role in their local communities than otherwise believed. Examining the artifacts associated with household maintenance activities has been especially useful in challenging stereotypes about women as powerless and passive in Israelite society.

It should be noted that the archaeologically derived information about women's substantial economic and sociopolitical contributions as well as their opportunities for supra-household leadership and camaraderie is probably age- and class-specific. That is, this information pertains largely to adult married women in peasant households. It is difficult to determine how many of the economic tasks and concomitant social interactions reconstructed for peasant women would have existed for elite women, who presumably had servants or slaves to carry out many laborious household chores. However, the higher social status of well-to-do women undoubtedly meant managerial control over female servants or slaves and perhaps over some male ones, too. Many of the epigraphic materials surveyed in §3.5 attest to commercial activities available only to elite women or to women managing households that could produce surpluses (see Prov 31:14–18, 24). As for women or girls in debt service or held as slaves, they, like men in those circumstances, would have experienced few of the opportunities noted for adult peasant women. Finally, another group of women, wage earners in the very largest towns or in the capital cities, have not been considered but must be mentioned. Very little relevant material has come from the capitals (Samaria and Jerusalem). Excavations of the largest towns may indicate that some women were employed in workshops producing textiles or other products. For example, the presence at Tell Taanek of enough loom weights in one room for at least three looms, all producing heavy-grade fabric, suggests a commercial workshop.[101] But neither the gender of the workers nor the social and economic meaning of that employment for their family lives has been determined.

A final comment concerns the relationship of women's roles in Israelite households to those of men. The labor of both women and men was essential for supplying the basic needs of food and clothing in a world without grocery stores or clothing shops.[102] As noted in §4.2.2, men produced many of the raw materials for food and clothing, and women transformed those materials into usable form. The tasks of the two genders differed but were complementary, a situation that typically signals the mutual respect of women and men—which is exactly what was reported for rural Afghanistan by the American woman quoted at the beginning of this study. In addition, this complementary labor situation (along with the participation of both women and men, albeit in different ways, in the social, economic, political, and religious life of their communities) signals a more balanced situation of gendered power within households than the Hebrew Bible reveals. The valuable and interdependent contributions of women and men to household and community involve what social scientists call a "classic partnership."[103] Men may act on behalf of the household in extra-household affairs; but women typically manage affairs within the household, controlling the location and sequence of maintenance activities.[104] Lineages may run along the male line; but women make it work, taking the initiative at critical times.[105] Several biblical texts that are arguably women's literature contain a phrase attesting to female household power.[106] In these passages about women, the family household is not designated in the usual way, by "house of the father," but rather by בית אם, which means "mother's household." This phrase identifies the basic unit of society with the "mother"—the Israelite woman responsible for its viability.

---

101. See Glenda Friend, *The Loom Weights* (vol. 3.2 of *Tell Taanek 1963–1960*; Birzeit, Palestine: Birzeit University, Palestine Institute of Archaeology, 1998), 10.

102. A limited market economy that made certain goods available commercially may have existed in Samaria and Jerusalem and in rudimentary form in the larger walled towns. But most households were largely self-sufficient; and even in settings where grain and fibers could perhaps be purchased, women still did much of the grinding and weaving.

103. Harriet Bradley, *Men's Work, Women's Work: A Sociological History of the Sexual Division of Labor in Employment* (Cambridge: Polity, 1989), 33–37.

104. Cassuto, "Bringing Home the Artifacts," 77.

105. Hieke, "Genealogy as a Means of Presenting History," in this volume.

106. These passages are in the Rebekah narrative (Gen 24:28), the story of Ruth (1:8), and the Song of Solomon (3:4; 8:2); cf. Prov 9:1 and 14:1. See Carol Meyers, " 'To Her Mother's House': Considering a Counterpart to the Israelite *Bêt 'āb*," in Jobling, Day, and Sheppard, *Bible and the Politics of Exegesis*, 39–51, 304–307.

THE STATUS OF WOMEN IN THE
LEGAL TEXTS OF THE ANCIENT NEAR EAST

Sophie Démare-Lafont
Université Panthéon-Assas Paris II and École pratique des hautes études

The abundance and variety of legal sources in cuneiform script are well known. These sources cover a chronological period extending over three thousand years, from the invention of writing around 3000 B.C.E. to the beginning of the Christian age. In addition to countless deeds dealing with such diverse areas as trade, loans, adoption, marriage, inheritance rights, and so on, several law codes have been preserved, including the famous Code of Hammurabi (king of Babylonia ca. 1750 B.C.E.). There are also royal edicts concerning, for example, the cancellation of debts or the organization of palace life, as well as trial records and administrative or private correspondence.

Despite these vast collections of documents comprising several hundreds of thousands of tablets, our knowledge about law in the ancient Near East is quite incomplete. The main source of ancient Near Eastern law is, in fact, the habits and customs of which only remainders and partial traces are found in the contracts. We must therefore acknowledge that we are dealing with an incomplete body of sources.

For a long time, scholars tended to see the Babylonian sources as the norm for the entire world of cuneiform script. The peculiarities noted in some regions, for example, in Nuzi (near Mosul),[1] were therefore considered indicative of uneducated marginal populations. The discovery of new Syrian sites and the publication of texts from Elba[2] and Mari[3] have modified this constant

---

1. On the legal sources from Nuzi, see Carlo Zaccagnini, "Nuzi," in *A History of Ancient Near Eastern Law* (ed. Raymond Westbrook; 2 vols.; HO 72; Leiden: Brill, 2003), 565–617.

2. Paolo Matthiae, *Aux origines de la Syrie: Ebla retrouvée* (Paris: Gallimard, 1996). The tablets have been published in the series Archivi Reali di Ebla: Testi (Rome) since 1981.

3. Jean-Marie Durand, *Les documents épistolaires du palais de Mari* (3 vols.; LAPO 16–18; Paris: Cerf, 1998–2000).

focus on Babylonia and revealed the specific cultural and religious variety of the sources. This statement is all the more important when it comes to the subject we are dealing with here: the legal status of women.

Most of the legal tablets concerning women present a homogenous and almost standardized picture of their legal situation. Even if this picture corresponds to a certain reality, it does not reflect all the possible situations. What we consider exceptions could be distortions that should be attributed to the written corpus. The more banal a situation is, the less necessary it is to put it into writing.[4] The women most frequently mentioned do not necessarily reflect the entire female population, but rather a group or several groups. Sociologically defined, they tend to live in cities or palaces and are generally members of wealthy families. We do not know much about female peasants, workers, or domestic servants. Nevertheless, some administrative texts present useful quantitative data (e.g., records of delivery of rations, the production rate of a workshop, lists of employees or of deportees). Today, these texts receive more attention from a sociohistorical point of view. Despite their uniformity and monotony, they provide important historical and sociological information about people who are not taken into consideration in the usual legal documents. Likewise, letters are useful sources that give us information about small details of daily life that never appear in the formulae of the contracts or in the provisions of the law codes.

We must therefore keep in mind that the legal texts convey only a partial picture of the true position of women. The view exhibited in legal documents needs to be completed and corrected with both literary and iconographic sources. Although scholars have attempted to do this, their endeavors often remained fruitless, since cross-checks are rare. Assyriological gender studies point to interesting paths,[5] but they are too specialized in fields far from legal concerns. In this essay we will limit ourselves to a general presentation of various aspects related to women's status and rights, mainly in the second millennium B.C.E., since most of the sources date from this period.

Speaking about women on the basis of legal texts leads us ultimately to speak primarily about men. Female subjects always appear in relation to a man, whether father, brother, master, or husband. This is also true for the royal families. Hence, we could consider women "eternal minors" subjected

---

4. Compared with the sociological reality of marriage, for example, the number of marriage contracts is rather small (around two to three hundred).

5. Most recently Rivkah Harris, *Gender and Aging in Mesopotamia: The "Gilgamesh Epic" and Other Ancient Literature* (Norman: University of Oklahoma Press, 2000); and Zainab Bahrani, *Women of Babylon: Gender and Representation in Mesopotamia* (London: Routledge, 2001).

to masculine power and at times treated like exchangeable objects, especially in the marital context. However, this picture needs to be qualified because, although it actually does represent one side of the female condition, it does not reflect the whole reality. The statute law depicts free women mainly in their family surroundings. However, other, more independent characters also appear in legal collections, such as prostitutes, widows, or "girlfriends." Let us look at a few examples:

> If a young married man has sexual relations with a prostitute from the street, and the judges order him not to go back to the prostitute, (and if) afterwards he divorces his first-ranking wife and gives the silver of her divorce settlement to her, (still) he will not marry the prostitute. (LL §30)[6]

> If a man strikes a prostitute causing her to abort her fetus, they shall assess him blow for blow, he shall make full payment of a life. (MAL A §52)[7]

> If a man has sexual relations with a widow without a formal written contract, he will not weigh and deliver any silver. (LU §11)[8]

> If a man should marry a widow without her formal binding agreement and she resides in his house for two years, she is a wife; she shall not leave. (MAL A §34)[9]

> If an unrelated man—neither her father, nor her brother, nor her son— should arrange to have a man's wife travel with him, then he shall swear an oath to the effect that he did not know that she is the wife of a man and he shall pay 7,200 shekels of lead to the woman's husband. If [he knows that she is the wife of a man], he shall pay damages and he shall swear, saying, "I did not fornicate with her." But if the man's wife should declare, "He did fornicate with me," since the man has already paid damages to the man (i.e., husband), he shall undergo the divine River Ordeal; there is no binding agreement. If he should refuse to undergo the divine River Ordeal, they shall treat him as the woman's husband treats his wife. (MAL A §22)[10]

---

6. Translation from Martha Roth, *Law Collections from Mesopotamia and Asia Minor* (SBLWAW 6; Atlanta: Scholars Press, 1995), 32. On MAL §40:66–87, see below §2.1. See the end of this essay for the list of abbreviations used.

7. Translation from ibid., 174.

8. Translation from ibid., 18.

9. Translation from ibid., 165.

10. Translation from ibid., 160. This sentence shows in *contrario* that an unmarried woman could travel with a man in order to entertain him. Such paramours are well-attested in the texts from Mari (see below).

Likewise, many emancipated females are proven to be behind masculine power. Moreover, legal deeds show that even married women have the legal power to conclude contracts in their own names. Although such texts are scarce, they prove that the daily life of women did not consist only of housework.

It is quite difficult to figure out how these various feminine archetypes are distributed within Mesopotamian society. As far as this point is concerned, historical research must be satisfied with suppositions. The housewife represents undoubtedly the social ideal and a clearly prevailing figure, but unmarried women and widows were not necessarily an exception or a minority.

1. THE SOCIAL STATUS OF WOMEN

The women most frequently mentioned in the cuneiform legal documents are the wives and daughters of wealthy and respected families. The laws are intended mainly for them. There are, however, other categories of women who appear less often in the contracts and, for this reason, are more difficult to place in the social structure. For example, slave-born women are rarely mentioned except within lists of prisoners and deportees. They must not be confused with servants who are temporarily subjected to the creditors of a father or husband but sooner or later regain their status of freedom.[11] The relations between a female slave and her mistress within the family may vary. The aging nurse who remains with her former ward is wrapped in affection. The female slave who, in lieu of her sterile mistress, has a child with the master becomes a dangerous rival. The Code of Ur-Nammu forbids her from comparing herself with her mistress:

> If a slave woman strikes someone acting with the authority of her mistress […]. (LU §26)[12]

---

11. Raymond Westbrook, "The Female Slave," in *Gender and Law in the Hebrew Bible and the Ancient Near East* (ed. Victor H. Matthews et al.; Sheffield: Sheffield Academic Press, 1998), 214–38.

12. Translation from Roth, *Law Collections*, 20. This paragraph is quite damaged, and its meaning is not clear. Discussion and bibliography in Sophie Démare-Lafont, *Femmes droit et justice dans l'Antiquité orientale: Contribution à l'étude du droit pénal au Proche-Orient ancien* (OBO 165; Fribourg: Vandenhoeck & Ruprecht, 1999), 316–19. Differently, Claus Wilcke, "Der Kodex Urnamma (CU): Versuch einer Rekonstruktion," in *Riches Hidden in Secret Places: Ancient Near Eastern Studies in Memory of Thorkild Jacobsen* (ed. Tzvi Abush; Winona Lake, Ind.: Eisenbrauns, 2002), 291–333, here 320: "Wenn (jemand) die ihrer Herrin gleich gemachte Sklavin schlägt…" (If [someone] strikes the slave woman who has been made equal of her mistress…).

The Bible illustrates this rivalry in the story of Sarah and Hagar (Gen 16).

Prostitutes undoubtedly occupy a lower position in the social hierarchy; nevertheless, they do have certain rights. The law protects them against violent abortion and recognizes their inheritance rights. They can request financial support from the married father of their child:

> If a man's wife does not bear him a child but a prostitute from the street does bear him a child, he shall provide grain, oil, and clothing rations for the prostitute, and the child whom the prostitute bore him shall be his heir; as long as his wife is alive, the prostitute will not reside in the house with his first-ranking wife. (LL §27)[13]

The "female travel companion"—a lady who accompanies and renders her services to a merchant on his journeys—is asked to stay away from the marital residence of her client. The decision of a king of Mari (ancient Syria) in the eighteenth century B.C.E. to set up his lovers in the palace instead of his wives provoked a great scandal, since the social positions of these two categories of women were thereby reversed.[14]

2. Laws for the Regulation of Family Life

2.1. Marriage

The standard Mesopotamian marriage was a two-step process leading to the conclusion of the marital bond.[15] First of all, the heads of the two families entered into an agreement that was formalized by the future husband, who offered a gift. Originally the gifts certainly were goods to be used at the wedding banquet (wool, animals, oil, etc.). In the second millennium B.C.E., they became small amounts of money given back to the groom after the wedding. This prior agreement constituted an inchoate marriage that existed for third parties but was as yet incomplete for the married couple. Consequently, this was not an engagement in today's sense. Each party could relinquish the agreement by paying compensation to the other. This phase could take place

---

13. Translation from Roth, *Law Collections*, 31.

14. Sophie Démare-Lafont, "Un 'cas royal' à l'époque de Mari," *RA* 91/2 (1997): 109–19, here 111.

15. Godfrey R. Driver and John C. Miles, *The Babylonian Laws* (2 vols.; Oxford: Clarendon, 1952–1955), 245–65; Raymond Westbrook, *Old Babylonian Marriage Law* (AfOB 23; Horn: Berger, 1988), 34–38.

when the people involved were still very young, around the age of seven for girls and fifteen for boys.[16]

The marriage became complete when the rights of the father of the bride were transferred to the husband. How this transfer occurred is not known: neither the consummation of the marriage, nor the public ceremonies with a banquet, nor the passage from the delivery of the wife in the house of her husband seem to provide a sufficient basis. Certain rites are mentioned, for example, the anointment or the obligation for the woman to wear the veil.[17] According to Assyrian law, married women were required to wear the veil in public at all times:

> A concubine who goes about in the main thoroughfare with her mistress is to be veiled. A married *qadiltu*-woman is to be veiled (when she goes about) in the main thoroughfare, but an unmarried one is to leave her head bare in the main thoroughfare, she shall not veil herself. A prostitute shall not be veiled, her head shall be bare. Whoever sees a veiled prostitute shall seize her, secure witnesses, and bring her to the palace entrance. They shall not take away her jewelry, but he who has seized her takes her clothing; they shall strike her 50 blows with rods; they shall pour hot pitch over her head. And if a man should see a veiled prostitute and release her, and does not bring her to the palace entrance, they shall strike that man 50 blows with rods; the one who informs against him shall take his clothing; they shall pierce his ears, thread them on a cord, tie it at his back; he shall perform the king's service for one full month. Slave women shall not be veiled, and he who should see a veiled slave woman shall seize her and bring her to the palace entrance; they shall cut off her ears; he who seizes her shall take her clothing. If a man should see a veiled slave woman but release her and not seize her, and does not bring her to the palace entrance, and they then prove the charges against him and find him guilty, they shall strike him 50 blows with rods; they shall pierce his ears, thread them on a cord, tie it at his back; the one who informs against him shall take his garments; he shall perform the king's service for one full month. (MAL A §40)[18]

---

16. It is supposed that girls were typically married at age fourteen (Martha Roth, "Age at Marriage and the Household: A Study of Neo-Babylonian and Neo-Assyrian Forms," *Comparative Studies in Societies and History* 29 [1987]: 737) or when they had become nubile (Claus Wilcke, "Familiengründung im alten Babylonien," in *Geschlechtsreife und Legitimation zur Zeugung* (ed. Ernst Wilhelm Müller; Freiburg im Breisgau: Alber, 1997), 241–44) and grooms at thirty (Roth, "Age at Marriage," 737).

17. See Sophie Démare-Lafont, "'À cause des anges': Le voile dans la culture juridique du Proche-Orient ancien," in *Etudes de droit privé en souvenir de Maryse Carlin* (ed. Olivier Vernier; Paris: Editions La Mémoire du Droit, 2008).

18. Translation from Roth, *Law Collections*, 168–69.

The legal vocabulary of marriage shows that the woman was considered an object more than a subject in the contract: the man "takes" the woman to be his wife; the woman is "given" to the man, without asking her personal consent; she must evidently come as a virgin, since her prior defloration could result in her repudiation.[19]

Marriage is envisioned in the context of monogamy, but that does not prevent the husband from having several wives. With the exception of the king, whose harem represents a visible sign of his political power,[20] polygamy is rarely documented. Some cases of bigamy are known from Babylonian contracts dating from the first half of the second millennium B.C.E.[21] They provide a hierarchical relationship between the two women: one is the servant of the other. In the end, only one woman bears the title of wife, and this confirms the monogamous structure of marriage. Moreover, the husband does not have permission to bring a slave-concubine into the household in order to have offspring.[22] All of these situations regulated by the laws are potential sources

---

19. See Démare-Lafont, *Femmes droit,* 45–59.

20. On the Syrian harem during the Amorite period, see Nele Ziegler, *Le harem de Zimrî-Lîm: La population féminine des palais d'après les archives royales de Mari* (Florilegium Marianum 4; Mémoires de NABU 5; Paris: SEPOA, 1999); eadem, "Le harem du vaincu," *RA* 93 (1999): 1–26.

21. Westbrook, *Marriage Law,* 103–11.

22. LH §§170–171: "But if the father during his lifetime should not declare to (or: concerning) the children whom the slave woman bore to him, 'My children,' after the father goes to his fate, the children of the slave woman will not divide the property of the paternal estate with the children of the first-ranking wife. The release of the slave woman and of her children shall be secured; the children of the first-ranking wife will not make claims of slavery against the children of the slave woman. The first-ranking wife shall take her dowry and the marriage settlement which her husband awarded to her in writing, and she shall continue to reside in her husband's dwelling; as long as she is alive she shall enjoy the use of it, but she may not sell it; her own estate shall belong (as inheritance) only to her own children.

"If her husband does not make a marriage settlement in her favor, they shall restore to her in full her dowry, and she shall take a share of the property of her husband's estate comparable in value to that of one heir. If her children pressure her in order to coerce her to depart from the house, the judges shall investigate her case and shall impose a penalty on the children; that woman will not depart from her husband's house. If that woman should decide on her own to depart, she shall leave for her children the marriage settlement which her husband gave to her; she shall take the dowry brought from her father's house and a husband of her choice shall marry her" (translation from Roth, *Law Collections,* 114).

LH §§144–145: "If a man marries a *nadītu,* and that *nadītu* gives a slave woman to her husband, and thus she provides children, but that man then decides to marry a *šugītu,* they will not permit that man to do so, he will not marry the *šugītu.*

"If a man marries a *nadītu,* and she does not provide him with children, and that man then decides to marry a *šugītu,* that man may marry the *šugītu* and bring her into his house;

of conflict within the families. The biblical story of Sarah and Hagar (Gen 16) is one of its most famous illustrations.

Wealthy families would give dowries to their daughters on their wedding day or when they entered a convent (in the case of nuns). The dowry included personal objects (clothing, jewelry, and equipment), oil, household instruments and furniture (tables, chairs, bed), and sometimes a female servant and a piece of land, but no money.[23] All these goods were listed on a tablet. In the case of edible goods, the quantities were indicated, so that, if necessary, they could be given back. The wife was the owner of her dowry, although it was administered by her husband. The buildings could not be sold, but they could be confiscated.

In addition to the dowry, the woman also occasionally received a marriage gift from her husband, probably after the birth of the first child.[24] This sum was used for her maintenance if her husband predeceased her and provided for the upbringing of the children by the widow. However, there were other legal means in order to achieve the same result. The Assyrians in the nineteenth century B.C.E., as well as the inhabitants of Emar (near Alep) or Nuzi (near Mosul) in the fourteenth century B.C.E., resorted to wills in which the wife was made "father and mother of the house."[25] This expression meant, with respect to the children, that the mother took the place of the deceased father. The fictive survival of the couple thus forbade any distribution of the inheritance. Hence, the heirs had to live together in joined ownership until the death of their mother. This measure protected the widow against expulsion from the marital residence, either by her own children or by her husband's family.[26] This statute of "father and mother" as well as the conventional dower (the husband's possessions due to the widow) were lost if the widow remarried a man who did not belong to the family of the deceased.

---

that *šugītu* should not aspire to equal status with the *nadītu*" (translation from Roth, *Law Collections*, 108–9).

Also see the contract from Sippar CT 8 37d: "Šahira, son of Bêlessunu, took Azatum (as a concubine) and she bore him five sons. Among the five sons, whom Azatum bore for Šahira, Šahira adopted Yakunum, his eldest son in the future, the sons of Azatum shall not be able to raise claims against Šahira. The have sworn the oath of Šamaš, Aya, Marduk and Hammurabi. Seven witnesses. Date" (my translation).

23. Westbrook, *Marriage Law*, 90–91; Stephanie Dalley, "Old Babylonian Dowries," *Iraq* 42 (1980): 53–74.

24. Westbrook, *Marriage Law*, 95–99.

25. Cécile Michel, "A propos d'un testament paléo-assyrien: Une femme de marchand 'père et mère' des capitaux," *RA* 94 (2000): 1–10, with bibliography.

26. Raymond Westbrook, "Social Justice and Creative Jurisprudence in Late Bronze Age Syria," *JESHO* 44 (2001): 36–38.

The married woman was responsible for any debts she contracted. Her legal capacity was therefore fully recognized: she could pledge marital property and freely dispose of the marital estate. Most frequently the husband was the one who acted, but sometimes she also took part in his undertakings. The prevalence of men in sale or loan contracts is thus a sociological reality and not a legal necessity.

The wife was also responsible for the debts incurred by her husband before their marriage, unless otherwise stated in the contract:

> If a woman who is residing in a man's house should have her husband agree by binding contract that no creditor of her husband shall seize her (for his debts)—if that man has a debt incurred before marrying that woman, his creditors will not seize his wife; and if that woman has a debt incurred before entering the man's house, her creditors will not seize her husband. (LH §151)[27]

Otherwise, her husband's creditor can make her liable for the debts and she must pay them by working or freely make a deposit from her own assets.

2.2. DISSOLUTION OF THE MARRIAGE

The woman has the same right as the man to divorce. At the beginning of the second millennium B.C.E., the marriage partners in Assyrian contracts had to make the same compensation payments.[28] In Babylonia, this situation seldom arose, since generally the clauses stipulated that the woman who asked for a divorce incurred the death penalty or paid quite high compensation.[29] These deterrents imply that from a sociological point of view divorce was a man's prerogative. An atypical provision qualifies this observation: §30 of Code of Lipit-Ishtar forbids the divorced husband from marrying a prostitute with whom he already had had intercourse while he was married. The right to divorce remained intact, but its morality was to a certain extent controlled by the lawgiver:

> If a young married man has sexual relations with a prostitute from the street, and the judges order him not to go back to the prostitute, (and if) afterwards

---

27. Translation from Roth, *Law Collections*, 110.
28. See Klaas Veenhof, "Old Assyrian Period," in Westbrook, *A History of Ancient Near Eastern Law*, 450–55.
29. See Westbrook, *Marriage Law*, 79–85.

he divorces his first-ranking wife and gives the silver of her divorce settlement to her, (still) he will not marry the prostitute. (LL §30)[30]

The dissolution of a marriage was accomplished by the *verba solemnia*: "You
are not my husband; you are not my wife." This statement was probably made
before witnesses. When the wife was repudiated without any fault on her part,
she received compensation and could take her dowry back. This did, however,
give rise to many problems, since the husband was often unable to return
the goods of the dowry or compensate their value.[31] If this duty could not be
fulfilled, the woman had the right to request an income in the form of goods,
such as regular rations of foodstuffs and clothing. According to the Laws of
Eshnunna (East of Iraq) from the eighteenth century B.C.E., if she had children, she could claim the marital residence and receive support to cover the
cost of their upbringing.[32]

The repudiation of a woman due to her own fault (bad behavior or adultery) implied that she was not to receive any financial compensation and had
to accept the loss of her dowry, which was not restored to her.

> If the wife of a man who is residing in the man's house should decide to leave,
> and she appropriates goods, squanders her household possessions, or dis-
> parages her husband, they shall charge and convict her; and if her husband
> should declare his intention to divorce her, then he shall divorce her; neither
> her travel expenses, nor her divorce settlement, nor anything else shall be
> given to her. If her husband should declare his intention to not divorce her,
> then her husband may marry another woman and that (first) woman shall
> reside in her husband's house as a slave woman. (LH §141)[33]

Absence of the husband for a long time because of his business or due to
desertion led to the dissolution of marriage. However, if a husband was cap-
tive in a distant country or was kept away in the service of the king, the marriage continued as long as the means of living permitted. Otherwise, the
Babylonian law allowed the woman to remarry, but when her first husband

---

30. Translation from Roth, *Law Collections*, 32. For a discussion and interpretation of
this article, see Démare-Lafont, *Femmes droit*, 29–30.

31. Klaas Veenhof, "The Relation between Royal Decrees and 'Law Codes' of the Old
Babylonian Period," *JEOL* 35–36 (1997–2000): 73–74.

32. LE §59: "If a man, after engendering children, divorces his wife and marries
another woman, they shall banish him from the house and the property and after her, who
… he shall go … the house." For the translation, see Roth, *Law Collections*, 68, 70 n. 32.

33. Translation from ibid., 107–8.

returned, he had the right to take her back.[34] The children from the second marriage remained with their father (LH §135). The Assyrian law gives the same principle, but the husband who had been absent had to find a wife of the same value for the second husband.

> If a woman is residing in her father's house, or her husband settles her in a house elsewhere, and her husband then travels abroad but does not leave her any oil, wool, clothing, or provisions, or anything else, and sends her no provisions from abroad—that woman shall still remain (the exclusive object of rights) for her husband for five years, she shall not reside with another husband. If she has sons, they shall be hired out and provide for their own sustenance; the woman shall wait for her husband, she shall not reside with another husband. If she has no sons, she shall wait for her husband for five years; at the onset of (?) six years, she shall reside with the husband of her choice; her (first) husband, upon returning, shall have no valid claim to her; she is clear for her second husband. If he is delayed beyond the five years but is not detained of his own intention, whether because a ... seized him and he fled or because he was falsely arrested and therefore he was detained, upon returning he shall so prove, he shall give a woman comparable to his wife (to her second husband) and take his wife. And if the king should send him to another country and he is delayed beyond the five years, his wife shall wait for him (indefinitely); she shall not go to reside with another husband. And furthermore, if she should reside with another husband before the five years are completed and should she bear children (to the second husband), because she did not wait in accordance with the agreement, but was taken in marriage (by another), her (first) husband, upon returning, shall take her and also her offspring. (MAL A §36)[35]

This is a typical feature of Assyrian law: the husband could totally disregard his wife's personality. In this way, he turned her into a component of his own person. In the same vein, a wife could be sold to pay her husband's debts, and he had the same right with a child or a slave. Similarly, a son could inherit the wife of his deceased father and marry her, provided, of course, that she was not his own mother.

> If a man either pours oil on her head or brings (dishes for) the banquet, (after which) the son to whom he assigned the wife either dies or flees, he

---

34. Several laws deal with this matter: LE §§29–30; LH §§30–31, 133–136; MAL A §§24, 36, 45. See Sophie Démare-Lafont, "L'absence dans les droits cunéiformes," in *Le monde de l'itinérance en Méditerranée de l'Antiquité à l'époque moderne* (ed. Claudia Moatti; Bordeaux: Ausonius Editions, 2009), 275–305.

35. Translation from Roth, *Law Collections*, 165–66.

shall give her in marriage to whichever of his remaining sons he wishes, from the oldest to the youngest of at least ten years of age. If the father is dead and the son to whom he assigned the wife is also dead, a son of the deceased son who is at least ten years old shall marry her. If the sons of the (dead) son are less than ten years old, if the father of the daughter wishes, he shall give his daughter (to one of them), but if he wishes he shall make a full and equal return (of gifts given). If there is no son, he shall return as much as he received, precious stones or anything not edible, in its full amount; but he shall not return anything edible. (MAL A §43)[36]

Even worse, the wife of a man who had raped a free young girl could be handed over to the father of the victim under the principle of retaliation (punishment through equal treatment).

If a man forcibly seizes and rapes a maiden who is residing in her father's house, [...] who is not betrothed (?), whose [womb (?)] is not opened, who is not married, and against whose father's house there is no outstanding claim—whether within the city or in the countryside, or at night whether in the main thoroughfare, or in a granary, or during the city festival—the father of the maiden shall take the wife of the fornicator of the maiden and hand her over to be raped; he shall not return her to her husband, but he shall take (and keep?) her; the father shall give his daughter who is the victim of fornication into the protection of the household of her fornicator. If he (the fornicator) has no wife, the fornicator shall give "triple" the silver as the value of the maiden to her father; her fornicator shall marry her; he shall not reject (?) her.[37] If the father does not desire it so, he shall receive "triple" silver for the maiden, and he shall give his daughter in marriage to whomever he chooses. (MAL A §55)[38]

This gruesome measure is based not on a notion of collective responsibility but on the intention to punish the only one who is guilty by extending his own person to that of his wife.

Thus, the legal texts exhibit an imposing contrast between the legal capacity of the wife, who can buy in her own name, lend money, and adopt, and, on the other hand, her complete lack of rights in certain situations, in which she is reduced to nothing more than an appendage of her husband. This distortion

---

36. Translation from ibid., 169–70.

37. Insertion made by Guillaume Cardascia, *Les lois assyriennes* (LAPO 2; Paris: Cerf, 1969), 249.

38. Translation from Roth, *Law Collections*, 174–75. Commentary in Démare-Lafont, *Femmes droit*, 145–57.

probably reflects the fact that matrimonial law was globally conceived by men and in their favor.

Nothing hindered widows and divorced women from remarrying. If the children were still very young, the woman had to wait until their upbringing had been completed or seek the permission of the judges.

> If a widow whose children are still young should decide to enter another's house, she will not enter without (the prior approval of) the judges. When she enters another's house, the judges shall investigate the estate of her former husband, and they shall entrust the estate of her former husband to her later husband and to that woman, and they shall have them record a tablet (inventorying the estate). They shall safeguard the estate and they shall raise the young children; they will not sell the household goods. Any buyer who buys the household goods of the children of a widow shall forfeit his silver; the property shall revert to its owner. (LH §177)[39]

According to the Assyrian law, a widow was someone who had neither a father nor a brother nor a son-in-law who could provide for her maintenance. Consequently, she was independent from the viewpoint of the law and could freely remarry after living in a marital relationship with a man for two years.

> If a man should marry a widow without her formal binding agreement and she resides in his house for two years, she is a wife; she shall not leave. (MAL A §34)[40]

The new husband received his wife's entire property when she moved in with him and, conversely, when he moved in with her.

> If a widow should enter into a man's house, whatever she brings with her belongs to her (new) husband; and if a man should enter into a woman's house, whatever he brings with him belongs to the woman. (MAL A §35)[41]

In this last case, the woman became the head of the household, which meant that she was in charge of the care of the children and the administration of the family estate, including inheritance arrangements. Therefore, the transmission of the family's property did not pass exclusively through men but also included women. Due to the lack of relevant documents, it is difficult to evaluate the role played by women in the bequeathal of inheritance. Nevertheless, it

---

39. Translation from Roth, *Law Collections*, 116.
40. Translation from ibid., 165.
41. Translation from ibid., 165.

is certain that the Assyrian law did not always attribute the primary position in a married couple to the husband.

2.3. INHERITANCE

The dowry provided for a daughter's marriage or for her entry into a convent was considered a share of inheritance; she therefore inherited nothing at her father's death. After she died, her dowry was distributed among her children. If she died childless, the dowry returned to her family.[42]

In the middle of the second millennium B.C.E., in some areas of Syria (Emar, near Alep) and Iraq (Nuzi, near Mosul), daughters were sometimes turned into sons in a will. Consequently, they had the same inheritance rights as the boys and assumed, among other things, the duty of taking care of the family's gods,[43] since as a rule the cult of the ancestors was assumed by the male heir.

3. WOMEN AND RELIGIOUS LIFE

Several categories of priestesses and nuns are mentioned in the legal texts. What their precise activity was and how they accomplished it is not always clear. Some of these women have been, no doubt erroneously, considered to be sacred prostitutes.[44] Princesses and daughters of aristocratic families could reach the prestigious rank of *entu*-priestess, who was considered to be the earthly wife of a god.[45] The most famous are the *nadītum*-nuns of Shamash or of Marduk, documented in Babylonia during the first half of the second millennium B.C.E.

The *nadītum*-nuns of Shamash had to remain unmarried and could not have children, since they were thought to be the secondary wives of the god and lived in monastic-like communities. They brought with them their dowry, which they managed like clever and determined business women.

---

42. On the inheritance rights of women, see Josef Klíma, "La position successorale de la fille dans la Babylonie ancienne," *ArOr* 18 (1955): 150–86; Zafrira Ben Barak, "The Legal Status of the Daughter as Heir in Nuzi and Emar," in *Society and Economy in the Eastern Mediterranean* (ed. Michael Heltzer; OLA 23; Leuven: Peeters, 1988), 87–97; Westbrook, *Marriage Law*, 89–102; Erich Ebeling, "Erbe, Erbrecht, Enterbung," *RlA* 2:458–62.

43. Westbrook, "Social Justice," 36–38.

44. Wilfried G. Lambert, "Prostitution," in *Außenseiter und Randgruppen: Beiträge zu einer Sozialgeschichte des Alten Orients* (ed. Volkert Haas; Xenia 32; Konstanz: Universitätsverlag, 1992), 141.

45. Johannes Renger, "Untersuchungen zum Priestertum in der altbabylonischen Zeit," *ZA* 58 (1967): 134–44.

The large number of conflicts with their brothers, who "forgot" to send them the incomes from their estates, reveals their strong personalities. After the death of such a priestess, her dowry generally returned to her family, except in cases where her father had assigned her its full ownership. They would often adopt nieces, who were themselves nuns and who then became their sole heir. If there was no dowry, they received the share of a child in the paternal estate.[46]

The nuns of Marduk could marry, but they could not bear children. They would ask a secondary wife, who was probably also consecrated, or a slave to give them offspring. Instead of a dowry, they received a third of a child's inheritance share from their father's estate.

All the priestesses, who were compelled to chastity—especially the *nadītus*—had to live a blameless life. The Laws of Hammurabi forbade them to open or to enter a tavern, under the penalty of being burned.

> If a *nadītu* or an *ugbabtu* who does not reside within the cloister should open a tavern or enter a tavern for some beer, they shall burn that woman. (LH §110)[47]

A probably similar behavior is punished in Lev 21:9. Under the general term "prostitute," the daughter of a priest brings the sentence of being burned at the stake upon herself.

On the other hand, the Laws of Hammurabi protect the reputation of priestesses and married women against slander. Someone who spread false accusations incurred flogging or enslavement.

> If a man causes a finger to be pointed in accusation against an *ugbabtu* or against a man's wife but cannot bring proof, they shall flog that man before the judges and they shall shave off half of his hair. (LH §127)[48]

---

46. On the position of the *nadītum*-sisters, see Rivkah Harris, "The *Naditu* Woman," in *Studies Presented to A. L. Oppenheim* (ed. Robert D. Biggs and John A. Brinkman; Chicago: University of Chicago Press, 1964), 106–35; Elizabeth C. Stone, "The Social Role of the *Naditu* Women in Old Babylonian Nippur," *JESHO* 25 (1982): 50–70.

47. Translation and commentary in Martha Roth, "The Priestess and the Tavern: LH § 110," in *Munuscula Mesopotamica: Festschrift für Johannes Renger* (ed. Barbara Böck, Eva Cancik-Kirschbaum, and Thomas Richter; AOAT 267; Münster: Ugarit-Verlag, 1999), 445–64.

48. Translation from Roth, *Law Collections*, 105.

The Assyrian law mentions another category of women (*qadiltu*) who devoted themselves to the cult of the god Adad. They were allowed to marry but were obliged to wear a veil in public, like all married women.[49]

Few religious offenses are attested in the legal sources. Some of these do concern women belonging to the secular society: those who commit sacrilege and blasphemy. In the first case, the Assyrian law stipulates that an oracle be consulted in order to set the penalty to be executed by a secular authority.

> If a woman, either a man's wife or a man's daughter, should enter into a temple and steal something from the sanctuary in the temple and either it is discovered in her possession or they prove the charges against her and find her guilty, [they shall perform (?)] a divination (?), they shall inquire of the deity; they shall treat her as the deity instructs them. (MAL A §1)[50]

Conversely, this same Assyrian collection stipulates that the married man who utters curses or steals something from a temple shall incur a secular penalty. He shall receive forty blows with a stick and must perform one month of corvée for the king.

> If a man [says ...] to another man in a quarrel, "You have spoken blasphemy, [...] and furthermore you have pilfered the temple," [...] they shall strike him 40 blows with rods; [he shall perform the king's service for x days]. (MAL N §1)[51]

According to the Babylonian court decisions, it seems that the punishment was a fine based on the value of the stolen goods and the status of the offender. There are no traces in the trial documents of the death penalty mentioned in the omen literature against the relapsed great priestess. The Assyrian laws stress that only the woman guilty of blasphemy is to be punished, not the rest of her family.

> If a woman, either a man's wife or a man's daughter, should speak something disgraceful or utter a blasphemy, that woman alone bears responsibility for her offense; they shall have no claim against her husband, her sons, or her daughters. (MAL A §2)[52]

---

49. MAL A §40 (see §2.1).
50. Translation from Roth, *Law Collections*, 155.
51. Translation from Roth, *Law Collections*, 190.
52. Translation from ibid., 155.

The more or less contemporary edict of an Assyrian king threatens a woman belonging to the royal harem with death, whatever her rank may be, if she wrongfully speaks the name of the great god Ashur or that of the king.

> (Any royal women), either the king's wives or other women [of the palace, who ...] fight among themselves and in their quarrel blasphemously swear by the name of the god, [...] he shall [(not)] enter; they shall cut the throat of the one who has [cursed (?)] the god Ashur; in their quarrel [...] ... [...] she shall not satisfy the claim.
> [If ... says: "..."] my life," for improper purposes [...; he shall] not [swear] by the name of the king in a quarrel; and even more so indeed he shall not swear by the name of the god. [... They shall kill a palace woman who swears] by the name of the god for improper purposes [...], they shall not spare her life. If a] palace [woman] should curse [...], or [should she curse] either a descendant of Tukulti-Ninurta, [or another member of the royal household, or an official of the] royal bedroom, [...] or an official of the stool, or if she should spitefully curse any woman who is beneath her in station, [...] carrying (a child?); they shall pierce the nose of the palace woman; they shall strike her [30 (?) blows with rods]. (Edict of Ninurta-apil-Ekur §§10–11, 17)[53]

4. WOMEN AND ECONOMIC LIFE

Most of the legal texts relating to trade, business, or economics generally speak about men but rarely mention women. The latter do, however, take an active part in the craft production and practice artistic or lucrative professions. The administrative texts contain lists indicating rations paid to women for their services as musicians, dancers, laundresses, or millers. In all of these cases, they work for an institution to which they belong, so they are not autonomous.

Work at home is probably the most widespread activity but also the most difficult to discern, since there are no sources to inform us about the productivity and workforce. In addition to the women who usually carried out the household tasks, wet nurses and prostitutes also worked at home. The former took the babies into their homes to breastfeed them. The Laws of Hammurabi forbade them from receiving two infants simultaneously because of the risk of childhood mortality and threatened to mutilate their breasts in the case of infringement.

> If a man gives his son to a wet nurse and that child then dies while in the care of the wet nurse, and the wet nurse then contracts to care for another child without the consent of his (the dead child's) father and mother, they shall

---

53. Translation from ibid., 201–3.

charge and convict her, and, because she contracted to care for another child without the consent of his father and mother, they shall cut off her breast. (LH §194)[54]

In Mesopotamia, weaving was typically a feminine activity. The workers either carried out their task in workshops for the palace or at home for their own use. In the nineteenth century B.C.E., the wives of Assyrian merchants belonged to the second category, although their production was not only destined for their families; it was also exported to Anatolia, in the context of the foreign trade organized by their husbands. The women received wages for this work. Furthermore, they represented their husbands when they were away traveling, in all possible commercial fields: they paid the taxes, loaded the caravans for the transport of goods, made loans, and so on. All of this indicates that they had access to the capital of the company. Nevertheless, they did not own the business with their husbands but rather had the status of a salaried employee.[55]

Another predominantly feminine profession in Mesopotamia was that of beer brewer,[56] which is connected with that of tavern owner: in the beer tavern the woman sold the beer she had made, as well as other foodstuffs, such as barley. She also extended credit. The law forbade her from raising the price of beer dishonestly by altering the exchange rate between barley and money. Moreover, she had to denounce any suspicious gatherings in her restaurant, under threat of the death penalty.

> If a woman innkeeper should refuse to accept grain for the price of beer but accepts (only) silver measured by the large weight, thereby reducing the value of beer in relation to the value of grain, they shall charge and convict that woman innkeeper and they shall cast her into the water.
> If there should be a woman innkeeper in whose house criminals congregate, and she does not seize those criminals and lead them off to the palace authorities, that woman innkeeper shall be killed. (LH §§108–109)[57]

---

54. Translation from ibid., 120. For the interpretation, see Guillaume Cardascia, "La nourrice coupable: § 194 du Code de Hammurabi," in *Mélanges à la mémoire de Marcel-Henri Prévost: Droit biblique: Interprétation rabbinique: Communautés et sociétés* (Paris: Presses universitaires de France, 1982), 67–84.

55. Klaas Veenhof, *Aspects of Old Assyrian Trade and Its Terminology* (SD 10; Leiden: Brill, 1972), 118.

56. Wolfgang Röllig, *Das Bier im alten Mesopotamien* (Berlin: Blaschker, 1970); Elena Cassin, "Note sur le 'commerce de carrefour' en Mésopotamie ancienne," *JESHO* 4 (1961): 164–67.

57. Translation from Roth, *Law Collections*, 101.

5. WOMEN IN CRIMINAL LAW[58]

A large part of the criminal law pertaining to the family belongs to the "household laws": the offended party is the father or the husband, whose honor has been tainted by the misdeed of, or against, one of his dependents. The laws consequently held that the punishment of certain offenses pertained to the head of the family, more or less framed by the public authorities.

The wife was mainly under the domestic jurisdiction of the husband, who had the right to punish her. This permitted him to whip her, tear her hair out, or mutilate her ears:

> In addition to the punishments for [a man's wife] that are [written] on the tablet, a man may [whip] his wife, pluck out her hair, mutilate her ears, or strike her, with impunity. (MAL A §59)[59]

Yet he had no right over life or death. Only an impulsive act was excused. The man who caught his wife with a lover could kill both culprits on the spot without being accused of murder.

> If a man should seize another man upon his wife and they prove the charges against him and find him guilty, they shall kill both of them; there is no liability for him (i.e., the husband). If he should seize him and bring him either before the king or the judges, and they prove the charges against him and find him guilty—if the woman's husband kills his wife, then he shall also kill the man; if he cuts off his wife's nose, he shall turn the man into a eunuch and they shall lacerate his entire face; but if [he wishes to release] his wife, he shall [release] the man. (MAL A §15)[60]

In the case of rape, the father could force the guilty man to marry his daughter in order to assure her a matrimonial future.[61] The Assyrian law admits the *actio noxalis*: in the case of theft or conspiracy in running away, the man had to hand his wife over to the family of the victim or redeem her:

> If a man's wife should steal something with a value greater than 300 shekels of lead from the house of another man, the owner of the stolen goods shall take an oath, saying, "I did not incite her, saying, 'Commit a theft in my

---

58. See, in general, Démare-Lafont, *Femmes droit*.

59. Translation from Roth, *Law Collections*, 175–76.

60. Translation from Roth, *Law Collections*, 158. Also see Démare-Lafont, *Femmes droit*, 67–72, 82–83.

61. MAL A §55: see §2.2.

house.'" If her husband is in agreement, he (her husband) shall hand over the stolen goods and he shall ransom her; he shall cut off her ears. If her husband does not agree to her ransom, the owner of the stolen goods shall take her and he shall cut off her nose. (MAL A §5)[62]

If a man's wife should withdraw herself from her husband and enter into the house of another Assyrian, either in that city or in any of the nearby towns, to a house which he assigns to her, residing with the mistress of the household, staying overnight three or four nights, and the householder is not aware that it is the wife of a man who is residing in his house, and later that woman is seized, the householder whose wife withdrew herself from him shall [mutilate] his wife and [not] take her back. As for the man's wife with whom his wife resided, they shall cut off her ears; if he pleases, her husband shall give 12,600 shekels of lead as her value, and, if he pleases, he shall take back his wife. However, if the householder knows that it is a man's wife who is residing in his house with his wife, he shall give "triple." And if he should deny (that he knew of her status), he shall declare, "I did not know," they shall undergo the divine River Ordeal. And if the man in whose house the wife of a man resided should refuse to undergo the divine River Ordeal, he shall give "triple"; if it is the man whose wife withdrew herself from him who should refuse to undergo the divine River Ordeal, he (in whose house she resided) is clear; he shall bear the expenses of the divine River Ordeal. However, if the man whose wife withdrew herself from him does not mutilate his wife, he shall take back his wife; no sanctions are imposed. (MAL A §24)[63]

Adultery is exclusively a feminine criminal action, and the guilt was placed mainly on the married woman. The lover, if he knew that she was married, was considered an accomplice.[64] The man was assumed to be acting in good faith. In other words, he ignored the marital status of the woman, if he met her in a tavern or on the street.

If a man should fornicate with another man's wife either in an inn or in the main thoroughfare, knowing that she is the wife of a man, they shall treat the fornicator as the man declares he wishes his wife to be treated. If he should fornicate with her without knowing that she is the wife of a man, the fornicator is clear; the man shall prove the charges against his wife and he shall treat her as he wishes. (MAL A §14)[65]

---

62. Translation from Roth, *Law Collections*, 156.
63. Translation from Roth, *Law Collections*, 161–162.
64. Démare-Lafont, *Femmes droit*, 29.
65. Translation from Roth, *Law Collections*, 158.

If the meeting occurs in an isolated place, such as in the mountains, it is supposed that the man raped the woman, because she may have called for help without receiving it.

> If a man seizes a woman in the mountain(s) (and rapes her), it is the man's offence, and he shall be put to death, but if he seizes her in (her) house, it is the woman's offence; the woman shall be put to death. If the (woman's) husband (lit. the man) finds them (in the act) and kills them, he has committed no offence. (HL §197)[66]

In an inhabited area, the woman must energetically defend herself in order to maintain the fact of rape.

> If a wife of a man should walk along the main thoroughfare and should a man seize her and say to her, "I want to have sex with you!"—she shall not consent but she shall protect herself; should he seize her by force and fornicate with her—whether they discover him upon the woman or witnesses later prove the charges against him that he fornicated with the woman they shall kill the man; there is no punishment for the woman. (MAL A §12)[67]

This criterion is not valid for a young girl who out of fear or subjugation has given herself to the rapist.[68]

Voluntary abortion and witchcraft seem to have been public crimes that led to a court trial and the death penalty. Such was the case, for example, in Assyria, where abortion was punished by impalement and the interdiction of burial:

> If a woman aborts her fetus by her own action and they then prove the charges against her and find her guilty, they shall impale her, they shall not bury her. If she dies as a result of aborting her fetus they shall impale her,

---

66. Translation from Harry A. Hoffner, *The Laws of the Hittites: A Critical Edition* (DMOA 23; Leiden: Brill, 1997), 156.

67. Translation from Roth, *Law Collections*, 157–58. See also the New Babylonian document BM 64153, which contains the testimony of two witnesses about a kidnapping (period of Nabonidus): "On 14 Nissan a man violently seized a woman and forced her to enter into the house of the son of B. that is in the street of the son of Z., across from the house of N. We heard the cries of protest of this woman and of her servant; she was forced to enter that house" (my translation); publication and commentary in Michael Jursa, "*Terdu*: Von Entführung in Babylon und Majestätsbeleidigung in Larsa," in *Studi sul Vicino Oriente Antico dedicati alla memoria di Luigi Cagni* (ed. Stefania Graziani et al.; Studi Asiatici Series Minor 16; Neapel: Istituto Universitario Orientale, 2000), 497–514, here 499.

68. MAL A §55 (see §2.2.).

they shall not bury her. If any persons should hide that woman because she aborted her fetus [...]. (MAL A §53)[69]

Incest was punished in several collections of laws. These took into consideration relationships between father and daughter, mother and son, father and son, father-in-law and daughter-in-law, brother-in-law and sister-in-law, stepson and stepmother, son-in-law and mother-in-law:

If a man should carnally know his daughter, they shall banish that man from the city. (LH §154)[70]

If a man, after his father's death, should lie with his mother, they shall burn both of them. (LH §157)[71]

If a man sins (sexually) with his own mother, it is an unpermitted sexual pairing. If a man sins (sexually) with (his) daughter, it is an unpermitted sexual pairing. If a man sins (sexually) with (his) son, it is an unpermitted sexual pairing. (HL §189)[72]

If a man selects a bride for his son and his son carnally knows her, after which he himself then lies with her and they seize him in the act, they shall bind that man and cast him into the water.

If a man selects a bride for his son and his son does not yet carnally know her, and he himself then lies with her, he shall weigh and deliver to her 30 shekels of silver; moreover, he shall restore to her whatever she brought from her father's house, and a husband of her choice shall marry her. (LH §§155–156)[73]

If a man sleeps with his brother's wife while his brother is alive, it is an unpermitted sexual pairing. (HL §195a)[74]

---

69. Translation from Roth, *Law Collections*, 174. On witchcraft, see MAL A §47: "If either a man or a woman should be discovered practicing witchcraft, and should they prove the charges against them and find them guilty, they shall kill the practitioner of witchcraft" (172).

70. Translation from ibid., 110.

71. Translation from ibid., 111.

72. Translation from Hoffner, *The Laws of the Hittites*, 149.

73. Translation from Roth, *Law Collections*, 110.

74. Translation from Hoffner, *The Laws of the Hittites*, 154.

> If a man, after his father's death, should be discovered in the lap of his (the father's) principal wife who had borne children, that man shall be disinherited from the paternal estate. (LH §158)[75]

> If a man sins (sexually) with his step-mother, it is not an offence. But if his father is (still) living, it is an unpermitted sexual pairing. (HL §190)[76]

> If he has the daughter (in marriage) and approaches her mother or her sister (sexually), it is an unpermitted sexual pairing. (HL §195C)[77]

Several of these cases are found in the long list in Leviticus (Lev 18). An acceptable case of incest exists in Mesopotamia and in the Bible, namely, the levirate marriage. This arrangement obliges or allows a childless widow to marry her brother-in-law in order to obtain an offspring that will be considered the child of her deceased husband. The aim of procreation justifies this exception, which eliminates the legal existence of the brother-in-law, since he is merely the procreator and not the father of the child to be born. This is the only case, in the context of family law, in which a man is reduced to being an object, and it helps us understand Boaz's hesitation toward Ruth's request (Ruth 4).[78]

Several cuneiform laws discuss slander by a third party against a wife or a daughter of a respected family.[79] Whoever cast doubt on their morality was punished by a fine or physical sanction (whipping, dishonoring marks). The married woman accused of adultery by her husband justified herself by taking an oath:

> If her husband accuses his own wife (of adultery), although she has not been seized lying with another male, she shall swear (to her innocence by) an oath by the god, and return to her house. (LH §131)[80]

She had to undergo the river ordeal to prove her guilt or innocence, if the accusation came from a public rumor.

---

75. Translation from Roth, *Law Collections*, 111.
76. Translation from Hoffner, *The Laws of the Hittites*, 150.
77. Translation from ibid., 154.
78. Raymond Westbrook, "The Law of the Biblical Levirate," *RIDA* 3/24 (1977): 65–87; Démare-Lafont, *Femmes droit*, 27–221.
79. Démare-Lafont, *Femmes droit*, 236–288.
80. Translation in M. Roth, *Law Collections*, 106.

If a man's wife should have a finger pointed against her in accusation involving another male, although she has not been seized lying with another male,
she shall submit to the divine River Ordeal for her husband. (LH §132)[81]

The Bible mentions a similar case in Num 5:11–31: the woman whose husband accused her of adultery had to undergo an "ordeal of jealousy."[82]

6. Conclusion

In all we have seen here, the legal position of women in the ancient Near
East was highly contradictory. They had a legal capacity and were not treated
as eternal minors, yet their social position largely determined the extent of
their rights. To be honorable or respected, they had to be submitted to a male
authority—whether father or husband or even an institution, such as the
temple or the palace. Criminal law clearly shows that the offenses to which
they were victim or those they had committed were felt as disturbances to
their immediate family or group. Therefore, they were not seen as fully legal
persons. Despite their civil legal independence, the criminal law perceived
women as appendages of their fathers or husbands.

Abbreviations of Law Codices

BM + N.	Tablets in British Museum + inventory number
CT	Cuneiform Texts from Babylonian Tablets in the British Museum (London)
HL	Hittite Laws
LE	Laws of Eshnunna
LH	Laws of Hammurabi
LL	Laws of Lipit-Ishtar
LU	Laws of Ur-Namma
MAL	Middle Assyrian Laws

---

81. Loc. cit.

82. On this topic, see Sophie Démare-Lafont, "L'interprétation de Nombres 5,31 à la
lumière des droits cunéiformes", in *La femme dans le Proche-Orient antique: Compte rendu
de la 33e Recontre Assyriologique Internationale (Paris, 7–10 July 1986)* (ed. Jean-Marie
Durand; Paris: ERC, 1987), 49–52.

Torah and Canon: Challenges and Perspectives

Donatella Scaiola
Pontifica Università Urbaniana

1. The Past Situation

1.1. Canon: Meaning of the Term and Notion

This contribution departs from the assumption that, before addressing the issue explicitly mentioned in the essay title, it is useful and necessary to first clarify some terminological and substantial elements concerning the meaning, notion, and definition of the term "canon."

1.1.1. Meaning of the Term

The term "canon" is used in many different ways that, starting from the basic meaning, evolve in various metaphorical senses.[1] The Greek word κανών means, first of all, a straight pole, from which many other uses of the term that convey the concept of "being straight" are derived. As a stick was used to hold certain items straight or to prove that other things were straight, κανών often denotes a plumb line. From this basic meaning, various metaphorical uses of the term are derived. The term indicates the *criterion* or *model* through which it is possible to determine the rectitude of opinions or actions. The Greeks, for example, spoke of an ideal or exemplary person as a canon of the good. The Alexandrine grammarians gave the name κανών to the collection of classical works considered worthy of being followed, as they were exemplary for their style. In art, "canon" is the standard of classical human anatomical propor-

---

1. Hermann Wolfgang Beyer, "κανών," *TDNT* 3:596–602; Robert Walter Funk, *Parables and Presence: Forms of the New Testament Tradition* (Philadelphia: Fortress, 1982), 151–53; Bruce Metzger, *The Canon of the New Testament: Its Origin, Development, and Significance* (Oxford: Clarendon, 1987), 289–93.

tions. In music, the monochord, on which all the other tonal relationships were set, was known as κανὼν μουσικός.

In the New Testament, κανών can be found in Gal 6:16 with the meaning norm or model, pertaining to acknowledged Christian behavior. On the other hand, the meaning of the word is debated in 2 Cor 10:3–16, and it may denote the geographical area where Paul had to operate.

The first patristic writers (Saint Clement of Rome, Clement of Alexandria, and so on) used the word in the sense of "rule" or "norm," one to which Christian life and teaching should conform. Over time, "canon" came to be used in the church to indicate something tangible, a sure and clearly defined decision, and also a person. Since around 300 C.E., the term also occurs in its plural form to designate the regulations or decrees promulgated by the councils and synods, for example, religious or monastic rules (Athanasius, Basil, Gregory of Nazianzus), or people living according to a particular ecclesiastical rule.

Another use of the term, this time about the subsequent designation of the books of Scripture, was the application of the word to a list or index. For example, the ten canons written by Eusebius for his edition of the four Gospels were not rules but systematically ordered lists of numerals corresponding to the numbered sections of the text of Gospels. It was possible to quickly recognize the parallel texts through these lists.

Eventually the term was also used to indicate the list of authoritative books for Christians, a documented use since the second half of the fourth century C.E. The first example is in the *Decrees of the Synod of Nicaea* by Athanasius, written after 350 C.E., in which it is said that the Shepherd of Hermas does not belong to the canon. In 363 C.E., the Council of Laodicea in Phrygia declared that only canonical books, as opposed to noncanonical books, could be read in the church. The use of the word *canon* recurs for the first time in the poem *Iambi ad Seleucum* to mean the entire collection of the holy books. It was composed around 380 C.E. by Amphilochius, bishop of Iconium, who, after listing the books of the Old and New Testaments, declared: "This is maybe the most reliable canon of Scriptures divinely inspired" (οὗτος ἀψευδέστατος κανὼν ἂν εἴη τῶν θεοπνεύστων γραφῶν).

In short, one could say that, in the first three centuries of the church, the word *canon* denoted internal law and the binding norm of faith for Christianity, while from the latter half of the fourth century it was used also to mean the sacred writings of the Old and New Testaments.

1.1.2. Notion of Canon

From what has previously been said, it is possible to ascertain some elements concerning the notion of canon:

►   "canon" is a technical term;

►   it is a late Christian term, even if it is a Jewish idea;

►   it means at once the "rule" of faith, the rule that determines the faith (the *norma normans*), and the "list" of books accepted as inspired Scripture (the *norma normata*); the latter meaning is prevalent;

►   there was a long process that culminated in the indication of the content of this list;

►   the list of holy books is the result of considered judgment, of a decision regarding which books were to be admitted and accepted and which excluded;[2]

►   the list of books was accepted or certified by one or more communities.

1.2. FORMATION AND CLOSURE OF JEWISH CANON

During the nineteenth and twentieth centuries, the theory that later became classical was developed.[3] It explained the development of the canonical process as follows:

(1) The Hebrew Bible would have been canonized in three different stages: the Pentateuch from 400 B.C.E.; the Prophets from 200 B.C.E. onwards; the third part in the Synod or Council of Yavneh[4] around 90 C.E. The term *canonized* involves something officially or authoritatively imposed upon certain literature.

(2) In addition, those who spoke of a gradual process[5] still considered the closure of the canon to be something imposed by an authoritative body

---

2. Considerations about the supposed secular character of Canticles and the possible contradictions that existed between a book and the prescriptions of the Torah (Ezek 40–48; Qoheleth; Proverbs) enter into the rabbinic debate concerning the inspiration of a book. The book of Esther was accused, moreover, of simply recounting the story of the marriage between a Jew and a pagan without condemning it in any way. For the New Testament, three criteria of canonicity were generally adopted: the apostolic origin of the writing, its liturgical use, and its orthodoxy.

3. In chronological order, Heinrich Hirsch Graetz, *Kohélet oder der salomonische Prediger* (Leipzig: Winter, 1871), 147–74; Samuel Davidson, *The Canon of the Bible* (London: H. S. King, 1877), 56–57; Frants Buhl, *Kanon und Text des Alten Testamentes* (Leipzig: Faber, 1891), 24; Herbert Edward Ryle, *The Canon of the Old Testament* (London: Macmillan, 1892), 196, 218.

4. This place is sometimes cited as Jamnia or Javne/Jabne.

5. See, for example, Harold Henry Rowley, *The Growth of the Old Testament* (London: Hutchinson, 1950), 170; Aage Bentzen, *Introduction to the Old Testament* (Copenhagen: Gad, 1948), 1, 31; Otto Eissfeldt, *The Old Testament: An Introduction, Including the Apoc-*

of Judaism, located in Yavneh.[6] The search for a closure of the canon gave expression to a corresponding search of lists in the ancient Hebrew literature outside the Tanak (the prologue to the translation of the book of Sirach; Philo, *Contempl.* 25; Josephus, *C. Ap.* 1.38–41; and Luke 24:44). Similarly, the work on the process of canonizations in the New Testament covered lists in Tertullian, Eusebius, the Muratorian fragment, and so on. These lists were considered valid indications about the closure of the canon for all of Judaism or for all of Christianity.

(3) The classical theory also explains the difference in content of the Masoretic Bible and the Greek Bible, as in the presence of books that Catholics call deuterocanonical in the Greek Bible, as well as the supposed opposition between a more restricted Palestinian canon and a broader Alexandrian canon.

2. The Present Situation

Against the backdrop of the present situation, we can mention four factors that have promoted (or caused) the generation of new interest in the canon.

(1) An important impetus came from the attempts made to elaborate *a* biblical theology that would overcome the dualism between the Old and the New Testament.

(2) The question concerning the "center of Scripture," or the center of the Old/New Testament, is linked to endeavors to elaborate *a* biblical theology. This question concerns the identification of the guidelines, of the main concepts that can be indicated as the (central) theological content of Scripture and of the Old and New Testaments. Among other things, single *concepts* (e.g., kingdom of God, election, covenant, and so on), and *typical forms* (e.g., the form/structure of the covenant) have been discussed.

(3) The Jewish-Christian dialogue is an important point in the canon debate. When Jews and Christians discuss their common scriptural foundation, it soon becomes apparent that *the* problem of Christian theology is that of the hermeneutics of the Old Testament. This problem in turn raises further questions about the relation between Christians and the Judaic world.

(4) On the basis of what has been remembered up to this point, it is now possible to mention one last element. This is on a different level compared to

---

rypha and Pseudepigrapha, and also the Works of Similar Type from Qumran: The History of the Formation of the Old Testament (trans. Peter R. Ackroyd; Oxford: Basil Blackwell, 1965), 568.

6. For a thorough analysis of the problem and the relevant documentation, refer to Jack P. Lewis, "Jamnia Revisited," in *The Canon Debate* (ed. Lee Martin McDonald and James A. Sanders; Peabody, Mass.: Hendrickson, 2002), 146–62.

those considered until now: interest in the canon has resulted in increased dissatisfaction with the historical-critical method. The value assigned to the canon, which considers the biblical text to be a normative entity, has resulted in the historical-critical method being questioned. Hence, it is subject to accusations of atomizing the text and failing to show special interest in its theology.

2.1. From the Classical Hypothesis to New Theories

The discovery of hundreds of ancient biblical manuscripts, which occurred in the middle of the twentieth century, has also forced critical science to reconsider the development of the canonical process. In fact, before the discovery of the Dead Sea scrolls, there was a self-evident awareness that the text of the Hebrew Bible was basically equivalent to the Masoretic Text.[7] The Samaritan Pentateuch and the Septuagint, the earliest Greek translation of the Bible, were typically only evoked when the Masoretic Text presented a problem. However, the Scrolls have highlighted a previously unsuspected stage in the history of the biblical text: a period in which the text of the books of Scripture was pluriform. Creative development of this was a precursor to the stage of a single text for every book. Qumran demonstrates that the textual form of many books was still in a stage of creative development (Samuel, Psalms), a situation that continued until at least 70 C.E., if not 132 C.E.

Against what has been said, it is necessary to modify the classical theory substantially. As for the Synod of Yavneh,[8] it is necessary to state that neither Flavius Josephus nor the ancient Christian literature refer to a Council of Yavneh or to any closure of the canon that occurred in that contest. From this point of view, we are completely dependent on a unique rabbinic text, m. Yad. 3:5, that mentions a discussion concerning some biblical books. It is, however, not a contemporary report; rather, it is a text that simply states that all Scriptures "make the hands impure,"[9] without defining their extension. Canticles and Qoheleth have been asserted to have this requisite, without any corroboratory authorities cited. Rabbi Judah states that Canticles has these qualities but also remarks that there is disagreement concerning Qoheleth. Rabbi Jose

---

7. The Masoretic Text is the edition of the Hebrew Bible commonly utilized in biblical studies. It is based on the Codex of Leningrad B19, a manuscript that contains all the Old Testament that belongs to the ancient tradition of the scribes of the family Ben Asher of Tiberias. Even though it is relatively recent (it was finished around the tenth century C.E.), it is considered reliable.

8. Lewis, "Jamnia Revisited," 153–59.

9. This expression is used in Judaism in order to denote inspired texts.

says that Qoheleth does not make the hands impure, although there is some dispute about Canticles.

In terms of this debate, Rabbi Simeon, in yet another text, adds that the school of Shammai adopted the most indulgent rule, while Hillel's was more rigid (m. 'Ed. 5:3). Rabbi Simeon b. Azzai claims to have heard of a tradition from the seventy-two elders who, on the day on which Rabbi Eleazar b. Azariah became chief of the assembly, affirmed that both Canticles and Qoheleth make the hands impure (m. Zebaḥ. 1:3; m. Yad. 4:1; b. Ber. 28a). However, the discussion about these two books does not end with Yavneh. In the second half of the second century C.E., Rabbi Simeon b. Menasia opposed the dominant notion by declaring that Qoheleth is essentially a book about the wisdom of Solomon (t. Yad. 2:14; b. Meg. 7a). Further doubts are voiced in the Qoh. Rab. 1:3; 11:9; Lev. Rab. 23; and 'Abot R. Nat. 1.

Moreover, today the hypothesis of an Alexandrian canon has been abandoned for the following reasons: (1) this hypothesis supposes that Alexandria had become the religious center of reference for the Jewish Diaspora; this is contradicted by historical sources, which include the Alexandrian sources; (2) the hypothesis of a Greek-Egyptian origin of the deuterocanonical books has had to be abandoned, as it has since been understood that some of these books were originally written in Greek; (3) moreover, the number of the books mentioned as Scripture by the authors of the New Testament and by the apostolic fathers corresponds to neither the rabbinic canon nor the so-called Alexandrian canon but exceeds both.

Finally, as for the process of canonization of the Jewish Bible, alternative theories have been proposed, yet none of these has successfully imposed itself. I will briefly mention three of them: (1) according to some, the process of canonization of the Jewish Bible, at least of the Torah and the Prophets, was already advanced in the Persian epoch;[10] (2) according to others, quite the contrary, the collection of the books of the Hebrew Bible as we know it has been established since 150 B.C.E.;[11] (3) according to yet others, ancient Juda-

---

10. Joseph Blenkinsopp, *Prophecy and Canon: A Contribution to the Study of the Jewish Origins* (University of Notre Dame, Center for the Study of Judaism and Christianity in Antiquity 3; Notre Dame, Ind.: University of Notre Dame Press, 1977); Odil Hannes Steck, *Der Abschluß der Prophetie im Alten Testament: Ein Versuch zur Frage der Vorgeschichte des Kanons* (Biblisch-theologische Studien 17; Neukirchen-Vluyn: Neukirchener, 1991); Stephen G. Dempster, "An 'Extraordinary Fact': Torah and Temple and the Contours of the Hebrew Canon," *TynBul* 48 (1997): 23–56, 191–218; Stephen B. Chapman, *The Law and the Prophets: A Study in Old Testament Canon Formation* (FAT 27; Tübingen: Mohr Siebeck, 2000).

11. Sid Zalman Leiman, *The Canonization of Hebrew Scripture: The Talmudic and Midrashic Evidence* (Hamden, Ct.: Archon, 1976); Roger Beckwith, *The Old Testament*

ism would not have fixed the definitive list of its Scriptures before the second century C.E.[12] Frankly, the dissent among these different hypotheses is more formal than real, since Brevard Childs and, above all, James A. Sanders have all enlarged the concept of canon. In brief, we can recall that, for Childs, the final stage of Scripture is normative and that the Old Testament is represented by the Masoretic Text. Moreover, the canon is a normative entity that must be studied as *norma normata*.

Childs focuses on the final form of the text but does not explain how various Christian canons arose and why the various communities for which the Bible functions as canon differ one from one another. Childs chose the most recent of all, the Protestant canon of the sixteenth century, as the canon of the Old Testament. This choice has been subject to criticism, as this canon corresponds, in content, to the Judaic canon alone and to no other canon of the first Christian communities.

According to Sanders, however, the two main features of Scripture as canon are its adhesion to the life and to the stability of the communities. Both the scribes and the ancient translators of the text sought to advance comprehension of the meaning of the text to their communities, even at the cost of making small changes or clarifying archaic expressions. Sanders thinks that adaptability has always been a primary trait of a canon, as, when speaking of a canon, the intended community must be specified. The concept of canon, in his opinion, cannot be limited to the final stage in the history of the formation of the Bible, even though it must be understood as part of the history of the transmission of the text itself. Text and canon go together. Sanders uses the adjective "canonical" in a very wide sense. It designates every piece of writing that has authority in the believing community, the traditions from which the canonical writings have originated, and the hermeneutics that the believing communities impose upon the writings and their traditions.[13]

Sanders pays more attention to the canonical process than to the final, consolidated form of the biblical text. Accordingly, he strongly supports the

---

Canon of the New Testament Church and Its Background in Early Judaism (Grand Rapids: Eerdmans, 1985); idem, "Formation of the Hebrew Bible," in *Mikra: Text, Translation, Reading and Interpretation of the Hebrew Bible in Ancient Judaism and Early Christianity* (ed. Martin Jan Mulder; CRINT 2; LJPSTT 1; Assen: Van Gorcum, 1988), 39–86; Arie van der Kooij, "The Canonization of Ancient Books Kept in the Temple of Jerusalem," in *Canonization and Decanonization* (ed. Arie van der Kooij and Karel van der Toorn; SHR 82; Leiden: Brill, 1998), 17–40.

12. Mauro Perani, "Il processo di canonizzazione della Bibbia ebraica: Nuove prospettive metodologiche," *RivB* 48 (2000): 385–400.

13. James A. Sanders, "Canon," *ABD* 1:847–51.

function of canon as *norma normans* of the believing community. This means that he concentrates on the function exerted by the canon in the groups in which it features in their identity.

2.2. Canon and Feminist Hermeneutics

Despite significant points of contact, there are also conflicts between "canonical criticism," in the sense adopted by Sanders, and feminist hermeneutics.[14]

2.2.1. Points of Contact

(1) One of Sanders's main contributions has been recalling attention to the process of canonization, trying to clarify this as far as possible. This process begins when a history or a text are repeated. One of the reasons why a story first becomes tradition and then canonical is its ability to adapt to new situations. For this reason, Sanders believes that one of the primary features of canon, as has been recalled, is its *adaptability,* along with its *stability.* The adaptability takes place on different levels. For example, it occurs when a primarily oral tradition (the creation, the exodus, and so on) is repeated and resignified or when other authoritative traditions are added to the first traditions. The importance of this process for feminist hermeneutics lies in the fact that the continuous adaptation of the text is a process in which feminist interpreters are also involved. "Canonical criticism" and feminist hermeneutics try to define the ways through which the canon can be adapted to our time. For feminist hermeneutics, making the canon adaptable means that the importance of gender has to be acknowledged as an aspect of interpretation and that women claim the right to participate (with free rein) to the interpretive process.

The attempt of feminist hermeneutics is not new: it seeks new ways to resignify the tradition, as ancient a process as the tradition itself. For example, Phyllis Trible employs the image of the Bible as a pilgrim, a metaphor comparable to Sanders's concept of the adaptability of the tradition taken up again in the canonical process.[15]

(2) Another aspect of the canon that Sanders has called attention to is the *multivalency* of the text. Sanders has shown that the same text can have

---

14. I intend to offer some basic remarks without pursuing the impossible aim for comprehensiveness, due to the diverse and nonhomogeneous nature of the subject and the specific tone of this contribution.

15. Phyllis Trible, *God and the Rhetoric of Sexuality* (OBT 2; Philadelphia: Fortress, 1978), 1.

different meanings in different contexts. The multivalency of the text is a characteristic that feminist biblical hermeneutics has taken on in different ways. For example, many authors agree with Sanders and reject an "objective" reading of the text;[16] they assert that the idea of gender makes a difference to the way a text is read and, hence, reaffirm the importance of the context. Actually, the gender and the experience of women influence the reading of a text, so women, in reading, produce a new context. These assumptions have allowed women to reinterpret the texts that were traditionally understood in a negative way in relation to them.[17]

(3) The *pluralism of the canon*: canon is pluralistic as it reflects the diversity of contexts and experiences through which Israel and the church have acknowledged the work of God.[18] This diversity is represented in the canon in many ways, among which one can mention the expression of various theologies/ideologies, the numerous literary genres, and the diversity of the social contexts from which the different works have originated.

In this pluralism, Sanders recognizes a critical principle in *monotheism*: through its diversity, the Bible states that there is an only one God at work.[19] In this manner, the Bible presents a process of auto-emendation that renders it impossible to make any language, experience, or culture absolute. Feminist hermeneutics, starting from the affirmation of monotheism, has shown that, from the refusal to absolutize any culture, the rejection of the oppressive patriarchal culture (recognizable both in the Bible and in our current institutions) is then justifiable. Feminists are committed to a movement of resistance against the current dominant ways of thought that still put the man in the center and relegate the woman to the margins. Feminists fight to affirm monotheism and to reaffirm that God is neither limited by, nor bound to, a patriarchal vision of the world and to its expression.

(4) Moreover, canonical criticism is based on the assumption, also shared by feminist hermeneutics, that the Bible belongs to particular communities of believers.[20]

---

16. Elisabeth Schüssler Fiorenza, *Bread Not Stone: The Challenge of Feminist Biblical Interpretations* (Boston: Beacon, 1984), 32.

17. For example, Trible (*God and the Rhetoric of Sexuality*, 72–143) rereads Gen 2–3 so as to give Eve a more positive function than that of traditional hermeneutics.

18. Sanders, "Canon," *ABD* 1:843–46.

19. Ibid., 1:843–44.

20. Sharon H. Ringe, "Biblical Authority and Interpretation," in *The Liberating Word* (ed. Letty M. Russell; Philadelphia: Westminster, 1976), 31–40; 37; Schüssler Fiorenza (*Bread Not Stone*, 1–22) insists on the fact that this community includes the community of women.

(5) Finally, Sanders introduces an important distinction between *text* and *Word of God*. Likewise, some feminists have tried to understand in what sense the Bible is the Word of God, especially because it has been used against women at times. Many feminists agree with Sanders that the locus of the divine revelation is the conjunction between text and context, not the text itself.[21] Yet they go on to further the discourse by saying that unless this conjunction of text and context functions in the sense of supporting the liberation of women from social and political oppression, the text cannot be understood as divine revelation and truth.

To conclude, the points of intersection between "canonical criticism" and feminist hermeneutics include:

▶   the adaptability of the text;
▶   its polyvalence;
▶   the importance of the context in interpretation;
▶   pluralism and monotheizing trends of the Bible; and
▶   the relation between text and the believing community.

2.2.2. Points of Contrast

(1) According to Sanders, one of the functions of the canon is that it acts as a *mirror* that reflects the image of one's identity.[22] This is problematic for feminist hermeneutics because the mirror reflects stories that deal with the experience of the faith of men. Therefore, women do not find an adequate reflection of their own experience of faith, and they refuse to consider themselves only in the way in which they are seen by men. It is not possible for women to find themselves in the mirror of Scripture when looking at the traditions that deal with women. There are obvious limitations: on the one hand, with regard to the amount of textual material available; on the other hand, because most of those were written by men about women. Therefore, the experience communicated is interpreted through patriarchal eyes.

---

21. James A. Sanders, "Hermeneutics in True and False Prophecy," in *Canon and Authority: Essays in the Old Testament Religion and Theology* (ed. George W. Coats and Burke O. Long; Philadelphia: Fortress, 1977), 21–41; Elisabeth Schüssler Fiorenza, *In Memory of Her: A Feminist Theological Reconstruction of Christian Origins* (Boston: Beacon, 1984), 34–35.

22. James A. Sanders, *Canon and Community: A Guide to Canonical Criticism* (Philadelphia: Fortress, 1984), 72.

(2) Radical feminists reject the Bible because of the *patriarchal structuring of Scripture*.[23]

(3) Finally, the process of canonization itself is complicated. It has promoted the selection of some texts and the exclusion of others. Feminist hermeneutics asserts that the process of selection has been conducted by those who had the power to exclude voices and traditions.[24] For example, Elisabeth Schüssler Fiorenza has suggested that the formation process of the canon of the New Testament has led to an increasing exclusion of women from ecclesiastical office. For this reason, the historical-exegetical work should maintain a distance from the writings of the biblical canon and explore alternative sources, such as apocryphal and pseudepigraphical texts of both Testaments and other contemporary documents (of iconographic and archaeological character also), in order to be able to reconstruct the type of life that women led in biblical times.

If one presumes, as Sanders asserts,[25] that the process of canonization has been carried out without malice, it is nevertheless necessary to take note of the fact that women's experiences of God have been practically excluded from Scriptures.

Therefore, it is possible to conclude that feminist criticism senses the need to revise canonical criticism at least for the following reasons:

► the inadequacy of canon as a "mirror" for women's identity;
► the patriarchal structuring of canon; and
► the exclusive character of the canonization process.

2.2.3. Final Conclusions

Finally, it is possible to say that, first of all, in feminist theology different meanings of the word "canon" are discussed, such as the meaning of "canon" as rule or norm to determine the truth of opinions. Even if a debate exists

---

23. It is possible to find a presentation of the positions of the diverse authors who share this approach in Carolyn Osiek, "The Feminist and the Bible: Hermeneutical Alternatives," in *Feminist Perspectives on Biblical Scholarship* (ed. Adela Yarbro Collina; SBLB-SNA 10; Chico, Calif.: Scholars Press, 1985), 93–105; and, more recently, in Luise Schottroff, "Feminist Exegetical Hermeneutics," in *Feminist Interpretation: The Bible in Women's Perspective* (ed. Luise Schottroff, Silvia Schroer, and Marie Theres Wacker; Minneapolis: Fortress, 1998), 38–40.

24. Schüssler Fiorenza, *In Memory of Her*, 53–56.

25. I essentially share this assumption, even if I am aware of the fact that many authors contest it, recalling the attention to the existence of sociopolitical criterions characterized, in their opinion, by a marked male chauvinism.

about how this norm of truth could be found in Scripture, feminist theological hermeneutics insists on the fact that the contemporary "criterion" to evaluate biblical texts should be structured through the fight for the liberation of
women—proposing, in practice, a "canon within the canon."

For some feminists, such as Rosemary Radford Ruether, the authoritative core of canon is constituted by the prophetic-messianic tradition; the rest
is subject to criticism in order to reveal its historical limits in the context of
a different sociocultural environment.[26] Others, such as Schüssler Fiorenza,
establish a comparable but different canon, stating that only non-male-chau-
vinist and nonandocentric traditions of the Bible have any revelatory power.
Schüssler Fiorenza adopts a particular concept of canon as criterion: a canon
that would confine the inspired truth and revelation to questions concerning
the salvation, freedom, and liberation of everyone, especially of women.[27] The
source of this canon is not Scripture but rather the community, in particular
the community of women who fight against oppression. Although Schüssler
Fiorenza's position is worthy of an in-depth, focused study, I do not develop
this here because she has concentrated her research on the New Testament
above all else. Considering the relevance that Schüssler Fiorenza has assumed,
I will nevertheless focus on the clarification of her particular point of view
on this subject. Schüssler Fiorenza has worked a great deal on the subject of
the authority of the Bible, which (as has previously been said) suffers from a
patriarchal structuring and has often been used as an authoritative instrument
to legitimate the oppression of women. On the other hand, the Bible has also
been used as a source of inspiration by marginalized people who have found
a foundation for their emancipatory struggles in it. The Bible has, in other
words, a contradictory character, as it is used both to justify the oppression of
the oppressed and also to support their liberation.

Schüssler Fiorenza's work consists of the elaboration of a third perspective, developing a model of biblical interpretation of a liberationist type. A
hermeneutics of liberation demands that the exegete connects biblical reading to liberation praxis. The life of the poor and the oppressed, in this case
the women, is seen as the locus of revelation. For Schüssler Fiorenza, the
Bible does not possess any intrinsic authority, but it is connected to a specific
community of reference: "The Bible is placed under the authority of feminist
experience."[28]

---

26. Rosemary Radford Ruether, *Sexism and God-Talk: Toward a Feminist Theology*
(Boston: Beacon, 1983), 12–46.
27. Schüssler Fiorenza, *Bread Not Stone*, 14.
28. Schüssler Fiorenza, *In Memory of Her*, 32.

The necessity of also referring to different sources from the strictly canonical ones, as well as the refusal of a series of texts that would sanction women's discrimination and subsequent marginalization, is thereby understandable.

Secondary to the meaning of the word, the meaning of "canon" as a model or type to be respected or imitated is discussed. Feminist hermeneutics rarely considers the books of the canon as unchangeable classics or models to be imitated, simply because the canon incorporates only a few texts that are liberating for women.

Theological feminist hermeneutics is, *in the end*, a critical hermeneutics that considers the Bible not a mythical archetype but a historical prototype that, unlike an archetype, is open to the possibility of transformation. When the Bible is considered a mythical archetype, its experiences and its (historically limited) texts are considered universal and normative for all times and all cultures. On the other hand, when the Bible is considered a historical prototype, it is seen as a model of faith and life. The prototype, as the archetype, is an original model, albeit subject to change.[29]

Within this perspective, biblical texts are placed under the authority of feminist experience.[30] A feminist-critical approach to Scripture cannot remain confined within the boundaries of the canon. It must transgress the canonical paradigm that would otherwise exclude, silence, marginalize, and, in the final analysis, declare apocryphal voices and visions not in line with the patriarchal and male chauvinist power that have selected the canonical texts.

2.3. RAISING NEW QUESTIONS

As we have seen, recent discussions about the formation of the canon have modified some well-known and widespread convictions. Therefore, currently we do not know exactly how, when, and by whom the list of books in the Hebrew Bible was compiled. From recent studies, however, emerges a conviction that there has only been a (Judaic) canon since the third to fourth centuries (or over a period of time that extends from the second to the sixth century C.E.). Irrespective of this, the emergence of a Jewish canon happened only after the Pharisaic-rabbinic branch became the dominant one. Until and even today, however, rabbis have been struggling for control of the normative

---

29. For a development of the question, see Anni Tsokinnen, "Elisabeth Schüssler Fiorenza on the Authority of the Bible," in *Holy Texts: Authority and Language = Heilige Texte: Authorität und Sprache = Textes sacrés: Authorité et Langue* (ed. Charlotte Methuen et al.; Yearbook of the European Society of Women in Theological Research 12; Leuven: Peeters, 2004), 133–42.

30. Tsokinnen, "Elisabeth Schüssler Fiorenza," 14.

text and accordingly utilize prescriptions related to the execution of the types of sacred scrolls suitable for the ritual.[31]

Set against the classical hypothesis that considers the canonical process to be linear and tripartite, today the situation of the history of the canon of this epoch is described in a more complex manner. This corresponds to the multiplicity of groups present in Judaism in the period before and after Christ. As David Carr says, "Just as there was a plurality of Jewish groups during this time [the Second Temple period], there seems to have been a plurality in conceptions of Scripture."[32]

In particular, Carr recognizes certain groups, such as the Samaritans, and other groups established in Palestine (e.g., the Sadducees) who would have focused their attention exclusively on the Torah, alongside others who also acknowledged the authority of the prophetic books. This enlarged "canon" would have been adopted, above all, by circles that operated outside the temple (such as the Pharisees, the community of Qumran, the first Christians).[33]

Second, the equivalence between Masoretic Text and original text cannot be asserted. As Emanuel Tov says:

> The text of the Bible is represented by the totality of its textual witnesses, and not primarily by one of them. Each Hebrew manuscript and ancient version represents a segment of the abstract entity that we call "the text of the Bible." One finds the "text of the Bible" everywhere and nowhere. I say "everywhere," because all manuscripts, from the ancient Qumran scrolls to the medieval Masoretic manuscripts, attest to it. I say "nowhere," because we cannot call a single source, extant or reconstructed, "the text of the Bible."[34]

Eugene Ulrich has already called attention to the fact that the book is canonical,[35] not its textual form, which can still be in evolution (such as the

31. Johann Meier, "Zur Frage des biblischen Kanons im Frühjudentum im Licht der Qumranfunde," *JBTh* 3 (1988): 146.

32. David McClain Carr, "Canonization in the Context of Community: An Outline of the Formation of the Tanakh and the Christian Bible," in *A Gift of God in Due Season: Essays on Scripture and Community in Honor of James A. Sanders* (ed. Richard D. Weis and David McClain Carr; JSOTSup 225; Sheffield: JSOT Press, 1996), 45.

33. Carr, "Canonization in the Context of Community," 48.

34. Emanuel Tov, "The Status of the Masoretic Text in Modern Text Editions of the Hebrew Bible: The Relevance of Canon," in McDonald and Sanders, *The Canon Debate*, 251.

35. Given that the canon concerns biblical books and not their specific textual forms, Eugene Ulrich believes that talk of a "canonical text" is incorrect and suggests instead that we use expressions such as "the text of a canonical book" (Eugene Ulrich, "The Canonical Process, Textual Criticism, and Latter Stages in the Composition of the Bible," in *"Sha'arei*

different outline of the Psalms) or indeed subject to changes bound to the needs of individual communities, for which it was normative (such as the different versions of the book of Jeremiah). On the other hand, this process is complete: the canon is a closed list of books. Therefore, provocations arising from critical feminist hermeneutics are unacceptable: the canon cannot be reopened; it represents a sort of limit (some books are excluded, others admitted). This limit cannot be overcome simply by departing from a legitimate need for liberation.[36]

Third, the terminology with which we opened this contribution needs further specification, against the backdrop of recent discussions. Ulrich, for example, considers the canon the definitive closed list of books that constitutes the authentic content of Scripture and refuses to speak of a canon of Scriptures at Qumran. According to him, it is true that there was a long process that led to the closure of the canon. He argues, however, that it would be anachronistic and a potential source of confusion to apply the term "canon" to indicate any stage along the trajectory (up until the end of the process). Before the establishment of the canon, one should rather speak of the "canonical process." This process involved various aspects; Ulrich mentions some of these:

► the process for which single traditions have been united and composed as books of the Bible;
► the process that has led similar books to be gathered together in groups or sections of the present canon;
► the process that has led different groups in Judaism to the supremacy of the part of canon that they believed to be the most important (the law or the prophets).[37]

Sanders has a different opinion, as we have already seen. Influenced by Sanders, Gerald Sheppard speaks of "canon 1" and "canon 2."[38] Canon 1 refers to texts or to authoritative people (e.g., Moses, Jesus) who lived primarily in the Jewish community and then in the Christian community, before being

---

Talmon": Studies in the Bible, Qumran, and the Ancient Near Eastern Presented to Shemaryahu Talmon [ed. Michael Fishbane and Emanuel Tov; Winona Lake, Ind.: Eisenbrauns, 1992], 272–73.

36. Similar discourse is valid for other approaches, as the Document of the Papal Biblical Commission on The Interpretation of the Bible in the Church.

37. Ulrich, "The Canonical Process," 268.

38. Gerald Sheppard, "True and False Prophecy within Scripture," in Canon, Theology, and Old Testament Interpretation: Essays in Honor of Brevard S. Childs (ed. Gene M. Tucker, David L. Peterson, and Robert R. Wilson; Philadelphia: Fortress, 1988), 262–82.

included in fixed lists (canon 2). Many texts, in different moments in time, became canon 1 in the early church without becoming canon 2 (e.g., 1 Enoch, 1 Clement, the Letter of Barnabas).

Sanders also highlights the need to distinguish between the two meanings of the word *canon*:

> Keeping in mind the two meanings of the word *canon*, authority and invari-
> ability, one should be careful to distinguish between the near stability of the
> Genesis-to-Kings complex B.C.E. and the dynamic character of a nascent col-
> lection of prophets. A canon begins to *take shape* first and foremost because
> a question of identity or authority has arisen, and a canon begins to *become
> unchangeable* or invariable somewhat later, after the question of identity has
> for the most part been settled.[39]

Other questions have emerged that also require answers. For example, What exactly is a biblical canon, and what function does it have? Does the canon only have the function of determining valid texts in a normative sense, or does it constitute a specific structure of sense, as a structured totality with a global message of its own? The scholarly community is divided on this point. Indeed, some believe the canon to be of interest only as a historical fact. As John Barton says, "The books of Scripture were not arranged in any particular order from which theological interpretations can be derived."[40]

According to others, such as Norbert Lohfink, a canon incorporates a plurality of books with a plurality of theologies, displays a need for unity of content, and excludes other texts. Since these three elements are connected, it follows that, above all, the canon must be defined based on and in light of the social function that it exerts.[41]

We believe that the order of the writings in the Bible could be understood as a reading key of either the whole or its single parts. From this perspective, the canon constitutes a structure of sense that emerges from the different order of the texts collected within, an arrangement that expresses an explicit intentionality. We also consider the organization of texts in the canon to assume one or more theological meanings, in relation to different environments or communities of reference.

---

39. James A. Sanders, *Torah and Canon* (Philadelphia: Fortress, 1972), 91.

40. John Barton, *Oracles of God: Perceptions of Ancient Prophecy in Israel after the Exile* (New York: Oxford University Press, 1988), 44.

41. Norbert Lohfink, "Alttestamentliche Wissenschaft als Theologie? 44 Thesen," in *Wieviel Systematik erlaubt die Schrift? Auf der Suche nach einer gesamtbiblischen Theologie* (ed. Frank-Lothar Hossfeld; QD 185; Freiburg: Herder, 2001), 39–40.

3. The Future

As has emerged from the previous remarks, some reassuring interpretations of the past have been denied on the basis of more recent reflection. Therefore, the general impression is that of living in a time of great uncertainty in which nothing is truly consolidated.

Moreover, speaking of "canon" obliges us to take themes connected to it into consideration. For example, it requires us to address the question of the relation between text (texts?) and canon, between canon and community. From this point of view, I have set forth my opinion concerning the impossibility of reopening or reconsidering the canon. But is it really a blind alley, or would the circular relation between text and community authorize this reconsideration? Sanders would say no, in light of the fact that the canon is adaptable, yet also established in a definitive manner.

If we return, finally, to Tov's provocative thesis, according to which "the biblical text" exists everywhere and nowhere, the following questions arise: What consequences does his thesis have for how we view the concept of the inspiration of the canonical text (or texts), for how we view the exegetical method, and on the highly charged debates about the relation between the two Testaments in the one Bible?

The relation between canon/canons and community also draws attention to the "canon in the canon," not only in scholarly exegesis but also in the practical-pastoral realm. As we all know, different Christian groups adopt this reading criterion in practice, predominantly where the Old Testament is concerned. Also, feminist scholarship is aware of this challenge and suggests various solutions. It is simply impossible to speak of a unified conception of "canon"; one must speak, rather, of many different conceptions. These, however, have far-reaching consequences regarding the type of exegetical methodology practiced (e.g., search for the "original" text, search for the extent of the canon, and so on).

In this light, research on canon and on lists of Holy Scriptures presents itself rather as a construction site; a solution capable of addressing all the various kinds of issues raised in this essay is currently not in sight.

Genealogy as a Means of Historical Representation in the Torah and the Role of Women in the Genealogical System*

Thomas Hieke
Johannes Gutenberg-Universität Mainz

1. Introduction: Problematization of Terms and Concepts

"God reveals himself in history," and "the Old Testament is a book of history." These theologically justified expressions lead to a fundamental dilemma: on the one hand, the Old Testament deals chiefly with the history of the people of Israel with its God; on the other hand, an analysis of this representation, made under the conditions of the modern conception of reality, indicates that, behind the exegetical tradition and the kerygmatic actualization, it has become practically impossible to recognize the facticity of what actually happened. Like all the other ancient sources, the Old Testament must be considered critically. This is the only way to determine intersubjectively the historical information that may be found in it: this implies knowledge of what occurred at a particular place and what did not occur.[1] The Bible

* I wish to thank Dr. Andrea Klug, both for her ample advice on the topics relative to Egyptology and for her correction of the manuscript. All the remaining discrepancies and errors are my responsibility alone.

1. On this and for the following exposé, see, among others, Jan-Christian Gertz, "Konstruierte Erinnerung: Alttestamentliche Historiographie im Spiegel von Archäologie und literarhistorischer Kritik am Fallbeispiel des salomonischen Königtums," *BTZ* 21 (2004): 3–5, with bibliography. On the rapport between fact and fiction, see also the contribution of Gerd Häfner, "Konstruktion und Referenz: Impulse aus der neueren geschichtstheoretischen Diskussion," in *Historiographie und fiktionales Erzählen: Zur Konstruktivität in Geschichtstheorie und Exegese* (ed. Knut Backhaus and Gerd Häfner; Biblisch-Theologische Studien 86; Neukirchen-Vluyn: Neukirchener, 2007), 67–96. Concerning this problem, see also the fundamental study of John Van Seters, *Prologue to History: The Yahwist as Historian in Genesis* (Louisville: Westminster John Knox, 1992), esp. 24–44.

shares with the historiography of antiquity and the ancient Near East the fact that its conception of "history" is not the same as that of modern or contemporary historiography:[2] biblical and ancient authors make no distinction between historical "facts" and the "exegetical" use of the sources. Of course, describing the Old Testament texts "exclusively" as "stories" and denying them any value as sources is a tendentious and methodically naïve ultimate demand. Yet it is better not to speak of Old Testament *Geschichtsschreibung* (historiography) and rather about its *Geschichtsdarstellung* (representation of history). Its historical value frequently does not manifest itself directly in the events it relates (and which occasionally prove to be fictional or constructed) but in the way it narrates them, or the manner it represents history and reflects God's action in it.[3] Therefore, the real challenge does not lie in indicating the fictional elements in many biblical "stories" but in describing how, in them and through the construction of memories, the identity of a solid relationship with God is outlined and an eternal message from God transmitted.[4]

These fundamental reflections, from a perspective of the theory of history, on the value and the quality of the historical representations in the Bible shall not be presented in depth here; on the contrary, the background will be presented as the focus on the presentation of Old Testament history in the form of *genealogies*, or rather a *genealogical system*. As Fitzenreiter writes, "The genealogical relationship is the joint of the historical draft... Through the "genealogical," the past becomes a logical part—the source—of the present.[5] Before considering the Bible itself, possible analogies will be sought in the surrounding ancient Egyptian, ancient Near Eastern, and Greek world.

---

2. Alongside Gertz's "Konstruierte Erinnerung," see also Donald B. Redford, *Pharaonic King-Lists, Annals and Day-Books: A Contribution to the Study of the Egyptian Sense of History* (The Society for the Study of Egyptian Antiquities Publication 4; Mississauga, Ont.: Benben, 1986), xiii. This fundamental question is also dealt with by Stuart D. Beeson, "Historiography Ancient and Modern: Fact and Fiction," in *Ancient and Modern Scriptural Historiography/ L'historiographie biblique, ancienne et moderne* (ed. George J. Brooke and Thomas Römer; BETL 207; Leuven: Leuven University Press, 2007), 3–11; and, in the same volume, Philip R. Davies, "'Another Country?' Biblical Texts and the Past," 13–24; and Christophe Nihan, "L'écrit sacerdotal entre mythe et histoire," 151–90.

3. Among others, see Beeson, "Historiography Ancient and Modern," 9.

4. See, among others, Davies, "Another Country," 19–20.

5. Martin Fitzenreiter, "Einleitung. Genealogie—Realität und Fiktion sozialer und kultureller Identität," in *Genealogie—Realität und Fiktion von Identität* (ed. Martin Fitzenreiter; Internet-Beiträge zur Ägyptologie und Sudanarchäologie 5; Berlin: Humboldt-Universität, 2005), 1 (unless otherwise indicated, all translations from languages other than English are mine); online: http://www2.hu-berlin.de/nilus/net-publications/ibaes5/

This does not suggest direct historical, religious, or even literary dependencies; the differences are often much greater than the similarities. However, the basic abstract idea appears in conjunction with the fact that relations between entities such as gods, kings, or peoples should be classified according to genealogical principles in many cultures. In a synchronic retrospection of cultural phenomena, analogies attract attention. Against this background, the specific profile of the biblical world—in which time periods and spaces are organized by means of genealogical family relations and their proximity or distance—stands out more clearly. The outer aspect in the patrilineages, that is, genealogies containing only men and going from father to son, may suggest a view exclusively reserved for men. However, the documents reveal that, in the biblical representation of history, women played a specific and very significant role. For this reason, this study will concentrate on the role of women in the genealogical system.

2. Ancient Egyptian, Ancient Near Eastern and Greek Surroundings

2.1. Egypt

The family structure as a community of sexes and a succession of generations is a basic anthropological experience that lends itself as an analogy useful for the organization of other relationships. Behind the "genealogical representation of history," there is possibly an essential idea that people returned to at various periods in different places: the arrangement of relationships between entities in the form of family histories and lines of descent. Such entities may be, for example, deities, but also protagonists of a history belonging to the distant past. An example known to us from ancient Egypt is the theogony of the nine gods that presents a principle of order of the first gods at the time the universe was created:

> From the first being Atum proceeds, through self-generation, the first sexually differentiated divine couple—Shu and Tefnut—they give birth to the next generation of gods Geb and Nut, and from this union of the god of earth and the goddess of heaven finally are born the siblings, Osiris, Seth, Isis and Nephthys, who bring the number to nine.[6]

---

publikation/ibaes5_fitzenreiter_einleitung.pdf. Fitzenreiter also discusses the fictionality, or reality, of the genealogical constructs in his contribution.

6. Erik Hornung, *Der Eine und die Vielen: Altägyptische Götterwelt* (6th ed.; Darmstadt: Primus, 2005), 236.

However, this ennead is neither the only principle of order of the world of the Egyptian gods nor a closed canonical system; it can be extended and modified.[7]

The genealogical order of the group of nine gods is interrupted after this number. Horus, the son of Isis and Osiris, and the four sons of Horus are not counted. It must be noted that Osiris's line would have ended with his death and dismemberment, had his sisters Isis and Nephthys not seen to his reconstitution, so Osiris and Isis, as his wife, can have a son: Horus. The initiative of the women, or of the goddesses, allows the maintenance, or rather prolongation, of the masculine genealogical line. This "basic model" shall reappear with the question of the role of women in Genesis (and related literature, such as the book of Ruth).

In Egypt, the mythical genealogy of the gods is prolonged through the earthly monarchy: the king of Egypt is recognized as the son of the sun-god and the king's mother and as "Horus": the new king and successor of the deceased king, who assumes the role of "Osiris." Thus, the monarchy in Egypt is the earthly representation of the world of the gods and has a fundamentally dynastic structure. The genealogical principle also extends its influence through political history.[8]

Consequently, Ludwig D. Morenz shows that the Theban king Mentuhotep (II) (Eleventh Dynasty, beginning of the second millennium B.C.E.), for example, was represented both as the descendant of the gods (Amun-Re or Month and Hathor) and as the successor of the regional Theban sovereigns. His status surpasses the latter, as he is depicted with a double crown as the pan-Egyptian king, at the beginning of the Middle Kingdom.[9] In the setting of Mentuhotep (II) as king, a genealogical program is developed for him in which his descent is attached, through three kings, all named Antef, to the

---

7. For example, through the replacement of Seth by Horus or that of Atum by other manifestations of the sun-god, or the precedence of another chief deity such as Ptah in Memphis. On this, see "The Theology of Memphis" (*ANET*, 4–6); Benedikt Rothöhler, "Neue Gedanken zum Denkmal memphitischer Theologie" (diss., Universität Heidelberg, 2004), online: http://www.ub.uni-heidelberg.de/archiv/7030; see also Van Seters, *Prologue to History*, 27.

8. On this subject, see the Turin king papyrus from the period of Ramesses II (Nineteenth Dynasty); see also Alan H. Gardiner, *The Royal Canon of Turin* (Oxford: Griffith Institute, 1959); Redford, *Pharaonic King-Lists*, 2–18; Van Seters, *Prologue to History*, 26–27, 36; fundamental reflections on the form of representation in Ludwig D. Morenz, "Die doppelte Benutzung von Genealogie im Rahmen der Legitimierungsstrategie für Menthu-hotep (II.) als gesamtägyptischer Herrscher," in Fitzenreiter, *Genealogie*, 109–12.

9. See Morenz, "Die doppelte Benutzung," 116, who explicitly refers to the analogy in Jesus' genealogy in Matt 1. For the following summary, see 119–20.

founder of the dynasty: Mentuhotep I, who is not mentioned in the contemporary sources. Consequently, it is suspected that this figure, if not invented, was only progressively stylized as a great sovereign by a local Theban ruler. The intention was "to give dynastic legitimacy to the ruling Theban house and to anchor the new monarchy's claim to pan-Egyptian sovereignty more solidly in history.[10]

In dealing with the topic of "genealogical representation of history," it is very instructive to ask how the signification of descent was conceived in ancient Egypt.[11] (1) To establish the identity of an individual, filiation is used probably from the Fifth Dynasty on. For this, either the name of the father or the names of both parents (in the Middle Kingdom and later) are given.[12] Moreover, in the Middle Kingdom (twentieth–eighteenth century B.C.E.) sometimes only the mother's name is cited. In the fourteenth century B.C.E., the princesses of Amarna, the daughters of king Amenophis IV Akhenaten, are also called "carnal daughter, loved by him (i.e., the king), born of the great royal wife Nefertiti."[13] The mention of the filiation (descent) from the mother is not evidence of a matrilineal concept, that is, suggesting that the lineage passes through the mothers. The indication of descent from the mother does not concern the lineage, which always runs through the fathers/men (patrilineal), but rather differentiation among the male descendants. The Egyptian king usually has other wives alongside his chief wife, and hence the naming of the mother serves the particular legitimization of the chief successor. Regional monarchs also practiced polygamy. So, since, as can be seen in the later texts, the children of the first marriage had greater inheritance rights than the children of following marriages, the naming of the mother was important for the clarification of the legal claims.

(2) This leads to the second function of the genealogical indication: the grounding of a moral or legal claim. Such a claim to a position,[14] in the kingdom or the priesthood, usually runs through the father. Now, when the ruling

---

10. Ibid., 120. See also Redford, *Pharaonic King-Lists*, 28.

11. For the following presentation, see Hellmut Brunner, "Abstammung," *LÄ* 1:13–18.

12. See Karl Jansen-Winkeln, "Die Entwicklung der genealogischen Informationen nach dem Neuen Reich," in Fitzenreiter, *Genealogie*, 138.

13. See Erika Feucht, "Mutter," *LÄ* 6:256.

14. On this, see the depiction of all the mayors of Meir on Uchhotep's (III) rock-cut tomb, which represents as many as fifty-nine ancestors, or predecessors of this office (with their wives). This depiction probably has the political function of strengthening and legitimizing the possibly unstable position of Uchhotep in Meir and putting before the eyes of the long-established families that the one who ordered this tomb "belongs to them." On this topic, see Wolfram Grajetzki, "Zwei Fallbeispiele für Genealogien im Mittleren Reich," in Fitzenreiter, *Genealogie*, 57–60; Redford, *Pharaonic King-Lists*, 158–59.

cast of a male lineage has died out, the dynasty ends. In the Old Kingdom, the link to the next dynasty is guaranteed through the feminine lineage, "the husband or son of the last king's daughter ascending to the throne."[15] Similarly, this does not constitute a "matrilineage" (see above); rather, it is a tentative means to maintain the continuity of the royal family.

(3) A third reason for the genealogical indication aims at elevating the reputation of the implicated person. In tombs, open to the public and where the memory of the buried dead is kept alive, the indication of long lists of ancestors may have served to draw attention to one's own "good name" and stress the tradition-consciousness of the family.[16] In later times, the lists use fictional names, especially when the number of the ancestors is great and extends back over several centuries. Precisely in the case of priests, the lineage has a significant role, since the consideration of the position is particularly pronounced. Such longer genealogies are documented notably from the Twenty-Second Dynasty (ca. 965–750 B.C.E.)[17] to the Hellenistic period; they legitimize the claims of priests and their families to positions and power.[18] The genealogies from the Twenty-Second Dynasty are perhaps not purely invented but rather represent the literary transcription of lists of descent first,

---

15. Feucht, "Mutter," 257. The older thesis that the right to the royal throne is transmitted through the feminine lineage of the royal family, i.e., implying that each king must legitimize himself by marrying the daughter of the preceding king, is rightly refuted by, among others, Gay Robins, *Women in Ancient Egypt* (London: British Museum Press, 1993), 26–27. Hence, for example, the wives of Thutmose III, Amenophis II, and Amenophis III would not be of royal descent.

16. See Grajetzki, "Zwei Fallbeispiele für Genealogien," 60–62; Jansen-Winkeln, "Die Entwicklung der genealogischen Informationen," 139; for the "family stelas," also see Martin Fitzenreiter, "Überlegungen zum Kontext der ‚Familienstelen' und ähnlicher Objekte," in Fitzenreiter, *Genealogie*, 69–96. Fitzenreiter considers the essential function of the family stelas to the documentation of a sacralization of relations between groups (85). The kinship, or genealogical bonds, do not necessarily constitute rapports of descent but rather regulate the dynamic of the contacts between social groups and individuals (92).

17. See Jansen-Winkeln, "Die Entwicklung der genealogischen Informationen," 137. He calculates that the use of longer genealogies began between the Twenty-First Dynasty and the end of the Third Intermediate Period (ca. tenth century B.C.E.) and that these longer genealogies reached an apogee from the Twenty-Second Dynasty to the Twenty-Sixth. The longest genealogy, with sixty generations, is found on the relief of a tomb from Saqqara. This predominantly concerns priestly genealogies, but this may depend on the sites of discoveries (temples) and be explained by the fact that there was practically no civil government during the Third Intermediate Period. See also Redford, *Pharaonic King-Lists*, 62–64.

18. See Robert R. Wilson, *Genealogy and History in the Biblical World* (YNER 7; New Haven: Yale University Press, 1977), 127; Fitzenreiter, "Überlegungen zum Kontext," 82; Jansen-Winkeln, "Die Entwicklung der genealogischen Informationen," 139.

transmitted orally over a long period of time (or better, of previous stages of transmission not conserved in writing).

The royal and priestly genealogies suggest that, in these cases, almost only men are mentioned.[19] In fact, women hardly appear in the primary literature on the history of ancient Egypt. The main reason for this lies in the fundamental and scarcely changing social structure, which is dominated by a king and the exclusively masculine priesthood and officialdom. There actually are priestesses in particular cultic forms. Thus, women belonging to the upper class can be called "priestesses of Hathor." The wife of the king Ahmose I, Ahmose-Nefertari (ca. 1575–1505), bears the title "God's Wife of Amun in Karnak." To fulfill the cultic obligations as "God's Spouse," she founds a community of priestesses. In the mythical vision of the world and of society, represented in the cult, as the human partner of the god Amun-Re, she looks after the royal descent of the king. However, it becomes clear that this was an exceptional role for a woman.

In the global review of her results, Gay Robins observes, in the introduction of her book *Women in Ancient Egypt*, "Thus women scarcely get a mention in political histories of Egypt."[20] Starting at creation, according to the vision of the world, male gods rule the land of Egypt, and in the course of history they are replaced by the male kings of the human race. These kings choose wives for themselves not exclusively from the royal families (in part, incestuous relationships) but also from the common classes. Often diplomatic reasons are involved. The fate of the women married in this way with the Egyptian court is uncertain and depends on the relations and the influence of their homeland in Egypt. Gay Robins summarizes:

> In fact, such women were little more than commodities to be traded for peace and alliance. They had no say in their fate, and yet they became important cogs in the workings of the international diplomatic system: while the system was run by men, the women were needed to make it work.[21]

When a child is born as a result of the relationship of the king with a woman, the child's gender determines his or her future: sons are potential successors to the throne, whereas daughters do not have such expectations. The normal path of the succession to the throne runs through the male line. In myths

---

19. See Jansen-Winkeln, "Die Entwicklung der genealogischen Informationen," 138: the fatherly lineage is predominant. The mother is named only when an important position is inherited through the motherly lineage or if the mother comes from a royal family.

20. Robins, *Women in Ancient Egypt*, 11. For the following presentation, 21.

21. Ibid., 36.

parallel to the concrete political world, this is represented by Horus (the living successor to the throne), who succeeds Osiris (the defunct predecessor) to the throne as king. According to this myth, there is no room for an official accession of women to the throne.[22]

When, nevertheless, women acceded to the royal throne, these constituted very exceptional cases that could occur if the king's mother[23] or his wife was able to impose her interests in the determination of the inheritance in a legitimate or conspiring way.[24] If the last male successor to the throne was still very young, the king's mother could effectively assume the government (including the cultic duties). This is illustrated by Ahhotep II, the mother of the founder of the Eighteenth Dynasty Ahmose, or his wife Ahmose-Nefertari (sixteenth century B.C.E.).

Probably the best-known example is that of Hatshepsut, the wife of Thutmose II (Eighteenth Dynasty). The latter had a son with his concubine, who officially reigned as Thutmose III from circa 1467 to 1413 B.C.E. During the first years of his reign, Hatshepsut assumed the government and adopted the royal iconography, which was constructed in accordance with the royal titles (for example, "Lady of Both Lands" [Upper and Lower Egypt]). She also presented offerings to the gods, an action usually reserved for kings. Toward the seventh year of the reign of Thutmose III, Hatshepsut renounced the title of queen, which had barely any political relevance, and instead used the five-part pharaonic title. On the commemorative monuments, she appears clothed as a king; she also has her divine descent represented in her mortuary temple in Thebes: the union of the god Amun-Re with her mother, Queen Ahmose, is followed by the birth of "King Hatshepsut." In documentation of her crowning, she legitimizes herself both by stating that Thutmose I chose her to succeed him and with a divine oracle. Scholars are not entirely certain how Hatshepsut was able to surmount tradition and how she was, as a woman, able to become "king"—with the acceptance of the male officialdom. Her strong

---

22. However, an integration of a queen may occur though Isis, the sister-wife of Osiris and mother of Horus. This is found under the Ptolemies, who include the queens as mothers of kings in the genealogies and also establish a place for the defunct sovereigns in the cult of the dead; on this, see Friederike Herklotz, "Der Ahnenkult bei den Ptolemäern," in Fitzenreiter, *Genealogie*, 161–62.

23. On the role of the king's mother and of the wives at the royal court in ancient Egypt, and especially on their influence over the politics in the New Kingdom, see the works of Silke Roth, *Die Königsmütter des alten Ägypten von der Frühzeit bis zum Ende der 12. Dynastie* (ÄAT 46; Wiesbaden: Harrassowitz, 2001); and eadem, *"Gebieterin aller Länder": Die Rolle der königlichen Frauen in der fiktiven und realen Außenpolitik des ägyptischen Neuen Reiches* (OBO 185; Fribourg: Universitätsverlag, 2002).

24. See Robins, *Women in Ancient Egypt*, 38, 42.

personality, along with her clever choice of officials who remained loyal to her, was surely decisive. From the twenty-second year on, Thutmose III reigned alone; Hatshepsut's end remains obscure. Even if, from time to time, women reigned for short periods at the end of dynasties,[25] the length of Hatshepsut's reign, which lasted twenty-two years, is indeed highly exceptional. As regent, she not only represented the real king but also assumed the actual male gender role in such a way that there were, in fact, two kings. This "jolt" to tradition had long-lasting consequences, and, after her death, while Thutmose III was still reigning, an attempt was made to reestablish "order" [ma'at], and her name was erased from the monuments.

Another equally exceptional, powerful, and apparently important woman was Nefertiti, the wife of Akhenaten, king of Amarna (ca. 1340–1324 B.C.E.). In depictions of her, she is wearing the crown, like the king. Her husband Akhenaten is assimilated with Shu, the son of the creator-god; Nefertiti assumes the role of Tefnut (daughter of the creator-god). Together with Aten, the unique god, they constitute the so-called "Triad of Amarna." The names of "King Hatshepsut," of Akhenaten king of Amarna, as well as those of his successors Smenkhkare, Tutankhamen, and Aye, are effaced in the Egyptian king lists.[26]

The normal roles of the royal wives was not as "occupants of the throne" but as representatives of the feminine principle of the universe through which the kingdom could renew itself; in practice, this means that they brought the successor to the throne into the world. All other forms of influence exercised by women constituted deviations from ideology and tradition.

---

25. Robins, *Women in Ancient Egypt*, 50–51, mentions three names, indicating that among there were only four women among the two to three hundred Egyptian kings.

26. Thus, for example, in the king list of the Eighteenth Dynasty (*TUAT* 1:541–44). Important enumerations of Egyptian kings are represented in the king lists from Abydos (First to Nineteenth Dynasty: Seti I), the Palermo stone (Predynastic Period to the Fifth Dynasty), the king list from Karnak (an inventory of the statues of kings that Thutmose III cleared away when the temple was built), the king list from Saqqara (a list of fifty-seven kings—approximately fifty names are conserved—revered by Ramesses II), and Turin King List (a fragmentary list from the time of Ramesses II). On the king lists, see Redford, *Pharaonic King-Lists*, 1–64. He emphasizes that these lists (with the exception of the Turin King List) did not have a "historical" or "historiographical" purpose but rather concerned cultic functions, for example, veneration of the ancestors (18).

2.2. The Ancient Near East

Ancient Mesopotamia, like ancient Egypt,[27] had great interest in the past. This manifested itself notably in king lists, chronicles, and annals as well as in the archiving of letters and books in the cuneiform libraries.[28] In spite of these "historiographical" genres, the reports are not neutral or "objective" but rather present particular perspectives, as in cases where the documents are not frankly partisan and so reveal the interests of each ruler.[29] The form in which history was represented in the genealogies plays only a minor role in this essay. Robert R. Wilson, in his study *Genealogy and History in the Biblical World*, notes that, prior to his work, there were no systematic studies of genealogies in the ancient Near East.[30] His work still constitutes an approach and a starting point for questions on this subject. Wilson consecrates his second chapter to the study of ancient Near Eastern genealogies[31] and discusses the findings of the Sumerian and Akkadian documents, as well as those of other Western Semitic areas such as Ugarit.

First of all, he establishes a basic distinction between the royal and non-royal genealogies. The genealogies in the royal inscriptions are all linear; that is, each genealogical line runs through only one ancestor on to the next generation (grandfather, father, son, grandson). Such genealogies are mostly found in the introduction of the inscriptions that connect royal titles and epithets. As a rule, the genealogies go through three generations, sometimes four. When they go further, the genealogies are no longer constructed with the usual formulas ("X son of Y son of Z"); instead, they have a very particular form. If several genealogies contain the same circle of people, then the phenomenon of "fluidity" (Wilson) appears between the different genealogies, that is, discrepancies between genealogies that should actually be identical or other variants of the father-son model. Among these variants, one finds what

---

27. The ancient historiographers (Herodotus, Theophrastus, and others) attest to the interest of the ancient Egyptians for the past with reference to well-known annals and lists; see Redford, *Pharaonic King-Lists*, 65.

28. See Ephraim A. Speiser, "Geschichtswissenschaft," *RlA* 3:217.

29. This is also true for the "Geschichtswissenschaft/Geschichtsschreibung" (study of history/historiography) in Hatti; see Heinrich Otten, "Geschichtswissenschaft in Hatti," *RlA* 3:220–21.

30. See Wilson, *Genealogy and History*, 56.

31. On this subject, see also Robert R. Wilson, "Between 'Azel' and 'Azel': Interpreting the Biblical Genealogies," *BA* 42 (1979): 13–18; then the short notices in Walter E. Aufrecht, "Genealogy and History in Ancient Israel," in *Ascribe to the Lord: Biblical and Other Studies in Memory of Peter C. Craigie* (ed. Lyle Eslinger and Glen Taylor; JSOTSup 67; Sheffield: JSOT Press, 1988), 206–11.

Wilson calls "telescoping." Thus, for example, in one genealogy of Esarhaddon, the names of the father and the grandfather are followed by the names of the founders of the dynasty (son and father), whereas the Assyrian king list indicates that, between them, at least sixty-two kings are left out. Hence the genealogy is collapsed through telescoping, and a direct relationship is established between the current ruler, via his father and grandfather, and the first ancestors of the dynastic foundation.[32] The function of such genealogies is not historiography, nor the simple recording of names, but the legitimization of the ruler who is governing at the moment of the redaction and of his lineage. Precisely at times of political instability and crisis-like changes, the genealogies become longer: in the face of unfaithful vassals and pretenders to the throne, the direct legitimacy of the present ruler must be explicitly emphasized. The genealogy is, however, not an element that need necessarily exist. It is not needed, for example, if the ruler derives his legitimacy directly from a deity or if the immediate predecessor is sufficiently legitimized so that, for the present king, a simple filiation (attestation of the father) suffices. If he is the son of a king genealogically attached to the tradition, his domination is also declared legitimate. Accordingly, genealogies do not appear with all kings, and they do not play an essential role in tradition: "the rulers were not interested in using royal genealogies, and for this reason it is unlikely that detailed genealogical information was preserved at all."[33] The Mesopotamian king lists are perhaps in the background of the genealogical information. These lists of kings—for example, the Sumerian king list, the list of the rulers of Lagash[34] or the Assyrian king list—only rarely contain genealogical indicators. They are not interested in transmitting concrete genealogies.

For instance, the Sumerian King List presents a succession of, in part, contemporary dynasties in different cities and formally describes how the monarchy passes from one city to another.[35] The last city mentioned is Isin, so that the political function of this list becomes clear: it legitimates the seat of the monarchy in the city of Isin. For this reason, the small number of genealogical aspects does not play a significant role. They are incidental and were

---

32. See Wilson, *Genealogy and History*, 64–65.

33. Ibid., 72.

34. On this subject, see, however, *TUAT* 1:329; and Edmond Sollberger, "The Rulers of Lagaš," *JCS* 21 (1967): 279–91. See also The Electronic Text Corpus of Sumerian Literature, online at: http://www-etcsl.orient.ox.ac.uk; Van Seters, *Prologue to History*, 64–66.

35. See *ANET*, 265–66; The Electronic Text Corpus of Sumerian Literature (http://etcsl.orinst.ox.ac.uk/cgi-bin/etcsl.cgi?text=t.2.1.1#); Van Seters, *Prologue to History*, 35–36, 62–64; Nihan, "L'écrit sacerdotal," 172–76.

left incomplete when no genealogical information was available. It is likely that independent genealogies never existed in this context.

The Assyrian King List contains, in its second part, a linear genealogy; whereas parts 1 and 3 are simple lists (without a genealogical indicator),[36] part 4 is a linear genealogy extended by the specification of the length of the reigns. In a comparison of the Assyrian king list with the corresponding inscriptions of the named kings, differences appear that must be attributed to the so-called phenomenon of "fluidity." These variations are motivated by the different functions: while the genealogies in the inscriptions support the legitimacy of the redacting king and thus represent the succession to the throne, which sometimes also passes from an older to a younger brother, the king list follows the regular succession from father to son and perhaps even establishes it when it does not correspond. This creates differences and rejections, which leads to the recognition that the main aim of the genealogical information is not exact historical descent but rather political organization. For the pursuit of this aim, genealogical successions are consciously modified or names are left out. Only in later times, when the genealogies had lost their direct political purpose, were "historical" chronicles written and transmitted as such.

The Genealogy of the Hammurapi Dynasty reveals another function of the genealogies: it first concerns a simple list of names, later placed into a sequence of epochal names and groups of persons.[37] In the end, it becomes clear that a series of invocations is presented: the redactor of the list or genealogy, the Babylonian king Ammisaduqa, wants to use it solely to accomplish the rite of offerings for the dead (kispu[m])[38] pertaining to all of his ancestors, in order to keep their memory alive and appease the spirits of the dead. For this, it is important to name *all* of them and not forget anyone—this explains the global epochs and the naming of groups. The detailed genealogical information is, therefore, unimportant, and for this same reason the genealogical indicators of relationships are largely left out.

In Mesopotamia, there are also records of nonroyal genealogies. They are primarily found in the form of information relative to the descent of the authors, which they insert with their names in the colophons of important texts. Alongside the normal filiation, as a part of the name, there are also genealogies featuring more generations in which the name can also indicate the tribe, that is, the forefather who founded the family. Wilson also explains the

---

36. See *ANET*, 564–66.

37. See Jacob J. Finkelstein, "The Genealogy of the Hammurapi Dynasty," *JCS* 20 (1966): 95–118.

38. On this, see also Alexander A. Fischer, *Tod und Jenseits im Alten Orient und Alten Testament* (Neukirchen-Vluyn: Neukirchener, 2005), 52–54.

exclusion of intermediary generations as an example of "telescoping."[39] In that case, it is also perhaps better to speak not of genealogies but of personal names presented in a genealogical form. Then the "forefather" can represent a particular guild (especially the author's trade)—instead of the family—along with its excellent reputation that the carrier of the name hence claims for himself. Long genealogies, especially of priests, serve to enhance the reputation and the influence of those concerned.

Genealogies play practically no role in Ugarit.[40] The function of Phoenician genealogies was apparently to identify groups of people; in the case of kings and priests, they also had a legitimizing purpose. Whereas Phoenician genealogies contain up to seven names, the related Punic genealogies were extended as far as the seventeenth generation. Hebrew, Moabite, and Aramaic inscriptions show concise genealogical information in the form of personal names with filiation (two generations) alone.

To sum up Wilson's observations, genealogies do not primarily serve historiography; rather, they have a "sociological" function. They are parts of personal names; they legitimize, in the political domain, the claim to the monarchy or an office; and they are a part of the cult of ancestors.[41] When, in the process of transmission, the genealogies lose their original function, they are interpreted as representations of historical information. This is also true when the genealogical details partially contradict the royal inscriptions with the same names in a different order. For later generations, the original function of genealogical information was no longer available. Therefore the genealogies were considered to be exact historical sources. From today's viewpoint, it is clear that the redaction of genealogies often shows great "fluidity." In these cases, the deviations have a political function, such as excluding a particular group of people or a "line" that does not fit into the political calculations.

The formal insertion of genealogical information into larger "narrative contexts" (royal inscriptions or king lists) shows that genealogies never serve to connect smaller narrative elements or constitute the structure of a story. Rather, genealogies seem to have been added to existing texts. Genealogical information is furnished only when it serves the purpose of the text's redaction. In the material analyzed by Wilson, no women are named. In view of this background, it is indeed remarkable that the figures of women play an important role in the *biblical* representation of history and also in the genealogical system of the Torah, as will be shown. Women appear, clearly profiled,

---

39. See Wilson, *Genealogy and History*, 115.
40. See ibid., 120. One Ugarit king list has been conserved (see *TUAT* 1:496–97).
41. See Wilson, *Genealogy and History*, 132.

in the foreground, as in the historical representations of ancient Egypt and the ancient Near East.

2.3. GREECE

Paula Philippson, in her study of the Greek myths, formulates a basic and very useful definition of genealogy as a historical representation:

> The original form in which the relation between the past, the present, and the future can be experienced as a unity in an obvious way is the generation (γένος). It represents simultaneously the tie of the ancestors with the living and future descendants and the connection, in the present, of mutually related living members. Hence, the *genos* assembles into *one unity* the multitude of the members in both the length and width of a temporal succession. This unity is determined by *one fact*—from the viewpoint of the recognizing subject: *conception*, which belongs to the original notion of *genos*, that the first ancestor continues to live in all the descendants. The original being that inhabits the ancestor is in itself timeless; it does not expire at the death of the ancestor but presents itself in his descendants, through the succession of time, in constantly new modifications. The form in which the *genos* comes to be represented is *genealogy*.[42]

This statement is made first in respect to Hesiod's *Theogony*, but it can certainly be generalized. This is what leads Wolfgang Speyer to write in his article "Genealogie" in *RAC*:

In all the peoples of the Mediterranean region, genealogy was first the report of succeeding generations of humans, gods, or divine beings proceeding from a holy original power. Given this, the conception of the genealogy is most closely related to the "mythical idea of origin." ... Hence, genealogy may possibly represent the first attempt to create a scientific and systematic naming structure. With the help of genealogy, people understood themselves and the visible world as products of an endless number of generations and thus referred the multiplicity of things and beings back to the divine One, the source of generation.[43]

---

42. Paula Philippson, *Untersuchungen über den griechischen Mythos* (Zürich: Rhein-Verlag, 1944), 7.

43. Wolfgang Speyer, "Genealogie," *RAC* 9:1146, 1148. For a summarizing global view of the phenomenon "genealogy," above all in the Greek, Hellenistic, and Roman cultures, see especially Jonathan M. Hall, *Ethnic Identity in Greek Antiquity* (Cambridge: Cambridge University Press, 1997); with special consideration of Homer and Hesiod, see, among others, Deborah Rae Davies, "Genealogy and Catalogue: Thematic Relevance and Nar-

The interest in these genealogies was probably immense in ancient Greece.[44]

The *Catalogue of Women* (Γυναικῶν Κατάλογος), an anonymous continuation of the *Theogony* by Hesiod of Ascra (ca. 700 B.C.E.), should be mentioned as a concrete example of a genealogical representation of history.[45] According to Martina Hirschberger, this work was probably written between 630 and 590 B.C.E.[46] The catalogue contains comprehensive genealogies that cover the entire heroic age and are interspersed by numerous narrative episodes and comments.[47]

> The *Catalogue of Women* offers ... a synthesis of genealogies of various regions, divided into five family trees that cover the entire heroic age, from Prometheus and the flood to the fall of the heroic race and the separation of the gods and the humans.[48]

The genealogies and narratives are incorporated into this frame, along with the further elaboration of totally independent epic cycles. The beginning already presents a clear connection with the *Theogony*: "The connection the catalogue establishes between goddesses and mortals in the *Theogony* (963–1018) concludes with the connection of gods with moral women, that is, of the

---

rative Elaboration in Homer and Hesiod" (Ph.D. diss., University of Michigan, 1992). For a series of other examples from the Greco-Roman cultural milieu, in relation with Jesus' genealogies, see Rodney T. Hood, "The Genealogies of Jesus," in *Early Christian Origins: Studies in Honor of Harold R. Willoughby* (ed. Allen Wikgren; Chicago: Quadrangle, 1961), 1–15. On examples from the Greek, Egyptian, and Persian cultures, in relation with the genealogies in 1 Chronicles, see Manfred Oeming, *Das wahre Israel: Die "genealogische Vorhalle" 1 Chronik 1–9* (BWANT 128; Stuttgart: Kohlhammer, 1990), 23–36.

44. Examples are found in Martina Hirschberger, *Gynaikōn Katalogos und Megalai Ēhoiai: Ein Kommentar zu den Fragmenten zweier hesiodeischer Epen* (Beiträge zur Altertumskunde 198; München: Saur, 2004), 63–70.

45. See Van Seters, *Prologue to History*, 177. Likewise, see the new study by Hirschberger, *Gynaikōn Katalogos*, as well as Richard Hunter, ed., *The Hesiodic Catalogue of Women: Constructions and Reconstructions* (Cambridge: Cambridge University Press, 2005).

46. See Hirschberger, *Gynaikōn Katalogos*, 49.

47. See Martin L. West, *The Hesiodic Catalogue of Women: Its Nature, Structure, and Origin* (Oxford: Clarendon, 1985), 3. West also provides many sketches of stemmata (genealogical tables) that systemize the relationships of descent (173–82). For the discussion concerning the Hesiodic *Catalogue of Women*, see Richard S. Hess, "The Genealogies of Genesis 1–11 and Comparative Literature," *Bib* 70 (1989): 251–53.

48. Hirschberger, *Gynaikōn Katalogos*, 67–68. For the contents, see the summary at 32–38.

Gynaikōn Katalogos.[49] This also explains the title and the subject of this work: its intention is to praise τὸ γυναικῶν φῦλον, "the race of women."[50] The women referred to are the most "outstanding" (ἄρισται), whose status is comparable to that of the heroes.[51] Thus, the catalogue can be called *heroogonia* in continuation of the *Theogony*.

The first fragment of the catalogue deals with "prehistory": Prometheus, as a son of the Titan Iapetos, constitutes the bond with Hesiod's *Theogony* and his *Erga*. With the story of the theft of fire, Prometheus represents the separation of the gods and the humans;[52] Deucalion, who survived the flood, belongs to this context. He has two daughters, Thyia and Pandora, as well as a son, Hellen. An entire collection of genealogies and stories starts with the son of Hellen, Aeolus, who has five daughters and seven sons. Complex connections of descent are mentioned, and the relationships between the daughters of humans and the gods, and also the apotheoses of women, are described. Alongside the Aeolians, the following four (shorter) family trees are named: the Inachus (i.e., the descendants of Io); the descendants of Callisto or Arcadians; the Atlanteans or "Children of the Pleiades"; and the Asopides. The end of the catalogue is most likely constituted by the wedding proposal to Helena and Zeus's plan: Tyndareus gives Helena in marriage to Menelaus; she gives birth to their daughter Hermione. After this, the epoch is broken off because Zeus puts an end to the heroic age and the sexual relationships between the gods and the humans.

The form of the representation with its two parts, the genealogy and the geography—that is, the portrayal of the lineage and of the local origin of the described people as the key to their identity—casts the style for early Greek historiography.[53] The genealogies are mostly segmented, grouped according to the lineage of siblings. The particular lineages are unimportant, since the catalogue is not intended to legitimate a dynastic line. Moreover, the gene-

---

49. Ibid., 164.

50. In this context, the Greek term φῦλον shows a remarkable similarity, in respect to the spectrum of meanings, with the Hebrew term *toledot* (תולדות, see below).

51. See Hirschberger, *Gynaikōn Katalogos*, 165.

52. According to other traditions, Prometheus formed the humans from clay (e.g., Ovid, *Metam.* 1.82–87).

53. See Van Seters, *Prologue to History*, 90. Other examples for the genealogical epic are given in Hirschberger, *Gynaikōn Katalogos*, 51–63. On this subject, see also her special study of the influence of the *Gynaikōn Katalogos* on Hecataeus's work and on the Ionic *Historíē* in Martina Hirschberger, "Genealogie und Geographie: Der hesiodeische Gynaikōn Katalogos als Vorläufer von Hekataios und der ionischen *Historíē*," *Antike Naturwissenschaft und ihre Rezeption* 14 (2004): 7–24. For a text edition, see Robert L. Fowler, *Early Greek Mythography* (Oxford: Oxford University Press, 2000), vol. 1.

alogies run through persons of both sexes, so that there are patrilineages as well as matrilineages. The endogamy between second- or third-degree relatives is quite frequent. From a formal point of view, expressions saying that the husband takes his wife home with horses and wagon point to virilocality (the woman lives in her father's house or in that of her husband). Uxorilocal marriages (where the man moves into the woman's home) are rare. When a child is born, normally both parents are mentioned, but from time to time there are purely patrilineal formulations (which, on the other hand, are very common in the Bible) such as "descending from him" or "he engendered." The choice of representing the patrilineal or matrilineal descent probably depends on considerations relative to narrative techniques. A clear insistence on the masculine lineage, as in the ancient Near Eastern and ancient Egyptian genealogical representations of history (king lists, etc.) is not found here. In spite of the stereotyped roles common in antiquity, the emphasis is evenly distributed; women are far more often clearly identified by their names; their contribution to the progression of the events is considerably more substantial and active. Furthermore, this concerns the heroic women of mythological prehistory; it is therefore impossible to draw conclusions about actual social facts and the concrete life of women in society, religion, and politics of Greek antiquity.

The epic genealogical representation is not intended to describe or legitimize the present situation but rather to depict the accomplishment of Zeus's plan in mythical prehistory.[54] Still, the *Gynaikōn Katalogos* also has a supertemporal message, which M. Hirschberger recapitulates: "In it genealogies and stories of mutually related landscapes are found and placed in the context of the heroic age. Through these ties between different local traditions, the *Catalogue* shows a Pan-Hellenic organization.[55] Thus, for example, in the meandering paths of the descendants of Io, who fled to Egypt due to Heras's jealously, two lineages lead back to Greece: from Io descend Phoenix, the eponym of the Phoenicians (and the father of Europa), as well as Danaus, the eponym of the Greeks, and Aegyptus, the eponym of the Egyptians. This serves simultaneously to refute the pretension of the Egyptians, who claim to be the first existing humans (Herodotus, *Hist.* 2.2.1), and to make the Egyptians, with their fascinating ancient culture, into a people of brothers of the Greeks. Hence, this shows a contemporary function, which probably also had political motives, of the genealogical form of historical representation. At the same time, this is an etiological construction of mythical prehistory. Through the proximity and the relationship between the gods and the humans during

---

54. See Hirschberger, *Gynaikōn Katalogos*, 65–67.
55. Ibid., 69.

the heroic age, the world is organized: after Zeus puts an end to this age, the world is as it is.

A similar combination of narratives and genealogical lists is found in the *Megalai Ēhoiai*, a work also attributed to Hesiod (ca. sixth century). The title is explained by the formula that serves to introduce a story or a genealogy, which also appears in the *Catalogue*: ἢ οἵη, "or a (woman) like....." Originally the formula made it possible, probably in the improvised oral epics, to pass from one story about women to the next.[56] This formula is the structuring principle of the *Megalai Ēhoiai*, which uses it to connect otherwise very dissimilar stories. In the *Catalogue*, on the contrary, the genealogies, not the formula, constitute the organizing and structuring element. The epics of the *Megalai Ēhoiai* transmit, among other things, genealogies of place eponyms, that is, the lineages of historical heroic founding figures of places and cities (e.g., Mycenae or Epidaurus).[57] Both works have only been preserved in a very fragmentary form.

The explanation of the world through the narration of the beginning—the organization of the universe through the elucidation of origins and sociopolitical relations in the form of intelligible genealogical relations—contains key notions that allow us to understand the functions of the genealogical representation of history. Essentially, these aspects also apply to the biblical representation of history expressed in the form of genealogies. This will now be considered more closely with regard to the Torah.

3. Genealogy as Means of Representation of History in the Torah

3.1. Preliminary Remarks concerning Content and Methodology

In the Torah, roughly three areas of historical representation can be distinguished. (1) The genealogical form of presentation constitutes the basic structure of Genesis in its final form and shapes the paradigm of the family history. The contacts and relationships are represented as family relations and descent lines. (2) The narratives concerning the experiences of the people of Israel, beginning with the departure from Egypt until the arrival in the steppes of Moab (Exodus to Numbers) are represented under the paradigm of proximity and distance relative to its God, YHWH, in which the gift of divine instruction and its accomplishment by the people are the main categories. (3) In Moses' discourses, as recapitulations of history and of divine instruction

---

56. Ibid., 30.
57. Ibid., 81–86.

(Deuteronomy), the narrated time is contracted on the last day of Moses' life, the contents are stylized as Moses' farewell discourses, and, with the account of his death, the conclusion of the revelation of divine instruction (Torah) is documented and sealed.

Given this, a study of genealogy as a means of representing history in the Torah can be limited essentially to Genesis. Another restriction can be made regarding the question of the diachronic analysis of the text: the underlying genealogical structure of Genesis is closely connected to the formation of the book (*Buchwerdung*) through the elaborated material. In the words of Naomi Steinberg, it can be said that "Genesis is a book whose plot is genealogy."[58] According to a large consensus, the different cycles concerning the main figures were long transmitted independently from one another. This can also be recognized in the fact that the stories can be understood and told separately. The different traditions and cycles are connected by means of a genealogical system that thus assembled them into a single book. So, the genealogical representation of history is a phenomenon at the level of the final text and is best recognized from the reader's viewpoint. Even if there is clearly a conscious conception behind the genealogical system, it would be impossible (in any reasonable scientific attempt) to describe the personalities of the authors and their intentions without resorting to speculation. To further the understanding of the phenomenon of the genealogical representation of history, it has proven fruitful to adopt a reader-oriented and text-centered approach.[59]

Readings of Genesis from the viewpoint of the genealogies show that the first book of the Bible is a firmly structured and solidly built literary work that can be read as a whole. The genealogical information constructs systems—the *toledot* system and the genealogical system—that form the supporting backbone of the book. Alongside formal descriptions of the linguistic means of representation, our intention is to grasp the interconnection of the genealogical and narrative passages, as well as the development of the systems.

---

58. Naomi Steinberg, "The Genealogical Framework of the Family Stories in Genesis," *Semeia* 46 (1989): 41.

59. The attempt to come close to historical figures in the texts of Genesis is an absolutely hopeless endeavor. As Irmtraud Fischer indicates, the texts "are not to be misunderstood as biographies of persons who lived at that time; rather, the narratives seek to present a theologically interpreted history of the beginnings of the people of Israel" ("Sara als Gründerin des Volkes Israel: Zur Befreiung einer aus männlichem Blick gezeichneten Erzählfigur aus dem Korsett des gender-bias in der Exegese," in *Sara lacht: Eine Erzmutter und ihre Geschichte* [ed. Rainer Kampling; Paderborn: Schöningh, 2004], 12).

3.2. The Formal Structuring of the Genealogical Information

A fundamental distinction exists between the segmented and linear genealogies. In the linear genealogies, each genealogical line runs through only one ancestor to the next generation (grandfather, father, son, grandson). In the segmented genealogies, there is one ancestor with several descendants and thus more than one genealogical line (father, several sons, who in turn have several sons).[60]

The existing material relative to the genealogical information in Genesis can be systemized into four elementary types:[61]

Abbreviation	Hebrew	Translation	Remark
toledot-type	תולדות	"succession of generations"	
yalad-type	ילד active	"bear, engender"	differentiated according to the verb formation, the verbal root (G/H), and the gender
	ילד passive + ל-	" X was born to Y"	differentiated according to the verb formation and verbal root (N/D pass)
ben-type	אב/אם (+ היה)	"father, mother"	*ben/em*- or *ben/ab*-type
	בן/בת (+ היה)	"son, daughter"	*ben/bat*- or *ben*-type
sibling-type	אח/אחות	"brother, sister"	

The important aspect here is how the genealogical relation is indicated.

(1) In the *toledot*-type, the Hebrew word *toledot* is used, which the NRSV usually translates as "the descendants of." However, this word has a wide range of meanings. Among other things, *toledot*, in the formula *toledot* NN, can also

---

60. See Thomas Hieke, "Genealogien," www.WiBiLex.de (2007); online: http://www.bibelwissenschaft.de/nc/wibilex/das-bibellexikon/details/quelle/WIBI/zeichen/g/referenz/19244/cache/b943f966470254a017db643207e3368f/; section 1.3.

61. See Thomas Hieke, *Die Genealogien der Genesis* (Herders Biblische Studien 39; Freiburg im Breisgau: Herder, 2003), 28–34.

signify the history of NN's descendants. Behind this word lies the root *yld* (*yalad*), which can mean, depending on the subject's gender, not only "engender" but also "bear."

(2) The second type, named in respect to this root the *yalad*-type, is characterized by the use of the verb *yalad*: the genealogical relation is hence expressed verbally in such a way that a man has *engendered* (grammatical masculine = *yalad*-type masc.) someone (most often his son, more rarely his daughter), whereas a woman has *born* (grammatical feminine = *yalad*-type fem.) someone (her son, her daughter). There is also a passive form used for men: X *was born* to Y.

(3) Unlike the second type, the third type is constructed *nominally*, that is, not with the verb *yalad* but with the nouns "father, mother, son, daughter." Most frequently the so-called filiation is featured; in other words, someone is presented as "the son of NN." This can be used to construct long chains. "Son" in Hebrew is *ben*, so this type is designated the *ben*-type.

(4) Type 4 is also constructed nominally, but here the relationships are not between generations, as in the *ben*-type, but within a same generation, between brothers and sisters. Hence the designation sibling-type.

An analysis of the *ben*-type and the *yalad*-type leads to the following observation: the *ben*-type is the more general indication and is thus used in a less specific way than the *yalad*-type. The verbal *yalad*-type is introduced in order to focus further on the genealogical system: in a text that combines segmented and linear genealogies, the *yalad*-type most often characterizes the *continuous* genealogical line. An example of such a complex text is found, for instance, in Exod 6:16–25. The genealogy of Levi is, first of all, segmented into three sons and one daughter, then the lines converge again. The *yalad*-type is used to mark the line that carries the focus. Both the use of the *yalad*-type fem. and the intensifying indication of the names of wives mark the most significant line: precisely the line leading to Aaron and Phinehas (as cipher for the priesthood).[62]

The elementary types mark and identify the genealogical information. Thus, it becomes possible to emphasize bonds and to connect the texts with one another. In the process of the reading, the genealogical system of Genesis, which determines its coherence, becomes visible. At the same time, the elementary types make it possible to prolong the genealogical system beyond the book of Genesis; the most important passages are Exod 6:14–25 and Num 3:1–4, as well as Ruth 4:18–22. Furthermore, in these continuations of the

---

62. See ibid., 216.

system, yet another focus and precision arise: through Exod 6 and Num 3 to the Aaronic priesthood, and through Ruth 4 to the Davidic monarchy.[63]

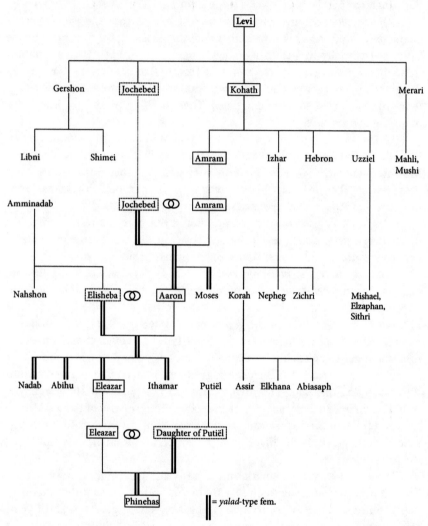

3.3. THE INTERCONNECTIONS OF THE NARRATIVE PASSAGES WITH THE GENEALOGICAL SYSTEM

The genealogical system is the chain from which the pearls of the narratives

---

63. See ibid., 338.

are suspended.[64] Often these narratives are also "pearls" in the metaphorical sense, since they can be understood as complete, independent units.[65] The actual connection of these units is provided *only* by the chief protagonists, especially through the dominant "fathers." Its coherence, in turn, is constituted *only* by the genealogical system.

The importance of the linguistic form of the genealogical system shows itself with the figure of Isaac: he does not belong to any genealogy in the strict sense; that is, he does not appear in any of the lists or enumerations in Genesis. His genealogical bonding occurs "only" through a genealogical narrative (Gen 21:1–8). Nevertheless, Isaac constitutes an important element in the *toledot*-system. Therefore, at the beginning of his *toledot*, the expression "Abraham engendered [הוֹלִיד] Isaac" is analogously repeated (Gen 25:19). With the particular *yalad*-type conjunction suffix masculine *hiphil* used here, a formal analogy with the genealogies in Gen 5 and 11 [וַיּוֹלֶד,וַיּוֹלִיד,וַהוֹלִיד], and notably with 11:27, "Terah engendered [הוֹלִיד] Abra(ha)m, Nahor, and Haran," occurs that introduces Isaac into the main line. The expression in Gen 25:19, which at first sight gives the impression of being a redundant gloss, is actually a necessary element in the chain for the construction of the genealogical system through the linguistic form of the elementary types.

If the true narrative coherence between each of the protagonists is thus provided by the family relationship, in the form of succeeding generations, this genealogical system is the decisive carrier of the aspects essential for the story and the theological message it transmits: the *blessing* and the *promises* of offspring and of a land.[66] The blessing and the promises are briefly expressed in Gen 12:1–3 and later reappear in diverse forms—tightly intertwined with the genealogical system. In this context, the blessing is always the same blessing that God gave at the creation. On the one hand, this is genealogically transmitted since the beginning (Gen 5:1–3) and is passed from one generation to another; on the other hand, however, it constantly needs God's intervention in order to be actualized and prolonged. In this, God shows that he

---

64. For the following presentation, see ibid., 339–43.

65. From the diachronic approach, this observation is used in particular in the so-called "hypothesis of narrative cycles," which departs from original thematically separated narrative cycles, and above all those relative to the main figures of the Pentateuch (Abraham, Jacob), each of which has its own history of development.

66. The *blessing* is a particular feature with respect to the promises of offspring and of a land. This also manifests itself in the fact that the blessing is present since the beginning of the creation (Gen 1). The fact that the blessing is not a part of the promises is shown by, among others, Rolf Rendtorff, *Das überlieferungsgeschichtliche Problem des Pentateuch* (Berlin: de Gruyter, 1977), 56.

is not moved by human facts and statutes (right of the firstborn) but rather proves—precisely in the numerous elections of sons born later (Isaac, Jacob, Joseph, Ephraim…)—to act as a God who freely and autonomously bestows his gifts. The *transmission* of the blessing, which God *actualizes*, is rooted in genealogy: first in the human lineage reaching from Adam to Noah and Terah, then accorded again personally to Abraham and his offspring (Gen 12). It is then transmitted, from Abraham's offspring, within the family until the twelve sons of Jacob/ Israel and finally directed to Levi, Aaron, and the priests, who in Num 6:22–27 receive the function of transmitting the blessing and whose existence is once again established on a genealogical basis.

The transmission of the numerous *offspring* through the genealogical system seems banal, yet precisely the concrete accomplishment of the promise of offspring entails considerable difficulties. Before the background of the regularly proceeding genealogies in Gen 5 and 11, the childlessness of Abraham and Sarah[67] is experienced as far more critical and dangerous: just when the progeny is promised, there is no male descendant (as yet). Along with sterility and childlessness, the early death of male descendants (Er and Onan, in Gen 38) or the deathly danger menacing male offspring (Ishmael in Gen 21; Isaac in Gen 22; Jacob's sons in Gen 42–43) further jeopardize the continuation of the genealogical system. It is God's continuous free, autonomous, unmerited intervention, which cannot be manipulated, that saves the chain of the generations. Thus, it is shown, through the perils and salvation of the genealogical system, that children are a promise made by God, who grants them as a gift. This idea is formulated with precision from a theological point of view in the short quarrel between Jacob and Rachel (Gen 30:1–2). God is the one who denies the fruit of the womb or opens the mother's womb (Gen 29:31)—this is the text's message. Finally, the genealogical system indeed does continue, in such a way that the promise of numerous offspring and of a great people is fulfilled in the transition from Genesis to Exodus, where Exod 1:7 suggests the fulfillment of the promise.

The aspect still missing from the book of Exodus and the Pentateuch as a whole is the fulfillment of the promise of the *land*. However, this aspect is also connected, in Genesis, with the genealogical system. From Adam to Jacob, only *one* main line is emphasized; that is, in each generation *one* son bears the focus and, consequently, the blessing and the promises of offspring and of the land. Jacob's twelve sons are the first heirs with equal rights. Although

---

67. Abraham and Sarah are first called Abram and Sarai; their names are changed in Gen 17:5, 15 by an act of God's sovereignty. For practical reasons, and with the exception of biblical quotations, the forms Abraham and Sarah will henceforth be used.

a higher or lower order is still indicated through the mothers and the for-mulations of the blessings (Gen 49), no tribe is decisively excluded from the promises. In fact, the lateral lines mentioned in the genealogical system of Genesis are excluded. This separation of lateral lines simultaneously implies that the Promised Land, where the ancestors still live as foreigners (e.g., Gen 26:3; 37:1), is free from inheritance claims. The text insists in several ways that the collateral lines settle *outside* the land (Gen 13:1–13: Lot; 21:21: Ishmael; 25:6: the sons of Keturah; 36:6–7: Esau). In the conception of the genealogical system, the land is therefore reserved for Jacob's descendants. This narrative ideal is made for outside the Torah, in the equally idealistic conception of the so-called "conquest" of the land.

Although the names in the genealogies are virtually all masculine, this does not mean that the *women* were invisible or insignificant. Indeed, the genealogical system in Genesis manifests the eminently important role of the women—even if, or precisely because, the system has a *patrilineal* structure. It depends on the women, whether they bear the hoped-for masculine prog-eny. Through this, their personal place is defined, but also, lastly, that of the patriarch, who—or whose lineage—is endangered by the absence of offspring (Abraham, Judah). When such a peril threatens a genealogical line, most often the women solve the problems though their creative initiatives (Sarah, Hagar, the daughters of Lot, Rebekah, Rachel, Tamar, Ruth). In these situa-tions, it is not always easy to see clearly the role that God plays; sometimes his approval is only recognized after the fact, when the male child who has been born becomes the blessing-bearer (examples are Rebekah and Jacob, Tamar and Perez). Another essential function of the women is the differentiation of the descendants (e.g., Adah and Zillah in Gen 4:19–24). In Abraham's case, Sarah is the chief wife who gives birth to the decisive offspring; in the case of Jacob's sons, the birth mother and her position with respect to Jacob decides the sons' order of rank. Finally, the origin of the women is also decisive for the election, or rejection, of each descendant in the genealogical system. The aim is an endogamous marriage within the same extended family group: the patriarchs contract endogamous marriages (vast accounts with Isaac, Gen 24, and Jacob, Gen 27:46; 28:1, thematic; see also Tob 4:12–13). Exogamous marital unions with "foreign" women (outside of one's own family, tribe, or people) lead to rejection (explicit with Esau). It is hard not to notice that, behind this recurrent theme, there is a pragmatic message in the text indicat-ing that, in the choice of a marriage partner, one's own genealogical identity must be kept. In this, the world of the postexilic period behind the text is perceptible. This paradigmatic stylization of a historical image of the ideal of the people's origin, as construed in Genesis, reveals the interweaving of these texts with the sociohistorical context of a particular time. The strong tendency in the postexilic community to protect its own identity by avoiding mixed marriages and to strengthen it through endogamous marital unions will be discussed later.

3.4. Interweaving and Precision of the Genealogical System in the Context of the Christian Bible

The appearance of specific elementary types in the genealogical system of Genesis outside of this book, on the one hand, creates a contextual incorporation in the Old Testament, or, better, of the entire Bible; on the other hand, it builds a bridge between the biblical genealogies, with the people and institutions they accentuate and the "origins"—in the widest sense—conceived in the book of Genesis.

The genealogical system has two kinds of furrows: the lineage passing through Judah, Perez, and the genealogy in Ruth 4:18–22 to David and, hence, into the dynastic *monarchy*; and the lineage running through Levi, Aaron, and the Levi-genealogy in Exod 6 (cf. Num 3) to Phinehas that founds the inherited Aaronic *priesthood*. The centering on "Judah" and "Levi" as ciphers for the monarchy and for the priesthood is confirmed in the reception of the genealogical system in 1 Chr 1–9, by the preeminent position afforded to Judah and the central place of Levi. The history of the extrabiblical reception (esp. in the Testament of the Twelve Patriarchs and in the literature of Qumran) shows that these two lineages were prolonged in early Judaism and, for example, in Qumran, oriented toward two eschatological expectations: a royal and a priestly Messiah.[68] Christianity adopts this genealogical conception by using genealogies to introduce Jesus into the biblical system: Matt 1:1 with the expression Βίβλος γενέσεως Ἰησοῦ Χριστοῦ ["Book of the genealogy of Jesus Christ"] constitutes a link precisely with Gen 2:4 LXX and Gen 5:1 and so to central points of the genealogical *toledot*-system,[69] adopting even the linguistic form (now in Greek).

The conceptual root of the priesthood (in early Judaism) and of the different notions of the Messiah, and also the biblical foundation of Christology, reach back to the book of Genesis. Consequently, they are implanted in the origins of the people of Israel, in the beginnings of humanity, and in the creation itself. Thus it becomes clear that the book of Genesis lays the foundation

---

68. See Hieke, *Die Genealogien der Genesis*, 270–277.

69. See Thomas Hieke, "BIBLOS GENESEOS: Matthäus 1,1 vom Buch Genesis her gelesen," in *The Biblical Canons* (ed. Henk Jan de Jonge and Jean-Marie Auwers; BETL 163; Leuven: University Press, 2003), 635–49; Martin Stowasser, "Die Genealogien Jesu im Evangelium des Matthäus und des Lukas," in Fitzenreiter, *Genealogie*, 183–96.

stone—in the truest sense of the word "genesis"—of concepts that are essential for the entire Bible. From the genealogical viewpoint alone, in this respect, the priesthood, the monarchy, and the messianic hopes must be mentioned, as well as the religious and ethnic identity of Judaism and, for Christianity, Christology, without implying completeness. Hence, retrospectively, Genesis has considerable conceptual importance in the canonical perspective as *the first book of the Bible.*[70]

4. THE ROLE OF THE WOMEN IN THE GENEALOGICAL SYSTEM

4.1. THE FINDINGS IN THE BOOK OF GENESIS AND IN RELATED PASSAGES

The genealogical system of the book of Genesis appears, at first sight, to be a purely masculine affair. The genealogical line is extended from father to son. However, the patrilinearity must not keep us from seeing that, at crucial points and in crises, the women in Genesis and beyond the book play a decisive role.[71] Karin Friis Plum formulates this in the following manner: "It may be said that the women enter the stage whenever something special happens—as the decisive crossroads of those in which the social relations are reflected."[72] This observation is not new (although it is not particularly old either). For this reason, the personalities and the roles of the women will be analyzed more closely, above all with respect to the genealogical system and their function and tasks.

---

70. On Genesis as the opening of the Torah, see Matthias Millard, *Die Genesis als Eröffnung der Tora: Kompositions- und auslegungsgeschichtliche Annäherungen an das erste Buch Mose* (WMANT 90; Neukirchen-Vluyn: Neukirchener, 2001).

71. Thanks to Irmtraud Fischer, who in numerous studies has time and again shown that, in a gender-fair interpretation of Genesis, it is not possible to speak only of stories of the fathers and exclusively consider the texts about men as high theology, while trivializing the texts concerning women as romantic. The women are the foundresses of Israel, just as the men are the founders; their actions, like those of the men, reflect the history of the People. See, among others, Irmtraud Fischer, *Die Erzeltern Israels: Feministisch-theologische Studien zu Genesis 12–36* (BZAW 222; Berlin: de Gruyter, 1994); eadem, "Zu einer genderfairen Interpretation der Erzeltern-Erzählungen," in *Studies in the Book of Genesis: Literature, Redaction and History* (ed. André Wénin; BETL 155; Leuven: University Press, 2001), 135–52; eadem, "Das Geschlecht als exegetisches Kriterium: Zu einer gender-fairen Interpretation der Erzeltern-Erzählungen," *CPB* 116 (2003): 2–9.

72. Karin Friis Plum, "Genealogy as Theology," *SJOT* 1 (1989): 73.

4.1.1. Mothers of the Cultural Achievements (Gen 4:17–24)

In Gen 4:17–24, Cain's wife remains unnamed, and likewise in the following linear genealogies only the names of men appear. The exception to this is the last member, Lamech, whose wives are both named: Adah and Zillah. They are the mothers of those who are presented as the founders of the human cultural achievements. This shows that the women had an essential function: they appear in places that require *differentiation*. The mention of women's names slows down the linear flow of the generations and indicates cultural progress and differentiation of humanity. Furthermore, a certain role model imposes itself in this passage: the women, with Eve as the prototype, are the mothers of all the living (Gen 3:20), who bring forth "life" in all its facets (and, hence, also mothers of all cultural achievements); the men, on the other hand, are associated with violence and death, just like Tubalcain, the armorer, and Lamech, who boastfully overflows with violent revenge. This violence necessitates a new beginning after the flood.

4.1.2 A New Beginning with Adam's Wife (Gen 4:25; 5:3)

In Gen 4:25, when Seth is born, Adam's wife is evoked without being named. This needs to be emphasized because, at the beginning of the strictly linear genealogy in Gen 5:3, no women are mentioned. Accordingly, Gen 4:25–26 also, in this sense, completes 5:1–3 (i.e., the content of 5:1–3 can suppose 4:25–26). The role of Adam's wife in 4:25 receives its significance only upon second consideration and with respect to the genealogical system: 4:25–26 (and then also 5:1-3) constitutes the new beginning of humanity after the fratricide and flight of Cain (and of his offspring). Likewise, 4:25–26 skips the facts related in 4:1–24 and refers back to the primeval history. However, according to both Gen 1 and 2, humanity's beginning always occurs through both a man *and* a woman. Therefore, it is important that Adam's wife be named when Seth is born—and Gen 5:3 also implies the presence of a woman. Since, in Gen 5, a patrilineal genealogy is presented, the woman in 5:3 is not named, due to the text's genre. However, this deficiency is made up for by the naming and functional incorporation of Adam's wife four verses earlier, in 4:25.

According to Gen 5:3, the patrilineal genealogy, typical of this genre, can be continued. In Gen 5; 10; and 11:10–26, no women are named, but with the expression "engendered sons *and daughters*," naturally, they are present. It is clear that the absolute namelessness of the women was already shocking for the book of Jubilees in its reception of Genesis; that is, it represented an open question. This is why Jubilees develops the role of the women and, along with their names, also expounds their roles for the narrative.[73]

4.1.3. Endogamy and Sterility (Gen 11:27–32)

An important turning point in both the genealogical system and the whole of the construction of the book of Genesis is Gen 11:27–32. Here women appear who have already been named.[74] In contrast to Gen 20:12, the fact that it is not mentioned that Sarah is Terah's daughter in this passage leaves an unresolved problem that is not expressed in the case of Nahor, Abraham's brother: precisely the question of the "proper" (= legitimate) marital union. With respect to Nahor, it is made clear that he marries within the family (endogamy) by marrying his collateral cousin, Milcah, the daughter of his father's brother. Sarah's origin, on the other hand, remains unclear; her genealogical origin is revealed later, in Gen 20:12. Another, even more evident point of tension is Sarah's barrenness, which places the genealogical system before a decisive problem.

4.1.4. The Problem of the Barrenness of the Female Ancestors

Another important function of the women in the genealogical system appears when the line of the promise is in danger of ending due to their barrenness. They (the women) take the *initiative* when extraordinary circumstances demand extraordinary resolutions. This becomes clear in the cases of Rebekah, Leah, Rachel, Tamar, Ruth, and, naturally, also in the case of Lot's daughters in Gen 19:30–38, whose names are not known. The women take the initiative in order to avert the menacing extinction of the patrilineal (!) genealogical line[75] and simultaneously to reinforce their own position. This is more than evident in Rachel's dramatic exclamation to Jacob: "Give me children, or I shall

---

73. See the more detailed study of Betsy Halpern Amaru, "The First Woman, Wives, and Mothers in Jubilees," *JBL* 113 (1994): 622.

74. In the preceding genealogy, Gen 11:10–26, in fact, only masculine names appear, although it is emphasized that each man "engendered sons *and daughters.*" So, logically, Terah's genealogy names four men and three women: Abraham, Nahor, Haran, Lot and Sarah, Milcah, Iscah. See Irmtraud Fischer, "Genesis 12–50: Die Ursprungsgeschichte Israels als Frauengeschichte," in *Kompendium Feministische Bibelauslegung* (ed. Luise Schottroff and Marie-Theres Wacker; 2nd ed.; Gütersloh: Kaiser/Gütersloher Verlagshaus, 1999), 13.

75. Another analogy is found in the initiative of Isis, who reconstitutes her dismembered brother Osiris, so that he and she can engender their son Horus and thus continue the masculine lineage (see above, on Egypt).

die!" (Gen 30:1). Within the patrilineal system, the women develop creative initiatives for self-assertion and the assurance of their social position.[76] The action of the women is a personal human initiative, not always in conformity with God's plan. Sarah's initiative with Hagar as the substitute mother, just as the behavior of Lot's daughters, is later rejected to a certain extent, in the course of the story: although Ishmael received the promises, he is expelled from the story. Moab and Benammi, ancestors of the peoples hostile to Israel, are discredited from the very beginning because of the incestuous relationship between Lot and his daughters. On the contrary, in the cases of Leah and Rachel, Tamar and Ruth, the central lineage of the promises continues, thanks to the initiative of these women, which is justified by a happy outcome.

4.1.5 But Bethuel Begat Rebekah (Gen 22:20–24; 24)

In Gen 22:20–24, the wives of Nahor, Abraham's brother, are explicitly named. Milcah and Iscah are, in the sense of a narrative equilibrium, the pendants of Sarah and Hagar. Functionally, these verses lead to Rebekah, Isaac's later wife, as well as to the number of sons: twelve, which Ishmael receives in the next generation. Only subsequently does this become the people of Israel in the third generation, with Jacob. This focus on Rebekah is clearly emphasized by a curious formulation: "But Bethuel begat Rebekah" (Gen 22:23). Irmtraud Fischer notes, "This is the only time in the story of the ancestors that it is said that a daughter was begat. Notices of procreation normally are only given for sons."[77] Thus, attention is called to Abraham and also to Rebekah, present in the preceding plotline, by the language of the genealogies.

　　Genesis 24 then relates in detail Isaac's search for a bride and Rebekah's courageous decision.[78] The chapter very subtly deals with the problematic of exogamous and endogamous marriages. Isaac's careful search for the right

---

76. See Fischer, *Die Erzeltern Israels*, 35, 99; Melissa Jackson, "Lot's Daughters and Tamar as Tricksters and the Patriarchal Narratives as Feminist Theology," *JSOT* 98 (2002): 33–35. See a very positive evaluation of Tamar's action, for example, by Benno Jacob, *Das erste Buch der Tora: Genesis* (Berlin: Schocken, 1934), 722–23.

77. Irmtraud Fischer, *Gottesstreiterinnen: Biblische Erzählungen über die Anfänge Israels* (2nd ed.; Stuttgart: Kohlhammer, 2000), 72; see also Fischer, *Die Erzeltern Israels*, 62.

78. On this, see Sharon P. Jeansonne, "Images of Rebekah: From Modern Interpretations to Biblical Portrayal," *BR* 34 (1989): 33, 46–47; then eadem, *The Women of Genesis: From Sarah to Potiphar's Wife* (Minneapolis: Fortress, 1990). For the reconstruction of the milieu of life behind Gen 24, see Susanne Gillmayr-Bucher, "Von welcher sozialen Wirklichkeit erzählt Gen 24?" *Protokolle zur Bibel* 7 (1998): 17–27; likewise eadem, "The Woman of Their Dreams: The Image of Rebekah in Genesis 24," in *The World of Genesis: Persons, Places, Perspectives* (ed. Philip R. Davies and David J. A. Clines; JSOTSup 257;

wife within his own family even calls for God's intervention in the form of a sign (24:14). This shows just how important the marital union with the "right" woman (especially from the endogamous perspective) is for the text. Genesis 24 also represents the ideal case of matchmaking and marriage contraction in the perspective of the Torah. The chapter simultaneously describes Rebekah's active role in the accomplishment of the divine plan of salvation: her decision allows the lineage of Abraham and Sarah to continue. Later on in the story, thanks to her action, the blessing is transmitted to the offspring chosen by God. Ultimately, she is the one, not Isaac, who makes the story advance (see below).

4.1.6. Farewell to Descendants From History (Gen 25:1–6, 12–18)

Genesis 25:1–6 evokes Abraham's third wife, Keturah, and in doing so once again shows the function of *differentiation* within Abraham's lineage. Abraham has many sons (eight in total), but *the* son, that is, the carrier of the line of promise, is defined by the *mother*: he is the only son of Sarah. The sons of Keturah are quickly enumerated in a list and distanced from the text's field of vision (25:6).

Isaac's brother, Ishmael, is dealt with in the same way as Keturah's sons, in that his lineage is also summed up in the form of a genealogy. A closer differentiation is not necessary, nor is any human initiative in a crisis. As this does not concern the problem of endogamy or exogamy, there is no need to evoke the women. The text hastily indicates Ishmael's offspring and then makes them into a "collateral lineage."

4.1.7. Ranking Offspring (Gen 27)

In the following course of the text, the couple Isaac and Rebekah is presented in great analogy with the parental couple, Abraham and Sarah. Although Rebekah is childless, like Sarah, this problem is solved much faster and does not require any human initiative from Rebekah. Her initiative in the ranking of the offspring only comes later when she incites Jacob to "lie" and induces him as the second-born son to steal his father's blessing intended for the firstborn (Gen 27).[79] Her actions disrupt their family life for a long time and prompt Jacob to flee to Haran. Rebekah disguises this flight with the necessity

---

Sheffield: Sheffield Academic Press 1998), 90–101; eadem, "Genesis 24—ein Mosaik aus Texten," in Wénin, *Studies in the Book of Genesis*, 521–32.

79. See Fischer, "Genesis 12–50," 18.

of finding the "right" wife for Jacob, that is, to introduce an endogamous marriage. Sharon P. Jeansonne presents her view of Rebekah as follows:

> The representation of Rebekah shows that women in Israel were viewed as persons who could make crucial decisions about their futures, whose prayers were acknowledged, who might know better than men what God designed, and who could appropriately take the steps necessary to support God's plans for the community.[80]

The rest of the story then makes clear "what God designed." Jacob's way is God's way. However, Rebekah was the one who decided who would be the heir in this generation, in the same way that Sarah settled the succession in the first generation by sending Ishmael and Hagar away (Gen 21)![81]

The opposite of Jacob—who flees to the east but, officially, is searching for a wife—is Esau; at his own risk and ostensibly against his parents' will, he entered into exogamous marriages (Gen 26:34–35). The narrative here explicitly evaluates and disqualifies Esau's behavior. Concerning this, Naomi Steinberg explains:

> Esau continues his father's lineage—but from outside the Israelite lineage— because he marries the "wrong" woman. ... Esau married a woman outside the appropriate kinship boundaries. His wife was from the line of Ishmael, whose mother was not from within the patrilineage of Terah. This is clear. What distinguishes Esau from Jacob is the character of their marriages. Rachel and Leah are correct wives for a son of the Abrahamic lineage because they are part of the collateral patrilineage of Nahor, as is Rebekah herself. But neither Mahalath, nor any of Esau's other wives (Gen 26.34; 28.9), is part of this descent line; thus, Esau's marriage choices render him illegible for inclusion in the Terahite patrilineage.[82]

Genesis 28:8–9 is a subsequent tentative approach made by Esau to regain his parent's benevolence through a third, endogamous marriage.

---

80. Jeansonne, "Images of Rebekah," 47.

81. See Irmtraud Fischer, "Den Frauen der Kochtopf—den Männern die hohe Politik? Zum Klischee der Geschlechterrollen in der Bibelauslegung am Beispiel der Erzeltern-Erzählungen," *CPB* 108 (1995): 136.

82. Naomi Steinberg, "Alliance or Descent? The Function of Marriage in Genesis," *JSOT* 51 (1991): 50. For critique of Steinberg's position, see R. Christopher Heard, *Dynamics of Diselection: Ambiguity in Genesis 12–36 and Ethnic Boundaries in Post-exilic Judah* (SemeiaSt 39; Atlanta: Society of Biblical Literature, 2001), 119–26.

4.1.8. The Construction of Jacob's House by Leah, Rachel, Zilpah, and Bilhah (Gen 29:31–30:24)

In Gen 29:31–30:24, it is evident that the women play the dominant role here. Leah and Rachel compete for the appropriation of their husband Jacob, whom they try to win over with masculine offspring (see 29:32, etc.). Thomas Meurer believes that the story in Gen 29:31–30:24 concerns "the existential challenge of the problem of barrenness against the background of the relationship between humans and God in the case of two feminine figures with a paradigmatic psychogram, which should be represented in an almost symbolic way."[83] From a theological point of view, it is worth noting the insistence upon the inaccessibility of the God who either grants or refuses the fruit of the womb, whose logic of action in favor of humans is not always immediately apparent, and the continuous experience of human contingency.[84] However, this does not as yet resolve the story completely, for the correlation with the context and the genealogical system of Genesis shows that the primary concern here is underlining the dominant and decisive participation of Jacob's wives in the construction of the "house of Israel:" Jacob's four wives are, as Irmtraud Fischer appropriately observes, the "foundresses of Israel."[85]

The male human conception—Jacob prefers Rachel and relegates Leah to the background—is reversed by a *divine initiative*: "When the Lord saw that Leah was hated, he opened her womb; but Rachel was barren" (Gen 29:31). In the course of the continuing competition, the question of the differentiation of Jacob's children arises, and the rank of the sons is a result of the rank of the mothers (the beloved wife versus the unloved wife and their respective servants). The order of the subsequent lists with the names of Jacob's twelve sons is always constructed with respect to their respective mothers. The aim of the enumeration is later shown by the perspective relative to the genealogical system formulated in Ruth 4:11. The people at the gate witness the juridical act of redemption accomplished by Boaz as well as the marriage of Boaz and Ruth and the formulation of the words of the blessing: "May the Lord make the woman, who is coming into your house, like Rachel and Leah, who together built up the house of Israel." Through the competition between the two wives, Leah and Rachel, the house of Israel is "constructed" as a differentiated people, or, as Karin R. Andriolo puts it:

---

83. See Thomas Meurer, "Der Gebärwettstreit zwischen Lea und Rahel," *BN* 107/108 (2001): 102.

84. See ibid., 106–8; quote, 106.

85. Fischer, "Genesis 12–50," 19.

male competition [= patrilineal descent, in which always only one son heads the line; at the end Jacob vs. Esau] generates the Jewish *lineage* as opposed to the peoples of the world, female competition [Leah vs. Rachel] generates the Jewish *people*. As male competition generates uniqueness within the diversity, female competition generates diversity within the uniqueness.[86]

These observations relating to Jacob's stories can be generalized to a certain degree and extended to the genealogical system of Genesis and the functions of men and women mentioned therein. Amongst the men, a decision must always be made: only one of the sons leads the line of the promises. "Male competition is exclusive, hence providing for homogeneity." As to the women, they give birth to sons having basically the same rights. "Female competition is inclusive, hence providing for heterogeneity." Yet in the case of Abraham and Isaac, a *differentiation* is necessary among the progeny, in the sense of a decision relative to the son of the line of promise. This is accomplished through the women: Sarah as chief wife predominates Hagar and Keturah; Rebekah, through her own initiative, sees to the decision in favor of Jacob as the carrier of the blessing of the firstborn. With Jacob's family, this kind of decision is no longer made; all the sons construct the house of Israel. First-birth no longer plays a role, and the rank of the mothers establishes the order of the sons. From the viewpoint of the history of origins, the higher or lower ranks within the people (dominance of Ephraim and Judah) are implied in the changing relationships with the narratives. For the topic women in the genealogical system of the book of Genesis, the principle aspect in the story of the origins of the pople of Israel, when the twelve sons are born, is that the women dominate and differentiate the progeny.

4.1.9. Women as Bridges Between Ethnic Groups (Gen 36)

In the chapter on Esau, Gen 36, a differentiation also occurs through the naming of Esau's wives, yet there is no competition for rank among the women or the sons (and grandsons) of Esau. The intention of this chapter is to fairly briefly present Esau's progeny and thus, at the same time, conclude the narrative concerning him. In this presentation, Esau's genealogy is described, up until the generation of his grandsons, as the genealogy of his wives. Each of the five named wives has her own genealogy; this emphasizes their integrative function for Edom and shows the variety of lines of descent of this neighboring people related to Israel. Genesis 36:12 mentions Timna, the concubine of

---

86. Karin R. Andriolo, "A Structural Analysis of Genealogy and Worldview in the Old Testament," *AmA* 75 (1973):1657–1669; 1668 (also the next two quotes).

Eliphaz, Esau's son. She serves as a family tie between Esau's genealogy and Seir's genealogy.[87] This brings up the subject of the family bond between Esau, the son of Isaac, and the land's inhabitants (Canaanites): Eliphaz follows his father's example and contracts an exogamous marriage. It is significant that this exogamous marriage leads to Israel's hereditary enemy: Amalek. In the end, it is obvious that the text completely rejects exogamous marriages.

4.1.10. Tamar in the Right, Judah in the Wrong (Gen 38)

Genesis *38*, the family history of Judah,[88] confronts masculine and feminine initiatives for securing the progeny once more. The (personal) initiative of the man, Judah, for the progression of his genealogical line, which initially corresponds exactly to the linguistic formulas used up to this point to express genealogical information, fails: his son Er, for whom Judah took a wife named Tamar, dies childless. Likewise Onan, who according to the principle of the levirate marriage (Deut 25:5–10) should have engendered a male descendant for Er with Tamar, yet simply exploited her sexuality. Tamar's feminine initiative to save her own life, and thus ensure the continuation of Judah's genealogical line, succeeded with the twins she had with Judah: Perez and Zerah.[89] The fact that the history of Judah's family is told precisely within the *toledot* of Jacob (Gen 37–50) is naturally not fortuitous; it is introduced here because this branch of Jacob's descendants is the most extended one—as far as to the kings of Israel. The genealogy in the book of Ruth (Ruth 4:18–22) is its most decisive link; the intertextual narrative binding force is carried by the numerous points of contact between the story of Ruth and that of Tamar.[90]

The story of Judah's family in Gen 38 can be considered an implicit rejection of exogamous marriages. Exactly why Er, the firstborn of Judah's marriage with the Canaanite daughter of Shua, displeased the Lord to the extent that he then had to die is an open question in this story. Does this contain a warning and a disapproval of Judah's unauthorized action in the form of

---

87. See Fischer, *Die Erzeltern Israels*, 61.

88. On this, see, among others, Eva Salm, *Juda und Tamar: Eine exegetische Studie zu Gen 38* (FB 76; Würzburg: Echter, 1996); Susan Niditch, "The Wronged Woman Righted: An Analysis of Genesis 38," *HTR* 72 (1979): 143–49.

89. The twins Perez and Zerah correspond to the sons Er and Onan, whom Judah had lost—a sign that Judah had been forgiven; see, for example, Judah Goldin, "The Youngest Son or Where Does Genesis 38 Belong," *JBL* 96 (1977): 30.

90. For details and more on the connection of Gen 38 with Ruth, see Harold Fisch, "Ruth and the Structure of Covenant History," *VT* 32 (1982): 430–31; Ramona Faye West, "Ruth: A Retelling of Genesis 38?" (Ph.D. diss., Southern Baptist Theological Seminary, 1987); Irmtraud Fischer, *Rut* (HTKAT; Freiburg im Breisgau: Herder, 2001), 20, 246–47, etc.

an exogamous marriage? The relative success of this matter—in the end, the twins Perez and Zerah continue Judah's lineage—depends exclusively on the initiative of the wife named Tamar and on the divine approval of this plan.[91]

Tamar's origin is never explicitly thematized in the Bible: the extrabiblical tradition in the book of Jubilees and in the Testaments of the Twelve Patriarchs continues weaving the narrative threads. The apocryphal texts also suppose that both Tamar (T. Jud 10:1) and her sister, Levi's wife, Milcah (Jub. 34:20; T. Levi 11:1), are descendants of Aram ben Kemuel ben Nahor ben Terah (Gen 22:21). This would guarantee the endogamous marriage, or ethnic relation, of the lineages of Levi and Judah, which were so important for the priesthood and the monarchy: "both tribes descended entirely from descendants of Abraham's father Terah."[92] Both the lineage of Judah, which led to the monarchy, and Levi's lineage, which led to the priesthood, would thus also be connected to Terah's descent *through the mother*. However, there is another Jewish tradition (among others, the Targum of Pseudo-Jonathan on Gen 38:6) that asserts that Tamar was a pagan or a proselyte (according to Philo, *Virt.* 220–222). Philo describes Tamar's origin with the words ἀπὸ τῆς Παλαιστίνης Συρίας (from Syro-Palestine), "which is simply a contemporary way of saying that she was a Canaanite."[93]

4.1.11. Not Counted but Valued (Gen 46:8–27; Exod 6:15)

In Gen 46:8–27, it is noteworthy that here also the women take on the task of structuring, differentiating, and establishing the order of rank among Jacob's sons and grandsons. The function of differentiation according to the wives Leah, Zilpah, Rachel, and Bilhah extends here to the third and even the fourth generation (Jacob's grandsons and great-grandsons). In Gen 46:10 and Exod 6:15, "Shaul, the son of a Canaanite woman," is evoked as Simeon's son—it must be supposed that the ethnical membership is indicated in the case of this wife of Simeon because this exogamous marriage is clearly the exception.

According to Gen 41:45, Asenath is the daughter of Potipheras, priest of On. Joseph's marriage with a non-Israelite, who is moreover the daughter of a priest "who serves the idols," is a fundamental problem that is solved in

---

91. Here Thomas Krüger represents a somewhat different interpretation; see his "Genesis 38—ein 'Lehrstück' alttestamentlicher Ethik," in *Konsequente Traditionsgeschichte: Festschrift für Klaus Baltzer zum 65. Geburtstag* (ed. Rüdiger Bartelmus et al.; OBO 126; Fribourg: Universitätsverlag, 1993), 205–26.

92. Richard J. Bauckham, "Tamar's Ancestry and Rahab's Marriage: Two Problems in the Matthean Genealogy," *NovT* 37 (1995): 317.

93. Ibid.

various ways. In the apocryphal novel Joseph and Asenath/Aseneth,[94] Asenath becomes the model case of conversion to faith in the one and only God.

4.1.12. The Women Mark the Line (Exod 6:16–27)

The evocation of women's names in Levi's genealogy (Exod 6:16–27) has yet another function: in these few verses many names appear, beneath which the promise line leading to Aaron and Moses (or Phinehas!) is in danger of ending. This line is emphasized and characterized by the mention of the names of the wives of men evoked in the line reaching from Levi to Phinehas. The naming of the wives also appears at points where it is truly important for the continuation of the narrative and the genealogical concept.

4.1.13. The Masculine Lineage in the Book about Women (Ruth 4:18–22)

Ruth 4:18–22 does not mention any women; it is exclusively a "masculine lineage in the book about Women."[95] However, this is not a reason to consider the passage secondary to the rest of the book; the close connections between the texts of Genesis and the book of Ruth rather suggest reading Ruth in the context of Genesis and, hence, considering the genealogy at the end of Ruth as a continuation of Genesis's genealogies. In this context, Ruth 4:15–17 is noteworthy: for Naomi, her daughter-in-law Ruth is "better than seven sons"; the feminine solidarity is of greater value to Naomi than an abundance (seven as the symbolic number of perfection) of male progeny.[96]

4.2. The Decisive Roles of Women in the Genealogical System

This makes it possible to present the following *summary* of the roles and tasks of women in the genealogical system.

---

94. On this, see, among others, Angela Standhartinger, "Joseph und Asenath: Vollkommene Braut oder himmlische Prophetin," in Schottroff and Wacker, *Kompendium Feministische Bibelauslegung*, 459–64, with more bibliography.

95. See Irmtraud Fischer, "Der Männerstammbaum im Frauenbuch: Überlegungen zum Schluss des Rutbuches (4,18–22)," in *"Ihr Völker alle, klatscht in die Hände!": Festschrift für Erhard S. Gerstenberger zum 65. Geburtstag* (ed. Rainer Kessler, Kerstin Ulrich, and Milton Schwantes; Münster: LIT, 1997).

96. See Fischer, *Rut*, 254.

4.2.1. Differentiation

Women come into play when it is necessary to open an exclusively unilin-eal-masculine, patrilineal genealogy and to introduce a differentiation in the progeny. Adah and Zillah are mentioned at the moment of the distribution of the human cultural achievements. Among Abraham's eight sons, the son of the promise is defined through his mother, Sarah, Abraham's chief wife. With Leah and Rachel and their servants, the house of Israel is constructed in a dif-ferentiated way. The rank of the mothers determines the rank of the sons and the grandsons.

4.2.2. Initiative

The women take the initiative in moments of crisis and especially when the genealogical reproduction is gravely endangered. This happens, on the one hand, in opposition to the divine plan (Sarah and Hagar) or in contravention to the divine law (the incest of Lot's daughters). On the other hand, the femi-nine initiative meets with divine approval, or later tolerance, with Rebekah, Tamar, and Ruth.

4.2.3. Matrimonial Unions: Endogamy versus Exogamy

The genealogical line that runs to the people of Israel and then continues in two separate branches (through Levi and Phinehas for the priesthood and through Judah, Perez, and David for the monarchy) is exclusively defined through men. However, they are not automatically in the sphere of the bless-ing; rather, their fate is decided by a "correct," namely, endogamous, marriage.[97] This problem naturally appears only after the differentiation of humanity into peoples and their spread over the entire earth, that is, with Abraham.[98] In Abraham's case, the endogamous origin of his wife Sarah is only added in Gen

---

97. See, among others, Terry J. Prewitt, "Kinship Structures and the Genesis Genealo-gies," *JNES* 40 (1981): 97; Robert A. Oden Jr., "Jacob as Father, Husband, and Nephew: Kinship Studies and the Patriarchal Narratives," *JBL* 102 (1983): 193.

98. His statement refers to the narrative course of the book of Genesis. From a histori-cal point of view, this topic (key word "Mischehenproblematik"), of course, only appears particularly relevant in the postexilic period; see, among others, Gerhard von Rad, *Das erste Buch Mose: Genesis* (ATD 2/4, Göttingen: Vandenhoeck & Ruprecht, 1964), 246; Daniel L. Smith-Christopher, "The Mixed Marriage Crisis in Ezra 9–10 and Nehemiah 13," in *Second Temple Studies: Temple Community in the Persian Period* (ed. Tamara C. Eskenazi and Kent H. Richards; JSOTSup 175; Sheffield: Sheffield Academic Press, 1994).

20:12 and related in the large and careful legendary idealized depiction in the story of his son Isaac (Gen 24). Esau excludes himself, in comparison to his brother Jacob, through his exogamous marriage. As to Jacob, he is sent to the other family branch, "in the east," the homeland of his mother Rebekah, in order to contract an endogamous union. Judah's exogamous marriage with the Canaanite Bat-Shua then at first remains without direct (masculine) off-spring. The fate of the third son, Shelah, is not mentioned initially (later, cf. Num 26:20; 1 Chr 2:3). Only in the case of Shaul, Simeon's son, is it said that his mother was a Canaanite—this union of Simeon seems to be an exception.

4.2.4. Excursus: Endogamy and Exogamy in the Genesis and Tobit

The book of Tobit explicitly notes that the patriarchs contracted endogamous marriages.[99] For this reason, Tobit gives the following advice to his son Tobias:

> Beware, my son, of all types of prohibited sexual intercourse! First of all: take a wife from among the descendants of your fathers! Do not marry a foreign woman, who is not of your father's tribe; for we are the sons of the prophets. Remember, my son, that Noah, Abraham, Isaac, and Jacob, our fathers of old, all took wives from among their brethren, and they were blessed in their children; their posterity will inherit the land. So now, my son, love your brethren, and in your heart do not disdain your brethren and the sons and daughters of your people by refusing to take a wife for yourself from among them. (Tob 4:12–13)[100]

From a paradigmatic point of view, behind this insistence on endogamous marriage in Genesis there is an appeal to identify with the line of the blessing and the promises, to discover their source and identity in this genealogical system, and to reflect one's own marital union and carefully choose a partner in one's own ethnic group. Hence, in this sense Genesis is not only a simple narrative; it is Torah, instruction, for the practical conduct of life. Under the paradigm of source analysis, Philippe Guillaume says this about the Priestly texts:

---

99. See Thomas Hieke, "Endogamy in the Book of Tobit, Genesis, and Ezra-Nehemiah," in *The Book of Tobit: Text, Tradition, Theology* (ed. Géza G. Xeravits and József Zsengellér; JSJSup 98; Leiden: Brill, 2005), 103–20. On the book of Tobit, see also the commentary by Helen Schüngel-Straumann, *Tobit* (HTKAT; Freiburg im Breisgau: Herder, 2000).

100. On this passage, see, among others, Merten Rabenau, *Studien zum Buch Tobit* (BZAW 220; Berlin: de Gruyter, 1994), 46–48, with references to many other parallel passages in extracanonical literature.

P is not encouraging young Jewish boys freshly arrived from Babylonia
to date Palestinian or Edomite girls. Jews should marry Golah cousins ...
Edomites should not intermarry with local Palestinians either. They should
now keep to Ishmaelite women. Therefore, P is reorganising Yehoud as
God separated a livable land out of an undifferentiated chaos. In so doing,
Edomites are sent back to Edom where they belong in order to intermarry
with their own Southern cousins. In doing so, they make room for the Aramaic wives and descendants of the returnees.[101]

The pragmatic background is therefore a particular tendency in the postexilic
community to preserve their own (ethnical and religious) identity by avoiding
mixed marriages.[102]

The same orientation as in the insistence on endogamy, or priestly control
over appropriate or prohibited marriages, also steers the story about Phinehas's jealous action in Num 25:6–18. In this, Jan Jaynes Quesada sees evidence
for the theological concept of people like Ezra—who, incidentally, is a descendant of Phinehas—and Nehemiah at the time of the Second Temple, who
for the benefit of a closed identity of the community strictly forbade mixed
marriages with non-Israelite women and vehemently supported endogamy.[103]
Quesada reads the narrative in Numbers as a "validating narrative for their
programme of endogamy."

In summary, Numbers 25 embodies a significant, empowering narrative
within the Torah that validates the Second Temple program of endogamy.
... The renunciation ... of all things foreign (especially women) seems to
have been a way for the Second Temple Judean community to ensure a clear
identity, under the premise that ethnic purity is a precondition for religious
fidelity.[104]

---

101. Philippe Guillaume, "'Beware of Foreskins': The Priestly Writer as Matchmaker
in Genesis 27,46–28,8," in *Jacob: Commentaire à plusieurs voix de Gen 25–36: Mélanges
offerts à Albert de Pury* (ed. Jean-Daniel Macchi and Thomas Römer; Geneva: Labor et
Fides, 2001), 76.

102. With William H. C. Propp, "Kinship in 2 Samuel 13," *CBQ* 55 (1993): 44: "however, for often ancestral legends feature forbidden relations, the better to establish the
purity of a lineage." See also Fischer, "Sara als Gründerin," 16.

103. On Ezra 9:1–4, see Thomas Hieke, *Die Bücher Esra und Nehemia* (Neuer Stuttgarter Kommentar/Altes Testament 9.2; Stuttgart: Katholisches Bibelwerk, 2005), 140–46;
especially the excursus on the socioeconomical background; on this, see also Tamara C.
Eskenazi, "Out from the Shadows: Biblical Women in the Postexilic Era," *JSOT* 54 (1992):
25–43.

104. Jan Jaynes Quesada, "Body Piercing: The Issue of Priestly Control over Acceptable Family Structure in the Book of Numbers," *BibInt* 10 (2002): 28, 35.

5. CONCLUSIONS

If we consider the form of the representation of history from the perspective of genealogical information and especially the question of the role of the women, the following picture appears: in ancient Egypt, the state and social order was dominated by male leaders, a situation that marked the myths as well as the inscriptions and visible testimonies. Women rarely occupied leading positions; when a woman did accede to the throne, she assumed the masculine stereotyped roles ("King Hatshepsut"). The genealogies played an important role for the dynastic principle, as well as for the legitimization of claims to a cultic or political office. Hence, the genealogy, as such, was considered less as a means of historiography. This was true for both Egypt and the ancient Near East: genealogies were to accomplish specific functions (legitimization, emphasis on dynastic ranking of the succession to the throne, veneration of the ancestors) and could for these purposes be modified ("fluidity") according to need. Only in later times did the tradition consider genealogical information to be a historical picture of bygone epochs. In ancient Greece, with the *Gynaikōn Katalogos*, a kind of genealogical representation of history appeared in which women were in the foreground. However, this concerned the great women of mythical prehistory, the heroines, and the narrative world revolved around relationships between gods and humans. This theme is briefly hinted at in Genesis, with Gen 6:1–4, but immediately rejected: Israel's origins do not lie in such myths but are rather related, in the strict context of the world, in the form of a family history of humans.

The biblical findings deviate, along with a series of other aspects, from the surrounding world of the ancient Near East and from antiquity. Precisely in the book of Genesis the genealogical representation of history occupies an unparalleled large amount of space. The genealogies, or the genealogical system, are the backbone and the structural principle of the book in its final form. Furthermore, women play a more important role here, especially in positions of leadership and decision-making, than they do in the testimonies from the world surrounding Israel. In the historical construction of the Torah, it becomes clear that women have a considerable share in the promise-line,[105] despite it running "nominally" through the men. With slight modification of a statement by Gay Robins quoted above, it could be said that, "while the system was run by men, the women were needed to make it work."[106] At essential points women give the story the right "twist." They take the initiative in crisis

---

105. See Plum, "Genealogy as Theology," 78.
106. Robins, *Women in Ancient Egypt*, 36.

situations; in accordance with their social position, the rank of the male progeny is differentiated. The choice of the "right" wife (among one's own people,
i.e., endogamical) also determines the subsequent destiny of the man.[107] Once
again, we see that the book of Genesis does not speak exclusively about the
"patriarchs" but rather about the "first parents" who contributed, each in his
or her own way, to the construction of the people of Israel (cf. Ruth 4:11).[108]

---

107. In ancient Egypt, kings not of royal descent who ascended to the throne after a
dynasty ended owing to no male offspring additionally tried to legitimate themselves by
marrying a princess from the royal family; see Brunner, "Abstammung," 14. On the other
hand, marrying a girl from a simple background and, on the contrary, rejecting the lineage and tradition could also be an expression of unlimited royal power, as in the case of
Amenophis III and his wife Tiye (17).

108. See Fischer, *Rut*, 247–48; eadem, "Genesis 12–50," 24; eadem, "Sara als Gründerin," 26.

Divine Image and Likeness: Women and Men in Genesis 1–3 as an Open System in the Context of Genesis 1–11

Mercedes Navarro Puerto
Escuela Feminista de Teologia de Andalucía and Universidad de Sevilla

1. Introduction

The first part of Genesis (chs. 1–11) continues to form part of the Western world's collective imagination, especially the stories of the creation. Many of the mythical-literary images that appear here are still used (e.g., the tree, the snake, the apple, the action of the woman eating, the divine prohibition, nudity, sexuality) as advertising gimmicks for seduction (in the secular world) and literally as a basis for the hierarchical subjugation of women to men (in the ecclesiastical religious world). These texts have also continually been the objects of study in Judeo-Christian exegesis, literature, and other "auxiliary" sciences of biblical study since the nineteenth century. Both male and female biblical experts, as well as women authors from other fields (whether feminists or not) are interested in them. In the recent past, we have witnessed a resurgence in this area.[1]

1.1. Narrative Analysis, Psychological Hermeneutics, and Gender Perspective

I use narrative analysis, psychological hermeneutics, and a gender perspective according to the following methodological principles.

(1) Narration and history are not opposed to each other, nor must they be so, especially when dealing with such old texts. I distinguish between two

---

1. Two volumes of Athalya Brenner, ed., *A Feminist Companion to the Bible* (FCB 1–2; 18 vols.; Sheffield: Sheffield Academic Press, 1993–2001), deal with Genesis in detail.

interconnected textual levels: the level of the story at which the plot unfolds (the narration itself), and the level of discourse at which the narrator and the reader (implicitly) relate to each other. The first level is that of action, characters, and plot. The second allows us the opportunity to investigate the contexts and historical undertones of the story (such as the documentary, social, archaeological, and epigraphical histories).

(2) Psychological hermeneutics and a gender-critical perspective are lenses through which I choose material, instruments, and orientation. Reflections on standpoints lend a scientific bent to studies and augment their objectivity, though they cannot, as we know through the history and the philosophy of science, ever be completely neutral.

(3) I will maintain a global psycho-anthropological perspective that, built upon the basis of the analysis of these ancient texts, transcends time, place, and culture (Western culture above all) through a critique of the symbols still in use.[2] I will study the texts in three parts and conclude with a psycho-anthropological interpretation of the results.

1.2. Genesis 1–3 within the Context of Genesis 1–11

1.2.1. General Context: Genesis 1–11

Many interpretations of Gen 1–11 exist. There are terms that permit us to establish a formal link with Gen 1–3 (man, land, heaven, the verb "to build," generations); There are also many themes that link the diverse stories to each other (the desire of people to debase their humanity; a divine monologue that shows fear of the consequences of certain human actions; schemes showing creation-destruction-rebuilding; a relationship between the expulsion from Eden to the earth and the dispersion of people through the lands; the importance of language; the cycle of generations that begins in 2:4a; the fall-punishment-recuperation sequence, among many others). Additionally, we see lines that advance the narrative of a proto-history (Gen 1–3) into a second phase (Gen 4–10), a moment of civilization in the construction of the city (Gen 4 and 11), and the change from a nomadic to a sedentary lifestyle. Within the perspective of my study, I am interested in perceiving and highlighting the

---

2. Western Judeo-Christian culture has for centuries transmitted to other places and cultures symbols that have been universalized and that reinforce the patriarchal pillars of the societies with which we are familiar. The inducement toward seduction unites, ironically, the woman to the snake-apple-tree, associating seduction with negative ethical content (shrewdness and astuteness, temptation, deceit…). This can be seen, e.g., in the American television series *Desperate Housewives*.

narrative advance of a creation and a humanity that, though commencing on the basis of equality, begin to diverge from this path. In Gen 1–11 this differentiation manifests itself in a relationship of paradoxical tension between chaos and order, a return to chaos followed by a reorganization. This differentiation, which in the beginning (Gen 1:1–30) establishes order by clearing the initial confusion of a world not yet created, is itself a producer of confusion and chaos that is resolved only as a new order emerges (stories in the garden of Eden, Cain and Abel, the flood, confusion of languages in Babel).

1.2.2. Genesis 1–3 in the General Context

In this work we will place special emphasis on Gen 1–3, in which the generations that culminate in 11:10 begin. We will proceed, in effect, from the general and ample (cosmic generations of heaven and earth) to the concrete and singular (generations of Abraham and the ancestry of Israel). From the general to the specific, Gen 1–3 marks the standard for a precise reading of the conflicts in which life unfolds. These first chapters set the reader on the correct path with the hermeneutical instrument of *complexity*, a main element of the positive and growing advance of life. These chapters break the ingenuity of the reader as he or she acknowledges a narrative train that does not turn back. The fundamental elements of a forward-oriented life are the *autonomy* and *freedom* that are first given here.

1.2.3. View of the Presence and Roles of Women in Genesis 1–11

Within this large context, the different figures of women play a very important role. This role, however, is interpreted more often than not in a negative way.[3] This begins with the creation of humans, male and female, man and woman, in God's image (Gen 1:26–29; 2–3). This section also includes the woman's disobedience of God's commands and the subsequent punishment: the expulsion of the humans from the garden of Eden. In Gen 4:1, the woman, now called Eve, gives birth to the first two sons, Cain and Abel, and interprets the name of her first son as "acquired from/with" YHWH. Women again have more importance in Gen 6:2–7, in which the relationship of the sons of God with the daughters of men is explained. This narrative is generally understood as the cause of the flood. After the covenant between God and humans, which

---

3. Differently, Irmtraud Fischer, "Donne nel Antico Testamento," in *Donne e Biblia: Soria ed esegesi* (ed. Adriana Valerio; La Bibbia nella Storia 21; Bologna: Edizione Dehoniane, 2006), 161–96, esp. 164–67.

ensures the continuity of creation, this part of Genesis (11:27–32) ends, as we said, with the generations of Abraham, where the name "Sarah" appears for the first time. It is possible to establish a type of continuity and advancement here, since women are present and active in three inaugural moments: the universal proto-history (Gen 1–3); the first general history (Gen 4–11); and the history of the Israelites' ancestors (Gen 11:27–32). In three of the four tales, the narrator closely links women and myths: in the beginnings of life (Gen 1–3) and with the union of gods and humans (Gen 4:1 and 6:2–7).

2. Narrative Analysis of Genesis 1

Genesis 1, the beginning of this particular book and of the Bible itself, is organized into two large sequences, each with various scenes, in a trajectory that extends from the "beginning" (בְּרֵאשִׁית) to history or "generations" (תּוֹלְדֹת). The creation takes place in the middle through a character that existed before the beginning of the book itself, before space, time, and beings were created.[4] The first sequence is responsible for setting the stage for the existence of life. The second introduces the life forms that begin to fill up the stage. We witness a growing dynamism and a progressive transformation that culminates in the creation of the human being and the seventh day. From a formal point of view, as relates to actions, the verb ברא ("to create," Gen 1:1, 21) delineates both sequences, marking a change in the form and dynamism of creation. In the second sequence, the verb בדל ("to separate, to divide") disappears and the verb ברך ("to bless") appears. The verbs עשׂה ("to make") and יצא ("to produce") are found very close together in 1:11–12 in the first sequence and in 1:24 in the second. These are the verbs that mark the creation of plant and human life and establish the continuity and qualitative progression of that life. Looking at this section from the point of view of the plot, one observes the different ways creation was carried out in each of the sequences: in a more static way in the first sequence, more dynamically in the second. Verse 26 marks a qualitative jump within the formal continuity (vocabulary and actions ברא, עשׂה, ברך).

The first sequence concerns itself with establishing the conditions necessary for the existence of life. The creation of the sun and the moon, which mark the seasons, finalizes and makes permanent that which began with the creation of light. The second sequence is then responsible for the creation of living beings, animals and humans, through three scenes and some final

---

4. See Ellen van Wolde, *Stories of the Beginning: Genesis 1–11 and Other Creation Stories* (London: SCM, 1996), 15.

summary and transition verses. The sentence "and Elohim saw all that he had made, and behold, it was very good," referencing the creation in its entirety on the sixth day, ends the second sequence and is followed by the summary and transition of Gen 2:1–4a.

This episode's perspective is life. The final summary takes the reader back to the beginning. The verb שבת ("to end, to rest") marks the end, and the noun תּוֹלְדוֹת ("genealogy, generations, origins") introduces a new level of continuity. The reader expects, then, that, after a rest, life will continue. In addition to the formal references, from the plot's perspective there is also a correspondence between Gen 1 and 2–3, where Gen 2:6 mentions the absence of the mist (אֵד) that rises from the land and evokes the deep waters (תְּהוֹם), the chaotic material with which God creates reality.[5]

2.1. The Evolution of Life toward Complexity

2.1.1. Principles of Narrative Progression in Genesis 1:1–2:4a

One sexist argument still active and present in today's collective unconscious is the attribution of a higher grade of perfection to that which is male and the masculine over all that is female and feminine. As we will see, this attribution can no longer be based on Gen 1:26–31 or on Gen 2–3. We find three main vectors (guiding principles) in the advancement of the action: (1) from the undifferentiated to the differentiated; (2) from the simple (large units) to the complex (smaller units); and (3) from the imperfect to the perfect, in a connected, relational, and interdependent advancement.

2.1.1.1. Narrative Progression from the Undifferentiated to the Differentiated

Differentiation is one of the guiding principles of creation, different in the initial phase and the final phase. In the first five days, this differentiation operates through separation, expressed with its own vocabulary: in 1:4, 18 we see the verb בדל ("to separate"), the particle בֵּין ... וּבֵין ("between ... and between"), and the terms "light–darkness" (1:4: וַיַּבְדֵּל אֱלֹהִים בֵּין הָאוֹר וּבֵין הַחֹשֶׁךְ; 1:18: וּלְהַבְדִּיל בֵּין הָאוֹר וּבֵין הַחֹשֶׁךְ) as indicative of the progress of differentiation.[6] After 1:18, the fifth day, this vocabulary disappears. The differentiation is now carried out in a different way. Only in the first instance, the biggest and most

---

5. See arguments in Terje Stordalen, "Man, Soil, Garden: Basic Plot in Genesis 2–3 Reconsidered," *JOST* 53 (1992): 15; and T. A. Perry, "A Poetics of Absence: The Structure and Meaning of Genesis 1.2," *JSOT* 58 (1993) 6.

6. The preposition בְּתוֹךְ ("in between") forms part of the vocabulary of separation.

explicitly expressed separation of light and darkness, which builds the frame
for this kind of differentiation, does Elohim appear as its subject. Are these
separations horizontal or vertical? According to the origin of the division, the
תְּהוֹם ("deepness, primordial waters"), the separation orients space and time
from east to west. The first advance follows in the direction of light, from the
east, the life, the dawn. Upon creating light, the east, Elohim separates it from
the darkness that stays to the west. In the ancient Near East, the west evoked
death and the east life. Elohim thus creates the space and time of life first. In a
second moment, when the waters from above and from below are separated,
the horizontal border of heaven is not yet created. The waters occupy a vertical space,[7] since we are dealing with waters that, like rain, inundate everything and leave no open spaces. In order to organize these different elements,
Elohim must create the continent, which causes us to think of that which
does not yet exist, absence (hollowness), and thereby the possibility of further
development. The advancement of the narrative, which creates the horizontal
dimension out of the vertical, is marked by the change in the subject controlling the act of separation: from Elohim to the earth. The rest of the separation
vocabulary is less explicit. "Between, in between…" indicates how the created
reality in turn carries out its own larger changes. The dynamic, then, progresses from the large and indeterminate to the concrete and specific, from
the vertical to the horizontal. It progresses from what was there before and
deadly (darkness) to that which gives life and comes next (light), from the
past (darkness) to the future (light). It is Elohim who begins this process, but
it is continued, indirectly, by the creatures themselves. Reality now produces
its own effects.

The manner of creation has been, up to this point, hierarchical, with
some "anomalies." In 1:19, for example, the reader is aware that the things
from above are dependent upon those from below, although hierarchical logic
would suggest that what is below should depend upon what is above. Heavens,
light, stars, water … these are created from the land's point of view, benefiting
all that is dry and, in relation to the oceans, what is wet, which will permit the
existence of life. Life, according to the order of the creation, is always found in
front, in the future, in the next sequence.

The logic of using separation to differentiate has its breaking point in
1:9, when Elohim orders the waters from below "to be gathered" (יִקָּווּ) in one
place. This gathering of the waters from below into one place has the effect of

---

7. I refer to Perry's arguments, "A Poetics of Absence," 5. Also for Gen 7:11 it must be
noted that תְּהוֹם is not horizontal; the cosmic primordial waters occupy the entire space
from top to bottom, that is, vertically.

distinguishing between what is dry and what is wet. Thus, the form of creation employed in this case is paradoxical and, at the same time, different from what came before. We now see that one can differentiate both by separating and by gathering together.

In the second sequence, from the fifth day onward (1:20), a new vocabulary emerges in regard to differentiation: the waters that "teem" (שָׁרְצוּ) with "living creatures" (נֶפֶשׁ חַיָּה) are ordered into existence, and the land animals, which must "grow, multiply and fill" (פְּרוּ וּרְבוּ וּמִלְאוּ), are "created" (ברא). Similarities appear: "according to their kind" (לְמִינֵהוּ), as does the divine action of "blessing" (ברך). The actions of growing, multiplying, and filling the waters and the land are in themselves differentiating, established on a principle of similarity (according to their kind) through the particle מִין, something that is in a certain way prolonged through the creation of the human being.

Upon creating the human being, the new verbs "to subdue" and "to rule" (כִבְשֻׁהָ וּרְדוּ; 1:28) are added to those of "to grow," "to multiply," and "to fill." These actions both differentiate and create a hierarchy. A paradox is also present here, though it is more visible in Gen 2: these orders and tasks must be realized by a human being, an earthling, an 'adam (אָדָם). The differentiation that operates in this generic human being is then carried out in continuity with the principle of advancing from the undifferentiated to the differentiated. In the case of the human being, as in those of other living beings, aquatic and land animals, differentiation is no longer carried out through direct separation but rather by distinctions derived from the reality that has been created (from the אָדָם, human, to the זָכָר, male, and the נְקֵבָה, female).

2.1.1.2. Narrative Progression from the Simple to the Complex

The second guiding principle in the creation is the progressive advancement from the simple to the complex, something closely united with what has already been discussed. The undifferentiated and large appear as more simple versions of reality. Successive differentiations then introduce complexity. Formally, the narrator hopes that the reader will perceive these differences in the apparently fixed and stereotypical outline of the narrative: "and Elohim said 'let there be....' And it was so. Elohim saw everything that he had made, and indeed, it was very good." Throughout the advancement some actions disappear and others appear, the style becomes indirect, and complexity is intensified from 1:20 onward.

Through this growing complexity, human beings take over the realities that have been created and begin to assume the sequence of creation themselves. Humans will share this same stage with land animals. With each new differentiation, complexity increases, and with it comes a greater possibility of conflict. All of this works to prepare the narrative for the environment of freedom that is soon to come. This is implicitly indicated in the narration through the indirect progressive style Elohim has used in his creation thus far. The reader notices that in the creation of the human being the divine figure changes the verbal mode from the imperative to the cohortative, thus signaling greater involvement: "let us make." There is a change from using words external to himself to using words that involve him in the process, something that supports the change in the style (the how) of his action: he makes humans in his image and shares with them dominance over what has been created.

2.1.1.3. Narrative Progression from the Imperfect to Perfect Imperfection

This progression, oriented toward the creation of the human being, is less obvious than those that precede it. Explicit vocabulary that would show this imperfect-perfect dualism does not exist. The narrative advance, however, allows for discussion of these terms, interpreting in the same sequence some of the words that are also included in the final phase of the creation. Thus, the addition of the adverb "very," which precedes "good" and marks a qualitative difference in divine judgment, allows for an understanding of the whole— more complex and perfect. It confirms what the narrative has shown in its progressive sequence. This sequence starts off from chaos, then installs order through a temporal rhythm and the fitting out (differentiating) of a space. It also leaves the stage open, however, although already full of life, to disorder caused by potential conflicts. It finally delineates a new order with the creation of a seventh day.

The particle מִן ("from, since, from this point on"), which marks a change in the manner of creating (from inanimate beings and plants to land animals and humans), helps us to understand the change from the imperfect to the perfectible. It indicates continuity through indirect progression of the new reality (land that becomes verdant of itself, waters that breed fish upon the divine command); it indicates, above all, change, since it does not come directly from the imperative but rather from the modality that accompanies it.

> Let the earth bring forth living creatures according to their kind: cattle and creeping things and beasts of the earth according to their kind; and it was so. Elohim made the beasts of the earth according to their kind, and the cattle according to their kind, and everything that creeps on the ground according to its kind. (Gen 1:24–25)

The expression "according to their kind" hints at similarity on the horizontal level.

The creation of the human being, in this model, implies another change with the disappearance of מִין and לְמִינֵהוּ, "according to." The dynamic of horizontal creation and the principle of similarity remain. The change, which is in reality a qualitative jump or narrative unfamiliarization,[8] is produced by the divine "let us make" (נַעֲשֶׂה) and the modality "according to our likeness" (בְּצַלְמֵנוּ כִּדְמוּתֵנוּ). The human species is connected then, with the divine *species* (if we allow ourselves license for such). What the similarity consists of is not mentioned;[9] the reader waits to receive more information later.

Perfection, then, is paradoxical. Humans are, on the one hand, closely related to other living creatures and, on the other hand—like all other creatures—connected to the horizontal and vertical differentiation. Just as species differ among themselves qualitatively and hierarchically, so do humans: they will differ among each other horizontally and hierarchically from the deity. The *species* comes before the animals. The *image* and *similarity* to the deity come before the humans. In this tale, equality and difference, parting from the manner of divine creation, are paradoxical. "Let us make ... in our image" establishes references and differences: references with the animals and their dependence on the environment (the plant world) and the deity; qualitative difference with the rest of what has been created and especially with the Creator. Toward *image* and *similarity* with Elohim are established reference and distance. The subject of the action, Elohim, installs the hierarchy. There is no derivation, only direct creation: "let us make."[10] This hierarchy or order from above that decides the level of similarity is carried out through the paradox. The human being will be similar accepting this distance, a perceptible type of difference. This will be one of the narrative threads of Gen 2–3.

This sequence and its conclusion make it seem as though Elohim intended a world order characterized by the absence of conflict and order without disorder. All of creation, with its rhythms and sequences, appears as a system,[11] apparently closed by the seventh day and with the narrator's information

---

8. The model suggested by the creation of living beings is, in effect, to create horizontal similarity by species. Each species reproduces in its own likeness, and differences exist between the species. This model creates an expectation in the reader, who foresees a human being differentiated *according to his species*.

9. Generally, similarity is associated with the immediately following verbs, "to subdue" and "to rule," which supposedly denote the purpose of creation. The reader, however, has not seen Elohim rule and subdue his creatures.

10. The creation does not come from nothing but rather from the chaos and the word. The creation of humans does not come from nothing here either but rather from all of the preceding creation.

11. It is so indicated in 2:4a upon ending with the phrase "these are the generations of the heavens and the earth."

about the divine action that "ends" (וַיִּשְׁבֹּת) everything that it had begun. But the creation of the seventh day itself constitutes a border in the system of creation, placing it as a moment of transition that, once completed, will allow for a new beginning, at the same point where everything had left off. On this day, interesting categories return to the story—the absence and the pause (in the temporal dimension) or the void and the empty space (in the special dimension). The reality that has been created is a live system and, as such, open. The phrase "this is the account of the heavens and the earth when they were created" (אֵלֶּה תּוֹלְדוֹת הַשָּׁמַיִם וְהָאָרֶץ) looks both backward and forward.

The supposed perfection of the end leaves many threads hanging, for example, the differentiating action of naming. Elohim does not give a name to either the living beings or to the humans.[12] He does not explicitly indicate, either, the purpose or objective united, on some occasions, to the action of name giving. Implicitly, one supposes that ruling and subduing form the humans' purpose, but in reality these remain inconclusive tasks that will be taken up again in Gen 2.

2.1.2. Narrative Transformations of the Creation Sequence

The transformations encountered in this sequence point in three directions: (1) the progressive autonomy of the reality that has been created; (2) the emergence of paradoxical dynamisms; and (3) the theology of the open system.

2.1.2.1. Progressive Autonomy of the Newly Created Reality

Each reality created by God's word starts and then establishes its own autonomy. The divine Subject does not install a system of control that would guarantee the good functioning of that which he has created. It is rather the reality itself that, in its progressive complexity, advances and implants its own control. Thus, if the waters do not remain in their designated places (if the distinction of land from water does not work, such as in the flood), plant and animal life can neither start nor continue. If the day–night and seasonal temporal rhythm (after the creation and naming of the moon) do not work by themselves, the rest of the created reality cannot function either. The autonomy of what has been created forms part of the internal system of control that has been established by the principles of differentiation, complexity, and learn-

---

12. He does not give them names, but he defines their activity by advancing their purpose (to grow, to multiply).

ing in the new reality.[13] This autonomy is the result of its good or bad functioning. Its progressive interdependence is paradoxical.[14] The order that is inherent in creation is broken once that which has been created runs by itself. Interrelationships then continuously create and re-create the order through the dependent autonomy and the autonomous dependency of what has been created. Elohim does not directly intervene in its functioning. At this point, the perception of the reader regarding the relationship between the narrative character of Elohim and the autonomy of the entire creation is very different. Dynamism advances and progression results from the mutual cooperation among the different areas of reality.

2.1.2.2. Emergence of Paradoxical Dynamisms

The dynamism of (mutual) interdependent autonomy is the prerequisite for the internal autonomy of the creation as a whole. It evokes another more general dynamism. This is a dynamism of creation that originates in an external, directive, and hierarchical imperative. It allows for the development of a system in which progression implies mediation, the inherent and mutual dependency. The narrative strategy of defamiliarization, which is activated specifically in the creation of the human being and the seventh day, is a base that supports this hypothesis. Concrete paradoxes mark and support dynamism, for example, joining the waters in order to separate them. Joining together in order to differentiate is, in its way, a basic evolutionary dynamism in all levels of life. Another example is the creation of the horizontal from the vertical, working interdependently in order to guarantee autonomy. In summary, the paradox is dynamism and at the same time is the result of the narrative progression.

2.1.2.3. Teleology of Creation as an Open System

At the end of this episode, goals and objectives have emerged, though some were included very early, for example, the function of light, of the moon and the sun. The divine creation is teleological, as are all of the paradoxical dyna-

---

13. Up to this point both readers and experts in exegesis and theology are in agreement. Disagreements arise upon the arrival of humans.

14. The great interdependence that lends a paradoxical fragility to the systematic order does not exist, and it is not by pure chance (although chance does have its place). It will be the freedom of humans, their capacity, thanks to their similarity to God and their ability to interrupt and to create disorder and chaos in the created world, who will provoke different orders that could become enormously destructive or enlighteningly creative.

misms that point toward an opening of the system. Creation, according to
Gen 1, is a progressive story, directional, heading toward a final point, but at
the same time open. The episode leaves certain narrative threads hanging and
presents an open creation, prepared and in need of continuation. Thereby
the dynamic guiding principles of progression, possibility of conflict, growth,
and development come into effect. The narrator does not set limits to this
openness.

2.1.3. Beginning (Gen 1:1–2) and Conclusion (1:26–2:4): Creation as Re-creation

The narrator beings with time, "in the beginning," followed by Elohim (Subject), and the action, the verb "to create." I understand this beginning, with
syntax and controversial translation,[15] as a principal sentence ("in the beginning Elohim created the heavens and the earth") that establishes inclusiveness
with the end of the episode and the beginning of the following (2:4b), due to
the editor's hand in the book. In 2:4 we find another temporal preposition that
unites beginning and continuity.

2.1.3.1. Original and Productive Earth (Gen 1:1)

This frame, in the voice of the narrator, is organized in two moments. The
first functions as the general title of the story. The spatial concept of heaven-
earth offers the reader a total perception of reality. The narrator then turns the
attention of his audience to the earth (an inverted literary link) and describes
the initial situation that will then progressively change before the reader's eyes.
The heavens are indirectly present in 1:2 through the onomatopoetic game
(שָׁמַיִם, מַיִם; "heavens," "water").[16] The "earth" הָאָרֶץ (grammatically feminine) is introduced for the first time in the voice of the narrator as opposed
to the "heavens" (grammatically masculine), although together they form a
whole. All posterior development must be understood using this section as a
key (אֵת הַשָּׁמַיִם וְאֵת הָאָרֶץ).

From this key we can understand the changes in the configuration of the
scenes, which originate in the original and productive earth. The term "earth,"
'erets (אֶרֶץ), is different from the posterior 'adamah (אֲדָמָה), which appears for
the first time in 1:25 and whose root means "red." When it is mentioned, just

---

15. For more information, see Claus Westermann, *Genesis 1–11: A Commentary*
(trans. John J. Scullion; Minneapolis: Augsburg Fortress, 1974), 94ff..

16. The term "heavens" (שָׁמַיִם) literally means "relative to the waters."

before the 'adam in 1:26ff., it links humans with the color red and foreshadows the narration of the formation of the first human as clay modeled by divine hands. The earth we see in the beginning has been changing color, as if it were a pictorial composition: from the black and white impressions (darkness = black, light = white), the earth has changed to the blue and green of the heavens, waters and land, and from these to the red of 'adam and 'adamah. The red evokes ideas of blood, which, in the Hebrew consciousness, is a sign of life. The stage has been animated and has acquired a successively complex color scheme. The land and the human being, both associated with the red of blood, appear alive in a different way than the other things that have been created. The association of the color red with blood and of blood with life also anticipates mortality (and with mortality, of course, come questions about continuity). The creation of the human couple as male and female responds, initially, to these implicit questions. The command "Be fruitful and multiply and fill the earth" (the 'erets) unites the beginning and the end, the original earth with the productive earth. The first, 'erets, includes the second, 'adamah.

2.1.3.2. Ruah and Creative Chaos (Gen 1:2)

Totality begins to unfold in the following description. The narrator, differing from what he will do in Gen 2, shows the situation of the earth through a series of paradoxes: "chaos" (תֹּהוּ), "void" (בֹּהוּ), and "darkness" (חֹשֶׁךְ)—all masculine terms with negative connotations. They create an expectation of change and transformation. This change, however, does not arrive immediately. The description and expectation are prolonged to include the "ruah of Elohim" (רוּחַ אֱלֹהִים). The ruah is linked to the deity (genitive link). The action of the ruah is of a divine and permanent nature (piel participle; מְרַחֶפֶת). She is not over the land, as the reader would expect, but "over the waters" (עַל־פְּנֵי הַמָּיִם), whose onomatopoeic relation with the heavens (מַיִם—שָׁמַיִם), still undifferentiated, indicates that he is making plans for the vertical whole.[17] The ruah precedes the word of Elohim. Her presence, described as "hovering," has disturbing connotations and foreshadows the action of transformation through change. It can be understood as "breath, wind, spirit, energy, movement" ... evoking life in its dynamism even when life still does not exist. In the narration, it has the function of maintaining expectation in the original situation, preparing for the differentiating word. Thus, the ruah is the principle of life.

---

17. The waters are not on the earth, as the dry-wet differentiation has not yet occurred. It is more logical to locate them in the vertical dimension, since there has still been no separation of earth and heaven.

She "hovers" over the chaos, void, and darkness, of all that which seems to be passively waiting for life to exist.

These connotations offer the reader an initial perception of the vitality whose signs are *relationship* (links), *dynamism* (air, wind, spirit), *energy* or *force*, and, lastly, *expectation*, which is a specific form of passivity. Within these one finds the latent paradoxes of passive movement and of dynamic passivity (expectation).

From 1:1 to 1:2 there is a subtle narrative progression that reveals yet another paradox: when the heavens and earth, in opposition to each other, make up everything that exists, the descriptive signs of the earth as chaos, void, and darkness are linked among themselves, forming a large negative whole. In a moment of narrative advancement, this situation is opposed due to the presence of the *ruah* of Elohim and her vertical action of hovering (paradox). The divine *ruah*, hovering over the deep waters (chaotic and dark), will act not only over the chaos but also inside and in front of it (עַל־פְּנֵי; "face to face"). The chaos, with the existence of the *ruah*, acquires connotations of possibility and develops into creative chaos.

One of the characteristics of constructive or creative chaos is its autopoietic capacity, which we can call the divine indirection. It is supported by the chaos, in front of and inside of which the divine *ruah* is coursing. The divine *ruah* and original chaos are inseparable. The *ruah* will act above (and toward) chaos, inside of and with chaos (this being understood as "the absence of," "the what is yet to be"). Elohim does not misuse a single element of the existent reality. He does not eliminate the darkness. Rather, he opposes it to light, creating the day-night rhythm at whose borders (evening-dawn) one sees a fluid and cooperative relationship between the two: they are united in the evening and are separated at the dawn. The divine *ruah* disappears when Elohim takes the stage. The undefined *ruah* gives way to an anthropomorphic image of deity: the divine act of creation is launched by the word.

2.1.3.3. When the End Is the Beginning (Gen 1:26–2:4a)

Two sequences are clearly distinguished here: the creation of humanity and the final conclusive summary of events.

Difference from Equality (Gen 1:26–31). The creation of humanity marks the most complex stage in the creative progression of this story. The complexity of this stage, however, is one that is reliant upon all that has come before. This story shows the human being to be the fruit of many interdependencies. But none of these, nor the stage itself, *produce* human life. This marks a qualitative jump implied in the act of creation of human beings. On the one hand, humanity's appearance in the creation implies continuity; on the other hand, something new is introduced.

- ▶ God gets involved due to his direct discourse—or, perhaps better, his internal monologue.[18] This is expressed by the cohortative "Let us make!" instead of an imperative that is directed to the external.
- ▶ The narrator informs about the modality as well as the purpose of the action to create human beings in the image of Elohim.
- ▶ The final evaluation "And indeed, it was very good!" starts with the humans but includes all of the creation.

From a narrative perspective this sequence is organized like the preceding sections:

- ▶ 1:26–27   creation of the human being in three stages (the divine word);
- ▶ 1:28–30ab   destiny and objective ("to…");
- ▶ 1:30c–31   realization and evaluation of the whole creation ("God saw everything that he had made, and, indeed, it was very good").

Creation of the Human Being (Gen 1:26–27).[19] The creation of humans develops through three narrative moments.

- ▶ "Elohim said, 'let us make humankind [אָדָם] in our image, according to our likeness'" (Gen 1:26a). Due to this direct discourse from Elohim, the essential, undifferentiated human being (אָדָם; without the article) comes into existence, just as in other sequences of the story[20] in which that which is still undifferentiated and generic becomes differentiated and specific.[21]

---

18. Elohim does not direct his comments toward anyone in this story.

19. This can be seen in my work *Barro y aliento: Exégesis y antropología narrativa de Gn. 2–3* (Madrid: San Pablo, 1993), 19ff.

20. Regarding the sequence of words, a similarity with 1:3 can be confirmed, when in the scene in which light is created the imperative appears + a noun with no article (יְהִי אוֹר, "let there be light"). The same appears here, only that the imperative is substituted by the cohortative with a noun with no article (נַעֲשֶׂה אָדָם).

21. The term אָדָם is new, and the word of Elohim does not associate it with 'adamah. Thus the narration prepares a second story in which the human being has the major role.

▶ "Elohim created humankind (הָאָדָם) in his image; in the image of God he created them" (Gen 1:27a). The narrator ascertains the creation of the undifferentiated, particular human being (אֹתוֹ; singular).[22]

▶ "Male [זָכָר] and female [נְקֵבָה] he created them"[23] (Gen 1:27b). The narrator informs the reader that the human being is differentiated into two sexes (אֹתָם; plural).

The narrative advance from the first to the third moment has to do with the emergence of the differentiated from the undifferentiated. The first thing that exists is common and generic, and from it begin to emerge things that are different and specific. The creation of the human being follows the rules of the entire process of creation. Second, we see that it is related to the process itself. The narrator tells the audience the *way* in which Elohim creates differences in the common and generic object. In this sense, when it comes to the creation of human beings, the order differs from that which we saw in the creation of the animals. In the latter, the expression "each according to their kind" appears once the type of life that was referred to had been created (although the species, just like the generic one here, seems to have come before). "According to" indicates the modality and, when it refers to the animals, also includes the blessing and the command to multiply. In the creation of the human being there is neither *species* nor before or after.[24] Quite the contrary, in the central stage, when humanity is still undifferentiated, the narrator provides the information that the human being in general is the image of the deity. Thus in the third place it has to do with Elohim. The narrator, at the end, uses the plural form to refer to the male and the female (אֹתָם), which recalls the plural forms both of Elohim (literally, "gods") and "let us make." Male and female (זָכָר וּנְקֵבָה) are similar to Elohim as is the generic human. The mention of the sexes is related to the divine blessing that comes right after and the imperative of "to multiply," "to fill the earth," and "to rule over creation." This last part, which is more developed, complex, complete, and emphasized, references the creation of animal life. The sexes are related, implicitly, to the species and thus destined to reproduce.

Let us for a moment pay attention to the terms צֶלֶם and דְמוּת, which we translate as "image" and "likeness." The first refers to a statue, alludes to a sign that makes present all that is absent. Said of the human being in relation

---

22. וַיִּבְרָא אֱלֹהִים אֶת־הָאָדָם בְּצַלְמוֹ בְּצֶלֶם אֱלֹהִים בָּרָא אֹתוֹ.

23. זָכָר וּנְקֵבָה בָּרָא אֹתָם, where זָכָר has to do with something pointed and sharp and נְקֵבָה with something hollow.

24. If "according to their kind" were mentioned, we could refer with more certainty to the animals, but only "male" and "female" are mentioned.

to Elohim, it indicates that each one of the possible humans will evoke the deity, bringing it to life, suggesting the presence of something that is absent. The human being, thus, is the evocation of the absent presence of the deity in the world. This general term specifies another, "likeness, similarity," which gives more depth to the first and constitutes a semantic whole in Hebrew. The creation through image and similarity is part of genealogy. The difference between genealogical references and those of image and likeness is founded in this union. The first refers to biological descent, whereas the second refers directly to creation. The reference to creation was thus made permanent in every human being, even before any type of genealogy existed (Gen 2:4a). Each human, whether Hebrew or of another race, man or woman, whatever his or her characteristics may be, through his or her humanity as created by Elohim, is the image and likeness of God, that is to say, the one who has provided for his presence in reality. From this point, everything is left open. This is confirmed by the narrator in reference to the beginning of this new state of reality that has been created. The audience that is listening or reading knows that it has begun, although they remain unaware of the consequences of such autonomy.[25]

The Seventh Day (Gen 2:1–4a). The preceding sequence's open ending is emphasized by the fact that it is the *sixth* day, symbolizing that which is unfinished and open. The *seventh*, which, on the other hand, symbolizes totality, is described as a day of rest using positive terms such as "to complete," "to finish," and "to rest," which contrast with the negative terms with which the second story began (Gen 2:5). The retrospective perspective from the seventh day shows the entire creative story to be open, with many aspects still unfinished in the process of realization through function given by Elohim to each of the creatures. Cessation and repose belong only to Elohim. This has an interesting effect: Elohim rests and views his work as finished and ready to follow its course alone. The end of work, thus, is not equivalent to the cessation of the creation process. The verbs related to Elohim show a systematic and continuous distancing that will allow him to evaluate his work. The seventh day connects with these moments, and, in this way, they enter into the dynamic of the creation. The fact that Elohim rests and blesses and sanctifies the seventh day does not immediately reach the humans. Nothing indicates that they must do the same or that creation itself should rest or stop. In fact, humans are not even discussed; only the cosmos in its all-encompassing dimension (heaven-

---

25. For example, in the previous narrative sequences, each stage prepared for the following, and its beginning (its autonomy) gave way to the next stage. Here, on the other hand, there is not information about what will follow. The editor has left this for the following chapters, although they will belong to a different tradition.

earth) is mentioned. This conclusion of the act of creation, which echoes the beginning, condenses the totality of all the transformations that have taken place. Israel has associated the creation story with the Sabbath. Whether the institutionalization of the Sabbath has taken place before the text was written or later remains unclear. Whatever the case, the relationship between the text and the institution are open to interpretation.

Linking Gen 1:1 and 2:1 through the words הַשָּׁמַיִם וְהָאָרֶץ ("the heavens and the earth") formally indicates the beginning and the end of the story at the same time as it emphasizes the final verses (Gen 2:1–4a). In 2:1, in contrast to the beginning, וְכָל־צְבָאָם (which can be translated as "and all their inhabitants" or "and all the cosmos"[26]) is added. In 2:4a the "generations," or *toledot* (תּוֹלְדוֹת), are also mentioned. The narrator again plays with the onomatopoeia of the words, thus drawing the audience's attention toward them. The words "seventh," "to finish–to rest," "cosmos" sound similar (צְבָאָם, וַיִּשְׁבֹּת, הַשְּׁבִיעִי).

The end of this section is arranged around information from the narrator about the culmination of all the divine creating activity and the blessing and sanctification of the seventh day (2:1–3), then a conclusion of sorts about the generations of the heavens and the earth. From a narrative perspective, the cessation of God's activity places the seventh day on a different level from those that precede it. The blessing of this day also occupies a different place than the blessing of the living things, for it links fecundity (1:28) and the divine rest (2:3). Creation does not rest, the rhythm of life does not stop, but the divine cessation does indeed have an effect over all that has been created. The seventh day, then, on a different level, allows the life cycle to be perceived in its own dynamism, in a continuous renewal toward the future. The timeline, in Elohim's case stopped for a day, allows for the perception of the continuity of life as a re-creation. In this ending we find, again, the *separation* which from the divine character's perspective, creates, blesses, and sanctifies a moment qualitatively different from the other parts of the creation. There is also a *link*, because, although different, the seventh day is connected to the sixth that came before and, as there is no eighth day, to the first through a repetition of the cycle from the beginning onward.

2.2. Demythologization of Space (Mother Earth) and Time (Sabbath)

The entire story, at the discourse level, offers comprehension that is not given on the narrative level alone. In the following we will take a brief look at the

---

26. It is thus translated by the Septuagint: καὶ πᾶς ὁ κόσμος αὐτῶν.

earth and how Israel's neighbors understood it in their stories and myths of origin, as well as at the seventh day as interpreted Sabbath and the polemics hidden therein.[27]

2.2.1. Mother Earth Undivinized

After many centuries of ups and downs in the relationship between humanity and nature, we witness here an attempt at the *reenchantment* and *remystification* of Gaia, Mother Earth. The religious and cultural Judeo-Christian tradition has interiorized a demystified and dedivinized relationship with nature, which also included women. Ecofeminism, though plural and diverse, is a breeding ground for efforts to remystify the earth and nature. On the other hand, Gen 1 returns us to our own tradition according to which all the aspects that form the natural world (הַשָּׁמַיִם וְהָאָרֶץ) are creation, respectively creatures (not just the dry land as the habitat of animated life, dependent upon the water). The text returns to us the unity, the cosmos as created reality. Genesis 1 does not divinize the stars or the sun or the moon, as did Egypt and other peoples; it also does not divinize the waters or any specific animal, as happened in Mesopotamia, nor does it suggest the reality of a struggle, as in Persian myths.[28] Rather, it says that the human being is created in the image and likeness of the deity, but it signals also an irreducible distance between the Creator (the *ruah* of Elohim; Elohim) and the creatures. Jewish monotheism has founded and preserved the autonomy of a reality in which nature and culture are hard to separate.

The earth as it appears in Gen 1 is part of a whole (heavens-earth), a space with life-giving possibilities (dry land as a place for plant, human, and animal life), but also subjugated to its Creator Elohim and to the beings whom Elohim made in his image. The earth is not a special creature; it does not have an autonomous role, and it does not appear with mythical or divine characteristics.[29] Such demystification and dedivinization play down the importance

---

27. Yairah Amit, *Hidden Polemics in Biblical Narrative* (Leiden: Brill 2000), 224ff.

28. See Xabier Pikaza, *Hombre y mujer en las grandes religiones* (Estella: Verbo Divino, 1996); and idem, *Diccionario de la Biblia: Historia y palabra* (Estella: Verbo Divino, 2007), 240.

29. Waters, for example, have a greater role, and in the narrator's treatment one perceives more easily the demythologization process. Water is a more complex and diversified element (primordial waters, waters above, seas…). In the second story, Gen 2:4b–3, on the other hand, the earth acquires a greater role (matter created in the hands of YHWH, a space in which the garden can grow…) and is a more condensed semantic term. The curse in Gen 3 causes us to think that behind everything there could be a divinization against which the text is reacting. Genesis 1, which is a later story, shows a more advanced and

of space and universalize it when moving to the temporal dimension. The theological background of the book of Genesis allows one to understand that the focus, which is at the beginning of the creation story on the original earth (protology), which has been divinized by Israel's neighbors, has moved to the end (eschatology) in the following stories. Mother Earth is turned into the promised land, with all the risks of resanctifying this idea.

The advantages that Gen 1 provides with its demytholized Earth have been diminished by moving the focus from the spatial dimension (divine and originating Mother Earth) to the temporal dimension (promised land). Due to the identification of women with nature[30] and men with culture and history (the timeline, due to the fact that the men beget sons and provide genealogy, the future and history of the people), patriarchy has been supported, in my opinion, even more than in other cultures surrounding Israel.

2.2.2. Demythologized Time

In the first part of the creation story, time forms part of the system in two senses. As the rhythm (sequence) of creation, time is dependent upon the divine word, which establishes its advancements and pauses. Time becomes continually more autonomous, as well as a specific element, which is especially noticeable on the seventh day.

At first, the temporal rhythm is exterior to the system. It does not belong to the system, and it does not come from the system but is instead progressively established by Elohim. The repetitive rhythm, however, constructs time as a necessary part of the creative system and mechanism. This is something that is perceived only in the following chapters when the human being, like the deity, has access to the word. Genesis 1 closely relates word-time and narrative-time pushing the new reality forward.

The story does not speak specifically of the Sabbath. The *sixth* day symbolizes that which is unfinished and still open to completion. On the level of discourse, the seventh day includes many questions, such as why the "seventh day" is mentioned rather than the Sabbath. The reasons that we see within the narrative do not exclude those outside of it. According to Yairah Amit, this is due to hidden polemics regarding the place of the Sabbath in the lives of the people.[31]

---

achieved demythologization process than Gen 2–3, in whose narrations one is better able to see its antiquity and mythical leftovers.

30. Probably due to the Israelites' fear of fertility cults.

31. According to Amit (*Hidden Polemics*, 225ff.), the unit of the seven days marked different happenings in Israel: the impurity of the birth (Lev 12:2); weddings (Gen 29:27–28;

The *seventh day* does not necessarily have to be identified with the Sabbath. The way, however, in which the narrator links the root *šbt* ("to cease, to rest") with *the seventh day,* among other aspects of the story, such as the similarity between what Elohim does and what the people do, suggests that the Sabbath is meant, although it is not mentioned explicitly. Thus, although it is formally a symbol with universal value, it becomes, indirectly, an element of identification for the people of Israel distinguishing them from those who surround them. Creation culminates on the seventh day. Time is given a role superior to that of space, due to the move from the spatial (the productive land) to the temporal that marks the line of the narrative, respectively, of history. Thus, the hierarchy of men (time, history) over women (space, nature) is placed in the foreground. This story line redefines the entire system of creation, because it is here that the narrator focuses his meaning.

Another question arises with regard to the traditional and even unconscious link between Sabbath and its function in the cyclical re-creation of order: Is there a link between the seventh day and its function and the function of females and males in the entire system of creation? The seventh day proves the victory of order (which began with one word that created time) over chaos (which is generally understood as undifferentiated space). Judaism sanctifies the Sabbath, preserving the balance from the threat of all types of chaos. Chaos, in the Hebrew Bible, appears associated with uncontrolled natural forces, unknown, feared, and disordered, linked above all to space. The institution of the Sabbath, supported in the story of the seventh day, however, not only celebrates the victory of order (time) over chaos (space) but also reinstitutes the value of the masculine over the feminine and downplays and demythologizes the creative system. The seventh day is a free day because it is reserved for Elohim. All work ceases in remembrance of the divine creating word. This pause leaves the created system in a parenthesis and allows humans to celebrate their similarity to the deity. The practical realization of the Sabbath, patriarchal in and of itself as well as a reinforcement of all that is patriarchal, does not block a return to its original meaning and, through this, to its possibilities.

As divine and human activity ceases, the structure that has been subjected to order throughout the week also stops. The human being now has

---

Judg 14:12); feasts (Exod 23:15) and cultic ceremonies (initiation of priests, Exod 29:30; Lev 8:33–35); the sanctification of the altar (Exod 29:37); and the dedication of the temple (1 Kgs 8:65–66), as well as the days of mourning (Gen 50:10; Job 2:13). The sequence of seven days, however, is not necessarily connected with the Sabbath but rather is based on a fixed model of ascending numbers whose final number is differentiated as a singularity or innovation.

the ability to continue demythologizing space and time during the seventh day—disassociating in order to associate. From a historical point of view, he or she can disassociate the temporal rhythm and the spatial order of the great godly creations that surround him or her (the stars, the land, the waters) in order to associate them to the deity's creating word. The internal imperfect perfection—the created autonomy—has an author and creator. This is neither inertia nor coincidence but rather a conscious and intended word.

In conclusion, a paradoxical relationship exists in respect to spatial-temporal movement. The final picture presents us with a frame prepared for cyclical repetition oriented toward the future. This is carried out through that which is fixed and yet moveable—stability and movement. The great separations that we have seen in the beginning set the stable frame (light–darkness, waters from under–waters from above, dry land–oceans and seas) in which all mobility takes place (days and seasons, plant and animal life, human life). Change and forward advancement can take place only within this paradoxical combination: mobile immobility or stable mobility. The entire unceasing process takes place within the general frame of the six days of the week; the seventh day is not counted here. The free day, the religious dimension, implicitly crosses the week through the complacent distancing of Elohim for whom each element is good. Explicitly, the cessation of the activity on the seventh day belongs to another level of created reality. It is the time and place of meaning. The complexity of life in its weekly movement of time, through the seventh day, is related to the similarity of humans to Elohim, especially because they are the only ones who can become conscious (distance themselves) and evaluate (everything is "very good"). The seventh day, set apart from the week, marks a distance from which evaluation is possible. It represents evaluation of meaning and conscience; it presents the overcoming of the inertia of life, and its message hints the readers implicitly to its creative and re-creative powers. The seventh day is a preliminary stopping of the world, realized through the human being, the only one able to be conscious of the cessation. In this dimension, there is no hierarchical gender discrimination.

Likeness is not explained. It is an enigma. The attentive reader, from the first moment, perceives with clarity and some logic the similarity of humans to the rest of creation, something unthinkable without the framework of mobile stability. The plural or differentiated human being is part of all the realities that were previously created, and Elohim presents this in his blessing. Nothing, however, indicates what it means to be made in the image and likeness of God. The audience perceives themselves being pushed forward, passing first through the seventh day. To escape normalized rhythm and obligations is an excess. To enter the seventh day, evoking completeness, is to overcome the lineal and to enter into the nonlineal, to change the logic of duties and rights, of cause and effect, for another logic changed to completeness, the useless and unproductive. If humans do not enter at the point in which the established order is broken, it will be difficult for them to make out the divine dimension, and, because of this, it will be difficult for them to enter into what is suggested by their possession of divine likeness and image. The seventh day has an implicit relationship with the time before the first creative command was delivered. It appeals paradoxically to this chaos, to the divine *ruah* related to the word. Beginning and end are constantly referring to each other. Without the seventh day, one could not examine the beginning, and without the beginning, the spatial-temporal order could not be appreciated. This can be seen only by breaking with the order. My hypothesis is that the meaning of divine image and how it is realized by Elohim is to be explained by the meaning of the seventh day.

2.2.3. The Complex and Paradoxical Frame of Life, from the Gender Perspective

The demythologization of space and time allows us to return again to the episode as a whole in order to contemplate the overall system and its characteristics.

In my opinion, we are able to establish a hermeneutical principle from which to read the entire sequence through the experience of the identity and human development processes of each gender (in our Western culture, clearly): separation and linking. If we read the story in these terms, as we have done gradually in our analysis, we will understand that the narration gives preference to the principle of relationships, links, interdependent dependence, and cooperation over the principles of division and separation. Both exist, but not with the same narrative weight in the plot's development. The final result is not an immediate and direct product of the divine word that separates but rather of a word that distinguishes, one moment separating and, most of the time, linking. Distinguishing and separating are not comparable in Gen 1. Mere separation and division do not produce complexity, nor do they allow for the continuity and innovation of life. Distinction through diversified connections, through internal mechanisms of interdependent autonomy, does, however, explain life's complexity and innovation.

Sociocultural gender attributes associate identity through separation to men and identity through continuity and relationships to women. Each one of these attributes is a very powerful force in the development both of history and of life. The predominance of separation is destructive, while cooperation and connection are constructive and of immense vital importance. It is irrefutable that without the cooperative principle, which basically exists because of women and their actions (and is also the archetypal principle of the feminine, in reality), life would be impossible. It has been shown that a good part of male education about certain attributes of masculinity, related to separation, has done a great deal of harm to them, to nature, to history, and to the cosmos. It must be emphasized again that we are not trying to separate the two principles but rather to relate them in another way to the identity and gender of each and to the identity and sequence of continued, renovated, and innovated life.[32]

There is another attribution from the "up is more, up is superior" idea.[33] This belief, belonging to fixed metaphorical outlines, has been projected upon the heaven-earth relationship and, associatively, to the man-woman relationship, something that supports the argument of the supposed divine command in Gen 3:16 (something that I will object to shortly). The texts of Gen 1 discount this thesis, however, since they show the heavens at the service of the earth, not the other way around. It is the earth that in some ways *rules* over the heavens. As relates to this order, another issue emerges: while the plants and animals of the water exist only through their surroundings, land animals and humans are on the land, between the heaven and the earth, in the space between the waters. Their autonomy and interdependence on their surroundings, thus, is of another type. Humans, in their upright position on the land and under the heavens, are also more vulnerable and unprotected, although, in the story, they are perceived by the reader as the best aspect of what has been created (yet another paradox). This logic, according to which that which comes later is better, is inverted in Gen 2 and 3. In reception history, *that which comes last* is very often considered to be *worst*. Thus, the general conclusion from Gen 2:25 is that the woman, if she appears after the man, must be derived from him and hence be less perfect than him. Likewise, the divine action that will expel the humans from the garden in Gen 3:24 is presented as a degradation of the beginning.

---

32. For more information on the masculine and feminine identities of men and women as they relate to the principles of separation and connection, see Nancy Chodorow, *The Power of Feelings* (New Haven: Yale University Press, 1999). In the scientific realm, see Fritjof Capra, *The Hidden Connections* (New York: Doubleday, 2002).

33. See George Lakoff and Mark Johnson, *Metaphors We Live By* (Chicago: University of Chicago Press, 1980).

3. THE WOMAN AND THE OPEN SYSTEM OF LIFE: NARRATIVE ANALYSIS OF GENESIS 2–3

The formal delineation of Genesis is created by the term אָדָם "human," which appears to both unite and separate the two stories of the creation from the posterior stories (Gen 1:27; 2:5; 4:1). Another word, "earth," is united to this term and to the name Elohim (associated with the new name YHWH). Some elements point toward continuity: the preposition בְּ links Gen 1:1 and 2:4b. In 1:1 בְּ introduces the "beginning" (רֵאשִׁית), and in 2:4b it introduces the "day" (יוֹם). The new story produces a *zoom* effect regarding time, space, and plotline. It proposes a transition from the panoramic to the detailed, from a fast pace to slow movement, and from the macro perspective to the micro. The narrative effect is a paradox of advancement through backtracking. Genesis 1 occupies six days that culminate on the seventh day—completeness. The story, from Elohim's character perspective, is closed; from the plot's perspective, however, it is still open. Genesis 2–3 occupies one day, interchangeable with the week that appeared in the first story. It seems to begin in the morning and to end in the afternoon (בַּגָּן לְרוּחַ הַיּוֹם).[34] In the second story, the slowness with which time passes allows for the focusing of attention on characters and actions and on the process or sequence itself.

The story is organized in three main episodes that are preceded by a long expository introduction and followed by a brief conclusion. The phrase "tree of life" (עֵץ הַחַיִּים) is formally included between the beginning and the end of the episodes. This tree, planted after YHWH Elohim creates humans, remains in the garden after their expulsion. Nothing is said about its actual function.[35] Both the trees, the tree of life and the tree of knowledge of good and evil, seem to have different functions and destinies.

The division into episodes, according to narrative criteria, is as follows:[36]

- ► 2:4b–6 narrative exposition;
- ► 2:7–25 episode 1: creation-introduction of humans by YHWH Elohim into the garden;
- ► 3:1–7 episode 2: human transgression of the divine command; and
- ► 3:8–24 episode 3: consequences of the humans' transgression and their expulsion by YHWH Elohim from the garden.

---

34. It is not coincidental that *ruah* רוּחַ appears at this moment in the narration, connecting Gen 1:1–2 with 3:8.

35. It is only mentioned in Gen 2:9; 3:22, 24.

36. See Navarro Puerto, *Barro y aliento*, 27–32.

The narrative plot unfolds through the correspondence of concentric inter-related circles, supported lexically in the similarities and differences between:

(1) YHWH Elohim and the tree of life—the humans and the tree of knowledge of good and evil;

(2) 'adamah (אֲדָמָה; earth)—'adam (אָדָם; human being); and

(3) 'ishah (אִשָּׁה; woman)—'ish (אִישׁ; man).

These interrelations, as we will see, are pushed forward through the conflicts in the plot, oriented toward a growing complexity that is first started by the woman.

3.1. THE EMERGENCE OF CONFLICT IN A CONTEXT OF COMPLEXITY

3.1.1. Genesis 2: More Difference Than Equality?

The action develops through a narrative emphasis on *absence*. This category, over a basis of negative terms and expressions, highlights the creation of the human being from clay and breath. The human being comes from the divine hands that model the clay (dust and water) and from the divine breath that goes from God's mouth to the "human's" (אָדָם) nostrils to convert it into a "living being" (נֶפֶשׁ חַיָּה). This episode (Gen 2:7–25), which is organized into various scenes and a descriptive pause relating to the rivers that go out from the garden, narrates the creation of this human in two moments: generic and undifferentiated; and differentiated into two sexes. The general narra-tive scheme of Gen 1 thus continues from large, barely differentiated, and less complex units to smaller, more differentiated, and complex, perfectible units. Complexity, here also, opens a path to conflict.

3.1.1.1. From the Generic Human Being (אָדָם) to Differentiated Human Beings (אִישׁ and אִשָּׁה)

The narrative process advances from YHWH Elohim's actions in creating the human. In this story, as relates to the one that precedes it, "to form" substitutes for "to create." In Gen 1 the divine character creates from chaos first the sur-roundings in which they will live and then the humans themselves. In Gen 2, the process is reversed: YHWH Elohim first creates the humans and then plants the garden. This act is preceded by the paradoxical absence: the "earth" and the hardly recognizable humidity that rises and permeates the earth. The earth-ground and the water exist in very primitive states. God creates the human from this material and later plants the garden. This sequence is impor-tant in order to be able to perceive the progression of the story that goes from the earth to the earth using three different terms: *'eres* (אֶרֶץ, 1:2; 2:1, 6); the 'adamah (אֲדָמָה,1:25; 2:5, 6, 7, 9, 19; 3:17, 19, 23; 4:3); and the "garden," gan (גַּן, 2:8), terms that will continue to be transformed. The garden, cultivated land brimming with life, is placed between two mentions of the earth. The 'adamah of the end of Gen 3 (3:19, 23) is not the same as the one at the beginning, since it has been transformed by the humans who have themselves been undergoing change while in the garden. The narrator shows the creatures, human beings, and YHWH Elohim in processes of evolution, an evolution that affects almost everything, except for the garden itself. The narrator links 'adam and 'adamah in its state of beginning and ending (from the earth, Gen 2:7, and returned to the earth, Gen 3:23),[37] and each will have an impact on the other. This impact produces a fundamental change: the generic 'adam from the beginning is transformed by God through the creation of the woman (אִשָּׁה). In this new stage there is another form of absence, thanks to YHWH Elohim.

YHWH Elohim's action (process of differentiation) is carried out in brief and progressive phases. In the first, the generic human is submerged (unconsciously) in sleep. Soon, a hole is opened, and from its צֵלָע ("breast, hole, rib, side…")[38] the "woman" (אִשָּׁה) is "made" (בנה) and then presented to the human being. The reader observes that that this generic human (אָדָם; 2:22b), although named as being equal, is not the same as the one we saw in 2:21 (as happens with the earth at the beginning and end of the episode). The relationship between lexical similarity and semantic difference leaves the text open to various interpretations. Some interpretations put emphasis on the lexical similarities and, through this emphasis, on the patriarchal and sexist conditions of the stories. Others would emphasize semantic difference, focusing thus on a less sexist change (though also androcentric).

The divine character has been covering the human being's needs by assuming a parental role (maternal-paternal) in the story: the garden, the food, the relationship with other living beings through the invitation to name them, the search for "the help meant for him" (עֵזֶר כְּנֶגְדּוֹ), which drives YHWH Elohim to construct a partner. The story's points of view and its changes indicate that the woman does not exist as a character either for YHWH Elohim or for the narrator. She is an object, first, of work-creation; she is brought, after, to the human being: he perceives her as similar through his words and focalization,

---

37. This is an inclusion in respect to the earth, but not in relation to the verbs. The verb "to form" from Gen 2:7 is not repeated in 3:23. It does not say "the earth from which he had been formed" but rather "taken." This difference shows that the narrator presents the human being as a divine creation. The verbs that he reserves for their creation are "to form" (2:7) and "to make" (2:22) in relation to their progressive complexity.

38. The term has more than one meaning, but its semantic line is clear.

and she is interpreted as taken by the *male*.[39] The reader, however, knows nothing about her, as the narrator fails to record her reactions, actions, or discourse.

The human character, generic and indirectly identified as male, is the subject of actions: the naming of the animals, not finding a helper suitable to him. He is also the subject of discourse about the discovery of the woman in the mirror (in reference to himself and his perceiving only the similarities to himself) as well as the narrator's report that the man will *leave* his father and his mother and *join* his wife so that they may be converted into one flesh. The woman, unlike the human male, does not exist as an autonomous character. The reader must notice, transversally, the narrative sequence of the two stories in respect to their deficiencies: less evolved/more evolved creation, less differentiated/more differentiated and perfectible creation. To lose the general perspective and to isolate it and its sequence would change the data and their meaning.

When the woman is constructed, the reader understands that YHWH Elohim has covered the need of the (generic) human with a helpmate for him (Gen 2:20), the *what*. In the *how*, there is a lot more information. The actions and performance of YHWH Elohim are not the same as those of the human. The divine character, in the narrator's focus, never names the man by his sex (as אִישׁ) but rather by his condition as a human being created from the earth ('*adam*, the earthling). The term "man" (אִישׁ) appears for the first time from the mouth of the human, naming himself before the new presence of the woman (emerging through the differentiation process), but his interpretation is the other way around. Instead of saying: I discover myself to be male because I perceive you to be female, he says, in a soliloquy, "She shall be called woman, because she was taken out of man." The hidden messages in the text are noteworthy: How does he know that being a human being and being male is the same thing? (Looking just at the narrative, they are not.) How does he know that she has been taken from him? (The narrative sends us back to '*adam* taken from '*adamah*, not to the '*ish* taken from '*adamah*, as this verb is not used anywhere in the process.) It could seem to be yet another collusion between '*adam* and YHWH Elohim, but it also could be understood as a narrative and psycho-perceptive deduction in line with the phase that follows.

---

39. The reader notices that she has not been taken from the *man* (אִישׁ) but from the *human being* (אָדָם). This leaves room for interpreting the onomatopoetic game between the terms *man-woman* (אִישׁ and אִשָּׁה) in their similarity, in parallel relation to the discovery that she is *bone of my bones and flesh of my flesh*. Part of my argumentation in *Barro*, 138–45.

We find support for this in the sequence of the different phases of creation. A material that is already in existence but is insufficient (chaos, empty land, a human without a helpmeet for him...) is the object of a divine action (word, hands, a breath, construction...) whose result is the creation of a new reality, progressively more differentiated and perfect. The entire process affects the initial material, but it also brings a framework of interdependence to all that is created. In this way the generic male human being deduces that the woman must have something to do with initial material, just as the narrator and YHWH Elohim deduce that the human being must be related to the earth by a play on phonetics. What the generic male human being does not discover is that the woman also is related to the earth.[40] The story, as it continues, puts the woman, and through her all of humanity, in another dimension. This new dimension will relate to the narrative themes of prohibition and transgression.

The conflict, in the narrative plot line relating to the creation of the humans as God's image but different from the deity emerges when the human acquires language and begins to differentiate like YHWH Elohim has done. In various parts of the story, then, conflicts linked to similarity and difference begin to appear.

3.1.1.2. The Significance of Genesis 2:24–25

We accept that in 2:24 the narrator intrudes in the story. The editor inserts him here intentionally, and because of this we need to know his function and be able to respond to questions about the antecedent of "therefore" (עַל־כֵּן)[41] and the meaning of the future tense in which the narrator expresses himself. What is the meaning of this sentence at this point of the plot, and what is its narrative function?

If the adverbial particle is referring to that which came just before, the narrator is informing his audience of an etiology, a consequence, at the same time, of the fact that the male has perceived and named the similarity of the woman to himself. A link would thus be established between the discovery and recognition of the similarities and the heterosexual pair, as indicated by the sequence "to cling" + "and be one flesh." The narrator places himself in line with the male's point of view by saying that the man will be joined to "*his* wife" (בְּאִשְׁתּוֹ). There has been a desire to find an allusion to fecundity in this verse, supported by the way that the two creation stories refer to life and

---

40. This is a curiosity, since the mythical-religious realm of Israel shows women and the earth to be closer than men and the earth.

41. See the parallelism with Gen 11:9, where the same expression is used in the context of a divine monologue.

its continuity on the basis of multiplication. The verb "to cling" (דבק) makes reference to a strong link, an alliance, in this sequence: "he will leave ... and cling to ... they will become"; the principal action, the two verbs, has the male as the subject, but the result, the third verb, is plural and includes the woman. The intrusion of the narrator both concludes and anticipates the heterosexual relationship. The posterior narrative unit will be concerned with the transmission of life, centered on fecundity. It does not appear explicitly here, where the emphasis of the narrator is on heterosexuality, important in and of itself because it places sexuality before the transgression. "Therefore" links "'adam will leave his father and his mother" with the plot. Who are the father and the mother? How can the intrusive narrator have been so careless as to leave this string untied in such a condensed story?

The sexual alliance between male and female is found in the midst of two occurrences: the discovery of similarity between the two humans in the question of sex, on one side, and the transgression and arrival at full consciousness of human autonomy and freedom, on the other. The narrator's intrusion points toward the future and anticipates what will take place outside the garden.[42]

Verse 25 insists on some of these aspects in their function as transitions between narrative units. They consist of vocabulary terms with high semantic value. The narrator uses the plural, anticipating the use that it will have in the following story. In the progression of these two stories, he mentions a negative lack from an ambiguous confirmation. "Nudity" (עֲרוּמִים) is a term that will be used in multiple-meaning wordplay, related with the "cunning" snake (עָרוּם). The narrator refers to the lack of a feeling of shame using negation. In the episode, let us remember, the negative particle (לֹא) appears at the beginning itself: in the voice of the narrator preparing the creation of the human (2:5); in the divine voice of the prohibition, or negative command, of eating fruit from the tree (2:17); in the voice of the generic human who says that he finds no helpmeet for him (2:20)—all of which come before the creation of woman. The negative particle precedes moments of progression in the narrative sequence of creation. At this moment, therefore, the reader is waiting for something to happen that will cause creation to progress yet again. Looked at in this light, the negative particle is paradoxically positive, anticipating advances in the creating process. It is only said once of the human being that he had *not* found a helpmeet for him.

---

42. In 4:1 (וְהָאָדָם יָדַע אֶת־חַוָּה אִשְׁתּוֹ) we find, in the narrator's voice using the woman-man relationship with the terms themselves and the difference in the verb "to know," the medium through which the heterosexual act is expressed, followed by conception and delivery.

These verses are positive for the reader and one's comprehension of the whole story. The narrator anticipates the relationship between nudity and shame from a narrative position superior to that of the characters. This causes a possible psychological and ethical valuation in the reader's mind before the characters themselves discover it (they were both naked, but they were not ashamed). This relationship also anticipates the possible conflict that will come with the humans' later realization.

With respect to content, it is possible that the strange mention of a father and mother, as agents who came before the humans, whom the male will have to leave, is linked in the narrative to the implicit role of the divine character.[43] If this is true, it would make sense that "therefore" refers to the anterior plot; the future tense of the verb "he will leave…" would then be an order, oriented toward the future, that implicitly welcomes the transgression that leads the humans to leave the garden and to acquire independence from the divine father-mother and from the house-garden-paradise, with the purpose of assuming the jobs and responsibilities of adult subjects. This implicit command to transgress, like 2:24 and 25, brings with it the framework of the male point of view. There are, however, certain anomalies that add to the complexity of this perspective.

Narrative logic has shown its profundity through the defamiliarizing distance of word games and supposedly obvious interpretation. The correlation between 'adam–'adamah indicates that the 'adamah came before and was materially necessary for the creation of 'adam. The correlation of the male, between 'ish and 'ishah, indicates that they refer to each other mutually, and thus refer, yet again, to 'adamah. The later identification between 'ishah and Eve as mother of the living indicates that it is not the 'ishah of the 'ish but rather the 'ish of the 'ishah, since it is she who gives life (hawwah), as did YHWH. All of these ('ishah–'ish, 'adamah–'adam, hawwah), to top it off, also refer to YHWH. The narrator of Gen 2:24–25 pronounces his "command" over 'adam, but the transgression will be subsequently first executed by the woman. What follows, in the light of such anticipation, changes because the male will join his woman once she has acquired autonomy. Autonomy, in this story, is equivalent to eating the fruit of the tree and giving it to the male to eat as well (inverting the terms of the supposed logic in which the male is the one who will give the female something to eat).[44] In fact, the man will cling to

43. The narrative absence or silence about ancestors in effect brings us back to he who gave life to the humans, who cared for them and accompanied them during this stage in the garden.

44. From a psycho-anthropological evolutionary point of view, the story plays with the interdependent relationships and does not allow these to be simplified and understood

the woman only outside of the garden in 4:1, using the verb ידע ("to know"), exactly the verb of transgression.

3.1.2. Genesis 2–3: The Function of Prohibition and Transgression

The emergence of the conflict in these stories can be attributed, almost in its entirety, to the woman's transgression, without noticing, of course, that the conflict truly begins with the divine prohibition. The reader could even perceive, if one extends one's perspective, that a tension (a potential conflict) is present from start to finish between the centrality of the earth and the centrality of the human being that is implicit at the beginning and explicit at the end in YHWH Elohim's damnation.

When we follow the sequence in relation to its actors and center our perspective on them, we discover three dimensions to the conflict: the *vertical* dimension in which the humans are measured against YHWH Elohim; the *depth* dimension in which the human being relates to himself (Gen 3:1–7); and the *horizontal* dimension in which the human actors relate with each other[45] and with the earth.

3.1.2.1. The Vertical Dimension of the Conflict: Genesis 2:9, 16–17; 3:8–24

The appearance (origin) of the conflict takes place in two moments, the first proleptic (2:9) and the second immediate (2:16–17).

First moment (2:9). The narrator informs the reader that YHWH Elohim has brought forth all kinds of beautiful trees bearing good fruit to eat. We should pay attention to the conjunctions here because, by causing ambiguities, they prepare for the conflict. Through the conjunction "and" the narrator unites and separates the tree of life, in the middle of the garden, and the tree of knowledge of good and evil from the garden as a whole. Thus, a certain ambi-

---

in only one way. In certain areas the man depends on the woman and in others the woman on the man. He will leave his parents (an act of autonomy) but will join a woman who, supposedly, will have already reached her independence (the text does not indicate that she has been given or sold or changed from another owner). She is his wife, but independent before he was.

45. Ellen Van Wolde also sees the entire story as preparation for the transgression (see *Van Wolde, Stories*, 45). The plot prepares the humans for life outside the garden. This means, the story acquires a specific function which evokes different stages of maturation. This is not the first biblical story based upon such a function. As relates to this idea, please see my work, "El paso del mar: nacer muriendo," in *Relectura del Éxodo* (ed. Isabel Gómez-Acebo et al.; En Clave de Mujer; Bilbao: Desclée de Brouwer, 2006), 85–143.

guity is introduced about the situation of the tree, and a first opposition is also introduced (from the whole) with the merism good-bad. The foundation (the ambiguity) is already in place.

The formal organization and the sequence of 2:9 can be followed through the thrice-mentioned noun "tree." The first time the expression is all-inclusive: "every tree," which surges from the earth thanks to the indirect action of the divine character. The narrator describes the scene by classifying the trees as pleasant to the sight and good for food. The second time, through the conjunction "and" (1), the narrator mentions the tree of life and tells about its place in the story's narrative space, in the midst of the garden, and, formally, in the midst of the verse and of the three times the word "tree" is mentioned. Through another conjunctive "and" (1), the narrator names the tree of knowledge of good and evil about which he gives no information.

Formally, the author calls his audience's attention toward the tree of life. Sequentially, he moves from more to less information. The story's audience can understand a variety of things from this.

(1) The description of all the trees includes the two that are later emphasized. The tree of life and the tree of knowledge of good and evil will be, thus, pleasant to look at and good to eat. Pleasure, a potential element of conflict, would also be associated with the two trees of the group that are emphasized. Pleasure and goodness appear in a positive way.

(2) The trees that are mentioned separately from the whole have their own connotations (including or not the general traits of the group). In fact, the tree of life is placed in the middle of the garden, and this centrality is open to many interpretations.

(3) This tree occupies the central space exclusively. This depends upon the interpretation of the conjunction that follows. The tree of knowledge of good and evil can be identified with the tree of life. It can occupy the central place, as does the tree of life being, as it were, a different tree. It can, lastly, be a different tree about which no one knows anything for the moment. [46]

Its brevity and the double conjunction give 2:9 a great deal of ambiguity and leave it open to many possibilities. One of its functions could be to involve the audience in its interpretation. Another could be to show the narrative paths that will shortly follow. It could also, however, have the function of inducing the conflict in the arena of discourse before bringing it fully into the story (as the narrator will later do in 2:24–25). The reader has more informa-

---

46. In this case the compactness of the area would be very high, since if it is the repository of all the knowledge there is, it would only be through acceding to the tree itself that one could know what it means to know good and evil.

tion and knowledge than the actors (except for the divine character and the narrator, with whom he can be allied). We are before a *prolepsis* of the conflict that goes from top to bottom and whose first recipient is the reader.

Pleasure, certainly, is an element of potential conflict, but even more so is the connotation of the last tree mentioned, which is to say, the opposition of *good–evil*. In agreement with the sapiential background of the story,[47] which refers back to the duality of opposites, we find ourselves, on the discourse level, facing the basic theme of choice and, because of this, of the possibility of freedom. In other moments of the Pentateuch and of sapiential literature, the people must choose between good and evil, but this choice supposes a space for freedom, conscience, and, above all, *knowledge*. Together with this clear and open duality we find another—more subtle and hidden—that will be fundamental: *life–death*. The opposition is not expressed between good–life and evil–death, but rather in each one of the trees, one of life (which hides its opposite, death) and another of good–evil, linked to knowledge. What is meant by this conjunctive linking?

In 2:9 itself, as viewed from the end, there is another anticipation of conflict: the trees in the garden are "pleasant to look at" (appealing) and "good to eat." The term "good" (טוֹב) is the same that is repeated in a *Leitmotiv* that speaks of the judgment that Elohim makes over his creation: "and Elohim saw that it was good." The verb "to see" (רָאה) appears in relation to "good" in Gen 1 as well as in 2:9 in order to classify the trees and is later seen in the narration of the action of the woman eating from the tree. The reader or listener must establish relations between terms and then check their variations and similarities.

"Pleasant" (נֶחְמָד) is used here in relation to sight as a characteristic of the trees that, as I see it, are included with all the others in 2:9. The sense of this link takes place when the woman wants to eat fruit from the tree of knowledge of good and evil. She perceives it to be "desirable to make one wise": "to see" (perception), "desire," and "knowledge"—a prolepsis of conflict.

Second moment (2:16–17). The divine character gives an order in direct discourse. In it he mentions what the human can do and what he cannot do. He can eat from all of the trees in the garden. He cannot eat from the tree of knowledge of good and evil because if he does he will surely die. First observa-

---

47. See Luis Alonso Schöckel, "Motivos sapienciales y de alianza en Gn 2–3," in *Hermenéutica de la Palabra III: Interpretación teológica de textos bíblicos* (ed. Luis Alonso Schöckel; Bilbao: Ediciones EGA, ed. Mensajero, 1991), 17–36. In the same line, with a global and innovative perspective, see Marinilla Perroni, "Gen. 1–3: Tre racconti brevi sulla nascita della deomcrazia," in *Mujeres ¿menos religión y más espiritualidad?* (ed. Mercedes Navarro Puerto and Mercedes Arriaga; Sevilla: Arcibel, 2010).

tion of 2:9: the tree of life is intentionally omitted when all the trees are mentioned, including that of knowledge of good and evil. Second observation: this omission is implicit because, if in 2:9 only life and/or death are discussed, here the possibility of death is mentioned explicitly as associated with the tree of knowledge. Opposition is mediated and implicit, an enigma whose resolution is found in the tree of knowledge. A paradoxical strategy is designed for the reader and the characters in the divine command: "ignore it by paying attention to it." To verbally introduce the possibility of death would be to introduce an element of conflict, something that would be garish in a supposedly perfect environment.

The reader at this point already knows that the tree is conflictive due to the good–evil opposition, and to this we now add the restrictive limitation that makes its conflictive nature more explicit. Nothing indicates that this tree does not have the characteristics of the others, that is to say, that it is not "pleasurable to look at and good for food." With that, the narrator foreshadows for the audience the woman's reaction after her conversation with the serpent and the variations with regard to the evaluation of the tree: on the one hand, it is given general characteristics, but at the same time it is individualized because of variations and focalization.

The divine prohibition's conflict is, additionally, conditional: "if you eat…, you will die." What is said here is just as important as what is not said. Is this a reversible order? Is it true that if the human does not eat he will not die? Why is this indicated in only one direction? Is YHWH Elohim trying to stop them from eating or from dying?

Beginning with this analysis, we can conclude that the conflict springs directly from the divine command, from the creator of this reality, when he forbids and establishes limits. We should analyze this command more closely. It supposes that, if the rest of the trees are pleasurable to look at and good for food, they support life. YHWH Elohim is excluded, but the human in the garden will need to eat from the trees in order to live. We can infer, thus, that the first part of the divine command, "you may freely eat of every tree of the garden," has the intention of giving life to the human, in agreement with the entire creation.

The second part, "in the day you shall eat of it, you shall surely die," is opposed to the preceding sentence on an explicit level. On the implicit level, will abstaining from eating from the tree of knowledge of good and evil mean that he will live? Another paradox is imposed: knowing good and evil is lethal. The two conflicts (to know good–evil and to live–die) are related. The reader finds an enigma on two levels: that of discourse and that of the story as it relates to the actors. How are they going to be able to solve this chain of conflicts?

3.1.2.2. The Conflict's Depth Dimension: Genesis 3:1–7

The conflict appears, again, on the discourse level when the narrator tells of the serpent's cunning and of its condition as a creature. This produces a change from verticality (from and going upward) to depth. The development and dynamism of the conflict takes place *in the same dynamic as communication*. The reader can infer that, in effect, communication contains the potential for conflict. Two actors are present here (the woman, grammatically feminine, and the serpent, grammatically masculine) whose communication takes place within the reference of Elohim's discourse. This allows the actors and the reader to verify the truth or falsity of communication. Thus, the readers become involved in the events. The conflict is developed on the cognitive level: the serpent distorts Elohim's discourse, and the woman corrects him. In the course of statements and responses, new information begins to appear, and thus the enigma acquires depth. This dialogue on the cognitive level reveals elements of conflict that remained hidden in the divine discourse: the reversibility of dying–living; the intention to be like gods; the relationship with the knowledge of good–evil; and the freedom to choose different options. The dimension of depth in this conflict is associated with interpretation and discernment.[48] On the content level, we should note the inference of suspicion and doubt in the woman when the serpent first speaks.

From the woman's point of view, the divine intention is that humans do not die ("not eat from the tree, not touch, otherwise we will die"). The paradox is cleared up if we identify the tree of which the woman speaks to be that which is in the center of the garden, that is, the tree of life. The paradox would consist of eating from the tree of life and then surely dying. The woman does not make the command reversible. Has she confused the two trees? Does she confuse them only to distinguish them correctly later? Is the serpent's trick to create this confusion between the tree of life and the tree of knowledge of good and evil? A great deal of interpretation can be derived from the association of both trees.[49] The resolution of the conflict in this episode passes

---

48. From the psychological perspective it is common to understand the dialogue between the woman and the serpent as a dramatization of the complexity of interior dialogue when facing enigmas and potential conflicts.

49. Anthropologically, one observes that the thirst for knowledge is insatiable, that knowledge and life are united together in quantity and quality and that this knowledge-life link is associated, ultimately, with a limitless, immortal life. The paradox lies in the links which presuppose risk and danger, for which it would not be strange to associate them with mortality. I find it interesting to associate these links with the figure of the original woman.

necessarily through the *transgression* of the command, and, depending on the interpretation that we give it, we will include this solution in the origin of the conflict itself. We will now examine the parallelisms and echoes between 2:9 and 3:6.

2:9: Out of the ground YHWH Elohim made to grow grow every tree that is *pleasant* to the sight and *good for food*; the tree of life also in the midst of the garden, and the tree of knowledge of good and evil.	3:6: So when the woman saw that the tree was *good* for *food*, and that it was a delight to the eyes, and that the tree was to be *desired* to make one wise.

The woman resolves the conflict by making concrete decisions, *choosing*:

(1) to eat, from the options "to eat–to not eat from the tree";
(2) to eat from the tree of knowledge of good–evil, from the options "all of the trees–the tree that is in the midst of the garden";
(3) to transgress, from the options "to obey or to disobey"; and
(4) to choose to live, without knowing that she is choosing to die, since in the end there is no real alternative.

The narrator, to tell of the woman's transgression, has put her in a point of view similar to that of YHWH Elohim before the trees of the garden. She, like God, sees that the tree is good for food and pleasant to look at (agreeable) and also to be desired *to make one wise*, an extra that refers to the property of the tree. There is, however, a difference: the woman *does not accept* the imposed limit but, paradoxically, when she does eat from the tree, it causes her to immediately understand the limits (nudity).

At this point the reader has various expectations for the consequences of the transgression: the humans can be like gods, possessing knowledge of good–evil; they can die (according to God's prohibition), or they can live forever and have their eyes can be opened (according to the serpent's alternative). The reader is involved in looking at the facts of such expectations since the humans, in effect, have had their eyes opened and understand that they are surely going to die (though not immediately) and that they will be like gods (3:22). It is important that the reader understands that in the narrative the dialogue is different *before* the transgression (the human being with himself) and *after* the disobedience (YHWH, verticality and humans, horizontality).

The trait of knowledge associated with the tree is central in the depth dimension of the conflict, as indicated by its function throughout the narration and according to the meaning of ידע ("to know"), which links knowledge to experience,[50] and the merism good–evil, which covers all reality. If to know good–evil one must have experience, it would not be possible to have access to this knowledge and to become similar to God without experience. If one does not eat from the tree, it is not possible to have experiential knowledge, and without this the freedom and autonomy enjoyed by the other creatures since Gen 1 is also impossible.

3.1.2.3. The Horizontal Dimension of the Conflict

The vertical dimension of the conflict, followed sequentially by its dimension of depth, culminates in the horizontal, vast dimension. We should go back in the narration to situate the origin of the relational conflict, when the human first expresses himself to the woman. Although recognition is established through similarity, the different levels of the text allow us to see how a new type of conflict emerges on the basis of asymmetry. At the discourse level, the readers know that the *male* and the *female* are both born from one of YHWH Elohim's actions. They also know that the diversification is made here using part of the undifferentiated and passive human. At the story level, however, the male says that the woman is so called because she has been taken from him, man. The readers know that this is not so and can infer a potential conflict in the asymmetry of origin that the man attributes to the woman. They can be left to come to their own conclusions and explain the traits of the relationship as they become more explicit. In the episode of the transgression, the symmetry is maintained, as it is the woman who takes the initiative. They both, woman and man, participate in the same act. The main difference is established in the last part. If in the dialogue with the serpent the woman has been active and present on behalf of both as a human totality or duality (thus indicated by the use of the plural), at the end the narrator, in the transgression, changes to the first-person singular form of the verb, thus manifesting a differentiated process. It is the woman who experiences a change. Nothing is said of the man. Does this difference have consequences in the scenes that follow? It certainly does when looking at the narrative, because the man uses the situation to remove himself from guilt and to place the blame on the woman.

In the dialogues between YHWH Elohim and the man and YHWH Elohim and the woman, there is a human distance. In the story, the humans never speak between themselves, and in this moment their communication is

---

50. We find this to be so in Deut 1:39; 2 Sam 19:36; and, among others, Eccl 1:8–10 from the manuscripts of Qumran.

indirect: the man speaks with God about the woman, but not with her. The woman does not even speak about her companion but rather about the serpent. The story is not directly interested in the relationship between the two people but rather in the relationship that they have with YHWH Elohim and with his command.[51] Indirectly, however, we can perceive something about these gender relationships in which, almost always, almost until the end, the humans share only a common name but do not have their own.

The man's sentence, "the woman whom you gave to be with me," indicates and foreshadows the kind of relationship that was established when God introduced her in 2:22–23, a gender relationship with conjugal connotations. The 'adam now tries to resolve a conflict that began in the verticality of the relationship with YHWH Elohim through a replacing of horizontality. Following the sentence we see that the sequence "the woman whom you gave to be with me → she gave me of the tree → and I ate" causes the final action to be dependent upon the fact that God gave him a woman. The distance between the sexes, in this case, moves toward negativity. The man accuses the woman in order to present himself as a victim. YHWH Elohim does not respond because the narrative function of the dialogue is none other than to make the humans talk about the fact that they have eaten. YHWH Elohim, in effect, does not even enter into this game. He speaks directly to the woman; he questions her almost as he does 'adam. These questions have the formal structure and rhetoric of an accusation in a forensic trial (rîb) and the goal of allowing the accused to defend himself. What is interesting here is the *way* each character defends himself/herself.

Strictly speaking, God does not blame either of the actors. The woman's question, however, has to do with what 'adam just said. Does YHWH Elohim's question, "What is this that you have done?" refer to feeding 'adam from the tree, or rather that she herself has eaten from the tree? This is ambiguous. If the latter is the case, the answer that the woman gives, "the serpent tricked me, and I ate," is correct. If the question, however, refers to the fact of giving the fruit to 'adam to eat, it will be necessary, to examine the serpent's seduction of the woman and, because of this, to return to the dialogue.

In the questioning of the serpent, the text is very condensed. "Because you have done this" refers to tricking the woman. Now the reader can understand that the true problem does not reside so much in the transgression as in the trickery of the serpent. Because of this, looking at the narrative, the

---

51. YHWH Elohim' s later words about the relationship between man and woman have been read as a direct consequence of asymmetry between the sexes, thus focusing the interest of the text on this. We will have the chance to show that other coherent readings can be made from what we are now examining.

reader should return to the scene 3:1–7 in order to figure out the key to the conflict and thus understand something of the enigma of the transgression. This key is not established on the horizontal level but rather on the vertical and depth levels.

The transgression seems inevitable, but is the serpent's trickery inevitable as well? From Gen 3:14 on, the words of YHWH Elohim emphasize the negative and difficult side of the conflict oriented now toward the future:[52] an enmity between the deceitful descendants of the serpent (goddesses), who want humans to seek immortality as God's image, and the lineage of the woman. This is an enmity between *immortal* descendants and finite and mortal humanity that can give life only by at the same time accepting the discontinuity of death. In the mouth of YHWH Elohim, this appears in terms of conflict: enmity or hostility and bruising of the serpent's head by the woman and the serpent lurking for the woman's heel.

To the woman, as relates to gender, YHWH Elohim emphasizes the conflict of her reproductive responsibilities and her tension with respect to the man. To the man, the gender conflict is emphasized in another way. The reason is "because you have listened to the voice of your wife." This can refer either to listening to the woman who "told him that he was naked" or to having chosen her voice over YHWH Elohim's and having "eaten" from the forbidden tree. All of this grows and extends the conflict from the man to the environment, just as it extends in the woman from her to her descendants. The interconnectedness of all that has been created appears yet again. After this sentence, the narrative tension diminishes. We see God act caringly toward and take care of his creatures. Despite this rough discourse, he makes them clothes from fur.

In 3:20, the man names the woman. Another paradox is produced: if name giving is an action that shows superiority and gives identity, in this case things are working backwards because in the name there is already a subversion of the origin. 'Adam situates the origin in name giving. The semantic sense of the given name indicates that she, "mother of all the living," is at the beginning of not only human life.[53] If 'adam is a living being, then he also must originate from her. From our twenty-first-century perspective, this difference of levels reveals a perpetual conflict between the sexes, but we cannot know if it was understood in the same way when the story was written.

---

52. This is indicated by the mention of the earth, a flashback to the "before" in the garden and a foreshadowing of the "after."

53. Readers of all epochs perceive in this sentence the background of original female deities, themselves part of the surroundings and the myths that the editor of the book of Genesis tries to demythologize and dedivinize in these stories.

The final verses show YHWH Elohim's ironic side when they inform the reader that the humans now are similar to him in one way, thanks only to the transgression. As if YHWH Elohim felt vulnerable and needed to protect another attribute of his deity, his immortality, he expels the humans from the garden and places cherubim as guards, a subtle word game (alliteration) that has a relationship with the serpent (their tongues).

With these last verses the narrator uses YHWH Elohim's direct discourse to tell the reader that the transgression has made the humans similar to YHWH himself and that this similarity is paradoxical because the differentiated knowledge reveals their immortality to them. He furthermore states that there are two trees that stand out in the garden. One of them, the tree of life, which the humans identified as the tree of knowledge of good and evil, is only YHWH Elohim's tree, the tree of immortality.

To summarize, when looking at the conflict and relationships, we can point out that there are asymmetrical relationships between YHWH and his creatures. The serpent–woman relationship is also asymmetrical, but in the opposite way. The relationship between man–woman is symmetrical and equal when it comes to their origin (the earth) and their "species," which is characterized by their similarity with God. It is asymmetrical, however, when the man claims to be the origin of humanity and blames the woman for the consequences of the transgression. In the final scenes there is distance and rupture even though YHWH Elohim makes them equal when he throws them out of the garden and returns them to earth. The readers perceive, at the end, that the many-dimensional conflict has originated, developed, and resolved itself in the garden, a space situated between two mentions of the earth, the first when it is presented as raw material, though hostile, and the second presented as damned material and thus denoted with a different type of hostility. The humans, at the end of the last episode inside the garden, expelled, are already prepared for the 'adamah.

In the punishing sentences of the man and the woman, there is a parallel relationship between labors of the earth and the act of labor in giving birth: both oriented toward life, take place in a hostile environment, and the fruits of each action are hard won. The differentiation of roles in and of themselves does not establish gender asymmetries. The painful action of the woman giving birth is located in symmetry with the action of hard work on the land. Life, thus, is removed from any possible idealization, since pain and hard labor mark the mortal human condition and their mediation. At the same time, however, life remains linked to the expectations of the divine and also to the similarity with the divine in the humans' work as co-creators. They work the land, know good and evil, are similar to God, and sustain a discontinuous (mortal) life.

3.1.2.4. Genesis 3:16b: And He Will Rule over You?

As an excursus, I am going to linger for a moment on the presumed divine command for the submission of woman to man, a question that is somewhat dependent upon the translation and interpretation of the verb used in the last part of the sentence (3:16b).[54] The author whose thoughts I follow, John J. Schmitt, starts from a study of the context of the story in order to decide if it is correct to translate the verb מָשַׁל as "to rule," that is to say, if it is suitable in the hierarchical sense. His analysis causes him to conclude that there really are no elements in the story that would justify the introduction of a vocabulary of commands, dominion, or subjection among the humans. The action, for example, of naming the animals is more an act of recognition than of domination. The cited verb has different meanings, and it is the context that can and should decide which is correct. Schmitt contemplates three possible meanings: the translation "to exercise dominion over," adopted in general by many translations (including the Septuagint and the Peshitta), is, according to him, already ideologically colored; "to mock," another documented translation, does not fit the context at all; and, finally, "to be equal to, to be like," is considered most suitable for the context of Gen 3. The meaning of מָשַׁל "to be like, to be equal to" appears in the niphal, hiphil and hithpael; "to use as a proverb, to speak allegorically" (qal and piel) and "to dominate, to have domination over" (qal and hiphil) are also represented in Phoenician and in Modern Hebrew. The sense of "to rule" appears in political contexts and in those of royal orders, contexts that are far removed from Gen 3:16 and for which reason they should be discarded. "To be equal to, to be similar to," on the other hand, expresses reciprocity and because of this fits the context and is the interpretation most faithful and respectful to the story. This would bring us to the following translation of the verse:

> Your desire (impulse) will be toward your husband, and he will feel the same way (will be similar to you, with you).

3.1.3. Genesis 3: The Paradox of Mortality

When we study Gen 1, we understand the importance of the paradox during the emergence of life. This importance also holds true in the second creation story. The process through which humans become acquainted with reality includes the paradox of evolving in life only through death and ending in

---

54. John J. Schmitt, "Like Eve, Like Adam: *mšl* in Gen. 3:16b," *Bib* 72 (1991): 1–22.

mortality only by first passing through life. Life appears at the end, as an open system, in the scene of expulsion from the garden, thanks to mortality. Interpretations of this section have been so marked by the paradox's mortal side that they have often forgotten its other part, which is the opening of life and its complexity. Because of this, the paradox's function has never been fully explained, and the novelties that could spring from it have not been explored. The interpretation of this last episode as a divine punishment has had the effect of hiding more interesting interpretations.[55]

The divine prohibition of eating from the tree of life and the tree of knowledge of good and evil is in itself paradoxical: ingesting life becomes a mortal act. The observation of reality confirms the divine command—as living undoubtedly implies dying. In this way, keeping in mind that the command is not reversible, the prohibition transforms itself into a warning (unthreatening) that in itself is impossible to follow. If the humans have come into life, how can they not eat from that tree? The complexity arises because neither the readers nor the characters know anything about this. If in truth it is only a tree of life, there is no reason not to eat from it. If it has other characteristics, it would be necessary to know about them first. This is an enigma. Since no more information about the tree is given, it is possible to understand the conjunction that separates it from that which follows (the tree of knowledge of good and evil) as a link of subordination. Only by agreeing to knowledge can the characters discover anything about the tree of life, about the mystery of life. When the woman eats from the tree and gives in to this knowledge, a dimension of the mystery is revealed to her. Very far from resolving the mystery, this dimension has the function of opening a complex and conflictive world, as we all of course understand.

The narrator, from the beginning, shows the profile of a divine character who is honest with his creatures, which is to say that he is paradoxical himself. The paradox is seen in the process through which human life is created. The reader or listener realizes as the story progresses that the process is positive and careful and that there is an abundance of symbols of vitality in a continuing and growing sequence. As the story advances, life in the garden grows, and the human being does, too, in an emerging progressive complexity. It is in this sense that we can explore the function of *nudity* in the story.

In the first episode, the reader has no information about how the human is presented. The first bit of information is given at the end of Gen 2, when the

---

55. The character through which these paradoxes of life through death and life as a complex open system can best be explored is the woman, and it is with her that we will work. I will focus on the paradox of Gen 3.

humans have been differentiated into genders and the man has recognized the woman as belonging to his species. Information about nudity is related to an absence of knowledge, something that signals the fact that in the following episode there will be a new advancement of life. The term is multipurpose. Its phonetic alliteration with "cunning" anticipates a link that is not further explained, that invites the active participation of the reader in its interpretation. Cunning, a trait linked to the serpent, informs the reader that this creature is in possession of knowledge. Without knowledge, there is no cunning. If the humans are naked and they do not know so, they therefore also lack cunning.

3.2. Discourse Level

Human life emerges and is sustained when knowledge or competence needed for life emerge and are transmitted. The story of Genesis says one thing about the quality of human life as linked to differentiated knowledge. The woman, as a representative of all that is human, has the choice between *differentiated and conflictive knowledge* and *undifferentiated knowledge of immortality*.[56] The divine forbiddance precedes the acquisition of this knowledge. The only way to realize the freedom that the humans have is to break with this command. But why does the story of creation relate these questions to the emergence of human life? The answer brings us to an extratextual connection that will allow us to examine the historical and cultural context in which the narrator seems to situate himself and from which he speaks to his audience. It is a background of religious practices and of reflections on wisdom, the temptation of idolatry, and the resulting abandonment of YHWH, a background of myths and stories of gods and goddesses who are active participants in creation, a background that is polemically referred to. Many of these reflect the interpretations that have been made and continue to be made about Gen 2–3. We will focus our attention on the information that relates to the serpent and the woman, which call forth a historical, cultural, and religious background of female deities.

3.2.1. YHWH (יהוה) and HWH (חַוָּה): The Demythologization of Eve

There are many terms in the story that sound similar to these: the Tetragrammaton (יהוה), the verb "to be" or "to become" (היה), the verb and the noun "to live, life" (חיה), and the name that the man imposes on his wife (חַוָּה).[57]

---

56. John Dominic Crossan, "Felix Culpa and Foenix Culprit: Comments of 'Direct and Third Person Discourse in the Narrative of the Fall' by Hugh C. White," *Semeia* 18 (1980): 107–11, especially 110.

57. Eve is not a typical name for Israelite women. Some believe that this is due to the

"Eva," *hawwah* (חַוָּה), is a noun that has been made an adjective, from the Phoenician-Canaanite root *hwt*, which can mean both "something living" and "vitality."[58] At the time of the writing of the book, it would have been easy to interchange the letters ו and the י. Although the root alludes to "life," if the ו is exchanged for a י, the similarity to the verbal root היה ("to be," a verb of identity) is surprising, as is its phonetic similarity to YHWH, the Tetragrammaton. In the second part of 3:20 there is a phonetic predisposition to this root (verb and adjective "living"). This information allows us to consider possible relationships between God, in reference to YHWH, and the woman, in reference to *hawwah*. God, YHWH, is possessor of immortal life and creator of human life as mortal and finite. The woman, Eve, *hawwah*, possesses this finite life given by God and is capable of generating life. Thus she is participating in creation. There is eternal and continuous life. The first, divine, is excluded from death; the second, to continue life and make the chain of succession possible, needs death. Later divine discourse emphasizes the painful, conflictive, and mortal side of the knowledge of good and evil, and it obviously links mortality to the life of the woman and, from her, human life.[59]

3.2.2. Reception of Female Deities in the Woman of Genesis 2–3

Different scholars believe that the serpent's motives, the woman as the first to succumb to his trickery, the tree of life, and YHWH Elohim's discourse of punishment to the humans would be unthinkable without a controversial and tense social, cultural, and religious background[60] in which different questions

---

foreign nature of the name. This is what Antonio Bonara opines in "La creazione: Il respire della vita e la madre dei viventi in Gen 2–3," *PSV* 5 (1982): 9–22. It does not seem to me, however, to be a convincing answer because this explanation presupposes, mistakenly, that Israel did not adopt Canaanite names, while the Hebrew Bible is full of them. My hypothesis is that the name was not used, regardless of its potential Phoenician-Canaanite root, due to its similarity to the Tetragrammaton, which was not pronounced because of its holiness.

58. Some scholars have tried to identify the Hebrew term *hawwah* with the Aramaic *hewya'*, which means "serpent," but there is no clear evidence for this. See A. J. Williams, "The Relationship of Genesis 3:20 to the Serpent," *ZAW* 89 (1977): 357–74. With all this, some authors (e.g., Vriezen) believe that there is a similarity between *hawwah* and the name given in Phoenician culture to the serpent-goddess.

59. It is part of patriarchal anthropology to consider women as closer to life and death. See also Isabel Gómez-Acebo, ed., *Relectura del Génesis* (Bilbao: DDB, 1997).

60. Thus G. Borgonovo, "La donna di Gen. 3 e le donne di Gen. 6,1–4: Il ruolo del femenino nell'eziologia metastorica," *RStB* 1–2 (1994): 71–99, found a highly apologetic context, a confrontation between two or more religious visions (the Baalistic and the Yahwistic) that could be expressed through the following questions: Which is the path of

such as the covenant, the cult, God, and the differentiation of roles by sex participate. There are, additionally, mythical motives that considerably predate the era of the audience being addressed by the narrator. These motives date back to cultures and religions, myths and symbols from Mesopotamia and Babylonia.

In old Babylonia female deities were often assigned the task of carrying out the divine decision to create the man. These were mother-goddesses such as Aruru, Mami, Nammu, Nihursanga, Nininsina, Ninah, and Nintu. Nintu, in the myth of Atrahasis, is also considered to be the *lady of all of the gods*. Ishtar, without a doubt, is important as well, as she is a warrior-goddess but also considered to be the goddess of love and fecundity. A *curiosity* for learning is attributed to her. Ishtar, pushed by a desire to know the conditions in which her sister Ereskigal is living, descends to hell. This descent brings with it a self-condemnation to death and causes the reality on earth to become out of balance. To reestablish equilibrium, she must leave someone, in her name, in hell. From this story we are interested in the relationship between the woman and her curiosity, even though in the myth this is considered to be a weakness and not a positive quality.

Mesopotamia's mythology, in the myth of Gilgamesh, exalts the wisdom of two courtesans. The first, the one who brings the savage Enkidu into civilization, is linked to culture, ethics, and religion. The other, Siduri, is seen as a cultic prostitute at the temple and related to sexuality.[61] The name of Ninti

---

knowledge that leads to life? Which god assures life and fecundity, the future and possession of the earth? According to Bogonovo, this text could not have been written without the problem of religious confrontation that developed in Canaan in the ninth-seventh centuries B.C.E., without the symbolic constellation instituted by Hosea over the baalistic cults and without the exhortation of Deuteronomy. He believes that this explains why the prophets of the eighth–seventh centuries B.C.E. did not pay attention to these texts, while others, such as those of the book Ben Sira (90–92), did. When Israel is identified with a woman (as an unfaithful spouse), the author continues, this explains why she is the first to disobey the divine prohibition, although the narrator quickly changes the symbolic register and introduces Adam so that the transgressor becomes the human couple. As he explains it, it is the same in the Canaanite Baalistic religion, where fecundity has an important role and women are important protagonists in the cults, unlike in Israel. It is my judgment that the author forces this explanation in some points and, in particular, in his conclusions, but he places himself in the position of those who believe that they see a background of controversial idolatry in the story, with some points in common with the prophetic tradition of Israel.

61. Luigi Cagni, "Miti di origine, miti de caduta e presenza del femminino nella loro tradizione interpretativa: Considerazione sui dati della traduzione sumerica e babilonese-assiria," *RStB* 1–2 (1994): 13–46. Ishtar, it should not be forgotten, is an ambiguous feminine deity, among other things, in her relationship with Tammuz, who is at once son and lover. Although there are profound differences with the figure of the woman in Gen 2–3,

(NIN.TI) from Gilgamesh is literally "woman of the rib" and "woman of life." It is not difficult to find an echo of a motif that would be familiar to the implicit reader in the scene of the creation of woman, Gen 2:21–22.

This tradition, which goes back to the second millennium B.C.E., relates the same name given to the woman, Eve, to a goddess called Hebat or Hepat in Hurrian.[62] She was considered to be the mother-goddess par excellence, and in the Amarna letters of the Jebusite king of Jerusalem she was called "servant of Hepat." This goddess invaded the Hittite pantheon as the supreme feminine goddess and entered Asia Minor around 1250 B.C.E. It was Puduhepas, consort of King Hattulisi, who is said to have introduced her cult and was herself the priestess of this goddess.[63] Hutena and Hutellura, also mythological creators of humanity, followed Hebat. Hebat is also associated with the Babylonian goddess Ishtar.[64] The name Hebat appeared in Hittite and Hurrian writings until a new linguistic group invaded Asia Minor and Hebat was joined to the Phrygian Cybele. This goddess, whose origins according to iconography date back to 5500 B.C.E., is also related to Eve. She maintained her identity for four centuries as the mother of gods and human beings. In Egypt, Eve was identified with Isis, an ancient goddess who was again recuperated during the Hellenistic period. Her cult was popular in the entire Mediterranean zone, including Ephesus, and she was also related to serpents.[65]

When looking at the goddess Hebat, we should emphasize, in addition to her name, her association with Hittite rituals. A woman who practiced these was known as a "wise woman" or "ancient woman." The relationship with wisdom and the association with a creating power (maternity), in the different versions, reveals a powerful deity of origins. The woman in Gen 2–3 thus evokes a background that links the female character with goddesses and the protagonists of myths related to wisdom, creation, and maternity understood as the origin of life, culture, and the sexual dimension of reality. The interpretation of these links depends more upon the concrete cultural factors of the empirical reader, in different historical periods, than on the evocations

---

some elements can be seen as part of the background. The Eve we see in 3:20 is considered to be the wife and mother of the man, because the sentence "she is the mother of all the living" includes him.

62. Richard Clark Kroeger and Catherine Clark Kroeger, *I Suffer Not a Woman: Rethinking 1 Timothy 2:11–15 in Light of Ancient Evidence* (Grand Rapids: Baker, 1992), 153. The Hurrian language has adopted the Semitic name Eve, not the other way around.

63. With the impetus and enthusiasm of this queen, the new deity was assimilated with the great sun-goddess Arina, the main goddess in the Hittite Pantheon. See *ANET*, 393 and 398.

64. *ANET*, 89, 205.

65. Apuleius, *Metamorphoses*, 11.3–4.

themselves. In some cases this will cause exaltation, and in others it will be more denigrating.[66]

3.2.3. The Traditions of the Serpent and the Demythologization of the Goddesses

Another main tradition in the background refers to the anticipatory evocations of the serpent. Let us remember a few things: God positions himself with regard to the relationship between the serpent and the woman; the *trick* refers to the fact that the mortal aspect of differentiated knowledge—the enigma of life—is hidden from the humans. The snake is linked to immortal life, while the woman believes that eating from the tree of knowledge of good and evil will bring her to immortality, though upon eating she will only discover mortality. Both the descendants of the immortal serpent and the mortal woman are opposed to each other in hostility. This hostility becomes a sort of *mark* on the human descendants. It is evident that the serpent as a character is not chosen at random as an association with the mysteries of the two episodes. When he condemns the serpent and reduces it to dust, YHWH Elohim inflicts the maximum humiliation upon it. Its deceit, which appeals to the deity as the only immortal, is greatly punished. What this deceit brings forth, however, will never be completely resolved because it is fated to follow at the heel of the woman and thus all humankind. It would not be difficult to associate the serpent with a deity.

---

66. This is indicated, for example, by the process of the negativization of the figure of Eve, in a line of late Jewish literature and in the first centuries of Christianity, including Paul. Together with a tradition in Judaism that saw and interpreted Eve as the first of the mothers of Israel (see Tg. Gen. 3:1), there are commentaries on Gen 2:22 that speak of Eve's beauty as a seductive element that drove the serpent to make her his own and to plan the murder of Adam (see Gen. Rab. 18:6 for 2:25 and 3:1). An echo of this goes back to Ireneaus in the second century (*Adversus haereses* 1.30.7). She was then considered to be a tempting, seductive figure who introduced evil into the world. In this respect, see Aristide Serra, "Valenze creative e distruttive della figura di Eva nel giudaismo antico," *RStB* 1–2 (1994): 179–99; and Romano Penna, "Il discorso paolino sulle origini umane alla luce di Gen. 1–3 e le sue funzioni semantiche," *RStB* 1–2 (1994): 233–39. See also Helen Schüngel-Straumann, *Die Frau am Anfang: Eva und die Folgen* (Frauenforum; Freiburg im Breisgau: Herder, 1989), who has been a pioneer in investigating this misogynistic reception history. Her monograph has been republished in various editions. See also Irmtraud Fischer, "Egalitär entworfen—hierarchisch gelebt: Zur Problemtaik des Geschlechterverältnisses und einer genderfairen Anthropologie im Alten Testament," in *Der Mensch im Alten Israel: Neue Forschungen zur alttestamentlichen Anthropologie* (ed. Bernd Janowski and Kathrin Liess; Herders Biblische Studien 59; Freiburg im Breisgau: Herder 2009), 265–98.

In Enuma Elish, the goddess Tiamat, within the myths of creation, is represented as a dragon or some form of a snake. In ancient myths she appears associated with a primordial and central tree (Etana, Gilgamesh, the tree of Huluppu), wrapping herself around its trunk.[67] The serpent could be considered the guardian of the tree and also the one who destroys it. The animal is generally considered to be a representation of the eternal battle between good and evil or, more appropriately, between order and chaos. The serpent is an ambiguous figure, symbolizing both death (snake bite) and curative powers (Num 21:4–9), seduction, sexuality, and fertility, with the ability to represent both the masculine (phallic symbol) and the feminine. In the Eastern Mediterranean, serpents are seen as guardians of cities.[68]

The serpent takes on multiple meanings in the myths of the ancient Near East. According to Joseph Campbell, four symbolic values are given to the snake. The first, *eternal youth*, is most likely supported by the shedding of skin. In Gilgamesh, it appears as a thief that robs the protagonist of the plant of life. Second, the snake appears linked to *wisdom*, as found in Egypt, where it is associated with the search for immortality.[69] In Gen 2–3 its astuteness is linked to knowledge or to an opening of eyes, synonymous with possessing wisdom,[70] a trait present in almost all cultures. Third, the snake is a symbol of *chaos*. In addition to Tiamat, in Ugaritic mythology Leviathan was repre-

---

67. This motif has been conserved in a large part of the pictorial Western Christian tradition in the representation of the scene of Gen 3:1–7. It is curious that, in spite of never mentioning the place where the dialogue between the woman and the snake takes place, and never explaining completely the relationship between the snake's spot and where the tree is, a paradigmatic scene has remained: a leafy tree, full of fruits, the snake wrapped around its trunk with its head facing the woman, who is standing with an apple of which she is just about to take a bite or has just bitten.

68. Lowell K. Handy, "Serpent," *ABD* 5:1113–17.

69. Linked with wisdom in the Egyptian context, the goddesses Thermuthis-Remenutet and Ma'at appear represented at times as a cobra like those seen on the crowns of the pharaohs. According to Merlin Stone, *When God Was a Woman* (San Diego: Harcourt Brace Jovanovich, 1976), the snake-goddess, Wadjet (from the pre-Dynastic period, patron of Lower Egypt whose main sanctuary was in Buto, in the Delta), was conserved in other later female deities. The most interesting of the Egyptian goddesses was Ma'at, who symbolized the order of the universe, all that was righteous and good. According to Stone (*When God Was a Woman*, 198ff.), the serpent in the ancient Near East was a feminine symbol rather than a phallic symbol and was associated with wisdom and vision more than with fertility. For more information on the relationship between goddesses and snakes, see Joseph Campbell, *The Masks of God* (New York: Arkana 1991).

70. In Jer 32:19 we read: "Great in council … for thine eyes are open upon all the ways of the sons of men: to give every one according to his ways, and according to the fruit of his doings" (עַל־כָּל־דַּרְכֵי בְּנֵי אָדָם לָתֵת לְאִישׁ כִּדְרָכָיו וְכִפְרִי מַעֲלָלָיו). The generic human

sented as an enormous snake. In Gen 2–3 the serpent does not appear as a contrast to chaos, but certainly, in a supposed attempt at order, he confuses the woman. Chaos, in this case, cannot be qualified in any way as negative in the good–evil opposition, since all of this takes place in a premoral environment in which YHWH Elohim himself has put the tree of knowledge. Fourth and last, the serpent can be considered a symbol of *fecundity and fertility*, as observed in the Canaanite context.

Other associations have to do with the episode of the bronze serpent in Num 21:4–9, erected by Moses to cure snake bites. This is also related to 2 Kgs 18:4, in which the king Hezekiah eliminates the snake from the temple in Jerusalem.[71] In the episode of the desert, the bronze snake is not a substitute for YHWH, nor does it appear to threaten YHWH's divine sovereignty. It is more likely that it would be in line with minor divinities, intermediaries, or mediators that have mundane functions such as curing the sick. The bronze serpent that was destroyed by Hezekiah was most likely a deity linked to curative powers and formed part of the Jewish pantheon. This is the only case in the Bible where the bronze serpent is linked to the image of a minor deity. There is no biblical evidence that connects the image of the bronze serpent with fertility cults. The most probable motifs linked to the serpent are those of wisdom, immortality, sexuality in general (not exclusively feminine), and fertility. These are plausible connections for the implicit reader both in the figure of the serpent and in the figure of the woman, who, like the snake, desires knowledge and immortality. Due to her name (Eve), she will be linked with the maternal role (fertility) and the process of converting order into chaos and then once again into order.

The implied reader in Gen 2–3 sees everything that in other cultural epochs had been associated with superhuman reality beginning to demythologize and then associates this with the emergence of humans. The task of demythologization in these evocations is, thus, more creative than destructive. The woman incorporates into herself attributes that in other contexts were given to gods, to superhuman beings. At the same time, the origin and quality of immortal life is reserved for YHWH only. Finally, let us not forget that in Gen 3:1–7 the woman, using the plural and the dual forms (as did the serpent), is the representative of diverse and differentiated humanity (man

---

is mentioned first and then the man (something that specifies the first, though it does not exclude the other gender).

71. As concerns Nehushtan, the name given to the bronze snake in the temple of Jerusalem, it has been speculated that he was a deity from the Jebusite cult in Jerusalem that David took over once again after conquering the city. It is not, however, easy to associate with the episode in the book of Numbers.

and woman). Humanity becomes *like* gods, having the knowledge of good and evil, but cannot be God. The woman and her lineage (*hawwah*) have forever chosen the path of the tree of life, guarded by nonhuman beings.

4. A New Story of Origins: Genesis 4:1–2, 17–24 and 6:1–4

The evolution of life in the context of its origins and in relation to woman reappears in three more texts, which we can examine only briefly. Eve gives birth to Cain and Abel in 4:1–2; two women, Adah and Zillah, appear in a masculine genealogy, 4:17–24, and the liaison between sons of gods and the daughters of human beings will in 6:1–4 become the reason for the flood, which is than followed by a re-creation.

4.1. The Divine Son: Genesis 4:1–2

Eve reappears in Gen 4:1. When it seemed as though her demythologization was complete, the narrator tells us that she gave birth to her first son, Cain. Eve herself explains his name with a new mythical allusion: "I have produced a man with YHWH." The explanation can be understood both as a rebellion against the father of the son and as a challenge to the definition of a patriarchal God in itself. As a rebellion against the man, she reestablishes the *order* of the beginning in the creative covenant with God: while the man, in Gen 2:23, has interpreted the woman as originating from him ("for out of the man this one was taken"), she now says the opposite, ironically confirming the name of Eve given by him: she creates a man with YHWH! The combination of the *'ish* ("man"), to name a newborn, and the verb *qnh* ("to produce, create, acquire"), used to speak of the creation of YHWH, allows for a background appearance of a heterosexual divine-human couple: Eve and YHWH. The alliance with humanity is established between God and the woman.

We can identify this character, her three actions, and her interior monologue with the woman in Gen 2–3 because of her name. The last episode introduced us to the woman in a double dimension. In the positive dimension she realizes her similarity to God in respect to knowledge, and in the negative or finite dimension she experiences suffering that will accompany the generations of life. The verbs "to be pregnant" (הרה) and "to give birth" (ילד) appeared in God's mouth and now return in the voice of the narrator, preceded by the verb of sexual knowledge, completing the divine word in 3:16. The knowledge acquired by Eve when she ate the fruit ("Behold, the human being is become as one of us, to know good and evil") is completed in the relational dimension of the couple and causes the generation of life. The text thus unites the act of knowing (ידע) with the sexual relationship and with human life (ילד, הרה). It suggests that the man actively fulfills this knowledge and the woman carries out her actions, thus confirming the differentiation of gender roles: the sexual initiative of the man and the giving birth to life of the woman.

There is an ellipsis in the text relating to the manner described by God in Gen 3:16, since nothing is said in Gen 4 about the fatigue and pain that Eve suffers when giving birth. The indirect consequences of finality and morality, however, are narrated. Genesis 4 tells of the experience of rupture (death) in the continuity of life, a type of death that originates in the human being (not in the circumstances). In Gen 4 we are witness to two human actions: that of the woman creating life with God's help and that of a man who produces death by defying YHWH. In this way the story presents us with two opposite characters and two opposite actions that still seem to be parallel: the woman gives life; the man, her son, takes it away. After the murder of Cain, we find ourselves with Eve giving birth to Seth. This second moment of the continuation of life is carried out after, and in spite of, the rupture that has come with death. The woman, however, in this hiatus does not appear. She is still connected, however, almost exclusively with the giving of life—almost exclusively, that is, because Eve displays knowledge in the act, a capacity for discernment and interpretation upon naming, not in identifying animals, but a human being. She begins, thus, cognitive mechanisms thanks to which knowledge will be possible. She carries out with her son what her husband had done with her: name giving. About the man, the narrator informs us; about the woman, we learn by her own interior monologue. Eve learned to interpret in her dialogue (or dramatized monologue) with the serpent. Now she advances in a direct interior monologue because the narrator wants his reader to enter into the interior world of the character.

4.1.1. Cain's Name

Cain's name has been the subject of many studies. In the Hebrew Bible there are other recurrences of the term (see Num 24:22; Judg 4:11; 2 Sam 21:16) whose meaning has been interpreted as "one who works metal," a metal forger, or "one who works with his hands" in a more general way. The root, in effect, has to do with metal workers, although the Hebrew could have chosen another of the many words for this type of work. The term must be understood in its context. There are people who think that it is a personal name that references a tribe. We can affirm, however, that Cain here is not the same as in 4:17ff., and it is not the same as the Kenites.

Keeping in mind the context of Gen 4:1–2, we can translate it more as "acquired," derived from the verb *qnh* (קנה) in the literal sense of "formed," a formed or, better said, "created," being, as translated by the verb in Prov 8:22.

This would explain the use of "man" (adult) or 'ish instead of "child" (יֶלֶד),
since 'ish is never used to refer to a newborn. The gender and the person have
already appeared supporting the narrator's sentence in Gen 2:15 and the man
in 2:23 (although in the latter case, we see this in an opposite way, since 'ish
comes from 'ishah). It also explains the concrete and exclusive reference to
YHWH, according to the already explained relationship with Eve (§3.2.1) cre-
ation/generation of life. The particle אֶת־ is more difficult because it is never
used as a mediation particle "with the help of." It could be interpreted in a
circumstantial sense ("with"), referring to the cooperation between YHWH
and the woman, where YHWH would be the co-subject, but it is always used
by God attending to the humans and not the other way around. The most adequate translation in the context would be "together with." The difficulty, however, continues, and this last explanation should not be considered definitive.

The parallelism between 2:23 and 4:1b lies in the reaction and narcissis-
tic relationship that the human establishes with the first being that is similar
to himself. In Gen 2–3 it was the man who began to build from this nar-
cissism; nothing is said of the woman. Here in 4:1, on the other hand, she
appears explicitly, with some questions that are difficult to answer: Why has
the woman not been able to structure her similarity with respect to the man
when she can do it in respect to the son?

4.2. GENESIS 4:17–24: ADAH AND ZILLAH

In 4:1 we have seen a recovery, in spiral, of the stories of the beginnings of
human life, which are followed by the well-known story of the first human
crime. The violence of two male brothers, Cain and Abel, is put in opposition
to the figure of Eve, who conceives children for this world in a close relationship with God himself. The woman generates life. The men kill life. The world
continues. In a dizzying rhythm, at the end of the terrible story of Cain, the
text of Genesis tells us of a genealogy that goes from fathers to sons. If up until
this moment the succession of generations emerge from Eve, continuing to
conceive and bear sons, now, in Gen 4:17–18, a list of male generations starting from Cain is introduced without citing the name of his wife. These people,
with Cain at the head, create and organize the city. Women become invisible.
Once the list ends, another narration begins that again advances the human
story. This time succession is narrated by women. The wives of Lamech appear,
conceive, and bear characters who will initiate culture.

The readers who have had the sensation of being present at beginnings
that have been based upon violence and death now find themselves again
with women who continue to transmit life. Everything seems to begin again.
Lamech's wives, Adah and Zillah, create sons. Adah gives birth to Jabal and

Jubal. Jabal is a shepherd, just like the murdered Abel. Jubal is the father of musicians. For her part, Zillah gives birth to Tubalcain, who makes tools of brass and iron, and to Naamah, his sister, of whom nothing is said about her trade. The shepherds and musicians initiate human culture and civilization. With the tool forger we see the origin of a new type of work that does not involve women. Once the text finishes describing the feminine task of giving birth, mentioned as an aside, Lamech takes the stage and sings a heroic song for his wives. In this song violence and vengeance are presented as the fundamental traits of heroism. Women and men are unable to find the common ground between them. The promise and possibility of life and a pacific and creative culture are threatened constantly by violence. The hero *uses* creativity. Music and rhythm, in the end, are tools at the service of vengeance, death, and the law of an eye for an eye.

We are able to deduce from the text:

(1) Men and women contribute to life and advance history in different ways: women give birth, in the greater majority to male children; men occupy themselves with civilization. The patriarchal point of view makes woman visible as those who create life by giving birth, while it shows men to be the generators of culture and civilization.

(2) Women and men seem to understand the continuity of life in different ways. Women see it as physical succession, men as creativity. The patriarchal point of view, in the biblical text, uses life given by women to feed the ego of heroes.

(3) Lastly, heroism is understood as vengeance, destruction, and death. Women appear as mute witnesses of this. What they think, feel, and want is left unknown.

4.3. DAUGHTERS OF MEN: GENESIS 6:1–4

What we have been able to deduce from Gen 4:17–24 brings us to an understanding of gender themes that is later repeated in another conflictive story. The entire fifth chapter of Genesis is dedicated to listing new genealogies. Thus we arrive at Gen 6, which begins with a summary in which the genealogical line (which is always masculine in Israel) enters a strange phrase:

> And it came to pass, when men began to multiply on the face of the earth ['adamah], and *daughters were born unto them* [emphasis added].

The narrator places himself clearly in the male point of view when he adds:

that the sons of God [Elohim, plural] saw that the daughters of human beings ['adam] were beautiful, and they took wives for themselves, whomever they chose.

The sons of gods may choose. They choose beautiful women for themselves. The result of cohabitation between the sons of gods and the daughters of men is the existence of *giants and warriors, the heroes.*

Claus Westermann, among others, believes that the goal of these verses is to describe the origin of the heroes as men of prestige or renown.[72] The genealogy in 6:1–2 is not, as normally happens, a genealogy of characters with their own names but rather a genealogy of groups. The warriors and giants are the result of the union of the two groups, the sons of gods and the daughters of men. Through narrative elements and aspects of Canaanite mythical culture (sons of gods, giants…) it is explained *from where* these warriors come, as they are very important to Israel's history, and also to humanity in general.

The story has only ever referred to a creature (and that indirectly) as "son/daughter of God/gods" (Elohim, plural) in Gen 4:1. The term 'elohim (Gen 1), different from YHWH (Gen 2–3), is used with frequency to underline what is common to the deity in his many forms and also to designate false gods. If this is so, then the expression with which we are working, given its context and difference from the rest of Genesis, brings us to consider it in a negative way. "Sons of" Elohim would be men with divine pretensions, a powerful *class* that would consider itself to be superior, with the possibility and opportunity to exercise its power. This display of power would be directed at women. The narrator places the reader squarely in the male point of view. They are the ones who "see" and then capriciously "take" women whom they consider to be beautiful.[73] What functions do these descendants of gods and giants have?

The sons of god are a potentially destructive *class* or category who take control of beautiful women without any respect to social or institutional limits that regulate sexual relationships and the chain of generations. The relationship between this abuse of power and destructive violence is interesting. The story criticizes, at the beginning of human history, the existence of warriors who are born from a possessive and unlimited masculine desire for beauty in women. The brief story in Gen 1–11, which occupies itself with human ori-

---

72. For more information on the mythological motives in this section, see Westermann, *Genesis.*

73. This is not the only sequence in biblical stories in which a powerful man *sees* a beautiful woman and *takes her* without any more consideration. This conduct is not approved of by YHWH. It is the typical behavior of characters such as the pharaoh (Gen 12:10) and kings such as David (2 Sam 11), a motif of patriarchal and monarchical stories.

gins, threats that come from violence, and the need for limits, presents powerful males as dangerous creatures and indicates that this background exists in
every warrior. YHWH intervenes by imposing limits of death, curtailing life's
time. He warns of the danger and possibility of extinguishing life "because the
earth was filled with violence." It is then that God sends the flood, so that the
world, the life it holds, and history can be born again in the waters. The story
about the sons of gods and the daughters of men indicates that warriors are a
dangerous class, the product of an uncontained desire that is manifest in the
way that they see women.

The entire story of Israel will show the close relationships between desire
and possession and between sex and violence against women. Some authors,
using a patriarchal logic, indicate that it is the beauty of the women that awak-
ens the desire of violent possession in men. The text, however, emphasizes the
fact that this is a male perception and a male point of view. The readers only
know what their point of view tells them about these women: that they were
beautiful and that they ended up as the wives of those who conquered them.
The guilt for the action is assumed by the recipient of the action. It is the men
themselves who have given weight to something as gratuitous and fortuitous
as the beauty of certain women. In the stories that follow in Genesis, the role
of the beauty of women such as Sarah, Rebekah, and Rachel, to name but a
few, is important for understanding this discussion. They are presented by the
narrator as threats to the stability of the patriarchs' family, while the patriarchs themselves are excused from guilt, requiring sympathy, complicity, or
an understanding pardon from the reader. On the other hand, the narrator
will call for the harsh judgment of female characters that, among their faults,
possess a beauty that alters the characters of the men who fall for them. Things
change radically when gender roles are reversed, and it is Joseph, the son of
Jacob, who is the beautiful one and the one who desires him is Potiphar's wife.

4.3.1. The Gender of Those Who See

Up to this point the relationships between *perception* and *beauty* present a
vivid contrast. In Gen 1 the one who *sees* is Elohim. Each time that creation
springs from his word, the text says that Elohim "sees" (ראה) and that what
he sees is "good" (טוב). Elohim sees the beauty of his work, he takes pleasure
in it, and then he abandons it freely to its own will. In Gen 3:6, the one who
"sees" (ראה) is the woman. She sees that the fruit of the tree of knowledge of
good and evil is "good" (טוב) to eat, pleasurable to look at, and desirable in her
quest for knowledge. She then "takes" (לקח) the apple, eats, and feeds the man.
Thanks to the sequence to see, to take, and to eat, the humans become similar
to Elohim in their possession of this knowledge of good and evil. Finally, the

sons of Elohim in Gen 6:1–4 "see" (ראה). They see "beautiful women" (תבט),
and they capriciously and freely "take" (לקח) them. That is to say, they take
them without their consent, and probably violently. The sequence of these
subjects' appearance is interesting: (1) God, (2) woman, (3) sons of gods. For
the last group, the women change from perceptive subjects (ones who can see)
to objects of perception (they are seen). There is a double consequence: they
are degraded and lose their status as "daughters of gods" or as being similar
to Elohim. Now they are "daughters of men." To summarize, some characters
are degraded while others are genealogically praised. The power to take is
sacrificed to men's perception. Women's beauty is given power, in exchange
for their appearance here as innocent victims. More than thirty centuries of
posterior history manifest the persistence of this dynamic.

Today's marketing testifies to the ambiguous lure that is some women's
beauty. We see that these women are given, deceitfully, incredible power, like
an alibi used to legitimize the insatiable and unlimited desire of men and their
possessive and violent control over women, who are thought of as *daughters
of men* compared to a gender still considered to be the descendant of giants
and gods. The masculine gender continues to appear as being superior to the
feminine. While men are still more genealogically linked to cultural heritage,
the female gender continues to be linked to the different dependencies that
being *daughters of men* supposes.

ON THE SIGNIFICANCE OF THE "WOMEN TEXTS" IN THE ANCESTRAL NARRATIVES

Irmtraud Fischer
Karl-Franzens-Universität Graz

The first book of the Bible, Genesis, is to be understood from its narrative thread within the Pentateuch as "prehistory" of the history of the people of Israel, which is later presented by the books of Exodus to Deuteronomy as a "biography of Moses." In Genesis, initial consideration is given in narrative form as to how the world came into being and what significance human beings have in it. Then the real living conditions are confronted with that ideal condition of the world created by God. The primeval history in Gen 1–11 is therefore largely to be read as a conglomerate of etiological narratives that attempts to explain in a variety of ways why the world is as it is, whereby three focal points are addressed: What is the relationship between God's good creation and the evil in the world? Out of the unity of creation, how does such a variety of peoples with their various languages and settlement areas come into being? Where is Israel geographically and genealogically located within this creation?

Genesis 12–36 then tells of the theological location of Israel by presenting the development of the nation and of the surrounding nations as stories of *one* family over several generations, toward which God turns himself in an incomparable manner.[1] The Joseph story (Gen 37–50) continues the plot with the same characters. On the one hand, it creates the geographical connection

---

1. The theses that are summarized in this essay are presented in detail in several of my publications; therefore, no references will be given to individual research results in the following: Irmtraud Fischer, *Die Erzeltern Israels: Feministisch-theologische Studien zu Genesis 12–36* (BZAW 222; Berlin: de Gruyter, 1994); eadem, *Women Who Wrestled with God: Biblical Stories of Israel's Beginnings* (trans. Linda M. Malony; Collegeville, Minn.: Liturgical Press, 2005); eadem, "Gen 10–36," in *Stuttgarter Altes Testament: Einheitsübersetzung mit Kommentar und Lexikon* (ed. Erich Zenger; 2nd ed.; Stuttgart: Katholisches Bibelwerk, 2004), 32–76. An abbreviated form is published in Italian: "Donne nel Antico Testamento,"

to the Exodus narratives beginning in Egypt; on the other, the development of the nation is presented genealogically by the fact that the twelve sons of Jacob become the ancestors of the twelve tribes of Israel. In the following, the historical-critical research tradition that has been dominant in analyzing Genesis up until now will be initially examined with regard to its gender implications; in addition, the problems of historical conclusions drawn on the basis of the presentation of biblical history will be pointed out. In a second section, the linking elements in Genesis will be presented. The third part presents in narrative form the gender-relevant aspects of the individual texts and the female figures of Genesis[2] and at the same time understands Genesis as the historically grown narrative context that interprets the story of Israel's beginnings in the context of its neighbors.

1. ISRAEL WRITES THE HISTORY OF ITS ORIGINS AS FAMILY HISTORIES

In the Western tradition of history writing, the presentation of history for the longest time was concentrated on the national-political events and the great, mostly male, personalities who characterized them. Only in the last half century has the significance of social history become more and more recognized, which corrects and supplements the historical notion of important,

---

in *Donne e Bibbia: Storia ed esegesi* (ed. Adriana Valerio; La Bibbia nella Storia 21; Bologna: Dehoniane, 2006), 161–96.

2. Overviews on the "women texts" (= texts in which women are principle figures in the action) of Genesis with gender awareness are found in the historical *Women's Bible*: Elizabeth Cady Stanton and the Revising Committee, *The Women's Bible* (New York: European Publishing, 1897; repr.: Seattle: Coalition Task Force on Women and Religion, 1974), 14–67, as well as in the book commentaries in Sharon P. Jeansonne, *The Women of Genesis: From Sarah to Potiphar's Wife* (Minneapolis: Fortress, 1990); Susan Niditch, "Genesis," in *The Women's Bible Commentary* (ed. Carol A. Newsom and Sharon H. Ringe; Louisville: Westminster John Knox, 1992), 10–25; Irmtraud Fischer, "Genesis 12–50: Die Ursprungsgeschichte Israels als Frauengeschichte," in *Kompendium Feministische Bibelauslegung* (ed. Luise Schottroff and Marie-Theres Wacker; 3rd ed.; Gütersloh: Gütersloher Verlagshaus, 2007), 12–25, as well as Tamara C. Eskenazi and Andrea L. Weiss, eds., *The Torah: A Women's Commentary* (New York: URJ, 2008). Essay collections on the subject include Isabel Gómez-Acebo et al., eds., *Relectura del Génesis* (En Clave de Mujer; 2nd ed.; Bilbao: Desclée de Brouwer, 1999); Athalya Brenner, ed., *A Feminist Companion to Genesis* (FCB 2; Sheffield: Sheffield Academic Press, 1993); eadem, ed., *Genesis* (FCB 2.1; Sheffield: Sheffield Academic Press, 1998); Alice Bach, ed., *Women in the Hebrew Bible: A Reader* (New York: Routledge, 1999). All the female names of people in Genesis are compiled in Carol L. Meyers, ed., *Women in Scripture: A Dictionary of Named and Unnamed Women in the Hebrew Bible, the Apocryphal/Deuterocanonical Books, and the New Testament* (New York: Houghton Mifflin, 2000).

war-waging men through the portrayal of the living conditions at all levels of the population. Women's studies also brings in gender-specific issues and sets as its goal to no longer allow the history of just half of humanity to be deemed "official history." It also does not want to portray the reconstructed history of women as a "compensating" history but rather to revise the entire portrayal of history, thus allowing it to become a history of *all* people.

For the longest time, the biblical presentation of the history of Israel's origins as stories of families had a very difficult time being accepted as a form of "historical writing" under these circumstances. In particular, the historical-critical research tradition of the last two centuries on the book of Genesis[3] was strongly focused on the principles of an androcentric-hierarchical presentation of history, in which it saw the patriarchs as historical figures who represented their clans as tribal heads but at the same time assessed the corresponding women figures as "accessories."[4] The reconstruction of the beginnings of Israel occurred with a massive gender bias, meaning that the narrative figures were granted varying historical significance depending on their gender. The sole criterion for that type of discriminating assessment of literary characters was gender.

1.1. Gender Bias in Research: From Patriarchs to Ancestors

The family narratives of Gen 12–36 that span over three generations were described up into the 1990s as "patriarchal narratives,"[5] even though nearly every second text introduces women as central figures of the plot. Solely the male narrative figures were made out to be addressee of the promise, even if the texts bear witness to the contrary and individual women figures such as Hagar (see Gen 16:10–12) are equally addressed for divine promises. The

---

3. A history of exegesis of the Pentateuch of the church fathers up into the 1960s is offered by Henri Cazelles and Jean-Paul Bouhot, *Il Pentateuco* (Biblioteca di Studi Biblici 4; Brescia: Paideia, 1968). A series of thematic collected volumes on the history of exegesis of individual texts of Genesis appeared in the series Themes in Biblical Narrative: Jewish and Christian Traditions (ed. Robert A. Kugler, Gerhard P. Luttikhuizen, and Loren T. Stuckenburck; Leiden: Brill, 1999–): 1. *Interpretations of the Flood* (1999); 2. *Paradise Interpreted* (1999); 3. *The Creation of Man and Woman* (2000); 4. *The Sacrifice of Isaac* (2002); 5. *Eve's Children* (2003); 6. *The Fall of the Angels* (2004); 7. *Sodom's Sin* (2004); 8. *The Creation of Heaven and Earth* (2004).

4. Martin Noth, *A History of Pentateuchal Traditions* (trans. Bernhard W. Anderson; Englewood Cliffs, N.J.: Prentice-Hall, 1972), 149.

5. This tradition is virtually widespread: English-language research speaks of "patriarchal narratives," the Spanish of "historia de los patriarcas," the Italian of "storia di patriarchi," and the German of "Patriarchen-Erzählungen."

deity, who turns not only to the men but also to the women (think of Hagar in Gen 16:21 or Rebekah in 25:19–26), was called the "God of the fathers," which according to the biblical evidence is to be documented at least through the label of "the God of Abraham, Isaac, and Jacob." For the longest time, research therefore spoke of the *patriarchal* narratives, in which the God of the *fathers* gives the promises to the *fathers*.

In my postdoctoral thesis I pointed out that this terminology is not only not in accordance with the text but also brings with it a narrowing of the perspective in reference to the texts to be treated: because they are narratives of the *fathers*, no independent significance is granted to the female narrative characters and the texts in which they figure.[6] I have therefore proposed "ancestral narratives" (*Erzeltern-Erzählungen*) as a more adequate term and encouraged references to be made to the "parents of Israel" when speaking of those individuals addressed by the promises. Those who plead that in Hebrew there are no gender-neutral relationship terms and therefore the plural of אָב, "father," אָבוֹת, is to be literally translated with "fathers," should take into account that Hebrew uses the masculine plural generically to indicate both male and female individuals. Since in generic languages a whole group of the female gender is presented grammatically as masculine due to a single male individual, translation into purely masculine forms in those languages in which there are also gender-neutral terms is incorrect. The term "fathers narratives" would therefore only be correct if in the texts only men were characters in the plot. The same translation strategy also applies to "brothers," which frequently means "siblings," or to "sons," which in most cases refers to "children."

1.2. GENDER AS A CATEGORY OF EXEGESIS

The perception that manifests itself in the terminology has repercussions on exegesis. While those texts that present men as the dominant figures of the plot are interpreted as an expression of political history writing, narratives about women are trivialized. Thus, for example, the texts about the dispute between the brothers Esau and Jacob are perceived as a manifestation of the conflict between the nations of Israel and Edom. If, however, a dispute takes place between women, the female figures are then stylized as quarrelsome, petty individuals whose only cares and aspirations concentrate on the struggle for their husbands and children.[7] According to this, the constant quarrels of

---

6. Fischer, *Die Erzeltern Israels*, 1–4.

7. See Hans Jochen Boecker, *1. Mose 25,12–37,1: Isaak und Jakob* (ZBKAT 1.3;

the two men about the birthright, which, beginning with the birth itself, are expressed in three different narratives (Gen 25:24–26; 25:27–34; 27:1–41), are to be read as a literary reflection of the national-historical conflict over supremacy in the region. The dispute between sisters in Gen 29:31–30:24, however, is only occasionally interpreted as a foundational text of the egalitarianly conceived "twelve tribes nation," which in the literary form of family narratives can come about only through twelve births in one generation.

While "men's texts" are entitled to a "double bottom" in significance, in the texts where women play a central role only a one-dimensional surface is perceived. It is simply the nature of family narratives that they deal with everyday problems and take place in the small circle of close relatives. Both men and women prepare meals in Genesis (e.g., Abraham and Sarah in Gen 18; Rebekah and Esau in Gen 27), work with the herds (both Jacob and Rachel are shepherds of Laban's cattle, according to Gen 29–30) and bemoan their childlessness (e.g., Abram[8] in Gen 15; Sarai in Gen 16), but it is only with the women that exegesis sees the presence of a gender-specific desire for children.[9] Thus it is seen that one's own ideas of gender roles lead to a different exegesis of the texts. They induce exegetes to interpret the women's texts "privately," since one wants to find what appears to correspond to today's female gender stereotypes. On the other hand, the narratives in question about men contradict the stated stereotypes, because neither the concern about children nor about daily meals is perceived as typically masculine. For these narratives, one therefore comes to the conclusion that there must be a deeper dimension that is "political," otherwise they would have to be only trivial stories. The exegetical tradition that takes the women stories of the ancestral narratives literally and thus interprets them in a fundamentalist way, thereby trivializing them, yet investigates the men stories from a historical-critical perspective and interprets them as a highly theological history of the origin of Israel and its neighbors should be brought to an end. It takes the category of gender as the sole and highest criterion of exegesis and measures with two gauges for

---

Zürich: Theologischer Verlag, 1992), 74–75, which characterizes the birthing contest of the two women Leah and Rachel with keywords such as "feminine passion" and "feminine intrigues."

8. Abram and Sarai are renamed Abraham and Sarah in Gen 17:5, 15; references beyond Genesis all speak of Abraham and Sarah. Accordingly, in this article reference is made to Sarai and Abram only where texts are introduced that use these names (Gen 11–17).

9. See Claus Westermann, *Genesis 12–36: A Commentary* (trans. John J. Scullion; Minneapolis: Augsburg, 1985), 314–15. For the significance of female sexuality and motherhood in Genesis, see Carmen Bernabé Ubieta, "El Génesis: Libro de orígenes y fundamentos," in Gómez-Acebo et al., eds., *Relectura del Génesis*, 127–33.

the genders.[10] Either we are to read all the narratives in Gen 12–36 as trivial literature or *all* texts write *a political national history of Israel* and its neighbors in the form of *family narratives*, as was customary in the ancient Near East.

2. Linking Elements between Narratives of Varying Origin

The ancestral narratives offer divergent material both from a chronological and a geographical perspective that allows one to conclude differing dates of origins and derivations. The disparate texts are linked by several elements: (1) the chronological sequence is created through the genealogical linking of the characters; (2) the geographical sites are linked through itinerant notes, so-called itineraries; (3) the theological connection is made through the passing on of the divine promises from one generation to the next; and finally, (4) the common grave traditions hold the narratives together that link the four ancestral generations from Gen 12–50. I will now briefly deal with these literary hinges in the following.

2.1. Genealogies

The detailed essay by Thomas Hieke in this volume is dedicated to the genealogies of the Pentateuch and their functions, such that only the essential aspects for the ancestral narratives will be briefly outlined here.

2.1.1. Linking Back to the Primeval History and Continuation in Exodus

The ancestors of Israel are linked through genealogies with both the primeval history and with the history of the people in Egypt: Abram's father Terah is the last member of the Semite family tree according to Gen 11:24–32. Through his father, Noah's firstborn son, Shem, links the story of the Israelite people not only with the flood narratives but also with the genealogical book of אָדָם, of "humankind" per se, because the genealogy of Adam in Gen 5 ends with Noah and the prospects for his sons (5:28–32). The connection to the Exodus narratives that play in Egypt is, on the one hand, present through the account of the migration structured as the genealogy of the family of Jacob in Gen 46:8–27 and, on the other hand, in taking up this account by naming the tribal heads in Exod 1:1–5, as well as the note that Israel had become a great nation in

---

10. For more detail on this cf. Irmtraud Fischer, "Das Geschlecht als exegetisches Kriterium: Zu einer genderfairen Interpretation der Erzeltern-Erzählungen," in *Studies in the Book of Genesis: Literature, Redaction and History* (ed. André Wénin; BETL 155; Leuven: University Press, 2001), 135–152; 147–150.

Egypt. In the texts of Genesis, genealogies thus have the main functions of linking generations and, in accordance with the double bottom of the texts, also peoples. They also have the narrative function of bridging long periods of time.

2.1.2. Genealogical Notes as an Indication of the Balance of Power of the Narrating Time

The genealogies of the Bible are not to be misinterpreted as family trees as we know them from European old and established families. Rather, they are indications of the shared social identities and balances of power of the time in which the texts originated, but not of that epoch of which they tell. This also explains the fact that the Bible itself at times offers several variations of one and the same family tree.[11] Since patriarchal cultures discriminate not only according to gender but also according to age and ethnicity, genealogies are to be read accordingly.

► The social group that stands behind the parents of a clan is more important than that which is represented in the generation of the children. What does it mean, therefore, when the Abraham anchored in Judah is more important than Jacob, the ancestral father of the northern kingdom?

► The merging of two ethnic groups into one is indicated through marriage (e.g., northern and southern kingdoms in the marriage of Isaac and Rebekah). The group that stands behind the mother is, as a rule, not the dominant one (the wives of Jacob-Israel coming from Aram).

► When social units are to be introduced as equals, this is expressed in the form of genealogical family stories as a sibling relationship (the egalitarianly conceived people of the twelve tribes is founded by twelve sons of one man with several wives).

Those hypotheses on the earliest history of the Pentateuch that counted on originally independently existing sources accepted the sequence of generations as the biblical historical outline presents them, mostly as the correlation already existing in the earliest texts.[12] More recent theses tend to propose a

---

11. A classic example for this is the family tree of Jesus in Matt 1 stylized according to the decimal system of the Genesis *toledot*, which freely deals with genealogical material but particularly through the stylization achieves the purpose of linking the youngest member back to the history of the nation.

12. For the distribution of women's texts over the Pentateuch sources, see Ubieta, "El Génesis," 114–18.

narrative cycle hypothesis in which the core of the Jacob cycle was passed down independently from the older texts of the Abraham-Sarah cycle.[13] Abraham as the ancestral father of the nation—and not Jacob/Israel, who carries the name of the nation—must therefore not be an old tradition but rather suggests a time of origin in which the southern kingdom of Judah had taken over dominance in the region after the downfall of the northern kingdom of Israel. The interface forms the newly created Rebekah-Isaac cycle, which consists mostly of retellings of the Abraham-Sarah cycle.[14] If, however, in this generation the mother is presented as more dominant than the father, this points to the ongoing importance continuing into the Persian period of that group that felt connected to the former "northern kingdom traditions."[15]

2.2. Itineraries and Settlement Areas

In reference to geographical connections, itineraries serve a similar function as attributed to the genealogies in social and chronological matters. The travel routes of the primeval ancestors link the individual local traditions with one another.

Through the note on the travels of the Terah family, as it is placed before the ancestral narratives in Gen 11:31, the *origins of the nation* that are symbolized in the beginnings of its ancestors are placed *outside of the land*. Israel is not autochthonous in its land but rather came there through the challenge of God and the obedience of its ancestors (Gen 12:1, 4–5). When the family of Abram follows God's command and passes on its journey such important locations in the north of Israel such as Shechem, Bethel, and Ai, they become linked from the outset with the ancestors of the nation; northern and southern kingdom traditions are introduced as a unit from the very beginning. When Abram builds altars at these places but does not offer up sacrifices on them, only prays, this suggests a narrative period in which the famous shrines of these cities are no longer functioning. It is thus unlikely that these connecting

---

13. Informative on the current status of research is Gary N. Knoppers and Bernard M. Levinson, eds., *The Pentateuch as Torah: New Models for Understanding Its Promulgation and Acceptance* (Winona Lake, Ind.: Eisenbrauns, 2007).

14. Thus the endangering of the ancestral woman as the reception of the abandonment narratives of Gen 12; 20 as well as the well disputes with Abimelech in the context of descriptions of the wealth of the ancestors.

15. The text about the matchmaking of Rebekah, certainly to be dated to the Persian period, which is to be read as a vote on the postexilic mixed-marriage issue, shows Rebekah in the dominant role, while Isaac only appears at the end of the narratives in a few verses virtually as the recipient.

texts originated prior to the downfall of the northern kingdom in 722 B.C.E. However, through the building of altars, the entire land that Abram is crossing is symbolically taken into possession for YHWH. In this way, the claim is upheld to parts of land that were lost as settlement areas.

This path that Abraham follows from east to west is also traversed a generation later by Rebekah. She, too, is prepared to leave her land to marry the son of the line of promise (Gen 24:1–9, 58–61). In the next generation Jacob returns back on this path again to flee from Esau. On the one hand, he wants to find refuge with his mother's brother (27:43–44) and, on the other, to take a wife from this family for the line that has moved into the promised land (28:1–7).[16] After Jacob and his wives had become a large family in the east, God calls them back into the land (31:3). Thus, the geographical arc from the promised land into Mesopotamia has been traversed multiple times, the land west of the Jordan all the way into the Negev installed as the right place for the life of the nation. The right women, however, come from the part of the family living in the east—a situation that existed only in Israel's history during the postexilic period, when the mixed-marriage problem also determined the identity of the nation.

But not only the *path into exile* and back finds its prefiguration in the ancestral narratives, but also the *exodus out of Egypt*. Abraham, after moving through the land, already immediately continues on to Egypt in order to avoid a famine (Gen 12:10–20) and there comes into conflict with the pharaoh. The Egyptian ruler is struck with plagues by YHWH (see נגע in Gen 12:17; Exod 11:1) to release Sarah out of the harem and to enable the couple to return to the promised land. In a similar situation in the second generation, the migration to Egypt is explicitly forbidden (Gen 26:2). The path to Egypt, which ultimately makes the exodus necessary, is again traversed three times: Joseph must traverse it since he has been sold into slavery by his brothers (37:36), and his brothers traverse it twice under the constraint of famine (42–43). In the end, Jacob's entire family as a nation is, as it were, invited to Egypt (45:9–28). When both Jacob and Joseph insist on being buried in the grave of their ancestors in the promised land, the latent longing for life in the land is codified for future generations (living in Diaspora) at least as an ideal.

The places visited by the ancestors on their travels thus represent in a nutshell all epochs and places of Israel's narrative history. The fate of the people is already prefigured in the ancestors—or said another way: what concerns

---

16. The two justifications that complement one another in the final text surely belong to different literary levels. See, e.g., J. Alberto Soggin, *Das Buch Genesis: Kommentar* (Darmstadt: Wissenschaftliche Buchgesellschaft, 1997), 357–60.

Israel as a whole is already told by the ancestors in the form of the national history as a family history. Even the exodus and exile are already sketched out in the ancestral narratives.

2.3. Promises

Another connecting line is produced by the promises,[17] which in the present-day final text is transferred from generation to generation. If through the patrilineal succession policy the main line of the genealogy is always determined by the man's firstborn son, the transfer of promises runs contrary to this. In none of the generations created through the linking of the traditions of the northern and southern kingdoms does the promise line transfer to the patriarch's firstborn son.[18] It is not Abraham's firstborn son Ishmael (Gen 16; 17; 21) who becomes the ancestral father of the nation of promise but rather Sarah's firstborn son, Isaac (21:12; 26:3–4). Isaac's favorite son Esau (25:28) does not have a very high regard for his birthright and sells it for some lentil stew (25:29–34). He is ultimately cheated out of his father's blessing, which passes on the legitimacy of the clan (27:30–40), but already the divine birth oracle knows of his secondary status (25:23–26). As if to emphasize the dominance of Jacob, the mother's second-born and favorite son (25:28), the transfer of the promises of the parents within the context of a divine appearance (28:12–15) is added in addition to these three etiological narratives of his superiority. Nearly all of the narratives about the return of Jacob's clan to the land link the narrative thread to the legitimization of the second born as the principal heir of the promise and of the blessing (31:3–4; 32:28–29 [Hebrew 32:29–30]; 33:16; 35:1–15).

In the fourth generation, through the birth of the twelve sons of Israel, the jump from the ancestors to the nation occurs. The legitimacy thus transfers from one main line to twelve egalitarian lines, the tribes. Nonetheless, even in this generation there is the formation of a main line: the elimination of the firstborn son Reuben is justified by his laying with his father's concubine

---

17. A compilation of all types of the promise is found in Claus Westermann, *Die Verheißungen an die Väter: Studien zur Vätergeschichte* (FRLANT 116; Göttingen: Vandenhoeck & Ruprecht, 1976). Synopses of all formulations of promises in Genesis are found in Rolf Rendtorff, *The Problem of the Process of Transmission in the Pentateuch* (trans. John. J. Scullion; JSOTSup 89; Sheffield: JSOT Press, 1990), 55–74.

18. This fact is suggested by Savina J. Teubal, *Sarah the Priestess: The First Matriarch of Genesis* (Athens: Swallow, 1984), as an indication of old writings that would have still testified to a matrilineal succession and that would have been eclipsed in the biblical texts through patriarchal redacting.

(Gen 35:22); the next-oldest brothers disqualify themselves through the escalation of vengeance against the Shechemites (34:30), to which Jacob refers in
his tribal blessing. Thus, only Judah remains as a potential main line of the
genealogy, whose founding is especially emphasized through its own narrative (Gen 38) and its dominance in the tribal blessing (49:8–12).

The updating of this narrative approach only occurs, of course, outside
the Pentateuch through the continuation of the Judah line as that group from
which the royal dynasty will come forth (Ruth 4:18–22; 1 Sam 16:1–13),
which again is given a promise (2 Sam 7:8–16). A second main line is shaped
through the Joseph story, which with the adoption and blessing of the two
sons of Joseph, Ephraim and Manasseh, ends with Jacob (Gen 48). The "house
of Joseph," which—in the narrated time, centuries later—characterizes the
northern kingdom of Israel, thus has a significant position. However, in the
overall biblical context, the Judean line is perceived as the dominant line of
promise.

The promises to the ancestors, in particular the promise of land, are
already taken up narratively in the Pentateuch. The clan, which had become
a great nation in Egypt (Exod 1:7), is promised freedom from the house of
slavery and the gift of land by reverting to the divine affirmations of Genesis
(3:13–17). The biblical narrative context of the Pentateuch thus presents the
forthcoming entry into the promised land in Deut 34 as the fulfillment of the
promise of land to the ancestors. Nevertheless, research is currently inten-
sively discussing whether the ancestors of Genesis were originally meant with
אָבוֹת, the parents of the book of Deuteronomy.[19]

2.4. BURIAL NOTES AND GRAVE TRADITIONS

If grave traditions were frequently viewed in historical-critical research as
time-honored, current Genesis research now assumes more of a late origina-
tion period for them. The ancestral narratives are also held together by the
burial place in the Cave of Machpelah near Hebron.[20] Since specific datings
and information about life spans are associated with the burial notes, they are
attributed to the Priestly texts of Genesis. The burial place is purchased by

---

19. See, for instance, Thomas Römer, *Israels Väter: Untersuchungen zur Väterthematik
im Deuteronomium und in der deuteronomistischen Tradition* (OBO 99; Fribourg: Universitätsverlag, 1990); Konrad Schmid, *Erzväter und Exodus: Untersuchungen zur doppelten
Begründung der Ursprünge Israels innerhalb der Geschichtsbücher des Alten Testaments*
(WMANT 81; Neukirchen-Vluyn: Neukirchener, 1999).

20. See Erhard Blum, *Die Komposition der Vätergeschichte* (WMANT 57; Neukirchen-
Vluyn: Neukirchener, 1984), 441–46.

Abraham for his deceased wife Sarah according to all the rules of Middle Eastern trade policy (Gen 23). Abraham (25:7–10), Isaac (35:27–29), and Jacob
(49:29–33) are then buried in it. According to Jacob's statements, both Leah
and Rebekah also rest in this family grave (49:31), in which he would like
to be buried as well. This grave tradition links the generations of the ancestors through a common place and thus forms another building block for a
consistent, ongoing family history over several generations. The gravesite of
Machpelah, which is presented very prominently in Genesis and in which
all members of the first three generations of the line of promise are buried
(except for Rachel, who died and was buried "on the way"), never comes up
again in the Bible. This suggests the suspicion that the entire tradition about
a common ancestral family grave is not a time-honored written tradition but
rather serves as a literary link to the quite disparate individual narratives with
regard to geography.

2.5. What Settlement Areas Disclose about the Origin of the Texts

Abraham's settlement area is stated as being in the south of Judah through the
towns of Hebron (Gen 13:18; 23:2, 19), Mamre (13:18; 18:1) and Beersheba
(21:25–34) as well as through the regions of the Negev (12:9; 13:1; 20:1) and
the southern end of the Dead Sea (13:10–12; 18:16–19, 29). He is thus clearly
the patriarch of the south.

However, the *places connected with Jacob* are all located in the area of the
northern kingdom. In Bethel, within the context of the vision of the stairway
to heaven, he is promised a return home, and after half a lifetime in a foreign land he does return there (Gen 28:10–22; 35:1–15). His first settlement
attempt in the land is localized in Shechem (Gen 34). The east Jordan land
situated to the north and partially in the northern kingdom's sphere of influence is crossed by Jacob starting from Gilead (31:21–54) via Mahanaim (32:1
[Hebrew 32:3]), Peniel (32:23–32 [33]), and Succoth (33:17). Only Rachel's
tomb and the return to the starting point of his wanderings link Jacob with
towns in the Judean region.

Isaac as the representative of the linking generation between the founding
families of the south and the north has, in accord with his literary function, *no
typical link to a place*. He awaits his wife, who is coming from Mesopotamia,
in Beer-lahai-roi (24:62), that place whose founding legend in 16:13–14 is tied
to Hagar's liberation. Otherwise, like his father before him, he is situated in
Beersheba (26:23–33; 28:10) and then—according to the complications surrounding the death blessing (Gen 27) narratively much too late—linked with
the young grave tradition in Hebron/Mamre (35:27).

3. The History of a Family in Four Generations

While the primeval history in Gen 1–11 condenses the time and covers whole epochs through large genealogies, time in the narratives of the remaining part of Genesis[21] is stretched over four generations, with an outlook to the fifth. In geographical terms, Israel traverses the entire path of its future history, from Mesopotamia to Egypt, multiple times and marks the Syro-Palestinian land bridge in the middle as land promised by God under oath.

3.1. Abraham-Sarah Cycle

The narrative cycle about the first generation[22] of the ancestors grows seamlessly from the end of the Semite family tree, from the notes about Terah's family and their travels. Narrative approaches for several build-ups of tension in the following "family saga" are embedded in the introduction of the Terah clan in Gen 11:27–32:

▶ Sarai, Abram's wife, is introduced as being infertile (11:30). All texts that discuss the topic of the ancestral couple's childlessness pick up this thread. These are de facto the biggest parts of Gen 12–21. In addition to the Hagar narratives (Gen 16; 21:8–21), this also includes Abram's complaints of not being able to see any realization of the promises without children (Gen 15, 17). Even for the abandonment narratives of Gen 12:10–20 and 20, the childlessness of the married couple is a prerequisite.

▶ Milcah, who is introduced with the genealogy of her father (Gen 11:29), and Nahor form the pivotal point of those narratives that play in the east, since the part of the family constituted by this couple does not move into the land. The sons of the line of promise get their wives from this clan. In this way, endogamy—marriage within the large

---

21. The Torah is divided into twelve sections in the synagogue reading, and there are also women's commentaries that follow suit, such as Yvonne Domhardt, Esther Orlow, and Eva Pruschy, eds., *Kol Ischa: Jüdische Frauen lesen die Tora* (2nd ed.; Zürich: Chronos, 2007); Elyse Goldstein, ed., *The Women's Torah Commentary: New Insights from Women Rabbis on the 54 Weekly Torah Portions* (Woodstock: Jewish Lights, 2008).

22. An easy-to-read overview on the texts about Sarah is given by Tammi J. Schneider, *Sarah: Mother of Nations* (New York: Continuum, 2004). Basic questions are compiled by Jean Louis Ska, "Essai sur la nature et la signification du cycle d'Abraham," in *Studies in the Book of Genesis: Literature, Redaction and History* (ed. André Wénin; BETL 155; Leuven: Leuven University Press, 2001), 153–77.

family consisting of several generations—is already set as a standard among the ancestors of Israel.

▶   The note that Abram's nephew Lot also moves into the land ultimately forms the starting point for the Lot narratives of Gen 13 and 19.

The narrative cycle begins when God calls Abram to leave his native land and to move to an unknown land on the basis of a promise (Gen 12:1). As a reward for obeying the command, Abram is promised he will receive the land and become a great nation there (12:2). This exodus of the family is given relevance for international law, because a blessing or curse for all on earth is decided by the position of Abram—and, as will be shown, of his family. While moving into the land, which does not come to a stop until the extreme-most south, in the Negev, the patriarch symbolically takes possession of the land for YHWH by building altars at central locations of the later northern kingdom. God then affirms the gift of this land for his descendants (12:7).

3.1.1. The Abandonment of the Ancestral Woman as the Abandonment of the Promises

When initial but grave difficulties crop up in this promised land, Abram leaves the Land to head toward Egypt. Genesis will also tell of avoiding famine in the Syro-Palestinian land bridge by heading to Egypt in the Joseph story (see Gen 42:5; 43:1), because the fertility of this land is not determined by rain but by the flooding of the Nile. Since the deity is not consulted when leaving the land, shortly before crossing the border Abram begins to fear that his beautiful wife could be desired and that attempts might be made to get rid of him. Abram's speech to his wife Sarai begins with a compliment (12:11b) in order to paint the blackest picture of the risk that she represents for him as his wife. Her survival is chiastically offset with his death:

> And they will kill me, but you they will allow to live! (Gen 12:12)

The narrative does not allow Sarai to answer, thus implying her victim status.[23] When the clan comes to Egypt, Sarai's extraordinary beauty is indeed affirmed. None of the Egyptians dares to touch the couple; instead, the woman is praised to the pharaoh, who then takes her into his house after paying a

_____

23. J. Cheryl Exum ("Who's Afraid of 'The Endangered Ancestress'?" in *The New Literary Criticism and the Hebrew Bible* [ed. J. Cheryl Exum and David J. A. Clines; JSOTSup 143; Sheffield: Sheffield Academic Press, 1993], 107–8) emphasizes the masculine perspective of the story.

princely bride-price. The Egyptian ruler does good things for Abram (12:16)—not a trace of unbridled desire, as Abram had feared in Egypt!

There is only one who is not in agreement with the integration of the ancestral woman into a foreign genealogical line: YHWH afflicts the pharaoh with great plagues because of Sarai, the wife of Abram (12:17). The deity of Israel intercedes not to get the patriarch back his wife but rather to save the woman under the promise. The foreign ruler then demands accountability from Abram as to why he made him risk adultery, a severe sin in the ancient Near East (12:18). It then becomes clear that the patriarch's strategy of passing his wife off as his sister is what caused the awkward situation. The fact that the pharaoh quotes *Abram's statement*, "She is my sister!"—and not that of Sarai, as Abram wanted to place in her mouth (12:13)—proves Sarai's innocence in the dilemma. However, the pharaoh is noble enough not to hurt a hair on the head of the man who had lied and cheated him. He gives him back his wife and arranges for them to be deported over the border under armed escort (12:19–20).

When they arrive in the land, there are conflicts between Lot and Abram due to the abundance of herds—apparently acquired through the bride-price paid for Sarai (12:16). Genesis 13 is the first of several narratives about disputes due to pastureland and wells, which all presume the stable wealth of the ancestral parents (21:22–34; 26:12–33). From the context, both the narrative about the abandonment of Sarai as well as that about the separation of Lot can be read as narratives about the abandonment of the promises: if Abram with Sarai abandons the divine promise of becoming a great nation, he is also disregarding the promise of the land by allowing Lot to select the region where he would like to live in the future. It is thus not surprising that YHWH has to renew the land promise with Abram after Lot chose the paradise-like Jordan Valley as his future dwelling area (13:14–18).

Since the promises to the ancestral parents have always been directed to the *fathers*, the narrative about the abandonment of the ancestral woman proves for the first time that not merely the patriarchs are addressed by the divine promises but rather the ancestral *parents*. Sarah is freed from a foreign harem as a bearer of the promise with whom the patriarch will fulfill the promise to become a great nation. But the narrative context presents a very similar story once again in Gen 20. From the narrated course of her life story, Sarah is no longer young and beautiful. She is an old woman who has just been promised the birth of a child in the next year, and it is in this year of pregnancy that her husband again abandons her while he is staying in Gerar as a stranger. Genesis 20 sets the accents of the narrative material somewhat differently than 12:10–20: Sarah becomes the "accessory," since the lie about the sibling relationship is also put into her mouth (20:5), and the lie becomes a half-truth since the two become half-siblings (20:12).[24] In addition, every suspicion that Sarah might have become the wife of the foreign ruler in his harem is removed because God himself prevents him from touching her (20:6). During the time while Sarah is in the harem, it is emphasized that God had struck Abimelech's household with infertility (20:18). In this way, any doubt about the paternity of Isaac, whose birth is told in the next section (21:1–7), is excluded.

Again this story tells of the abandonment of the ancestral woman, even if the risk of being integrated into a foreign genealogy no longer really exists here. In the third narrative that deals with this material, Isaac and Rebekah are the protagonists, Abimelech again the foreign ruler (Gen 26:1–11). In the story, the threat to the ancestral woman takes place more theoretically, since the foreign ruler already discovers before any contemplation of taking the woman into his household that the ancestral couple is not linked by the bonds of siblinghood but by the bonds of marriage. The crime of adultery is discussed more as a horrific possibility (26:10). To prevent this, the king places the couple under his personal protection by forbidding them from being touched (26:11).

Why is the same story told three times within fifteen chapters?[25] Traditional historical-critical research has explained this in terms of the composition of pentateuchal sources and the law of the passing down of saga, that the more unknown figure (Isaac) was the original[26] and the more famous (Abraham) appeals to all stories. Nonetheless, even with this explanation it begs the question of why this story in particular was considered so important that three versions have been preserved, while for others there are only one or two versions. Independent of the history of the origin of the three texts, which is not likely to be explained through source-like material, there must be a justification for this type of emphasis on a story that at first glance is not so important theologically, and one can in fact find it by taking an overall picture of the entire narrative cycle.

---

24. These interventions to alleviate the scandal presumably go back to a later redaction that sought to dress up the image of the ancestral parents. For more detail on Gen 20, see Fischer, *Die Erzeltern Israels*, 137–74.

25. On the problem of the double written traditions and their assessment for the history of the origin of the Pentateuch, see Aulikki Nahkola, *Double Narratives in the Old Testament: The Foundations of Method in Biblical Criticism* (BZAW 290; Berlin: de Gruyter, 2001).

26. See, e.g., Klaus Koch, *Was ist Formgeschichte? Methoden der Bibelexegese* (4th ed.; Neukirchen-Vluyn: Neukirchener, 1981), 154.

3.1.2. The Hagar Narratives

The two narratives about Hagar, Gen 16 and 21:8–21,[27] are inseparably linked with the motif of the ancestral woman's childlessness. According to 16:1–4, the infertile Sarai gives her husband her Egyptian slave for the purpose of surrogate motherhood. This legal arrangement of surrogate motherhood,[28] widely attested to in the ancient Near East, is not to be found anywhere in the legal texts of the Old Testament, yet it is found twice in the ancestral narratives: Rachel and Leah also made use of this option of coming to even more children, the only means by which the people of the twelve tribes can originate. What has to be seen from our perspective today as the exploitation of the female sexuality of enslaved women was a legitimate option in the ancient Near East of achieving legally recognized descendants without adoption. The success of the legal construction can then likely be spoken of when the surrogate mother is integrated into the family. This is the case with Bilhah and Zilpah, who in reference to their mistresses always remain in the status of the "slave" (שִׁפְחָה), while their legal position within the family, however, becomes that of אָמָה, the "maidservant."[29] However, for Hagar the integration into the family does not succeed: when Hagar notices that she is pregnant from the husband of her mistress, she becomes contemptible in Hagar's eyes. Hagar is thus not prepared to leave untouched the social gaps between slave and mistress.

---

27. The Hagar narratives have already been thoroughly examined at the final-text level by Phyllis Trible, *Texts of Terror: Literary-Feminist Readings of Biblical Narratives* (OBT 13; Philadelphia: Fortress, 1984). A reception history on the Hagar narratives up to the Reformation has been offered by John L. Thompson, *Writing the Wrongs: Women of the Old Testament among Biblical Commentators from Philo through the Reformation* (Oxford Studies in Historical Theology; Oxford: Oxford University Press, 2001), 17–99.

28. Savina J. Teubal, *Hagar the Egyptian: The Lost Tradition of the Matriarchs* (San Francisco: Harper, 1990), interprets the figures of Sarah and Hagar due to the widely attested legal arrangement in Mesopotamian legal texts (Code of Hammurabi 144–147) that highly ranked *nadītu* priestesses apparently had to remain childless and therefore could place their female slaves at the disposal of their husbands for surrogacy, as indications of matriarchal traditions of desert nomads that had been revised androcentrically in the legal texts. She understands both figures to be priestly, with the prerequisite for this of course being the assumption of very old written traditions that stretch far back into the second century B.C.E.

29. On this thesis, see Fischer, *Die Erzeltern Israels*, 91–97, as well as on the female slave texts of Genesis: Elisa Estévez López, "Las grandes ausentes: La memoria de las esclavas en los orígenes de Israel," in Gómez-Acebo et al., *Relectura del Génesis*, 221–67.

According to Exod 21:7–11, a female (Israelite) indebted slave with whom a free man of the slave-holding family had sexual contact could not be resold but instead had to be bought back. If the marital goods of food, clothing, and sexual intercourse were no longer granted to the slave, she had the right to go free without making payment. If one takes this arrangement into consideration, the appraisal of her mistress from Hagar's perspective certainly conforms to the written law: whoever has sexually recognized a slave woman can no longer treat her like a normal work slave. But this is precisely what Sarai and Abram do. The husband, who responds to his wife's command without question and whose child the slave woman is carrying, is not prepared to concede her the status of אָמָה but instead gives her back into the hand of her mistress without support. Sarai then oppresses Hagar so harshly that the slave woman runs away. The human attempt to assist in the fulfillment of the promise of a son has thus gone totally awry.

The death penalty is consistently applied in the legal policies of the ancient Near East for escape from slavery: whoever runs away is subject to death, as are those who do not bring the escaped slaves back to their masters.[30] Even if no such laws are found in the Old Testament, they are nonetheless to be assumed implicitly, since it is unlikely that slavery could have been maintained in the long term if an organized deprivation of liberty could have existed without force.

This legal historical background is to be borne in mind when the messenger of YHWH meets Hagar at a spring of water on the way from the Negev to her native land of Egypt and speaks to her (16:7–8). The fact that the angel addresses her with "Hagar, servant of Sarai," makes it clear that he knows about her escape. Nonetheless, he is the first to take her seriously as a person, since he calls her by her name and does not address her solely by her social status. On the one hand, he asks her about her origin, which Hagar answers truthfully by confessing her flight, and, on the other, about her future, to which the slave gives no answer. In the original narrative, which was likely redacted twice,[31] in response to Hagar's reply comes the affirmation, which was formulated anew with a second introduction to the speech in 16:11, that

---

30. A solid overview of the biblical legal provisions on slavery is offered by Innocenzo Cardellini, *Die biblischen "Sklaven"-Gesetze im Lichte des keilschriftlichen Sklavenrechts: Ein Beitrag zur Tradition, Überlieferung und Redaktion der alttestamentlichen Rechtstexte* (BBB 55; Königstein: Hanstein, 1981).

31. The speech introduction repeated three times does not conceal the redactions. See Mieke Bal, Fokkelien van Dijk-Hemmes, and Grietje van Ginneken, *Und Sara lachte...: Patriarchat und Widerstand in biblischen Geschichten* (Münster: Morgana Frauenbuchverlag, 1988), 29–50, which therefore speak of the "stammering messenger of God."

Hagar will bear a son. She is to give the child a memorial name, Ishmael, "God hears," to memorialize her deliverance from oppression. Verse 12 then introduces the fate of the freely born son who also lives in freedom in the image of the wild donkey. A double etiology forms the conclusion of the basic narrative, through which both the delivering deity as well as the place of the divine appearance conveyed by an angel is named. Both places, El-roi and Beer-lahai-roi, are brought in connection with "seeing," ראה, while the name of her son is linked to the deity with "hearing," שׁמע. All three etiologies are linked with El, while the remaining narrative uses the name YHWH for the deity. Whether it can be concluded from this that the etiologies are of an older origin and perhaps even stem from oral traditions is dubious. It could be that they all explain already-existing names that were acculturated into the Israelite religion with this story, similar to the case of Bethel in Gen 28:10–19.

Belonging to the redactional layer of this original deliverance narrative is the angel's command to return in 16:9, which conforms to the slave laws of the ancient Near East. In order to be able to tell the story a second time with different accents in Gen 21:8–21, Hagar's return to the house of slavery is an absolute prerequisite. The question of whether the promise speech of 16:10 inserted with another speech introduction also belongs to this layer must be answered in the negative. This verse fits better in the context of the redactional layer that idealizes the image of the ancestral parents in the advanced postexilic period and is visible both in Gen 20 and in 21:11–13.

The Priestly layer of the narrative is found in Gen 16:3, 15–16. It allows Hagar to become a social climber by Sarai giving her to her husband as a *wife*. The Priestly writing thus presumes the freeing of the slave, who then—without entanglements of social ranking—becomes pregnant and bears her husband his firstborn son. In this layer, which presumably originated independently from the other texts in Gen 16, the father names the son (16:15), since any etiology that could refer to deliverance must be lacking. The merging of the texts into the present-day Hagar narrative will have been done by the redactor who integrated the pre-Priestly material into the Priestly writing. The present-day final text has both a carrot and stick message for the oppressed slave: if she goes back and allows herself to be oppressed again, she gets a promise as has never before been granted to one of the ancestral women of the line of promise. However, the basic narrative has a universalistic approach to the deity of Israel's bequest of salvation: as Marie-Theres Wacker accurately ascertained, YHWH is also present in providing help to an Egyptian slave when leaving Israel—not just during Israel's exodus from Egypt.[32]

---

32. See Marie-Theres Wacker, "1. Mose 16 und 21: Hagar—die Befreite," in *32 aus-*

The second narrative of the expulsion of Hagar and Ishmael, who is now already a child, is told directly after the note on the weaning of the promised son Isaac. Sarah becomes aware that her son is not the firstborn son and therefore will not be the principal heir (21:9–10). In a twisting of the legal facts that the firstborn son of Abraham, Ishmael, would *co*-inherit with her son, she insists on the expulsion of Hagar, now called a maidservant. Abraham obeys, as previously in Gen 16:1–4, his wife's every word and expels his son and his son's mother the next morning. Hagar receives no settlement payment, only a ration of water and bread (21:14). If according to Gen 16:7 she was goal-directed and found the well on her own, according to 21:14 she wanders with her child dying of thirst lost in the desert, which is named after a well, Beersheba, but which she cannot seem to see. When the water in the skin runs out and the boy is about to die of thirst, Hagar raises up her voice in loud weeping (21:16). Virtually at the last moment, God saves the child by allowing an angel to come down from heaven to his aid, who then shows the mother the rescuing well. In the context of the salvation oracle of 21:17–18, she also receives the promise that her son will become a great nation. Ishmael pursues his further path through life as a free man, marries an Egyptian, and settles in the desert (21:20–21).

3.1.3. Sacrifice of Isaac versus Testing of the Abandoning Father

A twin text,[33] the narrative of the binding of Isaac, follows up this narrative of deliverance from the greatest need. If Abraham easily expels the one son hard-heartedly, he must now, with a heavy heart, sacrifice the other, the only remaining one after the expulsion of Ishmael: Isaac, his favorite son and the bearer of the promise (22:2). In both stories "Abraham rises in the morning" (וַיַּשְׁכֵּם אַבְרָהָם בַּבֹּקֶר, 21:14; 22:3) and "takes" (וַיִּקַּח) one of his sons to send him out of the house never to be seen again. Both times only one parent is alone on the road with the son, and both times the child is saved from death at the last moment because an angel speaks to the parent from heaven (וַיִּקְרָא מַלְאַךְ יי אֶל־ מִן־הַשָּׁמַיִם וַיֹּאמֶר, 21:17; 22:11). The angel then gives the par-

---

gewählte Bibeltexte für Gruppen, Gemeinden und Gottesdienste (vol. 1 of *Feministisch gelesen*; ed. Eva Renate Schmidt, Mieke Korenhof, and Renate Jost; 2nd ed.; Stuttgart: Kreuz, 1989), 28.

33. Blum, *Die Komposition der Vätergeschichte*, already discovered this. He labels Gen 21 the "dress rehearsal" for Gen 22, which in my estimation reduces the significance of the Hagar narrative. See the synopsis of both texts in Fischer, *Women Who Wrestled*, 40–43. The twin texts have a multitude of semantic commonalities as well as a similar structure; therefore, there must be references made between the two in their interpretation.

ents the instruction to save the boys with their own "hand" (יָד, 21:18; 22:12). Both parents ultimately receive a divine promise (21:18; 22:17–18). The story ends both times with information about the area where they will later live (21:20–21; 22:19).

The story of "the binding of Isaac," as Judaism calls it, or "the sacrifice of Isaac," as Christianity has called it through its typological-christological tradition of exegesis, is one of the most important texts in the reception history of the Hebrew Bible.[34] Time and again it has invited the identification of the elect people whose existence was threatened by pogroms and yet was rescued just in time. Time and again, particularly in the period after the Enlightenment, it has been denounced as a scandalous text[35] that reveals the supposedly cruel biblical image of God. If one reads the text as it stands in the Bible, the story does not deal with Isaac being threatened but rather with the father being tested (22:1). If he refuses to obey the command, nothing at all will happen to the son. This is because the deity does not want to sacrifice Isaac but to test whether Abraham is prepared to do to himself what he has already done to others. He has abandoned all the people around him: Sarah twice, by declaring her his sister and thus subjecting her to the risk of being integrated into a foreign genealogical line, and Hagar twice, since he was not man enough to stand by the woman carrying his child. With her he has abandoned his firstborn son twice and ultimately sends them away. Now God tests Abraham, who as an old man no longer has any realistic chance of having any more children, to see whether he is prepared to abandon his own future with his only son. The deity forces the patriarch to reconcile his social life, which looks more like a failure than a success, with his life of faith, in which despite all adversities he always believed anew in his God. Abraham passes the test by being prepared to follow this instruction directed against all earlier promises. If Sarah is absent in this story,[36] the reason for this is that she, who had been the driving force behind

---

34. The literature is compiled at Georg Steins, *Die "Bindung Isaaks" im Kanon (Gen 22): Grundlagen und Programm einer kanonisch-intertextuellen Lektüre: Mit einer Spezial-bibliographie zu Gen 22* (Herders Biblische Studien 20; Freiburg im Breisgau: Herder, 1999).

35. The history of exegesis of the text is broadly documented; in the German-speaking area alone, see, e.g., David Lerch, *Isaaks Opferung christlich gedeutet: Eine auslegungsge-schichtliche Untersuchung* (BHT 12; Tübingen: Mohr Siebeck, 1950); Lukas Kundert, *Die Opferung/Bindung Isaaks* (2 vols.; WMANT 78–79; Neukirchen-Vluyn: Neukirchener, 1998); Marion Keuchen, *Die "Opferung Isaaks" im 20. Jahrhundert auf der Theaterbühne: Auslegungsimpulse im Blick auf "Abrahams Zelt" (Theater Musentümpel–Andersonn) und "Gottesvergiftung" (Choralgraphisches Theater Heidelber—Grasmück)* (Altes Testament und Moderne 19; Münster: LIT, 2004).

36. Sebastian Brock, "Reading between the Lines: Sarah and the Sacrifice of Isaac

the expulsion of Hagar and Ishmael, had already been tested through being abandoned twice.

3.1.4. Birth Announcements (Gen 17 and 18:1–15)

In the Bible, birth announcements have an established form and are, with very few exceptions, always issued to the mother. They are usually imparted by God himself or one of his angels. They begin either with the announcement or discovery of the pregnancy, including a confirmation that a son will be born. His "expressive name" has usually already been determined by God and points to the fate of the mother, less often that of the father. The fact that the birth of a daughter is never promised can be explained, on the one hand, by the concentration on the patrilineality in a patriarchal society. On the other hand, the high regard given to sons results from the practice of patrilocal marriages whereby the daughters leave the home and are lost for the purpose of caring for their own parents in their old age. However, a marginalization of the female gender overall is revealed as the social impact.

In the Abraham-Sarah cycle a birth announcement for Ishmael is first given to Hagar in Gen 16:11–12. The older birth announcement for Isaac can be found in Gen 18:1–15. This story of the three men who visit Abraham and Sarah, which is very famous particularly in the reception of the Eastern churches due to the Trinitarian interpretation, combines a story of hospitality with an announcement of a birth. It begins with a dialogue between the men and Abraham (18:3–9) and ends as a dialogue between one of the men and Sarah (18:10–15). As Erhard Blum so aptly pointed out, a promise of such importance cannot be announced in the "'small talk' of anonymous 'men' "[37] but only in the speech of the one who makes it clear that he is God. If in the history of exegesis primarily Sarah has been repeatedly interpreted as an embarrassing figure,[38] the point of the narrative has been completely missed. She is not improperly eavesdropping on the men's conversations, but instead the interest of the men is focused on her, which is improper in a patriarchal society. She laughs because of the realistic estimation of her age and not because sexuality in old age was taboo or because she was laughing at God. The moment she realizes who the announcer is ("Is anything too wonderful for the Lord?" 18:14) her laughter gives way to faith, and she denies her

---

(Genesis, Chapter 22)," in *Women in Ancient Societies* (ed. Léonie J. Archer; London: Macmillan, 1994), 169–80.

37. Blum, *Die Komposition der Vätergeschichte*, 278.

38. See, e.g., Hermann Gunkel, *Genesis* (8th ed.; Göttingen: Vandenhoeck & Ruprecht, 1969), 197–98.

laughter, which ultimately gives Isaac his name (יִצְחָק-צחק). The fact that the deity insists on Sarah's laughter thus does not represent a severe reprimand but in fact the preparation of an etiology of the name Isaac determined by folk etymology.

In the present-day final text this birth announcement to the mother is preceded by the announcement to the father. Genesis 17, a text clearly characterized by Priestly influences, alienates the woman's experience in its position before Gen 18 by linking the birth announcement for the following year and laughter to explain the name Isaac to the father. If one considers that the Priestly writing (P) in the Abraham cycle consisted nearly entirely of genealogical notes and that Gen 17 was the only longer coherent text, a concentration on the father who names both sons can be seen overall in P, but this does not lessen the significance of Sarah. Like her husband, she is also given a new name (Gen 17:5, 15); *her* firstborn son is the promised son, not Abraham's firstborn son (16:3, 15–16; 17:18–21). If circumcision as a sign of the covenant is only personally borne by men, one can be glad of this in today's world, where there is broad awareness of the catastrophic consequences of female circumcision. However, the selection of a sign of the covenant[39] that is only visible on the male body is in fact an expression of a patriarchal culture in which the masculine represents the general state of things.

3.1.5. Lot's Rescued Daughters: Pure Blood or Abysmal Disgrace?

The Lot narratives (Gen 13–14; 18:16–19, 38) belong to those separation stories through which branch lines are eliminated from the direct line of promise. Lot chooses the paradise-like land in the Jordan Plain whose inhabitants, however, turn out to have deeply corrupt morals (Gen 19). The men who were so kindly received by Abraham and Sarah are threatened with rape in Sodom (19:5). Lot's offer to hand over his two virgin daughters for collective rape instead of his visitors demonstrates that this was not a case of homosexual men, but instead the custom of using sexuality for terrorizing purposes[40] (19:8). The integrity of the daughters is thus of less value than hospitality.

---

39. On this problem, see Judith Plaskow, *Standing again at Sinai: Judaism from a Feminist Perspective* (San Francisco: Harper, 1991), 82–83.

40. On this, see Ilse Müllner, "Tödliche Differenzen: Sexuelle Gewalt als Gewalt gegen Andere in Ri 19," in *Von der Wurzel getragen: Christlich-feministische Exegese in Auseinandersetzung mit Antijudaismus* (ed. Luise Schottroff and Marie-Theres Wacker; Biblical Interpretation Series 17; Leiden: Brill, 1996), 89. On the motif of sexual violence against outsiders, see Weston W. Fields, *Sodom and Gomorrah: History and Motif in Biblical Narrative* (JSOTSup 231; Sheffield: Sheffield Academic Press, 1997), 116–33.

Lot's two daughters are spared from the fate brought on them by their own father only because the divine visitors strike the men of Sodom with blindness (19:10–11).[41] However, with this episode that initially ends as a story of deliverance, the fate of Sodom is sealed. Only Lot is able to bring his family into safety prior to the destruction of the city. His wife, in fact, dares to look back, thus turning into a pillar of salt so characteristic for the region in the southern part of the Dead Sea (19:17–26).

The following scene, in which the father is alone with his two daughters (19:30–38), presupposes the absence of the mother. Exegesis does not agree on the interpretation of the double incest. While older research partially speaks of the "purity of the blood" or the courage of the daughters,[42] Elke Seifert suggests reading the story as a classic story of repression by an incestuous father.[43] Considering present-day court transcripts, she sees the same defense structure on the part of the perpetrators: alcohol was involved, the daughters wanted intercourse or even provoked it, and the mothers are not available to call upon for help. Even the story surrounding Lot's daughters can only partially cover up evidence of the crime. The incestuous names of the children Ammon ("of my people") and Moab ("from my father") speak volumes. Since these two nations were not exactly the most well-liked neighbors (see Deut 23:4) at the time of the final redaction of the Pentateuch, when decisions were also made on what to do with older stories, it can be assumed that the story is to be viewed critically even if explicit criticism of the incestuous creation of these nations is never expressed.[44] There is, however, one thing that the biblical text does not do, namely, "blame the victim," which absolutely cannot be said of the history of exegesis: Lot's daughters are never chastised for bearing the children.

---

41. On the problematic relationship between Lot and his daughters, see Mercedes Navarro Puerto, "Las extrañas del Génesis, tan parecidas y tan diferentes…," in Gómez-Acebo et al., *Relectura del Génesis*, 165–68.

42. See the compilation in James Alfred Loader, *A Tale of Two Cities: Sodom and Gomorrah in the Old Testament, Early Jewish and Christian Traditions* (CBET 1; Kampen: Kok, 1990), 45–46.

43. See Elke Seifert, *Tochter und Vater im Alten Testament: Eine ideologiekritische Untersuchung zur Verfügungsgewalt von Vätern über ihre Töchter* (Neukirchener Theologische Dissertationen und Habilitationen 9; Neukirchen-Vluyn: Neukirchener, 1997), 82–86.

44. A location of the Lot stories in the era of Ezra and Nehemiah is attempted by R. Christopher Heard, *Dynamics of Diselection: Ambiguity in Genesis 12–36 and Ethnic Boundaries in Post-exilic Judah* (SemeiaSt 39; Atlanta: Society of Biblical Literature, 2001), 172–74, whose book is devoted to the branch lines of the ancestral narratives.

3.2. Rebekah-Isaac Cycle

Research focusing on the history of passed-down written tradition, which considered Genesis to be a collection of legends, suspected it had found the original root of the double written traditions of abandoning the ancestral woman and the conflicts concerning wells in the "Isaac cycle," which are additionally found in the Abraham-Sarah cycle. However, increasing skepticism concerning an oral tradition that stayed constant over a long period of time has severely afflicted this thesis. Presumably the narrative cycle of the second-generation ancestors has been supplemented with a bridge function between the Abraham-Sarah cycle and the Jacob written tradition, which aims at the creation of the twelve tribes nation.

3.2.1. Rebekah as a Successor of Abraham (Gen 24)

Although in patrilineal societies genealogies are normally androcentric and in the ancestral narratives the line of promise is additionally presented in male succession, the genealogy of Milcah and Nahor points to Rebekah. The family tree is introduced as news brought to Abraham, whereby Rebekah and the ancestral father are linked from the very beginning.

According to this genealogical introduction, Rebekah is brought into the family at the initiative of Abraham. He sends a servant in search of a wife for his son, a woman who fulfills the same criteria as himself: she must be willing to leave her land to "go" (הלך) to the promised land as he did (cf. Gen 12:1; 24:7 with Rebekah's fulfillment in 24:58). The right marriage for Isaac would in fact be endogamous; that is, a wife from the same kin would have been ideal, but Abraham is willing to make trade-offs to the extent that life in the promised land is defined as a more important criterion. He makes Eliezer swear not to bring Isaac back to his own native land.

This exposition (24:1–9) already reveals that Gen 24, the so-called matchmaking narrative, represents a vote on the issue of mixed marriages, which was so important in the postexilic period. For this narrative the origin of the Diaspora defined as the true Israel is not decisive but rather the desire to move to the promised land to live there. It is thus only a conditional plea against mixed marriages and in this regard a middle position on this issue compared to the completely open position in the book of Ruth and the position strictly advocating ethnic purity in the books of Ezra and Nehemiah.

The matchmaking story is structured in a long-winded manner with a broadly sweeping style and large sections of repetition.[45] In addition to the

---

45. For a more extensive analysis of the text, see Susanne Gillmayr-Bucher, "וְהִנֵּה

criteria defined by Abraham, the servant—the only figure present in all scenes from beginning to end—adds an ethical criterion for the future wife of his master's son: she must be willing to give more than is demanded of her (24:14). Since the servant, typical of matchmaking narratives, sat down at the gender-specific meeting point in the city where Milcah and Nahor lived, at the well, he expects that the future bride will not only give him something to drink but all of his proverbial thirsty camels as well. In Rebekah, whose trek to the well is presented as an appearance (וְהִנֵּה רִבְקָה, 24:15: "behold, Rebekah..."), he not only finds a beautiful, untouched girl from the proper family (24:16) but also a hospitable woman who is willing to work and prepared to move to the promised land.

The certainly accurate social-historical details concerning the fact that a woman cannot bring a man home with her but that the guest must first be invited by a male member of the family are interesting in this context. A similar story is told in the next generation with Jacob and Rachel (cf. 24:28–31; 29:12–14). However, the family alone does not make the decision regarding the marriage. Instead, the bride is explicitly asked for her consent to leave her native land (24:50–58). The blessing that Rebekah as the bride receives from her family (24:60) has nearly the exact wording as the second affirmation by the angel in Gen 22:17. She is thus initially promised that which her father-in-law only received after he was gravely tested and passed, whereby Rebekah in turn is positioned as a successor of Abraham—and not his son Isaac.

The meeting of the engaged couple is told at a peculiar distance: Rebekah covers herself when she sees the lone man Isaac and descends from her camel.[46] Yet Isaac takes her into the tent of his mother, where his bride consoles him through his mother's death. The first story in this narrative cycle already proves that Rebekah is the strong woman on the side of a colorless man.

3.2.2. The Political Relevance of Pregnancy Complications

The imbalance of the characters also becomes clear in the story of the birth of the twins. The infertility of the ancestral woman seems to be a topos in the ancestral narratives (11:30; 25:21; 29:31) that belongs to the birth of the son to whom the promises will be passed on. In the case of Rebekah, no narrative is tied to this, just the note that Isaac prays for her (25:21) and that YHWH

רִבְקָה יֹצֵאת: Eine textlinguistische Untersuchung zu Gen 24" (Ph.D. diss., Universität Innsbruck, 1994).

46. For this section, see Magdalene L. Frettlöh, "Isaak und seine Mütter: Beobach-tungen zur exegetischen Verdrängung von Frauen am Beispiel von Gen 24,62–67," *EvT* 54 (1994): 427–52.

hears his prayers; the motif here is thus certainly not original. When Rebekah has complications with her pregnancy, she goes—apparently without her husband—to a sanctuary to inquire of YHWH. The note presupposes a working cult in a decentralized location. It is thoroughly possible that it suggests a tradition originally from the northern kingdom, for in the older narratives of the Jacob cycle Rebekah is depicted as the mother of Jacob and thus of Israel.

The oracle that Rebekah receives points to the national-political significance of her pregnancy: with her twins she is carrying two nations in her womb that are already fighting for supremacy over the other prior to birth. The younger brother will dominate over the older brother. The rivalry then continues in the birth scene. The younger brother, Jacob, is etymologically introduced as the "heel-holder"[47] for grabbing his brother's heel during birth. In terms of appearance and behavior, the two sons are as different as night and day. The rugged, natural boy Esau is accordingly referred to as his father's favorite son, while civilized Jacob is referred to as his mother's favorite son (25:27–28). Whether this corresponds to gender stereotypes is not to be answered here: Rebekah is aware of the dominance of the younger brother and purposefully supports him.

3.2.3. Rebekah's Abandonment: Isaac as a Successor of Abraham (Gen 26)

Two narratives are added between the texts about the struggle for the birthright and the paternal blessing, which are already familiar from the Abraham-Sarah cycle: the endangerment of the ancestral woman and the subsequent well conflicts. In this version of the abandonment narrative, the sister declaration does not pose a real threat but rather only a potential one to Rebekah (26:10–11). She already has children, whereby, on the one hand, the course of the narrative appears to be inhomogeneous. On the other hand, the dimension of abandoning the woman with whom the promised son must first be begotten is lost. Apparently chapter 26 in its entirety has the intention of positioning Rebekah and Isaac as successors of Abraham and Sarah. However, the couple is under the explicit protection and blessing of YHWH from the very beginning (26:2–5, 12, 22).

3.2.4. The Mother's Favorite Son Becomes the Patriarch (Gen 27)

As already seen in the first generation, the husband's firstborn son, who is normally the principal heir, does not enter into the line of promise, but

---

47. The proper name יַעֲקֹב, "Jacob," is associated with the root עקב, "hold by the heel."

instead the firstborn son of the female bearer of the promise. Rebekah enables her favorite son to receive his father's dying blessing through a deliberately planned, unscrupulous betrayal of her husband, who in this story is exclusively seen as the father of both sons. She risks the possibility of being cursed by the blind patriarch (27:12–13) and disguises Jacob as Esau (27:15–17). Her favorite son is to go to his father dressed up as Esau and give him his favorite meal of hunted game in order to then receive the blessing that passes on the legitimacy of the clan and the role of the patriarch. The blind father is suspicious since he hears Jacob's voice. Jacob must then repeat his false declaration multiple times until the father ultimately blesses him as his son Esau.

The blessing that Isaac ultimately bestows is involuntarily full of irony (27:28–29): he makes the "sons of his mother" subordinate to his supposed favorite son and does not know that he is blessing Rebekah's favorite son. She, who as a woman in a patriarchal society cannot pass down the legitimacy of the clan, has managed to ensure that her favorite son, to whom this was promised even before his birth, was blessed all the same.

Rebekah, however, pays a high price for this coup. She never sees her favorite son again, since he must flee from his cheated, vengeful brother. In the present-day final text Rebekah pleads in favor of an endogamous marriage as a pretext (27:46). This part of the chapter is apparently to be read as a vote on the issue of mixed marriages: the bearer of the promise must marry a woman from his own family. However, Isaac and Rebekah do not send Jacob to the brother of his grandfather Abraham, as one might expect in patrilineal societies, but instead to the brother of his mother Rebekah. The cross-cousin is thus presented as the ideal bride,[48] on the one hand, while, on the other hand, Rebekah is presented as the central figure whose genealogy is just as important as that of Abraham and Sarah.

3.3. JACOB AND HIS WIVES

The core of the narratives surrounding Jacob takes place either in the territory of the northern kingdom (Bethel, Shechem, Mahanaim, Peniel) or in Mesopotamia, where his mother's family remained. Jacob is originally the ancestral father of the northern kingdom, there is no doubt about that. Through his sons, however, Jacob becomes the ancestral father of the entire nation. The

---

48. On the legal implications of marriage in ancient Israel, see Angelo Tosato, *Il matrimonio israelitico: Una teoria generale, nuova prefazione, presentazione e bibliografia* (AnBib 100; Rome: Pontifical Biblical Institute, 2001); and Gordon Paul Hugenberger, *Marriage as a Covenant: A Study of Biblical Law and Ethics Governing Marriage Developed from the Perspective of Malachi* (VTSup 52; Leiden: Brill, 1994).

texts that particularly embed Judah into the Jacob narratives probably origi-nated after 701 B.C.E., when, as a result of the catastrophe of the downfall of the northern kingdom and the preservation of Jerusalem from the siege by the Assyrians, religious traditions were reexamined and reconceived and those of the southern and northern kingdom were merged.

3.3.1. Rachel the Shepherdess and Chosen Bride

As Jacob is fleeing from his cheated brother, God appears to him in a dream at Bethel in which he receives the confirmation that the promises of the ances-tors have been bestowed upon him (28:10–22). When Jacob arrives at the place where his mother's brother resides, his route—as in the case of the ser-vant in Gen 24—first takes him to the well. In fact, as if directed by divine guidance, he also meets the woman from the right family, who is to become his wife, at the well. However, Rachel is not engaged in the typical female activity of fetching water but instead is working as an unmarried woman as a shepherdess, a profession that her husband will assume after they are married. From Jacob's perspective, the narrator presents the encounter as love at first sight (Gen 29:11, 18, 20). Rachel subsequently grants him access to her father's house. Since the fugitive, unlike the servant in Gen 24, is unable to offer an adequate bride-price, Jacob offers to work as a shepherd for Laban's herds for seven years (Gen 29:15–19). The fact that these seven years seem like only a few days to Jacob (29:20) is meant to emphasize the intensity of his desire.

3.3.2. Leah's Marriage to Jacob: The Betrayer Is Betrayed at the Expense of the Wife

Jacob's desire, however, is satisfied in a completely inappropriate manner. In a motif reversal, as it were, the father of the bride betrays the betrayer who betrayed his father. Jacob, who pretended to be the older son, is now betrayed by Laban, who gives him the older daughter to be his wife before the desired younger daughter. The narrative further intensifies this by allowing Jacob to spend the wedding night with the wrong woman and thus making the outcry of the betrayed—similar to Esau's disappointment in Gen 27:33–36—seem all the more intense (29:25). Jacob is essentially repaid for his betrayal,[49] as it

---

49. On betrayal as a leitmotif, see Renate Andrea Klein, *Leseprozess als Bedeutun-gswandel: Eine rezeptionsästhetische Erzähltextanalyse der Jakobserzählungen der Genesis* (Arbeiten zur Bibel und ihrer Geschichte 11; Leipzig: Evangelische Verlagsanstalt, 2002), 182–83. This work is an example of the consistent application of the method of narrative analysis; however, she goes into only a few of the "women texts" in detail.

were, in the sense of cause and effect. The reader is not informed about how Leah or Rachel feels about their father's deception, thus pushing the two sisters into the role of victims. For the time being, the conflict is resolved when Jacob, who is supposed to be the lord over his relatives (Gen 27:29), agrees to work another seven years as a servant to pay the bride-price for Rachel, even though the two are married immediately.

In the constellation of the people in this story, which tells how Laban goes from a host to a betrayer as well as a retaliator for the injustice done to Isaac, it is striking that Laban's wife, the mother of Leah and Rachel, is absent. In contrast to the story about the matchmaking of Rebekah, in which the mother is the reference point of the household (cf. 24:28: "mother's house"), this woman does not appear in any of the long stories in Gen 29–31. It is uncertain as to whether her death should be silently presupposed or if it concerns a topos in which the mother is not present—or is even powerless—in stories in which the father wrongs the daughters (cf. Gen 19).

3.3.3. A Birthing Contest as a Struggle for the Promise to Become a Great Nation (Gen 29–30)

In many ways, the conflict that emerges from the bridal betrayal determines the first two decades of the new family. Jacob cannot come to terms with Leah as his involuntarily wedded wife and hates her because of her father's betrayal (29:31). To compensate for that, YHWH opens her womb, while Jacob's beloved Rachel is and remains barren. Here God is seen as the giver of fertility. If his gift fails to present itself, that person is infertile.

Leah's first four births are told in all of four verses. The unloved wife bears her husband one son after the other. When this series of births is concluded with the note that she stopped having children, this is not to be understood as temporary infertility but rather points to the fact that, after fulfilling his marital duty, which resulted in four sons, Jacob stops going to Leah (see 30:15–16 on this).

Leah names each of her four sons by pointing to her own fate with the children's names. Reuben (29:32) is essentially a cry of joy ("behold, a son!") confirming that YHWH has seen her affliction. To him she attaches her hope for Jacob's love. With the second son Simeon, the compensation for her lack of affection focuses on God having heard that she is not loved (29:33). With Levi, the naming is neutrally formulated ("he was named Levi"); however, with this name Leah once again points to her unreciprocated desire for Jacob. Of all namings, there is no reference to YHWH in the name of the ancestor of the priestly dynasty (29:34). The name of the fourth son has a conciliatory justification that exclusively expresses her gratitude to YHWH, as if Leah has finally come to terms, as it were, with the circumstances in her life (29:35).

After this peace, the next verse, Gen 30:1, brings action into the family constellation with a new narrative beginning. Rachel is dissatisfied with her situation as the beloved yet barren wife. She demands children from Jacob, which he repudiates by referring to the giver of fertility and the fact that he has fulfilled his own marital duties to the best of his ability: it is not he who is denying her children but YHWH. As a solution to this humiliating situation of childlessness in patriarchal societies, Rachel chooses the same strategy as Sarah. She gives Jacob her slave Bilhah as a surrogate mother and soon has two sons whose names express her own fate, not that of their biological mother. With the first son she feels justified by God; with the second son she feels victorious over her sister, who has many children. What is expressed in the name Naphtali in Gen 30:8 is not a quarrel between sisters but the founding of Israel. This becomes clear from the parallel verse in Gen 32:28 (Hebrew 32:29), in which Jacob is inaugurated as a "wrestler with God":[50]

Gen 30:8	Gen 32:28
Then Rachel said:	Then he said to Jacob:
Wrestlings with God	Your name (שְׁמֶךָ)
(נַפְתּוּלֵי אֱלֹהִים) have I	will no longer be Jacob,
wrestled (נִפְתַּלְתִּי עִם)	but Israel (יִשְׂרָאֵל),
with my sister,	for you have
yet I have prevailed (יָכֹלְתִּי)!	fought with (שָׂרִיתָ עִם)
And she called his name (שְׁמוֹ)	God (אֱלֹהִים) and with men
fighter, Naphtali (נַפְתָּלִי).	and have prevailed (וַתּוּכָל).

Like their husband, the two women wrestle with God. In Peniel, Jacob fights to cross over into the promised land, while Leah and Rachel fight for the founding of the house of Israel, for according to Ruth 4:11 it is the two women who built up the house of Israel. What is told in Gen 29–30 is not proof that the Bible saw women as "childbearing machines"; rather, the text is the founding legend of the egalitarianly organized people of the twelve tribes.

Twelve children are born to the family in the parental household of the women. In addition to Leah's four sons and Rachel's two juridical sons previously discussed, the two sons Gad and Asher are from Leah's maidservant Zilpah, as well as Issachar, with whom Leah became pregnant after selling the

---

50. For more detail on this, see Irmtraud Fischer, "Der erkämpfte Segen (Gen 32,23–33)," *BK* 58 (2003): 106.

mandrakes to Rachel (30:14–18). With this plant, which was regarded as a
homeopathic aphrodisiac, Leah purchases one single night with her husband
and immediately becomes pregnant again. After that another son, Zebulun,
is born, whose name once again (cf. 29:34; 30:20) indicates her hopes for her
husband to remain with her. Apparently this also occurs, for Leah becomes
pregnant yet again. With her seventh and final child, Leah gives birth to a girl.
Leah names her Dinah, but there is no justification for the name, which puts
the only daughter at a disadvantage compared to the sons.[51] Perhaps one can
conclude that the note about Dinah was added later in order to be able to tell
the story in Gen 34, in which Dinah plays a central role.

In the last of the births outside of the promised land, Joseph, Rachel's
long-hoped-for first son, is born. The name that she gives the child is nearly
disappointing, for she is impatiently waiting for the next child to follow: "May
YHWH add to me yet another son" (30:24). In fact, Rachel, who believed that
she would die without children (30:1), dies during the birth of her second
child. Benjamin is born in the land. On the way back to the ancestral homeland, Rachel's labor pains begin. She puts all of her strength into the birth of
her son, whom she then names Ben-Oni, "son of my vitality."[52] She dies after
childbirth near Bethlehem and is buried there as well. Rachel's tomb is the
only ancestral burial site that is also mentioned outside of Genesis, whereby
special historical significance is attributed to this tradition (1 Sam 10:2; cf. Jer
31:15).[53]

3.3.4. The Break with the Branch of the Family in the East: Another Female Narrative

What began as a contest between two main wives for the affection of the
same husband develops with each child into more of a wrestling with God for
descendants. After the episode about purchasing the mandrakes, no more is
said of a conflict between the sisters. On the contrary, Rachel and Leah work
together in the following story about the family's return to the promised land

---

51. For this contrast, see Navarro Puerto, "Las extrañas del Génesis," 169–72.

52. For this, see Stefanie Schäfer-Bossert, "Den Männern die Macht und der Frau
die Trauer? Ein kritischer Blick auf die Deutung von אוֹן—oder: Wie nennt Rahel ihren
Sohn?" in Feministische Hermeneutik und Erstes Testament: Analysen und Interpretationen
(ed. Hedwig Jahnow et al.; Stuttgart: Kohlhammer, 1994), 106–25.

53. On the great significance of Rachel in the Bible and Jewish reception history, see
Samuel H. Dresner, Rachel (Minneapolis: Fortress, 1994). For Rachel's tomb, see Susan
Starr Sered, "Rachel's Tomb and the Milk Grotto of the Virgin Mary: Two Women's Shrines
in Bethlehem," JFSR 2 (1986): 7–22.

(Gen 31). They agree on their assessment of their father: he is exploiting both his son-in-law as well as his own daughters. He constantly changed the working conditions for Jacob, and he used up the bride-price, which was apparently intended to serve as emergency provisions for the daughters in the event of being widowed or divorced (31:7–16).[54]

Leah and Rachel even consider themselves to be legitimate heirs to the wealth that has been transferred from Laban to Jacob (31:16) as a result of the successful breeding of the flocks (Gen 30:31–43). On the one hand, the text emphasizes how competent Jacob is at his work and that the prosperity of the young family is the result of hard work and God's blessing. On the other hand, it allows the self-confidence of the women to become apparent: in their original household in which the marriage is lived out irregularly in opposition to patrilocal customs, they and their children are entitled to the goods derived from the father (31:16). The fact that the two sisters claim the legitimacy of the succession in the family for themselves is also proven by the story about Rachel stealing the teraphim, which also tells of the daughters' ultimate separation from their father's household (31:19–55 [Hebrew 31:19–32:1]).

When the decision is made to emigrate and return[55] to the promised land, Rachel steals אֶת־הַתְּרָפִים אֲשֶׁר לְאָבִיהָ, "her father's teraphim" (Gen 31:19). What is meant by teraphim is not completely clear. From the episode in 1 Sam 19:13–16 it can be concluded that Michal places the teraphim in David's bed to hide his absence from his pursuers. This means that they can probably be imagined as larger, human-like figurines. Whether these idols represented deified ancestors cannot be determined with the necessary accuracy.[56] Laban at least calls them "my *elohim*," "my gods" (31:30). Apparently the teraphim are, however, in the possession of the respective main line of the genealogy. When Rachel steals her father's teraphim, she thus robs him—and thus his sons, who are her brothers—of the legitimacy of the clan. Ktziah Spanier pointed to the fact that the teraphim are found only in the narrative context of the northern kingdom, in the region of those tribes that trace back

---

54. Thus also Kenneth A. Mathews, *Genesis 11:27–50:26* (NAC 1B; Nashville: Broadman & Holman, 2005), 516, who points out that, in any case, the part of the inheritance that the women are speaking about is entitled only to male descendants.

55. In Gen 31:22–23, 25, leaving the land is presented as Jacob's flight and pursuit by Laban. The similarities that echo in Exod 14:5–9 were demonstrated by David W. Cotter, *Genesis* (Berit Olam: Studies in Hebrew Narrative and Poetry; Collegeville, Minn.: Liturgical Press, 2003), 236.

56. According to Niditch, "Genesis," 21.

to Rachel.[57] This episode at least (still?) sees the main line of the primeval ancestors in the northern kingdom.

It is not surprising that Laban is hurt by the loss. He and his sons immediately set out to pursue the family that has disappeared under the cover of night and to hold them accountable (31:22–30). Jacob apparently knows nothing about the theft of the teraphim, since he certainly would not have endangered his favorite wife through his declaration that the thief deserves to die (31:32). Rachel manages to use a trick to evade Laban's search. But the episode in which the woman sits on the household gods hidden under her camel's saddle and claims to be menstruating also has polemic traits (31:34–35): if the teraphim had any type of value or impact, they are in any case unclean as a result of this action and thus ineffective for cult rituals.

The question of whether Jacob's command in Gen 35:2 to remove the "foreign gods" (אֶת־אֱלֹהֵי הַנֵּכָר) before the vow of Bethel can be fulfilled has a literary connection to the story of the household idols is difficult to answer. The final text always connects the two episodes, since the legitimacy of the clan is not guaranteed through the possession of household gods in the promised land but rather through the transfer of the promises from the father to the son determined by God for this purpose.

The transfer of clan legitimacy into the promised land by taking along the household idols apparently has the effect that none of the sons will ever again go to one of his mother's brothers to get a wife. With this episode, the narrator severs the connection to the branch of the family remaining in the east. In the interwoven section about the separation from his daughters' kin, Laban becomes the "Aramean," the founding father of a nation with which Israel is related but with which there were many conflicts in the history of the northern kingdom.

The section on the final separation between Aram and Israel is structured not merely as a story about a covenant but instead as a story about women. The marriage contract with the daughters is seen as being equivalent with the establishment of the regional borders between the two peoples (31:44–55 [Hebrew 31:44-32:1]), now sealed with a covenant meal. The text even makes the part of the contract concerning the women the top priority. Since Jacob lived his married life in the household of his wives up until this point, the conclusion of the marriage contract at this point in time is not unusual. Of all people, the betraying father, whom Jacob can thank for his polygamy, insists when he is separated from his daughters that Jacob neither

---

57. See Ktziah Spanier, "Rachel's Theft of the Teraphim: Her Struggle for Family Primacy," *VT* 42 (1992): 404–12.

mistreat either of the wives nor take any other wives (31:50). The story ends with Laban's blessing over his daughters and grandchildren (31:55 [Hebrew 32:1]), whereby in this branch of the family the daughters are again emphasized before the sons, since there is never mention of a corresponding blessing over the male descendants.

3.4. The Fourth Generation: The Fate of the Twelve Tribes Nation Is Decided by Women

After the separation from the genealogical branch of Milcah and Nahor, the move to the promised land that is accompanied by wrestling with God takes place (Gen 32:22–32 [Hebrew 32:23–33]), which causes Jacob to become Israel. The reunion with his cheated brother, which Jacob feared and for which he took all precautions to ensure that his beloved Rachel would be best protected (33:1–7), takes place—after successfully wrestling with God—without any complications (Gen 33). The old conflicts have been resolved; the return to the place of departure at Bethel (35:1–15) and to his father and his burial (35:27–29) are possible, since Esau will settle outside of the promised land, in his wives' native land.

The suspense is built up in the stories of Gen 34–50 through the fate of the next generation, Jacob's children. Since Jacob's twelve sons make up the egalitarianly organized twelve tribes nation, no further main lines of the genealogy must be created from this generation. Nevertheless, stories are told that emphasize the dominance of individual "tribes,"[58] thus giving an account of historical dominations in the narrative.

3.4.1. Dinah and Her Brothers Simeon and Levi (Gen 34)

The first narrative that justifies Simeon and Levi being eliminated from the genealogical dominance begins as a story about the rape of Jacob's only daughter Dinah.[59] She went out to see (ראה) the *daughters* of the land, when

---

58. If older research was convinced of the historical existence of a twelve-tribe alliance (amphictyony; for this, see Martin Noth, *Das System der zwölf Stämme Israels* [Darmstadt: Wissenschaftliche Buchgesellschaft, 1966]), modern research is significantly more critical of this.

59. On this chapter, see the dissertation by Susanne Scholz, *Rape Plots: A Feminist Cultural Study of Genesis 34* (Studies in Biblical Literature 13; New York: Lang, 2000), which sees Dinah as the "key figure" (167) of the text. She reads the story of the act of violence committed against Jacob's daughter within the context of the case law on rape in Germany in the nineteenth century.

Shechem, the prince of the land, sees (ראה) her, takes her, lays with her, and violates her (34:1–2). This sequence of four narratives in 34:2 makes the rape seem like an imprudent and rash act. When it then says that he likes her, that he loves the young woman, that he speaks tenderly to her (34:3), and is then willing to pay any bride-price for her (34:11–12), the act of violence and its consequences are thus presented from the view of the perpetrator. The victim's perspective is never given a voice in the entire story; Dinah never has a chance to speak before her brothers, her father, Shechem, or his father. She is presented as a victim, and the act of violence committed against her becomes a matter of "honor" for the men.

Old Testament law has two different solutions for the criminal act of rape against an unmarried woman.[60] In the Book of the Covenant (Exod 22:15–16), where the word choice also could include the seduction of an inexperienced girl, the man is sentenced to pay the standard bride-price and must marry the woman unless her father refuses to permit it. In this way the young woman at least has the opportunity to vote against a marriage with a rapist, while this is not provided for according to Deut 22:28–29. In this legal policy the violently forced sexual relations automatically become a marriage, including all corresponding payments. The rapist must marry his victim and may never divorce her. Even though this guarantees a lifelong obligation to care for the woman, the woman at the same time loses any opportunity to free herself from the hands of her rapist.

In accordance with these policies,[61] the story of Dinah being raped is continued with negotiations on the bride-price. Dinah's father and brothers, who indeed consider this to be a violation of the family's honor, falsely enter into the negotiations and demand circumcision. The original text presumably demanded only that the groom be circumcised. A redactional layer[62] extended the circumcision demand and the intermarriage offer (34:9, 15–17) to all members of both groups, such that in the final text version of the story all of Shechem's men were circumcised and not only Shechem was condemned to the brothers' vengeance but all Shechemite men who were fevered and in pain following the procedure. The story about Dinah's rape and how it is avenged tells of a massacre against an entire ethnic group of which one member was guilty of attacking Jacob's family. In the narrative, Jacob's position is also criti-

---

60. For more detail on this, see the essay by Karin Finsterbusch in this volume.

61. Tikva Frymer-Kensky ("Virginity in the Bible," in *Gender and Law in the Hebrew Bible and the Ancient Near East* [ed. Victor H. Matthews, Bernard M. Levinson, and Tikva Frymer-Kensky; JSOTSup 262; Sheffield: Sheffield Academic Press, 1998], 86–96) has already read these three texts in conjunction with one another.

62. See the delineation in Fischer, *Women Who Wrestled*, 97–98.

cally opposed to the escalation of vengeance by the brothers. He urges them to restrain themselves, while mainly Simeon and Levi, Jacob's second- and third-born sons, invoke the argument of disgraced honor in their defense (34:7, 30–31). This opposition is also addressed in Jacob's tribal blessing in Gen 49:5–7, in which he condemns the act and even curses the two tribes, which are threatened with being scattered and dispersed among the other tribes.

The formulation בְּנוֹת הָאָרֶץ, "daughters of the land," in 34:1 could also, of course, indicate the undesirability of mixing with the local population (cf. Gen 27:46); however, this is by no means a technical term to refer to foreign women in the matter of mixed marriages. The history of exegesis has read Gen 34 as a plea for endogamous marriages. Levi, the founder of the priestly dynasty, is seen as a pioneer, just as his descendant Phinehas is cited as an authority by opponents of exogamous marriages.[63] In the book of Judith, Simeon is also declared a hero for avenging his sister's rape. In Judith's speech, Dinah stands for the sanctuary that is in danger of being violated, which the descendant of Simeon actually prevents by killing the general (Jdt 9:1–14, esp. 9:8).

3.4.2. Bilhah and Reuben (Gen 35:21–22)

While Jacob's second and third sons disqualify themselves for the leading role through the Dinah story, the firstborn son disqualifies himself through a short note about incest.

After the death of her mistress Rachel, Jacob apparently made Bilhah his "concubine" (פִּילֶגֶשׁ). Only here is Bilhah seen as a concubine. While Rachel was alive, she was Rachel's "slave" (שִׁפְחָה) and in her position within the family a "maidservant" (אָמָה) since she was brought into Jacob and Rachel's marriage as a surrogate mother. Sexual relations with concubines—in contrast to those with slaves and maidservants—are considered marriages, even if of a lesser legal status.[64] It can be assumed that they come about without paying a bride-price.

Reuben sleeps with this woman. There is nothing said of any consent on the part of Bilhah, so this incestuous act is not only a severe violation of the father's sphere but also a potential act of violence against his concubine. The only reaction reported is that Jacob heard of the act; the old patriarch remains

---

63. See Num 25; Ezra, the opponent of mixed marriages, traces his ancestry back to Phinehas; see Ezra 7:1–5.

64. On concubines, see Karen Engelken, *Frauen im Alten Israel: Eine begriffsgeschichtliche und sozialrechtliche Studie zur Stellung der Frau im Alten Testament* (BWANT 130; Stuttgart: Kohlhammer, 1990), 74–126.

strangely idle, similarly to how he acted after Dinah was raped. However, Jacob's judgment of the act becomes clear in the tribal blessing over Reuben: the firstfruits of his vigor rose up against his father with exuberant vitality (Gen 49:3–4). With this act and its valuation by the ancestral father, Reuben is explicitly disqualified for a leading role within the family, which he would have been entitled to as the firstborn son.

3.4.3. Tamar and Judah

In contrast to Jacob's first three sons with Leah, whose actions are also rebuked in the tribal blessings of Gen 49, two sons—Leah's fourth-born and Rachel's firstborn—are highlighted in longer stories. Rachel's son is presented as the one who will rescue Israel in the Joseph story. Judah is given a leading role both when Joseph is sold into slavery (Gen 37:26–27) as well as in the episode surrounding Rachel's second-born son Benjamin (43:1–10; 44:14–34). Something of a founding legend of the house of Judah is incorporated into the Joseph story in two attempts (Gen 38).[65]

Judah's first wife is introduced as the daughter of the Canaanite Shua (Gen 38:1–2). In Chezib, the "city of deception," she gives birth to three sons: Er, Onan, and Shelah (38:3–5). Judah arranges a marriage for his firstborn son to a woman without any genealogy but who instead is mentioned by the name of Tamar. Through this, Tamar and Judah are narratively linked to one another from the very beginning (38:6). Since the firstborn son Er dies prematurely,[66] Judah places his second-born son under the levirate obligation. According to Deut 25:5–10, this provides that, in the event of a still-undivided inheritance, a brother must beget a son with the widow of a brother who has died without children, so that the name of the late brother will be carried on. However, Onan, "the vital one," denies Tamar offspring, since this would catapult him from the position of the principal heir if he were to beget a son. The injustice that ultimately also leads to the death of this man who carries vitality in his name lies in the fact that, although he sleeps with Tamar, he practices coitus interruptus to deny her the entire reason why he is supposed to have sexual relations with her in the first place (Gen 38:8–9; Deut 25:5–6). YHWH also causes the death of this son of Judah (Gen 38:10). Since Judah's only remain-

---

65. Eva Salm, *Juda und Tamar: Eine exegetische Studie zu Gen 38* (FB 76; Würzburg: Echter, 1996), devoted her dissertation to the text. Phyllis A. Bird, *Missing Persons and Mistaken Identities: Women and Gender in Ancient Israel* (OBT; Minneapolis: Fortress, 1997), 202–8, addresses the aspect of prostitution in Gen 38.

66. In Gen 38:7, his name is to be understood as a play on words using the two consonants ע and ר: עֵר is evil, רַע.

ing son is not grown up yet and he assumes that Tamar is guilty of the deaths of both of his sons, he sends his daughter-in-law back to her father's house (38:11). With this action, Judah commits an injustice, since according to levirate law he can either release Tamar from the levirate obligation so that she is free to marry another man and start a family (see Deut 25:7–10), or he must care for the woman in his own household, if the demand of the levirate obligation is to be upheld. Yet even once his son Shelah is grown up, Judah still does not give him to Tamar (Gen 38:14).

Genesis 38:12–30 tells how Tamar personally gets from Judah what he denied her with the upheld levirate obligation: descendants. Almost as an excuse for Judah's behavior of going to a(n) (alleged) prostitute, an initial note is made informing the reader that his wife had died (38:12). Here he again meets the man who was mentioned in the context of meeting his wife (38:1, 12). Tamar is told that Judah is leaving the place where she and he are both known in order to go to shear the sheep (38:13). Starting in 38:14, readers are taken into a scene whose background remains unknown to Judah as a narrative figure. Tamar takes off her widow's clothes, veils herself so as not to be recognized, and sits down at the gate of Enaim ("dual fountain"). There she wants to appear to her father-in-law as a prostitute and seduce him. Research has pondered how Judah was able to identify the woman as a prostitute. It was certainly not the veil, which would only conceal what a prostitute wants to offer,[67] but instead the place where the woman is sitting alone: the gate is the men's gathering place; a single woman there is apparently identified by men as being available in exchange for money.

Tamar has assessed her father-in-law in a dramatically realistic way: he falls for the woman offering herself and immediately begins negotiations for the prostitute's wages (38:15–18). Since he apparently does not have the desired wage of the young goat with him, Tamar demands a triple pledge that will be able to clearly identify him. Judah does not recognize his daughter-in-law's masquerade and cluelessly leaves her with the most personal things that he has with him—comparable today to a credit card, mobile phone, and keychain. Even though he is aware of the risk of falling into disrepute, he does not resist the offer. He thus does not personally go to bring the wage and pick up the material signs of his identity but instead sends a friend. However, this friend must then find out that there was never a prostitute in Enaim and must return to Judah without achieving anything (38:20–23).

---

67. As already pointed out in Benno Jacob, *Das erste Buch der Tora: Genesis* (Berlin: Schocken, 1934), 715.

Tamar, apparently because what she did was justice for injustice (38:26), immediately becomes pregnant and continues to live as a decent widow in her parental house until her pregnancy becomes public and is reported to Judah. The two narrative figures who are directly linked to one another at the beginning of the story (38:6–11) apparently only interact via third parties any longer (38:13, 24), which is why Tamar also cunningly forces contact with Judah. Without finding out information about the more detailed living conditions of the daughter-in-law whom he damned to be a childless widow for life, Judah imposes the harshest possible sentence on her.

Tamar's wisdom is now proven yet again. She does not send Judah the pledge in order to resolve the issue within the family, but instead allows herself to be brought out for the death penalty to be performed so that she can then publicly[68] present the seal, staff, and cord belonging to the man by whom she is pregnant. In this way Judah cannot deny the paternity and must publicly reconcile with Tamar—which he also does (38:25–26).

Tamar used deception to obtain the goods of the levirate law, although the law does not entitle women to enforceable rights. She gives birth to twins, with the notes on the birth being structured similarly to those for Rebekah: Tamar's twins were also already fighting for the birthright while still in the womb. However, the midwife marks the firstborn son, who, as in the case of Esau and Jacob, later still will not be able to create the main line: in Ruth 4:18–22, the succession of generations of Judah is structured as the *toledot* of Perez, Tamar's second-born son, with David listed as the last member. With this narrative, the founding of the house of Judah is presented as the result of the will of a woman insistent upon justice. Even the names of Tamar's children point to the events during the birth, from which men in the ancient Near East were excluded. Ruth 4:12 also traces the founding of the "house of Perez" back to Tamar giving birth for Judah. The royal line thus thanks its existence to an unconventional woman who would not allow herself to be removed from the generational line.

3.4.4. Joseph, Potiphar's Wife, and Aseneth

As the story in Gen 38 serves to emphasize Judah as the line of promise, the Joseph story underscores the emphasis on the "house of Joseph," of "Ephraim and Manasseh," both designations that are used for the territory of the northern kingdom of Israel (see, e.g., Josh 17:17; Amos 5:6; Zech 10:6).

---

68. This is pointed out by Helen Schüngel-Straumann, "Tamar," *BK* 39 (1984): 154.

From the very beginning, Joseph is painted in a special light in the so-called Joseph story (Gen 37–50). Initially envied by his brothers for being the father's favorite son and ultimately sold into slavery, he becomes the one to rescue all of Israel by making the necessary provisions in Egypt to save Jacob's clan from starvation. Within the Joseph story there are three texts that are relevant for our question at hand: the story about Potiphar's wife; the marriage note regarding Joseph and Aseneth; and the account of the migration to Egypt.

In a reversal of the gender of the characters, Gen 39 tells of the abandonment of a member of the ancestral family (cf. the ancestral women in Gen 12:10–20; 20; 26:1–11), who is thus put into danger of being integrated into a foreign genealogical line. In Egypt, Joseph has the status of a purchased slave and is thus also bound to the orders of his master, including in sexual matters. His master could give him to a female slave, and as a slave he would be unable to have a choice in the matter. While Potiphar's wife, who is significantly not mentioned by name, is able to give the slave orders, according to ancient Near East marital law she is, however, not authorized to have sexual contact outside of her own marriage. The offense of adultery carries the risk of death, even more so if it is committed by someone who has no personal rights. In the story, Potiphar's wife is presented as the prototypic "strange woman" in the colors of an adulteress, as is also found, for instance, in Prov 1–9.[69] In the Joseph story, the seductive woman who desires the young foreigner and is not ashamed to betray her husband does not have her own role. As the antihero, she contrasts with the young and handsome yet at the same time loyal and God-fearing hero (39:2–6). Her external appearance is not mentioned; the narrator leaves it up to the reader to decide if she is beautiful or older than Joseph. The focus is only on her desire for him day after day, to which the unwavering man does not give in. Joseph attempts to argue as a wise man on ethical grounds, while the strange woman is guided only by her passion (39:7–12). When she does not get what she wants, her desire turns into hatred (39:13–20), and she attempts to destroy Joseph. In 2 Sam 13 a very similar abrupt change of unjust desire is told of Amnon, who wants to sleep with his

---

69. This correlation was already established by Athalya Brenner, *The Israelite Woman: Social Role and Literary Type in Biblical Narrative* (Biblical Seminar 2; Sheffield: JSOT Press, 1985), 111–12. Alice Bach (*Women, Seduction, and Betrayal in Biblical Narrative* [Cambridge: Cambridge University Press, 1997], 57) criticizes the exegesis that has stylized the woman as the "prototypic strange woman." Bach, who devotes herself to the narrative in detail (34–61), examines, among other things, the key words of the narrative and shows that the story works with a reversal of gender stereotypes: Joseph's body and the sexual desire of the woman are perceived.

half-sister Tamar and also does so against her will. There, too, the victim of a sexual attack argues using the ethics of Israel. However, as a woman she is unable to escape the rape (2 Sam 13:11–18).

Within the Joseph story, the story about Potiphar's wife acts as proof of the divine support for the wrongfully humiliated brother (Gen 37) and slave (Gen 39). It also demonstrates this man's wisdom, which truly unfolds in the provisions he takes against the long famine.

The account of the migration of Jacob's clan is structured as the genealogy of a nation in a nutshell in Gen 46:5–27. The members of the individual tribes are introduced as the "names of the children of Jacob who went to Egypt" in 46:8, but then—in accordance with the polygynous marriage of the ancestral father—structured according to his wives (46:15, 19, 22), whereby the list of Rachel's sons is framed by references to her (46:19, 22). The two maidservants Zilpah and Bilhah are each introduced in dependency to their mistresses (46:18, 25). The list also contains the names of exemplary women such as the daughter Dinah (46:15), the granddaughter Serah from the tribe of Asher (46:17), as well as a daughter-in-law who came along to Egypt from the tribe of Simeon (46:10) and Aseneth, the daughter-in-law from Egypt (46:20). The listing of these exemplary women emphasizes that an entire nation moved to Egypt and that only Joseph, who was already residing in Egypt, married an Egyptian woman. Israel's ethnic integrity is thus still constituted in the promised land as the introduction to the list insists through its emphasis on daughters and wives (46:5–7). However, in Egypt this group grows into a *great* nation (Exod 1:7–9).

Joseph's marriage to Aseneth is initiated by the pharaoh (41:45). She is introduced as the daughter of Potiphera, the priest of On. In the seven prosperous years Joseph begat two sons with her, Ephraim and Manasseh. According to the narrative perspective, the father and not the mother names the children, using their names to point to his own fate (41:50–52).

4. Why Is Such a Lead-In Written on the History of Israel?

The texts of the ancestral narratives are most certainly not all from a single source. How and when the individual texts were created, composed, and redacted is hotly disputed in present-day research on the Pentateuch. The old explanations of sources independent of one another, for which the abbreviations J, E, P, and D (Yahwist, Elohist, Priestly source, Deuteronomist) stand and that extend back to the early royal era, are outdated. They have become obsolete due to newer research on the historical circumstances in the early royal era.[70] It can thus be carefully formulated that the texts were worked on with certainty until far into the Persian era, the end point can be said to be before 400 B.C.E., and the latest start of the creation of the individual narratives can be said to be the time shortly before the downfall of the northern kingdom, since there were apparently independent traditions in the northern kingdom. Dealing with the catastrophe in the southern kingdom makes it necessary to synthesize the ancestral parents of the north (Jacob and Joseph traditions) with those of the south.

The genealogical construction of the dominance of the parents of the southern kingdom is possible after 722 B.C.E. at the earliest; it was probably first construed after 701 B.C.E., when Judah prevailed through the Assyrian crises. A considerable part of the narratives presupposes the processing of Israel's second major catastrophe, exile and the loss of people and land, as well as the destruction of Jerusalem. Within the Pentateuch, the lead-in of the ancestral narratives expresses hope that Israel will be able to preserve its land not because it observes the Torah but because the land is given to Israel exclusively as a promise from God. Despite all of the confusion and turmoil of history, which can also mean temporarily leaving or even losing the land, Israel as a nation is entitled to the land with the same name due to a sworn covenant (Gen 15). With these narratives that emerge from a general history of humankind (Gen 1–11), Israel's life in the promised land is written as firmly anchored in the primordial world order.[71] At the same time, the development of the nation is told in the form of family narratives as begetting and giving birth; the great importance of women is thus quite obvious. But the women are also bearers of the promise, and they also determine the inheritance succession of their sons. In this regard, the ancestral narratives can only be compared with the narratives about the beginnings of the kingdom.

---

70. On this see, for example, the best-selling monograph by Israel Finkelstein and Neil Asher Silberman, *The Bible Unearthed: Archaeology's New Vision of Ancient Israel and the Origin of Its Ancient Texts* (New York: Touchstone, 2001).

71. For more detail, see Irmtraud Fischer, "Israels Landbesitz als Verwirklichung der primordialen Weltordnung: Die Bedeutung des Landes in den Erzelternerzählungen," *Jahrbuch für Biblische Theologie* 23 (2008): 3–24.

THE FEMALE SAVIORS OF ISRAEL'S LIBERATOR: TWELVE "DAUGHTERS" IN EXODUS 1 AND 2

Jopie Siebert-Hommes
Universiteit van Amsterdam

1. TWELVE SONS

The book of Exodus describes how Moses liberates the people of Israel from oppression and slavery in Egypt. It is a men's book, undoubtedly: *sons* are in the foreground; *daughters* stay in the shadows. Right at the beginning, the major role of the sons is emphasized: their names are mentioned, all twelve of them:

> Reuben, Simeon, Levi, Judah, Issachar, Zebulun,
> Benjamin, Dan, Naphtali, Gad, Asher and Joseph,
> he was already in Egypt. (1:1)

Naming is an important issue in the Hebrew Bible. A person who is given a name is granted a role. Sometimes when someone assumes a new role, she or he receives a new name with it: Abram becomes Abraham, Sarai becomes Sarah, Jacob becomes Israel. The name the person receives is linked to the role that she or he is to play in history. The fact that the names of the twelve sons are mentioned so explicitly emphasizes that *they* are to be the leading figures in the ensuing events. They are the main characters in the fight of the "sons of Israel" against the Egyptians, the struggle between God and the pharaoh. Then, after they are liberated, these sons are guided through the desert. Women were also present, of course! However, the Hebrew text speaks rigidly about "*sons* of Israel." Further, because their names are mentioned in the beginning of the book, Exodus is named שמות in the Hebrew Bible: "Names."

The literary construction of the book of Exodus is divided in two main parts. The first part tells of slavery and liberation (chs. 1–15). The second part describes Israel's journey through the wilderness and deals with the question:

How shall we live together in the new land? The answer is found in the Ten Commandments (the rules and laws), in short: "to love God and your neighbor" (chs. 16–40). So the content of Exodus is twofold: first the liberation from Egypt, then the "words of life" pronounced by God in the wilderness. The first two chapters form the introduction to the overall book.

God or the pharaoh? … life or death? … This is the war to be waged. Will the sons live or die? The narrator gives expression to this dilemma through the words of the pharaoh:

If it is a son, you shall kill him. (1:16)

Why is the pharaoh so eager to kill the sons? Why just the sons? Would it not be better if he killed the girls and the women? Surely that would have been more effective![1] At the level of a historical representation, this would be the case. Here, however, we are dealing with a *theological* concept: the son is the bearer of the divine promise, as in the accounts of the patriarchs in the book of Genesis. It is upon him that the continuation of God's history depends. Consequently, the birth of a son is always a major event in the Bible. Sometimes it is even questionable whether there will be a son![2] The birth of a daughter, on the other hand, is usually not worth mentioning at all. Daughters are barely visible in the Bible; if they are mentioned, it is only in a minor role. There are scarcely any accounts about the birth of daughters. The sentence "She gave birth to a son" has no counterpart in report to the birth of a daughter. Where the birth of daughters is mentioned at all, it is only as a collective and as an addition to the birth of sons: "he begat sons and daughters. It rarely happens that a daughter appears as the subject of a story. Most commonly she is the object, sometimes even the "direct object," upon which the actions of the sons are concentrated.[3]

However, in the opening chapters of Exodus, *daughters* occupy a special position. This is remarkable and a striking exception to the aforementioned rule that sons are dominant and daughters are relegated to the background. The divine promise will undoubtedly be realized through the son, yet he is merely the passive object here. The actions take place around him, not through him. Daughters, on the contrary, are the *subject*: they assume an active role and appear to be of decisive importance for the stability of the divine promise.

---

1. See Phyllis Trible, "Depatriarchalizing in Biblical Interpretation," *JAAR* 41 (1973): 34.

2. See Gen 15:2; 18:11; 25:21; 29:31.

3. An example of this is Dinah, the daughter of Leah, in Gen 34. Although the story concerns her, she makes no contribution whatsoever. Her opinion is not sought, and what happens to her serves only to excuse the actions undertaken by the "sons."

It is fascinating to see how sons and daughters function within the literary structure of Exod 1 and 2.

1.1. MOSES THE LIBERATOR

First of all, the central position in the opening chapters of Exodus is assigned to Moses. He is the son who will liberate his people. The story of his birth is the core of the literary structure of the text. The other pericopes are arranged all around:

> prologue (1:1–7)
> > servitude (1:8–14)
> > the midwives (1:15–22)
> > > the birth of the liberator (2:1–10)
> > Moses in Egypt (2:11–15)
> > Moses in Midian (2:16–22)
> epilogue (2:23–25)

A short prologue is followed by two stories, one of which is about men, the other about women. Then, exactly in the center, the birth story of Moses. Thereupon two more stories follow—a men's story and a women's—and finally a short epilogue. The composition of these two chapters proves to be a closed unit in which each of the pericopes has its own remarkable structure.

The prologue (1:1–7) is framed by the expression "the sons of Israel." In 1:1 they are exclusively the descendants of Jacob; in 1:7 they have become a whole nation.

The following two pericopes prepare the birth story of Moses. The first one (1:8–14) deals with slavery and hard labor. Men are the main figures. We do not hear of any resistance. The second section (1:15–22), however, brings a surprising twist. The king of Egypt addresses women, midwives even! This theme is in direct contrast to the first, now it is about "giving birth," "fearing God," and "preserving life." Moreover, there is resistance now:

> The midwives did not do
> as the king of Egypt had ordered them. (1:17)

Although the two pericopes form a contrast in terms of content and theme, the structure exhibits a certain parallelism.

After the birth and rescue of Moses (exactly in the center of the two chapters), two pericopes follow: once again a men's story and a women's story. The men's story once again recounts servitude and violence: Moses witnesses the oppression of his brothers and kills the Egyptian. The women's story tells of the seven daughters of the priest Rehuel in Midian. They bring Moses into the house of their father, where he learns how to tend a flock until, after many years, he is called by God.

In the prologue, the sons of Israel are introduced; in the epilogue, God enters the stage. He sees and hears what is going on with the sons of Israel, and, with this, the change in Israel's fate begins.

As we have already said, in the middle we find the one son, Moses. He is the central figure in this story. But it is he who is threatened with death:

> Every son that is born,
> in the river you shall throw him. (1:22)

Will the son be alive or dead? Without sons,[4] the history of this nation has no future. Here, in the beginning of Exodus, the "sons of Israel" do not stand the slightest chance. They are forced into extreme servitude (1:13–14) or are already killed at birth (1:16). Accordingly, the history of Israel would come to an end.

2. Twelve Daughters

However, the history of Israel does not come to an end! In this very decisive moment, the future of Israel does not depend on sons but on daughters—and there are twelve daughters, too! While the twelve sons do *not* resist the measures of the pharaoh and allow themselves to be made into slaves, the twelve daughters do resist and make it possible for history to go on.

These daughters have, alongside the sons, a key position in these two opening chapters of Exodus. The words *son* and *daughter* are termed *Leitworte*. They arouse the readers' interest.[5] The structure of the text is determined by these two *Leitworte*, especially in 1:5–22 and 2:1–10. God's promise of life is

---

4. The fact that only the male children have to be killed is possibly related to "the patrilineal and patrilocal marriage form," which integrates the women into the family of the men. When a nation has a lack of men, it loses its identity in the society image. See Irmtraud Fischer, *Women Who Wrestled with God: Biblical Stories of Israel's Beginnings* (trans. Linda M. Malony; Collegeville, Minn.: Liturgical Press, 2005), 116.

5. The term *Leitwort* is taken from Martin Buber and Franz Rosenzweig, "Leitwort Style in Pentateuch Narrative," in *Scripture and Translation* (ed. Lawrence Rosenwald and Everett Fox; Bloomington: Indiana University Press 1994), 114: "By Leitwort I understand a word or root that is meaningfully repeated within a text or sequence of texts, those who attend to these repetitions will find a meaning of the text revealed or clarified, or at any rate made more emphatic."

indeed fulfilled with regard to the son, but he is only a passive object in this story: the developments occur around him. The daughters, on the other hand, are subjects: their actions are decisive for the future of the "sons of Israel." "It is a women's story, men are strikingly absent," observes Cheryl Exum, and she alludes to the inherent narrative irony: "Without Moses there would be no story, but without the initiative of these women, there would be no Moses!"[6]

The actual birth of Moses is recounted in an extremely sober fashion:

His mother conceived and bore a son. (Exod 2:2)

The boy does not have a name at this stage. This emphasizes the precarious situation of the newborn baby. Will he live at all?

Suddenly the daughter of the pharaoh appears right in the center of the pericope. She sees the child and has compassion. The verbs "to see" and "to have compassion" are decisive. From this very moment on, when the pharaoh's daughter *sees* the child and *shows compassion*, history begins to take a new direction. Thanks to her, the son remains alive.

But this daughter is not alone; she has eleven "sisters." Moses owes his very existence to twelve women. Because of them, he can live, grow up, and stay in Midian, where God will call him to lead the sons of Israel—represented by names at the beginning of the book—out of Egypt. This becomes possible due to the mediation of the twelve women. Their active intervention ensures that the history of Israel does not come to an end.

Who are these twelve? They are the two midwives; Moses' mother (who is called "daughter of Levi"); his sister; the pharaoh's daughter; and the seven daughters of the priest of Midian. Let us take a closer look at each of these figures, individually and collectively.

2.1. THE MIDWIVES

The first two women are introduced by name: Shiphrah and Puah. This is exceptional, as we see that the mighty pharaoh is left unnamed. Various commentators have attempted to reconstruct his name. The towns Pithom and Rameses are mentioned; perhaps it was Ramesses. We do not know. Some scholars suppose the name of the king to have been lost. Possibly. Yet the midwives have names! It seems plausible to see the monarch's anonymity as a narrative device. Has his name not been omitted on purpose? The unpretentious

---

6. J. Cheryl Exum, "You Shall Let Every Daughter Live: A study of Exodus 1.8–2.10," in *A Feminist Companion to Exodus to Deuteronomy* (FBC 6; ed. Athalya Brenner; Sheffield: Sheffield Academic Press 1994), 37–61; 52.

midwives have names: Shiphrah and Puah ("Beauty" and "Glow"). It is they who ensure that the children remain alive. The king, on the other hand, gives the order to kill, but he is shown to be powerless. His actions do not make his name. But the midwives make their names on account of their deeds.[7]

The actions of the midwives are introduced by a phrase indicating the framework within which they perform their task:

> The midwives feared God. (1:17; cf. 1:22)

We know from the book of Genesis that *to fear God* and *to kill* cannot possibly go together.[8] Anyone who fears God does not kill. This connection will also become clear to the pharaoh. He orders the midwives "to see," but instead of "seeing," the midwives "fear": they fear God. Here the Hebrew text provides a marvelous phonetic play on words that serves to underline the point of the story. In the Hebrew language, the expression "(you) see" [וראיתן] and "they fear" [ותיראן] are transcribed with the same letters but in a different order; they are inverted.[9] The midwives literally turn the whole affair the other way round. They do the exact opposite of what the pharaoh had ordered.

Remarkably, the pharaoh also makes a distinction regarding the gender of the newborn:

> If it is a son, put him to death;
> if it is a daughter, she shall live. (1:16)

The midwives, however, make no such distinction; they deal only with *children*:

> they allow the children to live. (1:17)

The midwives fear God and accordingly allow the children to live. There is no way they could kill a son!

The question as to whether the midwives were Egyptian or Hebrew women has often been posed, and opinions are diverse. The Hebrew text leaves both possibilities open. The Targumim and some Jewish exegetes of the Middle

---

7. The power of the pharaoh is opposed to the spirit and the inventiveness of the midwives, and the latter prove to be more powerful; so asserts Helen Schüngel-Straumann, *Anfänge feministischer Exegese: Gesammelte Beiträge, mit einem orientierenden Nachwort und einer Auswahlbibliographie* (Exegese in unserer Zeit 8; Münster: LIT, 2002), 263.

8. See Gen 20:11; 42:18.

9. Umberto M. D. Cassuto, *A Commentary on the Book of Exodus* (Jerusalem: Magnes, 1967), 14.

Ages assume that they were Hebrew. Translations such as the Septuagint and Vulgate and also Josephus (*Ant.* 2.206), suppose them to be Egyptians. Among modern interpreters, both views are found.

This story may very well have a thematic link to a myth about the Egyptian goddesses Isis and Nephtys, who were also midwives.[10] The authors of the text could feasibly have known of this myth. It tells how Isis and Nephtys were sent by the god Re in order to assist at the birth of the children of Rededjedet: "Let the children live!" It may well be that Shiphrah and Puah in Exodus are portrayed as Egyptian midwives who used their divine predecessors, Isis and Nephtys, as a model to exercise their duty.

The midwives in Exodus resemble the Egyptian goddesses, but they are not the same, as the story in Exodus is the exact opposite of that of the old Egyptian myth. While Re ordered Isis and Nephtys to let the children live, the pharaoh commands their death. Could it be that the pharaoh addresses Egyptian midwives? Jewish listeners know better. The names of Shiphrah and Puah sound pure Hebrew. Moreover, they fear God! They do not fear the god-king of Egypt; they disobey him. They let the children live, as Isis and Nephtys did.

Are the midwives Egyptian or Hebrew? The text of the Bible does not provide an unequivocal answer; both possibilities are left open. Perhaps this is intentional. There happens to be another curiosity in the command of the pharaoh, when he says:

> When you aid the Hebrew women in giving birth,
> see to the two stones. (1:16)

What could be meant by the expression "the two stones," as the literal rendering of the Hebrew text reads? We should probably think of two round stones that had a dual function at the delivery. First, they functioned as a kind of birthing stool upon which the woman in labor squatted or knelt in order to facilitate the delivery. Some ancient Near Eastern texts and relief drawings depict such a birthing stool being used in Egypt and elsewhere. Second, these stones indicate the place where, according to some texts, the child was laid after the delivery in order to see whether the baby would live or not. An Egyptian myth says that the god Thoth wrote the child's life span upon these stones.[11] According to this myth, the god had the power to decide whether the child would live or die. The two stones in Exod 1:16 above all indicate the place where the child came into the world, but the polysemy of the word

---

10. See the so-called Westcar Papyrus in T. Eric Peet, *A Comparative Study of the Literatures of Egypt, Palestine and Mesopotamia* (Eugene, Ore.: Wipf & Stock, 2007), 136.

11. Ibid., 112.

also brings the listener in touch with the context of this story. Here, at the two stones, the fate of the child is determined: Will the child live or die? The midwives decide to keep the children alive.

When the king demands an explanation and asks why they keep the children alive, they give a peculiar answer:

Not like the Egyptian women are the Hebrew women.
They are חיות. (1:19)

The meaning of the Hebrew word חיות is controversial.[12] It is a so-called *hapax legomenon*, a word that is found only once in the Bible. It is usually translated "vigorous, strong, lively." The word stem is related to the word חיות, used in the creation story to indicate the swarming of small, lively animals. Although these animals are not intended here, the word חיות has a clear connection with the verb חיה ("to live"). Therefore, the concept of *life* has to be recognized in the translation.

Furthermore, the word חיות may very well refer to the name of the first mother: Eve, חוה in Hebrew. Her name is an older form of the verb חיה ("to live"). Eve is named חוה by Adam, because she has become "the mother of all living" (Gen 3:20). Linguistically, our word חיות may be a plural form of this name. This raises the question of whether perhaps in Exod 1:19 the name of Eve, חוה, should also be recognized. In this event, the midwives' response should refer to the life-giving power of the first mother in the Bible, Eve. The Hebrew women are חיות; they are like Eve, life-producing, "mothers of all living."[13]

The first chapter of Exodus is full of references to the concept of "life." First, the pharaoh twice orders the daughters to be kept alive (1:16, 22). Then the narrator reports that the midwives keep *all* the children alive (1:17), after which the pharaoh asks *why* they kept the children alive (1:18). Furthermore, the midwives postulate that the mothers are חיות (life-producers; 1:19).

In addition to the word stem חיה ("life"), we find the stem ילד ("life-giving, giving birth") twelve times. The sons of Israel multiply and grow up in spite of everything. The mothers play a central role in this; they are of vital

---

12. See Jopie Siebert-Hommes, "Hebräerinnen sind חיות," in *"Dort ziehen Schiffe dahin...": Collected Communications to the XIVth Congress of the International Organization for the Study of the Old Testament, Paris 1992* (ed. Matthias Augustin and Klaus-Dietrich Schunk; BEATAJ 28; Frankfurt am Main: Lang 1996), 191–99.

13. See the chapter "Hebrew Women are Life Producers" in Jopie Siebert-Hommes, *Let the Daughters Live! The Literary Architecture of Exodus 1–2 as a Key for Interpretation* (Biblical Interpretation Series 37; Leiden: Brill, 1998), 101–10.

importance to the sons of Israel. They beget *life*, and with this they preserve
the history of God, the God of Life. Even the pharaoh cannot stop this.

The text seems to suggest that the midwives—who fear God—are aware
of this, as their answer is ambiguous and the meaning focuses on two areas.
To the king's ears, their answer sounds like an excuse: the Hebrew mothers
are "life-producing"; they have a quick childbirth and do not need a midwife.
However, anyone who hears this answer in its context sees that the text does
not primarily express an opinion on giving birth. The uncommon word חיות
is not particularly connected with the act of bearing but rather with the significant function of the biblical concept of "life." A Jewish commentary says that
the Hebrew mothers are "rulers of life."[14] Now, while the midwives keep the
children alive and the mothers are חיות (life-producers), Moses can be born.

2.2. The Daughter of Levi

The third woman is the mother of Moses. The way in which she is introduced
is somewhat surprising. Her name is not mentioned, neither is the name of the
father.[15] Moreover, the other characters in this story, the sister and the daughter of Pharaoh, remain unnamed. In this way, the spotlight is fully focused on
the only one who is named: Moses. This name, however, is not given by his
parents but by the Egyptian princess. With this he is *her* son. Will he thus be
an Egyptian?

Because of this question, it is significant that, right at the beginning,
another name is mentioned, indeed twice: Levi:

> A man of the house of Levi
> took the daughter of Levi. (2:1)

Moses' descent is important. The tribe of Levi has a special assignment concerning the Word of God, as the last book of the Torah states:

> The Levites observe your word and keep your covenant;
> they shall teach Jacob your judgments
> and Israel your Torah. (Deut 33:9–10)

---

14. Abraham S. Hartom, תורה, נביאם, כתובים (Tel Aviv: Tel Aviv University Press, 1973), 9.

15. However, within biblical tradition their names are known; see Exod 6:19; Num 26:59.

To Moses, as a descendant of Levi, this observation is particularly true: he will teach the Torah to his people.

There is a second remarkable detail: the *man* of the house of Levi is not said to take a *wife* of the house of Levi, but a *daughter*: "the daughter of Levi." Many scholars find it hard to understand why the mother of Moses is specified as a "daughter."[16] There are only a few translations that translate this literally:

There went a man of the house of Levi and took a daughter of Levi.[17]

So why is the mother of Moses specified as a "daughter of Levi"? This is a fascinating question, as she could not possibly have been a "physical" daughter of Levi. In such a case, she would have been a few hundred years old. Yet, would it not be more fitting to associate the designation "daughter of Levi" with the special function of "daughters" in this story, as there is a second daughter in this pericope: the daughter of the pharaoh? Both daughters act as the mother of Moses.[18] They stand side by side, which fits in very well with the whole composition of Exod 1–2, in which "daughters" play a prominent role. It is not without reason that in the command of the pharaoh to kill the sons, it is explicitly added: "Keep the daughters alive!" (1:22).

The daughter of Levi gives birth to the son; the daughter of the pharaoh adopts him and gives him a name. This name is not mentioned, as would be expected, at his birth but only after he has grown up with his mother:

When the child grew up,
she brought him to the daughter of the pharaoh;
he became *her* son, and *she* called his name Moses. (2:10)

At the place where, formally speaking, the name-giving belongs, it is stated that his mother saw him and saw that he was "good" (טוב; Exod 2:2).

---

16. See Martin Noth, *Das Zweite Buch Mose* (Göttingen: Vandenhoeck & Ruprecht, 1959), 13 n. 1: "The clearly erroneous text should perhaps be reconstructed: 'A woman from the house of Levi.'"

17. Martin Buber and Franz Rosenzweig, *Die fünf Bücher der Weisung: Verdeutscht von Martin Buber gemeinsam mit Franz Rosenzweig* (10th ed.; Heidelberg: Lambert Schneider, 1981), 154.

18. Athalya Brenner draws attention to the literary function of the "two-mothers pattern" found in various stories: "The two mothers complement each other" ("Female Social Behaviour: Two Descriptive Patterns within the 'Birth of the Hero' Paradigm," *VT* 36 [1986]: 260).

These words convey more than a simple remark about Moses' appearance. The rabbinical writings suggest an association with the light created by God on the first day:

God saw the light, that it was good [טוב]. (Gen 1:4)

Owing to the analogy between the two texts, the rabbis write: "When Moses was born, the whole house became flooded with light" (Exod. Rab. 2:2).

It seems quite likely that the word "good" (טוב) in Exodus contains a reference to Moses' future functioning. Just as God saw that the light was טוב, suitable for its function, so Moses' mother sees that her child is טוב, suitable for his mission. She decides to hide him—until the day comes when it is not possible to conceal him any more. Then she can no longer avoid the decree of the pharaoh:

Throw every son that is born
into the river! (1:22)

Into the river... Indeed, that is precisely what the daughter of Levi does. However, she does it in such a way that the threatening waters become a means of salvation. She constructs a little coffin, like Noah's ark (תבה).[19] Will her son survive the waters of death, as Noah once did?

The place where Moses, in his little ark, is laid is carefully indicated by the narrator: "in the reeds upon the shore of the river." The command of the pharaoh hangs ominously over this place, and it is the very place where the daughter of the pharaoh descends to bathe. Could we expect some form of salvation from her? Surely not! She is the daughter of the mighty monarch, after all! How could she stand against the express orders of her father? Initially, however, the sister of the child comes to the fore.

2.3. THE SISTER OF MOSES

Narrators and illustrators often sketch a romantic scene whereby Moses' sister remains at some distance in order to ensure that nothing goes wrong with her little brother among the rushes. However, is this the picture that the text intends to evoke?

His sister stood at a distance
in order to know what would be done to him. (2:4)

---

19. The same word is used for Noah's ark in Gen 6.

She stood at a distance. Of crucial importance is the verb "to stand," which is not the usual עָמַד, but a *hithpael* of the uncommon verb יצב, "to take one's stand firmly." This verb often indicates a particularly hopeless situation, a crisis in which no human help is available. For instance, in Exod 14:13, when Israel is under threat of extermination, the people are helpless. They are seized by panic: *before* them is the Red Sea, which means marsh and downfall; *behind* them the pharaoh approaches with his soldiers and horses. In this hopeless scenario, Moses also uses the verb יצב: "Take your stand!"

> Fear not, take your stand, stand firmly;
> then you shall see the salvation of the LORD. (Exod 14:13)

The verb יצב, "to take your stand, to stand firmly," in Exod 14 (on the shore of the sea) is related to salvation in the presence of God. Perhaps this is also the case in Exod 2 (on the shore of the river). The sister of Moses takes her stand (יצב) in order "to know what will be done to him," as the verbatim Hebrew text states. Can this "taking her stand" be read as her waiting to witness how God will save the child?

The following chapters describe God's tenfold intervention, as a result of which Israel is able finally to leave Egypt. The *beginning* of this exodus is situated here on the shore of the river, where Moses lies helplessly among the reeds. The exodus *ends* at the shore of the Red Sea, where the whole nation is rescued (Exod 15).

Moses' sister has no name here. Indeed, who is she? Is she the same person as "Miriam, the prophetess, the sister of Aaron," in Exod 15:20? The text does not make this clear. But if she were the same person, then she would be a witness at the beginning and end of this story: the rescue of Moses and the rescue of the entire nation (Exod 15:20–21). A "sister" forms an enclosing framework around the two waters of death. In the beginning, she takes her stand in order to *know* what will happen. In the end, on the other side of the water, she *knows* "what has been done"—and there she picks up her tambourine and praises the Lord.[20]

2.4. THE DAUGHTER OF THE PHARAOH

The rescue of Moses, however, requires another "daughter," namely, the daughter of the pharaoh. She is exactly in the middle of the birth story. Her role is exceptional. At the lowest point in the story, when the child has been

---

20. See also in this volume García Bachmann "Miriam, Primordial Political Figure in the Exodus."

committed to the waters of death and is unreachable, even to his sister, then the daughter of the pharaoh descends to the river. She sees the little ark in the midst of the rushes. A tense question is posed: What will she do?

For us, who know the outcome, it may be a matter of course that the daughter of the pharaoh saves the child; after all, she has compassion and wants to adopt the baby. But it is not that simple. It is even questionable whether she would have rescued the child at all, had the child's sister not been there!

Her father, the god-king of Egypt, had been determined to exterminate *all* the newborn sons of Israel. Would his daughter be in a position to disregard his command? Surely not! Certainly she has compassion, as the narrator states, and the boy is crying. The pharaoh's daughter is saying to herself:

> One of the Hebrew children is this … (2:6)

She knows exactly what is going on. This baby belongs to the Hebrews, to the "enemy people" that her father is going to extirpate. Could she ignore his orders? She hesitates, but then the sister of Moses comes forward, and *she* (Moses' sister) takes the initiative. She offers to help and chooses her words carefully:

> Shall I go and call *for you*
> a wet nurse from the Hebrew women,
> so that she can nurse the child *for you*? (2:7)

The twofold emphasis of the word "for you" is notable. It is as if the sister already assigns the child to the pharaoh's daughter; she speaks as though it were *her* child already. This is accepted by the pharaoh's daughter; she has no objections and simply says: "Go."

The daughter of the pharaoh has a central position in this pericope. She acts as the mother of the child and is also the one who gives him a name: Moses. Her explanation for this name is remarkable, since it does not concern the child but herself, as the name-giver:

> Out of the water I have drawn him. (2:10)

Like a "midwife," who allows the children to live (1:17), she draws him out of the stream, out of the deadly power of the water. As a mother, as if she herself has given birth to him, she names him: Moses.

> And he became her son. (2:10)

3. The Composition of the Text of Exodus 2:1–10

The harmonious literary composition of the text is underlined by the fact that *son*, *mother*, and *sister* occur concentrically around the *daughter of the pharaoh*:

> introduction: a man and the daughter of Levi (2:1)
>   birth of the *son* (no name; 2:2)
>   *mother* (surrenders the child; 2:3)
>   *sister* (distance; 2:4)
>   *daughter* of Pharaoh (sees; 2:5)
>   the *child!* (2:6a)
>   *daughter* of Pharaoh (has compassion; 2:6b)
>   *sister* (close by; 2:7–8)
>   *mother* (gets the child back; 2:9)
>   adoption of the *son* (name giving; 2:10)

The story of the birth of Moses turns out to be a thoroughly composed entity in which "the child" (2:6a) is exactly in the center,[21] not only thematically but also structurally. The word הילד (the child) is a *Leitwort* here. It occurs seven times in this pericope, exactly as frequently as מילדת (midwives), the *Leitwort* in the preceding pericope. This is remarkable, as the word "midwives" (מילדת) is from the same word stem as הילד (the child).

The story is framed by the word "son" (2:2, 10). Within it, we find the mother who gives up the child in 2:3 and gets him back in 2:9, then the sister who stands around helplessly in 2:4 yet comes closer in 2:7–8 and utters the right words at the right moment. In so doing, not only does she save the life of the child, but she also makes it possible for mother and child to be reunited. Nevertheless, the fate of Moses ultimately lies in the hands of the pharaoh's daughter. Indeed, although she gives him back to the mother, she personally assumes the responsibility for his upbringing, as she pays the mother for her duty: "I myself shall give you your wages" (2:9).

4. Death or Life?

After this, we hear nothing more about the pharaoh's daughter. This raises the question regarding her specific role in this story. Does she appear as a

---

21. Cassuto (*Commentary on the Book of Exodus*, 19) points out that the substantive "child" is mentioned another time after the pronominal suffix ה-. He believes that such a construction is not a "pleonastic or a later addition," but "a means of giving emphasis to a noun."

counterpart to her father? Although he is not mentioned in this pericope, he is nevertheless present in a menacing manner in the context of the central "death-life" theme. In contradiction to his words, "Throw him into the river!" (1:22), there are the words of his daughter: "Out of the water I have drawn him!" (2:10). The choice is between "death" or "life." Which of them will win?

In 1:15–22, the actions of the midwives prove to be the decisive factor for the outcome of the struggle. Whom will they fear: the king of Egypt or the God of Israel? In 2:1–10, the role of the pharaoh's daughter is decisive. Does she belong to the "kingdom of death," like her father? On the linguistic level of the text, there is no answer, yet on the narrative scene the actions of the daughter elucidate her stance: she has compassion! She rescues Moses out of the water, just like God will rescue the whole of Israel from out of the water (Exod 14).

5. To Midian

After the birth story of Moses, two stories follow: a men's story (2:11–15) and a women's story (2:16–22). The men's story takes place in a context of slavery again. Key words here are "knocking down" and "killing."[22] The main character is Moses. He grew up at the Egyptian court and now goes outward to look after his brothers, the sons of Israel. He witnesses their oppression and suffering under slave labor. In order to save one of his brothers, he kills an Egyptian foreman and buries his body in the sand. The following day he sees some of his brothers fighting each other and urges them to live in peace together. With both these actions, however, he achieves the opposite of his goal: he is threatened with death and forced to flee Egypt. Now his life has reached an impasse; everything has lead nowhere. What is to become of him? Will anyone ever hear of him again?

The second pericope, the women's story, is about liberation. Key words here are "drawing water" and "saturation." Here, once more, we encounter "daughters," seven at that! In contrast to the first five women, these seven are not linked to Moses in a "motherly" or "sisterly" way. This would not be appropriate to the context of the new situation: Moses has become a man. He is now entering a new phase in his life. The seven daughters take him into this new phase by bringing him into the house of their father, the priest of Midian. This place will prove to be of great importance to his future and destination.

---

22. Another keyword is אִישׁ ("man"). "Moses has grown out of the life-protecting company of the women into the brutal society of men." See Fischer, *Women Who Wrestled*, 123.

Thus far, Moses was an Egyptian prince, the son of the pharaoh's daughter. In this position, he acquired his name. He acts like an Egyptian, as the daughters of the priest say:

An Egyptian man has rescued us from the hands of the shepherds. (2:19)

He will remain an Egyptian until he is called by God, an event that is marked by the repeated "Moses, Moses!" (Exod 3:4). This calling is decisive; from this moment on he will take over the full meaning of his name: Moses, "the one who will draw out," Moses, the rescuer of Israel.

5.1. THE SEVEN DAUGHTERS OF THE PRIEST

Moses' encounter with the seven daughters occurs at a well. A meeting at a well is a common theme in the Bible; we find it in several instances.[23] The main character finds a well at the end of a journey. Just at that moment, a young woman, a "daughter," is coming to draw water, but there is a problem with the water-drawing. The man solves the problem and is then invited to her father's home. A marriage follows. Two stories are worth mentioning in this respect: Gen 24:1–61 and 29:1–30.

In Gen 24, the servant of Abraham is sitting at the well. He has the assignment of finding a wife for Isaac, the son of Abraham. Then Rebekah, the daughter of Bethuel, arrives to give her father's sheep water to drink. She shows concern for the stranger, lets him drink, and also fills the water troughs for his camels. In Exod 2, Moses is similarly sitting at the well, whereupon he also meets some daughters who have come to give water to their father's flock. In this story, however, things are the other way round than in Genesis: the daughters are not particularly concerned about the stranger, yet the stranger is concerned about the daughters. Moses fills the water troughs and lets the sheep brought by the daughters drink.

In Gen 29, the stranger at the well is Jacob. Just like Moses, he is running away, albeit from his brother Esau. Jacob meets his bride-to-be, Rachel, who comes to the well to give her father's flock a drink of water. Both Moses in Exodus and Jacob in Genesis are confronted with difficulties that arise in giving the flocks water. In the case of Moses, there are foreign shepherds who prevent the daughters giving water to their sheep. In the case of Jacob, there is a big stone over the opening of the well. Both Moses and Jacob resolve the

---

23. The well constitutes the gender-specific meeting place for women. See Fischer, *Women Who Wrestled*, 124.

problem with the well and thereby show their power. Hence both men make it possible for the daughters to give water to their father's flocks. The thematic similarity between the two stories is clear: the leading figures (Isaac, Jacob, Moses) find their future wives and a safe home after their flight due to an unforgivable deed (Jacob, Moses). Davies observes, "Moses re-enacts the histories of Jacob and the servant of Abraham."[24] He sees the similarity between Moses and the patriarchs "as the main point" in this story.[25] In his view, this pericope is about the question of Moses' identity.

6. MEN AND SONS, WOMEN AND DAUGHTERS

The text of Exod 1–2 connects the role of men and sons with "oppression," "bondage," and "death"[26]:

▶   The son must be killed (command of the pharaoh; 1:16, 22).
▶   Sons become slaves; they are forced into hard labor (1:11, 13, 14).
▶   Men fight, kill others, and murder each other (2:11, 12, 13).

Nevertheless, the sons are alive and fertile; they grow and multiply; they are numerous and strong (1:7, 9, 12, 20). How does this compare? Well, the text connects women and daughters with "salvation," "compassion," and "keeping alive":

▶   The daughters are allowed to live (the pharaoh's command 1:16, 22).
▶   The Hebrew women are חיות (life producers; 1:19).
▶   The midwives enable the children to live (1:17, 18).
▶   Levi's daughter and the pharaoh's daughter save Moses. They have compassion for him and ensure that he will be nursed.
▶   Seven daughters bring Moses into their father's home.
▶   One daughter, Zipporah, gives birth to a son: Moses is fertile, and his story goes on.

---

24. Gordon F. Davies, *Israel in Egypt: Reading Exodus 1–2* (JSOTSup 135; Sheffield: JSOT Press, 1992), 148. See also Fischer, *Women Who Wrestled*, 125: "The story in Midian places Moses within the horizon of experience and milieu of the patriarchs."

25. Davies, *Israel in Egypt*, 150.

26. James S. Ackerman draws attention to "[t]he general passivity of the Hebrews, pointing to the behind-the-scenes activity of the hidden God" ("The Literary Context of the Moses Birth Story [Exodus 1–2]," in *Literary Interpretations of Biblical Narratives* [ed. R. R. Kenneth Gros Louis et al.; Nashville: Abingdon, 1974], 90).

7. LET THE DAUGHTERS LIVE!

Moses is rescued and kept alive by women. After the pharaoh's daughter gave him his name—"Moses, he who draws out"—it already begins to become apparent what the aim of his life would be, namely, "liberation." In 2:11–15 he tries to liberate his brothers from the Egyptians. He also tries to teach his brothers how to live in peace with each other. Both attempts fail, as first one question must be answered: "Who has called you as a man who is chief and judge over us?" (Exod 2:14).

This is an important question. Moses has not yet been "called." He has to go to Midian for that. There, in the desert, he will be called by God. To that end, he must leave Egypt. After his double fiasco in Egypt, he is sitting at the well in Midian. It is here, still before his calling, that Moses is able to show what he will become: a savior. Standing up against injustice was not possible in Egypt until now, but here, in Midian, he comes through. He takes action against the shepherds who had chased away the women from the well and in doing so saves the seven daughters of the priest. These seven daughters are the counterpart of the five women who saved Moses earlier.

In the stories around the birth of Moses, daughters occupy a special place. This is already indicated in the formulation with which the pharaoh announces his order to the midwives:

> If it is a son, you shall kill him;
> if it is a daughter, she shall live! (1:16)

Half of the command, to kill the son, would have been sufficient. Twice, however, the text has the pharaoh order that the *daughter* is to live (1:16, 22). The first time he "says" it, to the midwives, to be sure. The second time he "commands" it, and with that he addresses the whole nation:

> Every son that is born, in the river you shall throw him,
> but every daughter: you shall allow to live! (1:22)

The choice of words fits the active role of daughters in this story. On the pharaoh's command—although in contrast to his intention—*they* make it possible, at this decisive moment, that history goes on. The future of the *twelve sons* of Israel depends on the one son who owes his birth and his life to the twelve women. Literally and metaphorically they keep his head above water. *Let the daughters live!*

Zipporah: The Vanishing of a Wife

Ursula Rapp
Universität Luzern

Zipporah is known as Moses' only wife. She is the daughter of a non-Israelite priest. She gives birth to two sons, Gershom and Eliezer, and at one point saves Moses' life. Although she is Moses' wife, not much is said about their relationship. Not a single dialogue is attributed to them. The sons are mentioned in passing, but they do not continue any kind of Mosaic heritage. Zipporah, unlike the women in the patriarchal narratives before her, is not a wife and mother engaged in political action. The only acts attributed to her are giving birth (Exod 2:22) and saving a life (4:24–26). Whoever wants to look for information about Zipporah's identity finds herself caught in a web of diverse and, in some cases, contradictory affirmations. According to Exod 2:15–22, she is a Midianite woman; therefore, Moses has a Midianite father-in-law, as Exod 3:1; 18:1–2, 5; and Num 10:29 indicate. In Num 12:1, it is said that Moses' wife is Cushite, and Judg 1:16 and 4:11 mention Moses' Cushite father-in-law. So, where does Zipporah come from, and why is her origin so unclear?

The name "Zipporah" is a feminine diminutive form of the Hebrew word for "bird" *zippor* (צפור). Consequently, Zipporah means "little bird." This name is particularly appropriate for her, because if we try to find her in the text she cannot be seized, just as a bird cannot be held.

The question imposes itself: Why, then, do the narratives say anything about her at all, and why is what is said so fragmentary? The hypothesis that the Zipporah tradition is ancient and therefore incomplete is plausible.[1] However, a "hermeneutic of suspicion" sets out from the idea that, if something was lost, this did not happen unintentionally. Above all, if contradictory information is transmitted, there are probably good reasons for it. The aim of

---

1. Thus, recently, for example, in Meik Gerhards, "Über die Herkunft der Frau des Mose," *VT* 55 (2005): 164 and *passim*.

this essay is to present these reasons. Hence, we must first discuss Zipporah's origin and then address the question of her role in Exod 4:24–26, where she saves Moses' life.

1. Zipporah's Identity

It cannot be assumed that Zipporah was a historical figure. Her identity is composed of bits of information presented in the texts that in the first instance have nothing to do with her marriage with Moses. The question is: Who is this figure apart from the marriage with Moses? What can be said about her ethnic and sociocultural background?

1.1. Zipporah's Origin

As noted at the beginning, the indications relative to Zipporah's ethnic origin diverge. In the following paragraphs, the suggestions concerning her origin shall be presented and their mutual connections considered. We shall see that Zipporah's origin is less enigmatic than it seems at first.

1.1.1. A Midianite Woman

Zipporah is named for the first time in Exod 2:21, where it is said that her father gave her to Moses to be his wife. This note is embedded in the account of Moses' flight from Pharaoh to Midian, after he killed an Egyptian (Exod 2:11–15). Moses' encounter with Zipporah is described as a meeting at a well, similar to those known from the "engagement narratives" (see Gen 24:10–32; 29:1–14). In comparison with these narratives, it is striking that Moses and Zipporah are not put in contact with one another. Moses does not notice Zipporah because, for example, she is particularly beautiful (as, for example, in Gen 24:16; 29:17), because she has come to the well alone, or because she needs his help to deal with the shepherds who are waiting at the well. In the scene at the well, Zipporah is not mentioned among the seven daughters of the Midianite priest. At first, she is merely the shepherdess of her father's animals and is named only when her father gives her to Moses to be his wife. It is not said why Jethro chooses precisely this daughter and not another one. It does not seem to matter.

Zipporah is not associated with Midian in any other texts, but twice in the book of Exodus (3:1; 18:1–2, 5) and once in Numbers (10:29) it is said that Moses had a Midianite father-in-law.

1.1.2. A Cushite Woman

In Num 12:1, Zipporah is called Moses' "Cushite wife": יתשהכ תשהא. The Septuagint has translated the expression with ἡ γυνὴ τῆς Αἰθιοπίσσης, thus laying the foundation stone for a long tradition relative to Moses' Ethiopian wife.[2] This was associated with an Ethiopian or Nubian and, in any case, black and African woman. The biblical basis for this association is the identification of יתשכ with Cush, that is, ancient Ethiopia.[3] The problem with this interpretation is that Ethiopia and Midian do not overlap geographically, so "Cush" does not permit any identification with the information concerning Zipporah's origin in the book of Genesis. Ancient Midian is most likely situated in northwestern Arabia, southern Transjordan.[4]

יתשכ "Cushite" can, however, also derive from the Cushite strip of land mentioned only in Hab 3:7, where it is evoked in a synonymous parallelism with Midian. In this case, Cushan may have been at least a part of Midian, or "Cushite" may also represent a people settled in a region of Midian. This reconstruction is supported by the fact that other passages of the Bible use "Cushite" to indicate the origin of people who do not come from Ethiopia.[5]

Now, why is Zipporah presented, in Num 12, not as a Midianite but rather as a Cushite woman? Midian has, at least since Num 25:1–3; 31; 32:4, 7 as well as after the conflicts in Josh 13:21; Isa 9:4 (Hebrew 9:3); 10:26 and the belligerent raids in Judg 6–8, an extremely bad reputation. Saying that Moses' wife is Cushite would, of course, not identify her as a Midianite, but it would not strip her of her Midianite identity. The term "Cushite woman" may therefore be considered a euphemism used to attribute a more appropriate marriage to Moses.[6]

---

2. This is suggested by most of the older commentaries, some of which then also stress the dark skin color, although there is no indication of that in the texts; see Josef Scharbert, *Numeri* (NEchtB; Würzburg: Echter, 1992), 52, and other references in Ursula Rapp, *Mirjam: Eine feministisch-rhetorische Lektüre der Mirjamtraditionen in der hebräischen Bibel* (BZAW 317; Berlin: de Gruyter, 2002), 65 nn. 121–22. See also recently, in a positive sense, Philip Lokel, "Moses and His Cushite Wife: Reading Numbers 12:1 with Undergraduate Students of Makerere University," *OTE* 19 (2006): 538–47, who sees in the Ethiopian woman a positive reference point for the African women who read the Bible.

3. See, e.g., Gen 10:6, 8; Isa 11:11; 20:3–5; 43:3; Ezek 29:19; Dan 11:3; Nah 3:9. See more references in Rapp, *Mirjam*, 64–65.

4. See Rapp, *Mirjam*, 66, with bibliography; recently also in Gerhards, "Über die Herkunft," 167–68.

5. Among these are people of different professional groups: 2 Sam 18:21; Jer 38:7.

6. See Rapp, *Mirjam*, 68. Similarly, Gerhards ("Über die Herkunft," 169–70) considers

1.1.3. The Kenite Woman

Although no passage calls Zipporah a "Kenite woman," Judg 1:16 and 4:11 speak about Moses' Kenite father-in-law. Here three considerations lead in a direction comparable to the description of Zipporah as a "Cushite woman."[7]

(1) There had been some contact between the Israelites and the Kenites. The two passages in the book of Judges indicate that Moses' father-in-law came from a region situated to the south of Judah. Judges 1:16 says that he settled in the region of the Kenites, south of Arad,[8] that is, close to the territory of Midian. The story of Heber the Kenite shows that, even after the wanderings in the desert, relations existed between Israel and the (semi)nomadic Kenites.

(2) In the etiological account of the Kenite tribe as Cain's descendants (Gen 4:1–16), it is said that, while Cain was forced to migrate, he nevertheless remained under God's special protection. This insistence on the relationship between God and the Kenites indicates a tie with Midian, since Israel's divinity comes from Midian. Therefore, Midian is very important for Israel's conception of God.

(3) The Kenites were not Israel's enemies. In 1 Sam 15:6, the Kenites are explicitly differentiated from the Amalekites and called friends of Israel.[9]

The localization of the settlement, the relationship with Israel's God, and the friendly attitude of the Kenites toward Israel have perhaps led to yet another euphemism with respect to Moses' Midianite relations.

In conclusion, concerning Zipporah's origin, it can be maintained that she was from the tribe of Midian. Given the hostilities between Midian and Israel, euphemisms relative to her origin, based on geographical and concrete facts, were probably introduced in order to veil the scandal of Moses' marriage with a Midianite woman.

1.2. ZIPPORAH WITH A PRIESTLY COMPETENCE AND FUNCTION

The question of Zipporah's social origin is part of the question concerning her identity. In Exod 2:21 she is presented with her six sisters as a shepherdess of her father's animals. This, first, allows us to conclude that Zipporah belongs to a sedentary or seminomadic milieu. However, additionally, in the short

---

Cushan a part of Midian. Therefore the expression "Cushite woman" is understood to be a "version" of Zipporah, the woman from Midian.

7. On the following argument, see Gerhards, "Über die Herkunft," 170–73.

8. About this settlement of the Kenites, see also 1 Sam 15:6; 27:10; 30:29.

9. Concerning the possible kinship of the Kenites and the Midianites, see also Werner H. Schmidt, *Exodus 1–6* (BKAT 2.1; Neukirchen-Vluyn: Neukirchener, 1988), 87–88.

episode about God's aggression against Moses (or Gershom), certain ritual competencies are attributed to her.

1.2.1. The Text of Exodus 4:24–26 and Its Difficulties

[24] On the way, at a place where they spent the night,
the LORD sought him and tried to kill *him*.[10]
[25] But Zipporah took a flint and cut off her son's foreskin
and touched *his* legs with it
and said,
"Truly you are a bridegroom of blood to me!"
[26] So he let *him* alone,
because she said,
"bridegroom of blood" by circumcision.

This text presents a number of difficulties.[11]

(1) Whom does God attack in 4:24? Both the verb in 24a הושגפיו ("seek") and the object in 24c המיתו ("let die, kill") have a suffix in the third-person masculine singular. However, it is not clear to whom this refers; it may be Gershom, the son of Moses and Zipporah, Moses himself,[12] or even Eliezer, the second son of Moses and Zipporah. Actually, we do not know if Eliezer was already born at the time of the return to Egypt.[13]

(2) The text contains other hazy points. For example, it is not clear in 4:25 whose legs Zipporah touches,[14] nor does the text say to whom she speaks. Furthermore, the term "bridegroom of blood" is not found in any other passage of the Hebrew Bible; therefore, its interpretation is problematic. Finally, we must ask ourselves if 4:26b is a posterior attempt to give an explanation or what other function it may have.[15]

---

10. In the translation, the pronominalizations with more than one meaning are indicated in italics.

11. See also the enumeration in Rita Burns, "Zipporah," *ABD* 6:1105; or Benno Jacob, *Das Buch Exodus* (Stuttgart: Calwer, 1997), 99–103; more detailed in Cornelis Houtman, *Ex 1,1–7,12* (vol. 1 of *Exodus*; Historical Commentary on the Old Testament; Kampen: Kok Pharos, 1993), 439–47.

12. See Burns, "Zipporah," 6:1105; Jacob, *Das Buch Exodus*, 99.

13. If Moses and Zipporah actually did separate at this point (see Jacob, *Das Buch Exodus*, 101) and Moses went to Egypt alone, then Eliezer must already have been born, since he is present at the family's next related meeting, in Exod 18.

14. Jacob (*Das Buch Exodus*, 100) reports that the Jewish tradition knows all the possible alternatives: the legs/genitals of the circumcised, of Moses, or of the assailant, who is then understood to be an angel.

15. See Burns, "Zipporah," 6:1105.

(3) The text does not say where Zipporah learned what she must do and how she acquired this ritual competence.

(4) Zipporah assumes the role of the Mohel, which is usually reserved for men.

1.2.2. Whom Does God Attack?

Arguments can be found to support both the aggression against the young Gershom and an attack aimed at Moses. On the one hand, aggression against *Gershom* is suggested by the killing of the firstborn, mentioned in 4:21–23. In this case, the suffix of וַיְבַקֵּשׁ הוּ ("sought *him*") in 4:24 would refer to the "first-born son" in 4:23. Consequently, 4:24 would be connected to the narrated discourse and not to the development of the action.

On the other hand, an attack against *Moses* is suggested by the narrative passage of 4:24–26, which speaks about Moses and God (4:24 is connected to the development of the action in 4:20–21, for 4:22–23 are narrated discourse).[16] The point of connection is then on the level of action in 4:21, where God speaks to Moses, or even in 4:18–20, where Moses' departure from Midian is announced.[17] Or Moses would be attacked as God's representative, as Jacob, the heir of God's promises, was in Gen 32:22–32 (Hebrew Gen 32:23–33). Moreover, the designation "bridegroom of blood" is not appropriate for Gershom.

The ambiguity of the text cannot be explained away. If Moses was indeed attacked, as most commentaries assume,[18] there are two possible reasons: either because he and/or his son have not yet been circumcised and God is angry; or, alternatively, only through the circumcision is he properly bound once and for all to his mission of leading Israel out of Egypt.[19] However, neither of these two reasons are found in the text.

Another solution, closer to the texts, appears when we consider the context: Moses' calling in Exod 3:1–4:23. Exodus 4 deals with Moses' doubt about his credibility in the eyes of the people of Israel. In the face of this,

---

16. On this, see Susan Ackerman, "Why Is Miriam Also among the Prophets? (And Is Zipporah among the Priests?)," *JBL* 121 (2002): 73.

17. See also Schmidt, *Exodus 1–6*, 220.

18. See, e.g., Jacob, *Das Buch Exodus*, 103; Schmidt, *Exodus 1–6*, 220; Houtman, *Ex 1,1–7,12*, 447.

19. A more detailed and global presentation of the different interpretations is found in Houtman, *Ex 1,1–7,12*, 439–47, or in Helen Schüngel-Straumann, "Mose und Zippora: Buch Exodus, Kapitel 2,4 und 18," in *Schön bist du und verlockend: Große Paare der Bibel* (ed. Herbert Haag; Freiburg: Herder, 2001), 154.

God announces legitimizing miracles and presents each of them to Moses (4:1–17). After this, Moses goes to Jethro's house, takes his wife and children,[20] and leaves (4:18–20). This scene is followed—directly before the scene of the attack—by the presentation of the last miracle intended for the night of the departure.

Since God hardens Pharaoh, Moses must announce that God is going to kill the firstborn sons of the Egyptians. The symbolic basis for this is the conception of Israel as God's firstborn son. This divine explanation is directly followed by God's attack, which leads to the circumcision of Moses' son. If we suppose that this constitutes the extension of a narrative, then the scene in Exod 4:24–26 is simply continued—as in the announcement of the other signs—indicating that God will actually realize what he has announced, that is, in this last case, the death of the firstborn sons.

Another element in this development is the fact that Israel will be saved by blood. So, God attacks the firstborn, and Zipporah saves him with *his* blood, not the blood of a lamb, as in the night of the exodus. This means that God attacks Gershom in order to represent the sign of the killing of the firstborn sons.[21]

1.2.3. The "Bridegroom of Blood"

Some commentaries note that, in Arabian territories, men had to be circumcised before their marriage and that *chattana*, "bridegroom," simply means "circumcised." This could be said just as well with respect to Moses or to his son. Of course, we must consider that in the biblical text there is no connection between the circumcision and the root חתן. The marital agreements, expressed by חתן in the *hithpael*, are always made by diverse social groups. חתן implies the reception of a man who does not belong to the same clan or social class as the woman. The formula signifies a marriage with an "outsider."[22]

---

20. It is not clear whether this refers to children of the flesh or to the single son, whose birth has already been related, and also includes the female farmhands and male servants. In 4:25 Zipporah takes "her son," which hints to the fact that she has only one. There is no mention of the birth of another son. Only in 18:4 is he mentioned with his name Eliezer (cf. 1 Chr 23:15, 17).

21. Similar interpretations appear in the Jewish tradition (see Jacob, *Das Buch Exodus*, 100). Schmidt also notes the connection with the rescue through blood (*Exodus 1–6*, 223).

22. Examples of marriages expressed with חתן and in which circumcision plays a role are the union of Jacob's family with the Shechemites in Gen 34, the aspired marriage of Samson with a woman of the uncircumcised Philistines (Judg 14:3; 15:6), and David's marriage with Michal for the bride-price of the Philistine foreskins (1 Sam 18:18, 21, 23, 26, 27). The marital alliance of different social groups indicated by the etymological root חתן,

This can be applied to Moses and Zipporah. When the father-in-law is called חֹתֵן, this also expresses Moses' introduction into the tribe of Midian and at the same time Moses' submission to Jethro,[23] which is also illustrated by the narrative when Moses watches over Jethro's sheep. The relationship that חתן is meant to express is characterized by religious tolerance and acceptance of the divinities and customs.

This implies that Zipporah speaks to Moses and calls him "bridegroom of blood." Now, does this mean that Gershom is attacked and circumcised, whereas Moses' legs are touched and he is called bridegroom of blood? Moreover, could this expression indicate that the marriage of Moses and Zipporah has a sociopolitical meaning? This cannot be clearly determined.

1.2.4. Zipporah's "Masculine" Role

The only clear affirmation is that Zipporah accomplishes the saving blood rite of circumcision. Biblical scholarship hardly reflects on this single certain affirmation.[24] Zipporah's role is only mentioned, as is stated, in so far as the circumcision accomplished by a woman is an ancient (and outdated and hence unimportant) tradition or an urgent necessity,[25] but certainly not a variant that would merit any further reflection in biblical scholarship.

As if mentioned just in passing, it is said that she saved the life of Moses or of her son. It is, however, precisely this saving, ritual role of the woman that should clearly remain in Israel's memory. Thus Zipporah finds herself, on the one hand, in the line of all the women who have saved Moses.[26] On the other hand, she exercises a priestly function[27] later taken over by the priests and then by the mohel. Certain commentaries note that Zipporah here assumes the role of her father, the priest: "If Zippora is seen as assuming her father's role as circumciser, should she also be seen as assuming in certain ways his

---

but without mention of circumcision, is also found in 1 Kgs 3, the note concerning Solomon's marriage with the daughter of Pharaoh, or also with the problematization of mixed marriages in Ezra 9:14. On this, see Allen Guenther, "A Typology of Israelite Marriage: Kinship, Socio-economic, and Religious Factors," *JSOT* 29 (2005): 390–396.

23. See Guenther, "A Typology of Israelite Marriage," 396.

24. The early tradition also completely left out the rescue by Zipporah and the blood rite; see Jub. 48; Josephus and Philo say absolutely nothing about this episode (see Houtman, *Ex 1,1–7,12*, 439).

25. The editing of a Midianite narrative is also considered (see Schmidt, *Exodus 1–6*, 226, with references; Houtman, *Ex 1,1–7,12*, 4).

26. See also Schüngel-Straumann, "Mose und Zippora," 154.

27. See Ackerman, "Why Is Miriam," 74.

role as priest?"[28] Since the blood rite strongly evokes the blood offerings (Exod 12:1–28; Josh 5:2–12), which were made only by the priests, Ackerman gives a positive answer to her question and characterizes Zipporah's role as "priestly-like."[29]

In addition, Zipporah is not the only woman of whom it is said that she circumcised her children. For example, 2 Macc 6:10 tells about women who circumcised their sons and thus consciously attested their observance of the Torah in opposition to the regime of Antiochus IV Epiphanes.[30] They had to expiate this by death. Likewise, 1 Macc 1:60 and 4 Macc 4:25 also say that the mothers were responsible for the circumcision and were the first to pay for this. Hence, we are not obliged to think that Zipporah as a circumcising mother appeared in later times to be an absurd relic of the most distant past.[31] On the contrary, this may be considered a sign of her piety. In any case, circumcision can still save lives or be seen as an encouragement to accept martyrdom that removes the sting of death.[32] The later literature of the period of

---

28. Ibid.

29. See ibid., 75. She attributes the role of a priest to Zipporah in the same degree as the role of prophet to Miriam. Moreover, these two "functions" are only valid within the time of the liminality represented by Exodus. Ackerman treats Miriam and Zipporah with Victor Turner's theory of "social drama." Within this sort of resolution of conflicts, the central phase of the crisis is particularly expressed by the status of "betwixt and between" on all the possible social and existential levels. This question cannot be further developed here. It should only be made clear that Ackerman is far from attributing to Miriam's prophecy the importance that it receives, for example, in Klara Butting, *Prophetinnen gefragt: Die Bedeutung der Prophetinnen im Kanon aus Tora und Prophetie* (Erev-Rav-Hefte: Biblisch-feministische Texte 3; Wittingen: Erev-Rav, 2001); Irmtraud Fischer, "The Authority of Miriam: A Feminist Rereading of Numbers 12 Prompted by Jewish Interpretation," in *Exodus and Deuteronomy: A Feminist Companion to the Bible* (ed. Athalya Brenner; trans. Barbara and Martin Rumschiedt; FBC 2/5; Sheffield: Sheffield Academic Pres, 2000), 159-73; repr. of "Die Autorität Mirjams: Eine feministische Relektüre von Num 12—angeregt durch das jüdische Lehrhaus," in *Anspruch und Widerspruch: Festschrift Evi Krobath zum 70. Geburtstag* (ed. Maria Halmer, Barbara Heyse-Schaefer, and Barbara Rauchwartner; Klagenfurt: Hermagoras, 2000), 23-38; eadem, *Gotteskünderinnen: Zu einer geschlechterfairen Deutung des Phänomens der Prophetie und der Prophetinnnen in der hebräischen Bibel* (Stuttgart: Kohlhammer, 2002), 72; or Rapp, *Mirjam*.

30. On this, see Toni Craven, "Women as Teachers of Torah," in *Passion, Vitality, and Foment: The Dynamics of Second Temple Judaism* (ed. Lamontte M. Luker; Harrisburg, Pa.: Trinity Press International, 2001), 282–89.

31. Thus, for example, Schmidt, *Exodus 1–6*, 218–19.

32. See Toni Craven, "Is That Fearfully Funny? Some Instances from the Apocryphal/Deuterocanonical Books," in *Are We Amused? Humour about Women in the Biblical Worlds* (ed. Athalya Brenner; JSOTSup 383; Bible in the Twenty-First Century Series 2; London: T&T Clark, 2003), 76.

the Maccabees speaks about this in a symbolic sense (cf. the discourse of the
mother of the seven martyrs in 2 Macc 7:29).

As concerns Zipporah's ritual role, we can conclude that by accomplishing the rite of circumcision she saved her husband, or son, from God's fatal aggression. She perhaps assumed her father's priestly ritual function. This reveals that the relationship between Moses and Zipporah was an ethnic-political "*chatan* relationship" between Midian and Israel. Over against the notion that this concerns an ancient custom, Zipporah may also be seen in connection with mothers of the late Hellenistic Period who circumcised their sons.

2. The Signification of the Marriage of Zipporah and Moses

Two texts (Exod 2:15–21; 18:1–6) speak about Moses' marriage, while Num 12 merely evokes it.

2.1. The Marital Agreement: Exodus 2:15–21

Zipporah appears in this text as a secondary narrative figure. Already in the opening scene of the marriage, she is mentioned only in passing. Generally in the well scenes (Gen 24:16; 29:17) the women are presented, and the qualities that make them desirable spouses are emphasized. At least one sentence is dedicated to this theme. In Zipporah's case, such a sentence is missing.[33]

After the introduction of the scene at the well (Exod 2:15) and after it has been said that Moses sat down beside it, there is no further mention of the women and their animals, but the text goes on to speak about a Midianite priest who has seven daughters. This is no coincidence: the women are presented as the daughters of a priest and not merely as shepherdesses. It is important that they are daughters of a priest. The name of the priest is mentioned only in 2:18, when his daughters speak to him.

When the daughters of the priest are annoyed by the shepherds, Moses helps them (2:19) by "saving" (נצל) them, drawing water, and watering their flock. The daughters tell their father about this, and he orders them to invite Moses to eat with them. Moses decides to stay and receives Zipporah to be his wife.

Immediately in the next verse, it is said that Zipporah gives birth to their son Gershom. Their son's name describes Moses' existence as a foreigner: Gershom means "for I have been an alien residing in a foreign land" (Exod 2:22).

---

33. See also Houtman, *Ex 1,1–7,12*, 315.

2.2. The Father(-in-Law) Unites the Family: Exodus 18:1–6

This scene tells that Jethro, Moses' father-in-law, hears about the wonders God worked during the exodus. After this, he goes to find Moses, taking his daughter and two grandsons with him, and meets him in the desert (18:5). Before anything happens, Jethro tells his son-in-law that he has brought his wife and sons with him. Zipporah and her sons only appear in the introduction to the two-part narrative consisting of Jethro's confession (18:1–12) and of his advice to Moses to delegate his powers of jurisdiction (18:13–27). While some commentators think that the aim of this narrative is only to bring the Moses' and Zipporah's family together,[34] others state that it has nothing to do with the family.[35] Several elements relating to the couple stand out:

(1) The text begins with Jethro, who is at the center of the narrative as Moses' father-in-law.

(2) Exodus 18:2 is the third text (after Exod 2:21; 4:25) in which Zipporah is named and presented as Moses' wife.

(3) The formulation אֶת־צִפֹּרָה אֵשֶׁת מֹשֶׁה אַחַר שִׁלּוּחֶיהָ (18:2) also merits reflection: Jethro "took Moses' wife, after she was sent." So, Zipporah is presented as Moses' wife, but what does "she was sent" mean? Does this indicate a divorce?

(4) Zipporah is presented as Moses' wife throughout the entire passage (18:2, 5, 6) and never as Jethro's daughter. Therefore, she has not returned to the premarital status of daughter; on the contrary, she continues to be associated with Moses.

(5) The sons are presented twice as Zipporah's children (18:3, 6) and once as Moses' (18:5). This is remarkable because paternity is one of the more important characteristics of identity and inheritance.

(6) Jethro, like his daughter, is associated with Moses. The text introduces him as Moses' father-in-law five times (18:1, 2, 5, 6, 7) but never as the father of Zipporah.

As far as family ties are concerned, Jethro and Zipporah are related to Moses and not to each other. The words "daughter" and "father," and also "husband," do not appear. Only the kinship with Moses is mentioned: *his* father-in-law and *his* wife. This puts the accent on the marital ties between the figures. None of these numerous references to family ties associates Zipporah with her father, to whom she would have returned after a divorce. The sons are

---

34. Cf. Jacob, *Das Buch Exodus*, 509.
35. Cf. Houtman, *Ex 1,1–7,12*, 394.

associated with Moses only when they receive their names; otherwise, they are Zipporah's sons.

How should we understand the expression in 18:2: שִׁלּוּחֶיהָ אַחַר "after she was sent"? שִׁלּוּחֶיהָ is a nominal construction in *piel*, in which it appears only three times in the entire Hebrew Bible and always—as here—in the plural form.[36] This term signifies a gift of release.

In 1 Kgs 9:16, שִׁלֻּחִים refers to the bridal gift the king gives to his daughter. Micah 1:14 is not set in the context of a marriage, but the term nevertheless refers to a gift of release (the *Bibel in gerechter Sprache* translates "Abschieds-gaben" ["departure gifts"]). שׁחל in *piel*, and other forms, can signify, among other things, that a man sends his wife away (i.e., he divorces himself from her); still, the expression שִׁלֻּחִים is not necessarily limited to that meaning only. It has to do with a departure. However, Exod 18:2 does not make clear whose departure is mentioned. Since Zipporah is constantly called the "wife of Moses"—and this expresses a steadfast marriage—the departure referred to may be that of Jethro, who has given her a gift of departure, as the testimonies of שִׁלֻּחִים suggest.[37]

In Exod 18:27, Moses says farewell only to his father-in-law, not to Zipporah. Does this mean that she stays with him? Since in the entire passage Moses has not paid attention to Zipporah, we cannot draw any conclusions from the silence of the text regarding this point. Another perspective appears when we consider the situation, once again, from the viewpoint of the marital typology with חֹתֵן. Jethro is called חֹתֵן of Moses four times in four verses, and the most remarkable aspect is Jethro's self-presentation, which is highlighted in many commentaries. Why does he need to tell Moses that he is his father-in-law? He must say it if he wants to express the special relationship between the two dissimilar tribes that has been sealed by the marriage. This is also why the text mentions Moses' submission and the pact of peace. In this passage, the marriage of Moses and Zipporah primarily receives a political meaning, precisely the peaceful relationship between Midian and Israel. So, once again political circumstances are treated in terms of a family story, in a way familiar to us from the stories of the patriarchs. This may also explain why the marital relationship is not more explicitly affirmed in Exod 18 and why Moses and Zipporah do not go on from there happily united; in fact, peaceful relations between Midian and Israel in the Hebrew Bible were practically impossible. This marriage remained difficult, perhaps even scandalous for political rea-

---

36. On the following, see Rapp, *Mirjam*, 75. Different in Fischer, "The Authority of Miriam," 164; eadem, *Gotteskünderinnen*, 72.

37. Different in Fischer, "The Authority of Miriam," 163, who, like Exod. Rab. 1:13, starts from the idea that Moses divorced Zipporah.

sons, and it was certainly not an exemplary marriage. Actually, since Zipporah was Midianite, she should not have been Moses' wife in the first place.

2.3. THE DAUGHTER IN THE SHADOW OF HER FATHER

Zipporah herself is mentioned in four passages (Exod 2:15–21; 4:24–26; 18:1–5; Num 12:1), and in seven of these verses she is either named or referred to as "the wife of Moses."[38] On the other hand, the father-in-law is evoked fifteen times[39] in seven passages (Exod 2:15–21; 3:1; 4:18; 18:1–12; Num 10:29; Judg 1:16; 4:11). Moses' father-in-law is clearly referred to more often than his wife, and often this observation has led to the conclusion that the woman was far less important to Moses than her Midianite provenance,[40] which was more or less relevant—depending on the interpretation. Some scholars maintain that Moses' relationship with Midian and, therefore, the origin of the veneration of YHWH should be stressed. Likewise, in that case the delegation of the jurisdiction in Exod 18 would also have a Midianite character and be important for understanding the Mosaic role.

Another interpretation emphasizes above all the marriage with a non-Israelite, be she Midianite, Cushite, or Kenite. This becomes significant especially in the postexilic context of the question of mixed marriages. This brings us to Num 12.

2.4. NUMBERS 12:1–2

Numbers 12:1–2 says:

> Miriam and Aaron spoke against Moses because of the Cushite woman whom he had married, for he had indeed married a Cushite woman; and they said, "Has God spoken really only to Moses? Has he not spoken to us also?" (NRSV)

These two verses introduce a short narrative. At the very beginning we must ask ourselves what Moses' marriage with a non-Israelite has to do with the reception of divine revelation. In fact, there is a connection if prophecy is understood in the later sense of prophecy as the interpretation of the Torah. In that case, this conflict concerns the question of knowing who has the author-

---

38. Exod 2:21–22; 4:25; 18:2, 5–6; Num 12:1.
39. Exod 2:18; 3:1; 4:18; 18:1–2, 5–6, 9–10, 12, 14, 17; Num 10:29; Judg 1:16; 4:11.
40. See George W. Coats, "Moses in Midian," *JBL* 92 (1973): 3–10.

ity legitimately to interpret the Torah:[41] Can Miriam and Aaron also do this or only Moses, as God's discourse in Num 12:6–8 clearly states? Next, what are the different positions represented, and who presents them? Concretely, if in Num 12 Moses' marriage with a non-Israelite is considered a problem, who is in favor of maintaining it, and who thinks it should be dissolved?

If we start with the idea that Moses' authority regarding the question of mixed marriages is claimed by Ezra and his polemics against mixed marriages, then Miriam—if she is at odds with Moses—is *in favor of* maintaining the mixed marriage. In that case, Miriam's argument would be this: even Moses had a non-Israelite wife. Precisely this fact would legitimize mixed marriages.[42]

Another way of reading of Num 12 consists in assuming that the marriage between Moses and Zipporah was not dissolved and, therefore, constitutes an even stronger argument for the defenders of mixed marriages.[43] The authors of Num 12, who write against this stance, which in fact is supported by Miriam, would consider Moses, in the sense of 12:6–8, as an absolute exception: only Moses speaks with God face to face, and he alone sees God's reflection, and only his marriage with the Cushite woman is legitimate.

In the end, both readings are possible, since Exod 18:1–5 does not say explicitly whether the marriage was maintained or dissolved. If it is true that the tradition of Moses' marriage with a Midianite woman is very ancient, as has often been affirmed, then it is even more plausible that there are several interpretations, since the relationship between the two, as we have seen, is not important for the Mosaic tradition. The significant aspects of the tie between Moses and Midian are the origin of Israel's God, the priestly father-in-law who perhaps has some connection with the veneration of this deity, and much later the question of the practice of mixed marriages.

---

41. Rainer Kessler understood Miriam as representative of prophecy in the postexilic period, Moses as the representative of the Torah, and Aaron in his function as priest, meaning that the three powers are symbolized in the figures of the siblings. See Rainer Kessler, "Mirjam und die Prophetie der Perserzeit," in *Gott an den Rändern: Sozialgeschichtliche Perspektiven auf die Bibel: Für Willy Schottroff zum 65. Geburtstag* (ed. Ulrike Bail and Renate Jost; Gütersloh: Gütersloher Verlagshaus/Christian Kaiser, 1996), 64–72.

42. On the contrary, Irmtraud Fischer interprets Exod 18:2 as the act of divorce. Consequently, Moses himself dissolved his marriage, and Miriam and Aaron criticize this in Num 12:1–2 (see Fischer, "The Authority of Miriam," 163–64; eadem, *Gotteskünderinnen*, 74).

43. I understand the text to mean that Miriam and Aaron plead for the maintenance of the mixed marriage and use Moses' standing marriage with a non-Israelite woman as an argument (see Rapp, *Mirjam*, 75–77, 186–87).

3. The Historicity and the Symbolic Power of Zipporah's Figure

Little can be said about Zipporah's historicity. The evaluation of her historicity will always resemble that of the historicity of Moses and Miriam. Whoever considers Moses a fictitious construction will think the same of Zipporah. On the other hand, whoever believes that the figure of Moses has a historical core will include Zipporah in it.[44] Indeed, there would hardly have been any reason at a later time for inventing a marriage with a non-Israelite,[45] unless the advocates of mixed marriages had wanted to attribute such a marriage to Moses. However, they were hardly strong enough to ensure that such a multifaceted tradition lasted. Moreover, if such reconstructions are correct, similar views would have been found in the prophetic texts; yet precisely these texts do not mention Zipporah. Alongside the impossibility of finding any interest behind Moses' mixed marriage, some exegetes stress that the disagreement over Zipporah's origin speaks in favor of the antiquity of this tradition.[46]

Whatever the conclusion to such speculations may be, I find the symbolic power of the figure of Zipporah far more important. One of the traits of her character is that the leader and legislator of the Pentateuch, the great prophet Moses, was married to a non-Israelite. Not a single text says anything about Moses having an Israelite wife. Thus, Moses is not only in the tradition of a Joseph. The image of Moses' mixed marriage is a standing criticism against a total seclusion over against the outside. It is valid for every community that recognizes these texts as holy. The texts that present Zipporah as a Midianite attest peaceful egalitarian relations between Midian and Israel, guaranteed by the bond of a *chatan* marriage.

In addition, Zipporah, as the one who saved Moses' life, is a woman instructed in the rituals and invested with priestly competence. If she had not intervened, Moses would have lost his life.

Finally, the question remains open whether Zipporah left her country for her husband or if she remained there. It has often been thought that Moses and Zipporah separated after the blood ritual and Moses continued his mission alone, with Aaron at his side. Zipporah is not implicated in her husband's affairs, nor is she gained to the cause of his people. At first, she remains faithful to herself and to her family and tradition. Only later is she brought back to Moses (Exod 18:2). Whether she stays, wants to stay, or is allowed to stay

---

44. See Gerhards, "Über die Herkunft," 162–64.
45. See ibid., 164.
46. See ibid., 169.

remains unresolved, and, as I suggested at the beginning, this truly fits the meaning of her name.

Miriam, Primordial Political Figure in the Exodus

Mercedes García Bachmann
Instituto Universitario ISEDET

1. Introduction

1.1. What Do We Know about Miriam?

Miriam is a deceptively simple character. Her name appears in seven Old Testament texts, which can be divided in two groups: those that contain information about her life (literary, not historical), and those that tell us something about later traditions but not about her. There is no consensus as to the meaning of her name, which might be related to the root מרר ("to be bitter") or to מרה ("to be a rebel").

It is notable that, at least on the popular level, the first mental association that one has with Miriam does not come from one of the seven mentions of her name but rather from her participation in the miraculous salvation of the newborn Moses (Exod 2). There "his sister" and "his mother" are anonymous.[1] The identification of this sister with Miriam comes mainly from other texts, especially Num 26:59. There are only two extensive texts about her: the just mentioned Exod 2 (which does not mention her name) and Num 12. Only in two texts does Miriam speak: Exod 2 and 15:20–21.[2] Two texts associate her with leprosy: Num 12 explains the origin of her marks, and in Deut 24:8–9 Miriam's example serves as a warning and exhortation to observe the dictate of the Levites. The news of her death in the desert (Num 20:1) must also be added to this list. The remaining text in the Torah that mentions

---

1. One of the difficulties regarding the exegesis of Exod 2 is how to reconstruct historical facts since the text has a clearly legendary slant.

2. Numbers 12:1–2 alludes to two themes that trouble Miriam and Aaron: concern over the marriage of Moses with a foreigner and the preeminence of Moses as the only one who can interpret the divine will (prophet). These two issues serve to initiate the chapter's events.

Miriam (Num 26:59) is a note about Jochebed, which leads us to infer that the event in Exod 2 really is part of Miriam's story. Outside of the Torah she is only mentioned twice, in Chronicles (1 Chr 5:29, a priestly genealogy like Num 26:59) and in the prophetic corpus (Mic 6:4, the only text in this corpus that mentions a prophetess by name).

1.2. How Do We Read the Texts?

There are many possible ways in which to interpret, classify, and present the texts about Miriam. But what would a person who was listening to or reading the Bible for the first time learn about Miriam's character? In a reading following the canonical ordering of texts, the main emphasis is on the narrative sequence and the readers: What do they perceive? What provokes the readers? What draws their attention? Such a reading, however, is difficult for anyone who is, for example, immersed in the Western culture and cannot read the story from a *tabula rasa* perspective. The fact already mentioned, that the most well-known text about Miriam is one that does *not* mention her name, is one of the evident difficulties of this approach. This approach, therefore, is not enough to reconstruct a reliable "life of Miriam."[3]

I am interested in a reading that focuses on the ideology(ies) of the text with which we are confronted in our reading, many times unconsciously. An ideological reading tries to uncover how reality is perceived and explained, especially in terms of the distribution of power, of honor and possession, and—especially in the case of religious texts—of divine approval or disapproval. Starting from these questions, I will present a reading of the texts according to the following classification:

(1) texts that allow us to construct a "life of Miriam" as a character of a text: Is there a coherent picture or not? (Within this section I will follow the order exodus, desert, death.)

(2) texts where Miriam is a negative or positive role model for her people: How is her character presented? Are these models consistent with or different from the picture presented in the texts studied in the first part? What ideological trajectories are visible?

It is necessary to remember time and again that any reading is done from a specific hermeneutical position, never from a blank or neutral point. In a

---

3. With the expression "life of Miriam," I am not referring to a historically precise biography but rather to that which becomes known about a character from reading texts about her. A discussion about her historicity would require much more space; moreover, it has to be taken into account that the texts were not written with the intention of presenting a detailed historiography.

liberation-theological approach, which closely links the texts to the life of the people and the life of the church, two fundamental attributes of Miriam's character that can be found in the biblical texts are emphasized. First, Miriam is part of a group of leaders. She is consequently not an isolated figure but appears in cooperation with other women, who complement her in her song (Exod 15:20). If we keep in mind the story of Exod 2:1–10, she appears with other women who keep Moses alive. In the two chapters of Numbers, in addition to being shown in close relation to her brothers, she is also closely related to the people, who wait for her during her exclusion from the camp and who rise against Aaron and Moses after her death. Additionally, Miriam's "sororization" with prominent figures, which means her inclusion in a genealogical line in a horizontal, not vertical, manner (sister, not daughter), contributes to this relationship of shared leadership. It can thus be perceived that Miriam is not a figure isolated from her companions or from her people. It is perhaps this that has saved her from oblivion. This emphasis on shared responsibility is more a hermeneutical concern of our days than the Bible's. Considering the aporias of our time, Miriam can teach us quite a lot.

Another characteristic of Miriam that is closely linked to the previous one is Miriam's place among strong patriarchal figures, including the deity YHWH. Being among them can be either an advantage or a problem. From a positive point of view, it allows for an emphasis on the fact that her adoration is directed toward YHWH, not toward Moses. Or, said in another way, no human should be put on a pedestal and adored together with YHWH, since YHWH's glory does not permit this. From Exodus onward there is a tendency either to put Moses on a pedestal and venerate him or to condemn him for having brought the people to the desert to be killed. This message is subtly transmitted when Exod 14:31b ("and the people believed in the LORD and his servant Moses") is juxtaposed with 15:21 (Miriam's invitation to sing to YHWH alone) and the quarrels in Num 11–12. On the negative side, Miriam's body ends up as the site of patriarchal confrontation between YHWH, the people, and their leaders.

1.3. How Will We Use the Existing Material?

Owing to various reasons, including length and relevance, not all these texts will in the following receive the same amount of space or attention. Since a complete chapter is dedicated to Exod 2 elsewhere in this volume, it will only be dealt with insofar as it is related to Miriam. In a certain sense, it is debatable if it should even be included in a study of "Miriam." It is a hero's legend, so it has its own characteristics, among which, of course, is the focus on the hero … who is not Miriam. In the same way, genealogies will be dealt with more briefly than the narrations of Numbers. It is impossible to include all the secondary literature that exists about these texts. Moreover, traditional commentaries, of course, do not guarantee greater information, since they do not focus on Miriam but rather on Moses or Aaron. Because of this, I will limit the use of traditional sources in favor of other resources more attuned to the type of reading that I intend to carry out here. The resources that will be most prevalent in this essay, more than can be acknowledged in the notes, can be divided into: (1) doctoral theses (Burns, Rapp, Butting); (2) different types of literary studies, including those that are structural (Jobling, Milgrom), those concerned with metric and Hebrew poetry (Cross and Freedman, Janzen), and those dealing with rhetoric (Trible, Janzen); and (3) essays about women (of different types, with different interests, which at times contradict each other) with a focus on gender issues (Fischer, Meyers, Ackerman, Gruber, Siebert-Hommes, and others).

2. Study of Texts and Themes

2.1. A "Canonical" Reading of Miriam

2.1.1. Meaningful Presence

In a sequential reading of the Bible, the first mention of Miriam appears in Exod 15:20:

> And Miriam the prophetess, the sister of Aaron, took the timbrel in her hand; and all the women went out after her with timbrels and dances.[4]

Anyone who has spent time in Sunday School will, however, associate the figure of Miriam with the childhood of Moses. Is such an association valid, or would it be better to eliminate that story from our revision of Miriam? The answer to this question depends upon what we look for in the texts. A canonical reading need not exclude it, since particular signals in the text suggest a link between Moses' unnamed sister in Exod 2 with Miriam the sister of Aaron and Moses. When the story reaches Exod 15:20 (having just heard the wonderful story of liberation from death represented by the pharaoh), the audience learns that Miriam, the prophetess, the sister of Aaron, took the timbrel: "Aha! This is the sister that we heard about before, who saved Moses from a premature death, but we did not know her name." The story continues.

---

4. Unless otherwise indicated, all translations of biblical texts are my own.

Now Miriam, like her brothers, is an adult and leader of the community. She interprets the exodus in her song and praises God. The stage in the desert begins, a period that will certainly not be easy for Moses, Aaron, the people, YHWH, or Miriam herself. During this stage the episodes relating to Miriam concern the questioning of authority uniquely attributed to Moses, Miriam's consequent leprosy, and, subsequently, her death in the desert (Num 20). Some chapters later, still during the time in the desert, the genealogical news that links Aaron, Moses, and Miriam appears. They are shown to be siblings born of Jochebed and Amram (Num 26:59). Up to this point that is all that could be said about Miriam if one were to write her biography and knew that the information contained in the Pentateuch were true. The remaining texts do not add anything to a "life of Miriam," since they build on this same information. This does not mean that the other texts are unimportant; it means, rather, that anyone listening to the biblical story for the first time would catch everything necessary to form her or his own idea of this character.

2.1.2. Meaningful Absences

The reading that I have just finished emphasizes what the texts say. There are many details lacking, however. For example, when Miriam appears as a daughter, she is anonymous (Exod 2), and when she has a name, it is only as a sister, not as a "daughter." If she really is older than Moses, following Exod 2, this text fails to mention her birth; the story begins with the marriage of one Levite to another and then passes directly to the conception and birth of Moses. We do not even know if Miriam married or had children. These are important facts in a patriarchal culture in which the most common function of a woman is just that, as wife and mother. We also do not have, at any point, information about her age: Was she old when she died? We could suppose that she was, as that is what happened to her "brothers." Numbers 20, however, does not call her "sister" and therefore does not allow conclusions about her age or belonging to this generation. Age is a sign of being blessed, so the mention of an exact age is important. With regard to Miriam, notes about her death as well as the mourning of her people about her are missing, unlike the situation with Aaron (Num 20:22–29) and Moses later on (Deut 34; cf. Num 27:15–23).

Why is all this information missing? Must these omissions all be seen as negative? This depends upon the reading of the text. The absence of "family" information could be indicative of the fact that what stayed in the memory of the people was not her role as wife and mother but rather that of singer and prophetess. This would explain why other facts were not included in the story. (This would not surprise us if she had been a man, but we are so accustomed to look for this information first that any absence of it is noticeable).

What is the goal or importance of such a canonical reading? In the first place, it has to be recognized that this is a very common reading among people from my cultural background, including our audience. Second, it is important to recognize this narrative trajectory because, I imagine, there is no greater pleasure for a narrator than to tell a story that enthralls and excites. The story of Miriam has these characteristics: born from Levite lineage on both sides, recognized as a prophetess, a strong leader of the people, she ends up with marks on her body, dies in the desert, and incites, with her death, the desanctification (of God? of the people? of Moses and Aaron?) whereby we can comprehend the lack of water, the rebellion, and the change of command that take place in Num 20.

In summary, as to the question of whether there is one coherent picture of Miriam, we can answer that the evidence does not provide us with such. Fundamental facts are missing, such as her birth, age, or familial status. We also do not have sufficient information about the development of her prophetic function throughout time or the possible implications of her priestly Levite origin. We can thus conclude that the picture with which we are presented is incomplete, though medially coherent in what it presents.

2.2. CRITICAL READING: MIRIAM AS PRIMORDIAL POLITICAL FIGURE IN THE EXODUS

In this section I will present some of the most important elements in the analysis of each text, as provided by different exegetes. The focus of my contribution is on Miriam as a primordial political figure in the exodus. I will thus begin with those texts that concern the exodus. Subsequently, I will discuss those texts that I consider to be most significant with regard to a political reading of Miriam's character. Prior to this, however, it is necessary to clarify what I understand by Miriam as a "political figure." First of all, we can conclude that in her role as a leader of the people on the path toward liberation, she, together with Moses and Aaron, was clearly one of the directors. This role is more obvious in the two texts in Numbers. Moreover, she appears as a political figure when she interprets the liberation from Egypt and the new life in the desert in a political way, as shown in her first important appearance in the story: "Sing to YHWH…" (Exod 15). Mercedes Navarro Puerto, on the other hand, considers a political Miriam from another perspective: due to narrative analysis, she interprets the crossing of the sea as a narrative that is particularly concerned with a question of national, political, and religious identity.[5]

---

5. Mercedes Navarro Puerto, "El paso del mar: Nacer muriendo," in *Relectura del*

2.2.1. Book of Exodus

2.2.1.1. Exodus 2:1–10

The story of Exod 2 places the child, later identified as Miriam, on the political stage, next to the pharaoh's daughter, negotiating with her in the search for a wet nurse.

Historical-critical exegesis is virtually unanimous in considering this chapter to be a legend destined to highlight the extraordinary origin of the hero, comparable to the Akkadian Sargon Legend. Because of its legendary character, we cannot expect historical information from this text. Exodus 2 should be read against the background of the totalitarian and demagogical measures taken by the pharaoh in Exod 1: the destruction of a people who, having lived in Egypt for generations, could eventually become an enemy: "they" and "we" are not the same for the pharaoh. Also, these genocidal measures should be read as an important element in the plot of Abraham's saga: the promise of a vast lineage has been fulfilled, and, paradoxically, this fulfillment puts it in danger. The family who went with Jacob to Egypt and stayed there, seventy people who came from him, have become a people who, according to the words of the pharoah in 1:9 "are more and mightier than we." Against this machinery of death, another plot is put into motion, but this one leads toward life. Without this plot formed by many people, Moses would not have become a man, supportive and faithful to his roots. The book of Exodus prioritizes, among these people, the midwives Shiphrah and Puah, Moses' anonymous mother and sister, the likewise anonymous daughter of the pharaoh, and, later, the daughters of the priest of Midian. Among these, only the chosen wife has a name. In a situation of state terrorism, however, the complicity of many people is necessary in order to keep a secret such as the hiding of Moses.[6] For example, the royal slaves who look for the basket and find it with the pharaoh's daughter; the cooks, servants, governesses, and

---

Éxodo (ed. Isabel Gómez Acebo et al.; En Clave de Mujer; Bilbao: Desclée de Brouwer, 2006), 112.

6. Jopie Siebert-Hommes, originally in "But If She Be a Daughter … She May Live! 'Daughters' and 'Sons' in Exodus 1–2," in *A Feminist Companion to Exodus to Deuteronomy* (ed. Athalya Brenner; FCB 6; Sheffield: Sheffield Academic Press, 1994), 62–74 (see also her contribution in this volume), speaks of the twelve daughters who help Moses as a counterpoint to the twelve sons of Jacob who form the basis of the people. The number twelve (male ancestors of the people and female saviors of Moses) has a symbolic importance. We can not fail to note, however, the gender asymmetry between these groups of twelve, nor can we forget the fact that other women are left out, such as the entire group related to the pharaoh's daughter, both by the river and in the palace.

other women who helped to raise Moses in the palace; and the Hebrews who did not denounce the concealment of the child even when, according to plot, their own families were in danger.[7]

Phyllis Trible is correct to identify Moses' sister as a bridge, as a mediator between the two very different (and also sociopolitically, economically, culturally, and religiously unequal) worlds of the pharaoh's daughter and the true family of Moses. She speaks of the daughter stopping at a distance to observe.[8] Trible emphasizes the narrative sequence, while my reading is sociopolitically oriented. Her observations are in any case noteworthy. The sister who in Exod 2 mediates between her mother and the Egyptian princess on the banks of the Nile will end her life as a mediator between diverse factions (Num 20).

For a number of years an established scholarly consensus has existed stating that the "exodus" can contain, in sum, some historical element, most definitely profoundly reworked from diverse experiences. Therefore, it is possible to speak of "exoduses" in the plural. That is to say, the different experiences of various witnesses have been shaped through the years into traditions linked to particular places or groups that were transmitted and reworked according to the new situations. Finally, they were placed in this key place where the promise made to Abraham's family of numerous descendants (Genesis) with their own land begins to be fulfilled.

What would be the saving experiences that form the content of these exoduses? Of course, we can enumerate the great feats, such as the miraculous crossing of a body of water (the "sea"), the escape of a group of slaves from imperial power, the food and the water that arrive unexpectedly when, humanly, there was nothing that could be done. The exoduses could also, however, be thought of as the Brazilian theologian Tânia Vieira Sampaio does. She focuses on Exod 1–15 from the perspective of the daily life of a home, interpersonal and social relations, and bodies:

> The many exoduses in the final text are bearers of the diversity of situations that constitute the human experience of desiring other worlds and other ways of organizing life. The exodus, thus, is announced as an invitation to

---

7. There are other stories, such as 1 Kgs 3, where "bad" mothers who have lost their own children prefer to inflict the same evil on others before saving the life of a living child. This is not the case in Exod 2.

8. Phyllis Trible, "Bringing Miriam Out of the Shadows," in Brenner, *Feminist Companion to Exodus*, 167. For a discussion about the incorporation of Miriam as a sister into the genealogy, see Irmtraud Fischer, *Gotteskünderinnen: Zu einer geschlechterfairen Deutung des Phänomens der Prophetie und der Prophetinnen in der Hebräischen Bibel* (Stuttgart: Kohlhammer, 2002), 67–68.

gratitude toward relationships, in the taste of the transitory, which accompanies the corporeal experience in the world.[9]

Seen from this viewpoint, an exodus would be a situation of retreat, a fleeing from death toward the possibility of life. The midwives, the Hebrew families themselves who reproduce in the face of socioeconomic oppression, the families who hide their sons from the pharaoh, the workers who request easier working conditions, even the Hebrews who refuse to accept a murderer—Moses—as their judge form part of these exoduses! Thinking in this way, as a small cluster of daily exoduses, it is not necessary to wonder about the historicity of the event nor even to try to explain the inexplicable that caused Miriam's song and so many other texts in the Hebrew Bible. Better, it invites us to celebrate not only the Plagues, the Collapse of the Egyptians and the Crossing of the Sea (capitalization shows their importance when seen as unique events), but also the creation of a plan to save a baby, the opportunity to obtain money from the pharaoh's daughter for raising one's own son at home, and the knowledge that someone in the palace will remind Moses that he is the brother of the Hebrew slaves who sweat beneath the sun making bricks, keeping ancestral language and culture alive against the danger of assimilation, preparing dough for the bread, asking the neighbor for a loan, gathering supplies, maintaining hope for a better world.... Seen in this way, in these exoduses there were many Miriams, anonymous and "unconscious" collaborators in God's plan.

I would like, finally, to underline that Trible's assessment of Miriam opens and closes with the crossing of the sea, locating itself in a kind of *inclusive place*, from the moment in which "she stood at a distance to see what would be done to him" with her brother laid in the ark, until she appears near to the sea.

2.2.1.2. Exodus 15:20–21

The Relationship of Exod 15:20–21 and 15:1–18. There are many opinions about this passage concerning its antiquity, the relation of these verses to those that precede it, its literary genre, and even its syntax. If it is true that 14:31 ends a prose story and a poem begins in Exod 15, I understand 14:1–15:21 as a semantic unit, even though it has internal divergences. In this way, the verses that specifically mention Miriam and the other women should

---

9. Tânia Mara Vieira Sampaio, "Un éxodo entre muchos otros éxodos: La belleza de lo transitorio oscurecida por el discurso de lo permanente. Una lectura de Éxodo 1–15," *RIBLA* 23 (1996): 87, my translation.

be seen in relation to the prose narration of the crossing of the sea and the son of Moses and the men.

The narration of the wonderful liberation culminates in 14:31, immediately following the introduction to a song that is attributed to Moses. This song continues until 15:18, closing with a doxology. Right after that, a verse in prose again speaks of the greatness of YHWH in the sea, giving way to Miriam's song. Part of the difficulty in identifying the literary genre of this poem comes from the fact that it includes a number of elements of different genres, without ever showing the typical literary form of just one.[10] In addition to prose (14:31; 15:19–21a) and poetry (15:1–18, 21b), in this text we also see the insertion of different narrative times. Because of this, it is very difficult to establish an adequate chronology of the events and, with them, the leading roles of the characters. If the proposal of Rabinowitz is correct, the temporal adverb in 15:1 indicates an action that began at the same time as the events that were already narrated.[11] In this case, Moses began to sing to YHWH while they were finishing their crossing of the sea. On the other hand, as Janzen proposes, Miriam's thanksgiving (15:20–21) also refers to an anterior event, to which it is linked by the literary tool of flashback and the narrative chain of *wayyiqtols*.[12] Thus the text offers a parallel between Moses and Miriam in order to indicate the simultaneity of their songs (neither song is "anterior" to the other). The text is chiastically structured by elements A-A' that are linked to Miriam and elements B-B' linked with Moses. In order to unite the elements with their respective match that came before, different literary resources are used. These indicated simultaneity (third column of the table). While, on the one hand, Moses and the men sing while they are cross-

---

10. See Brevard S. Childs, *The Book of Exodus: A Critical Theological Commentary* (Louisville: Westminster John Knox, 1974), 243–44. Rita J. Burns (*Exodus, Leviticus, Numbers* [Wilmington, Del.: Glazier, 1983], 114) considers it to be a song to the victorious warrior, similar to that found in Judg 11 or 1 Sam 18:6.

11. Isaac Rabinowitz ("אז Followed by Imperfect Verb-Form in Preterite Contexts: A Redactional Device in Biblical Hebrew," *VT* 34 [1984]: 53–62) states, among other things, about this verse: "The imperfect verb-form is used in these instances because the action is thought of as having taken place before the completion of, hence as incomplete relative to, the actions described as completed in the preceding context. The construction is resorted to as an efficient means of causing a reader or hearer to regard the ensuing additional textual material as temporally (though not sequentially) linked to the preceding textual statements, when the writer, editor or speaker does not wish to work in and to merge such additional material with that of the preceding text as given" (54).

12. The *wayyiqtol* is a Hebrew verbal form that is indicative of the narrative chain. See J. Gerald Janzen, "Song of Moses, Song of Miriam: Who Is Seconding Whom?" in Brenner, *Feminist Companion to Exodus*, 189–94.

ing the dry sea (parallelism achieved through the adverb אָז, which unites 14:31 and 15:1–18), on the other hand, the celebration of Miriam and the women is parallel to Exod 14:31. In this case the parallelism is not achieved through אָז but rather through the flashback.

A 14:26–29		Simultaneity:
	B 14:31 (climax of the story)	
	B' Moses' song (15:1–18)	אָז + imperfect 15:1
		flashback 15:19
A' Miriam's song 15:20–21		

There are various possibilities for the translation of the first words of 15:21 וַתַּעַן לָהֶם מִרְיָם. As Fischer emphasizes, the first meaning of the verb עֲנה is "to respond," although most interpretations translate "to sing." The *qal* of the verb עֲנה is rarely constructed with the preposition לְ; it is usually constructed with a direct object, the preposition בְ, or with pronoun suffixes— or it is unaccompanied. In the few cases in which it is accompanied by the preposition לְ, it also indicates the person about whom one is speaking: David, a vine, or YHWH.[13] In our case, לָהֶם (preposition + third-person masculine plural suffix) cannot mean "to them" (the people or the men) in the sense of singing *about* the people. Because of this, Fischer suggests reading it in the sense of "answering for them/in place of them." Thus Miriam takes on the prophetic function par excellence by mediating between the divine and the human and interpreting human reality in the light of divine reality and bringing the human word before God.[14]

---

13. See 1 Sam 29:5 (David); Num 21:17 (a well); Isa 27:2 (the vine); and Ps 147:7 (YHWH).

14. See Fischer, *Gotteskünderinnen*, 66–67. After Klara Butting, *Prophetinnen gefragt: Die Bedeutung der Prophetinnen im Kanon aus Tora und Prophetie* (Erev-Rav-Hefte: Biblisch-feministische texte 3; Wittingen: Erev-Rav, 2001), 38–44: Miriam calls them to sing, bringing the story to the present moment with her "prophetic imperative" to sing to the Lord.

This reading says nothing about the chronological origin of each text. It only explains the current literary arrangement: Is there one text that came before the other? Is it a matter of a refrain sung by Miriam, or, the other way around, Moses' answer to Miriam's invitation? What is being discussed in feminist discourses is whether the modern academic community can accept that the Bible considers both leaders to be equally important or if it prefers to think of the text as the submission of one through the editorial inclusion of a second character together with the first (and in this case, who would be the main actor). An important group of scholars, however, focus on this theme in a different way, considering Miriam's song to be probably older than Moses', though it functions in the canonical text as an antiphon in answer to the praise of the people guided by Moses.

Arguments in Favor of Moses' Song. The following are arguments for considering Moses' song as the original: the assignment of the song to Moses, given his preponderance in the narrated events; the importance of a man with illustrious credentials (in this case, Moses) for priests; and the fact that it was men who later revised (or created, according to how the process of the formation of the Pentateuch is understood) the texts and guarded the tradition of the Torah. There is also an unspoken argument: the primacy of Moses over Miriam is maintained by the weight of the traditional trajectory, that is to say, by appearing written, more or less supported in earlier quotes and being reproduced acritically as a given truth in many traditional commentaries throughout the ages.

Arguments in Favor of Miriam's Song. The most significant studies that push for the consideration of Miriam as the author of the original song are the following. Cross and Freedman, beginning with philology and the comparison of ancient Canaanite poetry, reach the conclusion that Miriam's is the oldest song and that 15:20–21 form its title, coming from another tradition.[15] On the other hand, among narrative analyses of Miriam, Phyllis Trible's is probably the oldest and still most used. Another important study is that which I have already cited by Janzen. This work concentrates on 15:1–21, trying to determine the relationship between the two songs through a study of the literary resources used. As many authors have noted, the North American trend tends to consider it to be very old, while recent European studies consider it

---

15. Frank Moore Cross Jr. and David N. Freedman, "The Song of Miriam," *JNES* 14 (1955): 237. Janzen, "Song of Moses," arrives at the same conclusion as Cross and Freedman but by using a different path.

to be postexilic. I believe that the text reflects very old elements, without this being an obstacle to, in the time of the definitive assembling of the Pentateuch (which I do consider to be postexilic), its being selected and even retouched, precisely because it responded to a need of that moment.

An additional element that should be considered to attribute the song of the crossing of the sea to Miriam is the fact that in the biblical tradition victory songs are almost always related to women who compose music, sing, dance, and play instruments.[16] These reasons (in addition to the fact that it is much easier to explain why Moses' name is added to hers) lead me, and many other scholars, to lean toward the conclusion that this text must be attributed to Miriam.

Miriam as Prophetess. We still must investigate the importance of her being called "a prophetess" and "the sister of Aaron." Opinions are much divided here as well. The first comprehensive work about Miriam is the doctoral dissertation of Rita Burns. She considers the nickname "prophetess" for Miriam to be something anachronistic that was added at a later time.[17] In her opinion, there were no prophets with the characteristics that ours acquire later during the premonarchic period; thus, the use of this term in such an early text must be a later, anachronistic addition. Though Burns's work deserves our gratitude for being a pioneer in research about Miriam, I do not share her conclusion about this point. Burns places too much emphasis on the absence of prophetic figures in the time of the march from Egypt; above all, she needlessly separates the cultic and priestly from the prophetic. It is enough for now to say that in biblical literature the prophetic figure is linked to different functions and thus the sense of the term is not unequivocal. Think, for example, of Elijah, Elisha, and other "men of God," prophets in ecstasy found by Saul, or even Samuel or Isaiah.

The interpretation of God's word for the people and especially for its governors was, without a doubt, one of its most important functions. In this

---

16. In addition to Miriam, we see an anonymous group of women who receive Saul and David (1 Sam 18:6) and the daughter of Jephthah receiving her father and his army (Judg 11:34); Jer 31:4 is a promise that in the future Israel will again go out and dance. We could also add the women dancing in Shiloh (Judg 20) and Deborah's song (Judg 5).

17. Rita J. Burns, *Has the Lord Indeed Spoken Only through Moses? A Study of the Biblical Portrait of Miriam* (SBLDS 84; Atlanta: Scholars Press, 1987), 41–79 (summary: 67); see also eadem, *Exodus, Leviticus, Numbers,* 115, where she considers that it is anachronistic because "the authentic prophetic activity is never attributable in Biblical texts." However, she bases this affirmation on her own analysis, which is unconvincing to me, that Miriam's activities (singing, dance, and musical execution in honor of the Divine Warrior) are cultic and not political and social (prophetic) activities.

sense, its use in Exodus is definitely anachronistic, since there were no governors—or better, since she herself was one of the "governors"! In this way, the
time of the judges or the period of greatest upheaval in the exilic and postexilic period could serve as a mirror to see Miriam as a prophet. In my opinion,
then, the problem is not in whether the term is used anachronistically in 15:20
but rather with what element of what is known about prophecy in the ancient
Near East we should compare Miriam. Although it is anachronistic, the fact
is that such an anachronism survived repeated editions of the Bible's material; different editors chose to associate her memory with prophecy (and with
dance and music).

I believe that an important key in Miriam's analysis as prophetess is her
role as an interpreter of God's word in the situation of that moment. This is
one of the principle characteristics of the prophetic movement, together with
intercession before YHWH. While intercession became a priestly prerogative, however, theological interpretation of public events and, especially, the
guardianship of fidelity to YHWH continued being prophetic functions. This
is precisely the reading of Miriam's song that I would like to emphasize. When,
in the moment of the sea crossing, she picks up the timbrel and calls the entire
community to sing to the victory of YHWH, she is theologically interpreting her present, her reality. She is "responding," responding to the events that
YHWH has carried out before the eyes of all the people, not only the men.
She is not only creating theology in the sense of reading the present in light of
the divine word. She is also correcting the community and Moses himself in
their tendency (the people's) to place their faith in Moses' person rather than
in YHWH. In effect, while 14:31 culminates with the note that the people,
after witnessing the great works of YHWH, believed in YHWH and in Moses
(וַיַּאֲמִינוּ בַּיהוָה וּבְמֹשֶׁה עַבְדּוֹ), Miriam's song calls them to praise only YHWH.
The doxological focus on Moses has been replaced, just as it should be!

Finally, Moses himself appears in the last two chapters of Deuteronomy
first singing and then blessing the people with a "testament" (Deut 33, another
ancient poem), and, after his death, the narrator dedicates the epitaph of the
unequal prophet to him (Deut 34:10–12). Further, Deborah is as much a
prophetess as a singer (Judg 4–5). It is certain that this seems to be more a
characteristic of Deuteronomy than of other sources, but it is indicative of the
fact that, for at least one of the important factions of Judaism, the association
of fathers and mothers with prophecy and poetry/music was not strange. The
same can be said about Chronicles, where the "sons of Levi" are the singers.

It seems, then, that there are enough elements to link Miriam with both
song and prophecy without doubting such a connection. What cannot be
determined because of a lack of information is her association with the
priesthood, although various scholars have tried. Her Levite lineage is well-

documented in the texts in which she appears as Aaron the priest's sister and therefore implicitly as Amram's (and Jochebed's) daughter, but we have no information about what this meant culturally or practically, if it meant anything. In this sense, Burns's effort is valuable for having brought attention to Miriam's connection with culture; perhaps one day new evidence will allow us to fully appreciate her conclusions, though at present they remain unconvincing.

Thus, the vision of Miriam that one would form from reading just the book of Exodus is that of a woman without her own family, mentioned in one text as Aaron's sister and in another as Moses'. She was a recognized leader of the community, prophetess, singer, dancer, and musician. We do not know the circumstances nor the timeline of her prophetic vocation, and we also do not know her exact burial place.[18] If we maintain the fiction that she is the anonymous sister in Exod 2:1–10, it shows that she knew at a very young age how to be a political bridge—between her Israelite (persecuted) family and the pharaoh's family.

2.3. The Book of Numbers

2.3.1. Numbers 12

Of what does the faithful leadership of YHWH's servants consist? What characteristics must one have? Which figure represents the ideal prophet? Should this prophet have priestly investiture, be a divine mediator, be masculine? In any case, is it necessary that there is a principle figure, a single leader, or is it possible to share such a position with other figures? Finally, what happens to those who challenge hegemonic power and lose the fight? These are some of the questions behind this story, which we will, unfortunately, not be able to discuss in detail.

2.3.1.1. The Context of Numbers 11–12

Numbers 12 cannot be understood without looking beyond it. It forms a structural and sensible unit with the preceding chapter. In order to delve deeper into our text, then, we must first understand the full unit to which it belongs. At the same time, Num 11–12 form part of a much larger structure

---

18. Marianne Wallach-Faller ("Mirjam—Schwester unter Brüdern," in eadem, *Die Frau im Tallit: Judentum feministisch gelesen* [ed. Doris Brodbeck and Yvonne Domhardt; Zürich: Chronos, 2000], 177–91) notes this difference in the treatment of Miriam as compared with Moses and Aaron.

covering a large number of episodes on the "infidelity" of the people: dismay, murmurings against YHWH or his leaders, apostasy, disobedience, fear, and more, from Exod 32 until Num 21.[19] Within this larger panorama, Miriam's figure grows as it diminishes. It grows in importance as a reference for the people, as will be argued below; it diminishes as Num 12 becomes just another episode, not even the worst, in the long story of disagreements between God and his people.

In reality, when looking at Num 11–12 as a unit, the true dimension of Miriam's challenge is perceived as part of a general movement of discontent:

(1) there is a general complaint from one part of the group that ends in a devouring fire (11:1–3);

(2) the "multitude" wants meat, tires of the manna, and ends up dead with the meat in its mouth (11:4–23, 31–34);

(3) Moses complains to God about the weight of leadership, doubts God's ability to supply meat for all the people, and loses his supremacy when God raises seventy elders (11:11–15, 24–30); and

(4) Miriam and Aaron's questioning of Moses ends with the punishment of Miriam and Aaron giving up before Moses and YHWH (12:1–2, 10–16).[20]

David Jobling, who highlights interrelations in Num 11–12, interprets the theme of Moses' leadership (a theme that is especially interesting to us, given Miriam's questioning of said leadership) as a complaint to YHWH that ends, like others that are similar, in Moses' own punishment. In any case, what is important for our study is that Miriam is only one among various people and groups who question or complain to YHWH (and to Moses) for reasons as diverse as being fed up with the manna or the idea of leadership. Against this backdrop, however, her figure is special, as she is the only woman to be individualized and punished. The narrator's lens focuses from an unspecified part of the camp to locate Miriam by name. This is one of the most common resources of androcentrism, individualizing a woman only when she is exceptional, and especially when her exceptionality is deserving of divine punishment.

---

19. In a concentric structure, the central theme is the most important. According to Philip J. Budd (*Numbers* [WBC 4; Waco, Tex.: Word, 1994], 162), the theme advances from apostasy to discontent and from discontent to open rebellion, with its center in the insubordination of the entire group.

20. David Jobling, "A Structural Analysis of Numbers 11–12," in idem, *The Sense of Biblical Narrative: Structural Analyses in the Hebrew Bible 1* (2nd ed.; JSOTSup 7; Sheffield: JSOT Press, 1986), 31–65.

Another very common resource in the maintenance of patriarchal structures is detected by Claudia Camp in one of her studies about the figure of the "estranged woman" in different texts of the Hebrew Bible.[21] It deals with the placement of the woman in a position on the fringe (according to Camp, the "double paradoxical role" of Miriam in Numbers). Being on the fringe is, by its very nature, ambiguous and thus fragile (although one can enjoy more mobility for the simple fact of being ambiguous). Miriam is, by lineage and right, an important part of the people, but at the same time, her Levite-priestly lineage is made invalid by being a woman. Her right as a prophetess ends with a forced week of isolation because of the ritual impurity incurred by leprosy. Belonging or being segregated is at the same time a physical theme (Who is in the center and who on the periphery?), an ethnic theme (Who belongs to Israel?) and a ritual theme (Who should be isolated from the camp for impurity?). Belonging to or being excluded from the people is always an important issue in a community, and it was especially important in the postexilic period, when certain groups tried to impose a refoundation for the people and their myths on the basis of the exclusion of impure, different "Miriams."[22]

2.3.1.2. A Detailed Study of Numbers 12

The Eruption of Conflict: 12:1–2. Syntactically, the narrative unit is limited to the *wayyiqtols* of 12:1 and 2:

And Miriam and Aaron spoke with [בְּ] Moses because of the Cushite woman,[23] for he had married a Cushite woman. And they said, "Has the

---

21. Claudia Camp, "Over Her Dead Body: The Estranged Woman and the Price of the Promised Land," *JNSL* 29 (2003): 1–13.

22. In Num 11–12, the exclusion is carried out through death (a fire that consumes part of the camp; eating quail) or isolation. Again, Miriam fares better than other rebel factions, but she is still the only woman who is singled out, distant, on the fringe.

23. There are many studies that prove that, if the term used is הַכֻּשִׁית ("the Cushite"), we are dealing with Zipporah, the daughter of the Midian priest, with whom Moses has been married (Exod 2). See the essay by Ursula Rapp in this volume. The reason for this possible association lies in Hab 3:7, where both terms are parallel. See also Irmtraud Fischer, "The Authority of Miriam: A Feminist Rereading of Numbers 12 Prompted by Jewish Interpretation," in *Exodus and Deuteronomy: A Feminist Companion to the Bible* (ed. Athalya Brenner; trans. Barbara and Martin Rumschiedt; FBC 2/5; Sheffield: Sheffield Academic Pres, 2000), 163–64; repr. of "Die Autorität Mirjams: Eine feministische Relektüre von Num 12—angeregt durch das jüdische Lehrhaus," in *Anspruch und Widerspruch: Festschrift Evi Krobath zum 70. Geburtstag* (ed. Maria Halmer, Barbara Heyse-Schaefer, and

YHWH indeed spoken only with [בְּ] Moses? Has he not spoken also with [בְּ] us?" And YHWH heard it.

In verse 3 there is a digression introduced by the conjunction and the proper name Moses.[24] These verses do not present classical textual difficulties. They do, however, resist unanimous interpretation for two reasons: (1) the multiple meanings of the preposition בְּ; and (2) the mixing of two different themes, both related to Moses: the foreign wife and unique or shared prophetic mediation.

When looking at (1), it is not clear that בְּ in its three appearances in 12:1–2 should be translated as "against," although the great majority of translations choose "Miriam spoke *against* Moses." In the following verses, this preposition also occurs various times. It is the ambivalence that creates suspense: "Oh! But did they speak with Moses because of the situation, or did they speak behind his back criticizing him? We will see the story continues...."

On the basis of a mini-chiastic structure, Ursula Rapp chooses the translation of בְּ as "about" for 12:1a and 8e and "to" for the verses that come between. I, however, in accord with Fischer, lean toward choosing only one translation for the combination דבר + ב in these verses: "to speak with." This indicates a direct conversation, without making any conclusion as to whether both speaking subjects are in agreement or not. In addition to the preposition בְּ is the fact that the text does not say that Miriam speaks *about* the woman but rather *because of* the woman (עַל־אֹדוֹת). If the object of her discourse has been the Ethiopian woman, the text would have used simply the preposition עַל, "about," a much more common term.[25] To my knowledge, the importance or lack thereof of עַל־אֹדוֹת has not yet been discussed sufficiently. Is it only a literary resource, or is it part of the plot? In any case, one thing is clear: the Cushite is the only one of the important characters who is involved who does not have her own voice or even a quote through a third person.[26]

Barbara Rauchwartner; Klagenfurt: Hermagoras, 2000), 27–28; eadem, *Gotteskünderinnen*, 71–73.

24. Ursual Rapp, *Mirjam: Eine Feministisch-Rhethorische Lektüre der Mirjamtexte in der hebräischen Bibel* (BZAW 317; Berlin: de Gruyter, 2002), 47–54, divides the chapter into the following units, based on various characters' changing of scenes: vv. 1–3, 4–10a, 10b–14e, and 15 a–c.

25. Two examples can help us to see more clearly the difference between עַל and עַל־אֹדות. Both are part of the same story in the desert. In Exod 18:8, Moses tells Jethro what YHWH did against Egypt *because of* (עַל אֹדת) Israel. In Num 13:24, the noun is explained "*because of* the bunch" (עַל אֹדת הָאֶשְׁכּוֹל) of grapes brought by the spies.

26. Jacqueline Williams notes that is not her condition as a wife that is in play but rather her condition as a Cushite, her primary identity ("'And She Became <Snow White>': Numbers 12:1–6," *OTE* [Johannesburg] 15 [2002]: 259).

What Is the Conflict? The possibility of naming the conflict is determined by the relationship between the reasons for the gossip of 12:1–2. Historical-critical exegesis considers the motives to have an independent origin that later appeared in our text. In this way, one tends to be chosen as the principal (prophesy) and the other as secondary; another alternative is to consider the existence of both motifs a result of redactional insertion, by pointing to the disappearance of the Cushite woman from the rest of the story.

If we were to understand the origin of the text, however, we would still not be able to explain why such incoherence was maintained. The traditional interpretations of the conflict include considerations of: (1) familial jealousy, including indignation over Moses having taken a new wife; (2) a xenophobic and racist reaction because Moses' wife is a black African (not Egyptian);[27] (3) jealousy because of Moses' special place in the community; and (4) an inability to speak to him directly about the problems (gossip behind his back).

There is a large androcentric tradition for which counteraction a lot of ink and a large amount of imaginative force would be necessary. I do not share the stereotypical explanations that make Miriam out to be a bitter woman, jealous of her sister-in-law, intriguing and incapable of expressing her opinion publicly—she would not be a prophetess! Further, although the process of "whitening" or "Europeanization" in the Bible has been denounced by many scholars and I share their concerns, I do not believe that this is the only conflict in the text. With Kessler, I tend to prefer an explanation against the background of the postexilic conflict in the priestly and political leadership of Judah.[28]

When asking which groups are backing Moses, Aaron, and Miriam in these texts, especially in Num 12 and in Mic 6, an answer that receives the major consensus is that which associates Moses with the Torah, Aaron with the priesthood, and Miriam with prophecy. During the exile and especially in the Jewish restoration with Ezra and Nehemiah, prophecy (Miriam) began to fall into discredit in favor of the Torah (Moses). This would explain why Miriam is designated as the one who must question Moses, although she was not alone in their function of criticism.

---

27. Williams ("And She Became," 266) considers this to be the motive that Miriam and Aaron had for rising up against Moses (that YHWH does *not* share), a motive that finds support by the text's redactor (and, if I understand it correctly, in the community that accompanies Miriam until her return to the camp).

28. See Rainer Kessler, "Mirjam und die Prophetie der Perserzeit," in *Gott an den Rändern: Sozialgeschichtliche Perspektiven auf die Bibel: Für Willy Schottroff zum 65. Geburtstag* (ed. Ulrike Bail and Renate Jost; Gütersloh: Gütersloher Verlagshaus/Christian Kaiser, 1996), 64–72.

Fischer adds another component to this conflict. The conflict is explained as a carelessness of Moses in one of his conjugal tasks with Zipporah (= the Cushite woman). Miriam has spoken *with* (not *against*) Moses about the problem. This is an especially interesting reading because it anticipates rabbinical literature and because it makes Miriam and Zipporah out to be united sisters-in-law and not enemies.[29]

This analysis can be complemented with another hypothesis that I will tentatively propose shortly, without the intention of rejecting other possible readings. It is known that Numbers takes up various stories from the book of Exodus and re-presents them with certain changes. To look at just one example, Num 11 takes up the arrival of quails sent so that the people can eat meat (Exod 16), and Num 20 repeats the idea of the need for water (Exod 17).

An important part of the narrative of Num 11–12 has to do, precisely, with the uniqueness or otherwise of Moses' leadership. The theme of leadership, thus, has already been part of Num 11 and *continues* (does not begin) in Num 12:1, despite the fact that Num 12 is rarely read this way. If our interpretation is correct, in 12:1 Miriam speaks with Moses because of the Cushite woman. In reality, she speaks with Moses about what his father-in-law had already advised him, according to Exod 18: the delegation of part of his responsibility to a trusted group of elders. Numbers 11–12 then, would be a "corrected" version of Exod 18, with the following important changes:

(1) shared responsibility is not seen positively, as it was in Exodus;

(2) the seventy designated men are not judges but rather prophets;

(3) the lessening of Moses' leadership caused by the seventy prophetic leaders is supported by Miriam in Num 12:1 and repealed in the following verses by YHWH;

(4) not only had the seventy leaders prophesied, but Miriam and Aaron had as well, as noted by the rhetorical question in Num 12:2; and

(5) the father-in-law does not appear implicitly but rather in the background through the mention of Moses' wife as the cause or reason for the discussion or argument between Moses and Miriam.[30]

---

29. Fischer, "The Authority of Miriam," 163, quotes Exod. Rab. 1:13 and shares the hypothesis of the postexilic conflict between groups related to the Torah and to the prophecy (see further below).

30. Butting, *Prophetinnen gefragt*, 70–73, discusses the parallel between Exod 17 and Num 20. Fischer, "The Authority of Miriam," 166, considers the relationship between Exod 18 and our text in relation to the controversy of mixed marriages. Rapp, *Mirjam*, 130, notes that both stories are related through the themes of Moses' marriage and the issue of leadership.

It would not even be out of line to suppose that Moses' Midianite wife herself could have been the one to suggest this, although later tradition will recall her father, Moses' father-in-law, as the advisor. It would not be the first case of an appropriation of ideas....[31]

To summarize, there are various hypotheses about the motive or motives of the conflict. Starting from a synchronic reading, I prefer to try to find only one reason that has to do both with the foreign wife and with Moses' leadership in 12:1–2. There are a variety of possible explanations. I can affirm that the strongest components are: (1) the postexilic resistance by those who had gone into exile to mixing with non-Jews; and (2) divergent models of leadership within this postexilic community retroactively applied to "Moses" and resisted by "Miriam" and "Aaron."

An Ardent Defense of Moses: 12:3–9. The beginning and the end of this section are composed of words from the narrator speaking of the Moses' personality (12:3) and of divine wrath (12:9). In 12:4 the narration begins again through a *wayyiqtol*, and it continues through 12:9. In the middle of this section the narrator puts a chiastic poetic speech in YHWH's mouth (directed at Miriam and Aaron) that has an apparently independent origin (12:6b–8).[32] YHWH's revelation to prophets (and prophetesses) other than Moses (visions and dreams, 12:6) is different from the manner in which his revelations to Moses are carried out (direct, face to face, 12:8). The center of the chiasmus, "Not so, with my servant Moses...," subordinates any other prophet to Moses. Let us repeat: only Moses, the servant of YHWH, is reliable over the entire house of God.

The passage ends with the confirmation of divine anger and with YHWH retiring from his presence. Thus, three elements are combined: the introduction that individualizes Moses as the most humble human being, his trait as the only face-to-face interlocutor with YHWH, and the divine anger against Miriam and Aaron at the end of this narrative section. It is a very effective combination, for it puts Moses on a pedestal, despite his manifest humility.

---

31. This last proposal would explain why the narrator does not name Jethro directly, given the high esteem that Exodus has for him (Exod 4:18; 18:1). But it could be as well a different tradition, since according to Num 10:29 Moses' father-in-law is Reuel ("the friend/companion of God"), not Jethro.

32. The Hebrew text of 12:6b cannot be translated as it has been preserved (literally, "If there is your [pl.] prophet, YHWH"). Moreover, the same word (מראה) in 12:6c and 8b is vocalized in a different way, implying that the terms should be translated in different ways ("vision" and "apparition"). About these verses, see John S. Kselman, "A Note on Numbers XII 6–8," *VT* 26 (1976): 502–4.

We must affirm, however, that here we are dealing with something more than just a legend about Moses' humility. The legend evolves because there is a strong tension between groups that are pro-Moses and groups that are against him. Evidently, the pro- Moses groups won the fight, but their rivals could leave, at least, tracks of their nonconformity with the very marked hegemony of a single leader.

Rhetorical Strategies

(1) הָאָדָם and הָאֲדָמָה (haʾadam—haʾadamah, the human—the ground). We will now see in more detail how this support is achieved rhetorically. In the introduction, the narrator leaves the chain of *wayyiqtol*s to affirm in 12:3 that

> the man Moses was very humble, more than any man who was on the face of the ground. (מִכֹּל הָאָדָם אֲשֶׁר עַל־פְּנֵי הָאֲדָמָה)

Independent of the ideological weight of such an affirmation, its construction catches my attention. The phrase הָאִישׁ מֹשֶׁה "the man/Moses" is not common, though it is also not unique.[33] The combination הָאָדָם and הָאֲדָמָה, the (generic) human being and the earth, the ground, however, is extraordinary.

The pairing of אָדָם and אֲדָמָה is very familiar to us from seeing it so many times in Gen 2–3. It is however, a relatively infrequent semantic unit in the Hebrew Bible. Outside of these texts, the combination of both elements is important in texts where there is a divine threat of total destruction, such as the story of the flood or one of the prophetic texts (e.g., Gen 6:1, 7; 9:21; Jer 7:20; Zeph 1:3; Hag 1:11). In all the places I have been able to find parallels, the only one that uses the exact same expression כֹּל הָאָדָם אֲשֶׁר עַל־פְּנֵי הָאֲדָמָה is Ezek 38:20.

Ezekiel 38:18–23 has been identified as a secondary oracle to 38:10–16, with clear references to Jer 4:23–26, another "cosmic cataclysm" that also includes the double אָדָם and אֲדָמָה[34] Ezekiel 38 and 39 announce YHWH's manifestations with the cosmic characteristics that will eventually cause all nations to recognize his divinity (38:23):

---

33. This expression appears in Exod 11:3 (referring to Moses!); Judg 17:5 (Micah); 1 Sam 1:21 (Elkanah); 1 Kgs 11:28 (Jeroboam); and Esth 9:4 (Mordecai).

34. Leslie C. Allen, *Ezekiel 20–48* (WBC 29; Waco, Tex.: Word, 1990), notes the semantic similarity regarding Ezek 38:18–23 and Jer 4:23–26. In this last text, however, the two terms appear in different verses.

Thus will I magnify myself and sanctify myself, and I will be known in the eyes of many nations, and they shall know that I am YHWH.[35]

I argue that the inclusion of the same phrase in only these two texts is not accidental but an important intertextual reference that, until now, had not been identified.

Let us not forget that the great narrative from Exodus to Deuteronomy has to do with a cosmic war in which YHWH fights for Israel against human and divine enemies: the pharaoh, Amalek, Gog, and others. In this war, the testimony of the people and their leaders is also in play, through their actions and words in favor or against their God: faith, obedience, vision—or complaints, infidelity, challenges. In order that, in Ezekiel's words, YHWH can show himself "magnified and sanctified ... and they will know that he is YHWH," one must recognize his chosen one, the one with whom God speaks face to face, the servant Moses, the most humble of all the humans on the ground, one who is well-established and in charge of the entire divine economy.[36] Moses' choice is not random. His recognition by the people, other leaders such as Aaron and Miriam included, is a condition of the recognition of YHWH as God and also as the Lord who can decide how he will manifest himself. He is the one who chose Moses as the one in whom he will confide. This is the next element that we will study.

(2) The Divine House. The fact that two of Moses' characteristics are put in YHWH's mouth also draws the reader's attention: his fidelity and responsibility over the entire house of God. What can these expressions mean? The participle *niphal* (passive) for the root אמן can mean "faithful, reliable" but also "to have been established" (e.g., Samuel as prophet, 1 Sam 3:20) or "to stand firm" (e.g., the promise of a "strong house" for Solomon, 1 Kgs 11:28). Are we then dealing with the fidelity of Moses or with God's decision to establish him? In other words, are we dealing with a quality that Moses possesses or with a decision made by the Lord over his servant? These are not necessarily the same thing.

The other expression, "in all my house" is troublesome: Is it innocent or charged with meaning? On the one hand, בַּיִת is so common that looking for

---

35. There are some texts in Ezekiel (7:2; 33:24, etc.) and Ps 146:3–4 that combine בֶּן־אָדָם, "human," with some reference to the earth, but these are not meaningful to our discussion.

36. This is not the place for a deep theological analysis, but it is at least important to call attention to the probable reasons for the connection of these texts. Both Ezekiel and Num 11–12 have a preoccupation with the sacred, the divine, the pure, and the danger of impurity.

it through a concordance is disorienting: it refers to lineage, a housing space, the temple of Jerusalem. On the other hand, בְּכָל־בֵּיתִי does not appear on any other occasion. בְּבֵיתִי, however, does appear nine times, of which two are of great interest for our discussion. In Isa 56:5 we see the divine promise of a name for the eunuchs who remain faithful to YHWH. This memorial will take place "in my house," presumably in the temple reconstructed after the exile. Better still, בְּבֵיתִי, coming directly from YHWH, appears in the Chronicles version of the promise made by Nathan to David: "I will settle him in my house and in my kingdom" (1 Chr 17:14). Again, I do not think this reference is by chance; with it, Moses receives extremely important support.

I would like to delve into the reasons for supposing an intertextual allusion and not mere coincidence. When a servant is put "over all the house," he has a considerable amount of power. Here we are not dealing with the dwelling space or the modern nuclear family but rather with YHWH's "family," of the royal house or its religious support, the temple. In this context, it is worth mentioning that Joseph himself, the son of Jacob, one of the twelve, evaluates the events that brought him to reunite with his brothers and with Jacob in Egypt, in the following words:

> God sent me before you to preserve for you a remnant on earth, and to keep alive for you many survivors. So it was not you who sent me here, but God; he has made me a father to Pharaoh, and lord of all his house and ruler over all the land of Egypt. (Gen 45:7–8 NRSV)

Joseph's assertion is corroborated by his own experience in Potiphar's house, of whom it says that

> From the time that he had made him overseer in his house [בְּבֵתוֹ], and over all that he had, that YHWH blessed the Egyptian's house for Joseph's sake [בִּגְלַל]; and the blessing of YHWH was upon all that he had in house [בְּכָל־ אֲשֶׁר־לוֹ בַּבַּיִת] and in the field. (Gen 39:5 NRSV[37])

Joseph was unjustly pursued in Potiphar's house, and Moses was questioned in the desert. Both were well-established in YHWH's house and are examples of fidelity to him. Both were closely connected to Egyptian power; they both married a foreigner (although in Joseph's case this was later on), and they were both protected by the deity when a woman opposed them. If at first glance the reasons behind the feminine opposition to the chosen character seem to

---

37. In all NRSV translations I have maintained YHWH as the divine name.

be very different in each case, they really are not: they always have to do with power![38]

All of these shared characteristics lead me to think that the narrator has the intention of connecting both stories, making Moses a new servant who is unjustly pursued and who does not seek revenge or answer back, loyal to YHWH in spite of everything and because of this praised by YHWH and restored to a place of honor.[39] Whatever the case, this theme deserves a deeper investigation than that allowed by the space we have here.

(3) Divine Wrath. Soon after his discourse, the writer introduces God's wrath and his direct question to Miriam and Aaron in 12:8. In the narrative, this news was already expected when the three were called together and the two guilty parties singled out, since the discourse seemed to verify God's anger. As we have already seen, this anger is part of the structure of all the stories of gossip, and it precedes the punishment (*supra*, Num 11–12). In the first episode of Num 11, its nearest parallel, three actions are united by *wayyqitols*:

and YHWH heard it, and his anger was kindled, and the fire of YHWH burned among them. (11:1)

Thus the connection between their gossip, God's wrath, and the punishment is made explicit. In episode three, on the other hand, the divine interpellation interrupts this causative chain. In the long interval between hearing the gossip and recognizing the anger, we see the inclusion of many other things: Moses' modesty (12:3), YHWH calling the three together in the tent and coming down in the cloud to meet them (12:4–5), and YHWH making clear that a hierarchy exists between them and that to question it is to provoke his wrath (12:6–8) and then his exit (12:9).

---

38. In Mercedes García Bachmann, "La excepción que confirma la regla: La mujer de Potifar y el acoso sexual (Génesis 39)," in *Ecce mulier: Homenaje a Irene Foulkes* (San José de Costa Rica: Universidad Bíblica Latinoamericana, 2005), 61–76, I have shown how the sexual harassment of Joseph by Potiphar's wife is related (as in so many everyday stories) to an imbalance of power. The wife does not resign herself to allowing all of Potiphar's house (her included?) to be in the hands of a foreign slave and not her own. Not knowing the reasons for Miriam's questioning, our texts do not allow us to determine to what measure Moses' power as leader crosses the sexual axis.

39. From what I know, only Jacob Milgrom associates both stories "the administration of the house of Israel is conferred to Moses just as were conferred to Eliezer (Gen 24:2) and to Joseph (Gen 39:4–5) the houses of Abraham and the Pharaoh respectively" (*Numbers: The Traditional Hebrew Text with the New JPS Translation* [JPS Torah Commentary; Philadelphia: Jewish Publication Society, 1990], 96). Note that Milgrom does not associate the story with Potiphar's house but rather directly with the pharaoh's palace.

Now, YHWH's wrath stands out in these verses as a rhetorical strategy, but it is not because of this that the reader's attention should be drawn from the wrath, or at least the discontent, as an important part of the plot of Num 11–12: YHWH's anger with the people, with Aaron and Miriam, and perhaps even with Moses; Moses' anger at the people and at YHWH for the weight of his responsibility; and the discontent of the people, of Joshua, Aaron, and Miriam for different reasons. It is, without a doubt, a recurring theme in these episodes.

Who Pays for Aaron and Miriam's Challenge to YHWH? (12:10–15)

Look! Miriam is a leper! I said in the introduction that I wanted to explore the ideological question of how reality is perceived and explained, especially in terms of a distribution of power, honor, consumer goods, and access to divine approval (support from the deity). In the previous section I studied the various rhetorical resources that were put at Moses' disposal above the other prophetic figures. Among these I noted the chiasmus of 12:6–8, where the center is the comparison of Moses with the others ("Not so with my servant Moses"); the cosmic war through the pair human-ground; the designation of Moses as controller of the divine economy; and the divine wrath added as if these other elements were not enough to show God's support for Moses. The balance of power, looked at in terms of honor and divine approval, leans strongly in favor of Moses. In the last verses we find the development of the question, Who pays for this?

It must be noted, however, that the events that continue the story after YHWH's exit and the cloud are only indirectly described as punishment after Aaron confesses "we have done foolishly, and we have sinned"; he asks for forgiveness and begs that Miriam not be consumed (12:11–12).

The passage is symbolically very rich for a number of reasons. On the one hand, it refers to the priest's task to confirm the purity or impurity of a person affected by leprosy.[40] In addition to his completion of this priestly task—a task that is taken very seriously—however, Aaron is separated by the writer from Miriam: those who up to this point had been a unit are from now on separated.[41]

---

40. It is well known that what tends to be translated in our Bibles as "leper" is not Hansen's disease. I will, however, use the term for convenience's sake, as there is a lack of other options ("affected by a flaky skin condition" is not practical). In any case, one should keep in mind that when the Bible deals with this it is not treated as a disease but rather as a condition of impurity, a social and ritual condition rather than a medical one. See in this volume the essay by Dorothea Erbele-Küster.

41. Aaron assumes co-responsibility in the sin but transfers it to Miriam, who has

This is the first thing that Aaron does:

Aaron looked upon Miriam, and, behold, she was leprous.

She is affected by a skin condition that makes her look "like one stillborn, whose flesh is half-consumed when it comes out of its mother's womb" (12:12). This is how she is described by Aaron when he intercedes on her behalf to Moses. The verb is a passivum divinum, with YHWH as the implicit agent.[42] This passage is not easy to interpret, although it does not contain textual difficulties. For one thing, it is hard to understand at what stage of suffering we find Miriam. A comparison with the laws of Lev 13–15 is of little help, since what is found there does not lend itself to our narration. According to Lev 13:4–6, there should be an isolation of one week to be sure that another breakout does not occur; according to 14:8, once the quarantine and corresponding rituals are over, the person can be reintegrated into the camp. Apparently, this is Miriam's situation. However, in her case neither sacrifices nor baths are mentioned (even less, of course, the process of shaving). It is noteworthy, however, that her leprosy occurs in the environment of the tent of meeting, a sacred place that is supposed to be protected by law from the impure.

If in this case the leprosy has already run its course and Miriam can again be considered pure once the quarantine ensures that there is no recurrence, what does Aaron's request for a cure to Moses, and of Moses to YHWH, mean? Outside of legal texts, the narratives in which lepers appear (of which none are women) are few in the Hebrew Bible.[43] Uzziah, king of Judah (2 Kgs 15:1–7; 2 Chr 26:20–21), therefore has to live in isolation, relinquishing the reign. Leprosy is understood as a life-long divine punishment.[44] There is another narrative about the Aramaic general Naaman, a foreigner. Elisha cures him

---

been punished. At the same time, the narrator continues to put distance between Aaron and Miriam and moves the man Aaron closer to Moses, as Rapp notes in *Mirjam*, 98–105; see also Butting, *Prophetinnen gefragt*, 63–64.

42. Stephen K. Sherwood, *Leviticus, Numbers, Deuteronomy* (Berit Olam; Collegeville, Minn.: Liturgical Press, 2002), 156.

43. There are four male lepers in a war story where, as a result of having to be outside the camp, the men end up discovering that the enemy camp is deserted (2 Kgs 7:1–20). In this case nothing is said about the cause of their leprosy nor if they were ever cured.

44. According to 2 Chr 26:16–23, Uzziah became conceited and took over the priestly right to burn incense in the temple. When the priests discovered him, still with the censer in his hand, he had leprosy on his forehead. In 2 Kgs 15:5, the narrator says of the same king (there referred to by another name) that "YHWH smote the king, so that he was a leper until the day of his death," for having allowed cultic places outside of Jerusalem ("the high places").

so that he knew that "there was a prophet in Israel." His leprosy passes on to Gehazi, Elisha's servant, and to his descendants forever, as a punishment for having challenged his master's decision not to charge for the miracle (2 Kgs 5).

Little can be taken from these stories to help us understand Miriam's leprosy better. Generally the leprosy is either permanent, or the cure is produced by immersions in the Jordan River. What we also see is that these stories all take place during the divided monarchy and are narrated in either Deuteronomy or Chronicles (there are no leprosy cures in the Prophets). In all of these there is a more or less evident relationship between human power and YHWH's glory, which is in some way questioned by the person affected by the leprosy.[45]

The feminine participle (מְצֹרַעַת), which also appears in another episode, can give us more clues in our interpretation. It appears in Exod 4:6, where God puts leprosy on Moses' hand and then immediately cures it. YHWH is trying to convince Moses of YHWH's divine power so that Moses, in turn, will convince the exploited, discouraged Israelites that YHWH can bring them out of slavery (Exod 4:7–8). The text does not tell us anything about the process of leprosy or the *status* of the purity or impurity of the afflicted. The leprosy occurs, however, as in Num 12, just when the affected person is in the presence of YHWH and when Moses' credibility as YHWH's ambassador is in question. In other words, in all of these stories the suffering (and the cure or not) of the leper is linked to acts that are perceived as hurtful (alternatively as favorable, when there is a cure) to the manifestation of divine glory.

The comparison of Miriam in 12:12 to a stillborn whose flesh is half-consumed is a powerful image. Does it refer literally to the way Miriam's skin looked before being cured? Does it refer to the flakes common to the skin of a newborn, which could look like the flakes of a leper's skin? Or should it not be interpreted literally? Commentaries tend to skip this aspect of the story. I, however, believe that there is a lot to be found here. This will become clearer after analyzing YHWH's response to Moses' request.

What is the "crime" for which she is punished? The notion of leprosy as a punishment is derived from various factors. On the structural level it comes from comparison, as we have already seen, with the other stories of gossip in Exodus–Numbers and especially in Num 11–12. It is also derived from a selection of certain textual clues (choosing some and ignoring others). On the one hand, we have the immediate confirmation of her leprosy after the divine wrath and YHWH's exit. We must note, however, that, in contrast to the first

---

45. Naaman is the exception; through his cure YHWH's cult will be brought to Damascus.

episode (Num 11:1–3), in this case there are no *wayyiqtols* that unite the three verbs with the subject God: to hear, to get mad, to punish. On the contrary, the chain is interrupted after mentioning the anger and the divine exit in 12:9:

> and the cloud went away from over the tent, and, behold, Miriam became leprous, white as snow. (12:10)

On the other hand, Aaron's confession, repentance, and request for intercession ("we have sinned!") from which YHWH agrees "to cure" Miriam encourage us to interpret, as do a majority of commentaries, that this is a punishment. Among the details that are ignored when one emphasizes the possible guilt of Miriam is the fact that God's wrath is against *them*, not against *her* (12:9). "They" are Miriam and Aaron, whom YHWH just put in their place as prophets of a lower rank than Moses.

In 12:14 Miriam is compared to a daughter whose father spits in her face. An analysis of ירק II, "to spit," does not offer enough elements to determine that leprosy was, indeed, punishment for a crime or sin. The verb appears outside of Num 12 in two laws. The law in Lev 15:8 establishes that whoever is spat upon by a man, who is then impure due to seminal fluid, will continue to be impure until nightfall. Nothing is said about whether this also applies to a woman. If it did, we could imagine many consequences for YHWH's image as father and as one who spits, but this is not the case. Anyway, nothing is said about the possible causes of Miriam's leprosy.

The other law, Deut 25:9, does indeed deal with part of our theme, indicating that the man who refuses the levirate will be spit upon by a widow as a signal of dishonor or scorn. This crime is not applicable to Miriam (additionally, little is said about YHWH). Again, nothing is said about the possible reason for Miriam's leprosy as a divine punishment.[46]

Note also that YHWH answers the request to cure Miriam (רפא, 12:13) with affirmations of a different kind, social, not medical:

> The outbreak is not an outbreak in the physical sense, but rather a social stigma. It can only be taken as true from the "correct" perspective. From this we also know that Miriam's mark is only externally visible. Her bodily self-perception is kept from us.[47]

---

46. The noun appears in Job 30:10 and in Isa 50:6. In both cases they are the complaints in the first person of an innocent suffering indirectly at YHWH's hands.

47. Rapp, *Mirjam*, 114, my translation.

In sum, the reading of Miriam's leprosy as a punishment is partially supported, on the one hand, by instances of the passive verb "to be affected by
leprosy" but not by the verb "to spit" in God's answer. The greatest relationship
to punishment is seen in the narrative, in its structure, and in all of the events
that continue (Aaron's confession of both their sins, the intercession of Aaron
and Moses to help cure Miriam, and YHWH's answer giving a week of isolation from the camp and her subsequent reincorporation with the people) to
be read as a unit in the linear sense.

The humiliation. In 12:14 we see that the cloud has left the tent and
YHWH speaks with Moses about Miriam (lamentably, God no longer speaks
directly with Miriam). It is not clear if Miriam and Aaron are listening to this
conversation or not, but this is not important here. Thus YHWH corroborates
what he just expressed, that he speaks face to face only with Moses. His answer
emphasizes a situation of humiliation through a fairly complicated explanation. The reason he gives is that, having been embarrassed because her father
spat on her, she should spend seven days separated until this shame passes. In
this way, she now must spend seven days outside the camp, after which time
she will be able to return.

The problem with this similarity is that we have no biblical testimonies
to help us understand it, since there is no instance in which ירק "to spit" has
a father, even less God, as its subject. Because of this, we have nothing to
use as a comparison. The status of impurity to the one who receives the spit
remains, in the only law that says anything to this respect, until nightfall of the
same day (see above). The best explanation, then, seems to be that Miriam was
immediately cured and that those days, coinciding with the week prescribed
in Lev 15, would be the "quarantine" period imposed by the priest until confirming a definitive cure for the leprous person. I would like to again point
out, however, that leprosy and humiliation are tools in the hands of different
patriarchal characters (including YHWH) used to put Miriam in her place
and exclude her socially until she silently reintegrates herself.

Miriam is readmitted. The narration ends by affirming that the people
did not move until Miriam joined them again after seven days. Like many
commentaries, I take this waiting period to be a sign of the people's love for
Miriam, whom they refuse to leave outside. The text does not indicate that
there was any obligation on their part to do this: neither YHWH nor Moses
gives any command, and there are no negative comments either. Considering that the narrative goal of the people is to arrive at the promised land, this
week's time in which they wait for her is very meaningful. It becomes even
more important when the news of her death is given, in Num 20, and the
rebellion begins. The readmission of Miriam to the group in Num 12:15 is an
important sign of restoration and respect for their leader. At the same time, it

is also another indication of Miriam's ambiguity and status. As Camp notes, the fact that the people do not continue while Miriam is excluded can be read in two ways: as an obligation of the people, since YHWH is also waiting for Miriam (which is expressed in his "occasional presence *outside* the tent"), or the opposite, the very fact that the people are waiting forces YHWH to wait before continuing the march. It could perhaps be affirmed, taking Trible's very incisive perspective, that her reinsertion in the people is also the occasion on which Miriam is cured upon returning to the company of other women.[48]

In the end, who pays for the challenge? At the end of these episodes of gossip, wrath, angry dialogues, and silences among YHWH, his leaders, and the people, a political hierarchy is clearly established. Despite his humility and his protests against leading a people whom he did not conceive, bear, or nurse (see 11:12), Moses gains even more power. Clearly this hierarchy is also religious and gender-specific. Its religiosity is marked, in the first place, by God's own words, but also by those chosen by the narrator to introduce his characters: Moses has nothing for which to repent (except, perhaps, for having asked for less responsibility), while Miriam and the group of people called "the mob" have to repent for everything, but they are not granted this opportunity. Aaron loses power in that he must give up the access he has to God to Moses ("Oh my lord, I beg you…," 12:11), but he is not punished and is a model of total repentance in spite of not having seduced anyone; the people, as a good group, are tepid.…

It is not just coincidental that this hierarchy is also permeated by gender, since it is instrumental to the patriarchal structure. The only individualized woman in the story, who could not be hidden behind a collective "people" or "mob," should be in the last place, after male leaders. She should be an example to other women who do not know their place, correctly punished and unrepentant. Miriam's unrepentant condition is due to the fact that, in addition to leprosy, she is mute (before her leprosy her questioning is at least cited in 12:2), and Aaron takes over the role as confessor of both their sins (12:11–12). In this way Aaron's strong repentance and Moses' also strong intercession for Miriam's return are achieved at the expense of Miriam's voice. We see both her own discursive silence and a narrative silence as well, since there is no omniscient relation of Miriam's reactions.

In search of a satisfactory interpretation. Why is there such anger against Miriam? What is there behind a narration that marks for life, humiliates, and

---

48. Camp, "Over Her Dead Body," 6–7; Trible, "Bringing Miriam," 174 notes that her confrontation with Moses in Num 12 is the occasion on which she has lost the company and female support.

silences one of the few female figures who is strong in her own right (not as wife or mother)? What interests were at play behind the struggle to exalt or punish figures who were dead and buried centuries before, and why are shocking images used in Num 12 to this end? The answers to these questions vary, and they are sometimes contradictory, but because of this they are very interesting, as they reflect the polyvalence of the text.

Philip Budd assigns these two chapters to the Yahwist and proposes that Moses' validation serves as a validation of David: "There [in Num 11] old men and prophets receive important and authentic places, but at the end the king is YHWH's man in a special sense and should not be spoken against."[49] It is hard to know if there was a Miriam in the Davidic period. In any case, the question remains: Was there no other prophetic, male leader of whom an example could have been made with punishment? Do we not have a group of characters here who make possible the reinforcement of androcentrism through the exemplification of punishment over the female body?

Also interpreting the story in relation to David, Adrien Bledstien reads it as a critical parable of the rape of Tamar, David's daughter. While in that story neither her father nor her brothers defended her (one of them, Amnon, is even the rapist), thanks to fraternal solidarity Miriam is defended by her brothers and restored after a period of exclusion for her humiliation.

Other interpretations prefer to see these episodes in light of the postexilic conflict over religious, social, cultural, and racial control. In the fight to gain the most hegemony possible in the new spaces given under Persia, many diverse interests were brought together related to racial purity, religious purification, the formation of the "canon," identity, and so on. It is not odd that in a moment of such conflict and instability discordant voices were found more and more outside the new configuration. As many biblical scholars note, this situation was a breeding ground for changing the foreign, the strange (that which does not correspond to the hegemony), the fringe, and the marginal—and among the different groups who were pushed to the edges, there were many women, many Miriams. Indeed,

> If the conflict is to be located in the days of the Persian rule, then Aaron clearly represents the priesthood and Miriam one of those prophetic groups that continue the work on the prophetic books.... The dominant group continuing that tradition of Moses would then be found in the group around Ezra, who, like Moses, traces his lineage back to priestly forefathers, and

---

49. Budd, *Numbers*, 138; he concludes that the story is perhaps functioning to legitimize the court's hiring of royal advisors. Also note the story in which Solomon instituted a new hierarch, Ahishar, עַל־הַבָּיִת, "over the house" (1 Kgs 4:6).

the one around Nehemiah, who, according to the narratives, works together with Ezra and the Levites (Neh 8:9–12) and, in full accord with the Deuteronomic tradition of Moses, binds the people to the Torah.[50]

This line of investigation allows for an explanation of the anger that the text pours upon Miriam. This is anger that, from the Moseses in Persian times, is used to quiet the Miriams with nothing more than the divine word. Miriams are not the only ones silenced, as postexilic Aarons (in this text, not in other traditions) suffer the same fate. The anger serves, from the point of view of these Aarons and Miriams, to be able to implant their resistance in a hegemonic model of leadership that does not leave room for complaints or the inclusion of "different people."[51] Thus, Miriam and the prophecy stay within the people but outside the camp—at least for the moment. Perhaps this is the price to be paid for fighting from within, when women choose to stay inside of patriarchal religious structures. Miriam, on the side of the people, argues that we are not all Moses: "His privileged position before God and his notable humanity [both belonging to Moses, in reference to his humility, v. 3] are not rules that just anyone may follow."[52] Miriam won the battle, but Jacob, upon fighting with the divine messenger, ends up with war wounds upon his body. No one can continue walking after such a war: a week of distancing from Moses and Aaron does not seem so bad in such circumstances!

We still must discuss at least two questions. The first is, Why are the two comparisons that the narrator chooses for Miriam that of a fetus that is dead when it leaves its mother's womb (Aaron's words) and that of a father who spits upon his daughter to humiliate her (YHWH's words)? The second question we must discuss is the possible relationship (or not) between these two images at the end of Num 12 and other images of a feminine YHWH, such as Moses' unburdening to YHWH in 11:12 (where Moses refuses to be the mother of the people whom he leads). Finally, we see the metaphor of the sea-crossing, where Miriam has the role of protagonist, as an image of birth.

Answers to these questions enter into the realm of interpretation. Of course, no interpretation will be universally satisfactory so I do not want to try to offer one to be taken as "the" answer. Looking at the appearance of

---

50. Fischer, "The Authority of Miriam," 165–66.

51. I recently used this text in a seminar on Roman Catholic theology with ecclesiastical communities as the base. One of the groups concluded: "If a Miriam confronts power, the power punishes her, and there is no way to escape unharmed, without leprosy, from a questioning of the prevailing religious system."

52. Translated directly from Fischer, "Die Autorität Mirjams," 33; the English translation in "The Authority of Miriam," 167 reads differently.

Miriam's skin and understanding the development of leprosy, with its effects
of discrimination and fear of the contagious person, perhaps what Aaron was
doing, when asking that Miriam be not like a dead fetus, was trying to establish the worst scenario possible in order to receive a lesser punishment from
God: "Okay, she will not be like a dead fetus, but she will pay as if ... as if ...
as if her father had spit upon her."[53] Metaphors are powerful tools, both to
explain the inexplicable and to invoke sensations and change ideas.

2.3.2. Numbers 20(:1–13)

In this chapter, the only explicit mention of Miriam is in 20:1, where her death
and burial are recorded:

> Then the sons of Israel, the whole congregation, came to the wilderness of
> Zin in the first month, and the people stayed at the sanctuary [בְּקָדֵשׁ, in
> Kadesh]. Now Miriam died there and was buried there.[54]

Kadesh is the first data accepted by historical biblical criticism when starting
a reconstruction of the "life" of Miriam. The news of her death in Kadesh is
what allows for connection, with a certain amount of historical probability,
to the tradition of a tomb belonging to a prophetess Miriam in the desert
of "Kadesh." Ironically, Kadesh in Num 20 is more a theological (not geographical) place, as Rapp has shown. It is not a triviality that Miriam's grave
is mentioned, for this kind of information is only given in the Hebrew Bible
with regard to significant persons. It is yet another piece of information that
confirms her as an important figure behind a few surviving mentions in the
Hebrew Bible.

Rapp has convincingly demonstrated that (the possibility of) death is
a central theme that unites the entire chapter. For this we must pass 20:1,
although Miriam still remains unnamed. The chapter is split into three sections, of which the first and third emphasize death:

20:1–13: death of Miriam and lack of water; Moses' and Aaron's lack of
    faith
20:14–21: detour around Edom's area
20:22–29: Aaron's death[55]

---

53. I thank Z. Carolina Insfrán for this suggestion.
54. Following Milgrom, *Numbers*, 164, who shows that חֹדֶשׁ here has the literal meaning of the new moon. The chronology of the year is a problem that we will not try to resolve.
55. Rapp, *Mirjam*, 239, slightly modified.

Between these two sections, the central one does not have any apparent connection with the others. Death does, however, threaten here as well, and the lack of water is insinuated as a possible cause of discomfort among both groups of people. For the analysis of the political figure of Miriam, the most important is the first pericope, with which we will now engage.

2.3.2.1. Lack of Water

> The Israelites, the whole congregation, came to the wilderness of Zin in the first month, and the people stayed at the sanctuary [בְּקָדֵשׁ, in Kadesh]. Now Miriam died there and was buried there. And there was no water for the congregation, and they assembled themselves against Moses and Aaron.

The start of the second verse is a digression in the discourse, as indicated by the interruption of the chain of *wayyiqtol*s. But it is an important digression! This is because, although little is explicitly said, it makes a link with themes that were enunciated before or that will soon be made clear. The central theme of the previous chapter is the ritual impurity incurred by people who were in contact with a cadaver. In this situation the people and their leaders would be quite worried once they realized that there was no water.[56] In addition, it is not just any body that is causing pollution but rather that of a woman—and, of course, not just any woman but one of the chosen leaders. Among the few commentaries that note this relationship, I would like to highlight Camp's. She argues that the rebellion of the people because of the lack of water and the pollution (that at least the most faithful of Miriam's followers, those who buried her would have incurred) does not end with the death of those who protest but rather with the death of the (pure or contaminated?) leaders.

The rebellion because of the lack of water has a clear parallel with Exod 17. There the lack of water, which is solved by a miracle, is a real problem. Here we see that what is in play is really the holiness (the unique character, the glory) of YHWH, something that has been darkened by Moses' and Aaron's disobedience. Thus the episode begins and ends with the holy and sacred, from the place where Miriam is buried (20:1) to the confirmation that God manifested his holiness (20:13). This interpretation is possible due to the fact that Moses' and Aaron's disobedience—disobedience that prevents their entrance into the promised land, no less!—is neither explained nor much less developed. It serves as an excuse for the manifestation of divine holiness and

---

56. Camp, "Over Her Dead Body," 5–11.

for the killing on the path of the last survivors of the incredulous and impatient generation, just at the end of the march through the desert.[57]

The redistribution of power after Miriam's burial is also attention-grabbing. Now that no one mediates between the people and their leaders, they will have to confront and resolve their differences by appealing only to YHWH. There will be a change in the leadership of the people, a change that generates much discomfort, especially at the moment of justifying actions before YHWH.

> The Estranged Woman—one of us, pushed out, corrupted, gathered in—had mediated the terrible theodicy of monotheism by providing an icon of evil apart from both God and men. At her death only these are left to blame. Will Miriam's brothers enter the promised land? Over her dead body.[58]

What then, does Num 20 add to a "life of Miriam"? It offers various indicators of her importance for the following generations. First, the fact that her death and burial were recorded is not a minor fact when we are dealing with stories of women in the Bible. Second, the lack of any mention of that death as related to some type of punishment is a very meaningful absence. In fact, not even Deut 24:8–9 connects her death with divine punishment (see more below), neither with the leprosy of Num 12, nor with the disobedience of her friends in the same chapter, nor with any other reason. In the third place, there is a semantic relationship between Miriam's death and the lack of water in the desert.[59] This relationship has been explored in many different ways, both from the historical-critical and the rabbinical literature and from feminist scholarship, which we cannot review again at this time. Thinking of a "life of Miriam," it does not add much, but it does once again confirm that there is a lot that remains only in the insinuations of biblical scribes.

---

57. Butting, *Prophetinnen gefragt*, 77, relates the death of Miriam with the manifestation of divine holiness, noting that the pronoun suffix "in/against them" (וַיִּקָּדֵשׁ בָּם) can refer both to the people as well as to Moses and Aaron. Cf. Rapp, *Mirjam*, 246–50.

58. Camp, "Over Her Dead Body," 11–12. Unfortunately, Camp does not enter into dialogue with any of the German-speaking authors brought to this discussion. I cannot help but think that such a dialogue would have been very fruitful. For example, Rapp (*Mirjam*, 249–51) would have spoken to her about the power of death condensed in Moses and Aaron and the transference of power to the people and their organization.

59. For rabbinical readings, see Wallach-Faller, "Mirjam"; and Alice Bach, "With a Song in Her Heart: Listening to Scholars Listening for Miriam," in Brenner, *Feminist Companion to Exodus*, 243–54; eadem, "Dreaming of Miriam's Well" in *A Feminist Companion to Exodus to Deuteronomy* (ed. Athalya Brenner; FCB 2/5; Sheffield: Sheffield Academic Press, 2000), 151–58.

2.3.3. Two Genealogies: Numbers 26:59 and 1 Chronicles 5:29

These two texts can be studied together, since both belong to genealogies, and both are interested in Aaron and his descendants, the priests.

This interest is clearest in 1 Chr 5:29 (6:3 NRSV), the briefest and probably most recent text about Miriam. It is part of a longer genealogy that says the least about the women in this family:[60]

> The children of Amram: Aaron, Moses, and Miriam. The children also of Aaron: Nadab, Abihu, Eleazar, and Ithamar.

Its parallel in Num 26:59 is also concerned with Aaron's family, which is why it also includes Levite credentials on the mother's side:

> And the name of Amram's wife was Jochebed, the daughter of Levi, whom she bore to Levi in Egypt, and she [Jochebed] bore unto Amram Aaron and Moses and Miriam their sister.

As Rapp notes, in this genealogy we perceive the remembrance of a matrilineal genealogy that has not been able to be totally erased, from the anonymous wife of Levi to Miriam.

Dry as all genealogical verses are, these texts are also full of information. They are the only texts that make the three leaders brothers and sister.[61] Additionally, they confirm that this tradition is of "brotherhood" in the sense of a relationship among equals, where no one is father or mother to anyone else. In any case, the order of naming always places Miriam last.

The most interesting part of these genealogies is that, in the middle of the men of the priestly caste, they have perpetuated the memory of a woman without making her into a sexual object. Perhaps the reason for this is connected with the postexilic structure, in which Levite families took over the priestly cults. It is certain that there is no direct information stating that Levite

---

60. Roddy Braun (*1 Chronicles* [WBC 14; Waco, Tex.: Word, 1986], 83) states that this genealogy "is the most extensive in priestly lineage found in the Old Testament and is, indeed, also the latest." Sara Japhet (*I and II Chronicles* [OTL; Louisville: Westminster John Knox, 1993], 149–50) notes that the inclusion of Miriam among the descendants of Kohat "can be considered the last move in the absorption of the Amramites."

61. Exod 15:20 joins Miriam and Aaron; Exod 6:20, however, joins only two men, ignoring Miriam. Num 11, Num 20, and Mic 6:4 do not establish familial relations between the three; finally, Exod 2:4, 7 mentions "his sister" (Moses') but without a name. Rapp (*Mirjam*, 374–76) calls attention to the fact that her participation as a sister, more than as a daughter, is highlighted.

women had an important role in certain cultural tasks such as song, but this is no reason to reject such a hypothesis, given the general lack of information about many women and their jobs, especially in relation to religion.[62] Within the Chronicles tradition there are various mentions of female singers. For example, 1 Chr 6 and 9 present different themes related with Levite families (among them "the singers") without specifying if women participated or in which areas. Ezra 2:65 // Neh 7:67 specifically mention male and female singers, but without specifying their lineage. Probably, given the priestly interest in the purity of each clan, they would have made space for the important fact of Levite lineage if the singers that they mention had belonged to this group (1 Chr 6). If, as I suppose, there was even space in the postexilic restructuring for certain Levite women to have a job similar to Miriam's in Exod 15 (the prophetess, the one who takes the timbrel, plays, dances, and directs the song while crossing the sea), then these are the women who preserved and transmitted Miriam's tradition. In that process, they could also be instrumental in the preservation of other Miriamite traditions, such as that of the leader who challenges Moses' priority and whose death undoes the death of her "brothers" in the desert.

2.4. CRITICAL READING: MIRIAM AS A MODEL FOR THE PEOPLE

Earlier I said that we would study texts according to the information they gave about the "life" of Miriam. Nevertheless, it is also necessary to address texts that reworked this information in a different tradition (making her into a model, whether positive or negative). The texts that will be studied now correspond to the second of these two categories. They do not add any new information about Miriam (her life or ministry, true or literary), but they use the information of other texts toward their own ends. Due to the fact that biblical science is on a path with no exit in reference to the dating of the majority of texts, it is virtually impossible to speak of certain traditions that are "anterior" or "posterior" to others without entering into an unending debate. We will avoid this, concentrating instead on the question of the ideological position of those texts that do not add more information to Miriam's life.[63]

---

62. With no apparent relationship to the Levite clan in Qoh 2:8 and 1 Sam 19:36, the male and female singers are part of the culture or entertainment repertoire. Finally, 2 Chr 35:25 mentions a more specific group of women, those who are in charge of lamentations for the dead.

63. A lack of consensus in the scholarly world about biblical dating makes any affirmation in this area virtually reckless, and since there is a limit on the number of reckless affirmations that an academic may permit himself or herself in a work, I reserve mine for

2.4.1. Deuteronomy 24:8–9

The reading of these two verses is the result of different editorial hands. This is indicated by the lack of clear context, the alternation between singular and plural in the addressee, the invocation of a legislative body already in existence, and the resource of the Levite priests in the middle of the exhortation:

> that you diligently observe and do according to all that the Levitical priests teach you; as I have commanded them, so you shall be careful to do. (24:8)

Moreover, there is an invocation of what YHWH "did to Miriam" (24:9), without a clear reference to what exactly, when, or where what happened to Miriam happened. Note additionally that it speaks of "the plague of leprosy" (נֶגַע־הַצָּרַעַת), an expression that is not found in Num 12 but in the laws of Lev 14:3, 54. However, we are not dealing with a law but with an exhortation based upon an anterior fact evidently known to the readers (and even more so to the female ones) and to an also-known ritual legislative body that the author wants to reinforce. In order to do this, the narrator refers to various elements:

(1) he instills fear by repeating Miriam's disgrace and her conduct ("remember...");

(2) he ignores the fact that the story to which he is appealing, Num 12, never speaks of Miriam's disobedience (nor of Aaron's, who is not even mentioned) of a determined law but rather to a questioning of (a part of) the religious status quo; and

(3) the entire book of Deuteronomy is, looking at the narrative, the discourse of Moses' farewell; before dying, in order to be buried in an unidentified place, he is declared a prophet like no other; this Moses, legislator, unequal prophet, and Levite, with all his weight, is on one side of the scale, while Miriam, a leper, is on the other.

There is, however, a much more important indicator that these verses invoke Miriam as an excuse in order to foster obedience toward the Levites. This is the fact that they are inserted in the middle of laws that have nothing to do with the problems of Numbers. Deuteronomy 24 groups together a number of laws relating to the family and the economy. In the first two the economic aspect is not immediately evident, although it is present (the remarriage of a

---

themes of more interest to me. When I speak of "ideological positions," I am thinking, among others, of the "trajectories" of Walter Brueggmann (e.g., in *A Social Reading of the Old Testament: Prophetic Approaches to Israel's Communal Life* [ed. Patrick D. Miller; Philadelphia: Fortress, 1994], 13–42; and more profound in his *Old Testament Theology: Essays on Structure, Theme and Text* [ed. Patrick D. Miller; Minneapolis: Fortress, 1992]).

woman who is divorced and the organizing of the house of a man who was recently wed, 24:1–5). Later, other different laws discuss economic protection of the poorest families, such as those of not taking a man's clothes though these have been given as the guarantee of a loan, of not going over for the second time the grapes in the vineyard or the olives in the orchard, and of not perverting justice in a court. Our verses are inserted, with no apparent relation, in the middle of all these laws.

It is possible that there has been a type of economic relationship among the laws of leprosy and the laws grouped in this chapter. If this is so, the connection is still not evident. In any case, if there is such a connection, we also do not know why they limited themselves and did not bring in such legislation, given the fact that the story of Num 12 says nothing about possible sacrifices or offerings from the cured leper.

If there is no economic intention in the insertion of this exhortation here, what is its function? It seems, simply, that it exists to instill fear, inducing obedience by appealing to an example of punishment.[64] Miriam turns out to be not only a dangerous example who should be neutralized as much as possible but also a negative example who should not be imitated for fear of receiving the same punishment. The fact that it is necessary to reinforce a forbiddance or a law so strongly is a sign that it did not have, when incorporated into and maintained in the legislation, the force needed to impose itself based upon its own worth.

2.4.2. Micah 6:1–8

The study of the literary unity of the book of Micah is not important for our analysis. What should be considered is that a great majority of commentaries make a cut at the end of chapter 5 (in many cases separating 1–5 into two blocks).[65] Thus, if we want a greater perspective, our attention should be centered on the two final chapters of the book, where there is much alternation between words of wisdom and of hope.[66]

---

64. See Peter C. Craigie, *The Book of Deuteronomy* (NICOT; Grand Rapids: Eerdmans, 1976), 308: "The exhortation to obey the law of leprosy is illustrated and emphasised through the call to remember (v. 9) the case of Miriam's leprosy and the procedure of purification with which the people dealt with it (Num. 12:9–16)."

65. Jesús M. Asurmendi Ruiz, "Miqueas," in *Comenatrio Bíblico Latinoamericano, AT II* (ed. Armando J. Levoratti, Estella: Verbo Divino, 2007), 524–525 enumerates between the causes for this separation in two blocks the difference in vocabulary and the different perspectives of the northern and southern kingdoms.

66. The fact that the prophetic books are part of a long writing-down process is not

Mayer Gruber relates in a recent article that from the feminist complaint to the prevalence of androcentric readings, there is a return to Micah. In Mic 7 there is an "individual lament" similar to many psalms. This is not a literary unit, and it is difficult to determine its exact division. The majority divides it into 7:1–7 and 8–20.[67] In Mic 7:8–10 a woman speaks (despite the fact that this type of evidence is often erased and ignored, for example, in translations) and quotes a dialogue of confrontation with another woman.[68] This dialogue has been interpreted as the joke of one of the enemies of Israel for Samaria or another city or region (both substantives are feminine in Hebrew). There is no reason, however, to discard Gruber's proposal, which deals with two prophetesses, one of whom is a prisoner and is tricked, in the way that Jeremiah was jailed and criticized by his enemies (Jer 26).

Within this ample framework, we will concentrate on 6:1–8, YHWH's complaint against Israel for its lack of compromise and fidelity.[69] In addition to textual difficulties, two factors that make the comprehension of the passage difficult are the changes in addressee and in the level of discourse in the message. From the first two verses we can know that YHWH has sent "me" (an unidentified first-person speaker) to proclaim a judicial lawsuit against Israel, where mountains will be YHWH's judges. But to which point does this quote

---

a new discovery: it is what generated historical criticism since its beginnings in the 19th century. On the other hand, all of Micah can also be read as the "prophetic announcement of YHWH's plans for the exaltation of Zion," as Marvin A. Sweeney proposes, *The Twelve Prophets* (Collegeville: Liturgical Press, 2000), 345, for Mic 1:2–7:20.

67. Mayer I. Gruber ("Women's Voices in the Book of Micah," *lectio difficilior* [2007]; online: http://www.lectio.unibe.ch/07_1/pdf/mayer_gruber_womans_voices.pdf) separates 7:1–7 from 8–20 and considers both Mic 6 and 7 to be the small book of a prophetess from the north, to be distinguished from Micah, the man from the south, in Mic 1–5. Attention is also called to the poetic beauty of 7:5–6, part of said lament, in which the gender and number of the nouns, actors, and actresses of daily life are mutually balanced: friend, lover, wife, daughter-in-law, enemies, etc. Gruber infers that this poem is the work of the prophetess, who is mocked by an enemy "in the second person feminine singular in Mic 7:10" (7).

68. If it were not for the fact that in this dialogue the enemy speaks to her in the second-person singular feminine, which in Hebrew has a different suffix than the masculine, we would not know that the one who speaks in the first person is also a woman.

69. Many commentaries separate these verses into two pericopes, e.g., Bruce K. Waltke, *A Commentary on Micah* (Grand Rapids: Eerdmans, 2007), 344–45, 366–71. Ralph L. Smith (*Micah–Malachi* [WBC 32; Waco, Tex.: Word, 1984], 51) considers that, "if verses 6–8 are related with verses 1–5, they provide Israel's answer to the implicit accusation against them." See also Delbert Hillers, *Micah: A Commentary on the Prophet Micah* (Hermeneia; Philadelphia: Fortress, 1984), 77.

continue? The next clear change at the discourse level occurs in 6:3, where YHWH presents his lawsuit against Israel in direct discourse:

> My people, what have I done to you and how have I wearied you? Answer Me.

The evidence that YHWH presents accuses Israel of impatience, disobedience, forgetfulness, or "infidelity" against him who has done so much for Israel. I detect an ironic tone in this case, where Israel can begin to feel aggravated or uncomfortable because of the magnificent benefits YHWH has given in its favor, such as having brought them out from the slavery of Egypt to freedom, given them Moses, Aaron, and Miriam, or having protected them from all evil (6:4–5). Again in 6:6–7 there is another change to the first-person singular:

> With what shall I come before YHWH and bow myself before God on high? Shall I come before him with burnt offerings, with calves of a year old? Will YHWH be pleased with thousands of rams or with ten thousands of rivers of oil? Shall I give my firstborn for my transgression, the fruit of my body for the sin of my soul? (NRSV)

These verses can be a righteous audience's answer that in its haste to respond to the accusation thinks immediately of offering abundant sacrifices. It could also be, however, the continuation of YHWH's (or his spokesperson's) discourse, citing the response of a loyal person. Perhaps he is ironically mocking the one who, in his haste to please YHWH, quickly makes a generous offer to quiet the prophetic voice and his own conscience. Or, even more radically, it could be the "system's" response, the priest's response, who for each sin makes a proposal of sacrifices. Finally, in 6:8 we see a response to the rapid and erroneous proposal of sacrifices in 6:6–7:

> A man has told you what is good,[70] and what does YHWH require of you but to do justice, to love kindness, and to walk humbly with your God?

---

70. The subject of the *hiphil* נגד "to tell" can be interpreted in two ways. The first, which considers this to be speaking of YHWH, has prevailed for the following reasons: (1) the antecedent subject in the beginning of the previous verse and its mention in the second hemistich of this same verse could also be considered to be doing "double duty"; (2) YHWH is circumstantial in the last infinitives of this verse. The other interpretation (for which I opt) was advanced, according to Gruber ("Women's Voices," 11 n. 17), already by Arnold Ehrlich at the beginning of the twentieth century. This involves taking אָדָם not as a vocative but rather as the subject of the causative verb: "a human/man has told you." What Gruber develops from this reading is the contrast of this anonymous prophetess of

Here it is the prophetess who makes a wonderful summary of what YHWH really hopes for: justice, loyalty, and fidelity to God's plan. These are enormous theological and biblical themes that the books of Micah, Isaiah, and Amos contextualize in a marvelous way.[71]

In addition to the textual and traditional difficulties in Micah, what really concerns our theme is the way in which the text uses Miriam's tradition. It is evident that it does not add anything to a possible "life" of this character. It says much less than any of the texts we have already studied. It is, however, a hermeneutic jewel, since it allows for the corroboration of Miriam's place with the two other major leaders, without relationship and with the single hierarchical move of placing her last. It also confirms that the traditions linked to Miriam's name are those of the exodus itself ("I brought you up from Egypt") and of the march through the desert ("My people remember what Balak did"). Between these two, "I sent before you Moses, Aaron, and Miriam" is equally applicable to the crossing of the sea and to the march through the desert. Miriam is a fringe figure, a key figure at the time when Israel was neither enslaved in Egypt nor ruler of its own land, neither a no-people situated in a strange land where they were considered a possible enemy (Exod 1) nor a people trained in God's path. In this middle, fringe stage, God is the agent who causes the march of the people, and Moses, Aaron, and Miriam appear as important but passive figures. What is more, as Fischer notes, these three ancestors of prophecy do not appear alone but are rather mentioned together with prophetic figures of another type, like Balaam and Micah.[72] The fact that Moses, Aaron, and Miriam are shown here to be figures on the edge and passive does not detract, in any case, from the fact that their messages are put in YHWH's mouth as one of Israel's saving events.

6:8 between what some man has prescribed ("a man has told you") and what YHWH wants ("what does YHWH require of you but…?").

71. We still must explain why, dealing with a confrontation between two prophetesses—a confrontation that leads, on the other hand, to a clearing up of the divine will in a very dark context—the one who talks is not identified as a woman when she is addressed in 6:1: "Arise!" There are, however, numerous examples in the Hebrew Bible of suffixes or verbs that are supposedly incorrect in their person. This is without counting the numerous cases of corrective editing that could very well have been applied to a text about a prophetess to make it more like the rest of the prophecies of the (male) prophet Micah.

72. Fischer (*Gotteskünderinnen*, 89–90) shows how Balaam and Miriam turn out to be a better prophet and prophetess than Moses, in the sense that they give YHWH the glory he deserves.

3. Conclusions

Given the available space, this section will be brief. Work with the texts themselves should never be replaced by hermeneutics or homiletics but should rather serve as their basis. I will now present some of the conclusions that come from said study on the basis of the text.

1. A figure of weight. The first conclusion that can be drawn from the study of the texts that mention Miriam is that she was an influential woman, valuable, with her own importance, "an excellent woman" (Prov 31:10). This comes in part from the role that is assigned to her in the texts: prophetess, musician, leader, the equal of Moses and Aaron, recognized by the people and by God. It also comes from the fact that later traditions in Chronicles did not eliminate her but rather assimilated her into one of the most recognized families, that of Levi. Different from other women (such as Zipporah) who disappear from the story, Miriam maintains a prominent place. This would not have been possible if she had not had behind her a group with enough influence to demand her remembrance. The only mention of Miriam in the Prophets is, precisely, a very significant mention in this respect.

A theme upon which I have only lightly touched is that of the role of other characters and their responsibility in the patriarchal transfer of power and renown. I refer above all to Joshua. Because he is not referred to in any of the texts in which Miriam appears, I have only mentioned him in passing. His intervention in Num 11 and, even more important, what the elimination of the great leaders of the older generation (Num 20) means for him do not make him an innocuous character. His character, as Fischer notes, lends support to his postexilic followers, who are more limited in their cosmovision than Moses himself is. On the same line, Moses' desire that all the people be prophetic, the prophecies of Joel 3 and of Mic 6, and even Miriam's questioning in Num 12 all form part of a more inclusive theological stream of thought that, even if it lost weight with Ezra's reform, did not disappear.

2. A relatively coherent figure. We know that it is impossible to create an exhaustive biography of Miriam. In reality, the nature of the biblical text itself makes this an impossible claim in reference to any character (including YHWH or Jesus himself). Thus we must resign ourselves to an incomplete mosaic. If we stay within the information that the texts give us, however (not in what they do *not* give), the mosaic is surprisingly coherent. For example, there is no uniformity in the genealogies with respect to her "brothers" or her "father and mother," but no text explicitly refutes these relations (though they do ignore them) or offers alternatives (different, for example, from the wife/ wives and father-in-law[s] of Moses, where there are various different and discordant traditions).

The same may be said of her characterizations as singer, prophetess, musician, or leader. If it is true that different texts take one (or some) of these traits and not all of them, it is also true that she is never presented in such a way as to make them incompatible. Numbers 12, which could be read very negatively because of her leprosy, also recognizes her prophetic gift, although it is subordinate to Moses'. Even Deut 24:8–9 uses Miriam's tradition of leprosy to instill fear and induce obedience, but it does it in a general, unspecific way.

3. A prophetic figure. With this expression I refer not only to the first title that she receives in the first text in which the reader finds her but also to the fact that Miriam is a character comparable to Jeremiah and other great biblical prophets. This is true in the sense that the she is presented as having the function of interpreting the situation in which she lives in light of the word of God. Such interpretation acquired different contextual and literary expressions: song, dance, and music when crossing the sea (Exod 15); a challenge to Moses' hegemony in the desert; a calling of attention to the need for coherence between what is lived and what is proclaimed in the case of Moses' foreign wife (Num 12); and even a mediation between the people, their other leaders, and the deity, evidenced when she is no longer available (Num 20). All of this is also expressed with great majesty and with less turbulence in Mic 6.

Interpreting the word of God brings with it risks, both on the part of the people and on the part of God. In some cases, such as that related in Num 12, it means that the word of God may correct its own prophet: "Why, then, were you my servants (Miriam and Aaron) not afraid to speak against my servant Moses?" says YHWH with wrath ... and Miriam contracts leprosy. It is clear that it would have been better for our constant fight against patriarchal hegemony if this correction had affected not only her (a woman) but also Aaron (a man and priest).

4. A figure to rescue from oblivion. I made the decision not to enter into discussion about the age of the different texts, given the complexity of the theme (it would have taken over the space reserved for Miriam) and the total lack of consensus at this moment among Hebrew Bible scholars regarding the world of ancient Israel and the formation of the canon. Without entering into these themes, however, tensions can be recognized behind the texts that have been analyzed. These tensions reflect very hard fights between groups with hegemonic and contra-hegemonic pretensions. As many scholars maintain, the postexilic time period is the most probable in the explanation of these tensions, given its pretension of purity and the influence of the priestly families.

In any case, the most important thing to rescue in this case is the fact that, with or without struggles, those who recognize themselves as Miriam's debtors managed to leave her mark on the texts. She was marked on her skin, humiliated and separated from the people for seven days, but present. She died and was buried in an unknown place but was mourned and remembered. Her birth and her name are ignored, but she has enough resources to save her "little brother's" life. She was robbed of her own song to YHWH, but even so intones it in antiphon in the most wonderful moment that the enslaved people witnessed during their liberation. Miriam, prophetess, singer, leader, deserves to be among the key figures in the sacred story of God's people.

Gender and Cult: "Pure" and "Impure" as Gender-Relevant Categories

Dorothea Erbele-Küster
Faculteit voor Protestantse Godgeleerdheid

Is impurity a question of gender? The reader who opens the Torah in the middle cannot avoid the impression that uncleanness has a female face. According to the postpartum prescription in Lev 12, a distinction between a male and a female newborn is to be made immediately after birth. The length of the time a woman is impure—that is, unsuitable for the cult—after the delivery depends on the child's sex. The separation of children into two biological genders is thus reflected in the woman's body and consequently in her relation to the cult. After the birth of a girl, she must abstain from the ceremonial events for twice as long than after a boy. Lev 12 says,

> If a woman conceives and bears a male child, she shall be cultically unclean seven days; as at the time of her menstruation, she shall be unclean. ... If she bears a female child, she shall be unclean two weeks, as in her menstruation; her time of blood purification shall be sixty-six days. (12:2, 5)

According to this passage, the uncleanness seems to be, as the title of this contribution suggests, a gender-relevant category. Alternatively, in more exact terms, the gender determines the period of the impurity, the cultic unfitness. This raises the question of the perspective from which a text such as Leviticus was written and the gender relation it implies. For example, it is noticeable that, in the context of the Leviticus prescriptions for the woman in childbed, the process of birth and its entire social reality, determined by miscarriage, stillbirth, and the risk to the mother's life,[1] is not considered.

---

1. See Carol L. Meyers, *Households and Holiness: The Religious Culture of Israelite Women* (Minneapolis: Fortress, 2005), 16–17.

This short look at a text from the prescriptions relative to purity in Leviticus already makes it clear that gender does not represent a biological entity but is always cultural-religiously mediated. Similarly, the concept, adopted only in the eighteenth century, that the body is a fixed entity with a so-called natural gender proves to be determined by the context. Body and gender are transmitted through culture and language. The perception of the world is structured by language, which is also constitutive for particular conceptions of body and gender. My intention here is to elucidate how gender is constructed with the help of the category "impurity" and to investigate its gender-political relevance. I will look at the texts' discursive power of definition. Therefore, I propose a gender-conscious rereading of the concept of gender in the laws of purity, both in biblical texts and beyond them.[2]

This study will focus on texts in which the question of purity, that is, suitability for cult worship, is intertwined with the question of gender. The determinations relative to the woman after childbirth, in Lev 12, and those surrounding bodily fluids in Lev 15 are a part of the rules concerning purity that span Lev 11–15. Formally, these rules are bracketed between the introductory notices: "YHWH spoke to Moses (and Aaron): Speak to the people of Israel" (Lev 11:1; 12:1; 13:1; 14:33; 15:1), and by the closing formulas: "This is the law pertaining to" (11:46; 12:7; 13:59; 14:32, 57; 15:32). The latter also gave them their names. Their content presents fundamental prescriptions relating to the choice of animals for food (Lev 11), skin diseases and mildew of textiles and houses (Lev 13–14), birth (Lev 12), and the secretion of sexual organs (Lev 15). Leviticus 12, with the woman in childbed, forms a bracket, with Lev 15, around the laws relating to skin disease in Lev 13 and 14. Leviticus 11–15 is, in turn, part of a larger textual section, Lev 11–26, which deals with purity and holiness.[3] The (gendered) body must be suitable for the cult ("pure"), in order to be able to approach God. It must reflect God's holiness. Body and gender grow out in the continuously evolving socioreligious practices.

Paradoxically, although these chapters of Leviticus were greatly reviled in Christianity, they have had strong effects in modern Judaism and Christianity and also the cultures influenced by them. This is true not only for the rites of

---

2. An exhaustive evaluation of the studies from the feminist, or gender-conscious, viewpoint is undertaken by Veronika Bachmann, "Die biblische Vorstellungswelt und deren geschlechterpolitische Dimension: Methodologische Überlegungen am Beispiel der ersttestamentlichen Kategorien 'rein' und 'unrein,'" *lectio difficilior* (2003); online: http://www.lectio.unibe.ch/03_2/bachmann.pdf.

3. See Frank Crüsemann, *Die Tora: Theologie und Sozialgeschichte des alttestamentlichen Gesetzes* (Munich: Kaiser, 1992), 325.

passage (such as circumcision in Judaism) and the absolution usually given to women after childbirth in the Roman Catholic Church, until Vatican II, but also for the conception of the body in general. Even in a recently published introduction to the philosophy of the body, biblical ideas about impurity are presented as examples of disdain for the body.[4] This is reason enough to investigate, by rereading these texts, how uncleanness is conceived and represented with the help of the category of gender.

This essay is composed of five sections. The first section considers the gender-neutral body (§1). In the two following sections, light is thrown on the construction of the gendered body, first the female (§2) and then the male body (§3). A subsection (§2.6) asks to what extent the concept of the female body's impurity, which so strongly influenced the history of reception, plays a role in the narrative texts and to which degree consequences of the laws of purity can be deduced in the frame of women's and men's daily lives. The question of im/purity as a gender-relevant factor, as formulated in the subtitle, constitutes the fourth section (§4). The conclusion presents remarks for further study on im/purity from the gender perspective (§5).

1. Gender-Neutral Discourse: Unity and Difference of the Two Sexes

In Leviticus, special attention is paid to the human body because it is seen in relation to holiness, which it can render unclean. This is why purity, or holiness, must be shown in the body. Although Lev 15 deals with the topic of gender-specific discharges, with reference to the gender-neutral term בָּשָׂר ("flesh"), a unified image of the body is created. Overall, the term is used in various ways in Lev 15: for the male and female body without specification of gender as a whole and also for the gendered male genitals and the female pubic region. In other texts, which order the purity of the sanctuary, the neutral term is used to represent male genitalia (see Exod 28:42; Lev 6:3; 12:3; 16:4). Since, in Lev 15:19—and only here—this term also designates a female pubic area, the vulva, we may infer that, clearly, the text attempts to understand the female and the male gendered body analogously. The *sexual differences* are hence *erased* by such gender-neutral terminology.

The observations suggest the conclusion that Lev 15, with its use of "flesh," considers the male body as normative. The Hebrew word for "flesh," or "body," is also used in texts that deal with circumcision: the "flesh of the foreskin" (cf. Lev 12 and Gen 17) is to be circumcised. Circumcision marks

---

4. See Michela Marzana, *Philosophie du corps (Que sais-je?)* (Paris: Vrin, 2007), 89–92.

a difference between the genders, although with "flesh" the author chose a word that bears a neutral concept of the body. The difference of gender is not applied to the body with the designation of the body parts but by means of different prepositions. In relation to women, the text speaks about the "flow *in* her body" (15:19), but, with respect to the male body, it says "*from/out of* his body" (15:2). The bodies of men and women are thus both differentiated from each another and seen as mutually corresponding. Both the female and the male bodies are at times ceremonially unclean (impure). In the use of the Hebrew word "flesh" in Lev 15, the unity and the difference of the two sexes are thus represented.

2. The Female Body in Its Menstrual Period

What do menstruant women and the land of Israel have in common? This strange question is posed here because, in God's discourse in Ezek 36:17, both are described as unclean and related to one another:

> Mortal, when the house of Israel lived on their own land, they defiled it with their ways and their deeds; their conduct in my sight was like the uncleanness of a woman in her menstrual period.

Here the devastated land is described with the specific term נִדָּה (*niddah*), which, in the laws of purity in Lev 15, expresses the state brought about by menstruation. In what follows, we will reread this term in order to explicate its meaning. We will see how difficult it is to translate, as it represents a specific cultic conception of the body. For this reason, it will be largely left untranslated here and simply transliterated.

The connection of the term *niddah* with menstruation and uncleanness in Ezekiel and other prophetic texts led to the identification of these two words. This was put into writing in the lexica,[5] in commentaries[6] and monographs on the topic,[7] and in translations of the Bible. A recent publication on menstrua-

---

5. See Wilhelm Gesenius, *Hebräisches und Aramäisches Wörterbuch zum Alten Testament: Bearbeitet von Frants Buhl* (17th ed.; Berlin: Springer, 1959), 487; and Geburgis Feld, "Menstruation," *Neues Bibel-Lexikon* (ed. Manfred Görg and Bernhard Lang; 3 vols; Zürich: Benzinger, 1991–2001), 2:773.

6. See Jacob Milgrom, *Leviticus 1–16: A New Translation with Introduction and Commentary* (AB 3; New York: Doubleday, 1996), 744; Erhard S. Gerstenberger, *Das dritte Buch Mose: Leviticus* (ATD 6; Göttingen: Vandenhoeck & Ruprecht, 1993), 180.

7. See Wilfried Paschen, *Rein und Unrein: Untersuchung zur biblischen Wortgeschichte* (SANT 24; Munich: Kösel, 1970), 27–28, who includes נִדָּה among the expressions for impurity; likewise, Veronika Bachmann, "Geschlecht und Un-/Reinheit: Zur feminist-

tion in the Old Testament uses both terms in a tautological sense and believes that this can be founded on "priestly texts."[8] The *Hebräisches und Aramäisches Wörterbuch zum Alten Testament* by Wilhelm Gesenius and Frants Buhl indicates, in the entry for נִדָּה, the primary meaning: "Abscheuliches, Unreines," that is, something that is repugnant, unclean.[9] With this definition, the dictionary suggests that the monthly bleeding is both repugnant and impure. Subdivisions are then introduced: (1) uncleanness of the female bleeding and (2) uncleanness in general; whereby the former sense mixes the levels of meaning, the physiological description of the bleeding and its qualification overlap. In the textbook edition of Wilhelm Koehler's and Walter Baumgarten's *Hebrew and Aramaic Lexicon of the Old Testament*, the article is divided into two subsections: (1) bleeding, menstruation of a woman and (2) separation, abomination, defilement."[10] In the *Theologisches Wörterbuch zum Alten Testament* (*ThWAT*), under נִדָּה, three fields of meaning are indicated: (1) uncleanness in relation to menstruation; (2) uncleanness in general, repugnance; (3) purification.[11] Here, too, uncleanness is considered to be the specific and dominant aspect of the definition. The *Dictionary of Classical Hebrew* (*DCH*) gives evidence of indecision over how *niddah* should be understood. It hesitates between the meaning "impurity" and "bleeding."[12] At the same time, the *DCH* suggests, as do the entries of the other lexica, that impurity is to be judged negatively.

However, is there evidence in the text to support this assimilation of impurity and menstruation? In the laws of purity, this term is only connected with uncleanness in Lev 15:26 "everything on which she sits shall be unclean, as in the uncleanness of her menstruation." Finally, *niddah*, in the constructive bond "water of the *niddah*" (cf. Num 19:9, 13, 20–21; 31:23), can be understood as not impure against the background of its use a cleaning substance. Moreover, it should also be noted that Hebrew usually employs the semantic field of טָמְאָה to describe impurity.

---

ischen Diskussion um die geschlechterpolitischen Implikationen des ersttestamentlichen Rein-Unrein-Denkens" (Lizentiatsarbeit, University of Fribourg, 2003).

8. See Taria S. Philip, *Menstruation and Childbirth in the Bible: Fertility and Impurity* (Studies in Biblical Literature 88; New York: Lang, 2006), 72: "The inherent nature of the impurity of menstrual blood is accepted in all priestly writings."

9. See Gesenius, *Hebräisches und Aramäisches Wörterbuch*, 487.

10. Wilhelm Koehler und Walter Baumgartner, *The Hebrew and Aramaic Lexicon of the Old Testament: Study Edition* (2 vols; Leiden: Brill, 2001), 673.

11. Jacob Milgrom, David Wright, and Heinz-Josef Fabry, "נִדָּה niddāh," *ThWAT* 5:252.

12. *DCH*, 621–24.

We will now deal with the questions raised by the review of the lexica by analyzing the passages containing *niddah*. This will reveal the semantic spectrum of the term. This will clearly show how the rapport between the female body and the cult is constructed.

2.1. BODILY, SOCIAL, OR CULTIC SEPARATION?

The two main etymological models of *niddah* that have been discussed present yet another question: Is *niddah* to be understood as a social or as a physiological separation?[13] The term derives either from the basic trunk (*qal*) of the root נדד, "leave, flee,"[14] or from the *piel* of נדה, "avoid, flee." Independent of the root preferred, the meanings only vary slightly and are practically synonymous: *niddah* (נִדָּה) is understood as rejection, distancing, and separation.

The intercultural comparison and, similarly, the later rabbinic texts have led to the general conclusion that women in ancient Israel were excluded from social life during their period of menstruation.[15] This thesis then serves in the discussion concerning the kind of "separation" as a circular argument in favor of understanding *niddah* as a social separation. However, this separation of women from the cult, or from the area of life of the men, does not necessarily have a punitive character.[16] Referring to "the" taboo relative to menstruation risks obscuring the nuances in the text. These stereotypes (drawn from the cultural comparisons and practice of the purity laws in circles of modern

---

13. See Stefan Schorch, *Euphemismen in der Hebräischen Bibel* (Orientalia Biblica Christiana 12; Wiesbaden: Harrassowitz, 2000), 164, and the review of the discussion in Moshe Greenberg, "The Etymology of nidda '(Menstrual) Impurity,'" in *Solving Riddles and Untying Knots: Biblical, Epigraphic, and Semitic Studies in Honour of J. C. Greenfield* (ed. Ziony Zevit et al.; Winona Lake, Ind.: Eisenbrauns, 1995), 69–77.

14. See Gesenius, *Hebräisches und Aramäisches Wörterbuch*, 487; BDB, 622.

15. See Erich Püschel, *Die Menstruation und ihre Tabus* (Stuttgart: Schattauer, 1988); Karel van der Toorn, *From Her Cradle to Her Grave: The Role of Religion in the Life of the Israelite and Babylonian Woman* (BiSe 23; Sheffield: JSOT Press, 1994); and Monika Fander, *Die Stellung der Frau im Markusevangelium: Unter besonderer Berücksichtigung kultur- und religionsgeschichtlicher Hintergründe* (Münsteraner Theologische Abhandlungen 8; Altenberge: Telos, 1989), 53, 183–85.

16. According to Thomas Buckley and Alma Gottlieb, "A Critical Appraisal of Theories of Menstrual Symbolism," in the introduction to *Blood Magic: The Anthropology of Menstruation* (ed. Thomas Buckley and Alma Gottlieb; Berkeley: University of California Press, 1988), 3–53: "In other cultures menstrual customs rather than subordinating women to men fearful of them, provide women with means of ensuring their own authority, influence and social control" (7). This is also emphasized by Deborah Klee, "Menstruation in the Hebrew Bible" (Ph.D. diss., Boston University, 1998), 26–36, in her intercultural comparison.

Judaism) have largely influenced the sense attributed to this Hebrew root for its linguistic usage in the Bible. The Sumerian expression, according to which a menstruant woman in Mesopotamia is called a *musukkatu*, a person marked as taboo (*asakku*),[17] requires the explication of the context where this occurred and what the taboo looked like.[18] In regard to Israel, at the time of the First and Second Testaments, there is no proof of such an isolation of women during or consequent to menstruation. On the one hand, the texts do not prescribe separation. The laws of purity more specifically concern those who enter into contact with the woman. Consequently, they imply social relations. On the other hand, there are some reference points in the few narrative passages concerning this subject, as we will see in the intertextual reflection at the end.

If the underlying verb "reject, abandon" represents the physical process, this term would then describe the bleeding, the separation of the blood.[19] This is expressed in Lev 15:19:

> When a woman has a discharge, her discharge is of blood from her body.

On the basis of this understanding of the lexeme נִדָּה as (blood) flow, the postulated variant of the meaning "impure" is inconceivable. The meaning of *niddah* cannot therefore be clearly determined by etymology alone; this is only possible through analysis of the contexts in which the word appears. The evolution through which this term has gone has cultic, moral, and religious-polemical dimensions.[20] I will briefly outline these in the following paragraphs.

2.2. *NIDDAH* AS A CULTIC TERM

The law relative to sexual discharges of the woman in Lev 15 is the starting point of the study, since this chapter, along with Lev 12, contains not only the largest number of occurrences (nine of fifteen) but also forges the content of

---

17. Thus Marten Stol, "Reinheid in Mesoptamië," *Phoenix* 4 (2002): 105.

18. See Klee, "Menstruation in the Hebrew Bible," 8–10; and Philip, *Menstruation and Childbirth*, 7–8.

19. See Milgrom, *Leviticus 1–16*, 745: "the word originally referred to the *discharge* or *elimination* of menstrual blood, which came to denote menstrual impurity and impurity in general"; Baruch A. Levine, *Leviticus: The JPS Torah Commentary* (Philadelphia: Jewish Publication Society, 1989), 97: "It does not connote impurity in and of itself but, rather, describes the physiological process of the flow of blood."

20. See Lucia Croce, "La nidda nel pensiero biblico e mišnico," *Egitto e vicino oriente* 6 (1983): 235–45.

the use of *niddah* with respect to the cultic state during menstruation. So, the (transmitted) application of *niddah* in the other passages presupposes Lev 15. The introductory verse about the secretion of the woman's body, Lev 15:19, says:

> When a woman has a discharge, her discharge is of blood from her body, she shall be in her *niddah* for seven days, and whoever touches her shall be unclean until the evening.

The formula "discharge of blood," which in this verse describes the woman's monthly bleeding as analogous with the "simple" outflow of the man (Lev 15:2–3), explicitly refers to the physiological process of the bleeding.

The expressions used for the extraordinarily long period of bleeding—"for many days, not at the time of the *niddah*" and "beyond the time of the *niddah*" (15:25b)—emphasize the temporal aspect of the *niddah* (as in Lev 12:2). The *niddah* lasts seven days, although the bleeding does not necessarily continue throughout this entire time. In the cultic texts, *niddah* becomes a technical term designating the state caused by bleeding that represents a threat to that which is holy. Owing to the lack of a cultic technical term, we can translate the word with "period," "menstrual bleeding," or "menstruation," which give it a stronger medical sense. Nevertheless, the term *niddah* cannot be translated by "menstruation" in all occurrences, since the bleeding is variable. Therefore, *niddah* is an abstract term that in many cases designates the seven-day state of separation from the cult as a result of bleeding.[21]

In Lev 15, *niddah* represents a *cultic term* drawing demarcation lines that is transposed, in a second step, to everyday processes and has produced, in the history of exegesis, a multitude of detailed prescriptions: whoever touches a woman during her menstrual period is unclean until evening; the same is also true for anything she has sat or laid on (15:20). Leviticus 15:19 does not explicitly say that the woman herself is impure. Verse 26 then adds as an explication: she is impure, "as in the uncleanness of her *niddah*." "Impurity," in the context of menstruation, is therefore evoked only through the combination of the two semantic fields. This excludes "impurity" as the original, or primary, sense of *niddah*. Thus it becomes clear that the lexica and commentaries adopted the secondary meaning as the primary one. How and why this happened will be discussed in the following paragraphs.

---

21. An analogous conclusion is reached by Moshe Greenberg, "The Etymology of nidda," 75. See also Klee, "Menstruation in the Hebrew Bible," 43, who substitutes "menstrual status" with "menstrual separation"; and David E. S. Stein, ed., *The Contemporary Torah: A Gender-Sensitive Adaption of the JPS Translation* (Philadelphia: Jewish Publication Society, 2006).

2.3. *NIDDAH* AS A SOCIORELIGIOUS TERM

The point in common of the following passages is that, while considering the menstruating woman, her state was construed not only as a cultic problem but also implicated in ethical questions. In the catalogue of sexual prohibitions, Lev 18:19 says:

> You shall not approach a woman to uncover her nakedness while she is in her menstrual uncleanness.

Whereas in Lev 15 sexual intercourse with a menstruating woman also renders the man cultically unclean for seven days, according to the verse just quoted from Lev 18 (cf. Lev 20), this act leads to his exclusion from the community of descent and cult. The moral and cultic questions are mutually related in this system of ordering. If Lev 15 concerns contact with contaminations, Lev 18 stipulates, with the help of prohibitions, that certain forms of conduct must be avoided at all costs and are liable to sanctions. Sexual contact with a woman during her menstrual period makes the land impure, just as sexual contact with the mother, sister, or the son's daughter does, and so on (see further Lev 18:6–19). A woman's abstinence during her *niddah* becomes a sign of difference vis-à-vis the neighboring peoples and their customs (18:3).

This use is presupposed by the book of Ezekiel, where 18:6b, in the context of a legal catalogue (18:5), draws a parallel between the exiled man who has sexual relations with his neighbor's wife and a menstruating woman:

> He does not defile his neighbor's wife or
> does not approach a woman during her menstrual period [*niddah*].

This is a curious combination. What do these two women have in common? Like the neighbor's wife, the woman is taboo during her menstrual period; even the man cannot control her sexuality. Analogously, the juridical speech in Ezek 22:10 alludes to the series of taboos in Lev 18 and 20, when it states:

> In you they uncover their fathers' nakedness;
> in you they violate women in their menstrual period [*niddah*].

Rereading both Ezek 22:10 and 18:6, it is thus not possible to speak of a disqualification of the menstruating woman; on the contrary, she receives special protection against violent abuse. The menstruating woman is seen as vulnerable. With an analogous formula, Ezek 18 says the neighbor's wife must not be made impure. The question of sexual contact becomes a matter of justice in Ezek 18:5. With the introduction of the cultic term into a legal or moral context, this term is transformed.[22] Although in Lev 15 moral or sexual abuse was not a problem, ethical and cultic categories can no longer be separated in these texts in Ezekiel and in Lev 18. From the moral sense, in certain texts, it is then deduced that *niddah* should be considered a pejorative term.

2.4. *NIDDAH* AS A PEJORATIVE OR POLEMICAL TERM

In Lev 20:11, 21; Ezek 7:19–20; 36:17; Ezra 9:10–11; and 2 Chr 29:5, *niddah* is used to denote religious, cultural, and ethnical differences. In this context, Ezekiel and Ezra attempt to use priestly ideas to overcome the contemporary crisis situation and to introduce the new constitution of a commonwealth. *Niddah* becomes the term designating whatever is outside of Israel's system, in as far as the texts infer that such a limit can be drawn. Toward the end of Ezra's penitential prayer, the flow of reading is practically stifled by the large number of terms describing the impurity of the land (Ezra 9:10b–11):

> For we have forsaken your commandments, which you commanded by your servants the prophets, saying, "The land that you are entering to possess is a contaminated land [*niddah*] with the contaminations [*niddah*] of the peoples of the land, with their abominations. They have filled it with their uncleanness."

Here *niddah* appears in the context of abomination and contamination. Whereas in Lev 18 contact with a woman in her *niddah* leads to the contamination of the land, in Ezra 9:11 the land itself is described as *niddah*. The catastrophe of the exile is, for Ezra, the result of these impurities (see also Ezek 36:17), yet this gives rise to the following question: What happened to the land such that it is described like this? After all, it is not stained. The lamentable moral state of the land is compared to a woman during her menstrual bleeding. The image carrier (the land) and the source of the image (the menstruating woman) are equally affected by this. Women are thus identified with impurity, and the condemnable state of the land is assimilated with a menstruating woman in such a way that impurity becomes a female image.

The solution proposed by Ezra with respect to mixed marriages and executed by the resolve of the community is correspondingly radical: he orders the dissolution of marriages with foreign women. As we can imagine, behind this program of social-rights matters lay the inheritance right. The desired

---

22. See Rachel Biale, *Women and Jewish Law: An Exploration of Women's Issues in Halakhic Sources* (New York: Schocken, 1984), 167: "Their connection to the laws of impurity was loosened and they became part of the laws regarding sexual transgressions."

outcome of the "divorce program" was most likely not achieved, as the aspired separation of Israelite men from the women of "others" makes it clear that what belongs to one's own and "the other" are intertwined. This is particularly noticeable in the children stemming from these marriages. Ezra 10:3 says that they must be sent away with the women.

Likewise, Ezek 7:19–20 uses *niddah* as a polemical accusation against the common religious policy, trying to draw a demarcation line motivated by the cult:

> They shall fling their silver into the streets;
> their gold shall be treated as contaminated [*niddah*].
> Their silver and gold cannot save them
> on the day of the wrath of YHWH.
> They shall not satisfy their hunger
> or fill their stomachs with it.
> For it was the stumbling block of their iniquity.
> From their beautiful ornament, in which they took pride,
> they made their abominable images, their detestable things;
> therefore I will make of it an object of contamination [*niddah*] to them.

In 7:19, the term *niddah* is used in parallel with "streets"; that which is *niddah* should not be inside but must be thrown out and separated from the realm of that which is holy. This does not necessarily impose the reverse conclusion, that women must be excluded from ordinary life during their menstrual periods.[23] It implies that whatever is *niddah* cannot be in the realm of that which is holy because it could damage it. The images of God are called "abominable images." God himself makes them *niddah* (7:20) in order to express their incompatibility with the holiness. In these passages *niddah* can be substitued with "contamination." There is a taboo on things that are designated *niddah*.

In the list of the sexual contacts to be condemned and punished in Lev 20:21, *niddah* is used with a devaluating tone:

> If a man takes a wife of his brother, it is taboo [*niddah*].

The logic here is inverted in comparison with Lev 18. While Lev 18:19 condemns sexual intercourse with a woman during menstruation (*niddah*), in Lev 20 sexual relations with the wife of one's brother is said to constitute *niddah*. A term that was employed as a neutral technical cultic expression for menstruation in Lev 12:2, 5; 15:19, 24–26 is analogous to "confusion of the

---

23. Thus Milgrom, *Leviticus 1–16*, 952.

levels of order" (20:12) or "shame" (20:14), for disqualification in Lev 20. Let us recall Ezek 36:17, quoted at the beginning, in which to denounce the impurity, presented in the comparative, indirect discourse as "like the impurity of the *niddah*," it is said that "their conduct in my sight was like the impurity of a woman in her menstrual period." If, in Lev 15, a woman is temporarily impure during her menstruation, then in the postexilic period she actually becomes the symbol of impurity.[24]

While in Leviticus cultic language is used to conserve the holiness of the sanctuary; in Ezra *niddah* becomes an ethno-political category. Likewise, in Lev 20; Ezek 7; 36; and 2 Chr 29 the term is used, in an indirect polemical discourse, to mark the difference. There is no evidence of a unilinear development; instead, divergent uses appear. The polemical, pejorative aspect of *niddah* was very efficacious. The use of *niddah* in Ezek 7:19 marks a decisive point in the transformation of the meaning, for the lexeme passed, through metaphorical use, from being a technical term designating a woman's state in relation to the cult to signifying a menstruating woman in the Hebrew of the Mishnah.

2.5. The Symbol System as Boundary Marker

The laws of purity represent a system of ordering. In this system the body serves as a microcosm around which the macrocosm constructs itself.[25] It symbolizes the society, or socioreligious conceptions, that in turn can be expressed in the rites or laws of purity. With the help of the body, boundaries are marked. Everything that leaves the body makes it impure. Yet, according to the laws of purity in Leviticus, examples of exceptions are saliva, urine, and excrement. Therefore, the rules cannot be explained with measures of hygiene alone, since, in this case, excrement would have also been introduced, as in Deut 23. We will now explicate how, or which, delimitations are established by the texts and their process of interpretation, as well the role gender plays in this.

---

24. This is the conclusion of Cruce, "La nidda," 242: "la donna, da impura per un breve periodo, diventa impura in quanto donna" (the woman who is impure for a short time becomes impure as woman).

25. See Mary Douglas, *Purity and Danger: An Analysis of the Concepts of Pollution and Taboo* (London: Routledge & Kegan Paul, 1966), 151–82.

2.5.1. *Niddah* as Cultic Boundary Marker

Niddah was coined in Lev 12 and 15 as a technical cultic term for the description of a woman's state due to menstruation that obliged her to stay away from the sanctuary. This condition of incompatibility with the cult lasted for seven days. The female cycle and the cult were therefore mutually related to each other through the term *niddah*.

The fundamental cultic meaning of the term also varies in its polemical use in Ezek 7:19–20, where it is said that everything affected by *niddah* must be removed from the sanctuary. Here a distinction is made between *niddah* itself and impurity.

2.5.2. *Niddah* as Physical Boundary Marker

The physiological details found in the texts relating to *niddah* are sparse. Leviticus 15 gives no indication of the duration of the complete female cycle or of the duration between the bleedings. Furthermore, the bleeding does not necessarily continue for seven days; only the dangerous condition created by the bleeding in relation to the cult lasts for seven days. Cultic impurity can arise independently from concrete material impurities, even after the bleeding has stopped. *Niddah* is therefore fundamentally not a physiological category. This is illustrated by the designation of a postpartum woman (i.e., after childbirth) as *niddah*. Nevertheless, at the same time, symbolic boundaries are inscribed on the woman's body.

2.5.3. *Niddah* as Gender Boundary Marker

The concept of *niddah* is reserved exclusively, in its use by the Hebrew Bible, for the description of women or female-gendered personifications. Then, in the Mishnah and in the Talmud, *niddah* designates the menstruation itself. There is no equivalent term for the state of the man after the discharge of semen—which is also polluting. In Qumran (CD 12:1–2; 4QMMT 45:10), this specifically female concept is likewise used with respect to the man, where the nocturnal emission is described as an impurity comparable to *niddah*.[26]

In Leviticus, however, only the impurity of the female body is doubly marked and designated with a particular term, which leads to the *othering* of

---

26. See Mayer I. Gruber, "Purity and Impurity in Halakhic Sources and Qumran Law," in *Wholly Woman—Holy Blood: A Feminist Critique of Purity and Impurity* (ed. Kristin De Troyer et al.; Harrisburg, Pa.: Trinity Press International, 2003), 71–72.

the woman. The physiological processes of the female body, determined by the hormones, become the metaphor for impurity, of what must be isolated. *Niddah* represents a one-sided category that establishes a boundary between the genders that can come to play a role in the constitution of identity, since the laws concerning im-/purity reflect the life cycle on a ritual level.[27] While female critics stress that the border was drawn by men and thus excludes women, Jewish women who observe the *niddah* laws are not the last to redefine them for themselves. They experience the observance of *niddah* as a connection with the tradition and, in this way, define themselves as Jewish and woman.

2.5.4. *Niddah* as an Ethnic and Religious Boundary Marker

The state during menstruation becomes a negative image, a symbol of society's decline, denounced by Ezra and Nehemiah. Due to this figurative use, the female body becomes a point of comparison for the postexilic society, because purity is extremely easy to define and control in the female body. *Niddah* thus becomes a category of ethnic delimitation.

The designation of the land as *niddah* in Ezra 9 is used to found the "prohibition of mixing." The expression introduces borders, in the postexilic literature of the Diaspora, between the culture and religion of the Hebrews and the culture of the "others" (i.e., Egyptians, Canaanites, Babylonians, Greeks, women and men), between the in-group and the out-group, and also between the male and the female sex.

In texts such as Ezek 7:19–20, *niddah* is used figuratively to defame a particular religious practice. Here the state of the women during their menstruation is evoked and used to mark the attendant social, ceremonial, and cultural exclusion. *Niddah* represents all that must be avoided; the term becomes an epitome of amorality. In Ezra and in Ezek 36:17–18, it is even used as a curse. This literature is a rhetorical response to the crisis situation of the community and the society, in the postexilic or Persian period, whereby boundaries must be introduced with reference to the notions of im-/purity from Leviticus. In this process, the female body is instrumentalized for religious and cultic demarcation. This process was to repeat itself in the course of (reception) history. Laws of purity become a moral regulation that attempts to get a hold of a situation, through the body (of the woman), over which the social body has no control. Moral conceptions and ideas about purity go hand in hand.

---

27. See Rachel Adler, "TUMAH and TAHARAH: Ends and Beginnings," in *The Jewish Woman: New Perspectives* (ed. Elizabeth Koltun; New York: Schocken, 1976), 63–71.

2.5.5. *NIDDAH* as Boundary Marker in Marital Sexual Life

In the Hebrew Bible already, the diverse prescriptions in Lev 15 can be understood as a discussion about the practice of the law of purity. Their details differentiate them from one another, while the introductory case to the chapter deals most broadly with the men's discharge. Finally, laws of purity can be constructeed as prescriptions for daily life in the praxis of interpretation. The measures for the men's discharge are transferred to the women's bleeding.[28]

The differentiations in rabbinic and talmudic literature reflect the transformation of the law of purity. The sexual intercourse of married couples was prohibited for up to fifteen days, that is, the days of the actual bleeding plus the seven following "white days."[29] In the Talmud, we already find the first explanations of these rules. This sexual continence is meant to increase the man's affection for his wife after the *niddah* (see b. Nid. 31b).

The transformation of cultic prescription into laws on morals and sex was promoted intertextually by Lev 18 and 20. There sexual intercourse with a menstruating woman is considered as sexual abuse. The destruction of the Second Temple in 70 C.E. led to change in the issue of cultic purity. "There was no access to Temple and thus no need for purification. The only person still subject to purification rite was the menstruant woman, not for reason of pollution and taboo but because of proscription of a sexual relationship which had nothing to do with purification for temple access."[30] In the course of the history of the reception of the prescriptions for daily life, the laws of purity among the cosmic cultic regulations in Lev 12 and 15 became "family laws,"[31] which concentrated on the regulation of the sexual life of the married couple. Yet, only some of these are actually valid for the Jewish woman.[32]

---

28. See David P. Wright, *The Disposal of Impurity: Elimination Rites in the Bible and in Hittite and Mesopotamian Literature* (SBLDS 101; Atlanta: Scholars Press, 1987).

29. See b. Nid. 66a and Evyatar Marienberg, *Niddah: Lorsque les juifs conceptualisent la menstruation* (Paris: Belles Lettres, 2003), 31–32, 133.

30. See Blue Greenberg, "Female Sexuality and Bodily Functions in the Jewish Tradition," in *Women, Religion and Sexuality: Studies on the Impact of Religious Teachings on Women* (ed. Jeanne Becher; Genf: WCC, 1990), 1–44, here 2.

31. See the presentation in Marienberg, *Niddah*, 40–41, 147–56, 275–79.

32. See Greenberg, "Female Sexuality," 28–29; she has personally studied these regulations and departs from the idea that outside of the Orthodox community only some women practice them. Pnina Navè Levinson ("Women and Sexuality: Traditions and Progress," in Becher, *Women, Religion and Sexuality*, 45) argues, in her introductory remarks, that most religious Jews (both men and women) situate themselves beyond the Orthodox groups. Hence, Reformed Judaism also emphasizes that menstruation is a private affair

2.6. Intertextuality in Narrative Texts

The reception of the term *niddah* in the prophetic texts, especially in meta-phorical application, has already been elucidated. The intention of the following excursus is simply to consider, in the form of an intertextual reflection with regard to the narrative texts, whether, here also the concept of the uncleanness of the female gendered body during menstruation plays a role. (This is regardless of the extent to which the cultic technical term *niddah* is used.) Furthermore, behind this stands the question as to whether the laws of purity were at least integrated into the writings that deal with the day-to-day practice of women. In the narrative texts, the phenomenon of menstrual bleeding or of the general female cycle has only a marginal role (Gen 18:11; 31:35; 2 Sam 11:2–5). The linguistic usage of the laws of purity is foreign to them. Genesis 31:35 and 2 Sam 11 stand out here because they are connected with the question of gender and impurity.

2.6.1. "The Way of Women Is upon Me" (Gen 31:35)

In order to hide the teraphim (the household gods of her father Laban), Rachel conceals them by sitting on them. She replies to her searching father that she cannot get up. The text in Gen 31:35b lets Rachel use an ambiguous formulation: "the way of women is upon me" (cf. the formulation in Gen 18:11). If Rachel's expression is understood as a euphemism for menstrual bleeding, this implies that she speaks figuratively owing to a taboo. With reference to Lev 15, the verse is interpreted in this sense. Hence, afraid of losing his purity by touching the things that[33] Rachel is sitting on, Laban avoids such contact and does not order her to get up. For him (as well as for Rachel!), it would be inconceivable to keep the teraphim, obviously of vital significance for all, in an unclean place. The strategy of the text is such that it does not present any clear evidence that Rachel has her period. In fact, she does not utter a single word about impurity. Moreover, this kind of fear of contact with contamination or danger is incompatible with the goodbye kiss that Laban later gives his daughter (Gen 32:1) or even with the thorough search of all the possessions and the tent. Indeed, according to Lev 15:19–21, both of these actions would have rendered him impure. Rachel's reasoning indicates a different sense. She does not say that Laban could be endangered by such contact; rather, she indicates

---

and does not prevent women from assuming religious duties. See Biale, *Women and Jewish Law,* 148, 158, 173–74.

33. Thus, for example, van der Toorn, *From Her Cradle,* 52–53, who concludes from this that the Leviticus laws of purity were deeply rooted in "popular belief."

that she cannot stand up because "the way of women" is upon her. However, in Lev 15 it is not said that women cannot, because of weakness, for instance, stand up during their menstruation period.

2.6.2. "She Was Purifying Herself after Her Period" (2 Sam 11:4)

In 2 Sam 11 we see, through David's eyes, a beautiful woman bathing not far from the king's house (11:2). A few verses later, after the account of David's sexual union with this woman, Bathsheba, wife of Uriah, the text says, "Now she was purifying herself after her period" (11:4). What does this notice refer to? It does not refer directly to the bathing David observed but rather to the sexual intercourse. The formulation in 11:4 recalls the priestly linguistic world, although the reference is unclear. Supposing that the expression does concern a bath of purification following the menstruation, it would not be a direct interpretation of Lev 15. The text there does not prescribe purification after menstruation; this only occurs later in postbiblical literature. The reference to Bathsheba's bath—in the sense of bath of purification—could be a subtle indication from the author that she did not become pregnant by her husband, since she had just had her period.

The rule derived from the prescriptions in Lev 15 stipulating that, after the expiration of the seven-day period of the unsuitability for the cult, the woman must wash is in conflict with Bathsheba's immediate pregnancy following a single act of intercourse, which is improbable at that moment. Nothing in the text suggests that 2 Sam 11, like the Mishnah, presupposes another seven days of separation following the end of the *niddah*.

At first sight, 2 Sam 11 evokes a context fashioned by Lev 11–15, but as has been shown, the references are not very specific. Consequently, the term "cultic abstinence/uncleanness" used, in fact, comes from cultic literature, although it is not found in combination with "purification" in the laws of purity. Perhaps an attempt was made in 2 Sam 11 to apply a term derived from the sacred space to everyday and private life. Finally, the extent to which the text has recourse to the system in Lev 15 remains unclear.

2.6.3. Narrative Texts beyond the Conceptual World of the Cult

No conclusions can be drawn from the narrative texts concerning the application of laws of purity from Lev 15, at the most from a negative point of view: a clear inscription in daily life cannot be established.[34] The texts do not use

---

34. See Feld, "Menstruation," 775, who asks critically "whether these texts [i.e., the

a unified terminology. The formulation in Gen 31 (cf. Gen 18) represents a euphemistic expression, although exactly what it covers is unclear. Likewise, no evident relation is established with menstruation. The silence surrounding this is perhaps part of the taboo. The expression, at the least, conceals physical phenomena.

Not only does the vocabulary of the narrative texts greatly differ from the laws of purity in Leviticus and from the prophetic texts they influenced, but the conceptual worlds are also different. Consequently, neither the narratives in Genesis nor the story in 2 Sam 11 represent interpretations of the legal texts. Moreover, nothing is said in these passages about isolation during menstruation or illness. The intertextual reflection of Lev 15 left aside, despite the fact that we are dealing with narrative literature, the everyday life of women during menstruation does not appear in the texts.

2.7. On the Relation between Text And Practice

Correspondingly, the importance of the Leviticus texts for everyday life is diversely assessed. Which practices reflect the laws of purity? Do they intend to provide instructions? Is the "ritual" prescription a historical religious,[35] ethnological, or form-critical category? How can we determine the rapport between the ritual and daily life? Wherever Leviticus is understood as a ritual agenda, it is in contradiction with the specific literary structure of the texts.[36] Not least, the completive character of the laws of purity shows that the latter are constructed according to the strict schema of a typical idealistic ritual text.

The variety of interpretations within Judaism shows that, in practice, the reader must always fill voids left open by the texts in order to guarantee a fitting application. The rabbinic writings attempt to do so by requiring that the woman bathe both after she has given birth and during menstruation (m. Nid. 4:3; 10:8; Miqw. 8:1, 5). The prescriptions relative to the size, the appearance,

---

laws of purification] were conceived by the authors with 'regard to daily existence and life in the household,'" as Gerstenberger, *Das dritte Buch Mose*, 118, supposes.

35. On impurity in the three monotheistic religions, cf. Maddalena Del Bianco Cotrozzi, *Precetti e riti di purità femminile nelle tre grandi religioni monoteiste* (Udine: Forum, 2004).

36. Erich Zenger, "Das Buch Leviticus als Teiltext der Tora/des Pentateuch: Eine synchrone Lektüre mit diachroner Perspektive," in *Leviticus als Buch* (ed. Heinz-Josef Fabry and Hans-Winfried Jüngling; BBB 119; Berlin/Bodenheim: Philo, 1999), 47–83; 71, who concludes because of the book's inherent system: *"die einseitige Deutung, das Buch Leviticus sei eine Sammlung kultischer Gesetze oder gar ein Handbuch für die Priesterausbildung, aus[zu]schließen"* [the unilateral interpretation that the Book of Leviticus is a collection of cultic laws or even a manual for the formation of priests must be excluded.]

and the affluence of water of the mikveh in the Jewish literature of the first centuries C.E. are to be understood against this background.

Enlisting the help of archaeology, scholars seeking extrabiblical evidence for the laws of purity in everyday life. Ritual baths of purification (mikvot) become more frequent only after the turn of the eras.[37] The explanation of the findings from the Second Temple is debated, because the baths can be understood in ways other than exclusively as a ritual interpretation of the laws of purity. The baths that have been excavated in the upper part of Jerusalem should also be seen in relation to personal hygiene, under the Hellenistic influence of the upper class. The archaeological findings suggest that the laws of purity are not reflected in the daily practice of ancient Israel. They are, rather, a later ideal[38] that, in turn, continues to determine the social history of Judaism even today. They are characteristically—like the laws' prescriptions for the construction of the sanctuary—divorced from reality, to an extent.

The rapport between text and practice is difficult to establish and requires a methodological discussion. In sum, the legal texts of the Old Testament are scarcely echoed in the narrative and prophetic literature. If the texts in Lev 12 and 15 do not represent practiced law, then what are they? This is how attempts to identify the texts as direct reflexes in "reality" frequently result in aporias. In contrast, the questions that can be, and have been, studied on the literary level are: How are the rules transmitted? What do they explain, and what do they not explain? Thus, the stylization in Leviticus rather indicates the text's programmatic character.

3. The Purity and Impurity of the Man

The chapter from the prescriptions relative to purity in Lev 15 (which has been so far the basis of our discusion) begins with regard to the sexual discharges of the man rather than the woman. The abnormal sexual discharges of the man (15:3b–15) constitute the prelude that is paralleled, in terms of the female gender, by the abnormal bleedings of the woman (15:25–30). For the two prescriptions pertaining to men, there are also two concerning women. There is consequently a great deal of discussion about the concentric structure of this chapter. The two inner sections are composed of the man's discharge of semen (15:16–17) and of the passage about the woman's menstrual bleeding

---

37. See Andrea M. Berlin, "Jewish Life before the Revolt: The Archaeological Evidence," *JSJ* 36 (2005): 452: "mikva'ot first appear in contexts of early mid first century B.C.E.; there is no evidence for installations in Jewish settlements before then."

38. See Meindert Dijkstra, "Schone Handen: Reinheid in de Culturen van de Levant," *Phoenix* 48 (2002): 91.

(15:19–24). They are grouped around the rule on sexual intercourse (15:18). These rules are framed by prescriptions concerning cases of "illness," although the text itself does not apply this category. Now, if the construction of the entire chapter of Lev 15 is considered, it is striking that the male genital discharge (15:3b–15) is not compared with ejaculation, while this is done with the menstrual bleeding of the women. Commentaries in this line that speak about unhealthy discharges do emphasize the distance, the incomparability, between the sexual discharge of the man and the menstruation of the woman.

3.1. The "Unusual" Discharges of the Man

In the introductory verse 2, an unspecified verb is used in regard to the man: "(out-)flow," which appears in the rest of the chapter in relation to both male and female bodies. No more details are given about the quality of the man's discharge; only the preposition "from"/"out" makes it clear that the delineation for secretion represents crossing bodily limits (see §1). The choice of this term for both genders in the text is elucidated in the explanation, when the gender-specific meaning is deciphered: (1) "Schleimfluss der Männer" (men's flow of mucus), which some commentaries or lexica identify in the sense of a medical specification of gonorrhoea benigna;[39] (2) "Blutfluss der Frauen"[40] (women's bleeding). This brings the medical viewpoint of the exegetes to light. They make a clear distinction between the male and female body. This analogous categorization of the diverse secretions such as the man's sexual (mucus) discharge and the woman's menstrual, or unusually long, bleeding seems to commentators often unintelligible. In fact, the text does not use the verb "flow" without specifying gender at all. In 15:19, with regard to the woman, additions such as the specification that the material secreted is blood make it evident that this concerns menstrual bleeding and, hence, a different sort of outflow than the man's.

With regard to the "abnormal" discharges, the text says: "When any man is a discharger, his member is discharging, he is impure." The personal pronoun in the expression of 15:2, "it/he is impure," can refer to either the discharge or the man. The question of whether the person or the discharge is declared "unclean" raises another general question: Does the text distinguish between the person and the discharge? The Hebrew formulation says that a

---

39. See Milgrom, *Leviticus 1–16*, 907; Koehler and Baumgartner, *Lexicon*, 255; and Gerstenberger, *Das dritte Buch Mose*, 187. Levine, *Leviticus*, 215, suggests that it is a urinary tract infection.

40. Gesenius, *Hebräisches und Aramäisches Wörterbuch*, 195; see also Koehler and Baumgartner, *Lexicon*, 266, 255.

person *is* a discharger; consequently, the person is defined by the secretion. The text should probably be understood with this double meaning.

3.2. DISCHARGES OF SEMEN

The second case deals with the discharge of semen: "If a man has an emission of semen" (15:16a). In comparison with the prescription about the man's sexual discharge (15:2–3) that opens the chapter, the construction relative to the emission of semen is completely different. There is no mention of (male) "flesh," and the physiological process is not described using the verb "flow." In the consecutive prescription of purification (15:17), it is said that "everything made of flesh" must be washed. Apparently "everything" was introduced in order to make it clear, in contrast to 15:3, where the word "flesh" designates only the male member, that in 15:17 the entire body is taken into consideration. Leviticus 15:16–17 speaks about the emission of semen. The genitive construction represents a concretely neutral technical term. The loss of semen makes the man cultically unclean for one day. The objects touched by the semen and the woman he was with are also impure until evening. However, the texts do not say why the emission of semen contaminates. Overall, the cultic aspect is emphasized.

The prescription concerning the proper behavior in a military camp in Deut 23:11 also regards the loss of semen. The camp must be kept holy so that YHWH does not leave it—that is the reasoning. The text mentions a "nocturnal event." This expression is peculiar and is understood as a euphemism for the emission of semen. After bathing, the man can return to the camp on the following evening. The conception of holiness is therefore reflected by the body. This passage shares a certain conceptual world with Lev 15, but, linguistically, it puts them into a different form. It is not clear whether 1 Sam 20:26 also refers to an emission of semen when Saul declares that David's absence is due to an "that" which has made him unclean and that prevents him from coming to the table for the evening meal. According to Lev 15, this would oblige only staying away from the cultic space, not necessarily from a banquet table.

Other texts, such as Num 5:2–3 (with respect to men and women) and Lev 22:4 and 2 Sam 3:29, which feature "flow" as a technical term, also presuppose Lev 15. Only 2 Sam 3:28–29 has a narrative context: David puts a curse over Joab and his (exclusively male?) house with a list of skin infections, sexual discharges, lameness, death by the sword, and lack of bread. Here, in contrast to Lev 13–15, skin infection and discharge do not primarily constitute impediments to the cult. Instead, they disturb the social and corporal equilibrium of the individual and of his community.

ニECOND

 OLcatrbusこ.

To summarize, it is noticeable that the man's unsuitability for the cult after ejaculation was received to only a limited extent inside and outside of the biblical texts.

4. "Unclean" or "in Conflict with the Cult" or "Ceremonially Abstinent"?

This section shall reread the categories of clean/unclean that constitute the foundation for this essay and that—as has been explicated—have a gender-specific expression. In today's everyday language, clean and unclean are primarily associated with physical hygiene and moral conceptions. However, in Leviticus, clean and unclean are used to describe the body in relation to the cult: according to Lev 11–15, a body is either in accordance to the cult or in conflict with the cult.

4.1. Misunderstandings

In numerous studies on this subject, the term "impure" receives precedence or emphasis, in direct contrast to "pure."[41] This corresponds entirely to the prescriptions in Leviticus, which barely say anything about purity. We could define purity negatively, as the absence of impurity. However, determining the rapport between the two Hebrew roots טמא ("unclean") and ("clean") and טהר is more complicated than the antithetical couplet of the translation "clean/unclean" suggests. In contrast to Greek and Latin and the European languages influenced by them, in Hebrew these two lexemes do not belong to the same family of words but derive from two completely independent roots. The many studies—and the title of this contribution also—have a basis whereby the "antithetical linguistic construction pure/impure follows the Greek Bible,"[42] which distinguishes between ἀκάθαρτος ("impure") and καθαρός ("pure"), rather than the Hebrew conception of the laws of purity in Leviticus. According to the Septuagint, "pure" represents the fundamental category, while "impure," marked by the privative prefix (α or un/im-), is its negation. However, in Hebrew this variation does not exist. Hence, it is incor-

---

41. Jean L'Hour, "L'Impur et le Saint dans le Premier Testament à partir du livre du Lévitique: Partie I: L'Impur et le Pur," *ZAW* 115 (2003): 524–37, understands, as the title and subtitle already clearly indicate, that impurity is a dominant category for Leviticus. See the review of the research on the conceptions of impurity in the Hebrew Bible and in Judaism in Jonathan Klawans, *Impurity and Sin in Ancient Judaism* (New York: Oxford University Press, 2000), 3–20.

42. Paschen, *Rein und Unrein*, 13, my translation.

rect to translate טָהוֹר with "pure" and טָמֵא with "impure."[43]Accordingly, I would like to make the case for alternative translations here, for example, "in conflict with the cult" or "dangerous for the cult," respectively, "ceremonial abstinence," words that have no negating particle and are not constructed as antitheses to "pure."

Both lexemes become intelligible only in relation to a third category, namely, holiness: "Everything that is in opposition to God's realm is impure. … purity makes it possible to enter into this realm."[44] Consequently, purity can be parallel to the holy (Lev 10:10; Ezek 22:26). The holy can be described in analogy to the impure as a dynamic reality, where the pure is static. Even if, at first sight, holiness appears to be the absolute opposite of impurity, both have similar characteristic structures; they share a common base. The holy can also have a contaminating effect (Lev 16:27–28; Num 19:7). Nevertheless, it remains part of a contrasting pair with "impure." The task of the priestly lineage consists, according to Leviticus, of separating the holy from the profane, the pure from the impure (Lev 10:10; cf. 11:47; 20:25).

In noncultic texts, "pure" seems to be the dominant category. Impurity is represented therein as a state deprived of purity, although the texts reveal differing types of negation (Gen 7:2, 8; Deut 23:11; 1 Sam 20:26). Language constructed with formulas, as in Leviticus, is therefore unrecognizable. In order to express a state of nonpurity, the negation of the Hebrew term for "pure" (טָהוֹר) is used, which makes the bipolarity stand out more clearly. In these noncultic texts, purity constitutes the background against which the opposite condition is qualified as "impure."

While "pure" in noncultic texts forms the dominant category, in the cultic texts the root "impure" has this function. The texts revolve around the conception of the state of suitablitity for the cult. Purity is secondary because impurity is contagious and can contaminate. Impurity dispenses a power that the prescriptions in Lev 12 and 15 attempt to neutralize. Consequently, these chapters note what must be done in order to negate the cultic unfitness, even though there is no detailed explanation of this condition. The common translations "impure" or "pure" motivate the association with materially perceptible conditions. "Pure" and "impure" are, in Lev 11–15, relational notions with regard to the cult.

---

43. See Ina Willi-Plein, *Opfer und Kult im alttestamentlichen Israel: Textbefragungen und Zwischenergebnisse* (SBS 153; Stuttgart: Katholisches Bibelwerk, 1993), 38.

44. Hans-Jürgen Hermisson, *Sprache und Ritus im Altisraelitischen Kult: Zur "Spiritualisierung" der Kultbegriffe im Alten Testament* (WMANT 19; Neukirchen-Vluyn: Neukirchener, 1965), 89.

4.2. Is Impurity a Material Reality?

Formulations such as "discharge of her impurity"[45] in Lev 15:25b, 30b or regarding "the impurity on/over a person" in 7:20 suggest that impurity is to be understood as material, at first sight. However, in the description of the woman's condition after childbirth in Lev 12, the blood is not taken as the reference point for the impurity. Should it be the reference point, then the conception of the impurity would have to be connected to the bleeding. However, the length of bleeding varies from one instance to another. Furthermore, it is highly debatable whether the bleeding lasts twice as long after the birth of a girl. The postpartum state of the ceremonially unfit woman cannot, therefore, be founded upon the bleeding. In this case, the time of the impurity and the duration of the bleeding could closely correlate, as stated in rabbinic explanations with formulations such as "after the last loss of blood she should count seven days" or "she has to be cult abstinent during the time of the bleeding and for the next seven days."[46] In Lev 12, the impurity seems to be constructed in reference to the woman's body, with direct consideration of physiological processes. The concept of impurity rather serves conversely to construct the body. Hence, it is constitutive for the perception of gender.

4.3. A Term with a Ritual Function

Over half of the occurrences of derivations from the root טמא ("impure") are found in the book of Leviticus.[47] The term "impure" is in the "priestly cultic texts a functional term"[48] that permits a statement about (un)suitablitity for the cult. Diverse assessments are made in Leviticus: sexual contact with a menstruant woman implies, according to Lev 15, that the status of *niddah* is only temporarily transferred to the man. According to Lev 18 and 20, this action merits death and has the consequence of exclusion from the community, as it pollutes the land. Does this mean that categories are blurred in Lev

---

45. See Bachmann, *Geschlecht und Un-/Reinheit*, 171: "all the days of the discharge of her impurity"; Gerstenberger, *Das dritte Buch Mose*, 180: "all the days of her impurity's discharge" (both my translation).

46. See b. Nid. 66a; Marienberg, *Niddah*, 31–32, 133–34.

47. See Paschen, *Rein und Unrein*, 27; L'Hour, *L'Impur et le Saint*, 526.

48. Theodor Seidl, "Rein und unrein," *Neues Bibel-Lexikon* (ed. Manfred Görg and Bernhard Lang; 3 vols.; Zürich: Benzinger, 1991–2001), 3:317, my translation. See also Geburgis Feld, "Leviticus: Das ABC der Schöpfung," in *Kompendium Feministische Bibelauslegung* (ed. Luise Schottroff and Marie-Theres Wacker; 2nd ed.; Gütersloh: Gütersloher Verlagshaus, 1999), 41.

18 and 20 and in the prophetic literature because questions of the cultic fitness determined by the body are dealt with at the same time as questions about sexual morals? This probably does not correspond to the thinking of the book, because for Leviticus both regulations imply protection against crossing boundaries.

In the exegetical literature, a distinction is made between partially inevitable pollutions and pollutions that are consequences of actions and, as such, forbidden.[49] Both groups have different characteristics: pollutions that come from external causes, such as contact with corpses or from the discharge of semen, can transmit their polluting force to a third party; indeed, they even, so to speak, radiate.[50] For this reason, measures should be taken to anticipate a threat to the sacred space. These pollutions are "contagious," but, at the same time, they can be cancelled with the help of purification rites such as waiting for a certain length of time or washing the body.

For Lev 11–15, "impure" is a cultic category that describes the status of an object in regard to the cult and the sanctuary. Hence, it is not a category that should produce disgust.[51] This is what the translations of the Hebrew term טָמֵא with "unsuitable for the cult," "unclean in cultic respect,"[52] "threatening for the cult," "cultically abstinent," or "in conflict with the cult" are intended to express.

4.4. IMPURITY AS A BOUNDARY MARKER

The laws of purity implement boundaries between inside and outside, between life and death, and, finally, between the genders. The bodily discharges pollute because bodily openings symbolize vulnerable places that are on the border of inside and outside. The laws of purity make it possible to define and conserve

---

49. David P. Wright, "Unclean and Clean: *Old Testament*," *ABD* 6:729–741; 729, speaks of "permitted impurity," "natural and necessary conditions" and "sinful situations"; Tikva Frymer-Kensky, "Pollution, Purification, and Purgation in Biblical Israel," in *The Word of the Lord Shall Go Forth: Essays in Honor of David Noel Friedmann* (ed. Carol L. Meyers et al.; Winona Lake, Indiana: Eisenbrauns, 1983), 399–414, differentiates "ritual pollutions" and "danger beliefs."

50. In the opposite sense, the "non-communicability" of pollution is evoked (cf. Wright, *The Disposal of Impurity*).

51. Cf. Mary Douglas, *Leviticus as Literature* (Oxford: Oxford University Press, 1999), 151: "Unclean is not a term of psychological horror and disgust, it is a technical term for the cult ... To import feelings into the translation falsifies, and creates more puzzles."

52. See Willi-Plein, *Opfer und Kult*, 25: "kultuntauglich"; in *Bibel in gerechter Sprache* (ed. Ulrike Bail et al.; 3rd ed.; Gütersloh: Gütersloher Verlagshaus, 2007) the expressions "kultunfähig" and "kultunrein" are frequently employed.

the order. In this sense, the cultic conception of the "woman's impurity during menstruation" was transformed in the crisis situations in the postexilic society and instrumentalized for ethnic, religious, delimitations.

The laws of purity concern basic life processes as well as the life-histori-cal border crossings.[53] The question is whether the prescriptions imposed the same limits on both genders or whether these limits had the same motivations.

It is often assumed that the prescriptions in Lev 11–15 also reinforce the boundary between life and death. A state that is life-threatening and belongs to the power of death would be "impure."[54] However, death is not explicitly referred to in the system of Lev 11–15. The contact with the dead is only dealt with in Lev 10:4–5; 21:11; 22:4; Num 6:6–7:9; 9:6–11; 19:14; 31:19–20, 24. In fact, commentators bring these categories forward because Israel's God is the God of life, and these laws aim to seize control over the realm of death.[55]

This system that draws a line between life and death receives a theological foundation. The different bodily discharges, contact with the dead, and skin infections are situated in this system. However, this cannot clearly explain the eczema-like changes affecting skin, textiles, and houses, which, according to Lev 13–14, do not lead to death. The loss of sperm is polluting because it represents a loss of life. Yet, this does not explain why the discharge of semen during sexual intercourse is also polluting, since it serves potential fecunda-tion, the generation of new life. Furthermore, only the man loses his semen, so the woman does not necessarily become impure. With reference to Lev 17:10–14, according to which life is in the blood, it is reasoned that the wom-an's genital bleeding is polluting.[56] The argument that the human being comes into contact with the realm of death when blood leaves the body is only plau-sible at the outset. Actually, life is also in the blood that is shed when the body is wounded—yet in this case it is not polluting according to Lev 11–15.

---

53. See Irmtraud Fischer, "Donne nel Antico Testamento," in *Donne e Bibbia* (ed. Adriana Valerio; Storia ed esegesi: La Bibbia nella Storia 21, Bologna: Edizioni Dehoniane, 2006), 186–87: "This epoch is not only the most significant one for literary development but also a time of polarization: while the priestly laws, with the categories of pure and impure, were distancing women more and more from regular participation in the life of the cult, there was an evident movement of opposition that found its expression in the forma-tion of the women's books in the Bible" (my translation).

54. See Paschen, *Rein und Unrein*, 60–64, who speaks about the "impurity of death" (60, 63); Milgrom, *Leviticus 1–16*, 766–67, 1000–1004; L'Hour, *L'Impur et le Saint*, 532.

55. Milgrom, *Leviticus 1–16*, 767: "The loss of vaginal blood and semen, both contain-ing seed, meant the diminution of life and, if unchecked, destruction and death. And it was a process unalterably opposed by Israel's God, the source of its life."

56. See ibid.

When the system of border-crossing alone is used to explain this, it is impossible to understand why not all the bodily discharges in the Leviticus system are polluting. Discharges from the body such as urine, perspiration, and excrement are not considered polluting in this system. Gender, with respect to sexuality, evidently plays a decisive role. Tears, for example, cannot be seen in relation to procreation and so are thus less apt to symbolize social relationships. Blood is only polluting in the context of reproduction when put in relation to cultic unsuitability. It is never said that blood itself is impure; on the contrary, it is associated with the notion of purity. An example of this is found in Lev 12:4, which speaks of "blood of purification." On the one hand, according to Lev 12 and 15, cultic impurity is gender-specific; on the other hand, cultic impurity constructs gender and has an ongoing discursive impact on it.

5. Im/Purity or Un/Suitability for the Cult in Gender Perspective

The rereadings in the previous section have shown the ambivalences of the category un-/clean in the laws of purity pertaining to the perception of the genders. Can this overcome the misogynous body-hostile reception of the laws inside and outside of the biblical texts?

5.1. Rereading of the Categories in Gender Perspective

Should the present contribution bear a different title? Instead of " 'Pure' and 'Impure' as Gender-Relevant Categories," should it be entitled "Unsuitability with Regard to the Cult as a Gender-Relevant Category"? Which points were made here by giving the female body in Lev 11–15 (through Lev 12) and in the biblical texts in general more space?

In this essay, the female body has been dealt with first in accordance with the emphasis upon the female body within and beyond the Bible, unlike the male body in Lev 15. The fact that translations played a decisive role in the reception history—in the context of exegesis also—has been illustrated with the category "impure." Indeed, the transmission of the texts implies certain preliminary decisions. A revision of Hebrew dictionaries and translations of the Bible in the gender perspective is therefore necessary.[57]

---

57. See the translations of the Bible that are attentive to this question: *Bibel in gerechter Sprache* and *The Contemporary Torah*. On this subject, see Dorothea Erbele-Küster, "Ungerechte Texte und gerechte Sprache: Überlegungen zur Hermeneutik des Bibelübersetzens," in *Die Bibel—übersetzt in gerechte Sprache? Grundlagen einer neuen Übersetzung* (ed. Helga Kuhlmann; Gütersloh: Gütersloher Verlagshaus, 2005), 222–34.

5.2. Impurity as Exclusion from the Cult

According to the Hebrew Bible, women assumed various roles in the realm of the cult, and, among these, a general distinction can be made between a professional role and lay elements.[58] So, a text such as Lev 12, with its demand that the mother of the newborn child offer a sacrifice after the expiration of her time of purification, presupposes the general active ceremonial participation of women.

The "churching of the mother," customary until Vatican II, is led back on this text. However, this ritual can be understood in ways other than as a rite of purification for the mother after having given birth. Instead, it can be described in connection with the more recent appearance of new women's rituals as a ritual of thanksgiving for the birth.[59]

For Lev 11–15, the Hebrew term for "unclean" is a cultic one that describes the status of an object with regard to the cult and the sanctuary. What does the temporary cultic unfitness of women (and men) imply in terms of their participation in the cult? As has already become clear, cultic impurity in the reception history of the laws of purity has primarily a female face. The fact that the sexual discharge of the woman receives particular emphasis as a special case, in order to refuse access to the sanctuary to women, is still maintained today.[60] Thus, with the recurrent cultic impurity of women during their menstruation and as a result of birth, their exclusion from priestly service was

---

58. Phyllis A. Bird, "The Place of Women in the Israelite Cult," in *Ancient Israelite Religion: Essays in Honor of Frank Moore Cross* (ed. Patrick D. Miller Jr., Paul D. Hanson, and S. Dean McBride; Philadelphia: Fortress, 1987), 397–19; repr. in Phyllis A. Bird, *Missing Persons and Mistaken Identities: Women and Gender in Ancient Israel* (Minneapolis: Fortress, 1997), 81–102. Bird distinguishes between "women in cultic service" and "women as worshipers"; an analogous distinction is made by Hennie J. Marsman, *Women in Ugarit and Israel: Their Social and Religious Position in the Context of the Ancient Near East* (OtSt 49; Leiden: Brill, 2003; repr., Atlanta: Society of Biblical Literature, 2009), i.e., between "women as religious specialists" and "women as worshipers." On the situation of women according to literary texts, see Dorothea Erbele-Küster, "Der Dienst der Frauen am Eingang des Zeltheiligtums (Exodus 38:8): Kultisch-religiöse Verortungen von Frauen in Exodus und Leviticus," in *The Interpretation of Exodus: Studies in Honour of Cornelis Houtman* (ed. Riemer Roukema et al.; CBET 44; Leuven: Peeters, 2006), 265–81.

59. See Grietje Dresen, "The Better Blood: On Sacrifice and the Churching of New Mothers in the Roman Catholic Tradition," in De Troyer et al., *Wholly Woman—Holy Blood*, 143–64.

60. The leader of a Korean Presbyterian Church has recently argued, with reference to Lev 15, that women in "his" church are excluded from the office of preaching. On the reception history in the West of the laws of Lev 15 regarding women, see *Wholly Woman—Holy Blood*.

both implicitly and explicitly justified. Yet, on the one hand, the Hebrew Bible gives no reason for reserving the priesthood to men; on the other hand, the argument is far more differentiated.

The supposition that women were ritually impure due to the system of Lev 11–15 during the majority of their life is, however, refuted by several points: the menstrual cycle of women in ancient Israel was not as regular as that of women in modern industrialized countries, with high-protein diets. There was a greater number of pregnancies and the monthly bleedings thereafter began later—among other things, in connection with the period of breastfeeding. Finally, menopause began earlier. As the intertextual reflection also showed, the prescriptions in Leviticus had hardly any influence on the narrative traditions. So we must critically ask to which extent they shaped everyday life. Here their utopian programmatic character must be stressed.

Moreover, it is stated that, even during the time of their ritual impurity, women were not completely excluded from participation in the cult.[61] Nowhere in Leviticus, nor in the purity laws of the Hebrew Bible, is it said that women are excluded from the cult or that they cannot assume nonofficial functions. According to this argument, men could also be excluded from the cult, since they regularly become ritually impure as well, for example, due to the discharge of semen.[62]

According to Lev 15, the female body, like the male body, is subject to periods of impurity, that is, cultic abstinence. However, when put the other way around, this also means that the gendered body is related to the cult. Furthermore, in contradiction to reception history, the female body is associated with purity and cultic suitability. Recently in gender-studies this has been formulated with respect to the female body in programmatic titles on the subject: *Households and Holiness: The Religious Culture of Israelite Women*,[63] *Menstrual Purity*, and *Wholly Woman—Holy Blood*.[64] Thus, a text such as Lev 12 speaks about a woman's "blood of purification." The reintegration ritual described there—as has already been explained above—simultaneously presupposes the general active participation of women in the cult.

---

61. Cf. Marsman, *Women in Ugarit and Israel*, 543–44.

62. Cf. Kristin De Troyer, "Blood: A Threat to Holiness or toward (Another) Holiness?" in *Wholly Woman—Holy Blood*, 45–64; 64: "Moreover, menstrual blood is not the only item on the lists of things that render a person unclean. Male semen—once out of the body—is on the list too."

63. See Meyers, *Households and Holiness*.

64. See Kristin De Troyer et al., eds., *Wholly Woman—Holy Blood*.

5.3. Gender, Body, and Identity

The cult in the purity regulations of Lev 12 and 15 moves the human body, both male and female, into the spotlight. In the history of interpretation, however, it seems that the male body, once circumcised, is free from impurity henceforth and thus put into a right relationship with God. The short note on circumcision in Lev 12 does not say who carries out the cutting. Given that this must be done on the eighth day, in Lev 12:3, following the seven days of being a danger to the cult, circumcision is associated with cultic suitability. Amidst the history of misogynous reception, the fact that the male body repeatedly becomes unsuitable for the cult until evening due to the discharge of semen has been neglected.

With respect to the relationship between gender and cult, another difference appears: the regulations say nothing about a specific ritual practiced by women after birth, for instance, the rites of washing and rubbing with salt evoked in Ezek 16:4. For girls or women, there is no ritual for the establishment of their sexual and religious identity analogous to the circumcision of the male descendants in the Hebrew Bible. However, in the reception of these laws, precisely in the Diaspora, the regular access of Jewish women to the mikveh after menstruation became a sign of their Jewish identity:[65] "To practice forms of menstrual abstention … allowed women to engage in the continuous observance of Torah, with and in their bodies."[66] Both rituals, that is, circumcision as well as the observance of the prescriptions of purity, repetitively construct gender and body. In the male body, the relationship with God, and relation to the cult, is engraved by a single act; in contrast, this occurs in the female body through the repeated observance of the laws of purity.

In Lev 12, the impurity with reference to the body of the woman seems to be constructed without any direct implication of the physiological processes. Indeed, on the contrary, the concept of impurity serves rather to construct the body and is constitutive for the perception of gender. Only the condition of cultic abstention of the female body is marked with a particular term and used in texts outside of the laws of purity in a metaphorical and pejorative sense.

---

65. See Rachel Wasserfall, "Menstruation and Identity: The Meaning of *Niddah* for Moroccan Women Immigrants to Israel," in *The People of the Body: Jews and Judaism from an Embodied Perspective* (ed. Howard Eilberg-Schwartz; New York: State University of New York Press, 1992), 309–27. Alongside this, there are other important rituals for women, for example the Bat Mitzvah. See also Katie Zezima, "A Place for a Ritual Cleansing of All Jews," *New York Times, Religion Journal* (July 3, 2004): 1–2.

66. Charlotte E. Fonrobert, *Menstrual Purity: Rabbinic and Christian Reconstructions of Biblical Gender* (Stanford, Calif.: Stanford University Press, 2000), 214.

This tendency, founded on the biblical texts, to mark the cultic impurity of the female body in particular is strengthened in reception history.

5.4. A CULTIC BODY BEYOND A CULT OF THE BODY[67]

However, as the texts relate the body to the cult, they describe cultic bodies beyond a cult of the body. The picture of the body in Lev 15 demonstrates gender differences and similarities. The texts in Leviticus present a world in which the gendered body, both male and female, is related to the cult and so to the holiness of God.

---

67. See Dorothea Erbele-Küster, *Body and Gender: Studies on Leviticus 12 and 15* (LHB/OTS; New York: Continuum, forthcoming).

Women between Subordination and Independence: Reflections on Gender-Related Legal Texts of the Torah

Karin Finsterbusch
Universität Koblenz-Landau

In recent years, researchers have given more attention to the gender-related legal texts in the Torah.[1] The many studies that have resulted reflect the large diversity of topics in these texts.[2] In this essay, two questions will guide the study of topics concerning gender in the legal texts of the Torah. The first question will consider statements *regarding* women (§1). Which statements are found in the legal texts, and how should these be assessed? After a short review of the findings (§1.1), focus will be placed on those texts dealing with

---

1. For very helpful comments on earlier versions of this manuscript, I would like to thank Udo Benzenhöfer, Irmtraud Fischer, Tal Ilan, and Norbert Lohfink.

2. See, for example, Phyllis Bird, "Images of Women in the Old Testament," in *Religion and Sexism: Images of Women in the Jewish and Christian Tradition* (ed. Rosemary Radford Ruether; New York: Simon & Schuster, 1974), 48ff.; Naomi A. Steinberg, "'Adam's and Eve's Daughters Are Many': Gender Roles in Ancient Israelite Society" (Ph.D. diss., Columbia University, 1984), 240ff.; Tikva Frymer-Kensky, "Gender and Law: An Introduction," in *Gender and Law in the Hebrew Bible and the Ancient Near East* (ed. Victor H. Matthews, Bernard M. Levinson, and Tikva Frymer-Kensky; JSOTSup 262; Sheffield: Sheffield Academic Press, 1998), 17–24; Raymond Westbrook, *Property and the Family in Biblical Law* (JSOTSup 113; Sheffield: JSOT Press, 1991); Mayer I. Gruber, "Women in the Cult according to the Priestly Code," in *The Motherhood of God and Other Studies* (ed. Mayer I. Gruber; Atlanta: Scholars Press, 1992), 49–68; Carolyn Pressler, *The View of Women Found in the Deuteronomic Family Laws* (Berlin: de Gruyter, 1993); Elke Seifert, *Tochter und Vater im Alten Testament: Eine ideologiekritische Untersuchung zur Verfügungsgewalt von Vätern über ihre Töchter* (Neukirchen-Vluyn: Neukirchener, 1997), 195–234; Rhonda J. Burnette-Bletsch, "My Bone and My Flesh: The Agrarian Family in Biblical Law" (Ph.D. diss., Duke University, 1998); Cheryl B. Anderson, *Women, Ideology, and Violence: Critical Theory and the Construction of Gender in the Book of the Covenant and the Deuteronomic Law* (London: T&T Clark, 2004).

the manumission of both men and women slaves (§1.2.), because in my view it has become evident that there are hitherto underestimated variations in the legal texts with the regard to the conception of women's roles. The second focal question, which has not yet been sufficiently dealt with in the feminist theological context, is of overriding importance, since it asks whether the authors of the legal texts were also referring to women in their use of the common address "you" (singular and plural: אתה/אתם), that is, whether women were *legal subjects* (§2). Here, for pragmatic reasons, I shall consider only the three major law codes of the Torah: the Covenant Code in Exod 20:20–23:33 (§2.1), the Deuteronomic Code in Deut 12–26 (§2.2) and the Holiness Code in Lev 17–26 (§2.3). As far as methodology is concerned, it should be noted that, despite their editorial revisions, these collections of laws may be regarded as meaningful literary units rather than independent fragments. Each represents a particular "world" based on different specific conditions.[3] This understanding is essential in approaching the topic. Indeed, these different "worlds" considerably influenced the roles women played, or should have played, in each particular circumstance. Furthermore, let us insist here on the fact that these roles were not necessarily identical to those that women in fact did play.[4] An important consequence of this is the great variation in women's roles in the law codes (§3).

---

3. Consequently, the statements relating to gender in the different codes should be studied independently (see below, §1.2 and §2.). Otherwise the variations in respect to women's roles are obscured, unlike the thesis advanced by Anderson in *Women, Ideology, and Violence*. Likewise, findings relating to legal and nonlegal texts should first be presented separately; see Bird, "Images of Women in the Old Testament," 47–48.

4. See also Carolyn Pressler, "Wives and Daughters, Bond and Free: Views of Women in the Slave Laws of Exodus 21,2–11," in Matthews, Levinson, and Frymer-Kensky, *Gender and Law*, 148. For a reconstruction of the daily life of women in ancient Israel, see, e.g., Carol L. Meyers, *Discovering Eve: Ancient Israelite Women in Context* (New York: Oxford University Press, 1988); eadem, "Everyday Life: Women in the Period of the Hebrew Bible," in *The Women's Bible Commentary* (ed. Carol A. Newsom and Sharon H. Ringe; Louisville: Westminster John Knox, 1992), 244–51; Nahman Avigad, "The Contribution of Hebrew Seals to an Understanding of Israelite Religion and Society," in *Ancient Israelite Religion: Essays in Honour of Frank Moore Cross* (ed. Patrick D. Miller Jr. et al.; Philadelphia: Fortress, 1987), 195–208; Tamara C. Eskenazi, "Out from the Shadows: Biblical Women in the Postexilic Erea," *JSOT* 54 (1992): 25–43; Bernhard Lang, "Women's Work, Household and Property in Two Mediterranean Societies," *VT* 54 (2004): 188–207.

1. Statements in the Legal Texts of the Torah Regarding Women

1.1. Women as Objects: Review of the Primary Gender-Related Legal Texts

Women mainly appear as objects in the legal texts of the Torah; that is, the laws make stipulations *regarding them*. The major texts are briefly presented in the following passages.

Certain texts dealing with *slavery* are gender-related. Such texts are found in the Book of the Covenant, in the Deuteronomic Code, and in the Holiness Code. The laws on the liberation of slaves (Exod 21:2–11; Deut 15:12–18; Lev 25:39–55) will be considered separately (in §1.2). Here Lev 19:20–22 is pertinent. These verses deal with the case of sexual relations of a man with an engaged female slave. The relationship is described exclusively from the man's standpoint and presupposes an act of rape. It is to be noted that the case does not result in the death penalty, which usually applies in the event of adultery. Moreover, the cultic consequences of the offense are determined. According to 19:22, the man must elicit "forgiveness" by presenting a guilt offering. From today's viewpoint, as Erhard Gerstenberger has rightly emphasized, this way of handling the violation of an engaged woman is intolerable.[5]

In the *legislation on the cult*, certain points particularly discriminate against women. The prescriptions concerning what is "clean and unclean" lead to women being excluded from the cultic community more often than men. Girls and women are valued, in monetary terms, less than boys and men (e.g., Lev 27:3–4). The genealogical succession allows only men to become priests. However, there were women among cultic personnel: according to Exod 38:8, women could serve as prophets at the sanctuary.[6]

The findings relating to the *inheritance right* are complex. Deuteronomy 21:15–17 indicates that only sons may receive the family inheritance. The father must pass the greatest part of the inheritance on to his firstborn son. An inheritance right for widows is not mentioned in any biblical legal text, although there is historical proof of such a right from the Persian period.[7]

---

5. Erhart S. Gerstenberger, *Das dritte Buch Mose: Leviticus* (ATD 6; Göttingen: Vandenhoeck & Ruprecht, 1993), 250.

6. On this, see below, §2.3.

7. This is proven by documents in the archives of the Jewish community of Elephantine; see Rainer Kessler, "Die Sklavin als Ehefrau: Zur Stellung der ʾāmāh," *VT* 52 (2002): 506. In some biblical and postbiblical narratives, it is assumed that childless widows inherit. Such was the case with Naomi and Judith, for example; on this subject, see Willy Schottroff, "Die Armut der Witwen," in *Schuld und Schulden: Biblische Traditionen in gegenwärtigen Kon-*

An inheritance right for daughters is only introduced by the "case" of the five daughters of Zelophehad (Num 27:1–11). According to Num 27:7–8, if a man does not have a son, his daughter may receive the inheritance. Consequently, in such circumstances, the daughter has full right of disposal over the inheritance. Should a man die childless, the inheritance shall be given to his closest male relative. In Num 36:1–12, a form of addition is introduced that modifies what was said in the case of Zelophehad's daughters in Num 27: the daughters can receive the inheritance only if they marry men from their clan. According to 27:6–7, this is intended to ensure that the heritage remains in the clan. Indeed, the daughters of Zelophehad do marry their cousins, as 27:11 states. Accordingly, the inheritance really is transmitted to the descendants of the closest male relative.

The legal texts also speak about *sexual violence* against women. The ruling of the Holiness Code concerning the engaged female slave has already been mentioned. Exodus 22:15–16 indicates that the man who seduces an unengaged virgin must pay the bride's dowry to her father as compensation and is obliged to marry her. However, the father has the right not to give his daughter's hand in marriage to the man. Exodus 22:15–16 is not an incidental text among the laws in the Book of the Covenant that concern damage requiring compensation. The Deuteronomic Code also presents a similar case, which is handled from the perspective of men's rights to compensation.[8] According to Deut 22:28–29, the man who rapes an unengaged virgin must pay her father fifty shekels of silver. In addition, he must marry the girl and is not allowed to divorce her for as long as he lives. This law was in all probability conceived by its authors as "protection"; it was meant, on the one hand, to assure that the raped girl would not remain unmarried in the house of her parents; on the other hand, the prohibition to divorce was to guarantee perpetual social security.[9] Deuteronomy 22:23–27 deals with the case of the violation of an

---

flikten (ed. Marlene Crüsemann and Willy Schottroff; Munich: Kaiser, 1992), 78ff.; Frank S. Frick, "Widows in the Hebrew Bible: A Transactional Approach," in *A Feminist Companion to Exodus to Deuteronomy* (ed. Athalya Brenner; FCB 6; Sheffield: Sheffield Academic Press, 1994), 148ff.; Christa Schäfer-Lichtenberger, "Beobachtungen zur Rechtsstellung der Frau in der alttestamentlichen Überlieferung," *WuD* 24 (1997): 111; Irmtraud Fischer, *Rut* (HTKAT; Freiburg im Breisgau: Herder, 2001), 56–57, 236.

8. See Irmtraud Fischer, *Die Erzeltern Israels: Feministisch-theologische Studien zu Genesis 12–26* (BZAW 222; Berlin: de Gruyter, 1994), 85–86; Seifert, *Tochter und Vater*, 197ff.

9. Cf. Pressler, *The View of Women*, 41; Eckart Otto, *Gottes Recht als Menschenrecht: Rechts- und literaturhistorische Studien zum Deuteronomium* (Wiesbaden: Harrassowitz, 2002), 250. It is questionable whether women could actually *experience* such a law as protection, against Seifert, *Tochter und Vater*, 200, 211.

engaged virgin. However, the violation is only recognized "in the open country" because in the city she could call for help and be heard (22:24). Clearly,
this is a dubious argument.

The implication of the model of the patriarchal family represented in the
law codes of the Torah includes the fact that a woman's *sexuality* was *controlled*
by the man to whom she was subordinated, typically either her father or her
husband. This is shown by Exod 22:15–16, a text mentioned earlier: if a man
lies with an unengaged girl, he must pay the bride's dowry to her father as
compensation; if a husband discovers that his bride is not a virgin, she shall
be stoned (Deut 22:13–21).[10] The father is responsible for his daughter's virginity: it is a part of the "honor" of his house and a condition of a marriage
appropriate to her standing. The husband has an exclusive right to his wife's
sexuality; however, this right does not apply the other way around.

Let us note yet another viewpoint in the context of the quoted texts: these
texts do not give a young woman the possibility of choosing her husband; he
should be *chosen* for her by the male head of the family (usually the father).[11]
Women's approval is of no importance to the author. This may imply, for
example, that, on the basis of Deut 22:29 a raped woman is bound for life to a
man she despises.[12]

When a woman gets married, she must leave her parents' house and
move in with her husband. On account of the *patrilocal marriage*, the woman
ceases to be a work force in the house of her parents, in particular in order
to help them in their old age. The bride's dowry that the husband must pay to
his wife's father (Exod 22:25) should be understood as compensation for the
woman's family.[13]

Several legal texts take *polygyny* into consideration. This means that a
man may be married to several women, but a woman can be married to only
one man. The demand for women's exclusive marital faithfulness probably has
something to do primarily with paternity.[14] *Adultery* is punished by the death

---

10. Interestingly, proof must be provided by a girl's parents (both father and mother!):
"The case of the slandered bride and the case of the rebellious son (Deut 21; 22) both
present circumstances in which children endanger their parents' honor and wellbeing, the
daughter by lack of chastity and the son by drunkenness and profligacy" (Tikva Frymer-
Kensky, "Virginity in the Bible," in Matthews, Levinson, and Frymer-Kensky, *Gender and
Law*, 95).

11. There is an exception to this in Num 36:6.

12. See Fischer, *Die Erzeltern Israels*, 86; Seifert, *Tochter und Vater*, 198, 200.

13. See Fischer, *Die Erzeltern Israels*, 81.

14. This probably explains why a female prisoner of war, destined to be married, must
live in isolation for a month (Deut 21:10–14), see Harold C. Washington, " 'Lest He Die in
the Battle and Another Man Take Her': Violence and the Construction of Gender in the

penalty in the case of a man who destroys another's marriage and of a woman who breaks up her own marriage.[15] In unproven cases, or should suspicion be hardened by a divine ordeal (Num 5:11–31), the husband may rightfully let himself be divorced from his wife, as Eckart Otto has shown.[16] Numbers 5:11–31 should at least briefly be considered. If a man is seized by the "spirit of jealousy" (5:14) and suspects that his wife is guilty of adultery, he can oblige her to undergo a divine ordeal. This kind of ordeal, known not only in Israel,[17] was clearly a magical ritual. The frightening consequences of the legal text in Num 5:11–31 admit the possibility for jealous husbands to act in accordance with their feelings while women are left defenseless in the face of their husband's jealousy.

A married couple can be divorced. According to Deut 24:1–4, *men* may ask for a divorce, but the legal texts of the Bible do not grant free women this right. Hence, the biblical legislation once again contradicts "reality": from a historical perspective, since the Persian period there is proof that free women have had such a right.[18] According to Exod 21:11, the woman who is a slave because of indebtedness has a kind of right to divorce because, if her husband neglects his marital obligations, she can leave the house as a free woman. A woman who receives a certificate of divorce can remarry.

If a man dies without leaving behind a son, Deut 25:5–10 indicates that his brother should marry his widow.[19] The firstborn son of this union counts as the son (and hence the heir) of the deceased. Of course, the brother of the deceased cannot be forced into the *levirate marriage*. However, according to Deut 25:5–10, the levirate marriage is a right of the childless widow that she can take to court. If this right is refused, the widow can publicly denounce

---

Laws of Deuteronomy 20–22," in Matthews, Levinson, and Frymer-Kensky, *Gender and Law*, 206; Anderson, *Women, Ideology, and Violence*, 47-48.

15. Lev 20:18; Deut 22:20–21, 22–23. See also the commandments of the Decalogue in Exod 20:14 and Deut 5:18.

16. See Otto, *Gottes Recht als Menschenrecht*, 261–62; also idem, *Theologische Ethik des Alten Testaments* (Stuttgart: Kohlhammer, 1994), 39ff.

17. See Thomas Staubli, *Die Bücher Levitikus, Numeri* (Neuer Stuttgarter Kommentar: Altes Testament 3; Stuttgart: Katholisches Bibelwerk, 1996), 221–23; Jaeyoung Jeon, "Two Laws in the Sotah Passage (Num. v 11–31)," *VT* 57 (1997): 192–93.

18. This proof appears in documents in the archives of the Jewish community of Elephantine; see Bezalel Porten and Ada Yardeni, *Contracts* (vol. 2 of *Textbook of Aramaic Documents from Ancient Egypt*; Winona Lake, Ind.: Eisenbrauns, 1989), 30–33; Eskenazi, "Out from the Shadows," 28ff.

19. The levirate is also mentioned in Gen 38 and Ruth 4; on the significant differences between the three biblical sources and for a discussion about the meaning and the intention of the Levirate, see especially Westbrook, *Property and the Family*, 69ff.

her brother-in-law. Being a widow, according to legal texts, is a grim fate for a woman. This view is not surprising, since the aforementioned law of inheritance does not consider widows. The request to care for or not to oppress (Exod 22:21; Deut 14:29; 24:17, 19) *personae miserabiles*, including widows, is often reiterated. Here I wish to add only that, according to Lev 21, the laws concerning marriage are stricter for priests: Lev 21:14 indicates that a high priest cannot marry a widow, and Lev 21:7 states that a priest cannot marry a divorced woman.

Just how difficult it is to appreciate the outlined findings is shown by the various endeavors of exegetical literature.[20] I would like to stress only two points. First, the topics involving women are selective in the legal texts of the Torah. As already noted, the biblical legal texts say nothing about the inheritance right of widows, which is historically documented since the Persian period. Let us consider two other significant examples. In the documents of the ancient Near East, the most frequently evoked case of enslavement because of indebtedness, that is, the enslavement of a daughter as a work force, is not explicitly dealt with. Likewise, in the narratives of the Hebrew Bible, the well-documented case of marriage with a concubine (פילגש) is not mentioned.

---

20. Steinberg ("Adam's and Eve's Daughters," 250, 262–63) and Burnette-Bletsch ("My Bone and My Flesh," 270–71, 343–46, 362) insist in their studies on the balanced distribution of roles between men and women in the legal texts of the Bible. This appreciation is excessively one-sided; see Anderson, *Women, Ideology, and Violence*, 49: "For example, both Steinberg and Burnette-Bletsch point to parity in the laws concerning parental authority (Deut 21:18–21) and procreation (Deut 24:5) to substantiate their conclusions. Therefore, these two scholars find male and female roles to be interdependent and symmetrical. The existence of such inclusive laws, however, should not preclude recognition that exclusive laws also exist. Such exclusive laws mandate that a women could be killed for the lack of virginity (Deut 22:13–21) when the absence of virginity is not an offense for a male." The family laws are considered from a juridical historical point of view by Eckart Otto, "False Weights in the Scales of Biblical Justice? Different Views of Women from Patriarchal Hierarchy to Religious Equality in the Book of Deuteronomy," in Matthews, Levinson, and Frymer-Kensky, *Gender and Law*, 140, with the following result: "The family laws in the Book of Deuteronomy had a progressive and protective attitude to the legal status of women. They were deeply concerned with the restriction of male predominance. This did by no means imply that these provisions really overcame the patrilineal and patriarchal pattern of Judean society, but they were intended to install women even in matters of family law as legal subjects vested with rights and titles of their own that were not derived from rights and decisions of men." It must, however, be critically observed as Frymer-Kensky does: "I wonder, however, whether Deuteronomy's restriction of the dominance of one male (husband or father) over a woman really restricts male predominance when power is vested in a council of males or in a patriarchal state" ("Gender and Law," 22); see also the critique by Fischer, *Die Erzeltern Israels*, 86 n. 53.

This leads us to ask how the biblical law collections should be understood. Are they legal manuals containing common legislation intended to guide the determination of rights,[21] so that the authors did not need to discuss "customary law"? Do the law codes really validate rights or present merely scholarly reflections?[22] Did the authors want to insist less on "justice" and rather make use of the collections to construct identity?[23] In my opinion, as shall now be shown, at least the Deuteronomic Code and Holiness Code certainly had the intention of constructing identity.

Second, above all the family laws show that, in respect to women's roles in the families organized on the basis of the patriarchal model, despite some differences in detail, there is a "basic consensus" that is also accepted by the authors of other law collections of the ancient Near East. As such, the laws support the traditional family structures in such a way that the interests of the families are essentially identified with those of the male heads.[24] Indeed, it is possible to recognize attempts to protect the dependent family members (for example, by the penalties for rape). However, the perspectives of women are not taken into consideration here, their status of dependency is not questioned, and there is no reflection on the highly decisive issue of their physical and psychic integrity. Without undermining this "basic consensus," there are parts of the legal texts of the Torah that reveal quite different positions with respect to women's roles.

1.2. Women as Slaves in the Mirror of the Manumission Laws of the Torah

This section will deal in particular with the laws on the manumission of male and female salves (Exod 21:2–11; Deut 15:12–18; Lev 25:39–55). As texts such as Jer 34:8–22 and Neh 5:1–5 show, slavery was not an exception in Israel before and after the exile. Hence, it is not surprising to find several laws dealing with this subject in the law codes of the Torah. Interestingly, their state-

---

21. This is suggested in reference to the Book of the Covenant by Ludger Schwienhorst-Schönberger, *Das Bundesbuch (Ex 20,22–23,33): Studien zu seiner Entstehung und Theologie* (BZAW 188; Berlin: de Gruyter, 1990), 406–7.

22. See Norbert Lohfink, "Fortschreibung? Zur Technik von Rechtsrevisionen im deuteronomistischen Bereich, erörtert an Deuteronomium 12, Ex 21,2–11 und Dtn 15,12–18," in *Studien zum Deuteronomium und zur deuteronomistischen Literatur IV* (ed. Norbert Lohfink; SBAB 31; Stuttgart: Katholisches Bibelwerk, 2000), 180 and 188–89.

23. See Anderson, *Women, Ideology, and Violence*, 11ff.

24. See also Bird, "Images of Women in the Old Testament," 51; Pressler, *The View of Women*, 114.

ments about women as slaves differ. Now, the intention is not only to show the differences in relation to women's roles but also to investigate the reasons behind them. Let us first of all look at the manumission law in the Book of the Covenant, Exod 21:2–11.[25]

2 When you buy a male Hebrew slave, he shall serve six years,
but in the seventh he shall go out a free person, without debt.
3 If he comes in single, he shall go out single;
if he comes in married, then his wife shall go out with him.
4 If his master gives him a wife and she bears him sons or daughters,
the wife and her children shall be the master's, and he shall go out alone.
5 But if the slave declares, "I love my master, my wife, and my children;
I will not go out a free person,"
6 then his master shall bring him before God.
He shall be brought to the door or the doorpost;
and his master shall pierce his ear with an awl;
and he shall serve him for life.
7 When a man sells his daughter as a slave,
she shall not go out as the male slaves do.
8 If she does not please her master,
who designated her for himself,[26]
then he shall let her be redeemed;
he shall have no right to sell her to a foreign people,
since he has dealt unfairly with her.
9 If he designates her for his son,
he shall deal with her as with a daughter.
10 If he takes another wife to himself,
he shall not diminish the food, clothing, or marital rights of the first wife.
11 And if he does not do these three things for her,
she shall go out without debt, without payment of money.

The law opens with the perspective of the buyer: if an Israelite buys another Israelite as a "(male) slave" (עֶבֶד), the latter shall be set free in the seventh year without a debt. The accent in Exod 21:2–6 is on the man who is a slave because

---

25. Exod 21:2–11 is the oldest recognizable biblical manumission law; see especially Bernard M. Levinson, "The Birth of the Lemma: The Restrictive Reinterpretation of the Covenant Code's Manumission Law by the Holiness Code (Leviticus 25,44–46)," *JBL* 124 (2005): 617–39.

26. With Qere לוֹ (against Ketiv לֹא); see also Martin Buber and Franz Rosenzweig, *Die Schrift: Bd. 1: Die fünf Bücher der Weisung* (Darmstadt: Wissenschaftliche Buchgesellschaft, 1987), s.v.; Etan Levine, "On Exodus 21,10 'Onah and Biblical Marriage," *ZABR* 5 (1999): 137; Bernard S. Jackson, *Wisdom-Laws: A Study of the Mishpatim of Exodus 21:1–22:16* (Oxford: Oxford University Press, 2006), 80.

of indebtedness; women are considered principally as wives of the עבד. If this man is married, he shall be bought, as 21:3b says (in all cases?), along with his wife and probably their children, should they have any. The family clearly lives on the buyer's property, and the wife and probably the children as well must be set free with the slave in the seventh year. Verse 4 deals with the case of an unmarried slave to whom the buyer assigns a woman. This supposes, as Karen Engelken has rightly observed, that the Israelite may possess several male and female slaves.[27] In this case, the Israelite can evidently not only dispose of the labor of his male and female slaves but also freely determine their relationships. To this extent, men and women are totally dependent.

The female slave temporarily designated by the buyer for sexual relations[28] is along with her children the property of the master. The text does not say whether this concerns a Hebrew or non-Hebrew female slave. In my opinion, there are no reasons whatsoever to preclude the possibility of a Hebrew slave.[29] Hence, 21:2–6 are not to be understood as inclusive.[30] That is to say, in light of these precepts, the Hebrew female slave cannot be freed in the seventh year as the Hebrew male slave can.[31]

In Exod 21:7–11, the focus shifts. This passage deals with the case of a daughter sold by her father as a "(female) slave" (אמה) with the option to become the wife[32] of either the buyer or his son. First, we must consider the

---

27. Karen Engelken, *Frauen im Alten Israel: Eine begriffsgeschichtliche und sozialrechtliche Studie zur Stellung der Frau im Alten Testament* (BWANT 130; Stuttgart: Kohlhammer, 1990), 150.

28. It is not question of a marriage; on this, see Fischer, *Die Erzeltern Israels*, 78–80, 102.

29. See also Frank Crüsemann, *Die Tora: Theologie und Sozialgeschichte des alttestamentlichen Gesetzes* (2nd ed.; Gütersloh: Kaiser/Gütersloher Verlagshaus, 1997), 186–87. Differently, John Van Seters, "The Law of the Hebrew Slave," *ZAW* 108 (1996): 541; Jackson, *Wisdom-Laws*, 89.

30. Lohfink ("Fortschreibung," 189) and Otto ("False Weights," 142), for example, argue in favor of a (women-)inclusive understanding of 21:2–6. Pressler ("Wives and Daughters," 167) thinks that 21:2–6 apply to "some bondswomen": "We would expect a widow, abandoned wife or the like who sells herself as a general household slave to be treated like the male slaves, and released."

31. See also Engelken, *Frauen im Alten Israel*, 150; Christoph Dohmen, *Exodus 19–40* (HTKAT; Freiburg im Breisgau: Herder, 2004), 161.

32. With Kessler, "Die Sklavin als Ehefrau." Generally commentaries erroneously assume that the slave could only be a secondary wife or a concubine; see, e.g., Pressler, "Wives and Daughters," 163; Raymond Westbrook, "The Female Slave," in Matthews, Levinson, and Frymer-Kensky, *Gender and Law*, 218–19 and 236–37; David L. Baker, "Concubines and Conjugal Rights: ענה in Exodus 21:10 and Deuteronomy 21:14," *ZABR* 13 (2007): 89.

extreme implications (at least from today's point of view) of this case for the daughter. Her sexuality can quite legally be bought and sold; it may be traded as a "commercial product." Throughout her entire life, the sold daughter has no right to dispose of even her most personal affairs.

Now, it is highly instructive to view which fact in relation to the status of the sold daughter is of the greatest interest to the author. According to 21:10, it is not permitted with regard to a slave who has become a wife to reduce the food, clothing, or sexual relations (עונה)[33] if another wife is taken. The last point is in particular striking—it is found neither in any other law of the Bible nor in the ancient Near East.[34] In this context, Christoph Dohmen has convincingly shown that the sexual relations still give the female slave the chance to become a mother.[35] Thus, this law takes the status of a woman (free or slave) as a mother into account, a fact that, as many biblical narratives clearly show, had great importance in the society of ancient Israel.

The law concerning the manumission of male and female slaves in the Deuteronomic Law, comparable to that in the Book of the Covenant, says the following (Deut 15:12–18):

[12] If a member of your community [אח! literally, "if your brother/sister"],
whether a Hebrew man or a Hebrew woman, is sold to you
and works for you six years,
in the seventh year you shall set that person free.
[13] And when you send a male slave out from you a free person,
you shall not send him out empty-handed.
[14] Provide liberally out of your flock,
your threshing floor, and your wine press,
  thus giving to him some of the bounty with which YHWH your God has
    blessed you.
[15] Remember that you were a slave in the land of Egypt,
and YHWH your God redeemed you;
for this reason I lay this command upon you today.
[16] But if he says to you, "I will not go out from you,"
because he loves you and your household, since he is well off with you,
[17] then you shall take an awl and thrust it through his earlobe into the door,
and he shall be your slave forever.
You shall do the same with regard to your female slave.
[18] Do not consider it a hardship when you send them out from you free
    persons,

---

33. For this interpretation of עונה, see in particular Levine, "On Exodus 21,10," 150.
34. Ibid., 137–38.
35. Dohmen, Exodus 19–40, 162, with reference to Ina Willi-Plein.

because for six years they have given you services worth the wages of hired
    laborers,
and YHWH your God will bless you in all that you do.

In 15:12 and 17, the perspective of the Hebrew female slave is clearly presented. This needs explanation, because the Deuteronomic social precepts relating to the את[36] normally do not explicitly mention the perspective of women. Although I cannot give detailed reasons here, I do not base my reasoning on the idea that the double reference to the female slave is in 15:12 and 17 a later addition.[37] Likewise, I find the conclusion drawn, for example, by Phyllis Bird to be unconvincing, in that in laws referring to both men and women, the authors of the legal texts explicitly mention women.[38] In all probability, the consideration of both sexes in Deut 15:12–18 derives from the following reason: the author wanted to make it unmistakably clear, in delineation of the law in the Book of the Covenant, that in the case of slavery for indebtedness, the same rights apply to both sexes, that is, the same obligations of the "you" in relation to indebted male and female slaves.[39] This also implies that, according to the Deuteronomic legislation, the labor of a woman may be sold but not, as in the Book of the Covenant, her sexuality.

The emphasis with regard to slavery, which is so different from that of the Book of the Covenant, especially concerning the status of the female slave, is

---

36. This noun is usually translated by the undifferentiated word "brother." However, as Deut 15:12 indicates, את can signify brother and/or sister; see also Jer 34:14–16. Actually, the signification of this noun must be determined independently according to each law. On this question, see also Irmtraud Fischer, "Zwischen Kahlschlag, Durchforstung und neuer Pflanzung: Zu einigen Aspekten Feministischer Exegese und ihrer Relevanz für eine Theologie des Alten Testaments," in *Theologie und Exegese des Alten Testaments/der Hebräischen Bibel: Zwischenbilanz und Zukunftsperspektiven* (ed. Bernd Janowski; SBS 200; Stuttgart: Katholisches Bibelwerk, 2005), 52.

37. With Lohfink, "Fortschreibung," 183, 190; against Innocenzo Cardellini, *Die biblischen "Sklaven"-Gesetze im Lichte des keilschriftlichen Sklavenrechts: Ein Beitrag zur Tradition, Überlieferung und Redaktion der alttestamentlichen Rechtstexte* (BBB 55; Königstein/Ts: Hanstein, 1981), 275, 368–69; Eleonore Reuter, *Kultzentralisation: Entstehung und Theologie von Dtn 12* (Frankfurt am Main: Hain, 1993), 147–48.

38. Phyllis Bird, "Translating Sexist Language as a Theological and Cultural Problem," *USQR* 42 (1988): 92–93; similarly Schäfer-Lichtenberger, "Beobachtungen zur Rechtsstellung der Frau," 103. Skepticism over Bird's thesis is also expressed by Georg Braulik, "Durften auch Frauen in Israel opfern? Beobachtungen zur Sinn- und Festgestalt des Opfers im Deuteronomium," in *Studien zum Deuteronomium und seiner Nachgeschichte* (ed. Georg Braulik; SBAB 33; Stuttgart: Katholisches Bibelwerk, 2001), 85–86 n. 90.

39. See also Tikva Frymer-Kensky, "Deuteronomy," in *The Women's Bible Commentary* (ed. Carol A. Newsom and Sharon H. Ringe; Louisville: Westminster John Knox, 1992), 54.

tied to the Deuteronomic conception of society. This conception represents the ideal of a society whose members live together (as far as possible) freely and without poverty. The Deuteronomic laws relating to impoverished free families of farmers are intended to limit the extent of their indebtedness.[40] The final stage in the process of impoverishment is that of enslavement because of indebtedness. In this respect, Deut 15:12–18 clearly instructs the "you" to make a new life in freedom possible for the members of these families (men and women) by giving them start-up capital at the end of their time as slaves (15:18). A decisive role is played, in this context, by the theology of the exodus. According to 15:15, the condition of slavery belongs irrevocably to the past, since YHWH himself freed the "you" from slavery in Egypt. The "you" refers, as it is to be demonstrated (§2.2), to both men and women. Given this, in Deuteronomy's conception of the world slavery can only be a temporary condition for both Hebrew men and women. The permanent state of slavery is permitted in 15:16 to only a certain extent and as an exception.

In the Holiness Code, the legislative text of interest is set in the context of the prescription for the year of jubilee, in Lev 25. Here, merely an extract is quoted:

> [39] If any who are dependent on you become [literally, "if your brother become"] so impoverished that they sell themselves to you,
> you shall not make them serve as slaves.
> [40] They shall remain with you as hired or bound laborers.
> They shall serve with you until the year of the jubilee.
> [41] Then they and their children with them shall be free from your authority;
> they shall go back to their own family and return to their ancestral property.
> [42] For they are my servants (the children of Israel),
> whom I brought out of the land of Egypt;
> they shall not be sold as slaves are sold.
> [43] You shall not rule over them with harshness
> but shall fear your God.
> [44] As for the male and female slaves whom you may have,
> it is from the nations around you
> that you may acquire male and female slaves.
> [45] You may also acquire them from among the aliens residing with you,
> and from their families that are with you, who have been born in your land,

---

40. The poor in the Deuteronomic system do not include orphans, widows, foreigners, and Levitical families, as shown by Norbert Lohfink, "Das deuteronomische Gesetz in der Endgestalt: Entwurf einer Gesellschaft ohne marginale Gruppen," in *Studien zum Deuteronomium und zur deuteronomistischen Literatur III* (ed. Norbert Lohfink; SBAB 20; Stuttgart: Katholisches Bibelwerk, 1995), 205–18.

and they may be your property.
[46] You may keep them as a possession for your children after you, to inherit
as property.
Forever—them—may you make serve as slaves,
but as for your fellow Israelites, no one shall rule over the other with harshness.

This law is based on the case of an impoverished male Hebrew farmer who
has been obliged to leave his property and his clan in order to sell himself to
a wealthy Israelite. Verse 40 stipulates that he is not to be treated like a slave
but rather like an employee or bound laborer. This is a significant initial step
toward the abolition of slavery in general and its transformation into salaried
employment.[41] Verse 41 establishes norms for the case of a farmer who either
has a family or founds one during his "time of service," which can last up to
forty-nine years. Accordingly, his children and almost certainly also his wife
(who is not mentioned)[42] are to be liberated with him in the Year of Jubilee.

These determinations, rather different in comparison with Exod 21:2–11
and Deut 15:12–18, are tied to the following theological reflections of the
authors of this law. The members of the people of Israel are considered, as
one can deduce from the exodus, exclusively as *slaves of YHWH* (Lev 25:42);
they cannot be *slaves of human beings*. Accordingly, the "brother" can only be
employed as a salaried worker or tenant, not as a slave. In addition, YHWH
is recognized as the true master of the land who shared it out to the clans on
a kind of long-term lease (Lev 25:23). Each Year of Jubilee, the "original" relations are to be reestablished, and thus the impoverished farmers along with
their families may return in freedom to the property of their ancestors and
to their clans. On the basis of these theological reasons, unlike those of Exod
21:4–6 and Deut 15:16–17, neither the farmer nor his wife or children can

---

41. See also Alfred Cholewinski, *Heiligkeitsgesetz und Deuteronomium: Eine vergleichende Studie* (AnBib 66; Rome: Biblical Institute Press, 1976), 236–37; and Crüsemann,
Tora, 353.

42. See also 15:54. Cardellini comments on 25:41a that the man and his sons were
to be set free in the Jubilee Year (*Die biblischen "Sklaven"-Gesetze*, 290); in this sense also
Klaus Grünwaldt, *Das Heiligkeitsgesetz Leviticus 17–26: Ursprüngliche Gestalt, Tradition
und Theologie* (Berlin: de Gruyter, 1999), 330. The question of the wives and daughters
is not even raised. Not very plausible, in my opinion, is the thesis presented by Gregory
C. Chirichigno, *Debt-Slavery in Israel and the Ancient Near East* (JSOTSup 141; Sheffield:
JSOT Press, 1993), 328ff.; and Adrian Schenker, "The Biblical Legislation on the Release of
Slaves: The Road from Exodus to Leviticus," *JSOT* 78 (1998): 33: "This rule for the jubilee
does not therefore apply to all categories of slaves, but only to that of married Israelites who
have (male) children."

permanently remain in a state of dependency. Only non-Hebrew female and male slaves may be regarded as the "possession" of their Israelite owners; only they may be made to serve as slaves forever (25:45b).[43] It is also permissable to dominate them with "harshness" (פרך). In light of Lev 25:39–46, they are entirely unprotected from a theological and juridical point of view.

There are indeed now some questions to be asked regarding the wording of the law concerning the role and status of (Hebrew) women. If a sold farmer has a wife or takes another one during his time of service, should the family live on the buyer's land or its own land, which is practically leased to the family? What "status" does this farmer's family have? Must his wife and children work without recompense for the owner?[44]

In addition, the question arises as to whether Lev 25:39–46 is to be understood inclusively, that is, whether the law can be applied analogously to a "sister."[45] The possibility of such an analogy is refuted by the fact that 25:44 (like 25:6) clearly mentions both the עבד (male slave) *and* the אמה (female slave). This is evidence that, if 25:39–43 indeed included both men and women Israelites, this distinction would also be made in the formulation. Hence, if the Holiness Code, unlike Deut 15:12–18, does not provide for the case of a Hebrew woman who sells herself, it should be possible to present reasons for this. Interestingly, it is remarkable that, in Hebrew, there is no feminine form that corresponds to the masculine salaried worker (כירש).[46] On the other hand, texts such as Prov 31:15 and Ruth 2:8 could certainly be understood to imply that young women among the working personnel (נערות) were paid.[47] For the Priestly authors of legal texts, was the conception of the remuneration *ad personam* connected with salaried employment incompatible with their

---

43. See especially Levinson, "The Birth of the Lemma," 623–25.

44. There is little mention of the servitude of women in the biblical texts, hence it is largely invisible, although there is an exception in 1 Sam 8:13; on this topic, see Willy Schottroff, "Der Zugriff des Königs auf die Töchter: Zur Fronarbeit von Frauen im alten Israel," in *Gerechtigkeit lernen: Beiträge zur biblischen Sozialgeschichte* (ed. Frank Crüsemann et al.; Theologische Bücherei 94; Gütersloh: Kaiser/Gütersloher Verlagshaus, 1999), 94–114.

45. This is supposed by Pressler, "Wives and Daughters," 169; differently by, for example, Engelken, *Frauen im Alten Israel*, 155; and Sara Japhet, "The Relationship between the Legal Corpora in the Pentateuch of Manumission Laws," in *Studies in the Bible* (ed. Sara Japhet; Scripta Hierosolymitana 31; Jerusalem: Magnes, 1986), 83, 88.

46. Exod 2:9 is the only exception, since the pharaoh's daughter promises recompense (כרש) to the woman who will nurse her adopted son.

47. On the נערות in Prov 31:15, see Christine Roy Yoder, *Wisdom as a Woman of Substance: A Socioeconomic Reading of Proverbs 1–9 and 31:10–31* (BZAW 304; Berlin: de Gruyter, 2001), 86–87; on the נערות in Ruth 2–3 see Fischer, *Rut*, 163–64.

vision of society or of women?[48] In any case, it should be borne in mind that the wife of the farmer was rendered "invisible" in the course of the phrasing of this manumission law.

2. "You" (Singular and Plural) in the Law Codes of the Torah

First of all, it must be emphasized that the form of address in the legal texts of the Bible is chiefly masculine: the masculine forms of "you" (singular אתה and plural אתם) predominate. Now, as we know, this "you," both in singular and plural, not only indicates the gender but may also be used as a neutral or inclusively.[49] In the following section I will examine how "you" both singular and plural is to be understood in the legal texts. I will consider examples from the three major law codes of the Torah: the Book of the Covenant, the Deuteronomic Code, and the Holiness Code.

2.1. "You" in the Book of Covenant (Exod 20:22–23:33)

The findings relating to the addressees in the Book of the Covenant are fairly homogenous.[50] In the Book of the Covenant, women are explicitly mentioned, although only in terms of *how they are to be treated* (for example, as female slaves, mothers, daughters, and widows). Nothing specifically indicates that women are considered inclusively as addressees. In other words, not only are the laws formulated without exception with the usual masculine terminology, but they are also conceived from the masculine perspective or represent a masculine point of view. To use an expression coined by Athalya Brenner and Fokkelien van Dijk-Hemmes, "M (masculine/male) voices" are heard.[51]

---

48. For a comparable "conservative" position, see Sir 25:22.

49. This also applies to the addressees of the texts occasionally called בני ישראל ("sons" or "children" of Israel); see Silvia Schroer, "Auf dem Weg zu einer feministischen Rekonstruktion der Geschichte Israels," in *Feministische Exegese: Forschungserträge zur Bibel aus der Perspektive von Frauen* (ed. Luise Schottroff et al.; Darmstadt: Primus, 1997), 90; and Dorothea Erbele-Küster, "Der Dienst der Frauen am Eingang des Zeltheiligtums (Exodus 38,8): Kultisch-religiöse Verortungen von Frauen in Exodus und Leviticus," in *The Interpretation of Exodus: Studies in Honour of Cornelis Houtman* (ed. Riemer Roukema et al.; Leuven: Peeters, 2006), 275–79.

50. See also Drorah O'Donnell Setel, "Exodus," in Newsom and Ringe, *The Women's Bible Commentary*, 2634; and Susanne Scholz, "Exodus: Was Befreiung aus 'seiner' Sicht bedeutet...," in Schottroff and Wacker, *Kompendium Feministische Bibelauslegung*, 35–37.

51. Athalya Brenner and Fokkelien van Dijk-Hemmes, *On Gendering Texts: Female and Male Voices in the Hebrew Bible* (Leiden: Brill, 1993), 8.

Exodus 22:20–26 serves as an example.[52] The passage contains a series of social prescriptions. Here it will suffice to quote only 22:22–24:

> 22 You shall not abuse any widow or orphan.
> 23 If you do abuse them (one of these persons), (and) when they cry out to me,
> I will surely heed their cry
> 24 and my wrath will burn,
> and I will kill you with the sword,
> and your wives shall become widows and your children fatherless.

The formulation of "your wives" and "your children" in 22:24b is instructive. It concerns the wives and children of the addressees in the event of the latter becoming oppressors. This remark shows quite clearly that, in the Book of the Covenant, women are not directly addressed as persons who should or could practice God's commandments.

Let us make an observation relating to a "difficult" passage. The quotation is taken from the festival calendar in Exod 23:14–19:

> 14 Three festivals in the year *you* shall hold for me.
> 15 You shall observe the Festival of Unleavened Bread:
> you shall eat unleavened bread for seven days....
> 17 Three times in the year all *your* males shall appear before YHWH.

Verse 14 constitutes the introduction. Verses 15–16 contain the prescriptions pertaining to the three pilgrimage festivals, and verse 17 practically concludes the unit. Verses 14 and 17 are connected linguistically, for example, by the formula "three X in the year" (23:14: שלוש רגלים בשנה ["three festivals in the year"]; 23:17: שלוש פעמים בשנה ["three times in the year"]).[53] In terms of content, it can be said that the general prescription of 23:14 is made explicit in 23:17. Concerning the question of the addressees, there are essentially two possible interpretations in this context. The first possible interpretation can be expressed as follows: in 23:14, the meaning of "you" remains open with respect to Israelite women and men; then, in 23:17, the formula "all your

---

52. Another example is Exod 23:12: On the seventh day, alongside the beasts of burden, "you, the son [!] of your female farmhand, and the resident alien" shall rest. According to Dohmen, this text concerns "people who are particularly affected by [agricultural] labor" (*Exodus 19–40*, 187, my translation). With respect to Ruth 2, this interpretation is questionable.

53. See also Schwienhorst-Schönberger, *Das Bundesbuch*, 402–3; Dohmen, *Exodus 19–40*, 188.

males" (i.e., your = man and woman) limits the prescription of appearing before YHWH in the (local) sanctuary for men. According to the second possible interpretation, "you" in 23:14 addresses Israelite men. Then, in 23:17, the accent of the formulation "all your males" (your = man) is on "all": "*all* your males" [כל זכורך] without exception shall appear before YHWH. The addressees must ensure this, for example, in their role as fathers who care for their sons. It is not easy to choose between these two alternatives. In reference to a comparable formula, in the so-called "Minor Book of the Covenant" (Exod 34:10–26), in Exod 34:23, the second interpretation appears plausible in any case.[54] Accordingly, the author did not intend with the formulation in 23:17 "all your males" (כל זכורך) to exclude women, as they were overlooked in the calendar of festivals from the outset.

The Book of the Covenant is situated, synchronically, in the context of the Sinai pericope: it is YHWH's word addressed to Moses, which Moses must transmit to the people (Exod 24:3). According to the narrative, before YHWH begins to speak on Mount Sinai, some preparations are necessary. Among other things, it is said that Moses gives orders to the people. In this context, Exod 19:14–15 is instructive:

> [14] So Moses went down from the mountain to the people.
> He consecrated the people, and they washed their clothes.
> [15] And he said to the people, "Prepare for the third day;
> do not go near a woman."

Verse 15 says that Moses speaks to the "people" (עם), but in fact he only addresses himself to the adult, masculine part of the people, as 19:15b clearly indicates.[55] Now, it is clear that the scene at Sinai cannot be imagined without women. However, 19:15 shows that the author, or editor, of this text was not interested in the perspective of women and concealed it. On this point, the findings relating to the Book of the Covenant coincide with its narrative context.

---

54. "You" in Exod 34:23, as the formulation in the context shows (34:20: "All the first-born of your children"), is clearly masculine; on this, see Karin Finsterbusch, "The First-Born between Sacrifice and Redemption in the Hebrew Bible," in *Human Sacrifice in Jewish and Christian tradition* (ed. Karin Finsterbusch et al.; Leiden: Brill, 2007), 96.

55. See also Moshe Weinfeld, *Deuteronomy and the Deuteronomic School* (Oxford: Clarendon, 1983), 291; Bird, "Images of Women in the Old Testament," 50; Judith Plaskow, *Standing Again at Sinai: Judaism from a Feminist Perspective* (San Francisco: Harper, 1991); O'Donnell Setel, "Exodus," 29–33; Athalya Brenner, "An Afterword: The Decalogue—Am I an Adressee?" in Brenner, *A Feminist Companion to Exodus*, 256; Scholz, "Exodus," 34–35; Erbele-Küster, "Der Dienst der Frauen," 277 n. 44.

Let us explicitly insist here that one should not draw conclusions from the totally masculine perspective that, in the view of the authors and the editors, the laws collected in the Book of the Covenant had no relevance for women.[56] To state it clearly, they certainly did not believe that a woman had the right to kill someone. However, in this respect, there is a "void" in the Book of the Covenant and in its narrative context. Women do not appear as persons who actively observe the laws in the world of the Book of the Covenant. The existence of an alternative to this "void" in biblical law codes appears notably in the Book of Deuteronomy.

2.2. "YOU" IN THE DEUTERONOMIC CODE (DEUT 12–26)

In the Deuteronomic family laws, "you" is used exclusively to designate men: the adult Hebrew man is addressed in terms of his role as father or husband. However, in addition to this use, it is also possible to account for an inclusive use in the Deuteronomic Code. According to the thesis presented here, in the world of the Deuteronomic Code, or of Deuteronomy, women and men are often spoken to in a similar manner.[57] A "revealing passage" appears in Deut 24:8–9, the law concerning leprosy:

> [8] Guard against an outbreak of a leprous skin disease by being very careful; you shall carefully observe whatever the Levitical priests instruct you, just as I have commanded them. [9] Remember what YHWH your God did to Miriam on your journey out of Egypt.

Verse 8 contains cautions in the event of "leprosy" (נגע הצרעת): the sick are to carefully follow the instructions of the Levitical priests. According to verse 9, the stricken "you" must remember how YHWH treated Miriam during the flight from Egypt (see the narrative in Num 12). The sense of this recollection can be interpreted in different ways. Georg Braulik thinks that Miriam's fate is intended as a warning against disobedience.[58] Jeffrey H. Tigay reasons: "So perhaps the point is to show that nobody is immune, so that people wouldn't

---

56. Pressler, *The View of Women*, 110, also emphasizes: "The fact that the laws in the Book of the Covenant are couched in masculine language does not mean that those laws would not have applied to women also." Nevertheless, as the following presentation shall show, it is not possible to support her evaluation of the Deuteronomic findings: "Deuteronomy's gender specific language may be simply a matter of style" (110).

57. See also Frymer-Kensky, "Deuteronomy," 53–54; Crüsemann, *Tora*, 294; Angelika Engelmann, "Deuteronomium: Recht und Gerechtigkeit für Frauen im Gesetz," in Schottroff and Wacker, *Kompendium Feministische Bibelauslegung*, 69.

58. Georg Braulik, *Deuteronomium II: 16,18–34,12* (NEchtB; Würzburg: Echter,

assume 'it can't happen to me' and fail to consult a priest regarding a potentially 'leprous' skin affection."[59] Ursula Rapp suggests that Miriam could well
be presented as a negative example in relation to the recognition of Moses'
authority.[60] Whatever the case may be, according to the narrative Miriam
became leprous, and so, in this context, she is an example of a person struck
by leprosy. Thus, the reference to Miriam makes it near evident that both the
plural and the singular forms of "you" in verses 8–9 also include women.
Hence, we need to assume that the inclusive language in the legal texts of
Deuteronomy is essentially a matter of course.

In this context, the cultic legislation is also instructive. The Deuteronomic legislation explicitly stipulates several times who shall take part in the
sacrificial meals at the central sanctuary in Jerusalem during the pilgrimage
festivals. The shortest lists say, "you [singular] and your household" (Deut
14:26; 15:20) or "you [plural] and your household" (12:7). In some passages
the members of the "household" are enumerated: sons and daughters as well
as male and female slaves. Depending on the context, the lists sometimes
also include Levites, the alien, the widow, and the orphan in addition to the
family members (Deut 12:12, 18; 16:11, 14; 26:11). It is striking that there is
absolutely no mention of the wives in these enumerations of the family members. In principle, this may be interpreted in two ways. On the one hand, the
women could have gone unmentioned because they had to stay behind to
take care of the house and carry out necessary work during the pilgrimage
festivals. However, this interpretation is refuted by a text within the context
of the Deuteronomic Code: Deut 31:9–13. This passage orders the people to
come to Jerusalem every seventh year for the Festival of Booths, and women
are explicitly mentioned in 31:12. Now, there is no indication in Deuteronomy
that the women were to come to Jerusalem for the Festival of Booths only
every seven years.

The second possible interpretation is more plausible: the wives do not
appear on the lists because, like the men, they are included in the "you" being
addressed.[61] The implications of this assumption have been described by
Georg Braulik as follows: Deuteronomy emancipates the free women and lifts

---

1992), 180. See also Phyllis Trible, "Bringing Miriam Out of the Shadows," in Brenner, *A
Feminist Companion to Exodus*, 178.

59. Jeffrey H. Tigay, *Deuteronomy: The Traditional Hebrew Text with the New JPS
Translation* (JPS Torah Commentary; Philadelphia: Jewish Publication Society, 1996), 225.

60. Ursula Rapp, *Mirjam: Eine feministisch-rhetorische Lektüre der Mirjamtexte in der
hebräischen Bibel* (BZAW 317; Berlin: de Gruyter, 2002), 198.

61. See also Weinfeld, *Deuteronomy and the Deuteronomic School*, 291; Crüsemann,
Tora, 293.

them to the level of their husbands by giving them the same rights in the cult.[62] Therefore, as Braulik rightly concludes, a wife can exercise the following activities at the sanctuary as independently as her husband: present burnt offerings (Deut 12:14); prepare sacrifices on YHWH's altar and pour the blood of sacrifices over YHWH's altar (12:27); offer a tithe of all the harvest (14:22); consecrate all the firstborn males to YHWH (15:19); present a voluntary offering (16:10); bring the firstfruits of the ground and the basket before YHWH and prostate herself (26:10).

However, a central text contradicts this "liberal" position: the summarizing regulation in Deut 16:16–17 relating to the pilgrimage festivals:

> Three times a year all your males shall appear before YHWH your God at the place that he will choose: at the Festival of Unleavened Bread, at the Festival of Weeks, and at the Festival of Booths. They shall not appear before YHWH empty-handed; all shall give as they are able, according to the blessing of YHWH your God that he has given you.

These verses are reminiscent of an older formulation in the Book of the Covenant (Exod 23:17) and in the Minor Book of the Covenant (Exod 34:23). The Deut 16:16–17 unit might be considered a Deuteronomistic addition[63] appended to a more ancient tradition with the intent of largely limiting women's roles in the cult. Accordingly, pilgrimages and sacrifices are henceforth to be obligatory only for the male portion of the people of Israel ("your"[64]): women, at best, retain the possibility of voluntary participation in the cult.[65] However, there is no corroborating evidence for this critical literary judgment. Moshe Weinfeld suggests: "According to the BC [Book of the Covenant] law only males are obliged to make the pilgrimage to 'behold' the face of the Lord, whereas the author of Deuteronomy, who is familiar with this law and even cites it on one occasion (16:16), has extended its application to all members of

---

62. Braulik, "Durften auch Frauen in Israel opfern," 84. The same opinion is held by Otto, "False Weights," 143. For the following presentation, see Braulik, "Durften auch Frauen in Israel opfern," 86–87.

63. This is the opinion of Horst-Dietrich Preuss, *Deuteronomium* (EdF 164; Darmstadt: Wissenschaftliche Buchgesellschaft, 1982), 53.

64. The "you" in Deut 16:16–17, unlike in Exod 23:14–17 and Exod 34:23, should be defined as inclusive.

65. Verse 16a is interpreted in this sense by Reuter, *Kultzentralisation*, 150; Otto, *Gottes Recht als Menschenrecht*, 267 n. 754; Udo Rüterswörden, *Deuteronomium* (Neuer Stuttgarter Kommentar: Altes Testament 4; Stuttgart: Katholisches Bibelwerk, 2006), 110.

the Israelite household, male and female alike (16:11 and 12)."[66] The ancient law in the Book of the Covenant could have been understood, from the perspective of the author of Deut 16:16–17, as a kind of "minimal prescription," in this sense it would not have contradicted his own position.

Now I would like to consider another text in which "you" clearly seems to apply exclusively to men. This text belongs to the unit of Deut 13:7–12:

> [7] If anyone secretly entices you—even if it is your brother, your father's son or your mother's son, or your own son or daughter, or the wife you embrace [literally, "the wife of your bosom"], or your most intimate friend—saying, "Let us go worship other gods," whom neither you nor your ancestors have known, … [9] you must not yield to or heed any such persons. Show them no pity or compassion and do not shield them. [10] But you shall surely kill them; your own hand shall be first against them to execute them, and afterwards the hand of all the people. …

The formulation "the wife of your bosom" (אשת חיקך), in 13:7 reveals in this passage that "you" has the profile of an adult male. Yet a closer look at the argumentation actually shows that there is no intention of exclusiveness; the text offers only an example. Men and women are included on the enticer's side so it is not presumed that only men would be enticed. The brother is mentioned on the side of the enticer, and, from the perspective of the argumentation, it is impossible to think that this does not also concern the sister. This fact is indeed interesting, since it indicates that the content of the text clearly extends beyond the masculine profile of the addressees. In other words, a sufficient number of references to the exemplary character of the argumentation were built into the text.[67] Indeed, the text clearly shows that the exemplary argumentation is presented from the masculine perspective. The feminine perspective must be *deduced*; things are never conceived the other way around.

The question of the addressees becomes even clearer from a synchronic viewpoint, when it is considered in the light of central texts in the context of Deut 12–26. Two short examples shall suffice.

Deuteronomy 29–30 deals with the conclusion of the covenant in Moab; here is a passage from Deut 29:

---

66. Weinfeld, *Deuteronomy and the Deuteronomic School*, 291–92; see also Gruber, "Women in the Cult," 51.

67. See also Deut 17:2–3. On the interpretation of Deut 13:7, see especially Bernard M. Levinson, "Textual Criticism, Assyriology, and the History of Interpretation: Deuteronomy 13:7a as a Text Case in Method," in *"The Right Chorale": Studies in Biblical Law and Interpretation* (FAT 54, Tübingen: Mohr Siebeck, 2008), 112–44.

[9] You stand assembled today, all of you, before YHWH your God—the leaders of your tribes, your elders, and your officials, all the men of Israel, [10] your children, your women, and the aliens who are in your camp, both those who cut your wood and those who draw your water—[11] to enter into the covenant of YHWH your God, sworn by an oath, which YHWH your God is making with you today, [12] in order that he may establish you today as his people and that he may be your God, as he promised you and as he swore to your ancestors, to Abraham, to Isaac, and to Jacob. [13] I am making this covenant, sworn by an oath, not only with you who stand here with us today before YHWH our God, [14] but also with those who are not here with us today. [15] You know how we lived in the land of Egypt and how we came through the midst of the nations through which you passed. [16] You have seen their detestable things, the filthy idols of wood and stone, of silver and gold, that were among them. [17] It may be that there is among you a man or woman, or a family or tribe, whose heart is already turning away from YHWH our God to serve the gods of those nations....

Deuteronomy 29:9–14 presents the protocol of a ceremony of oath-taking, in the form of a performative speech. In contrast with the Sinai pericope, this passage enumerates, from several points of view, whom the covenant is to be made with: all social classes, women and men of all ages, the kinfolk of Israel and also aliens. The covenant is sealed, as the context reveals, on the basis of the Deuteronomic law transmitted to the people. The scope of Deut 29:9–14 completely excludes interpreting the laws as though they were only addressing the masculine part of Israel.

The following sermon of Moses (29:15–20) intends to assure that the consent of the heart (לֵב) be joined to the participation in the ceremony that seals the covenant. Here children are naturally left out, as they are not yet able to do this. Verse 17 first mentions man and woman as the smallest entity of the people, then the bigger entities: the family and the tribe. The explicit reference to man *and* woman is not fortuitous; it manifests the understanding that in the religion's "functioning" the participation of both sexes is equally important.

The covenant is made only once, but the laws must be transmitted and observed in each generation. This is the subject of Deut 31:9–13, already referred to above, which also explicitly mentions women:

[9] Then Moses wrote down this law and gave it to the priests, the sons of Levi, who carried the ark of the covenant of YHWH, and to all the elders of Israel. [10] Moses commanded them: "Every seventh year, in the scheduled year of remission, during the Festival of Booths, [11] when all Israel comes to appear before YHWH your God at the place that he will choose, you shall read this law before all Israel in their hearing. [12] Assemble the people—men, women, and children, as well as the aliens residing in your towns—so that they may

hear and learn to fear YHWH your God and to observe diligently all the words of this law, [13] and so that their children, who have not known it, may hear and learn to fear YHWH your God, as long as you live in the land that you are crossing over the Jordan to possess."

The Deuteronomic Torah (Deut 5–26; 28; 32)[68] is the foundation for the existence and the identity of the people. Therefore, it must be listened to and learned by men and women in the context of a regular collective, festive ritual of learning (31:12). This means that women must also learn the laws of the Torah that in fact exclusively address a masculine "you." It also means that women, like men, must learn the laws that do not directly concern their gender (for example, the prescriptions relating to clothing in Deut 22:5).[69]

The children are of course present during the learning ritual. Those who are still too young to learn what the texts involve must at least learn to fear God (31:13a). In addition to the collective learning ritual during the Festival of Booths in the seventh year, other programmatic texts in Deuteronomy indicate that both father and mother had the responsibility of teaching their children the law in everyday life: girls as well as boys (Deut 6:7, 20–25).[70]

On the whole, the Deuteronomic/Deuteronomistic authors probably took no interest in women as such.[71] Nevertheless, certain texts of theirs clearly reflect the recognition that religious identity could only be gained and maintained through the active participation of Israel's women.

2.3. "You" in the Holiness Code (Lev 17–26)

In the Holiness Code are units whose addressees must be identified as exclusively masculine for reasons of content, for example, the explanations of the permitted and forbidden sexual relations in Lev 18 and 20. In addition, some prescriptions apply particularly to men, such as not marring the edge of the beard in the context of mourning rites (Lev 19:27). Certain passages apply exclusively to priests (e.g., Lev 21). Other texts, according to their content, could be addressed to men and women alike (e.g., several prescriptions of

---

68. On this, see Karin Finsterbusch, *Weisung für Israel: Studien zu religiösem Lehren und Lernen im Deuteronomium und in seinem Umfeld* (FAT 44; Tübingen: Mohr Siebeck, 2005), 288, 297.

69. See also Deut 23:18. See as well Otto, "False Weight," 144–45.

70. Karin Finsterbusch, "Die kollektive Identität und die Kinder: Bemerkungen zu einem Programm im Buch Deuteronomium," *JBTh* 17 (2002): 103ff.

71. See also Pressler, *The View of Women*, 111 ("the laws are not concerned with women qua women at all").

the "individual ethical program"[72] in Lev 19 or the instructions of the festival calendar in Lev 23). Actually, there are only a few indications of an inclusive "you" in the Holiness Code itself. This merits several remarks.

First of all, attention should be given to a negative finding: in the festival calendar of the Holiness Code (Lev 23) there is no prescription analogous to Exod 23:17; 34:23 and Deut 16:16–17, that is, no law obliging the masculine part of Israel to participate in the festivals. Does this "nonenunciation" indicate that the calendar of festivals in Lev 23 is addressed to both women and men?[73]

In this respect, a "revealing verse" is found in Lev 26, which concludes the Holiness Code, namely, verse 26:

> When I break your staff of bread, ten women shall bake your bread in a single oven, and they shall dole out your bread by weight; and though you eat, you shall not be satisfied.

The text does not say "ten of your women," but rather ten women shall bake "your bread." I find it inconceivable that the women must bake bread for the group being addressed without belonging to it. Therefore, "your" is to be understood as inclusive not only in this verse but in the entire context. Depending on how the addressees act in relation to the laws, Lev 26 pronounces on them blessings or curses. The "you" that is so often ordered to act by prescriptions in the Holiness Code cannot therefore be defined as fundamentally masculine.

On the basis of a text in the festival calendar (Lev 23), the question should now be posed whether the inclusive understanding of "you" (singular and plural) makes sense, especially with regard to the priestly laws in the literary context of the Holiness Code. Verses 37–38, which may be described as a kind of "signature" and probably initially concluded the festival calendar,[74] say:

> These are the appointed festivals of YHWH, which you shall celebrate as times of holy convocation [מקראי קדש],[75] for presenting to YHWH

---

72. Otto, *Theologische Ethik des Alten Testaments*, 243ff.

73. Also see Grünwaldt, *Das Heiligkeitsgesetz Leviticus 17–26*, 295 n. 875.

74. See Gerstenberger, *Das dritte Buch Mose*, 299, 301ff., and Grünwaldt, *Das Heiligkeitsgesetz Leviticus 17–26*, 77–78.

75. According to Gerstenberger (*Das dritte Buch Mose*, 323), the festivals in Lev 23 are not to be understood as pilgrimage festivals. Andreas Ruwe (*"Heiligkeitsgesetz" und "Priesterschrift": Literaturgeschichtliche und rechtssystematische Untersuchungen zu Leviticus 17,1–26,2* [FAT 26; Tübingen: Mohr Siebeck, 1999], 320–21) believes that only the Festival of Booths was conceived as a pilgrimage festival.

offerings by fire—burnt offerings and grain offerings, sacrifices and drink offerings, each on its proper day—apart from the Sabbaths of YHWH, and apart from your gifts, and apart from all your votive offerings, and apart from all your freewill offerings, which you give to YHWH.

If these verses were inclusive, women and men alike must have been able to bear the responsibility for the ordered sacrifices. Is this credible in the light of the priestly prescriptions relating to sacrifices? As we know, Lev 12:6–7; 15:29–30 and Num 5:6–8 explicitly order women to present an animal for a holocaust and a sin offering to the priest in particular situations. Numbers 6:2 indicates that men and women may make the Nazirite vow in the same way. According to Num 30, women can make vows.[76] Furthermore, in an instructive contribution entitled "Women in the Cult according to the Priestly Code," Mayer I. Gruber makes a plausible case that formulations in the context of the prescriptions relating to offerings, such as Lev 2:1 (ונפש כי תקריב ["when anyone wants to offer"]) or 4:27 (נפש אחת ... מעם הארץ ["any one of the people of the land"]) are meant to be gender-neutral. Accordingly, men and women may make offerings—naturally, within the limits imposed on them as laity. If these considerations are correct, nothing in the context impedes understanding Lev 23:37–38 inclusively and interpreting the orders relating to the festivals in Lev 23 as directed at both men and women alike. Moreover, Dorothea Erbele-Küster presents an argument in favor of this interpretation. She suggests that the formula בני ישראל in 23:34 and 23:42–44 applies to both men and women and should consequently be understood to mean "*children of Israel*."[77] To conclude, at least in some textual units in the Holiness Code,

---

76. Actually, the father, the fiancé, and the husband have the right to cancel the vows of their daughter, fiancée, and wife; on the contrary, the vows of a widow or of a divorced woman cannot be contested. On Num 30, see Jione Havea, *Elusions of Control: Biblical Law on the Words of Women* (SemeiaSt 41; Atlanta: Society of Biblical Literature, 2003); for women's vows in the Hebrew Bible, see Karel van der Toorn, *From Her Cradle to Her Grave: The Role of Religion in the Life of the Israelite and the Babylonian Woman* (Biblical Seminar 23; Sheffield: JSOT Press, 1994), 97–102; Fokkelien van Dijk-Hemmes, "Traces of Women's Texts in the Hebrew Bible," in Brenner and van Dijk-Hemmes, *On Gendering Texts*, 91–92.

77. Erbele-Küster, "Der Dienst der Frauen," 277. Somewhat differently, Jan Joosten, *People and Land in the Holiness Code: An Exegetical Study of the Ideational Framework of the Law in Leviticus 17–26* (VTSup 67; Leiden: Brill, 1996), 31–32, states: "The intention behind the use of the phrase בני ישראל is not, therefore, to exclude women—as if they should not hear or keep the laws—but rather to subsume them under the person of the man in whose household they live. The Israelite men are addressed, not so much as individuals, but in their quality as head of the family." Joosten concentrates on Lev 18 in particular.

women as well as men are addressed and ordered to accomplish the same tasks.

What could the reason be for such an open position? Is the determining difference, as Phyillis Bird suggests,[78] in respect to the cultic prescriptions, for example, not so much that between men and women but rather essentially between the laity and the priesthood? Is the concept of holiness that dominates the world of the Holiness Code applicable only if it refers to all the people living in the land of Israel, that is, the kinfolk of Israel as well as the aliens,[79] men as well as women?

Here I would like to add another closing comment concerning the priestly texts. As noted in §1.1, they generally do not have a reputation of being particularly friendly toward women. Be that as it may, the findings are probably less "exclusive" than they seem to be at first sight. In a study of Exod 38:8, Irmtraud Fischer has convincingly shown that the activity described in this verse is to be understood as a transmission of word and revelation the women carry out *at* (not *in front of*) the entrance of the tent of meeting.[80] Accordingly, we must allow for the fact that the priestly legislation presupposed women in cultic functions.

3. Concluding Considerations

The authors of the biblical laws share a common assumption: their point of departure is a patriarchal model of the family whose principal head is male. This is tied to an extreme image of women that can especially be detected in the biblical family laws. The women are subordinated to the masculine power of disposition. For example, they do not have any say in the decision as to who

---

78. Phyllis Bird, "The Place of Women in the Israelite Cultus," in *Ancient Israelite Religion: Essays in Honour of Frank Moore Cross* (ed. Patrick D. Miller Jr., Paul D. Hanson, and S. Dean McBride; Philadelphia: Fortress, 1987), 411.

79. See Crüsemann, *Tora*, 345: "The same proximity to the shrine makes people even beyond Israel ultimately equal" (my translation). The aliens must at least observe a part of the laws; so Joosten, *People and Land*, 63ff.

80. Irmtraud Fischer, *Gender-faire Exegese: Gesammelte Beiträge zur Reflexion des Genderbias und seiner Auswirkungen in der Übersetzung und Auslegung von biblischen Texten* (Münster: LIT, 2004), 50–62; see also Marie-Theres Wacker, "'Religionsgeschichte Israels' oder 'Theologie des Alten Testaments'—(k)eine Alternative? Anmerkungen aus feministisch-exegetischer Sicht," *JBTh* 10 (1995): 147. Prophetesses at the sanctuary could have been Isaiah's wife (Isa 8:1–4) and Noadiah (Neh 6); on this, see Irmtraud Fischer, *Gotteskünderinnen: Zu einer geschlechterfairen Deutung des Phänomens der Prophetie und der Prophetinnen in der Hebräischen Bibel* (Stuttgart: Kohlhammer, 2002), 205ff., 262ff.

their partner in life shall be, and their physical and psychological integrity is not taken into consideration.

Interestingly, it is possible to see, in spite of this "basic conception," that the diverse law codes differ considerably with regard to the conception of women's roles. This has been shown by the analysis of the manumission laws and through the definition of the "you" addressed to in the major law codes of the Torah (Covenant Code, Deuteronomic Code, and Holiness Code). In summary, here are the key points listed once again.

The manumission law in the Covenant Code represents a "conservative" position. A father can sell his daughter as a slave with the option that, as a slave, she shall become the wife of the buyer or his son; a slave-owner can give a female slave to a male slave for sexual relations. The possibility of being liberated in the seventh year is explicitly granted only to a man who is a slave because of indebtedness. According to the Deuteronomic manumission law, only (adult) women and men may sell themselves (!), in terms of their labor (!), for six years. The corresponding law in the Holiness Code stipulates that a Hebrew "slave" is to be treated like a salaried worker; this kind of role obviously does not provide for women. The wife of a "slave," whose existence is determined by the reference to children, remains invisible in the formulation of the law.

Concerning the definition of "you" (singular and plural), especially notable with regard to the exclusive position (which leaves women aside) of the Book of the Covenant and the rather open position of the Holiness Code (in my opinion, there is an inclusive tendency in at least a few passages) are the findings in the Deuteronomic Code in the book of Deuteronomy. Here we can recognize many passages containing inclusive language in reference to "you" (singular and plural). This language has vast implications. The same rights are granted to woman and man in the cult. Consequently, like a man, the woman can present offerings independently. Moreover, as the Deuteronomic texts show in the context of the legal code, both men and women are obliged to listen to the Torah and to learn it during the Festival of Booths in the seventh year. This means that women, just like men, must know the text of the whole Deuteronomic Code! Likewise, both are responsible for educating their children with respect to the law.

The reasons for these differences are diverse. Social situations to which the law codes react certainly play a role. On the other hand, in the case of the Deuteronomic Code and the Holiness Code, the ideal of society presented by the authors of these collections was reflected upon and elaborated from a theological point of view during a particular period. In the world of the Deuteronomic Code, the developed ideal presents a society whose members live together in freedom and without poverty. A consequence of this is that the duration of slavery is limited for both men and women. Also, with reference to the collective experience of slavery in Egypt and YHWH's redemption, start-up capital must be given to the male and female slaves for their lives in liberty. The conception of society is part of the program of reforms undertaken in Judah toward the end of the seventh century, after the period of Assyrian domination, and elaborated during the exile. This program was intended to reestablish and found the religious identity of the people. Together with the unquestioned insertion of women in the patriarchal family structure, it is most likely that the granting of equal rights and obligations in the cult and in the education of children are attributable to the understanding that a lasting religious reform cannot succeed without the widespread support of women.

In the Holiness Code one finds a sixth-century reaction to the experiences of the loss of Judah's sovereignty, the exile, and the return of some exiled families. The authors of this code do not elaborate the ideal of a society without poverty but rather a program for reconciliation between rich and poor. Here one of the consequences is that, with reference to the exodus by which YHWH showed himself as the sole Lord of Israel, true slavery is transformed into provisional salaried labor. This possibility is not considered for women. This program had no need for "salaried" women (or wives), who did indeed exist during the exilic and postexilic period. Moreover, such an image of women apparently also went too far for the authors of this law. Nevertheless, the concept of holiness did perhaps imply the open-mindedness in regard to women that we have discovered in the Holiness Code: all Israel must be "holy." This means that the "you," to whom certain forms of behavior are referred, could not really be exclusively masculine.

Bibliography

For abbreviations, see http://www.bibleandwomen.org.

Ackerman, James. "The Literary Context of the Moses Birth Story (Exodus 1–2)." Pages 74–119 in *Literary Interpretations of Biblical Narratives*. Edited by Kenneth R. R. Gros Louis et al. Nashville: Abingdon, 1974.

Ackerman, Susan. "Why Is Miriam Also among the Prophets? (And Is Zipporah among the Priests?)." *JBL* 121 (2002): 47–80

Adler, Rachel. "Tumah and Taharah: Ends and Beginnings." Pages 63–71 in *The Jewish Woman: New Perspectives*. Edited by Elizabeth Koltun. New York: Schocken, 1976.

Allen, Leslie C. *Ezekiel 20–48*. WBC 29. Waco, Tex.: Word, 1990.

Allison, Penelope M., ed. *The Archaeology of Household Activities*. London: Routledge, 1999.

Alonso Schökel, Luis. *Hermenéutica de la Palabra III: Interpretación teológica de textos bíblicos*. Bilbao: Ediciones EGA, 1991.

Alsean, Alicia, Assumpcio Malgosa, und Carles Simo. "Looking into the Demography of an Iron Age Population in the Western Mediterranean: I. Mortality." *American Journal of Physical Anthropology* 110 (1999): 285–301.

Amit, Yairah, *Hidden Polemics in Biblical Narrative*. Leiden: Brill, 2000.

"An Afghan Love Affair." Interview with Nancy Hatch Dupree in The Story. American Public Media (16 May 2007). Online: http://thestory.org/archive/the_story_251_An_Afghan_Love_Affair.mp3/view.

Anderson, Bernhard W. "The Song of Miriam Poetically and Theologically Considered." Pages 283–96 in *Directions in Biblical Hebrew Poetry*. Edited by David J. A. Clines and Philip R. Davies. Sheffield: Sheffield Academic Press, 1987.

Anderson, Cheryl B. *Women, Ideology, and Violence: Critical Theory and the Construction of Gender in the Book of the Covenant and the Deuteronomic Law*. JSOTSup 394. London: T&T Clark, 2004.

Andriolo, Karin R. "A Structural Analysis of Genealogy and Worldview in the Old Testament." *American Anthropologist* 75 (1973): 1657–69.

Apuleius. *Metamorphosen oder der Goldene Esel: Lateinisch und Deutsch von Rudolf Helm*. Schriften und Quellen der Alten Welt 1. Berlin: Akademie-Verlag, 1957.

Assmann, Jan. *Das kulturelle Gedächtnis: Schrift, Erinnerung und politische Identität in frühen Hochkulturen*. 5th ed. Munich: Beck, 2005.

Asurmendi Ruiz, Jesús María. "Miqueas." Pages 523–537 in *Libros proféticos y sapienciales*. Vol. 2. of *Comentario bíblico latinoamericano: Antiguo Testamento*. Edited by Armando J. Levoratti. Estella: Verbo Divino, 2007.

Asociación de Teólogas Españolas, ed. *Aletheia*. 4 vols. Estella: Verbo Divino, 2006–2009.

Aufrecht, Walter E. "Genealogy and History in Ancient Israel." Pages 205–35 in *Ascribe to the Lord: Biblical and Other Studies in Memory of Peter C. Craigie*. Edited by Lyle Eslinger and Glen Taylor. JSOTSup 67. Sheffield: JSOT Press, 1988.

Avigad, Nahman. *Bullae and Seals from a Post-exilic Judean Archive*. Qedem 4. Jerusalem: Institute of Archaeology, Hebrew University of Jerusalem, 1976.

———. "The Contribution of Hebrew Seals to an Understanding of Israelite Religion and Society." Pages 195–208 in *Ancient Israelite Religion: Essays in Honor of Frank Moore Cross*. Edited by Patrick D. Miller Jr., Paul D. Hanson and S. Dean McBride. Philadelphia: Fortress, 1987.

Avigad, Nahman, and Benjamin Sass. *Corpus of West Semitic Stamp Seals*. Jerusalem: Israel Academy of Sciences and Humanities, Israel Exploration Society, and Institute of Archaeology, Hebrew University of Jerusalem, 1997.

Bach, Alice. "Dreaming of Miriam's Well." Pages 151–58 in *Exodus to Deuteronomy: A Feminist Companion to the Bible*. Edited by Athalya Brenner. FCB 2/5. Sheffield: Sheffield Academic Press, 2000.

———. "With a Song in Her Heart: Listening to Scholars Listening for Miriam." Pages 243–54 in *A Feminist Companion to Exodus to Deuteronomy*. Edited by Athalya Brenner. FCB 6. Sheffield: Sheffield Academic Press, 1994.

———. *Women, Seduction, and Betrayal in Biblical Narrative*. Cambridge: Cambridge University Press, 1997.

———, ed. *Women in the Hebrew Bible: A Reader*. New York: Routledge, 1999.

Bachmann, Veronika. "Die biblische Vorstellungswelt und deren geschlechterpolitische Dimension: Methodologische Überlegungen am Beispiel der ersttestamentlichen Kategorien 'rein' und 'unrein.'" *lectio difficilior* 2 (2003). Online: http://www.lectio.unibe.ch/03_2/bachmann.pdf.

———. "Geschlecht und Un-/Reinheit: Zur feministischen Diskussion um die geschlechterpolitischen Implikationen des ersttestamentlichen Rein-Unrein-Denkens." Lizentiatsarbeit, Universität Fribourg, 2003.

Backhaus, Knut, und Gerd Häfner. *Historiographie und fiktionales Erzählen: Zur Konstruktivität in Geschichtstheorie und Exegese*. Biblisch-Theologische Studien 86. Neukirchen-Vluyn: Neukirchener, 2007.

Bahrani, Zainab, *Women of Babylon: Gender and Representation in Mesopotamia*. London: Routledge, 2001.

Bail, Ulrike, et al., eds. *Bibel in gerechter Sprache*. 3rd ed. Gütersloh: Gütersloher Verlagshaus, 2007.

Baker, David L. "Concubines and Conjugal Rights: עֹנָה in Exodus 21:10 and Deuteronomy 21:14." *ZABR* 13 (2007): 87–101.

Bal, Mieke, Fokkelien van Dijk-Hemmes, and Grietje van Ginneken. *Und Sara lachte...: Patriarchat und Widerstand in biblischen Geschichten*. Münster: Morgana Frauenbuchverlag, 1988.

Barber, Elizabeth Wayland. *Women's Work: The First 20,000 Years—Women, Cloth, and Society in Early Times*. New York: Norton, 1994.

Barkay, Gabriel, Marilyn J. Lumberg, Andrew G. Vaughan, and Bruce Zuckerman. "The Amulets from Ketef Hinnom: A New Edition and Evaluation." *BASOR* 334 (2004): 41–71.

Barton, John, *Oracles of God: Perceptions of Ancient Prophecy in Israel after the Exile*. New York: Oxford University Press, 1988.

Bauckham, Richard J. "Tamar's Ancestry and Rahab's Marriage: Two Problems in the Matthean Genealogy." *NovT* 37 (1995): 313–29.

Beckwith, Roger. "Formation of the Hebrew Bible." Pages 39–86 in *Mikra: Text, Translation, Reading and Interpretation of the Hebrew Bible in Ancient Judaism and Early Christianity*. Edited by Martin Jan Mulder. CRINT 2; LJPSTT 1. Assen: van Gorcum, 1988.

———. *The Old Testament Canon of the New Testament Church and Its Background in Early Judaism*. Grand Rapids: Eerdmans, 1985.

Beeson, Stuart D. "Historiography Ancient and Modern: Fact and Fiction." Pages 3–11 in *Ancient and Modern Scriptural Historiography/L'historiographie biblique, ancienne et moderne*. Edited by George J. Brooke und Thomas Römer. BETL 207. Leuven: Leuven University Press, 2007.

Ben Barak, Zafrira. "The Legal Status of the Daughter as Heir in Nuzi and Emar." Pages 87–97 in *Society and Economy in the Eastern Mediterranean*. Edited by Michael Heltzer. OLA 23. Leuven: Peeters, 1988.

Bentzen, Aage. *Introduction to the Old Testament*. 2 vols. Kopenhagen: Gad, 1948.

Berlin, Andrea M. "Jewish Life before the Revolt: The Archeological Evidence." *JSJ* 36 (2005): 417–70.

Bernabé Ubieta, Carmen. "El Génesis: Libro de orígenes y fundamentos." Pages 111–54 in *Relectura del Génesis*. Edited by Isabel Gómez-Acebo et al. 2nd ed. En Clave de Mujer. Bilbao: Desclée de Brouwer, 1999.

Beyer, Hermann Wolfgang. "κανών." *TDNT* 3:596–602.

Biale, Rachel. *Women and Jewish Law: An Exploration of Women's Issues in Halakhic Sources*. New York: Schocken, 1984.

Bird, Phyllis A. "'Frauenarbeit' und die Sphäre des Religiösen im alten Israel: Überlegungen zu Kontinuität und Diskontinuität in häuslichen und kultischen Rollen anhand von Trauerriten." Pages 23–35 in *Geschlechterdifferenz, Ritual und Religion*. Edited by Elmar Klinger. Würzburg: Echter, 2003.

———. "Images of Women in the Old Testament." Pages 41–88in *Religion and Sexism: Images of Women in the Jewish and Christian Traditions*. Edited by Rosemary Radford Ruether. New York: Simon & Schuster, 1974.

———. "Israelite Religion and the Faith of Israel's Daughters." Pages 97–108, 311–17 in *The Bible and the Politics of Exegesis: Essays in Honor of Norman K. Gottwald on His Sixty-Fifth Birthday*. Edited by David Jobling, Peggy Day, and Gerald T. Sheppard. Cleveland: Pilgrim, 1991.

———. *Missing Persons and Mistaken Identities: Women and Gender in Ancient Israel*. OBT. Minneapolis: Fortress, 1997.

————. "The Place of Women in the Israelite Cultus." Pages 397–419 in *Ancient Israelite Religion: Essays in Honor of Frank Moore Cross*. Edited by Patrick D. Miller Jr., Paul D. Hanson, and S. Dean McBride. Philadelphia: Fortress, 1987.

————. "Translating Sexist Language as Theological and Cultural Problem." *USQR* 42 (1988): 89–95.

Bledstein, Adrien. "Family Matters: A Multidimensional Reading of Miriam's Humiliation and Healing." *BR* 46 (2001): 55–61.

Blenkinsopp, Joseph. *Prophecy and Canon: A Contribution to the Study of the Jewish Origins*. University of Notre Dame, Center for the Study of Judaism and Christianity in Antiquity 3. Notre Dame, Ind.: University of Notre Dame Press, 1977.

Bloch-Smith, Elizabeth. *Judahite Burial Practices and Beliefs about the Dead*. JSOTSup 123. Sheffield: JSOT Press, 1992.

Blum, Erhard, *Die Komposition der Vätergeschichte*. WMANT 57. Neukirchen-Vluyn: Neukirchener, 1984.

Boecker, Hans Jochen. *1. Mose 25,12–37,1: Isaak und Jakob*. ZBKAT 1.3. Zürich: Theologischer Verlag, 1992.

Bonora, Antonio. "La creazione: Il respiro della vita e la madre dei viventi in Gn 2–3." *Parola Spirito e Vita* 5 (1982): 9–22.

Bordreuil, Pierre, Felice Israel, and Dennis Pardee. "King's Command and Widow's Plea: Two New Hebrew Ostraca of the Biblical Period." *Near Eastern Archaeology* 61 (1998): 2–13.

Borger, Rykle. "Der Codex Hammurapi." Pages 39–80 in *Rechtsbücher*. Edited by Rykle Borger et al. TUAT 1.1. Gütersloh: Gütersloher Verlagshaus, 1982.

————. "Die mittelassyrischen Gesetze." Pages 80–92 in *Rechtsbücher*. Edited by Rykle Borger et al. TUAT 1.1. Gütersloh: Gütersloher Verlagshaus, 1982.

Borgonovo, Gianantonio. "La donna di Gen 3 e le donne di Gen 6,1–4: Il ruolo del feminino nell'eziologia metastorica." *RStB* 1–2 (1994): 71–99.

Bowser, Brenda, and John Q. Patton. "Domestic Spaces as Public Spaces: An Ethnoarchaeological Case Study of Houses, Gender, and Politics in the Ecuadorian Amazon." *Journal of Archaeological Method and Theory* 11 (2004): 157–81.

Bradley, Harriet. *Men's Work, Women's Work: A Sociological History of the Sexual Division of Labor in Employment*. Cambridge: Polity, 1989.

Brandt, Peter. *Endgestalten des Kanons: Das Arrangement der Schriften Israels in der jüdischen und christlichen Bibel*. BBB 131. Berlin: Philo, 2001.

Braulik, Georg. *Deuteronomium II: 16,18–34,12*. NEchtB 28. Würzburg: Echter, 1992.

————. "Durften auch Frauen in Israel opfern? Beobachtungen zur Sinn- und Festgestalt des Opfers im Deuteronomium." Pages 59–89 in idem, *Studien zum Deuteronomium und seiner Nachgeschichte*. SBAB 33. Stuttgart: Katholisches Bibelwerk, 2001.

Braun, Roddy. *1 Chronicles*. WBC 14. Waco, Tex.: Word, 1986.

Breasted, James H., Jr. *Egyptian Servant Statues*. Bollingen Series 13. Washington, D.C.: Bollingen Foundation, 1948.

Brenner, Athalya. "An Afterword: The Decalogue—Am I an Adressee?" Pages 255–58 in *A Feminist Companion to Exodus to Deuteronomy*. Edited by Athalya Brenner. FCB 6. Sheffield: Sheffield Academic Press, 1994.

———. "Female Social Behaviour: Two Descriptive Patterns within the 'Birth of the Hero' Paradigm." *VT* 36 (1986): 257–73.

———. *The Israelite Woman: Social Role and Literary Type in Biblical Narrative.* Biblical Seminar 2. Sheffield: JSOT Press, 1985.

———, ed. *A Feminist Companion to Genesis.* FCB 2. Sheffield: Sheffield Academic Press, 1993.

———, ed. *Genesis.* FCB 2/1. Sheffield: Sheffield Academic Press, 1998.

Brenner, Athalya, and Fokkelien van Dijk-Hemmes. *On Gendering Texts: Female and Male Voices in the Hebrew Bible.* Biblical Interpretation Series 1. Leiden: Brill, 1993.

Brock, Sebastian. "Reading between the Lines: Sarah and the Sacrifice of Isaac (Genesis, Chapter 22)." Pages 169–80 in *Women in Ancient Societies.* Edited by Léonie J. Archer. London: MacMillan, 1994.

Brown, Francis, Samuel R. Driver and Charles A. Briggs. *A Hebrew and English Lexicon of the Old Testament.* Oxford: Clarendon, 1907. [= BDB]

Brueggemann, Walter. *A Social Reading of the Old Testament: Prophetic Approaches to Israel's Communal Life.* Edited by Patrick D. Miller. Philadelphia: Fortress, 1994.

Brunner, Hellmut. "Abstammung." *LÄ* 1:13–18.

Brunner-Traut, Emma. *Die altägyptischen Scherbenbilder (Bildostraka) der deutschen Museen und Sammlungen.* Wiesbaden: Steiner, 1956.

Buber, Martin, and Franz Rosenzweig. "Leitwort Style in Pentateuch Narrative." Pages 114–28 in Martin Buber and Franz Rosenzweig, *Scripture and Translation.* Edited by Lawrence Rosenwald und Everett Fox. Indiana Studies in Biblical Literature. Bloomington: Indiana University Press, 1994.

———. *Die Schrift: Bd. 1: Die fünf Bücher der Weisung: Verdeutscht von Martin Buber gemeinsam mit Franz Rosenzweig.* 12th ed. Darmstadt: Wissenschaftliche Buchgesellschaft, 1997.

Buckley, Thomas, and Alma Gottlieb. "A Critical Appraisal of Theories of Menstrual Symbolism." Pages 3–53in *Blood Magic: The Anthropology of Menstruation.* Edited by Thomas Buckley and Alma Gottlieb. Berkeley: University of California Press, 1988.

Budd, Philip J. *Numbers.* WBC 5. Waco, Tex.: Word, 1994.

Buhl, Frants. *Kanon und Text des Alten Testamentes.* Leipzig: Faber, 1891.

Burnette-Bletsch, Rhonda J. "My Bone and My Flesh: The Agrarian Family in Biblical Law." PhD. diss., Duke University, 1998.

Burns, Rita J. *Exodus, Leviticus, Numbers.* Wilmington, Del.: Glazier, 1983.

———. *Has the Lord Indeed Spoken Only through Moses? A Study of the Biblical Portrait of Miriam.* SBLDS 84. Atlanta: Scholars Press, 1987.

———. "Zipporah." *ABD* 6:1105.

Butting, Klara. *Prophetinnen gefragt: Die Bedeutung der Prophetinnen im Kanon aus Tora und Prophetie.* Erev-Rav-Hefte: Biblisch-feministische Texte 3. Wittingen: Erev-Rav, 2001.

Cagni, Luigi. "Miti di origine, miti di caduta e presenza del femminino nella loro tradizione interpretativa: Considerazione sui dati della tradizione sumerica e babilonese-assiria." *RStB* 1–2 (1994): 13–46.

Camp, Claudia. "Over Her Dead Body: The Estranged Woman and the Price of the Promised Land." *JNSL* 29 (2003): 1–13.

Campbell, Joseph. *The Masks of God.* New York: Arkana 1991.

Capra, Fritjof. *The Hidden Connections.* New York: Doubleday, 2002.

Cardascia, Guillaume. *Les lois assyriennes.* LAPO 2. Paris: Cerf, 1969.

———. "La nourrice coupable: §194 du Code de Hammurabi." Pages 67–84 in *Mélanges à la mémoire de Marcel-Henri Prévost: Droit biblique: Interprétation rabbinique: Communautés et société.* Paris: Presses universitaires de France, 1982.

Cardellini, Innocenzo. *Die biblischen "Sklaven"-Gesetze im Lichte des keilschriftlichen Sklavenrechts: Ein Beitrag zur Tradition, Überlieferung und Redaktion der alttestamentlichen Rechtstexte.* BBB 55. Königstein: Hanstein, 1981.

Carr, David McClain. "Canonization in the Context of Community: An Outline of the Formation of the Tanakh and the Christian Bible." Pages 22–64 in *A Gift of God in Due Season: Essays on Scripture and Community in Honor of James A. Sanders.* Edited by Richard D. Weis and David McClain Carr. JSOTSup 225. Sheffield: JSOT Press, 1996.

Carter, Charles E. "Ethnoarchaeology." *OEANE* 2:280–284.

Cassin, Elena. "Note sur le 'commerce de carrefour' en Mésopotamie ancienne." *JESHO* 4 (1961): 164–67.

Cassuto, Deborah. "Bringing Home the Artifacts: A Social Interpretation of Loom Weights in Context." Pages 63–78 in *The World of Women in the Ancient and Classical Near East.* Edited by Beth Alpert Nakhai. Newcastle-upon-Tyne: Cambridge Scholars, 2008.

Cassuto, Umberto M. D. *A Commentary on the Book of Exodus.* Jerusalem: Magnes, 1967.

Cazelles, Henri, and Jean-Paul Bouhot. *Il Pentateuco.* Biblioteca di Studi Biblici 4. Brescia: Paideia, 1968.

Chapman, Stephen B. *The Law and the Prophets: A Study in Old Testament Canon Formation.* FAT 27. Tübingen: Mohr Siebeck, 2000.

Childs, Brevard S. *The Book of Exodus: A Critical Theological Commentary.* Louisville: Westminster John Knox, 1974.

Chirichigno, Gregory C. *Debt-Slavery in Israel and the Ancient Near East.* JSOTSup 141. Sheffield: JSOT Press, 1993.

Chodorov, Nancy. *The Power of Feelings.* New Haven: Yale University Press, 1999.

Cholewinski, Alfred. *Heiligkeitsgesetz und Deuteronomium: Eine vergleichende Studie.* An Bib 66. Rome: Biblical Institute Press, 1976.

Clark Kroeger, Richard, and Catherine Clark Kroeger. *I Suffer Not a Woman: Rethinking 1 Timothy 2:11–15 in Light of Ancient Evidence.* Grand Rapids: Baker, 1992.

Clines, David J. A. ed. *The Dictionary of Classical Hebrew.* Sheffield: Sheffield Academic Press, 1993–. [= *DCH*]

Coats, George W. "Humility and Honor: A Moses Legend in Numbers 12." Pages 97–107in *Art and Meaning: Rhetoric in Biblical Literature.* Edited by David J. A. Clines, David M. Gunn, and Alan J. Hauser. JSOTSup 19. Sheffield: Sheffield Academic Press, 1982.

———. "Legendary Motifs in the Moses Death Reports." *CBQ* 39 (1977): 34–44.

———. "Moses in Midian." *JBL* 92 (1973): 3–10.

Cotter, David W. *Genesis*. Berit Olam: Studies in Hebrew Narrative and Poetry. Collegeville, Minn.: Liturgical Press, 2003.

Craigie, Peter C. *The Book of Deuteronomy*. NICOT. Grand Rapids: Eerdmans, 1976.

Craven, Toni, "Is That Fearfully Funny? Some Instances from the Apocryphal/ Deuterocanonical Books." Pages 65–78 in *Are We Amused? Humour about Women in the Biblical Worlds*. Edited by Athalya Brenner. JSOTSup 383; Bible in the Twenty-First Century Series 2; London: T&T Clark, 2003.

———. "Women as Teachers of Torah." Pages 275–289 in *Passion, Vitality, and Foment: The Dynamics of Second Temple Judaism*. Edited by Lamontte M. Luker. Harrisburg, Pa.: Trinity Press International, 2001.

Croce, Lucia. "La nidda nel pensiero biblico e mišnico." *Egitto e vicino oriente* 6 (1983): 235– 45.

Cross, Frank Moore, Jr. and David Noel Freedman. "The Song of Miriam." *JNES* 14 (1955): 237–50.

Crossan, Jean Dominic. "Felix Culpa and Foenix Culprit: Comments of 'Direct and Third Person Discourse in the Narrative of the Fall' by Hugh C. White." *Semeia* 18 (1980): 107–11.

Crüsemann, Frank. *Die Tora: Theologie und Sozialgeschichte des alttestamentlichen Gesetzes*. 2nd ed. Gütersloh: Gütersloher Verlagshaus, 1997.

Dalley, Stephanie. "Old Babylonian Dowries." *Iraq* 42 (1980): 53–74.

Daum, Annette. "Blaming the Jews for the Death of the Goddess." *Lilith* 7 (1980): 12–13.

Daviau, P. M. Michèle. *Houses and Their Furnishings in Bronze Age Palestine: Domestic Activity Areas and Artifact Distribution in the Middle and Late Bronze Age*. JSOT/ ASOR Monograph Series 8. Sheffield: Sheffield Academic Press, 1993.

Davidson, Samuel. *The Canon of the Bible*. London: H. S. King, 1877.

Davies, Deborah Rae. "Genealogy and Catalogue: Thematic Relevance and Narrative Elaboration in Homer and Hesiod." Ph.D. diss., University of Michigan, 1992.

Davies, Gordon F. *Israel in Egypt: Reading Exodus 1–2*. JSOTSup 135. Sheffield: JSOT Press, 1992.

Davies, Philip R. "'Another Country?' Biblical Texts and the Past." Pages 13–24 in *Ancient and Modern Scriptural Historiography/L'historiographie biblique, ancienne et moderne*. Edited by George J. Brooke und Thomas Römer. BETL 207. Leuven: University Press, 2007.

Dayagi-Mendels, Michal. *Perfumes and Cosmetics in the Ancient World*. Jerusalem: Israel Museum, 1989.

Del Bianco Cotrozzi, Maddalena. *Precetti e riti di purità femminile nelle tre grandi religioni monoteiste*. Udine: Forum, 2004.

Démare-Lafont, Sophie. "L'absence dans les droits cunéiformes." Pages 275–305 in *Le monde de l'itinérance en Méditerranée de l'Antiquité à l'époque moderne: Procédures de contrôle et d'identification*. Edited by Claudia Moatti et al. Etudes 22. Bordeaux: Ausonius, 2009.

———. "Un 'cas royal' à l'époque de Mari." *RA* 91 (1997): 109–19.

———. "'A cause des anges': Le voile dans la culture juridique du Proche-Orient ancien." Pages 235–53 in *Etudes d'histoire du droit privé en souvenir de Maryse Carlin*. Edited by Olivier Vernier, Michel Bottin, and Marc Ortolani. Paris: Editions La Mémoire du Droit, 2008.

———. *Femmes, droit et justice dans l'Antiquité orientale: Contribution à l'étude du droit pénal au Proche-Orient ancien*. OBO 165; Fribourg: Editions Universitaires, 1999.

———. "L'interprétation de Nombres 5,31 à la lumière des droits cunéiformes." Pages 49–52 in *La femme dans le Proche-Orient antique: Compte rendu de la 33e Recontre Assyriologique Internationale (Paris, 7–10 juillet 1986)*. Edited by Jean-Marie Durand; Paris: ERC, 1987.

Dempster, Stephen G. "An 'Extraordinary Fact': Torah and Temple and the Contours of the Hebrew Canon." *TynBul* 48 (1997): 23–56, 191–218.

Derriks, Claire. *Les miroirs cariatides égyptiens en bronze: Typologie, chronologie et symbolique*. Münchener Ägyptologische Studien 51. Mainz: Zabern, 2001.

De Troyer, Kristin. "Blood: A Threat to Holiness or toward (Another) Holiness?" Pages 45–64 in *Wholly Woman—Holy Blood: A Feminist Critique of Purity and Impurity*. Edited by Kristin De Troyer et al. SAC. Harrisburg, Pa.: Trinity Press International, 2003.

De Troyer, Kristin, et al., eds. *Wholly Woman—Holy Blood: A Feminist Critique of Purity and Impurity*. SAC. Harrisburg, Pa.: Trinity Press International, 2003.

Deutsch, Robert. *Messages from the Past: Hebrew Bullae from the Time of Isaiah through the Destruction of the First Temple*. Tel Aviv: Archaeological Center, 1999.

Deutsch, Robert, and Michael Heltzer. *New Epigraphic Evidence from the Biblical Period*. Tel Aviv: Archaeological Center, 1995.

Dijk-Hemmes, Fokkelien van. "Some Recent Views on the Presentation of the Song of Miriam." Pages 200–206 in *A Feminist Companion to Exodus to Deutreronomy*. Edited by Athalya Brenner. FCB 6. Sheffield: Sheffield Academic Press, 1994.

———. "Traces of Women's Texts in the Hebrew Bible." Pages 17–109 in Athalya Brenner and Fokkelien van Dijk-Hemmes, *On Gendering Texts: Female and Male Voices in the Hebrew Bible*. Biblical Interpretation Series 1. Leiden: Brill, 1993.

Dijkstra, Meindert. "Schone Handen: Reinheid in de Culturen van de Levant." *Phoenix* 48 (2002): 73–92.

Dohmen, Christoph. *Exodus 19–40*. HTKAT; Freiburg im Breisgau: Herder, 2004.

Domhardt, Yvonne. Esther Orlow, and Eva Pruschy, eds. *Kol Ischa: Jüdische Frauen lesen die Tora*. 2nd ed. Zürich: Chronos, 2007.

Douglas, Mary. *Leviticus as Literature* (Oxford: Oxford University Press, 1999.

———. *Purity and Danger: An Analysis of the Concepts of Pollution and Taboo*. London: Routledge & Kegan Paul, 1966.

Dresen, Grietje. "The Better Blood: On Sacrifice and the Churching of New Mothers in the Roman Catholic Tradition." Pages 143–64 in *Wholly Woman—Holy Blood: A Feminist Critique of Purity and Impurity*. Edited by Kristin De Troyer et al. SAC. Harrisburg, Pa.: Trinity Press International, 2003.

Dresner, Samuel H. *Rachel*. Minneapolis: Fortress, 1994.

Driver, Godfrey R., and John C. Miles. *The Babylonian Laws*. 2 vols. Oxford: Clarendon, 1952–1955.

Durand, Jean-Marie. *Les documents épistolaires du palais de Mari*. 3 vols. LAPO 16–18. Paris: Cerf, 1998–2000.

Ebeling, Erich. "Erbe, Erbrecht, Enterbung." *RlA* 2:458–62.

Ehrman, Bart D. *Lost Christianities: The Battle for Scripture and the Faiths We Never Knew*. Oxford: Oxford University Press, 2005.

——. *The Orthodox Corruption of Scripture: The Effect of Early Christological Controversies on the Text of the New Testament*. Oxford: Oxford University Press, 1996.

Eissfeldt, Otto, *The Old Testament: An Introduction, Including the Apocrypha and Pseudoepigrapha, and also the Works of Similar Type from Qumran: The History of the Formation of the Old Testament*. Translated by Peter R. Ackroyd. Oxford: Basil Blackwell, 1965.

Engelken, Karen. *Frauen im Alten Israel: Eine begriffsgeschichtliche und sozialrechtliche Studie zur Stellung der Frau im Alten Testament*. BWANT 130. Stuttgart: Kohlhammer, 1990.

Engelmann, Angelika, "Deuteronomium: Recht und Gerechtigkeit für Frauen im Gesetz." Pages 67–79 in *Kompendium Feministische Bibelauslegung*. Edited by Luise Schottroff and Marie-Theres Wacker. Gütersloh: Gütersloher Verlagshaus, 1998.

Erbele-Küster, Dorothea. "Der Dienst der Frauen am Eingang des Zeltheiligtums (Exodus 38:8): Kultisch-religiöse Verortungen von Frauen in Exodus und Leviticus." Pages 265–81 in *The Interpretation of Exodus: Studies in Honour of Cornelis Houtman*. Edited by Riemer Roukema. CBET 44. Leuven: Peeters, 2006.

——. "Hat dieser Körper ein Geschlecht? Die Bestimmungen der Wöchnerin in Lev 12." Pages 101–8 in *Theologie des Alten Testaments aus der Perspektive von Frauen*. Edited by Manfred Oeming; Beiträge zum Verstehen der Bibel 1. Münster: LIT, 2003.

——. "Körperkult und Kultkörper: Variationen über Leviticus 12 und 15." Pages 17–30 in *Körper-Kulte: Wahrnehmung von Leiblichkeit in Theologie, Religions- und Kulturwissenschaften*. Edited by Christina aus der Au and David Plüss. Christentum und Kultur 6. Zürich: Theologischer Verlag Zürich, 2007.

——. "Ungerechte Texte und gerechte Sprache: Überlegungen zur Hermeneutik des Bibelübersetzens." Pages 222–34 in *Die Bibel—übersetzt in gerechte Sprache? Grundlagen einer neuen Übersetzung*. Edited by Helga Kuhlmann. Gütersloh: Gütersloher Verlagshaus, 2005.

Eskenazi, Tamara Cohn. "Out from the Shadows: Biblical Women in the Postexilic Era." *JSOT* 54 (1992): 25–43.

Eskenazi, Tamara Cohn, and Andrea L. Weiss, eds. *The Torah: A Women's Commentary*. New York: URJ Press, 2008.

Estévez López, Elisa. "Las grandes ausentes: La memoria de las esclavas en los orígenes de Israel." Pages 221–67 in *Relectura del Génesis*. Edited by Isabel Gómez-Acebo et al. 2nd ed. En Clave de Mujer; Bilbao: Desclée de Brouwer, 1999.

Exum, J. Cheryl. "Second Thoughts about Secondary Characters: Women in Exodus 1.8–2.10." Pages 75–87 in *A Feminist Companion to Exodus to Deuteronomy*. Edited by Athalya Brenner. FCB 6. Sheffield: Sheffield Academic Press, 1994.

——. "Who's Afraid of 'The Endangered Ancestress'?." Pages 91–113 in *The New Literary Criticism and the Hebrew Bible*. Edited by J. Cheryl Exum and David J. A. Clines. JSOTSup 143. Sheffield: Sheffield Academic Press, 1993.

——. "You Shall Let Every Daughter Live: A Study of Exodus 1.8–2.10." Pages 37–61 in *A Feminist Companion to Exodus to Deuteronomy*. Edited by Athalya Brenner. FCB 6. Sheffield: Sheffield Academic Press, 1994.

Fander, Monika. *Die Stellung der Frau im Markusevangelium: Unter besonderer Berücksichtigung kultur- und religionsgeschichtlicher Hintergründe*. Münsteraner Theologische Arbeiten 8. Altenberge: Telos, 1989.

Faust, Avraham. "Differences in Family Structure between Cities and Villages in Iron II." *TA* 26 (1999): 233–50.

——. "The Rural Community in Ancient Israel during Iron Age II." *BASOR* 317 (2000): 17–39.

Faust, Avraham, and Ze'ev Safrai. "Salvage Excavations as a Source for Reconstructing Settlement History in Ancient Israel." *PEQ* 137 (2005): 139–58.

Feld, Geburgis. "Leviticus: Das ABC der Schöpfung." Pages 40–53 in *Kompendium Feministische Bibelauslegung*. Edited by Luise Schottroff and Marie-Theres Wacker. 2nd ed. Gütersloh: Gütersloher Verlagshaus, 1999.

——. "Menstruation." Pages 773–76 in vol. 2 of *Neues Bibel-Lexikon*. Edited by Manfred Görg and Bernhard Lang. 3 vols. Zürich: Benzinger, 1991–2001.

Feucht, Erika. "Mutter." *LÄ* 6:253–63.

Fields, Weston W. *Sodom and Gomorrah: History and Motif in Biblical Narrative*. JSOTSup 231. Sheffield: Sheffield Academic Press, 1997.

Finkelstein, Israel, and Neil Asher Silberman. *The Bible Unearthed: Archaeology's New Vision of Ancient Israel and the Origin of Its Sacred Texts*. New York: Touchstone, 2001.

Finkelstein, Jacob J. "The Genealogy of the Hammurapi Dynasty." *JCS* 20 (1966): 95–118.

Finsterbusch, Karin. "The First-Born between Sacrifice and Redemption in the Hebrew Bible." Pages 87–108 in *Human Sacrifice in Jewish and Christian Tradition*. Edited by Karin Finsterbusch et al. Studies in the History of Religions 112. Leiden: Brill, 2007.

——. "Die kollektive Identität und die Kinder: Bemerkungen zu einem Programm im Buch Deuteronomium." *JBTh* 17 (2002): 99–120.

——. *Weisung für Israel: Studien zu religiösem Lehren und Lernen im Deuteronomium und in seinem Umfeld*. FAT 44. Tübingen: Mohr Siebeck, 2005.

Fisch, Harold. "Ruth and the Structure of Covenant History." *VT* 32 (1982): 425–37.

Fischer, Alexander A. *Tod und Jenseits im Alten Orient und Alten Testament*. Neukirchen-Vluyn: Neukirchener, 2005.

Fischer, Irmtraud. "Die Autorität Mirjams: Eine feministische Relektüre von Num 12 – angeregt durch das jüdische Lehrhaus." Pages 23–38 in *Anspruch und Widerspruch: Festschrift für Evi Krobath zum 70. Geburtstag*. Edited by Maria Halmer,

Barbara Heyse-Schaefer, and Barbara Rauchwarter. Klagenfurt: Hermagoras, 2000.

———. "The Authority of Miriam: A Feminist Rereading of Numbers 12 Prompted by Jewish Interpretation." Pages 159–73 in *Exodus to Deuteronomy: A Feminist Companion to the Bible.* Edited by Athalya Brenner. FCB 2/5. Sheffield: Sheffield Academic Press, 2000.

———. "Donne nel Antico Testamento." Pages 161–96 in *Donne e Bibbia: Storia ed esegesi.* Edited by Adriana Valerio. La Bibbia nella Storia 21. Bologna: Edizioni Dehoniane, 2006.

———. "Egalitär entworfen—hierarchisch gelebt: Zur Problematik des Geschlechterverhältnisses und einer genderfairen Anthropologie im Alten Testament." Pages 265–98 in *Der Mensch im Alten Israel: Neue Forschungen zur alttestamentlichen Anthropologie.* Edited by Bernd Janowski und Kathrin Liess. Herders Biblische Studien 59. Freiburg im Breisgau: Herder, 2009.

———. "Erinnern als Movens der Schriftwerdung und der Schriftauslegung: Woran und warum sich Israel nach dem Zeugnis der Hebräischen Bibel erinnert und wieso dies für unsere heutige Erinnerung relevant ist." Pages 11–25 in *Erinnern: Erkundungen zu einer theologischen Basiskategorie.* Edited by Paul Petzel and Norbert Reck. Darmstadt: Wissenschaftliche Buchgesellschaft, 2003.

———. "Der erkämpfte Segen (Gen 32,23–33)." *BK* 58 (2003): 100–107.

———. *Die Erzeltern Israels: Feministisch-theologische Studien zu Genesis 12–36.* BZAW 222. Berlin: de Gruyter, 1994.

———. "Den Frauen der Kochtopf—den Männern die hohe Politik? Zum Klischee der Geschlechterrollen in der Bibelauslegung am Beispiel der Erzeltern-Erzählungen." *Christlich-pädagogische Blätter* 108 (1995): 134–38.

———. "Gen 10–36." Pages 32–76in *Stuttgarter Altes Testament: Einheitsübersetzung mit Kommentar und Lexikon.* Edited by Erich Zenger. 2nd ed. Stuttgart: Katholisches Bibelwerk, 2004.

———. *Gender-faire Exegese: Gesammelte Beiträge zur Reflexion des Genderbias und seiner Auswirkungen in der Übersetzung und Auslegung von biblischen Texten.* Exegese in unserer Zeit 14. Münster: LIT, 2004.

———. "Genesis 12–50: Die Ursprungsgeschichte Israels als Frauengeschichte." Pages 12–25 in *Kompendium Feministische Bibelauslegung.* Edited by Luise Schottroff and Marie-Theres Wacker. Gütersloh: Gütersloher Verlagshaus, 2nd ed., 1999; 3rd ed., 2007.

———. "Das Geschlecht als exegetisches Kriterium: Zu einer gender-fairen Interpretation der Erzeltern-Erzählungen." Pages 135–52 in *Studies in the Book of Genesis: Literature, Redaction and History.* Edited by André Wénin. BETL 155. Leuven: Leuven University Press, 2001.

———. "Das Geschlecht als exegetisches Kriterium: Zu einer gender-fairen Interpretation der Erzeltern-Erzählungen." *Christlich-pädagogische Blätter* 116 (2003): 2–9.

———. *Gotteskünderinnen: Zu einer geschlechterfairen Deutung des Phänomens der Prophetie und der Prophetinnen in der Hebräischen Bibel.* Stuttgart: Kohlhammer, 2002.

——. *Gottesstreiterinnen: Biblische Erzählungen über die Anfänge Israels*. Stuttgart: Kohlhammer, 2nd ed., 2000; 3rd ed., 2006.

——. "Israels Landbesitz als Verwirklichung der primordialen Weltordnung: Die Bedeutung des Landes in den Erzelternerzählungen." *JBTh* 23 (2008): 3–24.

——. "Der Männerstammbaum im Frauenbuch: Überlegungen zum Schluss des Rutbuches (4,18–22)." Pages 195–213 in *"Ihr Völker alle, klatscht in die Hände!"*: *Festschrift für Erhard S. Gerstenberger zum 65. Geburtstag*. Edited by Rainer Kessler, Kerstin Ulrich, and Milton Schwantes. Exegese in unserer Zeit 3; Münster: LIT, 1997.

——. *Rut*. HTKAT. Freiburg im Breisgau: Herder, 2001.

——. "Sara als Gründerin des Volkes Israel: Zur Befreiung einer aus männlichem Blick gezeichneten Erzählfigur aus dem Korsett des *gender-bias* in der Exegese." Pages 11–26 in *Sara lacht: Eine Erzmutter und ihre Geschichte: Zur Interpretation und Rezeption der Sara-Erzählung*. Edited by Rainer Kampling. Paderborn: Schöningh, 2004.

——. "Was kostet der Exodus? Monetäre Metaphern für die zentrale Rettungserfahrung Israels in einer Welt der Sklaverei." *JBTh* 21 (2006): 25–44.

——. "Zwischen Kahlschlag, Durchforstung und neuer Pflanzung: Zu einigen Aspekten Feministischer Exegese und ihrer Relevanz für eine Theologie des Alten Testaments." Pages 41–72 in *Theologie und Exegese des Alten Testaments/der Hebräischen Bibel: Zwischenbilanz und Zukunftsperspektiven*. Edited by Bernd Janowski. SBS 200. Stuttgart: Katholisches Bibelwerk, 2005.

Fitzenreiter, Martin. "Einleitung. Genealogie—Realität und Fiktion sozialer und kultureller Identität." Pages 1–10 in *Genealogie—Realität und Fiktion von Identität*. Edited by Martin Fitzenreiter. Internet-Beiträge zur Ägyptologie und Sudanarchäologie 5. Berlin: Humboldt-Universität, 2005. Online: http://www2.hu-berlin.de/nilus/net-publications/ibaes5/publikation/ibaes5_fitzenreiter_einleitung.pdf.

——. "Überlegungen zum Kontext der 'Familienstelen' und ähnlicher Objekte." Pages 69–96 in *Genealogie—Realität und Fiktion von Identität*. Edited by Martin Fitzenreiter. Internet-Beiträge zur Ägyptologie und Sudanarchäologie 5. Berlin: Humboldt-Universität, 2005. Online: http://www2.rz.hu-berlin.de/nilus/net-publications/ibaes5/publikation/ibaes5_fitzenreiter_familienstelen.pdf.

——, ed. *Genealogie—Realität und Fiktion von Identität*. Edited by Martin Fitzenreiter. Internet-Beiträge zur Ägyptologie und Sudanarchäologie 5. Berlin: Humboldt-Universität, 2005. Online: http://www2.rz.hu-berlin.de/nilus/net-publications/ibaes5/.

Fonrobert, Charlotte E. *Menstrual Purity: Rabbinic and Christian Reconstructions of Biblical Gender*. Contraversions: Jews and Other Differences. Stanford, Calif.: Stanford University Press, 2000.

Foust, Michael, comp. "Archeological Find Linked to Another Obscure O.T. Figure." *Baptist Press* (1 February 2008). Online: http://www.bpnews.net/bpnews.asp?id=27307.

Fowler, Robert L. *Early Greek Mythography*. Vol. 1. Oxford: Oxford University Press, 2000.

Frettlöh, Magdalene L. "Isaak und seine Mütter: Beobachtungen zur exegetischen Verdrängung von Frauen am Beispiel von Gen 24,62–67." *EvT* 54 (1994): 427–52.

Frick, Frank S. "Widows in the Hebrew Bible: A Transactional Approach." Pages 139–151 in *A Feminist Companion to Exodus to Deuteronomy*. Edited by Athalya Brenner. FCB 6. Sheffield: Sheffield Academic Press, 1994.

Friend, Glenda. *The Loom Weights*. Tell Taanek 1963–1968 3.2; Birzeit: Birzeit University, Palestine Institute of Archaeology, 1998.

Frier, Bruce W. "Roman Life Expectancy: Ulpian's Evidence." *HSCP* 86 (1982): 213–51.

Frymer-Kensky, Tikva. "Deuteronomy." Pages 52–62 in *The Women's Bible Commentary*. Edited by Carol A. Newsom and Sharon H. Ringe. Louisville: Westminster John Knox, 1992.

———. "Gender and Law: An Introduction." Pages 17–24 in *Gender and Law in the Hebrew Bible and the Ancient Near East*. Edited by Victor H. Matthews, Bernard M. Levinson, and Tikva Frymer-Kensky. JSOTSup 262. Sheffield: Sheffield Academic Press, 1998.

———. "Pollution, Purification, and Purgation in Biblical Israel." Pages 399–414 in *The Word of the Lord Shall Go Forth: Essays in Honor of David Noel Freedman in Celebration of His 60th Birthday*. Edited by Carol L. Meyers et al. Winona Lake, Ind.: Eisenbrauns, 1983.

———. "Virginity in the Bible." Pages 79–96 in *Gender and Law in the Hebrew Bible and the Ancient Near East*. Edited by Victor H. Matthews, Bernard M. Levinson, and Tikva Frymer-Kensky. JSOTSup 262. Sheffield: Sheffield Academic Press, 1998.

Funk, Robert Walter. *Parables and Presence: Forms of the New Testament Tradition*. Philadelphia: Fortress, 1982.

Ganslmayr, Herbert. *Aphrodites Schwestern und christliches Zypern: 9000 Jahre Kultur Zyperns: Ausstellungskatalog*. Bremen: Übersee-Museum, 1987.

García Bachmann, Mercedes. "La excepción que confirma la regla: La mujer de Potifar y el acoso sexual (Génesis 39)." Pages 61–76 in *Ecce mulier: Homenaje a Irene Foulkes*. San José de Costa Rica: Universidad Bíblica Latinoamericana, 2005.

Gardiner, Alan H. *The Royal Canon of Turin*. Oxford: Griffith Institute, 1959.

Gerhards, Meik. "Über die Herkunft der Frau des Mose." *VT* 55 (2005): 162–75.

Gerstenberger, Erhard S. *Das dritte Buch Mose: Leviticus*. ATD 6. Göttingen: Vandenhoeck & Ruprecht, 1993.

Gertz, Jan-Christian. "Konstruierte Erinnerung: Alttestamentliche Historiographie im Spiegel von Archäologie und literarhistorischer Kritik am Fallbeispiel des salomonischen Königtums." *BTZ* 21 (2004): 3–29.

Gesenius, Wilhelm. *Hebräisches und Aramäisches Wörterbuch zum Alten Testament: Bearbeitet von Frants Buhl*. 17th ed. Berlin: Springer, 1959.

Gilchrist, Roberta. *Gender and Archaeology: Contesting the Past*. London: Routledge, 1999.

Giles, Madeline. "Human and Animal Remains: Appendix B." Pages 318–22 in *Lachish IV (Tell ed-Duweir): The Bronze Age*. Edited by Olga Tufnell et al. Wellcome-Marston Archaelogical Research Expedition to the Near East Publications 4. London: Oxford University Press, 1958.

Gillmayr-Bucher, Susanne. "Genesis 24—ein Mosaik aus Texten." Pages 521–32 in *Studies in the Book of Genesis: Literature, Redaction and History.* Edited by André Wénin. BETL 155. Leuven: Leuven University Press, 2001.

———. "The Woman of Their Dreams: The Image of Rebekah in Genesis 24." Pages 90–101 in *The World of Genesis: Persons, Places, Perspectives.* Edited by Philip R. Davies und David J. A. Clines. JSOTSup 257. Sheffield: Sheffield Academic Press 1998.

———. "Von welcher sozialen Wirklichkeit erzählt Gen 24?" *Protokolle zur Bibel* 7 (1998): 17–27.

———. "וְהִנֵּה רִבְקָה יֹצֵאת: Eine textlinguistische Untersuchung zu Gen 24." Ph.D. diss., Universität Innsbruck, 1994.

Gössmann, Elisabeth, ed. *Das wohlgelahrte Frauenzimmer.* 8 vols with a special volume. Archiv für philosophie- und theologiegeschichtliche Frauenforschung. Munich: Iudicium, 1984– 2004.

Goldin, Judah. "The Youngest Son or Where Does Genesis 38 Belong." *JBL* 96 (1977): 27–44.

Goldstein, Elyse, ed. *The Women's Torah Commentary: New Insights from Women Rabbis on the 54 Weekly Torah Portions.* Woodstock: Jewish Lights Publishing, 2008.

Gómez-Acebo, Isabel, ed. *Relectura del Éxodo.* En Clave de Mujer. Bilbao: Desclée de Brouwer, 2006.

———. *Relectura del Génesis.* En Clave de Mujer. Bilbao: Desclée de Brouwer, 1997; 2nd ed., 1999.

Graetz, Heinrich Hirsch. *Kohélet oder der salomonische Prediger.* Leipzig: Winter, 1871.

Grajetzki, Wolfram. "Zwei Fallbeispiele für Genealogien im Mittleren Reich." Pages 57–68 in in *Genealogie—Realität und Fiktion von Identität.* Edited by Martin Fitzenreiter. Internet-Beiträge zur Ägyptologie und Sudanarchäologie 5. Berlin: Humboldt-Universität, 2005. Online: http://www2.rz.hu-berlin.de/nilus/net-publications/ibaes5/publikation/ibaes5_grajetzki_fallbeispiele.pdf.

Greenberg, Blue. "Female Sexuality and Bodily Functions in the Jewish Tradition." Pages 1–44 in *Women, Religion and Sexuality: Studies on the Impact of Religious Teachings on Women.* Edited by Jeanne Becher. Geneva: WCC Publications, 1990.

Greenberg, Moshe. "The Etymology of נִדָּה '(Menstrual) Impurity.'" Pages 69–77 in Solving Riddles and Untying Knots: Biblical, Epigraphic, and Semitic Studies in Honor of J. C. Greenfield. Edited by Ziony Zevit et al. Winona Lake, Ind.: Eisenbrauns, 1995.

Gruber, Mayer I. "Purity and Impurity in Halakhic Sources and Qumran Law." Pages 65–76 in *Wholly Woman—Holy Blood: A Feminist Critique of Purity and Impurity.* Edited by Kristin De Troyer et al. SAC. Harrisburg, Pa.: Trinity Press International, 2003.

———. "Women in the Cult according to the Priestly Code." Pages 49–68 in *The Motherhood of God and Other Studies.* Edited by Mayer I. Gruber. Atlanta: Scholars Press, 1992.

——. "Women's Voices in the Book of Micah." *lectio difficilior* 1 (2007). Online: http://www.lectio.unibe.ch/07_1/mayer_gruber_womens_voices.htm.

Grünwaldt, Klaus. *Das Heiligkeitsgesetz Leviticus 17–26: Ursprüngliche Gestalt, Tradition und Theologie.* BZAW 271; Berlin: de Gruyter, 1999.

Guenther, Allen. "A Typology of Israelite Marriage: Kinship, Socio-economic, and Religious Factors." *JSOT* 29 (2005): 387–407.

Guillaume, Philippe. "'Beware of Foreskins': The Priestly Writer as Matchmaker in Genesis 27,46–28,8." Pages 69–76 in *Jacob: Commentaire à plusieurs voix de Gen 25–36: Mélanges offerts à Albert de Pury.* Edited by Jean-Daniel Macchi and Thomas Römer. Le monde de la Bible 44. Geneva: Labor et Fides, 2001.

Gunkel, Hermann. *Genesis.* 8th ed. Göttinger Handkommentar zum Alten Testament 1.1. Göttingen: Vandenhoeck & Ruprecht, 1969.

Häfner, Gerd. "Konstruktion und Referenz: Impulse aus der neueren geschichtstheoretischen Diskussion." Pages 67–96 in Knut Backhaus und Gerd Häfner, *Historiographie und fiktionales Erzählen: Zur Konstruktivität in Geschichtstheorie und Exegese.* Biblisch-Theologische Studien 86. Neukirchen-Vluyn: Neukirchener, 2007.

Halbwachs, Maurice. *Das kollektive Gedächtnis.* Frankfurt: Fischer, 1991.

Hall, Jonathan M. *Ethnic Identity in Greek Antiquity.* Cambridge: University Press, 1997.

Halpern Amaru, Betsy. "The First Woman, Wives, and Mothers in Jubilees." *JBL* 113 (1994): 609–26.

Handy, Lowell K. "Serpent." *ABD* 5:1113–17.

Hardin, James W. *Households and the Use of Domestic Space at Iron II Tell Halif: An Archaeology of Destruction.* Reports of the Lahav Research Project 2. Winona Lake, Ind.: Eisenbrauns, 2009.

Harris, Rivkah. *Gender and Aging in Mesopotamia: The "Gilgamesh Epic" and Other Ancient Literature.* Norman: University of Oklahoma Press, 2000.

——. "The *Naditu* Woman." Pages 106–35 in *Studies Presented to A. L. Oppenheim.* Edited by Robert D. Biggs and John A. Brinkman. Chicago: University Press, 1964.

Hartom, Abraham S. תורה, נביאם, כתובים. Tel Aviv: Tel Aviv University Press, 1973.

Havea, Jione. *Elusions of Control: Biblical Law on the Words of Women.* SemeiaSt 41. Atlanta: Society of Biblical Literature, 2003.

Heard, R. Christopher, *Dynamics of Diselection: Ambiguity in Genesis 12–36 and Ethnic Boundaries in Post-Exilic Judah.* SemeiaSt 39. Atlanta: Society of Biblical Literature, 2001.

Herklotz, Friederike. "Der Ahnenkult bei den Ptolemäern." Pages 155–64 in *Genealogie—Realität und Fiktion von Identität.* Edited by Martin Fitzenreiter. Internet-Beiträge zur Ägyptologie und Sudanarchäologie 5. Berlin: Humboldt-Universität, 2005. Online: http://www2.rz.hu-berlin.de/nilus/net-publications/ibaes5/publikation/ibaes5_herklotz_ptolemaeer.pdf.

Hermisson, Hans-Jürgen. *Sprache und Ritus im altisraelitischen Kult: Zur "Spiritualisierung" der Kultbegriffe im Alten Testament.* WMANT 19; Neukirchen-Vluyn: Neukirchener, 1965.

Hernando, Almudenda. "¿Por qué la Historia no ha valorado las actividades de man-tenimiento?" Pages 115–33 in *Dones i activitats de mantinement en temps de canvi.* Edited by Paloma González Marcén, Sandra Montón Subías, and Marina Picazo Gurina. Treballs d'Arqueologia 11. Barcelona: Universitat Autònoma de Barcelona, 2005.

Hess, Richard S. "The Genealogies of Genesis 1–11 and Comparative Literature." *Bib* 70 (1989): 241–254

Hieke, Thomas. "BIBLOS GENESEOS: Matthäus 1,1 vom Buch Genesis her gelesen." Pages 635–49 in *The Biblical Canons.* Edited by Henk Jan de Jonge and Jean-Marie Auwers. BETL 163. Leuven: Leuven University Press, 2003.

———. *Die Bücher Esra und Nehemia.* Neuer Stuttgarter Kommentar: Altes Testament 9.2. Stuttgart: Katholisches Bibelwerk, 2005.

———. Endogamy in the Book of Tobit, Genesis, and Ezra-Nehemiah." Pages 103–20 in *The Book of Tobit: Text, Tradition, Theology: Papers of the First International Conference on the Deuterocanonical Books, Pápa, Hungary, 20–21 May 2004.* Edited by Géza G. Xeravits and József Zsengellér. JSJSup 98. Leiden: Brill, 2005.

———. "Genealogien." www.WiBiLex.de (2007). Online: http://www.bibelwissen-schaft.de/nc/wibilex/das-bibellexikon/details/quelle/WIBI/zeichen/g/refer-enz/19244/cache/b943f966470254a017db643207e3368f/.

———. *Die Genealogien der Genesis.* Herders Biblische Studien 39. Freiburg im Breis-gau: Herder, 2003.

Hillers, Delbert R. *Micah: A Commentary on the Book of the Prophet Micah.* Herme-neia. Philadelphia: Fortress, 1984.

Hirschberger, Martina. "Genealogie und Geographie—Der hesiodeische Gynaikōn Katalogos als Vorläufer von Hekataios und der ionischen *Historíē*." *Antike Natur-wissenschaft und ihre Rezeption* 14 (2004): 7–24.

———. *Gynaikōn Katalogos und Megalai Ēhoiai: Ein Kommentar zu den Fragmenten zweier hesiodeischer Epen.* Beiträge zur Altertumskunde 198. Munich: Saur, 2004.

Holladay, John S., Jr. "House, Israelite." *ABD* 3:308–18.

Hood, Rodney T. "The Genealogies of Jesus." Pages 1–15 in *Early Christian Origins: Studies in Honor of Harold R. Willoughby.* Edited by Allen Wikgren. Chicago: Quadrangle, 1961.

Hornung, Erik. *Der Eine und die Vielen: Altägyptische Götterwelt.* 6th ed. Darmstadt: Primus, 2005.

Houtman, Cornelis. *Ex 1,1–7,12.* Vol. 1 of *Exodus.* Historical Commentary on the Old Testament. Kampen: Kok Pharos, 1993.

Hugenberger, Gordon Paul. *Marriage as a Covenant: A Study of Biblical Law and Ethics Governing Marriage Developed from the Perspective of Malachi.* VTSup 52. Leiden: Brill, 1994.

Hunter, Richard, ed. *The Hesiodic Catalogue of Women: Constructions and Reconstruc-tions.* Cambridge: University Press, 2005.

Jackson, Bernard S. *Wisdom-Laws: A Study of the Mishpatim of Exodus 21:1–22:16.* Oxford: Oxford University Press, 2006.

Jackson, John R. "Enjoying the Fruit of One's Labor: Attitudes toward Male Work and Workers in the Hebrew Bible." Ph.D. diss., Duke University, 2005.

Jackson, Melissa. "Lot's Daughters and Tamar as Tricksters and the Patriarchal Narratives as Feminist Theology." *JSOT* 98 (2002): 29–46.

Jacob, Benno. *Das Buch Exodus*. Stuttgart: Calwer, 1997.

———. *Das erste Buch der Tora: Genesis*. Berlin: Schocken, 1934.

Jansen-Winkeln, Karl. "Die Entwicklung der genealogischen Informationen nach dem Neuen Reich." Pages 137–46 in *Genealogie—Realität und Fiktion von Identität*. Edited by Martin Fitzenreiter. Internet-Beiträge zur Ägyptologie und Sudanarchäologie 5. Berlin: Humboldt-Universität, 2005. Online: http://www2.rz.hu-berlin.de/nilus/net-publications/ibaes5/publikation/ibaes5_jansen-winkeln_entwicklung.pdf.

Janzen, J. Gerald. "Song of Moses, Song of Miriam: Who Is Seconding Whom?" *CBQ* 54 (1992): 211–220. Repr. as pages 187–99 in *A Feminist Companion to Exodus to Deuteronomy*. Edited by Athalya Brenner. FCB 6. Sheffield: Sheffield Academic Press, 1994.

Japhet, Sara. *I and II Chronicles: A Commentary*. OTL. Louisville: Westminster John Knox, 1993.

———. "The Relationship between the Legal Corpora in the Pentateuch in Light of Manumission Laws." Pages 63–89 in *Studies in the Bible*. Edited by Sara Japhet. Scripta Hierosolymitana 31. Jerusalem: Magnes, 1986.

Jeansonne, Sharon P. "Images of Rebekah: From Modern Interpretations to Biblical Portrayal." *BR* 34 (1989): 33–52.

———. *The Women of Genesis: From Sarah to Potiphar's Wife*. Minneapolis: Fortress, 1990.

Jeon, Jaeyoung. "Two Laws in the Sotah Passage (Num. v 11–31)." *VT* 57 (1997): 181–207.

Jobling, David. "A Structural Analysis of Numbers 11–12." Pages 31–65 in idem, *The Sense of Biblical Narrative: Structural Analyses in the Hebrew Bible 1*. 2nd ed. JSOTSup 7. Sheffield: JSOT Press, 1986.

Joosten, Jan. *People and Land in the Holiness Code: An Exegetical Study of the Ideational Framework of the Law in Leviticus 17–26*. VTSup 67. Leiden: Brill, 1996.

Jursa, Michael. "*Terdu*: Von Entführung in Babylon und Majestätsbeleidigung in Larsa." Pages 497–514 in *Studi sul Vicino Oriente Antico dedicati alla memoria di Luigi Cagni*. Edited by Simonetta Graziani et al. Series Minor 61. Neapel: Dipartimento di Studi Asiatici, Istituto Universitario Orientale, 2000.

Keel, Othmar. *Das Böcklein in der Milch seiner Mutter und Verwandtes*. OBO 33. Fribourg: Universitätsverlag, 1980.

———. *Deine Blicke sind Tauben: Zur Metaphorik des Hohen Liedes*. SBS 114/115. Stuttgart: Katholisches Bibelwerk, 1984.

———. *Gott weiblich: Eine verborgene Seite des biblischen Gottes*. Fribourg: Academic Press, 2008.

———. *Jahwe-Visionen und Siegelkunst: Eine neue Deutung der Majestätsschilderungen in Jes 6, Ez 1 und 10 und Sach4*. SBS 84/85. Stuttgart: Katholisches Bibelwerk, 1977.

———. *Jahwes Entgegnung an Ijob: Eine Deutung von Ijob 38–41 vor dem Hintergrund der zeitgenössischen Bildkunst.* FRLANT 121. Göttingen: Vandenhoeck & Ruprecht, 1978.

———. *Das Recht der Bilder gesehen zu werden: Drei Fallstudien zur Methode der Interpretation altorientalischer Bilder.* OBO 122. Fribourg: Universitätsverlag, 1992.

———. *The Symbolism of the Biblical World: Ancient Near Eastern Iconography and the Book of Psalms.* Translated by Timothy J. Hallett. London: SPCK, 1978.

———. *Die Welt der altorientalischen Bildsymbolik: Am Beispiel der Psalmen.* 5th ed. Göttingen: Vandenhoeck & Ruprecht, 1996.

Keel, Othmar, and Silvia Schroer. *Eva—Mutter alles Lebendigen: Frauen- und Göttinnenidole aus dem Alten Orient.* 3rd ed. Fribourg: Academic Press, 2010.

———. *Schöpfung: Biblische Theologien im Kontext altorientalischer Religionen.* 2nd ed. Göttingen: Vandenhoeck & Ruprecht, 2008.

Keel, Othmar, and Christoph Uehlinger. *Gods, Goddesses and Images of God in Ancient Israel.* Minneapolis: Fortress 1998.

———. *Göttinnen, Götter und Gottessymbole.* 5th ed. QD 134. Freiburg im Breisgau: Herder, 2001.

Kellenbach, Katharina von. *Anti-Judaism in Feminist Religious Writings.* AAR Cultural Criticism Series 1. Atlanta: Scholars Press, 1994.

Kessler, Rainer. "Mirjam und die Prophetie der Perserzeit." Pages 64–72 in *Gott an den Rändern: Sozialgeschichtliche Perspektiven auf die Bibel: Für Willy Schottroff zum 65. Geburtstag.* Edited by Ulrike Bail und Renate Jost. Gütersloh: Gütersloher Verlagshaus, 1996.

———. "Die Sklavin als Ehefrau: Zur Stellung der ʾāmāh." *VT* 52 (2002): 501–12.

Keuchen, Marion. *Die "Opferung Isaaks" im 20. Jahrhundert auf der Theaterbühne: Auslegungsimpulse im Blick auf "Abrahams Zelt" (Theater Musentümpel-Andersonn) und "Gottesvergiftung" (Choralgraphisches Theater Heidelberg-Grasmück).* Altes Testament und Moderne 19. Münster: LIT, 2004.

King, Karen L. *What Is Gnosticism?* Cambridge: Harvard University Press, 2005.

King, Philip J., and Lawrence E. Stager. *Life in Biblical Israel.* Library of Ancient Israel. Louisville: Westminster John Knox, 2001.

Klauck, Hans-Josef, et al., eds. *The Encyclopedia of the Bible and Its Reception.* Berlin: de Gruyter, 2009–.

Klawans, Jonathan. *Impurity and Sin in Ancient Judaism.* New York: Oxford University Press, 2000.

Klee, Deborah. "Menstruation in the Hebrew Bible." Ph.D. diss., Boston University, 1998.

Klein, Renate Andrea. *Leseprozess als Bedeutungswandel: Eine rezeptionsästhetische Erzähltextanalyse der Jakobserzählungen der Genesis.* Arbeiten zur Bibel und ihrer Geschichte 11. Leipzig: Evangelische Verlagsanstalt, 2002.

Klíma, Josef. "La position successorale de la fille dans la Babylonie ancienne." *ArOr* 18 (1955): 150–86.

Knoppers, Gary N., and Bernard M. Levinson, eds. *The Pentateuch as Torah: New Models for Understanding Its Promulgation and Acceptance.* Winona Lake, Ind.: Eisenbrauns, 2007.

Koch, Klaus. *Was ist Formgeschichte? Methoden der Bibelexegese.* 4th ed. Neukirchen-Vluyn: Neukirchener, 1981.

Koehler, Wilhelm, and Walter Baumgartner. *The Hebrew and Aramaic Lexicon of the Old Testament: Study Edition.* 2 vols. Leiden: Brill, 2001.

Kooij, Arie van der. "The Canonization of Ancient Books Kept in the Temple of Jerusalem." Pages 17–40 in *Canonization and Decanonization: Papers Presented to the International Conference of the Leiden Institute for the Study of Religions (LISOR) Held at Leiden 9–10 January 1997.* Edited by Arie van der Kooij and Karel van der Toorn. SHR 82. Leiden: Brill, 1998.

Kraeling, Emil G. *The Brooklyn Museum Aramaic Papyri: New Discoveries of the Fifth Century BC from the Jewish Colony at Elephantine.* New Haven: Yale University Press, 1953.

Kramer, Carol. *Ethnoarchaeology: Implications of Ethnography for Archaeology.* New York: Columbia University Press, 1979.

———. *Village Ethnoarchaeology: Rural Iran in Archaeological Perspective.* New York: New York Academic Press, 1982.

Krüger, Thomas. "Genesis 38—ein 'Lehrstück' alttestamentlicher Ethik." Pages 205–26 in *Konsequente Traditionsgeschichte: Festschrift für Klaus Baltzer zum 65. Geburtstag.* Edited by Rüdiger Bartelmus et al. OBO 126. Fribourg: Universitätsverlag, 1993.

Kselman, John S. "A Note on Numbers XII 6–8." *VT* 26 (1976): 502–4.

Kundert, Lukas. *Die Opferung/Bindung Isaaks.* 2 vols. WMANT 78–79. Neukirchen-Vluyn: Neukirchener, 1998.

Lakoff, George, and Mark Johnson. *Metaphors We Live By.* Chicago: University of Chicago Press, 1980.

Lambert, Wilfried G. "Prostitution." Pages 127–57 in *Außenseiter und Randgruppen: Beiträge zu einer Sozialgeschichte des Alten Orients.* Edited by Volkert Haas. Xenia 32. Konstanz: Universitätsverlag, 1992.

Laqueur, Thomas. *Auf den Leib geschrieben: Die Inszenierung der Geschlechter von der Antike bis Freud.* Munich: Deutscher Taschenbuch Verlag, 1996.

Lang, Bernhard. "Women's Work, Household and Property in Two Mediterranean Societies." *VT* 54 (2004): 188–207.

Leiman, Sid Zalman. *The Canonization of Hebrew Scripture: The Talmudic and Midrashic Evidence.* Transactions of the Connecticut Academy of Arts and Scienes 47. Hamden, Ct.: Archon, 1976.

Lenski, Gerhard E. *Power and Privilege: A Theory of Social Stratification.* Chapel Hill: University of North Carolina Press, 1984.

Lerch, David. *Isaaks Opferung christlich gedeutet: Eine auslegungsgeschichtliche Untersuchung.* BHT 12. Tübingen: Mohr Siebeck, 1950.

Levine, Baruch A. "The Biblical 'Town' as Reality and Typology: Evaluating Biblical References to Towns and Their Functions." Pages 421–53 in *Urbanization and Land Ownership in the Ancient Near East.* Edited by Michael Hudson and Baruch A. Levine. Peabody Museum Bulletin 7. Cambridge: Peabody Museum of Archaeology and Ethnology, Harvard University Press, 1999.

———. *Leviticus*. JPS Torah Commentary. Philadelphia: Jewish Publication Society, 1989.

Levine, Etan. "On Exodus 21,10 '*Onah* and Biblical Marriage." *ZABR* 5 (1999): 133–64.

Levinson, Bernard M. "The Birth of the Lemma: The Restrictive Reinterpretation of the Covenant Code's Manumission Law by the Holiness Code (Leviticus 25,44–46)." *JBL* 124 (2005): 617–39.

Levinson, Pnina Navè, "Women and Sexuality: Traditions and Progress." Pages 45–63 in *Women, Religion and Sexuality: Studies on the Impact of Religious Teachings on Women*. Edited by Jeanne Becher. Geneva: WCC Publications, 1990.

Levy, Thomas E. "Preface." Pages x–xvi in *The Archaeology of Society in the Holy Land*. Edited by Thomas E. Levy. New York: Facts on File, 1995.

Lewis, Jack P. "Jamnia Revisited." Pages 146–62 in *The Canon Debate*. Edited by Lee Martin McDonald and James A. Sanders. Peabody, Mass.: Hendrickson, 2002.

L'Hour, Jean. "L'Impur et le Saint dans le Premier Testament à partir du livre du Lévitique: Partie I: L'Impur et le Pur." *ZAW* 115 (2003): 524–37.

———. "L'Impur et le Saint dans le Premier Testament à partir du livre du Lévitique: Partie II: Le Saint et sa rencontre avec l'Impur et le Pur." *ZAW* 116 (2004): 33–54.

Lilyquist, Christine. *Ancient Egyptian Mirrors from the Earliest Times through the Middle Kingdom*. Münchener Ägyptologische Studien 27. Munich: Deutscher Kunstverlag, 1979.

Loader, James Alfred. *A Tale of Two Cities: Sodom and Gomorrah in the Old Testament, Early Jewish and Christian Traditions*. CBET 1. Kampen: Kok, 1990.

Lohfink, Norbert. "Alttestamentliche Wissenschaft als Theologie? 44 Thesen." Pages 39–49 in *Wieviel Systematik erlaubt die Schrift? Auf der Suche nach einer gesamtbiblischen Theologie*. Edited by Frank-Lothar Hossfeld. QD 185. Freiburg im Breisgau: Herder, 2001.

———. "Das deuteronomische Gesetz in der Endgestalt: Entwurf einer Gesellschaft ohne marginale Gruppen." Pages 205–18 in *Studien zum Deuteronomium und zur deuteronomistischen Literatur III*. Edited by Norbert Lohfink. SBAB 20. Stuttgart: Katholisches Bibelwerk, 1995.

———. "Fortschreibung? Zur Technik von Rechtsrevisionen im deuteronomistischen Bereich, erörtert an Deuteronomium 12, Ex 21,2–11 und Dtn 15,12–18." Pages 163–203 in Norbert Lohfink, *Studien zum Deuteronomium und zur deuteronomistischen Literatur IV*. SBAB 31. Stuttgart: Katholisches Bibelwerk, 2000.

Lokel, Philip. "Moses and His Cushite Wife: Reading Numbers 12:1 with Undergraduate Students of Makerere University." *OTE* 19 (2006): 538–47.

London, Gloria. *Women Potters of Cyprus*. Video. Nicosia: Tetraktys Film Productions, 2000.

Lutz, Hanns-Martin, Hermann Timm, und Eike Christian Hirsch, eds. *Altes Testament: Einführungen, Texte, Kommentare*. 8th ed. Munich: Piper, 1992.

Lutzmann, Heiner. "Aus den Gesetzen des Königs Lipit Eschtar von Isin." Pages 23–31 in *Rechtsbücher*. Edited by Rykle Borger et al. TUAT 1.1. Gütersloh: Gütersloher Verlagshaus, 1982.

Luz, Ulrich. *Das Evangelium nach Matthäus*. 4 vols. EKKNT 1. Neukirchen-Vluyn: Neukirchener, 1985–2002.

Lyon, William John, and Jorunn Økland, eds. *The Way the World Ends? The Apocalypse of John in Culture and Ideology*. Bible in the Modern World 19. Sheffield: Sheffield Phoenix, 2009.

Maier, Johann. "Zur Frage des biblischen Kanons im Frühjudentum im Licht der Qumranfunde." *JBTh* 3 (1988): 143–54.

Marienberg, Evyatar. *Niddah: Lorsque les juifs conceptualisent la menstruation*. Paris: Belles Lettres, 2003.

Marsman, Hennie J. *Women in Ugarit and Israel: Their Social and Religious Position in the Context of the Ancient Near East*. OtSt 49. Leiden: Brill, 2003. Repr., Atlanta: Society of Biblical Literature, 2009.

Marx, Alfred. "L'impureté selon P: Une lecture théologique." *Bib* 82 (2001): 363–84.

Marzana, Michela. *Philosophie du corps (Que sais-je?)* Paris: Vrin, 2007.

Mathews, Kenneth A. *Genesis 11:27–50:26*. New American Commentary 1B. Nashville: Broadman & Holman, 2005.

Matthiae, Paolo, *Aux origines de la Syrie: Ebla retrouvée*. Paris: Gallimard, 1996.

Mazar, Amihai. *From the Late Bronze Age IIB to the Medieval Period*. Excavations at Tel Beth-Shan 1989–1996 1. Jerusalem: Israel Exploration Society and Institute of Archaeology, Hebrew University of Jerusalem, 2006.

McNutt, Paula M. *Reconstructing the Society of Ancient Israel*. Library of Ancient Israel. Louisville: Westminster John Knox, 1999.

Methuen, Charlotte. "Stranger in a Strange Land: Reflections on History and Identity." Pages 41–68 in *Feministische Zugänge zu Geschichte und Religion*. Edited by Angela Berlis und Charlotte Methuen. Jahrbuch der Europäischen Gesellschaft für theologische Forschung von Frauen 8. Leuven: Peeters, 2000.

Metzger, Bruce. *The Canon of the New Testament: Its Origin, Development, and Significance*. Oxford: Clarendon, 1987.

Meurer, Thomas. "Der Gebärwettstreit zwischen Lea und Rahel." *BN* 107/108 (2001): 93–108.

Meyers, Carol L. "Contributing to Continuity: Women and Sacrifice in Ancient Israel." In *Women and the Gift: Beyond the Given and the All-Giving*. Edited by Morny Joy. Bloomington: Indiana University Press, forthcoming.

———. *Discovering Eve: Ancient Israelite Women in Context*. New York: Oxford University Press, 1988)

———. "Engendering Syro-Palestinian Archaeology: Reasons and Resources." *Near Eastern Archaeology* 66 (2003): 185–97.

———. "Everyday Life: Women in the Period of the Hebrew Bible." Pages 244–51 in *The Women's Bible Commentary*. Edited by Carol A. Newsom and Sharon H. Ringe. Louisville: Westminster John Knox, 1992.

———. *Exodus*. New Cambridge Bible Commentary. Cambridge: Cambridge University Press, 2005.

———. "The Family in Early Israel." Pages 1–47 in Leo G. Perdue, Joseph Blenkinsopp, John J. Collins, and Carol Meyers, *Families in Ancient Israel*. Louisville: Westminster John Knox, 1997.

———. "Having Their Space and Eating There Too: Bread Production and Female Power in Ancient Israelite Households." *Nashim* 5 (2002): 14–44.

——. *Households and Holiness: The Religious Culture of Israelite Women*. Facets Books. Minneapolis: Fortress, 2005.

——. "Material Remains and Social Relations: Women's Culture in Agrarian Households of the Iron Age." Pages 425–44 in *Symbiosis, Symbolism, and the Power of the Past: Canaan, Ancient Israel, and Their Neighbors from the Early Bronze Age through Roman Palaestina*. Edited by William G. Dever and Seymour Gitin. Winona Lake, Ind.: Eisenbrauns, 2003.

——. "Miriam the Musician." Pages 207–30 in *A Feminist Companion to Exodus to Deutreronomy*. Edited by Athalya Brenner. FCB 6. Sheffield: Sheffield Academic Press, 1994.

——. "Of Drums and Damsels: Women's Performance in Ancient Israel." *BA* 54 (1991): 16–27.

——. "Recovering Objects Re-visioning Subjects: Archaeology and Feminist Biblical Study." Pages 270–84 in *A Feminist Companion to Reading the Bible: Approaches, Methods, and Strategies*. Edited by Athalya Brenner and Carole Fontaine. Sheffield: Sheffield Academic Press, 1997.

——. " 'To Her Mother's House': Considering a Counterpart to the Israelite *Bêt 'āb*." Pages 39–51 and 304–7 in *The Bible and the Politics of Exegesis: Essays in Honor of Norman K. Gottwald on His Sixty-Fifth Birthday*. Edited by David Jobling, Peggy L. Day, and Gerald T. Sheppard. Cleveland: Pilgrim, 1991.

——. "Women in the OT." *NIDB* 5:891–92.

——. " 'Women of the Neighborhood' (Ruth 4.17): Informal Female Networks in Ancient Israel." Pages 110–27 in *Ruth and Esther*. Edited by Athalya Brenner. FCB 2/3. Sheffield: Sheffield Academic Press, 1999.

——, ed. *Women in Scripture: A Dictionary of Named and Unnamed Women in the Hebrew Bible, the Apocryphal/Deuterocanonical Books, and the New Testament*. New York: Houghton Mifflin, 2000.

Meyers, Eric M. "The Shelomith Seal and the Judean Restoration: Some Additional Considerations." *ErIsr* 18 (1985): 33–38.

Michel, Cécile. "A propos d'un testament paléo-assyrien: Une femme de marchand 'père et mère' des capitaux." *RA* 94 (2000): 1–10.

Milano, Andrea. *Donne e amore nella Bibbia: Eros, agape, persona*. Bologna: Edizioni Dehoniane, 2008.

——, ed. *Misoginia: La donna vista e malvista nella cultura occidentale*. Rom: Edizioni Dehoniane, 1992.

Milgrom, Jacob. *Leviticus 1–16: A New Translation with Introduction and Commentary*. AB 3. New York: Doubleday, 1996.

——. *Numbers: The Traditional Hebrew Text with the New JPS Translation*. JPS Torah Commentary. Philadelphia: Jewish Publication Society, 1990.

——. "The Structures of Numbers: Chapters 11–12 and 13–14 and Their Redaction: Preliminary Gropings." Pages 49–61 in *Judaic Perspectives on Ancient Israel*. Edited by Jacob Neusner, Baruch A. Levine, and Ernest S. Frerichs. Philadelphia: Fortress, 1987.

Milgrom, Jacob, David Wright, and Heinz-Josef Fabry. "נִדָּה niddāh." *ThWAT* 5:250–53.

Millard, Matthias. *Die Genesis als Eröffnung der Tora: Kompositions- und auslegungsge-schichtliche Annäherungen an das erste Buch Mose.* WMANT 90. Neukirchen-Vluyn: Neukirchener, 2001.

Molleson, Theya. "The Eloquent Bones of Abu Hureyra." *Scientific American* 271 (1994): 70–75

Morenz, Ludwig D., "Die doppelte Benutzung von Genealogie im Rahmen der Legitimierungsstrategie für Menthu-hotep (II.) als gesamtägyptischer Herrscher." Pages 109–24 in *Genealogie—Realität und Fiktion von Identität.* Edited by Martin Fitzenreiter. Internet-Beiträge zur Ägyptologie und Sudanarchäologie 5. Berlin: Humboldt-Universität, 2005. Online: http://www2.rz.hu-berlin.de/nilus/net-publications/ibaes5/publikation/ibaes5_morenz_menthu-hotep.pdf.

Moreschini, Claudio, and Enrico Norelli. *Handbuch der antiken christlichen Literatur.* Gütersloh: Gütersloher Verlagshaus, 2007.

Müllner, Ilse. "Tödliche Differenzen: Sexuelle Gewalt als Gewalt gegen Andere in Ri 19." Pages 81–100 in *Von der Wurzel getragen: Christlich-feministische Exegese in Auseinandersetzung mit Antijudaismus.* Edited by Luise Schottroff and Marie-Theres Wacker. Biblical Interpretation Series 17. Leiden: Brill, 1996.

Murdock, George P., and Catherine Provost. "Factors in the Division of Labor by Sex: A Cross-Cultural Analysis." *Ethnology* 12 (1973): 203–25.

Nahkola, Aulikki, *Double Narratives in the Old Testament: The Foundations of Method in Biblical Criticism.* BZAW 290. Berlin: de Gruyter, 2001.

Navarro Puerto, Mercedes. *Barro y aliento: Exégesis y antropología narrativa de Gn 2–3.* Madrid: San Pablo, 1993.

———. "Las extrañas del Génesis, tan parecidas y tan diferentes..." Pages 155–219 in *Relectura del Génesis.* Edited by Isabel Gómez-Acebo et al. 2nd ed. En Clave de Mujer. Bilbao: Desclée de Brouwer, 1999.

———. "El paso del mar: nacer muriendo." Pages 85–143 in *Relectura del Éxodo.* Edited by Isabel Gómez-Acebo et al. En Clave de Mujer. Bilbao: Desclée de Brouwer, 2006.

Naveh, Joseph. "Hebrew and Aramaic Inscriptions." Pages 1–14 in *Inscriptions.* Vol. 6 of *Excavations at the City of David 1978–1985, Directed by Yigal Shiloh.* Edited by Donald T. Ariel. Qedem 41. Jerusalem: Institute of Archaeology, Hebrew University of Jerusalem, 2000.

Nelson, Sarah Milledge. *Gender in Archaeology: Analyzing Power and Prestige.* 2nd ed. Gender and Archaeology 9. Walnut Creek, Calif.: AltaMira, 2004.

———, ed. *Handbook of Gender in Archaeology.* Lanham, Md.: AltaMira, 2006.

Niditch, Susan. "Genesis." Pages 10–25 in *The Women's Bible Commentary.* Edited by Carol A. Newsom and Sharon H. Ringe. Louisville: Westminster John Knox, 1992.

———. "The Wronged Woman Righted: An Analysis of Genesis 38." *HTR* 72 (1979): 143–49.

Nihan, Christophe. "L'écrit sacerdotal entre mythe et histoire." Pages 151–90 in *Ancient and Modern Scriptural Historiography/L'historiographie biblique, ancienne et moderne.* Edited by George J. Brooke and Thomas Römer. BETL 207. Leuven: Leuven University Press, 2007.

Noth, Martin. *A History of Pentateuchal Traditions*. Translated by Bernhard W. Anderson. Englewood Cliffs, N.J.: Prentice-Hall, 1972.

———. *Das System der zwölf Stämme Israels*. Darmstadt: Wissenschaftliche Buchgesellschaft, 1966.

———. *Das Zweite Buch Mose: Exodus*. Das Alte Testament Deutsch 5. Göttingen: Vandenhoeck & Ruprecht, 1959.

O'Connor, Kathleen M. "The Feminist Movement Meets the Old Testament." Pages 3–24 in *Engaging the Bible in a Gendered World: An Introduction to Feminist Biblical Interpretation in Honor of Katharine Doob Sakenfeld*. Edited by Linda Day and Carolyn Pressler. Louisville: Westminster John Knox, 2006),

Oden, Robert A., Jr. "Jacob as Father, Husband, and Nephew: Kinship Studies and the Patriarchal Narratives." *JBL* 102 (1983): 189–205.

O'Donnell Setel, Drorah. "Exodus." Pages 26–35 in *The Women's Bible Commentary*. Edited by Carol A. Newsom and Sharon H. Ringe. Louisville: Westminster John Knox, 1992.

Oeming, Manfred. *Das wahre Israel: Die "genealogische Vorhalle" 1 Chronik 1–9*. BWANT 128. Stuttgart: Kohlhammer, 1990.

Økland, Jorunn. "Donne interpreti della Bibbia nella tradizione protestanti." Pages 99–116 in *Donne e Bibbia: Storia ed esegesi*. Edited by Adriana Valerio. La Bibbia nella Storia 21. Bologna: Edizioni Dehoniane, 2006.

———. "Nature, Revelation and Gender Hierarchy in Paul and His Early Modern Interpreters." Pages 31–48 in *Gender, Religion, Human Rights in Europe*. Edited by Kari Børresen und Sara Cabibbo. Rome: Herder, 2006.

Osiek, Carolyn. "The Feminist and the Bible: Hermeneutical Alternatives." Pages 93–105 in *Feminist Perspectives on Biblical Scholarship*. Edited by Adela Yarbro Collins. SBLBSNA 10. Chico, Calif.: Scholars Press, 1985.

Otten, Heinrich. "Geschichtswissenschaft in Hatti." *RlA* 3:220–21.

Otto, Eckart. "False Weights in the Scales of Biblical Justice? Different Views of Women from Patriarchal Hierarchy to Religious Equality in the Book of Deuteronomy." Pages 128–46 in *Gender and Law in the Hebrew Bible and the Ancient Near East*. Edited by Victor H. Matthews, Bernard M. Levinson, and Tikva Frymer-Kensky. JSOTSup 262. Sheffield: Sheffield Academic Press, 1998.

———. *Gottes Recht als Menschenrecht: Rechts- und literaturhistorische Studien zum Deuteronomium*. Wiesbaden: Harrassowitz, 2002.

———. *Theologische Ethik des Alten Testaments*. Theologische Wissenschaft 3.2. Stuttgart: Kohlhammer, 1994

Paschen, Wilfried. *Rein und Unrein: Untersuchung zur biblischen Wortgeschichte*. SANT 24. Munich: Kösel, 1970.

Paz, Sarit. *Drums, Women, and Goddesses: Drumming and Gender in Iron Age II Israel*. OBO 232. Fribourg: Academic Press, 2007.

Peet, T. Eric. *A Comparative Study of the Literatures of Egypt, Palestine and Mesopotamia: Egypt's Contribution to the Literatures of the Ancient World*. The Ancient Near East: Classical Studies. Eugene, Ore.: Wipf & Stock, 2007.

Penna, Romano. "Il discorso paolino sulle origini umane alla luce di Gen 1–3 e le sue funzioni semantiche." *RStB* 1–2 (1994): 233–239.

Perani, Mauro. "Il processo di canonizzazione della Bibbia ebraica: Nuove prospettive metodologiche." *RivB* 48 (2000): 385–400.

Perroni, Marinella. "Gen 1–3: Tre racconti brevi sulla nascita della democrazia." In *Mujeres ¿menos religión y más espiritualidad?* Edited by Mercedes Navarro Puerto and Mercedes Arriaga. Sevilla: Arcibel, 2010.

Perry, T. A. "A Poetics of Absence: The Structure and Meaning of Genesis 1.2." *JSOT* 58 (1993): 3–11.

Peterson, Jane. *Sexual Revolutions: Gender and Labor at the Dawn of Agriculture.* Gender and Archaeology 4. Walnut Creek, Calif.: AltaMira, 2002.

Philip, Taria S. *Menstruation and Childbirth in the Bible: Fertility and Impurity.* Studies in Biblical Literature 88. New York: Lang, 2006.

Philippson, Paula. *Untersuchungen über den griechischen Mythos.* Zürich: Rhein-Verlag, 1944.

Pikaza, Xabier. *Diccionario de la Biblia: Historia y palabra.* Diccionarios Maior; Estella: Verbo Divino, 2007.

———. *Hombre y mujer en las grandes religiones.* Estella: Verbo Divino, 1996.

Plaskow, Judith. "Blaming the Jews for the Birth of Patriarchy." Pages 298–302 in *Nice Jewish Girls: A Lesbian Anthology.* Edited by Evelyn Torton Beck. Crossing Press Feminist Series. Trumansburg, N.Y.: Crossing, 1982.

———. "Christian Feminism and Anti-Judaism." *Cross Currents* 33 (1978): 306–9.

———. *Standing again at Sinai: Judaism from a Feminist Perspective.* San Francisco: Harper, 1991.

———. *Und wieder stehen wir am Sinai: Eine jüdisch-feministische Theologie.* Luzern: Exodus, 1992.

Plum, Karin Friis. "Genealogy as Theology." *SJOT* 1 (1989): 66–92.

Porten, Bezalel, and Ada Yardeni. *Contracts.* Vol. 2 of *Textbook of Aramaic Documents from Ancient Egypt.* Winona Lake, Ind.: Eisenbrauns, 1989.

Portugali, Yuval. "'Arim, Banot, Migrashim, and Haṣerim: The Spatial Organization of *Eretz-Israel* in the Twelfth–Tenth Centuries BCE according to the Bible" [Hebrew]. *ErIsr* 17 (1983): 282–90.

Pressler, Carolyn. "Sexual Violence and Deuteronomic Law." Pages 102–12 in *A Feminist Companion to Exodus to Deuteronomy.* Edited by Athalya Brenner. FCB 6. Sheffield: Sheffield Academic Press, 1994.

———. *The View of Women Found in the Deuteronomic Family Laws.* BZAW 216. Berlin: de Gruyter, 1993.

———. "Wives and Daughters, Bond and Free: Views of Women in the Slave Laws of Exodus 21,2–11." Pages 147–72 in *Gender and Law in the Hebrew Bible and the Ancient Near East.* Edited by Victor H. Matthews, Bernard M. Levinson, and Tikva Frymer-Kensky. JSOTSup 262. Sheffield: Sheffield Academic Press, 1998.

Preuss, Horst-Dietrich. *Deuteronomium.* EdF 164. Darmstadt: Wissenschaftliche Buchgesellschaft, 1982.

Prewitt, Terry J. "Kinship Structures and the Genesis Genealogies." *JNES* 40 (1981): 87–98.

Propp, William H. C. "Kinship in 2 Samuel 13." *CBQ* 55 (1993): 39–53.

Püschel, Erich. *Die Menstruation und ihre Tabus.* Stuttgart: Schattauer, 1988.

Quesada, Jan Jaynes. "Body Piercing: The Issue of Priestly Control over Acceptable Family Structure in the Book of Numbers." *BibInt* 10 (2002): 24–35.

Rabenau, Merten. *Studien zum Buch Tobit*. BZAW 220. Berlin: de Gruyter, 1994.

Rabinowitz, Isaac. "*āz* Followed by Imperfect Verb-Form in Preterite Contexts: A Redactional Device in Biblical Hebrew." *VT* 34 (1984): 53–62.

Rad, Gerhard von. *Das erste Buch Mose: Genesis*. ATD 2/4. Göttingen: Vandenhoeck & Ruprecht, 1964.

Räisänen, Heikki. "The Effective 'History' of the Bible: A Challenge to Biblical Scholarship." *SJT* 45 (1992): 303–24.

Rapoport, Amos. "Spatial Organization and the Built Environment." Pages 460–502 in *Companion Encyclopedia of Anthropology*. Edited by Tim Ingold. London: Routledge, 1994.

Rapp, Ursula. "The Heritage of Old Testament Impurity Laws: Gender as a Question of How to Focus on Women." Pages 29–40 in *Gender und Religion: European Studies*. Edited by Kari E. Børresen, Sara Cabibbo, and Edith Specht. Quaderni 2. Rom: Carocci, 2001.

———. *Mirjam: Eine feministisch-rhetorische Lektüre der Mirjamtexte in der hebräischen Bibel*. BZAW 317. Berlin: de Gruyter, 2002.

Redfield, Robert. *Peasant Society and Culture: An Anthropological Approach to Civilization*. Chicago: University of Chicago Press, 1956.

Redford, Donald B. *Pharaonic King-Lists, Annals and Day-Books: A Contribution to the Study of the Egyptian Sense of History*. The Society for the Study of Egyptian Antiquities Publications 4. Mississauga, Ont.: Benben, 1986.

Reisner, George A., Clarence S. Fisher, and David G. Lyon. *Harvard Excavations at Samaria, 1908–1910*. 2 vols. Cambridge: Harvard University Press, 1924.

Rendtorff, Rolf. *The Problem of the Process of Transmission in the Pentateuch*. Translated by John J. Scullion. JSOTSup 89. Sheffield: JSOT Press, 1990.

———. *Das überlieferungsgeschichtliche Problem des Pentateuch*. BZAW 147. Berlin: de Gruyter, 1977.

Renger, Johannes. "Untersuchungen zum Priestertum in der altbabylonischen Zeit." *ZA* 58 (1967): 110–88.

Reuter, Eleonore. *Kultzentralisation: Entstehung und Theologie von Dtn 12*. BBB 87; Frankfurt: Hain, 1993.

Riché, Pierre, and Guy Lobrichon, eds. *Bible de tous les Temps*. 8 vols. Paris: Beauchesne, 1984–1989.

Ringe, Sharon H. "Biblical Authority and Interpretation." Pages 31–40 in *The Liberating Word: A Guide to Non-sexist Interpretation of the Bible*. Edited by Letty M. Russell. Philadelphia: Westminster, 1976.

Robins, Gay. *Women in Ancient Egypt*. London: British Museum Press, 1993.

Röllig, Wolfgang. *Das Bier im alten Mesopotamien*. Berlin: Blaschker, 1970.

Römer, Thomas. *Israels Väter: Untersuchungen zur Väterthematik im Deuteronomium und in der deuteronomistischen Tradition*. OBO 99. Fribourg: Universitätsverlag, 1990.

Römer, Willem H. P. "Aus den Gesetzen des Königs Urnammu von Ur." Pages 17–23 in *Rechtsbücher*. Edited by Rykle Borger et al. TUAT 1.1. Gütersloh: Gütersloher Verlagshaus, 1982.

Rogers, Susan Carol. "Female Forms of Power and the Myth of Male Dominance: A Model of Female/Male Interaction in Peasant Society." *American Ethnologist* 2 (1975): 727–56.

Rollston, Christopher A. "Prosography and the יזבל Seal." *IEJ* 59 (2009): 86–91.

Romero, Margarita Sánchez. "Women, Maintenance Activities and Space." Pages 178–182 in *SOMA 2001: Symposium on Mediterranean Archaeology: Proceedings of the Fifth Annual Meeting of Postgraduate Researchers, the University of Liverpool, 23–23 February 2001*. Edited by Georgina Muskett, Aikaterini Koltsida, and Mercourios Georgiadis. BAR International Series 1040. Oxford: Archaeopress, 2002.

Roth, Martha. "Age at Marriage and the Household: A Study of Neo-Babylonian and Neo-Assyrian Forms." *Comparative Studies in Societies and History* 29 (1987): 715–47.

———. *Law Collections from Mesopotamia and Asia Minor*. SBLWAW 6. Atlanta: Scholars Press, 1995.

———. "The Priestess and the Tavern: LH § 110." Pages 445–64 in *Munuscula Mesopotamica: Festschrift für Johannes Renger*. Edited by Barbara Böck, Eva Cancik-Kirschbaum, and Thomas Richter. AOAT 267. Münster: Ugarit-Verlag, 1999.

Roth, Silke. *"Gebieterin aller Länder": Die Rolle der königlichen Frauen in der fiktiven und realen Außenpolitik des ägyptischen Neuen Reiches*. OBO 185. Fribourg: Universitätsverlag, 2002.

———. *Die Königsmütter des alten Ägypten von der Frühzeit bis zum Ende der 12. Dynastie*. Ägypten und Altes Testament 46. Wiesbaden: Harrassowitz, 2001.

Rothöhler, Benedikt. Neue Gedanken zum Denkmal memphitischer Theologie. Diss., Universität Heidelberg, 2004. Online: http://www.ub.uni-heidelberg.de/archiv/7030.

Rowley, Harold Henry. *The Growth of the Old Testament*. Hutchinson's University Library: Christian Religion 45. London: Hutchinson, 1950.

Ruether, Rosemary Radford. *Sexism and God-Talk: Toward a Feminist Theology*. Boston: Beacon, 1983.

Rüterswörden, Udo, *Das Buch Deuteronomium*. Neuer Stuttgarter Kommentar: Altes Testament 4. Stuttgart: Katholisches Bibelwerk, 2006.

Ruwe, Andreas. *"Heiligkeitsgesetz" und "Priesterschrift": Literaturgeschichtliche und rechtssystematische Untersuchungen zu Leviticus 17,1–26,2*. FAT 26. Tübingen: Mohr Siebeck, 1999.

Ryle, Herbert Edward. *The Canon of the Old Testament: An Essay on the Gradual Growth and Formation of the Hebrew Canon of Scripture*. London: Macmillan, 1892.

Salm, Eva. *Juda und Tamar: Eine exegetische Studie zu Gen 38*. FB 76. Würzburg: Echter, 1996.

Sanders, James A. "Canon." *ABD* 1:837–52.

———. *Canon and Community: A Guide to Canonical Criticism*. Philadelphia: Fortress, 1984.

———. "Hermeneutics in True and False Prophecy." Pages 21–41 in *Canon and Authority: Essays in Old Testament Religion and Theology.* Edited by George W. Coats and Burke O. Long. Philadelphia: Fortress, 1977.

———. *Torah and Canon.* Philadelphia: Fortress, 1972.

Satran, David. "Apocrypha/Pseudepigrapha. II. Old Testament." *RPP* 1:308.

Sawyer, John. "The Place of Reception-History in a Post-Modern Bible Commentary." Online: http://www.bbibcomm.net/news/sawyer.html.

Schäfer-Bossert, Stefanie. "Den Männern die Macht und der Frau die Trauer? Ein kritischer Blick auf die Deutung von אוֹן—oder: Wie nennt Rahel ihren Sohn?" Pages 106–25 in *Feministische Hermeneutik und Erstes Testament: Analysen und Interpretationen.* Edited by Hedwig Jahnow et al. Stuttgart: Kohlhammer, 1994.

Schäfer-Lichtenberger, Christa. "Beobachtungen zur Rechtsstellung der Frau in der alttestamentlichen Überlieferung." *WD* 24 (1997): 95–120.

Scharbert, Josef. *Numeri.* NechtB. Würzburg: Echter, 1992.

Schenker, Adrian. "The Biblical Legislation on the Release of Slaves: The Road from Exodus to Leviticus." *JSOT* 78 (1998): 23–41.

Schmid, Konrad, *Erzväter und Exodus: Untersuchungen zur doppelten Begründung der Ursprünge Israels innerhalb der Geschichtsbücher des Alten Testaments.* WMANT 81. Neukirchen-Vluyn: Neukirchener, 1999.

Schmidt, Eva Renate, Mieke Korenhof, and Renate Jost, eds. *Feministisch gelesen: Ausgewählte Bibeltexte für Gruppen, Gemeinden und Gottesdienste.* 2 vols. Stuttgart: Kreuz-Verlag, 1988/89.

Schmidt, Werner H. *Exodus 1–6.* BKAT 2.1. Neukirchen-Vluyn: Neukirchener, 1988.

Schmitt, John J. "Like Eve, Like Adam: *mšl* in Gen 3,16." *Bib* 72 (1991): 1–22.

Schneider, Tammi J. *Sarah: Mother of Nations.* New York: Continuum, 2004.

Scholz, Susanne. "The Complexities of 'His' Liberation Talk: A Literary Feminist Reading of the Book of Exodus." Pages 20–40 in *A Feminist Companion to Exodus to Deuteronomy.* Edited by Athalya Brenner. FCB 2.5. Sheffield: Sheffield Academic Press, 2000.

———. "Exodus: Was Befreiung aus 'seiner' Sicht bedeutet...." Pages 26–39 in *Kompendium Feministische Bibelauslegung.* Edited by Luise Schottroff and Marie-Theres Wacker. Gütersloh: Gütersloher Verlagshaus, 1998.

———. *Rape Plots: A Feminist Cultural Study of Genesis 34.* Studies in Biblical Literature 13. New York: Lang, 2000.

Schorch, Stefan. *Euphemismen in der Hebräischen Bibel.* Orientalia Biblica et Christiana 12. Wiesbaden: Harrassowitz, 2000.

Schottroff, Luise. "Auf dem Weg zu einer feministischen Rekonstruktion der Geschichte des frühen Christentums." Pages 173–248 in Luise Schottroff, Silvia Schroer, and Marie-Theres Wacker, *Feministische Exegese: Forschungserträge zur Bibel aus der Perspektive von Frauen.* Darmstadt: Primus, 1997.

Schottroff, Luise, and Marie-Theres Wacker, eds. *Kompendium Feministische Bibelauslegung.* 3rd ed. Gütersloh: Gütersloher Verlagshaus, 2007.

Schottroff, Willy. "Die Armut der Witwen." Pages 54–89 in *Schuld und Schulden: Biblische Traditionen in gegenwärtigen Konflikten.* Edited by Marlene Crüsemann and Willy Schottroff. Kaiser Taschenbücher 121. Munich: Kaiser, 1992.

—. "Der Zugriff des Königs auf die Töchter: Zur Fronarbeit von Frauen im alten Israel." Pages 94–114 in *Gerechtigkeit lernen: Beiträge zur biblischen Sozialgeschichte*. Edited by Frank Crüsemann et al. Theologische Bücherei 94. Gütersloh: Gütersloher Verlagshaus, 1999.

Schroer, Silvia. "Auf dem Weg zu einer feministischen Rekonstruktion der Geschichte Israels." Pages 83–172 in Luise Schottroff, Silvia Schroer, and Marie-Theres Wacker, *Feministische Exegese: Forschungserträge zur Bibel aus der Perspektive von Frauen*. Darmstadt: Primus, 1997.

—. "Gender and Iconography from the Viewpoint of a Feminist Biblical Scholar." *lectio difficilior* 2 (2008). Online: www.lectio.unibe.ch/08_2/Silvia_Schroer_Gender_and_Iconography.html.

—. "Häusliche und außerhäusliche religiöse Kompetenzen israelitischer Frauen—am Beispiel von Totenklage und Totenbefragung." *lectio difficilior* 1 (2002). Online: http://www.lectio.unibe.ch/02_1/schroer.htm.

—. *Die Mittelbronzezeit*. Vol. 2 of *Die Ikonographie Palästinas/Israels und der Alte Orient: Eine Religionsgeschichte in Bildern*. Fribourg: Academic Press, 2008.

—. *In Israel gab es Bilder: Nachrichten von darstellender Kunst im Alten Testament*. OBO 74. Fribourg: Universitätsverlag, 1987.

—. "'Under the Shadow of Your Wings': The Metaphor of God's Wings in the Psalms, Exodus 19.4, Deuteronomy 32.11 and Malachi 3.20, as Seen through the Perspectives of Feminism and History of Religion." Pages 264–82 in *Wisdom and Psalms*. Edited by Athalya Brenner and Carol R. Fontaine. FCB 2/2. Sheffield: Sheffield Academic Press, 1998.

Schroer, Silvia, and Othmar Keel. *Vom ausgehenden Mesolithikum bis zur Frühbronzezeit*. Vol. 1 of *Die Ikonographie Palästinas/Israels und der Alte Orient: Eine Religionsgeschichte in Bildern*. Fribourg: Academic Press, 2005.

Schroer, Silvia, and Thomas Staubli. *Body Symbolism in the Bible*. Collegeville, Minn.: Liturgical Press, 2001.

—. *Die Körpersymbolik der Bibel*. 2nd ed. Darmstadt: Wissenschaftliche Buchgesellschaft, 2005.

Schuler, Einar von. "Hethitische Rechtsbücher." Pages 96–123 in *Rechtsbücher*. Edited by Rykle Borger et al. TUAT 1.1. Gütersloh: Gütersloher Verlagshaus, 1982.

Schüngel-Straumann, Helen. *Anfänge feministischer Exegese: Gesammelte Beiträge, mit einem orientierenden Nachwort und einer Auswahlbibliographie*. Exegese in unserer Zeit 8. Münster: LIT, 2002.

—. "Mose und Zippora: Buch Exodus, Kapitel 2,4 und 18." Pages 152–56 in *Schön bist du und verlockend: Große Paare der Bibel*. Edited by Herbert Haag. Freiburg im Breisgau: Herder, 2001.

—. *Die Frau am Anfang: Eva und die Folgen*. Frauenforum. Freiburg im Breisgau: Herder, 1989. 2nd ed. Exegese in unserer Zeit 6. Münster: LIT, 1997.

—. "Tamar." *BK* 39 (1984): 148–57.

—. *Tobit*. HTKAT. Freiburg im Breisgau: Herder, 2000.

Schüssler Fiorenza, Elisabeth. *Bread, Not Stone: The Challenge of Feminist Biblical Interpretation*. Boston: Beacon, 1984.

———. *In Memory of Her: A Feminist Theological Reconstruction of Christian Origins.* New York: Crossroad, 1983.

———. "Introduction: Transforming the Legacy of *The Woman's Bible*." Pages 1–24 in *A Feminist Introduction.* Vol. 1 of *Searching the Scriptures.* Edited by Elisabeth Schüssler Fiorenza. London: SCM, 1995.

———, ed. *A Feminist Commentary.* Vol. 2 of *Searching the Scriptures.* London: SCM, 1994.

———, ed. *A Feminist Introduction.* Vol. 1 of *Searching the Scriptures.* London: SCM, 1994.

Schwienhorst-Schönberger, Ludger. *Das Bundesbuch (Ex 20,22–23,33): Studien zu seiner Entstehung und Theologie.* BZAW 188. Berlin: de Gruyter, 1990.

Seidl, Theodor. "Rein und unrein." Pages 315–20 in vol. 3 of *Neues Bibel-Lexikon.* Edited by Manfred Görg und Bernhard Lang. 3 vols. Zürich: Benzinger, 1991–2001.

Seifert, Elke. *Tochter und Vater im Alten Testament: Eine ideologiekritische Untersuchung zur Verfügungsgewalt von Vätern über ihre Töchter.* Neukirchener Theologische Dissertationen und Habilitationen 9. Neukirchen-Vluyn: Neukirchener, 1997.

Serra, Aristide. "Valenze creative e distruttive della figura di Eva nel giudaismo antico." *RStB* 1–2 (1994): 179–99.

Sheppard, Gerald. "True and False Prophecy within Scripture." Pages 262–82 in *Canon, Theology, and Old Testament Interpretation: Essays in Honor of Brevard S. Childs.* Edited by Gene M. Tucker, David L. Petersen, and Robert R. Wilson. Philadelphia: Fortress, 1988.

Sherwood, Stephen K. *Leviticus, Numbers, Deuteronomy.* Berit Olam. Collegeville, Minn.: Liturgical Press, 2002.

Siebert-Hommes, Jopie. "But If She Be a Daughter … She May Live! 'Daughters' and 'Sons' in Exodus 1–2." Pages 62–74 in *A Feminist Companion to Exodus to Deuteronomy.* Edited by Athalya Brenner. FCB 6. Sheffield: Sheffield Academic Press, 1994.

———. "Die Geburtsgeschichte des Mose innerhalb des Erzählzusammenhangs von Exodus I und II." *VT* 42 (1992): 398–404.

———. "Hebräerinnen sind chaiot." Pages 191–99 in *"Dort ziehen Schiffe dahin…": Paris 1992.* Edited by Matthias Augustin und Klaus-Dietrich Schunck. BEATAJ 28. Frankfurt: Lang, 1996.

———. *Let the Daughters Live! The Literary Architecture of Exodus 1–2 as a Key for Interpretation.* Biblical Interpretation Series 37. Leiden: Brill, 1998.

Siegele-Wenschkewitz, Leonore. *Verdrängte Vergangenheit, die uns bedrängt: Feministische Theologie in der Verantwortung für die Geschichte.* Kaiser Taschenbücher 29. Munich: Kaiser, 1988.

Ska, Jean Louis. "Essai sur la nature et la signification du cycle d'Abraham." Pages 153–77 in *Studies in the Book of Genesis: Literature, Redaction and History.* Edited by André Wénin. BETL 155. Leuven: University Press, 2001.

Smith, Ralph L. *Micah–Malachi.* WBC 32. Waco, Tex.: Word, 1984.

Smith-Christopher, Daniel L., "The Mixed Marriage Crisis in Ezra 9–10 and Nehemia 13." Pages 243–65 in *Second Temple Studies 2: Temple and Community in the Persian Period*. Edited by Tamara C. Eskenazi and Kent H. Richards. JSOTSup 175. Sheffield: Sheffield Academic Press, 1994.

Soggin, J. Alberto. *Das Buch Genesis: Kommentar*. Darmstadt: Wissenschaftliche Buchgesellschaft, 1997.

Sollberger, Edmond, "The Rulers of Lagaš." *JCS* 21 (1967): 279–91.

Solvang, Elna K. *A Woman's Place Is in the House: Royal Women of Judah and Their Involvement in the House of David*. JSOTSup 349. Sheffield: Sheffield Academic Press, 2003.

Spanier, Ktziah. "Rachel's Theft of the Teraphim: Her Struggle for Family Primacy." *VT* 42 (1992): 404–12.

Speiser, Ephraim A. "Geschichtswissenschaft." *RlA* 3:216–20.

Speyer, Wolfgang. "Genealogie." *RAC* 9:1145–1268.

Stager, Lawrence E., "The Archaeology of the Family in Ancient Israel." *BASOR* 260 (1985): 1–35.

Standhartinger, Angela, "Joseph und Aseneth: Vollkommene Braut oder himmlische Prophetin." Pages 459–64 in *Kompendium Feministische Bibelauslegung*. Edited by Luise Schottroff and Marie-Theres Wacker. 2nd ed. Gütersloh: Gütersloher Verlagshaus, 1999.

Stanton, Elizabeth Cady, and the Revising Committee. *The Women's Bible*. New York: European Publishing, 1897; Repr., Seattle: Coalition Task Force on Women and Religion, 1974.

Starr Sered, Susan. "Rachel's Tomb and the Milk Grotto of the Virgin Mary: Two Women's Shrines in Bethlehem." *JFSR* 2 (1986): 7–22.

Staubli, Thomas. *Die Bücher Levitikus, Numeri*. Neuer Stuttgarter Kommentar: Altes Testament 3. Stuttgart: Katholisches Bibelwerk, 1996.

Steck, Odil Hannes. *Der Abschluß der Prophetie im Alten Testament: Ein Versuch zur Frage der Vorgeschichte des Kanons*. Biblisch-theologische Studien 17. Neukirchen-Vluyn: Neukirchener, 1991.

Stein, David E. S. "Dictionary of Gender in the Torah." Pages 393–412 in *The Contemporary Torah: A Gender-Sensitive Adaptation of the JPS Translation*. Edited by David E. S. Stein. Philadelphia: Jewish Publication Society, 2006.

———, ed. *The Contemporary Torah: A Gender-Sensitive Adaption of the JPS Translation*. Philadelphia: Jewish Publication Society, 2006.

Steinberg, Naomi. "'Adam's and Eve's Daughters Are Many': Gender Roles in Ancient Israelite Society." Ph.D. diss., Columbia University, 1984.

———. "Alliance or Descent? The Function of Marriage in Genesis." *JSOT* 51 (1991): 45–55.

———. The Genealogical Framework of the Family Stories in Genesis." *Semeia* 46 (1989): 41–50.

Steins, Georg. *Die "Bindung Isaaks" im Kanon (Gen 22): Grundlagen und Programm einer kanonisch-intertextuellen Lektüre: Mit einer Spezialbibliographie zu Gen 22*. Herders Biblische Studien 20. Freiburg im Breisgau: Herder, 1999.

Stol, Marten. "Reinheid in Mesoptamië." *Phoenix* 48 (2002): 103–7.

Stone, Elizabeth C. "The Social Role of the *Naditu* Women in Old Babylonian Nippur." *JESHO* 25 (1982): 50–70.

Stone, Merlin. *When God Was a Woman*. San Diego: Harcourt Brace Jovanovich, 1976.

Stordalen, Terje. "Man, Soil, Garden: Basic Plot in Genesis 2–3 Reconsidered." *JSOT* 53 (1992): 3–26.

Stowasser, Martin. "Die Genealogien Jesu im Evangelium des Matthäus und des Lukas." Pages 183–96 in *Genealogie—Realität und Fiktion von Identität*. Edited by Martin Fitzenreiter. Internet-Beiträge zur Ägyptologie und Sudanarchäologie 5. Berlin: Humboldt-Universität, 2005. Online: http://www2.rz.hu-berlin.de/nilus/net-publications/ibaes5/publikation/ibaes5_stowasser_jesu.pdf.

Strack, Hermann L., and Paul Billerbeck. *Kommentar zum Neuen Testament aus Talmud und Midrasch*. 4 vols. Munich: Beck, 1922–1928.

Sugimoto, David T. *Female Figurines with a Disk from the Southern Levant and the Formation of Monotheism*. Tokyo: Keio University Press, 2008.

Sweeney, Marvin A. *The Twelve Prophets*. Berit Olam. Collegeville, Minn.: Liturgical Press, 2000.

Taschl-Erber, Andrea. *Maria von Magdala—erste Apostolin? Joh 20,1–18: Tradition und Relecture*. Herders Biblische Studien 51. Freiburg im Breisgau: Herder, 2007.

Teubal, Savina J. Hagar the Egyptian: The Lost Tradition of the Matriarchs. San Francisco: Harper, 1990.

———. *Sarah the Priestess: The First Matriarch of Genesis*. Athens: Swallow Press, 1984.

Thompson, John L. *Writing the Wrongs: Women of the Old Testament among Biblical Commentators from Philo through the Reformation*. Oxford Studies in Historical Theology. Oxford: Oxford University Press, 2001.

Tigay, Jeffrey H. *Deuteronomy: The Traditional Hebrew Text with the New JPS Translation*. JPS Torah Commentary. Philadelphia: Jewish Publication Society, 1996.

Toorn, Karel van der. *From Her Cradle to Her Grave: The Role of Religion in the Life of the Israelite and the Babylonian Woman*. Biblical Seminar 23. Sheffield: JSOT Press, 1994.

Tosato, Angelo. *Il matrimonio israelitico: Una teoria generale, nuova prefazione, presentazione e bibliografia*. AnBib 100. Rome: Pontifical Biblical Institute, 2001.

Tov, Emanuel. "The Status of the Masoretic Text in Modern Text Editions of the Hebrew Bible: The Relevance of Canon." Pages 234–51 in *The Canon Debate*. Edited by Lee Martin McDonald and James A. Sanders. Peabody, Mass.: Hendrickson, 2002.

Trebolle Barrera, Julio. *La Biblia judía y la Biblia cristiana: Introducción a la historia de la Biblia*. Colleccion estructuras y procesos: Serie religión. Madrid: Trotta, 1993.

Trible, Phyllis. "Bringing Miriam Out of the Shadows." Pages 166–86 in *A Feminist Companion to Exodus to Deuteronomy*. Edited by Athalya Brenner. FCB 6. Sheffield: Sheffield Academic Press, 1994.

———. "Depatriarchalizing in Biblical Interpretation." *JAAR* 41 (1973): 30–48.

———. *God and the Rhetoric of Sexuality*. OBT 2. Philadelphia: Fortress, 1978.

———. *Texts of Terror: Literary-Feminist Readings of Biblical Narratives*. 2nd ed. OBT 13. Philadelphia: Fortress, 1985.

Tsokkinen, Anni. "Elisabeth Schüssler Fiorenza on the Authority of the Bible." Pages 133–42 in *Holy Texts: Authority and Language = Heilige Texte: Autorität und Sprache = Textes Sacrés: Autorité et Langue*. Edited by Charlotte Methuen et al. Yearbook of the European Society of Women in Theological Research 12. Leuven: Peeters, 2004.

Ulrich, Eugene. "The Canonical Process, Textual Criticism, and Latter Stages in the Composition of the Bible." Pages 267–91 in *"Sha'arei Talmon": Studies in the Bible, Qumran, and the Ancient Near East Presented to Shemaryahu Talmon*. Edited by Michael Fishbane und Emanuel Tov. Winona Lake, Ind.: Eisenbrauns, 1992.

Valerio, Adriana, ed. *Donne e Bibbia: Storia ed esegesi*. La Bibbia nella Storia 21. Bologna: Edizioni Dehoniane, 2006.

Valerio, Adriana, Francesco Santi, and Claudio Leonardi, eds. *La Bibbia nel'interpretazione delle donne*. Millennio medievale 34. Florenz: Il Galluzzo, 2002.

Van Seters, John. "The Law of the Hebrew Slave." *ZAW* 108 (1996): 534–46.

———. *Prologue to History: The Yahwist as Historian in Genesis*. Louisville: Westminster John Knox, 1992.

Veenhof, Klaas. *Aspects of Old Assyrian Trade and Its Terminology*. SD 10. Leiden: Brill, 1972.

———. "Old Assyrian Period." Pages 431–83 in *A History of Ancient Near Eastern Law*. Edited by Raymond Westbrook. 2 vols. Handbook of Oriental Studies 72. Leiden: Brill, 2003.

———. "The Relation between Royal Decrees and 'Law Codes' of the Old Babylonian Period." *JEOL* 35–36 (1997–2000): 49–83.

Vieira Sampaio, Tania Mara. "Un éxodo entre muchos otros éxodos: La belleza de lo transitorio oscurecida por el discurso de lo permanente: Una lectura de Exodo 1–15." *RIBLA* 23 (1996): 75–87.

Wacker, Marie-Theres. "Mirjam." Pages 44–52 in *Zwischen Ohnmacht und Befreiung: Biblische Frauengestalten*. Edited by Karin Walter. Reihe Frauenforum. Freiburg im Breisgau: Herder, 1988.

———. "Mirjam—Schwester unter Brüdern." Pages 177–91 in eadem, *Die Frau im Tallit: Judentum feministisch gelesen*. Edited by Doris Brodbeck and Yvonne Domhardt. Zürich: Chronos, 2000.

———. "1. Mose 16 und 21: Hagar—die Befreite." Pages 25–32 in vol. 1 of *Feministisch gelesen: 32 ausgewählte Bibeltexte für Gruppen, Gemeinden und Gottesdienste*. Edited by Eva Renate Schmidt, Mieke Korenhof, and Renate Jost. 2nd ed. Stuttgart: Kreuz, 1989.

———. " 'Religionsgeschichte Israels' oder 'Theologie des Alten Testaments'—(k)eine Alternative? Anmerkungen aus feministisch-exegetischer Sicht." *JBTh* 10 (1995): 129–55.

Wallach-Faller, Marianne. "Mirjam—Schwester unter Brüdern." Pages 177–91 in eadem, *Die Frau im Tallit: Judentum feministisch gelesen*. Edited by Doris Brodbeck and Yvonne Domhardt. Zürich: Chronos, 2000.

Waltke, Bruce K. *A Commentary on Micah*. Grand Rapids: Eerdmans, 2007.

Washington, Harold C. " 'Lest He Die in the Battle and Another Man Take Her': Violence and the Construction of Gender in the Laws of Deuteronomy 20–22." Pages 185–213 in *Gender and Law in the Hebrew Bible and the Ancient Near East*. Edited by Victor H. Matthews, Bernard M. Levinson, and Tikva Frymer-Kensky. JSOTSup 262. Sheffield: Sheffield Academic Press, 1998.

Wasserfall, Rachel. "Menstruation and Identity: The Meaning of Niddah for Moroccan Women Immigrants to Israel." Pages 309–27 in *People of the Body: Jews and Judaism from an Embodied Perspective*. Edited by Howard Eilberg-Schwartz. The Body in Culture, History, and Religion. New York: State University of New York Press, 1992.

Watson, Patty Jo. *Archaeological Ethnography in Western Iran*. Viking Fund Publications in Anthropology 57. Tucson: University of Arizona Press, 1979.

Weidner, Ernst. "Hof- und Harems-Erlasse assyrischer Könige aus dem 2. Jahrtausend v. Chr." *AfO* 17 (1954–1956): 257–93.

Weinfeld, Moshe. *Deuteronomy and the Deuteronomic School*. Oxford: Clarendon, 1983.

West, Martin L. *The Hesiodic Catalogue of Women: Its Nature, Structure, and Origins*. Oxford: Clarendon, 1985.

West, Ramona Faye. "Ruth: A Retelling of Genesis 38?" Ph.D. diss., Southern Baptist Theological Seminary, 1987.

Westbrook, Raymond. "The Female Slave." Pages 214–38 in *Gender and Law in the Hebrew Bible and the Ancient Near East*. Edited by Victor H. Matthews, Bernard M. Levinson, and Tikva Frymer-Kensky. JSOTSup 262. Sheffield: Sheffield Academic Press, 1998.

———. "The Law of the Biblical Levirate." *RIDA* 24 (1977): 65–87.

———. *Old Babylonian Marriage Law*. AfOB 23. Horn: Berger, 1988.

———. *Property and the Family in Biblical Law*. JSOTSup 113. Sheffield: JSOT Press, 1991.

———. "Social Justice and Creative Jurisprudence in Late Bronze Age Syria." *JESHO* 44 (2001): 22–43.

Westermann, Claus. *Genesis 1–11: A Commentary*. Translated by John J. Scullion. Minneapolis: Augsburg Fortress, 1974.

———. *Genesis 12–36: A Commentary*. Translated by John J. Scullion. Minneapolis: Augsburg, 1985.

———. *Die Verheißungen an die Väter: Studien zur Vätergeschichte*. FRLANT 116. Göttingen: Vandenhoeck & Ruprecht, 1976.

Whitekettle, Richard. "Leviticus 12 and the Israelite Women: Ritual Process, Liminality and the Womb." *ZAW* 107 (1995): 393–408.

Wilcke, Claus. "Familiengründung im alten Babylonien." Pages 213–317 in *Geschlechtsreife und Legitimation zur Zeugung*. Edited by Ernst Wilhelm Müller. Freiburg im Breisgau: Alber, 1997.

———. "Der Kodex Urnamma (CU): Versuch einer Rekonstruktion." Pages 291–333 in *Riches Hidden in Secret Places: Ancient Near Eastern Studies in Memory of Thorkild Jacobsen*. Edited by Tzvi Abush. Winona Lake, Ind.: Eisenbrauns, 2002.

Wilkinson, Alix. *Ancient Egyptian Jewellery*. Methuen's Handbooks of Archaeology. London: Methuen, 1971.

Willett, Elizabeth A. R. "Women and Household Shrines in Ancient Israel." Ph.D. diss., University of Arizona, 1999.

Williams, A. J. "The Relationship of Genesis 3:20 to the Serpent." *ZAW* 89 (1977): 357–74.

Williams, Jacqueline. "'And She Became <Snow White>: Numbers 12:1–16." *OTE* 15 (2002): 259–68.

Willi-Plein, Ina. *Opfer und Kult im alttestamentlichen Israel: Textbefragungen und Zwischenergebnisse*. SBS 153. Stuttgart: Katholisches Bibelwerk, 1993.

Wilson, Robert R. "Between 'Azel' and 'Azel': Interpreting the Biblical Genealogies." *BA* 42 (1979): 11–22.

———. *Genealogy and History in the Biblical World*. Yale Near Eastern Researches 7. New Haven: Yale University Press, 1977.

Winter, Urs. *Frau und Göttin: Exegetische und ikonographische Studien zum weiblichen Gottesbild im alten Israel und dessen Umwelt*. 2nd ed. OBO 53. Fribourg: Universitätsverlag, 1987.

Wolde, Ellen van. *Stories of the Beginning: Genesis 1–11 and Other Creation Stories*. London: SCM, 1996.

Wright, David P. *The Disposal of Impurity: Elimination Rites in the Bible and in Hittite and Mesopotamian Literature*. SBLDS 101. Atlanta: Scholars Press, 1987.

———. "Unclean and Clean: Old Testament." *ABD* 6:729–41.

Yoder, Christine Roy. *Wisdom as a Woman of Substance: A Socioeconomic Reading of Proverbs 1–9 and 31:10–31*. BZAW 304. Berlin: de Gruyter, 2001.

Zaccagnini, Carlo. "Nuzi." Pages 565–617 in *A History of Ancient Near Eastern Law*. Edited by Raymond Westbrook. 2 vols. Handbook of Oriental Studies 72. Leiden: Brill, 2003.

Zenger, Erich. "Das Buch Leviticus als Teiltext der Tora/des Pentateuch: Eine synchrone Lektüre mit diachroner Perspektive." Pages 47–83 in *Leviticus als Buch*. Edited by Heinz-Josef Fabry and Hans-Winfried Jüngling. BBB 119. Berlin: Philo, 1999.

———. *Das Erste Testament: Die jüdische Bibel und die Christen*. 5th ed. Düsseldorf: Patmos, 1995.

Zevit, Ziony. *The Religions of Ancient Israel: A Synthesis of Parallactic Approaches*. London: Continuum, 2001.

Zezima, Katie. "A Place for a Ritual Cleansing of All Jews." *New York Times, Religion Journal* (July 3, 2004): 1–2.

Ziegler, Nele. *Le harem de Zimrî-Lîm: La population féminine des palais d'après les archives royales de Mari*. Florilegium Marianum 4; Mémoires de NABU 5. Paris: SEPOA, 1999.

———. "Le harem du vaincu." *RA* 93 (1999): 1–26.

Zwickel, Wolfgang. *Frauenalltag im biblischen Israel*. Stuttgart: Katholisches Bibelwerk, 2005.

CONTRIBUTORS

Sophie Démare-Lafont, Professor, Université Panthéon-Assas Paris II and École pratique des hautes études, Paris, France

Dorothea Erbele-Küster, Professor, Faculteit voor Protestantse Godgeleerdheid, Brussels, Belgium, and Protestantse Theologische Universiteit, The Netherlands

Karin Finsterbusch, Professor and Chair, Instituts für Evangelische Theologie, Universität Koblenz-Landau, Germany

Irmtraud Fischer, Professor, Institut für Alttestamentliche Bibelwissenschaft, Karl-Franzens-Universität Graz, Austria

Mercedes García Bachmann, Professor, Instituto Universitario ISEDET, Buenos Aires, Argentina

Thomas Hieke, Professor, Abteilung Altes Testament, Johannes Gutenberg-Universität Mainz, Germany

Carol Meyers, Professor, Department of Religion, Duke University, Durham, North Carolina, U.S.A.

Mercedes Navarro Puerto, Professor, Escuela Feminista de Teologia de Andalucía, and Facultad de Filología, Universidad de Sevilla, Spain

Jorunn Økland, Professor and Director, Centre for Gender Research, University of Oslo, Norway

Ursula Rapp, Assistant Professor, Exegese des Alten Testaments, Universität Luzern, Switzerland

Donatella Scaiola, Extraordinary Professor, Facoltà di Missiologia, Pontifica Università Urbaniana, Rome, Italy

Silvia Schroer, Professor, Institut für Bibelwissenschaft, Universität Bern, Switzerland

Jopie Siebert-Hommes, Assistant Professor (retired), Universiteit van Amsterdam, The Netherlands

Andrea Taschl-Erber, Assistant Professor, Katholisch-Theologische Fakultät, Universität Wien, Austria

Adriana Valerio, Professor, Dipartimento di Discipline Storiche, Università degli Studi di Napoli Federico II, Naples, Italy

INDEX OF ANCIENT SOURCES

GREEK AND LATIN AUTHORS

The twenty-one volumes of The Bible and Women project, to be published simultaneously in German, English, Italian, and Spanish, will present a reception history of the Bible and its cultural history, focusing on gender-relevant biblical themes, biblical female characters, and the women who throughout history have read, appropriated, and interpreted the Bible in text and image. At the center of the project stand a number of related interests:

- female literary figures within the Bible and the reception of such figures within the history of exegesis by male and female interpreters
- gender-specific social and cultural contexts in the areas and periods in which the biblical books emerged
- women who interpreted the Bible in particular eras and faith traditions
- women to whom biblical texts or their interpretation are attributed
- gender-relevant texts (e.g., legal codes) and themes (e.g., purity–impurity)
- the treatment of female biblical characters and gender-relevant issues in art

1. Hebrew Bible/Old Testament

1.1. Torah: Irmtraud Fischer and Mercedes Navarro Puerto, eds., with Andrea Taschl-Erber

1.2. Prophets: Irmtraud Fischer and Athalya Brenner, eds.

1.3. Writings: Nuria Calduch-Benages and Christl Maier, eds.

2. New Testament

2.1. Gospels: Narratives and History: Mercedes Navarro Puerto and Marinella Perroni, eds.

2.2. New Testament Letters: Jorunn Økland and Elisa Estévez López, eds.

3. Pseudepigrapha and Apocryphal Writings

3.1. Jewish Pseudepigrapha and Apocrypha: Marie-Theres Wacker and Kristin De Troyer, eds.

3.2. Apocryphal Writings of Early Christianity: Silke Petersen and Caroline Vander Stichele, eds.

4. Jewish Interpretation

4.1. Talmud: Tal Ilan and Charlotte Elisheva Fonrobert, eds.

4.2. Jewish Middle Ages and Modern Times: Susannah Heschel and Gerhard Langer, eds.

5. Patristic Period

5.1. Church Fathers: Kari Elisabeth Børresen and Emanuela Prinzivalli, eds.

5.2. Women's Texts of the Early Church: Eva Synek and Elena Giannarelli, eds.

6. Middle Ages and the Early Modern Era

6.1. Early Middle Ages: Franca Ela Consolino and Judith Herrin, eds.

6.2. High Middle Ages: Kari Elisabeth Børresen and Adriana Valerio, eds.

6.3. "The Women's Renaissance" (Querelle des femmes): Ángela Muñoz Fernandez and Valeria Ferrari Schiefer, eds.

7. Era of Reform and Revolution

7.1. Reformation and Counter-Reformation in Northern and Central Europe: Charlotte Methuen and Tarald Rasmussen, eds.

7.2. Reformation and Counter-Reformation in Southern Europe: Adriana Valerio and Maria Laura Giordano, eds.

7.3. Enlightenment and Restoration: Ute Gause and Marina Caffiero, eds.

8. The So-Called "Long" Nineteenth Century

8.1. Finding Themselves: Women and the Bible in the Nineteenth Century: Angela Berlis, ed.

8.2. Departing for Modernity versus Clinging to the Outdated: Women's Biblical Hermeneutics in the Context of Modern Times: Ruth Albrecht and Michaela Sohn-Kronthaler, eds.

9. The Twentieth Century and the Present

9.1. Scholarship and Movement: Feminist Biblical Studies in the Twentieth Century: Elisabeth Schüssler Fiorenza, ed.

9.2. Current Trends: Maria Cristina Bartolomei and Jorunn Økland, eds.

CPSIA information can be obtained at www.ICGtesting.com
Printed in the USA
LVOW112205061111

253741LV00001B/1/P